36.75

DICTIONARY
OF
INTERNATIONAL
TRADE
4th Edition

This book is dedicated to the memory of my father
Allen Joseph Hinkelman
who taught me the meaning of many words.

DICTIONARY
OF
INTERNATIONAL
TRADE
4th Edition

Handbook of the Global Trade Community
Includes 12 Key Appendices

Edward G. Hinkelman

with contributions by:
Karla Shippey, J.D. • Stacey Padrick • Alexandra Woznick
Sibylla Putzi • John O'Conor • U.S. Department of Commerce
International Chamber of Commerce (ICC) • Sea Land Shipping
IATA (International Air Transport Association)
Air Transport Association (of the US) • CIGNA Worldwide
Insurance Company of North America • World Bank
Swiss Bank Corporation • Hapag Lloyd (America) Inc.
Wells Fargo HSBC Trade Bank

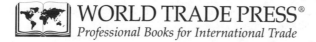

WORLD TRADE PRESS®
Professional Books for International Trade

World Trade Press
1450 Grant Avenue, Suite 204
Novato, California 94945 USA
Tel: [1] (415) 898-1124; Fax: [1] (415) 898-1080
Order Line (U.S. credit card sales only) [1] (800) 833-8586
Email: worldpress@aol.com
www.worldtradepress.com
www.globalroadwarrior.com
Edward G. Hinkelman Email: egh@worldtradepress.com

Disclaimer
This publication is designed to provide information concerning the terminology used in international trade and the businesses that support international trade. It is sold with the understanding that the publisher is not engaged in rendering legal or any other professional service. If legal advice or other expert assistance is required, the services of a competent professional should be sought.

Library of Congress Cataloging-in-Publication Data:

Hinkelman, Edward G., 1947—
      Dictionary of International Trade: Handbook of the Global Trade Community,
   Includes 12 Key Appendices / Edward G. Hinkelman; with contributions
  by Karla Shippey ... [et al.]. -- 4rd Edition
      p. cm.
   Includes bibliographical references.
   ISBN 1-885073-84-4 (alk. paper)
    1. International trade --Dictionaries. 2. United States--Commerce Dictionaries. I. Title.
HF1373.H55   2000
382´.03--dc21
                                         00-024675
                                       CIP

Printed in the United States of America

Table of Contents

A

abandonment
(shipping/insurance) (a) The act of refusing delivery of a shipment so badly damaged in transit that it is worthless. (b) Damage to a vessel that is so severe that it is considered a constructive total loss. *See* constructive total loss.

abbrochment
(law) The purchase at wholesale of all merchandise that is intended to be sold in a particular retail market for the purpose of controlling that market.

about
(banking) In connection with letters of credit, "about" means a tolerance of plus/minus 10% regarding the letter of credit value, unit price or the quantity of the goods, depending on the context in which the tolerance is mentioned.

absolute advantage
(economics) An advantage of one nation or area over another in the costs of manufacturing an item in terms of used resources.

absorption
(economics) Investment and consumption purchases by households, businesses and governments, both domestic and imported. When absorption exceeds production, the excess is the country's current account deficit. *See* current account.
(shipping) The assumption by one carrier of the special charges of another carrier generally without increasing charges to the shipper.

accelerated tariff elimination
(customs) The gradual reduction of import duties over time. Accelerated tariff elimination is often a feature of free trade agreements. The North American Free Trade Agreement (NAFTA) is an example of a trade agreement with accelerated tariff elimination.

acceptance
(law) (a) An unconditional assent to an offer. (b) An assent to an offer conditioned on only minor changes that do not affect any material terms of the offer. *See* counteroffer; offer.
(shipping) Receipt by the consignee of a shipment thus terminating the common carrier liability.
(banking) A time draft (bill of exchange) on the face of which the drawee has written "accepted" over his signature. The date and place payable are also indicated. The person accepting the draft is known as the acceptor. Note: The drawee's signature alone is a valid acceptance and is usually made across the left margin of the bill of exchange. *See* bill of exchange; bank acceptance.

acceptance letter of credit
(banking) A letter of credit which, in addition to other required documents, requires presentation of a term draft drawn on the bank nominated as the accepting bank under the letter of credit. *See* acceptance; bank acceptance; letter of credit.

accepted draft
(banking) A bill of exchange accepted by the drawee (acceptor) by putting his signature (acceptance) on its face. In doing so, he commits himself to pay the bill upon presentation at maturity. *See* acceptance; bank acceptance; bill of exchange.

accepting bank
(banking) A bank who by signing a time draft accepts responsibility to pay when the draft becomes due. In this case the bank is the drawee (party asked to pay the draft), but only becomes the acceptor (party accepting responsibility to pay) upon acceptance (signing the draft). *See* acceptance; bill of exchange.

acceptor
(banking) The party that signs a draft or obligation, thereby agreeing to pay the stated sum at maturity. *See* acceptance; bill of exchange.

accession
The process by which a country becomes a member of an international agreement, such as the World Trade Organization (WTO), the GATT or the European Community (EC). Accession to the WTO involves negotiations to determine the specific obligations a nonmember country must undertake before it will be entitled to membership benefits. *See also* accessions.

accessions
(law) (a) Goods that are affixed to and become part of other goods. Examples include semiconductors that are inserted into computers, parts that are added onto vehicles, and dials that are used in watches. (b) A nation's acceptance of a treaty already made between other countries. *See also* accession.

A

accessorial charges

(shipping) Charges made for additional, special, or supplemental services, normally over and above the line haul services.

accessorial services

(shipping) Services performed by a shipping line or airline in addition to the normal transportation service. Common accessorial services include advancement of charges, pickup, delivery, C.O.D. service, signature service and storage.

accommodation

(law) An action by one individual or legal entity (the accommodation party) that is taken as a favor, without any consideration, for another individual or legal entity (the accommodated party). An **accommodation note or paper** is a commercial instrument of debt that is issued by or for an accommodated party (who is expected to pay the debt) and that contains the name of the accommodation party. A person may make an accommodation, for example, to help another party raise money or obtain credit. An accommodation party is usually treated like a surety, who is responsible for the performance of the accommodated party. The distinction between an accommodation and a surety is that an accommodation is made without consideration, that is, it is freely given. *See* surety.

accord and satisfaction

(law) A means of discharging a contract or cause of action by which the parties agree (the accord) to alter their obligations and then perform (the satisfaction) the new obligations. A seller who cannot, for example, obtain red fabric dye according to contract specifications and threatens to breach the contract may enter into an accord and satisfaction with the buyer to provide blue-dyed fabric for a slightly lower price.

account number

(shipping) An identifying number issued by a carrier's accounting office to identify a shipper and/or consignee. The number helps ensure accurate invoicing procedures and customer traffic activity.

account party

(banking) The party that instructs a bank (issuing bank) to open a letter of credit. The account party is usually the buyer or importer. *See* letter of credit.

accounts payable

(accounting) A current liability representing the amount owed by an individual or a business to a creditor(s) for merchandise or services purchased on an open account or short-term credit. *See also* accounts receivable.

accounts receivable

(accounting) Money owed a business enterprise for merchandise or services bought on open account. *See also* accounts payable.

accrual of obligation

(law) The time at which an obligation matures or vests, requiring the obligor to perform. In a contract between a buyer and seller, for example, the seller's obligation to deliver goods may accrue when the buyer tenders payment in full. Alternatively, if the contract specifies a date for delivery of the goods, the seller's obligation accrues at that date, even if the buyer tenders payment before or after that date.

acquisition

The purchase of complete or majority ownership in a business enterprise, usually by another business enterprise.

Act of God

An act of nature beyond man's control such as lightning, flood, earthquake or hurricane. Many shipping and other performance contracts include a "force majeure" clause which excuses a party who breaches the contract due to acts of God. *See* force majeure.

action ex contractu

(law) A legal action for breach of a promise stated in an express or implied contract.

action ex delicto

(law) (a) A legal action for a breach of a duty that is not stated in a contract but arises from the contract. A seller of goods, for example, who represents that the goods can be used for a certain purpose has a duty to furnish goods that can be so used, even if that duty is not stated in the contract. If the seller fails to provide such goods, the seller breaches that duty and the buyer has an action ex delicto based on the seller's fraudulent representation. (b) A legal action that arises from a wrongful act, such as fraud.

added-value tax

See value-added tax.

address of record

(law) The official or primary location for an individual, company, or other organization.

adhesion contract

(law) Contract with standard, often printed, terms for sale of goods and services offered to consumers who usually cannot negotiate any of the terms and cannot acquire the product unless they agree to the terms.

adjustment

(general) The refund or replacement of lost or damaged goods by either the seller or by an insurance carrier.

(insurance) The settlement of an insurance claim.

(U.S. government) The negative impact of increased import competition to U.S. businesses. *See* adjustment assistance.

adjustment assistance

(U.S.) Financial, training and reemployment technical assistance to workers, and technical assistance to firms and industries, to help them cope with adjustment difficulties arising from increased import competition. The objective of the assistance is usually to help an industry to become more competitive in the same line of production, or to move into other economic activities. The aid to workers can take the form of training (to qualify the affected individuals for employment in new or expanding industries), relocation allowances (to help them move from areas characterized by high unemployment to areas where employment may be available) or unemployment compensation (to tide them over while they are searching for new jobs). The aid to firms can take the form of technical assistance through Trade Adjustment Assistance Centers located throughout the United States. Industry-wide technical assistance also is available through the Trade Adjustment Assistance program. The benefits of increased trade to an importing country generally exceed the costs of adjustment, but the benefits are widely shared and the adjustment costs are sometimes narrowly—and some would say unfairly—concentrated on a few domestic producers and communities. Adjustment assistance can also be designed to facilitate structural shifts of resources from less productive to more productive industries, contributing further to greater economic efficiency and improved standards of living. *See* Trade Adjustment Assistance Centers.

Administrative Exception Notes (AEN)

A listing of strategic commodities that member nations of the Coordinating Committee on Multilateral Export Controls (CoCom) may approve for export on their own, but must notify CoCom after the fact. CoCom is an informal organization of 17 nations that cooperatively restrict strategic exports to controlled countries. CoCom controls exports at three levels, depending on the item and the proposed destination. At the lowest level, "national

discretion" (also called "administrative exception"), a member nation may approve the export on its own, but CoCom must be notified after the fact. Administrative exception notes are appended to list categories describing commodities that can be approved solely at national discretion.

See Coordinating Committee on Multilateral Export Controls.

administrative notes

See Administrative Exception Notes.

Administrative Protective Order (APO)

(U.S. law) An Administrative Protective Order, APO, is used to protect proprietary data that is obtained during an administrative proceeding. Within the U.S. Department of Commerce, APO is most frequently used in connection with antidumping and countervailing duty investigations to prohibit opposing counsel from releasing data. The term is also applied in connection with civil enforcement of export control laws to protect against the disclosure of information provided by companies being investigated for violations. *See* dumping; countervailing duties.

admiralty

(law/shipping) Any civil or criminal issue having to do with maritime law.

admiralty court

(law/shipping) A court of law that has jurisdiction over maritime legal issues. These generally include ocean shipping, collisions of vessels, charters, contracts and damage to cargo.

admission temporaire

(customs) The free entry of goods normally dutiable. *See* ATA Carnet.

Admission Temporaire/ Temporary Admission Carnet

See ATA Carnet.

ad valorem

Literally: according to value.

(general) Any charge, tax, or duty that is applied as a percentage of value.

(taxation) A tax calculated on the value of the property subject to the tax.

(shipping) A freight rate set at a certain percentage of the declared value of an article.

(U.S. Customs) Ad valorem duty. A duty assessed as a percentage rate or value of the imported merchandise. For example 5% ad valorem. *See* specific rate of duty; compound rate of duty; tariff.

advance against collection
(banking) A short term loan or credit extended to the seller (usually the exporter) by the seller's bank once a draft has been accepted by the buyer (generally the importer) of the seller's goods. Once the buyer pays, the loan is paid off. If the buyer does not pay the draft, the seller must still make good on the loan. *See* bill of exchange.

advance arrangements
(shipping) The shipment of certain classes of commodities—examples: gold, precious gems, furs, live animals, human remains and oversized shipments—require arrangements in advance with carriers.

Advanced Technology Products (ATP)
(U.S.) About 500 of some 22,000 commodity classification codes used in reporting U.S. merchandise trade are identified as "advanced technology" codes and they meet the following criteria: (1) The code contains products whose technology is from a recognized high technology field (e.g., biotechnology); (2) These products represent leading edge technology in that field; and (3) Such products constitute a significant part of all items covered in the selected classification code.

advancement of charges
(shipping) A service under which a shipping line or airline, in some instances, pays incidental charges arising before or after a shipment or airhaul. Examples include cartage and warehousing costs. These charges can be in advance for the convenience of either the shipper or the receiver.

advice
(banking) The term "advice" connotes several types of forms used on the banking field. Generally speaking, an advice is a form of letter that relates or acknowledges a certain activity or result with regard to a customer's relations with a bank. Examples include credit advice, debit advice, advice of payment and advice of execution. In commercial transactions, information on a business transaction such as shipment of goods.

(banking/letters of credit) The forwarding of a letter of credit, or an amendment to a letter of credit to the seller, or beneficiary of the credit, by the advising bank (seller's bank).

See issuance; letter of credit; amendment.

advice of fate
(banking) A bank's notification of the status of a collection which is still outstanding.

advised credit
(banking) A letter of credit whose terms and conditions have been confirmed by a bank. *See* letter of credit; confirmed letter of credit.

advising bank
(banking) The bank (also referred to as the seller's or exporter's bank) which receives a letter of credit or amendment to a letter of credit from the issuing bank (the buyer's bank) and forwards it to the beneficiary (seller/exporter) of the credit. *See* letter of credit; confirming bank; issuing bank.

Advisory Committee on Export Policy
(U.S. government) The ACEP is an interagency dispute resolution body that operates at the Assistant Secretary level. ACEP is chaired by the U.S. Department of Commerce; membership includes the Departments of Defense, Energy and State, the Arms Control and Disarmament Agency, and the intelligence community. Disputes not resolved by the ACEP must be addressed by the cabinet-level Export Administration Review Board within specific time frames set forth under National Security Directive #53. *See* National Security Directive #53; Export Administration Review Board.

Advisory Committee on Trade Policy and Negotiations
(U.S. government) The ACTPN is a group (membership of 45; two-year terms) appointed by the President to provide advice on matters of trade policy and related issues, including trade agreements. The 1974 Trade Act requires the ACTPN's establishment and broad representation of key economic sectors affected by trade. Below the ACTPN are seven policy committees: SPAC (Services Policy Advisory Committee), INPAC (Investment Policy Advisory Committee), IGPAC (Intergovernmental Policy Advisory Committee), IPAC (Industry Policy Advisory Committee), APAC (Agriculture Policy Advisory Committee), LPAC (Labor Policy Advisory Committee) and DPAC (Defense Policy Advisory Committee). Below the policy committees are sectoral, technical and functional advisory committees.

See Industry Consultations Program.

advisory notes
See Administrative Exception Notes.

affiliate
A business enterprise located in one country which is directly or indirectly owned or controlled by a person of another country.

(U.S.) A business enterprise located in one country which is directly or indirectly owned or controlled by a person of another country to the extent of 10 percent or more of its voting securities for an incorporated business enterprise, or an equivalent interest for an unincorporated business enterprise, including a branch. For outward investment, the affiliate is referred to as a "foreign affiliate"; for inward investment, it is referred to as a "U.S. affiliate." *See* direct (foreign) investment; foreign direct investment in the United States; affiliated foreign group.

affiliated foreign group
(U.S.) An affiliated foreign group means (a) the foreign parent, (b) any foreign person, proceeding up the foreign parent's ownership chain, which owns more than 50 percent of the person below it up to and including that person which is not owned more than 50 percent by another foreign person and (c) any foreign person, proceeding down the ownership chain(s) of each of these members, which is owned more than 50 percent by the person above it. *See* direct (foreign) investment; foreign direct investment in the United States; affiliate; foreign-owned affiliate in the U.S.

affreightment
(shipping) The hiring or chartering of all or part of a vessel for the transport of goods.

affreightment contract
(shipping/law) A contract with a shipowner to hire all or part of a ship for transporting goods.

afghani
The currency of Afghanistan. 1 Af = 100 puls.

afloat
(shipping) Refers to a shipment of cargo which is currently onboard a vessel between ports (as opposed to on land).

African, Caribbean and Pacific Countries (ACP)
Developing countries which are designated beneficiaries under the Lome Convention. *See* Lome Convention.

African Development Bank (AfDB)
The AfDB, established in 1963, provides financing through direct loans to African member states to cover the foreign exchange costs incurred in Bank-approved development projects in those countries. Fifty-one African countries are members and ordinarily receive loans. The Republic of South Africa is currently the only African country not a member. Address: African Development Bank, Rue Joseph Anoma, 01 BP 1387, Abidjan 01, Cote d'Ivoire; Tel: [225] 20-44-44; Telex: 23717; Fax: [225] 20-40-06; http://www.afdb.org.

African Development Foundation
An independent, nonprofit U.S. government corporation established to provide financial assistance to grass-roots organizations in Africa. ADF became operational in 1984. Address: African Development Foundation, 1400 Eye Street NW, 10th Floor, Washington, DC 20005 USA; Tel: [1] (202) 673-3916; http://www.adf.gov.

aft
(shipping) Direction toward the stern of the vessel (ship or aircraft).

after date
(banking) A notation used on financial instruments (such as drafts or bills of exchange) to fix the maturity date as a fixed number of days past the date of drawing of the draft. For example, if a draft stipulates "60 days after date," it means that the draft is due (payable) 60 days after the date it was drawn. This has the effect of fixing the date of maturity of the draft, independent of the date of acceptance of the draft. *See* acceptance; drawee; bill of exchange.

after sight
(banking) A notation on a draft that indicates that payment is due a fixed number of days after the draft has been presented to the drawee. For example, "30 days after sight" means that the drawee has 30 days from the date of presentation of the draft to make payment. *See* acceptance; drawee; bill of exchange.

agency
(law) A relationship between one individual or legal entity (the agent) who represents, acts on behalf of, and binds another individual or legal entity (the principal) in accordance with the principal's request or instruction. In some countries, agency is more narrowly defined as a relationship created only by a written agreement or a power of attorney, entered into by a principal and a person who is designated to act for the principal within the limits of the written document creating the agency. *See* agent; principal; power of attorney.

(a) An **express agency** is established by a written or oral agreement between the parties. An express agency is created, for example, when a seller orally contracts with a sales representative to sell products or when a company makes a written power of attorney to authorize a person to act on its behalf. (b) An **implied agency** arises as a result of the conduct of the parties. If a seller's assistant, for example, sometimes deals with customers, a

A

court may determine from that conduct that an implied agency exists between the seller and the assistant. (c) An **agency by estoppel** is imposed by law when an agent acts without authority, but the principal leads a third person to conclude reasonably that the agent had authority and to rely on that conclusion. If a seller, for example, informs a buyer that the seller's representative is authorized to negotiate any contract terms for the seller, a court may decide that an agency by estoppel existed, that the contract should be enforced, and that the seller cannot avoid performing the contract by claiming that the representative in fact had no authority. (d) An **agency del credere** arises when a principal entrusts goods, documents, or securities to an agent who has broad authority to collect from a buyer and who may be liable for ensuring that the buyer is solvent. A sales representative, for example, who is given goods and who is authorized to receive payment from buyers is an agent del credere. (e) An **exclusive agency** is an arrangement with an agent under which the principal agrees not to sell property to a purchaser found by another agent. If a seller of green and red shoes, for example, gives a sales representative an exclusive agency to sell the green shoes in a particular country, the seller is not permitted to sell those shoes through any other representative in the same country. The seller may, however, authorize other agents to sell red shoes in that country. (f) A **universal agency** authorizes the agent to do every transaction that a principal can legally delegate. A principal who will be traveling for some time may, for example, give an agent authority to deal with all business and personal transactions for the principal during that absence. (g) A **general agency** authorizes an agent to do all acts related to the principal's business, which may include negotiating contracts, establishing credit, advertising, arranging for shipping and setting up overseas offices and outlets. (h) A **special agency** gives an agent limited powers to conduct one transaction or a specific series of transactions. A contract with a representative to secure the sale of certain components to a particular factory creates a special agency.*See* agent; principal; power of attorney.

agency by estoppel
See agency.

agency del credere
See agency.

Agency for International Development
(U.S. government) A unit of the United States International Development Cooperation Agency. AID administers U.S. foreign economic and humanitarian assistance programs in the developing world, Central and Eastern Europe, and the Commonwealth of Independent States. Among the economic programs are those that foster employment growth, and that promote use of clean and efficient energy and environmental technologies. Maintains economic, social and demographic statistics for many developing countries. AID has field missions and representatives in approximately 70 developing countries in Africa, Latin America, the Caribbean and the Near East. Address: Agency for International Development, Ronald Reagan Building, 1300 Pennsylvania Avenue, NW; Washington, DC 20523 USA; Tel: [1] (202) 712-4320; www.info.usaid.gov. *See* Center for Trade and Investment Services; International Development Cooperation Agency.

agent
(law) An individual or legal entity authorized to act on behalf of another individual or legal entity (the principal). An agent's authorized actions will bind the principal. A sales representative, for example, is an agent of the seller. *See* agency; principal; power of attorney.

agent ad litem
(shipping/law) An agent who acts on behalf of a principal in prosecuting or defending a lawsuit.

agent bank
(banking) (a) Bank acting for a foreign bank. (b) Bank handling administration of a loan in a syndicated credit.

Agent/Distributor Service (ADS)
(U.S. government) An International Trade Administration (ITA) fee-based service which locates foreign import agents and distributors for U.S. exporters. ADS provides a custom search overseas for interested and qualified foreign representatives on behalf of a U.S. exporter. Officers abroad conduct the search and prepare a report identifying up to six foreign prospects that have examined the U.S. firm's product literature and have expressed interest in representing the U.S. firm's products. Contact the nearest Department of Commerce District Office or call [1] (800) USA-TRADE. *See* United States Department of Commerce.

A

aggregated shipments

(shipping) Numerous shipments from different shippers to one consignee that are consolidated and treated as a single consignment.

agreed valuation

(shipping) The value of a shipment agreed upon by the shipper and carrier to secure a specific rate and/or liability.

agriculture export connections

(U.S. government) The U.S. Foreign Agriculture Service through AgExport Connections (formerly Agriculture Information and Marketing Services) provides services designed to help U.S. exporters of agricultural products make direct contact with foreign buyers. Services include: Trade Leads—compiled by overseas offices and retrievable from the Economic Bulletin Board; Buyer Alert—publication for U.S. exporters to advertise their products; and Foreign Buyer Lists. Contact: Trade Assistance and Promotions Office, USDA, Foreign Agriculture Service, 1400 Independence Avenue, SW Stop 1004, Washington, DC 20250-1052 USA; Tel: [1] (202) 720-7420; Fax: [1] (202) 720-9728; http://www.fas.usda.gov.

airbill

See air waybill.

air cargo

(shipping) Any property (freight, mail, express) carried or to be carried in an aircraft. Does not include passenger baggage.

aircraft pallet

(shipping) The use of a platform or pallet (in air freight usually from 3/4" to 2" thick) upon which a unitized shipment rests or on which goods are assembled and secured before being loaded as a unit onto an aircraft. Most carriers offer container discounts for palletized loads.

Palletization results in more efficient use of space aboard freighter aircraft and better cargo handling, particularly when used as part of mechanized systems employing such other advances as pallet loaders and pallet transporters. The **pallet loader** is a device employing one or more vertical lift platforms for the mechanical loading or unloading of palletized freight at planeside.

The **pallet transporter** is a vehicle for the movement of loaded pallets between the aircraft and the freight terminal or truck dock. Sometimes the functions of both the pallet loader and pallet transporter are combined into a single vehicle. *See also* pallet.

air express

(shipping) A term used to describe expedited handling of air freight service. *See* priority air freight; air freight.

air freight

(shipping) A service providing for the air transport of goods. The volume of air freight has been increasing significantly due to: (1) decreased shipping time, (2) greater inventory control for just-in-time manufacturing and stocking, (3) generally superior condition of goods upon arrival, and (4) for certain commodities, lower shipping costs.

air freight forwarder

(shipping) A freight forwarder for shipments by air. Air freight forwarders serve a dual role. The air freight forwarders are, to the shipper, an indirect carrier because they receive freight from various shippers under one tariff, usually consolidating the goods into a larger unit, which is then tendered to an airline. To the airlines, the air freight forwarder is a shipper. An air freight forwarder is ordinarily classed as an indirect air carrier; however, many air freight forwarders operate their own aircraft. *See* freight forwarder.

airmail

(shipping) The term "airmail" as a class of mail, is used only in international postal service. Within the United States, the U.S. Postal Service moves all first class mail, priority mail, and express mail by air where doing so will expedite delivery.

air parcel post

(shipping) A term commonly used for priority mail which consists of first class mail weighing more than 13 ounces. Priority mail is another economical and expedited service for the shipping of parcels by air.

Airport Mail Facility (AMF)

(shipping) A U.S. Postal Service facility located on or adjacent to an airport. AMFs are primarily engaged in the dispatch, receipt, and transfer of mail directly with air carriers.

air waybill (airbill)

(shipping) A shipping document used by the airlines for air freight. It is a contract for carriage that includes carrier conditions of carriage including such items as limits of liability and claims procedures. The air waybill also contains shipping instructions to airlines, a description of the commodity and applicable transportation charges. Air waybills are used by many truckers as through documents for coordinated air/truck service.

Air waybills are not negotiable. The airline industry has adopted a standard formatted air waybill that accommodates both domestic and international traffic. The standard document was designed to enhance the application of modern computerized systems to air freight processing for both the carrier and the shipper. *See* bill of lading; negotiable.

airworthiness certification
(shipping) Documentation to show that an aircraft or components comply with all the airworthiness requirements related to its use as laid down by the regulatory authorities for the country in which the aircraft is registered.

Aksjeselskap (A/S)
(Norway) Designation for a joint stock company with limited personal liability to shareholders. See Business Entities Appendix.

Aktiebolag (AB)
(Finland, Sweden) Designation for a joint stock company with limited personal liability to shareholders. See Business Entities Appendix.

Aktiengesellschaft (AG)
(Austria, Germany, Switzerland, Liechtenstein) Designation for a joint stock company with limited personal liability to shareholders. See Business Entities Appendix.

Aktieselskab (A/S)
(Denmark) Designation for a joint stock company with limited personal liability to shareholders.

Alcohol, Tobacco and Firearms (ATF)
See Bureau of Alcohol, Tobacco and Firearms.

alienable
(law) The capacity to be transferred or conveyed. Interests in real or personal property, for example, are alienable.

aliquot
(law) A fractional share. A court, for example, may award damages aliquot against several parties who breached a contract, meaning that each must pay a proportionate share of the damages. Aliquot liability differs from joint and several liability, in that the latter refers to whether the breaching parties may be sued and held liable together or individually. *See* joint and several liability.

all-cargo aircraft
(shipping) An aircraft for the carriage of cargo only, rather than the combination of passengers and cargo. The all-cargo aircraft will carry cargo in bulk or container in the main deck as well as in the lower deck of the aircraft. It may include a scheduled and/or nonscheduled service.

all risk
(insurance) Extensive insurance coverage of cargo, including coverage due to external causes such as fire, collision, pilferage etc., but usually excluding "special" risks such as those resulting from acts of war, labor strikes and the perishing of goods, and from internal damage due to faulty packaging, decay or loss of market.

All risk insurance covers only physical loss or damage from external cause(s) and specifically affirms the exclusion of war risks and strikes and riots unless covered by endorsement. These losses are excluded, either by expressed exclusions, conditions or warranties written into the policy or by implied conditions or warranties that are read into every marine policy by legal interpretation.

An "all risks" policy may expressly exclude certain types of damage such as marring and scratching of unboxed automobiles or bending and twisting entirely or unless amounting to a specified percentage or amount.

Also, certain perils such as war and strikes, riots and civil commotions are commonly excluded, but these perils can be and usually are reinstated, at least in part, by special endorsement or by a separate policy.

The "all risk" clause is a logical extension of the broader forms of "with average" coverage. The all risk clause generally reads:

"To cover against all risks of physical loss or damage from any external cause irrespective of percentage, but excluding, nevertheless, the risk of war, strikes, riots, seizure, detention and other risks excluded by the F.C.&S. (Free of Capture and Seizure) Warranty and the S.R.&C.C. (Strikes, Riots and Civil Commotion) Warranty in this policy, excepting to the extent that such risk are specifically covered by endorsement."

(air shipments) All risk insurance of air shipments usually excludes loss due to cold or changes in atmospheric pressure. *See* average; with average; free of particular average; inherent vice, war risk; strikes, riots and civil commotion.

allowance
An amount paid or credited by a seller as a refund or reimbursement due to any one of a number of causes including: faulty packaging, shipment of goods which do not meet buyer's specifications, a late shipment, etc.

A

alongside
(shipping) A phrase referring to the side of a ship. (a) Goods to be delivered "alongside" are to be placed on the dock or lighter within reach of the transport ship's tackle so that they can be loaded aboard the ship. (b) Goods delivered to the port of embarkation, but without loading fees.

alternative tariff
(shipping) A tariff containing two or more rates from and to the same points, on the same goods, with authority to use the one which produces the lowest charge.

amendment
(law/general) An addition, deletion, or change in a legal document.
(banking/letters of credit) A change in the terms and conditions of a letter of credit (e.g., extension of the letter of credit's validity period, shipping deadline, etc.), usually to meet the needs of the seller. The seller requests an amendment of the buyer who, if he agrees, instructs his bank (the issuing bank) to issue the amendment. The issuing bank informs the seller's bank (the advising bank) who then notifies the seller of the amendment. In the case of irrevocable letters of credit, amendments may only be made with the agreement of all parties to the transaction. *See* letter of credit.

American Arbitration Association
A private not-for-profit organization formed in 1926 to encourage the use of arbitration in the settlement of disputes. Address: American Arbitration Association, 1633 Broadway, 10th Floor, New York NY 10019 USA; Tel: [1] (212) 484-4181; Fax: [1] (212) 382-2606; http://www.adr.org. *See* arbitration.

American Association of Exporters and Importers
(U.S.) A trade association which advises members of legislation regarding importing and exporting, and fights against protectionism. Also hosts seminars and conferences for importers and exporters. Address: American Association of Exporters and Importers, 11 W. 42nd St., 30th Floor, New York, NY 10036 USA; Tel: [1] (212) 944-2230; Fax: [1] (212) 382-2606; http://www.aaei.org.

American Institute in Taiwan
A non-profit corporation that represents U.S. interests in Taiwan in lieu of an embassy. In 1979, the United States terminated formal diplomatic relations with Taiwan when it recognized the People's Republic of China as the sole legal government of China.

The AIT was authorized to continue commercial, cultural and other relations between the U.S. and Taiwan. Address: American Institute in Taiwan, 7, Lane 134, Section 3, Hsin Yi Road, Taipei, 106, Taiwan; Tel: (2) 709-2000; Telex: 78523890 US-TRADE; Fax: (2) 701-4216; http://ait.org.tw/.

American National Standards
A set of product standards established by the American National Standards Institute (ANSI). *See* American National Standards Institute. *See also* International Standards Organization.

American National Standards Institute (ANSI)
An organization that develops and publishes a set of voluntary product standards called the American National Standards. In addition to product standards, ANSI publishes a guide to unit-load and transportation package sizes for containers. ANSI is also an influential member of the ISO (International Standards Organization). Address: American National Standards Institute, 11 West 42nd Street, New York, NY 10036 USA; Tel: [1] (212) 642-4900. *See also* International Standards Organization; http://web.ansi.org/default_js.htm.

American option
(banking/foreign exchange) A foreign exchange option containing a provision to the effect that it can be exercised at any time between the date of writing and the expiration date. *See also* European option.

American Traders Index (ATI)
A compilation of individual U.S. & Foreign Commercial Service (US&FCS) domestic client files, for use by overseas posts to generate mailing lists. *See* United States and Foreign Commercial Service.

amidships
(shipping) At or in the middle of a vessel. Because a ship's movement is less in the middle of the vessel, shippers will sometimes specify that fragile freight be placed amidships.

amortization
(banking) (a) The gradual extinguishment of any amount over a period of time (e.g., the retirement of a debt). (b) A reduction of the book value of a fixed asset.

analysis certificate
See certificate of analysis.

ancillary equipment
(shipping) Equipment used to build up a palletized load or to convey a unit load device outside an aircraft. *See* aircraft pallet.

A

Andean Group

An alliance of Latin American countries formed in 1969 to promote regional economic integration among medium-sized countries. Members include Bolivia, Colombia, Ecuador, Peru and Venezuela. Address: Andean Group, Avenida Paseo de la Republica 3895, Casilla Postal 18-1177, Lima 18, Peru; Tel: [51] (14) 41-4212; Telex: 20104 PE; Fax: [51] (14) 42-0911.

Andean Trade Initiative (ATI)

(U.S.) A U.S. government initiative providing for assistance for alternative economic development to the drug producing countries of Bolivia, Colombia, Ecuador and Peru. The (U.S.) Andean Trade Preference Act of 1991 proposes the designation of ten years of duty-free treatment for most goods produced in one or a combination of these four countries. Currently, none of the four ATI countries has received formal designation as a beneficiary.

Animal and Plant Health Inspection Service (APHIS)

(U.S. government) A U.S. government agency attached to the U.S. Department of Agriculture which has the responsibility of inspecting and certifying animals, plants and related products for import to or export from the United States. APHIS is also responsible for the inspection of animal and plant product processing facilities both in the United States and in countries that export to the United States. Address: Animal and Plant Health Inspection Service, 4700 River Road, Riverdale, MD 20782 USA; Tel: [1] (301) 734-7799; Fax: [1] (301) 734-5221 ;http://www.aphis.usda.gov. *See also* phytosanitary inspection certificate.

animal containers

(shipping) The use of air freight as a means of transporting household pets led to the development of special containers designed to provide adequate protection and air circulation. Such containers may be purchased or rented from many air carriers.

annual basis

(accounting) Statistical shifting of data that are for a period less than 12 months in order to estimate the full results for an entire year. To be accurate the processing should consider the effect of the seasonal variation.

antidumping

(customs) Antidumping, as a reference to the system of laws to remedy dumping, is defined as the converse of dumping. *See* dumping; antidumping duties; General Agreement on Tariffs and Trade; Antidumping Act of 1974.

Antidumping Act of 1974

(U.S. law) Legislation designed to prevent the sales of goods at a lower price than exists in the goods' country or origin. The U.S. Treasury Department determines whether imported products are being sold at a "less than fair value" in the United States. Should it be determined that the domestic industry is harmed by the imports, extra duties can be imposed. *See* countervailing duties; dumping.

Antidumping/Countervailing Duty System

(U.S. Customs) A part of the U.S. Customs' Automated Commercial System, containing a case reference database and a statistical reporting system to capture data for International Trade Commission reports on antidumping and countervailing duties assessed and paid.
See dumping; countervailing duties.

antidumping duties

(customs) Duties assessed on imported merchandise of a class or kind that is sold at a price less than the fair market value. Fair market value of merchandise is defined as the price at which it is normally sold in the manufacturer's home market. *See* dumping; countervailing duties.

antidumping petition

(customs) A claim filed on behalf of a U.S. industry alleging that imported merchandise is being sold in the United States at "less than fair value," and that sales of such merchandise is causing or threatening injury to, or retarding the establishment of a U.S. industry. *See* dumping; countervailing duties.

any quantity

(shipping) A cargo rating that applies to an article regardless of weight (i.e., in any quantity).

apparent good order and condition

(shipping) A statement, on a bill of lading or other shipping document, indicating that the shipment is available for shipment or delivery with no apparent damage.

appraiser, customs

(U.S. Customs) An individual authorized by the U.S. Customs Service (Department of Treasury) to examine and determine the value of imported merchandise.

appreciation

(foreign exchange) An increase in the value of the currency of one nation in relation to the currency of another nation.

approval basis

(banking/letters of credit) If documents containing discrepancies are presented to the nominated bank under a letter of credit, the bank can forward the documents to the issuing bank for approval, with the beneficiary's agreement. Because of the risk of loss in transit and delays resulting in interest loss, however, it is recommended that the beneficiary first try to correct the documents; but, if that is not possible, the beneficiary asks the nominated bank to contact the issuing bank for authorization to accept the discrepancies.

approximately
See about.

appurtenance
(law) An accessory that is connected to primary property, and that is adapted to be used with that property, and that generally is intended to be permanently affixed to that property. Appurtenances to a ship, for example, may include cranes attached to the ship for loading and unloading cargo. An easement for access to land is considered an appurtenance to that land. Industrial machinery that is affixed to a factory facility is an appurtenance to the building.

apron
(shipping) The area of an airport where aircraft are parked for loading and unloading of cargo or passengers.

Arab League
A regional alliance established in March 1945 which aims to improve relations among Arab nations. Headquarters are located in Cairo, Egypt. Members include: Algeria, Bahrain, Djibouti, Egypt, Iraq, Jordan, Kuwait, Lebanon, Libya, Mauritania, Morocco, Oman, Qatar, Saudi Arabia, Somalia, Sudan, Syria, Tunisia, United Arab Emirates and Yemen. Address: Arab League, Arab League Building, Tahrir Square, Cairo, Egypt; Tel: [20] (2) 575-0511; Telex: 92111; Fax: [20] (2) 577-5626.

Arab Maghreb Union (AMU)
A regional alliance established in February 1989 with the goal of joining the Gulf Cooperation Council and other states in a common market. AMU members include: Algeria, Morocco, Tunisia, Libya and Mauritania. Address: Union du Maghreb Arabe, c/o Office du President, Tunis, Tunisia.

arbiter
See arbitration.

arbitrage
(banking/finance/foreign exchange) The simultaneous buying and selling (or borrowing and lending) of identical securities, currencies, or commodities in two or more markets in order to take advantage of price differentials. See also hedging.

arbitrage, space
(banking/finance/foreign exchange) The simultaneous buying and selling (or borrowing and lending) of identical securities, currencies, or commodities in two or more locations in order to take advantage of price differentials.

arbitrage, time
(banking/finance/foreign exchange) The simultaneous buying and selling (or borrowing and lending) of identical securities, currencies, or options at different maturity dates in order to take advantage of price differentials.

arbitrageur
(finance) A person systematically engaged in arbitrage dealing.

arbitration
(law) The resolution of a dispute between two parties through a voluntary or contractually required hearing and determination by an impartial third party. The impartial third party is called the arbiter or arbitrator and is chosen by a higher or disinterested body, or by the two parties in dispute. In the United States, the main arbitration body is the American Arbitration Association, 140 West 51st Street, New York, NY 10020 USA; Tel: [1] (212) 484-4000. Internationally, the main arbitration body is the International Chamber of Commerce (ICC), 38 Cours Albert 1[er], 75008 Paris, France; Tel: (1) 49-53-28-28; Fax: (1) 49-53- 29-42. For the U.S. representative of the ICC, contact: U.S. Council for International Business, 1212 Avenue of the Americas, New York, NY 10036 USA; Tel: [1] (212) 354-4480. *See* arbitration clause; American Arbitration Association; International Chamber of Commerce.

arbitration clause
(law) A contract clause included in many international contracts stating for example:
"Any controversy or claim arising out of or relating to this contract, or the breach thereof, shall be settled by arbitration in accordance with the Commercial Arbitration Rules of the American Arbitration Association, and judgment upon the award rendered by the arbitrator(s) may be entered in any court having jurisdiction thereof." *See* arbitration; American Arbitration Association; International Chamber of Commerce.

Arms Control and Disarmament Agency
(U.S.) An independent agency within the U.S. State Department which reviews dual-use license appli-

A

cations from a non-proliferation perspective—anything that could impact on the proliferation of missiles, chemical and biological weapons, and nuclear weapons. The agency was created in 1961, has about 200-to-250 staff and has a fairly substantial and growing technology transfer and export control function. The Director is the principal arms control adviser to the Secretary of State, the President and the (NSC) on: conventional arms transfer; commercial sales of munitions; nuclear, missile, chemical and biological warfare; East-West military munitions issues; Coordinating Committee on Multilateral Export Controls (CoCom); and negotiating Memorandums of Understanding (MOUs) with the third world on strategic trade. *See* United States Department of State.

arrival notice

(shipping) A notice furnished to consignee and shipping broker alerting them to the projected arrival of freight and availability of freight for pickup.

arrivals

(customs) Imported goods which have been placed in a bonded warehouse for which duty has not been paid.

articles of extraordinary value (AEV)

(shipping) Commodities identified as high value items, requiring special care in shipping.

Asian Development Bank (ADB)

The ADB was formed in 1966 to foster economic growth and cooperation in Asia and to help accelerate economic development of members. Address: Asian Development Bank, PO Box 789, Manila Central Post Office, 0980 Manila, Philippines; Tel: [63] (2) 632-4444; Fax: [63] (2) 636-2444; http://www.adb.org.

Asia Pacific Economic Cooperation (APEC)

An informal grouping of Asia Pacific countries that provides a forum for ministerial level discussion of a broad range of economic issues. APEC includes the six ASEAN countries (Brunei, Indonesia, Malaysia, Philippines, Singapore and Thailand), plus: Australia, Canada, China, Hong Kong, Japan, South Korea, Taiwan and the United States. The Secretariat is located in Singapore. Address: 438 Alexandra Road, #14-00, Alexandra Point, Singapore 119958; Tel: [65] 276-1880; Fax: [65] 276-1775; http://www.apecsec.org.sg/.

as is

(law) A term indicating that goods offered for sale are without warranty or guarantee. The purchaser has no recourse to the vendor for quality of the goods.

ask(ed) price; market price

(finance) The price at which a security or commodity is quoted or offered for sale.

assailing thieves

(insurance) A reference to an insurance policy clause covering the forcible taking rather than the clandestine theft or mere pilferage of goods.

assembly service

(shipping) A service under which an airline assembles shipments from many shippers and transports them as one shipment to one receiver.

assessment

(customs) The imposition of antidumping duties on imported merchandise. *See* dumping; antidumping duties; countervailing duties.

assign

(law) To transfer or make over to another party.

assignee

(law) One to whom a right or property is transferred. *See also* assignor; assignment.

assignment

(law/shipping/banking) The transfer of rights, title, interest and benefits of a contract or financial instrument to a third party.

(banking/letters of credit) The beneficiary of a letter of credit is entitled to assign his/her claims to any of the proceeds that he/she may be entitled to, or portions thereof, to a third party. Usually the beneficiary informs the issuing or advising bank that his/her claims or particle claims under the letter of credit were assigned and asks the bank to advise the assignee (third party) that it has acknowledged the assignment. The validity of the assignment is not dependent on bank approval. In contrast, the transfer requires the agreement of the nominated bank. An assignment is possible regardless of whether the letter of credit is transferable. *See* letter of credit.

assignment of proceeds

See assignment.

assignor

(law) One by whom a right or property is transferred. *See also* assignee; assignment.

assist

(U.S. Customs) Any of a number of items that an importer provides directly or indirectly, free of charge, or at a reduced cost, for use in the production or sale of merchandise for export to the United States.

Assists are computed as part of the transaction value upon which duty is charged, when the duty rate is a percentage of the value of the merchandise. Examples of assists are: materials, components, parts and similar items incorporated in the imported merchandise; tools, dies, molds and similar items used in producing the imported merchandise; engineering, development, artwork, design work and plans and sketches that are undertaken outside the United States. Engineering is not treated as an assist if the service or work is: (1) performed by a person domiciled within the United States, (2) performed while that person is acting as an employee or agent of the buyer of the imported merchandise, and (3) incidental to other engineering, development, artwork, design work, or plans or sketches undertaken within the United States. *See* valuation; transaction value; deductive value; computed value.

Association of Southeast Asian Nations (ASEAN)

ASEAN was established in 1967 to promote political, economic and social cooperation among its six member countries: Indonesia, Malaysia, Philippines, Singapore, Thailand and Brunei. Address: Association of Southeast Asian Nations, Jalan Sisingamangaraja, Jakarta-12110, Indonesia; Tel: [62] (21) 726-2991; Fax: [62] (21) 739-8234; http://www.asean.or.id.

assumpsit

(law) An assumption or undertaking by one person (the promisor) to perform an act for, or to pay a sum to, another person (the promisee), often without express agreement from the promisee to perform an act or remit consideration in return. An assumpsit is created, for example, when one person employs another without any written agreement as to compensation. In such an arrangement, the law will imply a duty to pay reasonable wages. An assumpsit also arises when one person receives money that belongs to another, in which event the law implies a duty to remit the sum to the owner.

(a) An **express assumpsit** is one in which the promisor states the assumption in distinct and definite language. A person who agrees to work for another on certain tasks for a specified time has made an express assumpsit.

(b) An **implied assumpsit** is one in which a promise is inferred by law from the conduct of a party or the circumstances of the case. If, without any express statement, a person begins working for

another who knows and does not object to that work, a court may find that an implied assumpsit has arisen.

(c) An **action in assumpsit** is a court action to recover damages for breach of an oral or other informal contract. A seller who delivers goods to a buyer based on an oral contract and who does not receive payment may recover the proceeds in an action in assumpsit.

assurance

(insurance) British term for insurance.

assurance of performance

(law) A declaration intended to induce one contracting party to have full confidence in the other's performance. Pledges and sureties are forms of assurances.

assured

(insurance) The individual, company or entity which is insured.

astern

(shipping) (a) Behind a ship or aircraft, (b) Towards the back of a ship or aircraft, (c) Backwards, as in the movement of a ship.

ATA Carnet

(customs) ATA stands for the combined French and English words "Admission Temporair/Temporary Admission." An ATA Carnet is an international customs document which may be used for the temporary duty-free admission of certain goods into a country in lieu of the usual customs documents required. The carnet serves as a guarantee against the payment of customs duties which may become due on goods temporarily imported and not re-exported. Quota compliance may be required on certain types of merchandise. ATA textile carnets are subject to quota and visa requirements.

The ATA Convention of 1961 authorized the ATA Carnet to replace the ECS ("Echantillons Commerciaux/Commercial Samples") Carnet that was created by a 1956 convention sponsored by the Customs Cooperation Council.

ATA Carnets are issued by National Chambers of Commerce affiliated with the Paris-based International Chamber of Commerce (ICC). These associations guarantee the payment of duties to local customs authorities should goods imported under cover of a foreign-issued carnet not be re-exported.

The issuing and guaranteeing organization in the United States is: U.S. Council, International Chamber of Commerce, 1212 Avenue of the Americas, New York, NY 10036 USA; Tel: [1] (212) 354-4480.

A

Additional information can be obtained from The Roanoke Companies, agents for the U.S. Council for International Business. Address: The Roanoke Companies, 1930 Thoreau Drive, Suite 101, Schaumburg, IL 60173 USA; Tel: [1] (800) ROANOKE, [1] (847) 490-5940.
See also International Chamber of Commerce; carnet.

athwartships
(shipping) Across a vessel from side to side.

at sight
(banking) Terms of a financial instrument which is payable upon presentation or demand. A bill of exchange may be made payable, for example, at sight or after sight, which (respectively) means it is payable upon presentation or demand, or within a particular period after demand is made. *See* bill of exchange.

attachment
(law) Legal process for seizing property before a judgment to secure the payment of damages if awarded. A party who sues for damages for breach of contract may request, for example, that the court issue an order freezing all transfers of specific property owned by the breaching party pending resolution of the dispute.

attendant accompanying shipments
(shipping) Sometimes attendants accompany cargo shipments as when grooms or veterinarians accompany race horses or other live animals. This service requires advance arrangements with a shipping company or airline.

at-the-money
(foreign exchange/finance) A call or put option is at-the-money when the price of the underlying instrument is equivalent or very near to the strike price. *See* option; call option; put option.

attorn
(law) To agree to turn over or transfer money or goods to an individual or legal entity other than the party who was to originally receive them. A company that has bought out another legal entity may seek an attornment from a supplier who had an outstanding contract with the former entity, and if the supplier attorns, the company can obtain goods on the same terms as were agreed to with the former entity.

attorney-in-fact
(law) A person authorized to transact business generally or to perform a designated task of a nonlegal nature on behalf of another individual or legal entity. An attorney-in-fact is a type of agent. In many countries, this authority must be conferred by a written power of attorney. If a company buys goods from a foreign firm, for example, and agrees to place sufficient funds for the purchase in an escrow account, the buyer may authorize an attorney-in-fact in that foreign country to disburse the escrow funds on receiving verification from the buyer that the goods are satisfactory. A business enterprise may also authorize an attorney-in-fact to testify to facts on the company's behalf in arbitration or legal proceedings held in a foreign country. *See* agent; agency; power of attorney.

audit
(general) A formal examination of records or documents—usually financial documents.

(shipping) The formal examination of freight bills to determine their accuracy.

Australia Group (AG)
An informal forum through which 20 industrialized nations cooperate to curb proliferation of chemical and biological weapons through a supply approach. The AG's first meeting, held at the Australian Embassy in Paris in June 1986, was attended by Australia, Canada, Japan, New Zealand, the United States, and the ten member nations of the European Community. Membership has expanded to include Norway, Portugal, Spain, Switzerland, Austria, and representatives of the European Commission, the European Community's executive arm.

austral
The currency of Argentina. 1A=100 centavos.

authentication
(law) The act of certifying that a written document is genuine, credible, and reliable. An authentication is performed by an authorized person who attests that the document is in proper legal form and is executed by a person identified as having authority to do so. In many countries, persons authorized to authenticate documents include consulate officials, notaries public, and judicial officers.

Automated Broker Interface (ABI)
(U.S. Customs) ABI, a part of U.S. Customs' Automated Commercial System, permits transmission of data pertaining to merchandise being imported into the U.S. directly to U.S. Customs. Qualified participants include customs brokers, importers, carriers, port authorities, and independent data processing companies referred to as service centers. To use ABI, send a letter of intent to the District Director of Customs or to your nearest district Custom's Office. *See* Automated Commercial System.

Automated Clearinghouse (ACH)
(U.S. Customs) ACH is a feature of the Automated Broker Interface which is a part of Customs' Automated Commercial System. The ACH combines elements of bank lock box arrangements with electronic funds transfer services to replace cash or check for payment of estimated duties, taxes, and fees on imported merchandise. *See* Automated Commercial System.

Automated Commercial System
(U.S. Customs) The ACS is a joint public-private sector computerized data processing and telecommunications system linking customhouses, members of the import trade community, and other government agencies with the Customs computer. Trade users file import data electronically, receive needed information on cargo status, and query Customs files to prepare submissions. Duties, taxes, and fees may be paid by electronic statement, through a Treasury-approved clearinghouse bank. ACS contains the import data used by Census to prepare U.S. foreign trade statistics. ACS began operating in February 1984 and includes: (1) the Automated Broker Interface, (2) the Census Interface System, (3) the Automated Manifest Systems, (4) the Bond System, (5) the In-Bond System, (6) the Cargo Selectivity System, (7) the Line Release System, (8) the Collections System, (9) the Security System, (10) the Quota System, (11) the Entry Summary Selectivity System, (12) the Entry Summary System, (13) the Automated Information Exchange, (14) the Anti-dumping/Countervailing Duty System, (15) the Firms system, (16) the Liquidation System, (17) the Drawback System, (18) the Fines, Penalties, and Forfeitures System, and (19) the Protest System. *See* United States Customs Service.

Automated Information Exchange
(U.S. Customs) AIES, a part of Customs' Automated Commercial System, allows for exchange of classification and value information between field units and headquarters.
See Automated Commercial System.

Automated Manifest Systems (AMS)
(U.S. Customs) AMS, a part of Customs' Automated Commercial System (ACS), controls imported merchandise from the time a carrier's cargo manifest is electronically transmitted to Customs until control is relinquished to another segment of the ACS. *See* Automated Commercial System.

Auto Parts Advisory Committee
(U.S.) Established by an amendment to the Trade Act to set up an advisory committee to the U.S. Department of Commerce for dealing with U.S.-Japan trade issues involving the auto parts industry. Address: Auto Parts Advisory Committee, Chairman, Robert Cole, V.P. of Governmental Affairs, Kaifer Chemical Corporation, 655 15th Street, NW Suite 200, Washington, DC 2005; Tel: [1] (202) 638-2020.

availability
(banking/letters of credit) In letters of credit, refers to the availability of documents in exchange for payment of the amount stated in the letter of credit. Availability options are:

(1) By **sight payment**: payment on receipt of the documents by the issuing bank or the bank nominated in the letter of credit.

(2) By **deferred payment**: payment after a period specified in the letter of credit, often calculated as number of days after the date of presentation of the documents or after the shipping date.

(3) By **acceptance**: acceptance of a draft (to be presented together with other documents) by the issuing bank or by the bank nominated in the letter of credit, and the payment thereof at maturity.

(4) By **negotiation**: meaning the giving of value by the nominated bank to the beneficiary for the documents presented, subject to receipt of cover from the issuing bank.

See letter of credit; bill of exchange; negotiation.

aval
(banking) Payment of a bill of exchange, which is the responsibility of the drawee, can be either completely or partially guaranteed via an aval (joint and several guarantee), where the guarantor places his/her signature on the draft either alone or with corresponding explanation "per aval" or "as guarantor." If other information is lacking, the guarantor commits him/herself on behalf of the issuer. *See* bill of exchange.

average
(insurance) A loss to a shipment of goods that is less than a total loss. It comes from the French word avarie, which means "damage to ship or cargo," (and ultimately from the Arabic word awarijah, which means "merchandise damaged by sea water").

(a) A **particular average** is an insurance loss that affects specific interests only.

(b) A **general average** is an insurance loss that affects all cargo interests on board the vessel as well as the ship herself.

See also particular average; general average; with average; free of particular average; deductible average.

avoidance of contract

(law) The legal cancellation of a contract because an event occurs that makes performance of the contract terms impossible or inequitable and that releases the parties from their obligations. *See* commercial frustration; commercial impracticability; force majeure.

avoirdupois

(measure) (a) French for "having weight." (b) A system of weight measurement based on the pound of 16 ounces and the ounce of 16 drams. Refer to Weights and Measures in the Appendix.

Background Notes

A series of publications by the U.S. State Department providing an overview of a country's history, people, political conditions, economy, and foreign relations. Also includes map of country and travel notes. Available from: Superintendent of Documents, U.S. Government Printing Office, Washington, DC 20402; P.O. Box 371954, Pittsburgh PA 15250-7954 USA; http://www.access.gpo.gov/su_docs. To receive catalog, contact U.S. Fax Watch: [1] (202) 512-1716.

back haul

(shipping) To haul a shipment back over part of a route which it has traveled.

back order

That portion of an order that cannot be delivered at the scheduled time, but will be delivered at a later date when available. Also, to restock requested out-of-stock items.

back-to-back borrowing

(banking) The process whereby a bank brings together a borrower and a lender so that they agree on a loan contract.

back-to-back letter of credit

(banking) A new letter of credit opened in favor of another beneficiary on the basis of an already existing, non-transferable letter of credit. For example, a British merchant agrees to buy cotton in Egypt for sale to a Belgian shirtmaker. The Belgian establishes a non-transferable letter of credit for payment to the British merchant who then uses the strength of the letter of credit as a security with his bank for opening a letter of credit to finance payment to the Egyptian. *See* letter of credit.

back-to-back loan

(banking) Operations whereby a loan is made in one currency in one country against a loan in another currency in another country (e.g., a U.S. dollar loan in the U.S. against a pounds sterling loan in the U.K.).

bad faith

(law) The intent to mislead or deceive (mala fides). It does not include misleading by an honest, inadvertent or uncalled-for misstatement.

bagged cargo

(shipping) Goods shipped in sacks.

baht

The currency of Thailand. 1B=100 satangs.

bailment

(law) A delivery of goods or personal property by one person (the bailor) to another (the bailee) on an express or implied contract and for a particular purpose related to the goods while in possession of the bailee, who has a duty to redeliver them to the bailor or otherwise dispose of them in accordance with the bailor's instructions once the purpose has been accomplished. A bailment arises, for example, when a seller delivers goods to a shipping company with instructions to transport them to a buyer at a certain destination.

(a) A **bailment for hire** is a bailment contract in which the bailor agrees to compensate the bailee. A shipping contract is usually a bailment for hire because the shipper transports the goods for a fee.

(b) A **special bailment** is one in which the law imposes greater duties and liabilities on the bailee than are ordinarily imposed on other bailees. Common carriers, for example, are special bailees, because the law imposes extra duties of due care with regard to the property and persons transported than are required of private carriers. *See* carrier.

balanced economy

(economics) A condition of national finances in which imports and exports are equal.

balance of payments

(economics) A statement identifying all the economic and financial transactions between companies, banks, private households and public authorities of one nation with those of other nations of the world over a specific time period. A transaction is defined as the transfer of ownership of something that has an economic value measurable in monetary terms from residents of one country to residents of another.

The transfer may involve: (1) goods, which consist of tangible and visible commodities or products; (2) services, which consist of intangible economic outputs, which usually must be produced, transferred, and consumed at the same time and in the same place; (3) income on investments; and (4) financial claims on, and liabilities to, the rest of the world, including changes in a country's reserve assets held by the central monetary authorities. A transaction may also involve a gift, which is the provision by one party of something of economic

value to another party without something of economic value being received in return.

International transactions are recorded in the balance of payments on the basis of the double-entry principle used in business accounting, in which each transaction gives rise to two offsetting entries of equal value so that, in principle, the resulting credit and debit entries always balance. Transactions are generally valued at market prices and are, to the extent possible, recorded when a change of ownership occurs.

These transactions are divided into two broad groups: current account and capital account. The **current account** includes exports and imports of goods, services (including investment income) and unilateral transfers. The **capital account** includes financial flows related to international direct investment, investment in government and private securities, international bank transactions and changes in official gold holdings and foreign exchange reserves.

(IMF) The International Monetary Fund (IMF), which strives for international comparability, defines the balance of payments as "a statistical statement for a given period showing (1) transactions in goods, services and income between an economy and the rest of the world, (2) changes of ownership and other changes in that economy's monetary gold, special drawing rights (SDRs) and claims on and liabilities to the rest of the world, and (3) unrequited transfers and counterpart entries that are needed to balance, in the accounting sense, any entries for the foregoing transactions and changes which are not mutually offsetting."

(U.S.) The six balances that are currently published quarterly concerning the U.S. balance of payments are:

(1) The **balance on merchandise trade**, which measures the net transfer of merchandise exports and imports (which differs in some ways from the trade balance published monthly by the Bureau of the Census);

(2) The **balance on services**, which measures the net transfer of services, such as travel, other transportation, and business, professional, and other technical services (this balance was redefined in 1990 to exclude investment income);

(3) The **balance on investment income**, which measures the net transfer income on direct and portfolio investments;

(4) The **balance on goods, services and income**, which measures the net transfer of merchandise plus services and income on direct and

B

portfolio investment (this balance is equivalent to the pre-1990 balance on goods and services; it is also conceptually comparable to net exports of goods and services included in GNP);
(5) The **balance on unilateral transfers** (net), which measures the net value of gifts, contributions, government grants to foreign countries and other unrequited transfers;
(6) The **balance on current account** (widely used for analysis and forecasting) which measures transactions in goods, services, income and unilateral transfers between residents and nonresidents.

balance of trade
(economics) The difference between a country's imports and exports over a set period. (a) A **balance of trade deficit** is when a country imports more than it exports. (b) A **balance of trade surplus** is when a country exports more than it imports.

balance on ...
See balance of payments.

balboa
The currency of Panama. 1B=100 centesimos.

bale
(shipping) A large bundle of compressed, bound and usually wrapped goods, such as cotton.

bale cargo
(shipping) Bulky cargo shipped in bales, usually of burlap.

ballast
(shipping) Heavy material strategically placed on a ship to improve its trim or stability. In most vessels water is used as ballast.

bandwidth
(Internet) The volume of data that can be transmitted through a given computer connection measured in bits-per-second. An increase in bandwidth means that more data can be transferred in the same or less time. Standard computer modems operate at a bandwidth between 28.8 and 56 k (kilobits per second. A DSL (Digital Subscriber Line) operates at a bandwidth of between 256 to 300 k.

bank acceptance
(banking) A bill of exchange drawn on or accepted by a bank to pay specific bills for one of its customers when the bill become due. Depending on the bank's creditworthiness, the acceptance becomes a financial instrument which can be discounted for immediate payment. *See* bill of exchange.

bank affiliate export trading company
(U.S.) An export trading company partially or wholly owned by a banking institution as provided under the U.S. Export Trading Company Act. *See* export trading company; Export Trading Company Act.

bank draft
(banking) A check drawn by one bank against funds deposited to its account in another bank.

banker's bank
(banking) A bank that is established by mutual consent by independent and unaffiliated banks to provide a clearinghouse for financial transactions.

banker's draft
(banking) A draft payable on demand and drawn by, or on behalf of, a bank upon itself. A banker's draft is considered cash and cannot be returned unpaid.

Bank for International Settlements (BIS)
(banking) Established in 1930, this organization was designed to foster cooperation among world central banks, to seek opportunities for development of financial activity among governments and to serve as an agent involving the transfer of payments. Address: Bank for International Settlements, Centralbahnplatz 2, CH-4002 Basel, Switzerland; Tel: [41] (61) 280-8080; Fax: [41] (61) 280-9100; http://www.bis.org.

bank guarantee
(banking) Unilateral contract between a bank as guarantor and a beneficiary as warrantee in which the bank commits itself to pay a certain sum if a third party fails to perform or if any other specified event resulting in a default fails to take place. *See* letter of credit.

bank holding company
(banking) Any company which directly or indirectly owns or controls, with power to vote, more than five percent of voting shares of each of one or more other banks.

bank holiday
(banking) A day on which banks are closed.

bank note
(banking) Paper issued by the central bank, redeemable as money and considered to be full legal tender.

bank note rate
(banking/foreign exchange) Exchange rate used in bank note dealing.

bank release
(banking) A document issued by a bank, after it has been paid or given an acceptance, giving authority to a person to take delivery of goods.

bankruptcy
(law) (a) The status of an individual or legal entity who does not have the financial resources needed to pay debts as they come due. (b) The legal proceedings for declaring bankruptcy and discharging or restructuring debts. Laws related to these proceedings vary greatly among different countries. In the United States, bankruptcy proceedings are brought before bankruptcy courts. In some countries, a bankruptcy is dealt with through administrative agencies and a bankrupt person must first attempt to make a composition with creditors. *See* composition with creditors.

Bank Wire Service
(banking) A private wire service linking over 250 banks through the facilities of Western Union. This service serves as a message system for transfer of funds and information for the member banks.

banque d'affaires
(banking) A French bank involved in long-term financing and in the ownership of companies, usually industrial firms. Synonymous with merchant bank.

bareboat charter
(shipping) A charter of a vessel where the charter party has the right to use his own master and crew on the vessel.

barge
(shipping) A flat bottomed inland cargo vessel with or without propulsion usually used on rivers and canals.

barratry
(shipping) The willful misconduct of ship's master or crew including theft, intentional casting away of vessel, or any breach of trust with dishonest intent.

barter
The direct exchange of goods for other goods without the use of money as a medium of exchange and without the involvement of a third party. *See also* countertrade.

Basel Convention
The Basel Convention restricts trade in hazardous waste, some non-hazardous wastes, solid wastes and incinerator ash. It was adopted in 1989 by a United Nations-sponsored conference of 116 nations in Basel, Switzerland. Twenty nations must ratify the treaty before it goes into effect.

basing point
(shipping) A point (location) which is used in constructing through rates between other points.

basing rate
(shipping) A rate used only for the purpose of constructing other rates.

basket of currencies
(banking/foreign exchange) A means of establishing value for a composite unit consisting of the currencies of designated nations. Each currency is represented in proportion to its value in relation to the total. The European Currency Unit, for example, is a weighted average of the currencies of the European Community member nations, used as a unit of value in transactions among businesses in the member countries. *See* European Currency Unit.

battens
(shipping) The protruding fixtures of the inside walls of a vessel's hold which keep cargo away from the walls of the vessel, or to fasten the cargo to the walls of the vessel.

baud
(Internet) The measurement of the transmission speed of a computer modem expressed in bits per second.

bearer
(general) The person in possession.
(banking/finance/law/shipping) A person who possesses a bearer document and who is entitled to payment of funds or transfer of title to property on presentation of the document to the payee or transferor. A buyer, for example, who presents bearer documents of title (such as a bill of lading) to a shipper that transported the goods is entitled to receive the shipment. A seller who presents to a bank a negotiable instrument, such as a check, that is payable to the bearer is entitled to payment of the funds. *See* bearer document; endorsement.

bearer document
(banking/finance/law/shipping) A negotiable instrument, commercial paper, document of title, or security that is issued payable or transferable on demand to the individual who holds the instrument, or one that is endorsed in blank. A bearer document authorizes the payment of funds or the transfer of property to the bearer when the bearer presents the document to the person, such as a bank or a shipper, that is holding the funds or property. *See* bearer; endorsement.

bearer instrument
See bearer document.

B

beggar-thy-neighbor policy

(economics) A course of action through which a country tries to reduce unemployment and increase domestic output by raising tariffs and instituting non-tariff barriers that impede imports, or by accomplishing the same objective through competitive devaluation. Countries that pursued such policies in the early 1930's found that other countries retaliated by raising their own barriers against imports, which, by reducing export markets, tended to worsen the economic difficulties that precipitated the initial protectionist action. The Smoot-Hawley Tariff Act of 1930 is often cited as a conspicuous example of this approach.

Belgium, Netherlands, Luxembourg Economic Union (BENELUX)

A cooperative organization formed by Belgium, The Netherlands and Luxembourg to encourage economic activity among the three nations. It has eight committees addressing such areas as economic relations, agriculture, commerce, industry, customs and social affairs. Address: BENELUX, 39 rue de la Régence, 1000 Brussels, Belgium; Tel: [32] (2) 519-38-11; Fax: [32] (2) 513-42-06.

belly pits or holds

(shipping) Compartments located beneath the cabin of an aircraft and used for the carriage of cargo and passenger baggage.

beneficiary

(banking/letter of credit) The individual or company in whose favor a letter of credit is opened.

(insurance) The person or legal entity named to receive the proceeds or benefits of an insurance policy.

BENELUX

See Belgium, Netherlands, Luxembourg Economic Union.

Berne Convention for the Protection of Literary and Artistic Works

Formal name: The International Union for the Protection of Literary and Artistic Works. Also called the Berne Union. A part of the World Intellectual Property Organization. An international agreement that was concluded in Berne, Switzerland, by representatives of participating countries which provides copyright, patent, trademark and other intellectual property protection to countries that are signatories to the convention. *See* World Intellectual Property Organization; copyright; patent; trademark; service mark.

berth

(shipping) The place beside a wharf, pier or quay where a vessel is secured and can be loaded or unloaded of its cargo.

Besloten Vennootschap met Beperkte Aansprakelijkheid (B.V.B.A.)

(Belgium/Netherlands) Designation for a private limited liability corporation with limited liability to shareholders.

bid bond

Guarantee established in connection with international tenders. Guarantees fulfillment of the offer, i.e. that the contract will be signed if awarded. *See* bond; tender.

bilateral investment treaty (BIT)

(foreign investment) A treaty between two countries with the goals of ensuring investments abroad of national or most favored nation treatment; prohibiting the imposition of performance requirements; and allowing the investor to engage top management in a foreign country without regard to nationality. BITs ensure the right to make investment-related transfers and guarantee that expropriation takes place only in accordance with accepted international law. BITs also guarantee access by an investing party to impartial and binding international arbitration for dispute settlement.

bilateral steel agreements

(trade agreement) Agreements between governments to reduce or eliminate state intervention—that is, domestic subsidies and market barriers, in the production and sale of steel. The U.S. has negotiated ten BSAs with major steel trading partners.

bilateral trade

(economics) The commerce between two countries.

bilateral trade agreement

A formal or informal agreement involving commerce between two countries. Such agreements sometimes list the quantities of specific goods that may be exchanged between participating countries within a given period.

bill

(law) (a) A written statement of contract terms. (b) A listing of items in a transaction or demand. (c) A promissory obligation for the payment of money. (d) An account for goods sold, services, rendered, or work completed.
See bill of . . .; bill of lading.

billed weight
(shipping) The weight shown in a waybill or freight bill.

billing third party
(shipping) The invoicing of transportation charges to other than shipper or consignee.

bill of adventure
(law) A written certificate used if goods are shipped under the name of a merchant, shipmaster, or shipowner. It certifies that the property and risk in the goods belong to a person other than the shipper and that the shipper is accountable to that other person for only the proceeds.

bill of credit
(law) A written statement, commonly used by business travelers, given by one individual or legal entity to another, to authorize the recipient to receive or collect money from a foreign correspondent, such as a bank in the recipient's country. *See also* letter of credit.

bill of exchange
(banking) An unconditional order in writing, signed by a person (drawer) such as a buyer, and addressed to another person (drawee), typically a bank, ordering the drawee to pay a stated sum of money to yet another person (payee), often a seller, on demand or at a fixed or determinable future time.

The most common versions of a bill of exchange are:

(a) A **draft**, wherein the drawer instructs the drawee to pay a certain amount to a named person, usually in payment for the transfer of goods or services. **Sight drafts** are payable when presented. **Time drafts** (also called usance drafts) are payable at a future fixed (specific) date or determinable (30, 60, 90 days etc.) date. Time drafts are used as a financing tool (as with Documents against Acceptance, D/A terms) to give the buyer time to pay for his purchase.

(b) A **promissory note**, wherein the issuer promises to pay a certain amount.

bill of health
(general) A certificate issued by port or customs authorities attesting to the health of the crew and passengers of a vessel or airplane upon arrival or departure from the port.

(a) A **clean bill of health** is issued by authorities when no contagious disease(s) has been found,

(b) A **suspected bill of health** is issued when no contagious disease(s) has been found, but authorities fear that one may develop, and

(c) A **foul bill of health** is issued when a contagious disease has been found.

In the cases of issuance of a suspected bill of health or a foul bill of health, the vessel, airplane, or its passengers must enter a quarantine. *See* quarantine.

bill of lading
(shipping) A document issued by a carrier to a shipper, signed by the captain, agent, or owner of a vessel, furnishing written evidence regarding receipt of the goods (cargo), the conditions on which transportation is made (contract of carriage), and the engagement to deliver goods at the prescribed port of destination to the lawful holder of the bill of lading.

A bill of lading is, therefore, both a receipt for merchandise and a contract to deliver it as freight. There are a number of different types of bills of lading.

(a) A **straight bill of lading** indicates that the shipper will deliver the goods to the consignee. The document itself does not give title to the goods (non-negotiable). The consignee need only identify himself to claim the goods. A straight bill of lading is often used when payment for the goods has been made in advance.

(b) A **shipper's order bill of lading** is a title document to the goods, issued "to the order of" a party, usually the shipper, whose endorsement is required to effect its negotiation. Because it is negotiable, a shipper's order bill of lading can be bought, sold, or traded while goods are in transit and is commonly used for letter-of-credit transactions. The buyer usually needs the original or a copy as proof of ownership to take possession of the goods.

(c) An **air waybill** is a form of bill of lading used for the air transport of goods and is not negotiable. *See* air waybill for a fuller explanation.

(d) A **clean bill of lading** is a bill of lading where the carrier has noted that the merchandise has been received in apparent good condition (no apparent damage, loss, etc.) and which does not bear such notations as "Shipper's Load and Count," etc.

(e) A **claused bill of lading** is a bill of lading which contains notations which specify deficient condition(s) of the goods and/or packaging.

bill of parcels
(law) A statement that lists the descriptions and prices of goods in a parcel and that is sent to the buyer with the goods. This bill is often referred to as a packing slip.

B

bill of sale
(law) A written document by which an individual or legal entity assigns or transfers title to goods to another.

bill of sight
(U.S. Customs) A document used by U.S. Customs that permits a consignee of goods to see them before paying duties.

bill-to party
(shipping) Refers to the party designated on a bill of lading as the one responsible for payment of the freight charges; this can be the shipper, freight forwarder, consignee, or another person.

binder
(insurance) A document certifying temporary insurance coverage. A binder is issued by an insurance company or its agent pending the issuance of an insurance policy.

binding decisions
(U.S. Customs) A binding tariff classification ruling (decision), which can be relied upon for placing or accepting orders or for making other business determinations. May be obtained by writing to a local Customs district director or to the Area Director of Customs, New York Seaport, 6 World Trade Center, New York, NY 10048. The rulings will be binding at all ports of entry unless revoked by the Customs Service's Office of Regulations and Rulings. Note that while the port and district offices of Customs are, for many purposes, your best sources of information, informal information obtained on tariff classification is not binding.

biological agents
A biologically active material. Several classes of biological agents have been identified according to their degree of pathogenic hazard, and are unilaterally controlled by various governments. In the United States applications to export certain biological agents are referred to the Department of State and the intelligence community on a case-by-case basis.

biomedical materials
(shipping) Items that can cause human disease (infectious/etiological agent). (UN CLASS 6) Examples are live virus vaccines and etiologic agents. Hazards/precautions are: may be ignited if carrier is flammable; contact may cause infection/disease; and damage to outer container may not affect inner container.

birr
The currency of Ethiopia. 1Br (or 1E$)=100 cents.

black market
Buying or selling of products and commodities, or engaging in exchange of foreign currencies in violation of government restrictions.

blank endorsement
(law/banking/shipping) The signature or endorsement of a person or firm on any negotiable instrument (such as a check, draft or bill of lading), usually on the reverse of the document, without designating another person to whom the endorsement is made. The document therefore becomes bearer paper. In shipping, for example, the holder of a blank endorsed bill of lading can take possession of the merchandise. *See* endorsement; bearer document.

blanket rate
(shipping) (a) A rate applicable from and/or to a group of points; (b) A special single rate applicable to different articles in a single shipment.

blockade
The act of preventing commercial exchange with a country or port, usually during wartime, by physically preventing carriers from entering a specific port or nation. *See also* embargo.

blocking or bracing
(shipping) Wood or metal supports to keep shipments in place in or on containers.

board foot (fbm, BF, bd ft)
(measurement) A unit of measurement used for lumber. One board foot is 12 inches by 12 inches by 1 inch, or one square foot of lumber one inch thick.

bolivar
The currency of Venezuela. 1B=100 centimos.

boliviano
The currency of Bolivia. 1$b=100 centavos.

bona fide
(law) In or with good faith, honesty and sincerity. A bona fide purchaser, for example, is one who buys goods for value and without knowledge of fraud or unfair dealing in the transaction. Knowledge of fraud or unfair dealing may be implied if the facts are such that the purchaser should have reasonably known that the transaction involved deceit, such as when goods that are susceptible to copyright piracy are provided without product documentation as to their origin.

bond
(general) An interest-bearing certificate of debt, usually issued in series, by which the issuer obli-

gates itself to pay the principal amount at a specified time and to pay interest periodically,

(banking) An instrument used as proof of a debt.

(finance) The obligation to answer for the debt of another person.

(insurance) A contract between a principal and a surety (insurance company or their agent) which is obtained to insure performance of an obligation (often imposed by law or regulation).

(U.S. Customs) A bond required by the federal government in connection with the payment of duties or to produce documentation. U.S. Customs entries must be accompanied by evidence that a surety bond is posted with Customs to cover any potential duties, taxes and penalties which may accrue. Bonds may be secured through a resident U.S. surety company, but may also be posted in the form of United States money or certain United States government obligations. In the event that a customs broker is employed for the purpose of making entry, the broker may permit the use of his or her bond to provide the required coverage. *See* bond system; surety; in bond.

bonded

(U.S. Customs) Goods stored under supervision of customs until the import duties are paid or the goods are exported.

bonded exchange

(foreign exchange) Foreign exchange which cannot be freely converted into other currencies. *See* foreign exchange.

bonded stores

(customs) A place (usually a secured storeroom) on a vessel or airplane where non-customs entered goods are placed under seal until the vessel leaves the port or country.

bonded terminal

(customs) An airline terminal approved by the U.S. Treasury Department for storage of goods until Customs duties are paid or the goods are otherwise properly released.

bonded warehouse

(U.S. Customs) A warehouse owned by persons approved by the Treasury Department, and under bond or guarantee for the strict observance of the revenue laws of the United States; utilized for storing goods until duties are paid or goods are otherwise properly released. Payment of customs duties is deferred until the goods enter the Customs Territory of the United States. The goods are not subject to duties if reshipped to foreign points. *See* bond; in bond.

bond of indemnity

(shipping) An agreement made with a carrier relieving it from liability for any action on its part for which it would otherwise be liable.

bond system

(U.S. Customs) A part of the U.S. Customs' Automated Commercial System, provides information on bond coverage. A Customs bond is a contract between a principal, usually an importer, and a surety which is obtained to insure performance of an obligation imposed by law or regulation. The bond covers potential loss of duties, taxes, and penalties for specific types of transactions. Customs is the contract beneficiary. *See* Automated Commercial System.

booking

(shipping) The act of recording arrangements for the movement of goods by vessel.

bordereau

(insurance) (a) A method of reporting shipments to an insurance company under an open insurance policy. (b) An insurance form, similar to a declaration, which provides for insurance coverage of multiple shipments within a prescribed reporting period, usually a month.

This form calls for the name of the vessel and sailing date, points of shipment and destination, nature of commodity, the amount of insurance desired, and the number of the open policy under which the shipment is made. The bordereau form is prepared by the assured and is forwarded within a prescribed reporting period, usually monthly. The forms are forwarded to the insurance agent or broker for transmission to the insurance company. The premium is billed monthly in accordance with the schedule of rates provided by the policy.

The bordereau is generally not used in cases where evidence of insurance must be supplied to a customer, to banks or to other third parties in order to permit collection of claims abroad. This calls for a special marine policy, occasionally referred to as a certificate. The bordereau, therefore, is mainly used for import shipments, not export shipments.

See special marine policy. *See also* declaration.

bounties or grants

Payments by governments to producers of goods, often to strengthen their competitive position.

bow

(shipping) The front of a vessel.

box 30 **Dictionary of**

B

box

(shipping) Colloquial term referring to a trailer, semi-trailer or container.

box car

(shipping) A closed freight car.

boycott

A refusal to deal commercially or otherwise with a person, firm or country.

breakage

(a) A monetary allowance or credit that a manufacturer agrees to give a buyer to compensate for damage caused to goods during transit or storage. (b) A fractional amount due as part of a payment to a party, such as pennies that result from a computation of interest on a loan or deposit.

breakbulk

(shipping) To unload and distribute a portion or all of the contents of a consolidated shipment for delivery or reconsignment.

breakbulk cargo

(shipping) Cargo which is shipped as a unit but which is not containerized. Examples are any unitized cargo placed on pallets, or in boxes.

breakbulk vessel

(shipping) A general cargo vessel designed to efficiently handle breakbulk loads. Breakbulk cargo vessels are usually self-sustaining in that they have their own loading and unloading machinery.

break-even point

(banking/foreign exchange) The price of a financial instrument at which the option buyer recovers the premium, meaning that he makes neither a loss nor a gain. In the case of a call option, the break-even point is the exercise price plus the premium, and in the case of a put option, the exercise price minus the premium. *See* option; call option; put option.

Bretton-Woods Agreement of 1944

(banking/foreign exchange) Articles of agreement adopted by the international monetary conference of 44 nations which met at Bretton Woods, New Hampshire. The International Monetary Fund and the International Bank for Reconstruction and Development were created as a result of this agreement. The Fund's major responsibility is to maintain orderly currency practices in international trade, while the Bank's function is to facilitate extension of long-term investments for productive purposes. Periodic meetings are held at Bretton Woods to amend the original agreement.

See Bretton-Woods System; International Monetary Fund; International Bank for Reconstruction and Development.

Bretton-Woods System

(banking/foreign exchange) A system of fixed exchange rates with fluctuation grids, in which every member of the International Monetary Fund (IMF) sets a specific parity for its currency relative to gold or the dollar, and undertaking to keep fluctuations within ±1% of parity by central bank market interventions.

See Bretton-Woods Agreement of 1944; International Monetary Fund; International Bank for Reconstruction and Development.

bribe

A payment resulting in the payer's receiving some right, benefit, or preference to which he has no legal right and which he would not have obtained except with the payment of the money. A bribe is a criminal offense in most countries, but may not be a criminal offense in a home country if committed in a foreign country. *See* Foreign Corrupt Practices Act.

British High Commission (BHC)

(diplomacy) The term British High Commission (BHC, or High Commission, HC, or Her Majesty's High Commission, HMHC) is used in lieu of "embassy" in Commonwealth countries.

broken cross rates; triangular arbitrage

(banking/foreign exchange) A forward foreign exchange arrangement which is not for a standard maturity period. Standard periods are: 1 week; 2 weeks; 1, 2, 3, 6 and 12 months.

(banking/foreign exchange) In foreign exchange, disparity among three or more rates; e.g., if DM 1=30 cents and FF 1.5 while FF 1=22 cents, a Deutschmark will bring 30 cents if converted directly but 33 cents if converted first into francs and then into dollars.

broker

An individual or firm that acts as an intermediary, often between a buyer and seller, usually for a commission. Often an agent.
(a) **Customs broker**—An individual or firm licensed to enter and clear goods through Customs for another individual or firm. *See* customs broker.
(b) **Insurance broker**—An individual or firm which acts as an intermediary between an insurance company and the insured. *See* insurance broker.

brokerage license, domestic

(U.S.) Authority granted by the U.S. Interstate Commerce Commission to persons to engage in the business of arranging for transportation of persons or property in interstate commerce.

browser
(Internet) A computer program used to access and search the Internet (World Wide Web).

Brussels Tariff Nomenclature
(customs) A once widely used international tariff classification system which preceded the Customs Cooperation Council Nomenclature (CCCN) and the Harmonized System Nomenclature (HS). *See* Harmonized Tariff Schedule; Customs Cooperation Council Nomenclature.

bulk cargo
(shipping) Cargo that consists entirely of one commodity and is usually shipped without packaging. Examples of bulk cargo are grain, ore and oil.

bulk carrier
(shipping) A vessel specifically designed to transport bulk cargo. There are two types of bulk carriers: those designed to transport dry bulk cargo such as grain or ore, and those designed to transport liquid bulk cargo such as oil.

bulk container
(shipping) An ocean or air freigh container designed to ship dry bulk cargo such as malt. Bulk fluid cargo such as chemicals and fruit juices are shipped in tank containers. Bulk cargo such as ore, grain, and crude oil are generally shipped in specialized bulk cargo ships rather than in containers.

bulk freight
(shipping) Freight not in packages or containers. For example: grain, ore, timber.

bulkhead
(shipping) (a) A partition separating one part of a ship between decks from another. (b) A structure to resist the pressure of earth or water.

bulk liquids
(shipping) Liquid cargo shipped in intermodal tank containers.

bulk sale or transfer
(law) A transfer of substantially all of the inventory or property of an enterprise to one individual or legal entity in a single transaction not in the ordinary course of the business of the enterprise. In some countries, bulk sales and transfers are regulated by law in an effort to reduce the potential for defrauding creditors through this type of transaction.

bulk solids
(shipping) Dry cargo shipped loose in containers.

Bundesbank
(banking) Established in 1875, the central bank of Germany, located in Frankfurt.

bunker
(shipping) A compartment on a ship for storage of fuel.

bunker adjustment factor (BAF)
(shipping) An adjustment in shipping charges to offset price fluctuations in the cost of bunker fuel.

bunker charge
See bunker adjustment factor.

bunker fuel
(shipping) The fuel used to power a ship.

Bureau of Alcohol, Tobacco and Firearms (ATF)
(U.S. government) An agency of the U.S. Department of Treasury, the ATF regulates the alcohol, firearms and explosives industry, ensures the collection of federal taxes imposed on alcohol and tobacco, investigates violations of federal firearms, explosives and tobacco laws. Address: Bureau of Alcohol, Tobacco and Firearms, Department of the Treasury, 650 Massachusetts Ave. NW, Washington, DC 20226 USA; Tel: [1] (202) 927-7777; http://www.atf.treas.gov.

Bureau of Customs
See United States Customs Service.

Bureau of Export Administration (BEX)
(U.S. government) Responsible for control of exports for reasons of national security, foreign policy and short supply. Licenses on controlled exports are issued and seminars on U.S. export regulations are held domestically and overseas. Address: Bureau of Export Administration, Office of Public Affairs, Room 3897, 14th Street and Constitution Avenue NW, Washington, DC 20226 USA; Tel: [1] (202) 482-2721; http://www.bxa.doc.gov.

Bureau of International Expositions
An international organization established by the Paris Convention of 1928 to regulate the conduct and scheduling of international expositions in which foreign nations are officially invited to participate. The BIE divides international expositions into different categories and types and requires each member nation to observe specified minimum time intervals in scheduling each of these categories and types of operations. Under BIE rules, member nations may not ordinarily participate in an international exposition unless the exposition has been approved by the BIE. The U.S. became a member of the BIE in April 1968. Federal partici-

pation in a recognized international exposition requires specific authorization by the Congress, based on the President's finding that participation is in the national interest.

Business Executive Enforcement Team
(U.S. government) A channel for private sector U.S. business executives to discuss export control enforcement matters with the Bureau of Export Administration. *See* Bureau of Export Administration.

Buy American acts
U.S. federal and state government statutes that give a preference to U.S. produced goods in government contracts. These statutes are designed to protect domestic industry and labor, but tend to increase the price paid for goods and services government agencies buy. *See also* non-tariff barriers or measures; trade barriers.

buyback
(economics) A form of countertrade that involves the exportation of technological know-how, specialized machinery and the construction of an entire factory in exchange for a set percentage of the factory's production over a five to twenty-five year period. Buyback is also known as compensation trading. *See* countertrade.

buying rate (bid rate)
(banking/foreign exchange) Rate at which a bank is prepared to buy foreign exchange or to accept deposits. The opposite of selling (or asked) rate.

C

cabotage
(shipping) Coast-wide water transportation, navigation or trade between ports of a nation. Many nations, like the U.S., have cabotage laws which require domestic owned vessels to perform domestic interport water transportation service.

Cairns Group
An informal association of agricultural exporting countries established in August 1986. Members include: Argentina, Australia, Brazil, Canada, Chile, Colombia, Hungary, Indonesia, Malaysia, New Zealand, Philippines, Thailand and Uruguay. Address: Cairns Group, c/o Department of Foreign Affairs and Trade, Bag 8, Queen Victoria Terrace, Canberra, ACT 2600, Australia; http://www.dfat.gov.au/trade/negotiations/cairns_group.

call
(banking) A demand of payment on a loan, often as a result of non-compliance on the part of the borrower to the terms and conditions of the loan.

call in a contract
(law) (a) Demanding payment on a contract. A seller, for example, may be entitled under the contract terms to demand payment at the time the goods are ready to ship. (b) Submitting a formal, usually written, notice to collect payment on a contract. A seller who has not received payment, for example, may send a written letter to the buyer demanding remittance of the funds owed—that is calling in the contract.

call money
(banking/finance/foreign exchange) Currency lent by banks on a very short-term basis, which can be called the same day, at one day's notice or at two days' notice. Called overnight money in Great Britain and Federal funds in the United States.

call option
(banking/finance/foreign exchange) The right (but not the obligation) to buy a fixed amount of a commodity, security or currency from the option writer (option seller) at a predetermined rate and/or exercise price within a specified time limit. *See* option; put option; American Option; European Option.

Calvo Doctrine
(foreign investment) The Calvo Doctrine (or principle) holds that jurisdiction in international invest-

ment disputes lies with the country in which the investment is located; thus, the investor has no recourse but to use the local courts. The principle, named after an Argentinian jurist, has been applied throughout Latin America and other areas of the world.

Canadian Commercial Corporation
(Canada) The prime contractor in government-to-government sales transactions, facilitating exports of a wide range of goods and services from Canadian sources. In response to requests from foreign governments and international agencies for individual products or services, CCC identifies Canadian firms capable of meeting the customer's requirements, executes prime as well as back-to-back contracts, and follows through with contract management, inspection, acceptance, and payment. Address: Canadian Commercial Corporation (CCC), Metropolitan Centre, 11th Floor, 50 O'Connor St., Ottawa, ON K1A 0S6, Canada; Tel: [1] (613) 996-0034; Fax: [1] (613) 995-2121; http://www.ccc.com.

cap
(banking/finance/foreign exchange) On borrowed funds with an interest rate which is tied to the market rate, an upside limit or cap can be agreed upon, i.e. against payment of a premium, an upper interest rate limit is agreed upon, which will not be exceeded even if the market rate rises above the stated level.

capacity to contract
(law) Legal competency to make a contract. A party has capacity to contract if he or she has attained the age required by law and has the mental ability to understand the nature of contract obligations.

capital account
(economics) Juxtaposition of the long and short-term capital imports and exports of a country. *See* balance of payments.

capital flight
(economics) The transfer of money or other financial resources from one country to another as a hedge against inflation or poor economic or political conditions.

capital goods
(economics) Manufactured goods that are for productive industrial use. For example: machine tools. *See also* consumer goods.

capital market
(finance) The market for buying and selling long-term loanable funds, in the form of bonds, mortgages and the like. Unlike the money market, where short-term funds are traded, the capital market tends to center on well-organized institutions such as the stock exchange. However, there is no clear-cut distinction between the two other than that capital market loans are generally used by businesses, financial institutions and governments to buy capital goods whereas money-market loans generally fill a temporary need for working capital.

capital movements
(economics) (a) The international payments of a nation. (b) A nation's short and long-term claims and liabilities, which are entered into vis-a-vis foreign countries, including repayment of foreign debt, direct investments, portfolio investments and purchase of private real estate.

captain's protest
(shipping) A document prepared by the captain of a vessel on arrival at port, showing unusual conditions encountered during voyage. Generally, a captain's protest is prepared to relieve the ship owner of any liability for any loss to cargo, thus requiring cargo owners to look to insurance companies for reimbursement.

cargo
(shipping) Merchandise hauled by transportation lines.

cargo agent
(shipping) An agent appointed by an airline or shipping line to solicit and process international air and ocean freight for shipments. Cargo agents are paid commissions by the airline or shipping line.

cargo aircraft
See all-cargo aircraft.

cargo manifest
(shipping) A list of a ship's cargo or passengers, but without a listing of charges.

cargo, N.O.S.
(shipping) Articles not otherwise specifically provided for. In determining the freight rate, a general category of articles for shipment.

cargo selectivity system
(U.S. Customs) A part of U.S. Customs' Automated Commercial System, specifies the type of examination (intensive or general) to be conducted for imported merchandise. The type of examination is based on database selectivity criteria such as assessments of risk by filer, consignee, tariff number,

country of origin, and manufacturer/shipper. A first time consignee is always selected for an intensive examination. An alert is also generated in cargo selectivity the first time a consignee files an entry in a port with a particular tariff number, country of origin, or manufacturer/shipper. *See* Automated Commercial System.

cargo tonnage
(shipping) The weight of a shipment or of a ship's total cargo expressed in tons.

Caribbean Basin Economic Recovery Act (CBERA)
(U.S.) The CBERA affords nonreciprocal tariff preferences by the United States to developing countries in the Caribbean Basin area to aid their economic development and to diversify and expand their production and exports. The CBERA applies to merchandise entered, or withdrawn from warehouse for consumption, on or after January 1, 1984. This tariff preference program has no expiration date. *See* Caribbean Basin Initiative.

Caribbean Basin Initiative (CBI)
(U.S.) A program providing for the duty-free entry into the United States of merchandise from designated beneficiary countries or territories in the Caribbean Basin.

This program was enacted by the United States as the Caribbean Basin Economic Recovery Act and became effective January 1, 1984.

The purpose of the program is to increase economic aid and trade preferences for twenty-eight states of the Caribbean region. The Caribbean Basin Economic Recovery Act provided for twelve years of duty-free treatment of most goods produced in the Caribbean region. The Initiative was extended permanently (CBI II), by the Customs and Trade Act of August 1990. The 23 countries include Antigua and Barbuda, the Bahamas, Barbados, Belize, the British Virgin Islands, Costa Rica, Dominica, the Dominican Republic, El Salvador, Grenada, Guatemala, Guyana, Honduras, Jamaica, Montserrat, the Netherlands Antilles, Nicaragua, Panama, St. Christopher-Nevis, St. Lucia, St. Vincent and the Grenadines, Trinidad and Tobago. The following countries may be eligible for CBI benefits but have not formally requested designation: Anguilla, Cayman Islands, Suriname, and the Turks and Caicos Islands.

Caribbean Common Market (CARICOM)
A regional trade alliance composed of 13 English speaking Caribbean nations. Its purpose is to further economic development and increase social and cultural cooperation among member nations.

Members include Antigua and Barbuda, the Bahamas, Barbados, Belize, Dominica, Grenada, Guyana, Jamaica, Montserrat, St. Kitts-Nevis, St. Lucia, St. Vincent and the Grenadines, and Trinidad and Tobago). Address: Caribbean Common Market, Bank of Guyana Building, PO Box 10827, Georgetown, Guyana; Tel: [592] (2) 69-281; Telex: 2263; Fax: [592] (2) 66-091.

carnet
(customs) A customs document permitting the holder to carry or send merchandise temporarily into certain foreign countries (for display, demonstration, or similar purposes) without paying duties or posting bonds. *See* ATA Carnet.

Carriage and Insurance Paid To (...named port of destination) (CIP)
(Incoterms 2000) An international trade term of sale in which, for the quoted price, the seller/exporter clears the goods for export, delivers them to the carrier, and is responsible for paying for carriage and insurance to the named port of destination. However, once the goods are delivered to the carrier, the buyer is responsible for all additional costs.

In Incoterms 2000 the seller is also responsible for the costs of unloading, customs clearance, duties, and other costs if such costs are included in the cost of carriage such as in small package courier delivery. The seller is responsible for procuring and paying for insurance cover.

The CIP term is valid for any form of transport including multimodal

The "named port of destination" in CIP and all "C" Incoterms 2000 is domestic to the buyer, but is not necessarily the final delivery point.

The Carriage and Insurance Paid To term is often used in sales where the shipment is by air freight, containerized ocean freight, courier shipments of small parcels, and in "ro-ro" (roll-on, roll-off) shipments of motor vehicles.

A "carrier" can be a shipping line, airline, trucking firm, railway or also an individual or firm who undertakes to procure carriage by any of the above methods of transport including multimodal. Therefore, a person, such as a freight forwarder, can act as a "carrier" under this term.

If subsequent carriers are used for the carriage to the agreed destination, the risk passes when the goods have been delivered to the first carrier.
See Guide to Incoterms 2000 Appendix.

Carriage of Goods by Sea Act of 1936
(shipping) A U.S. law which, among other provisions, establishes statutory responsibility for the

carrier's liability for certain types of damage. Where the COGSA applies, general speaking, the vessel or carrier is responsible for damage resulting from negligence in the loading, stowing and discharge of cargo. It is not responsible for damage resulting from errors of navigation or management of the ship, from unseaworthiness of the vessel (unless caused by lack of due diligence to make it seaworthy), or from perils of the sea, fire, and a number of other listed causes. The burden of proof in establishing fault will rest at times upon the shipper and at times upon the carrier.

The degree to which a steamship company can be held responsible for damage sustained by a specific shipment is frequently difficult to determine. COGSA applies to import and export shipments and, by agreement, to much U.S. coastwise and intercoastal business a well.

Carriage Paid To (...named port of destination) (CPT)

(Incoterms 2000) An international trade term of sale in which, for the quoted price, the seller/exporter/manufacturer clears the goods for export, delivers them to the carrier, and is responsible for paying for carriage to the named port of destination. However, once the seller delivers the goods to the carrier, the buyer becomes responsible for all additional costs.

In Incoterms 2000 the seller is also responsible for the costs of unloading, customs clearance, duties, and other costs if such costs are included in the cost of carriage such as in small package courier delivery.

The seller is not responsible for procuring and paying for insurance cover.

The CPT term is valid for any form of transport including multimodal.

The "named port of destination" in CPT and all "C" Incoterms 2000 is domestic to the buyer, but is not necessarily the final delivery point.

The Carriage Paid To term is often used in sales where the shipment is by air freight, containerized ocean freight, courier shipments of small parcels, and in "ro-ro" (roll-on, roll-off) shipments of motor vehicles.

A "carrier" can be a shipping line, airline, trucking firm, railway or also an individual or firm who undertakes to procure carriage by any of the above methods of transport including multimodal. Therefore, a person, such as a freight forwarder, can act as a "carrier" under this term.

If subsequent carriers are used for the carriage to the agreed destination, the risk passes when the goods have been delivered to the first carrier.
See Guide to Incoterms 2000 Appendix.

carrier

(law/shipping) An individual or legal entity that is in the business of transporting passengers or goods for hire. Shipping lines, airlines, trucking companies, and railroad companies are all carriers.

Note: The worldwide acceptance of Incoterms 1990 (and now Incoterms 2000) has resulted in an expanded definition of "carrier." In the older and more limited definition, only shipping lines, airlines, trucking companies and railroad companies are carriers. However, the significant increase in multimodal transport and integrated logistics has placed freight forwarders into the position of "carrier." In the definition above, a freight forwarder is a "legal entity that is in the business of transporting goods." The ICC (International Chamber of Commerce) has established the folowing definition:

(ICC definition) "Carrier means any person who, in a contract of carriage, undertakes to perform or to procure the performance of transport by rail, road, air, sea, inland waterway or by combination of such modes." Within the context of this definition, when a buyer nominates a freight forwarder to receive the goods, such as in the FCA (Free Carrier) Incoterm, the seller fulfills his obligation to deliver the goods by delivering to that person.

(a) A **common carrier** is one that by law must convey passengers or goods without refusal, provided the party requesting conveyance has paid the charge for transport.

(b) A **private or contract carrier** is one that transports only those persons or goods that it selects.

(U.S. shipping) By U.S. government regulation a common carrier publishes stated rates for carriage and must accept any passengers or goods for transport so long as space is available and the published rate is paid.

carrier's certificate

(U.S. Customs) A document issued by a shipping company, addressed to a District Director of Customs, which certifies that a named individual is the owner or consignee of the articles listed in the certificate. This document is often the "evidence of right to make entry" required by U.S. Customs for an individual to clear goods through Customs. *See also* evidence of right to make entry.

C

cartage agent
(shipping) A ground service operator who provides pickup and delivery of freight in areas not served directly by an air or ocean carrier.

cartage/drayage
(shipping) (a) The local transport of goods. (b) The charge(s) made for hauling freight on carts, drays or trucks.

cartel
An organization of independent producers formed to regulate the production, pricing, or marketing practices of its members in order to limit competition and maximize their market power.

casco
(insurance) Marine insurance coverage on the hull of a ship.

casus major
(law/shipping) A major casualty that is usually accidental, such as a flood or shipwreck.

catalog & video; catalog exhibitions
(U.S.) A U.S. International Trade Administration program promoting low-cost exhibits of U.S. firms' catalogs and videos, offering small, less-experienced companies an opportunity to test overseas markets for their products without travel. The International Trade Administration promotes exhibitions, provides staff fluent in the local language to answer questions, and forwards all trade leads to participating firms. Contact: Trade Fairs and Exhibitions; Tel: [1] (800) USA-TRADE. *See also* International Trade Administration.

category groups
Groupings of controlled products. *See* export control classification number.

cause of action
(law) Facts that give a party a right to seek a judicial remedy against another individual or legal entity.

caveat emptor
(law) Latin for "Let the buyer beware." The purchaser buys at his own risk.

cedi
The currency of Ghana. 1¢=100 pesewas.

cell
(shipping) The on board stowage space for one shipping container on a ship

cells
(shipping) The modular construction system on board a cellular shipping vessel designed to allow containers to be stowed securely one on top of another with vertical bracing at the four corners.

cellular vessel
(shipping) A special use shipping vessel designed for the efficient stowage of ocean containers one on top of the other with vertical bracing at the four corners.

Census Interface System
(U.S. Customs) A part of U.S. Customs' Automated Commercial System, which includes edits and validations provided by the Bureau of the Census to allow for the accurate and timely collection and submission of entry summary data. Census Interface is accomplished through Automated Broker Interface entry summary transmissions. *See* Automated Commercial System.

Center for Trade and Investment Services
(U.S.) CTIS is the focal point in the Agency for International Development (AID) for the collection and dissemination of information on the agency's programs and activities that support international private enterprise in the developing countries where AID operates. CTIS is a full service, comprehensive "one-stop-shop" for information about AID's trade and investment programs and business opportunities in countries served by AID. The center's objective is to further economic development abroad by facilitating increased business activity between the private sectors of AID-assisted countries and the U.S. Address: Agency for International Development, G/EGAD/BD-Global Technology Network, 1300 Pennsylvania Avenue, Washington, DC 20523 USA; Tel: [1] 800-USAID4U; Fax: [1] (202) 216-3526; general AID information: http://www.info.usaid.gov; Global Network Technology: http://www.usgtn.org.

Central American Common Market
A regional trade alliance established in July 1991 comprised of Honduras, Guatemala, El Salvador, Nicaragua and Costa Rica. The common market covers all products traded within the region as of 1992. A second step toward regional integration will be the establishment of a common external tariff. Panama is becoming progressively more involved in the regional integration discussions. Address: Central American Common Market, 4A Avda 10-25, Zona 14, Apdo Postal 1237, 01901, Guatemala City, Guatemala; Tel: [502] (2) 682-151; Telex: 5676; Fax: [502] (2) 681-071.

central bank
(banking) The only institution which has the right to issue bank notes and which constitutes the mon-

etary and credit policy authority of a currency zone. Apart from this, it supplies the economy with money and credit, regulates domestic and foreign payments transactions and maintains internal and external monetary stability.

certificate of analysis

A document issued by a recognized organization or governmental authority confirming the quality and composition of goods listed in the certificate. Certificates of analysis are often required by authorities in importing countries for animal and plant products for consumption and for pharmaceuticals. *See* certificate of inspection; phytosanitary inspection certificate.

certificate of inspection

A document certifying that merchandise (such as perishable goods) was in good condition at the time of inspection, usually immediately prior to shipment. Pre-shipment inspection is a requirement for importation of goods into many developing countries. Often used interchangeably with certificate of analysis. *See* phytosanatary inspection certificate; certificate of analysis.

certificate of insurance

See insurance certificate.

certificate of manufacture

A document (often notarized) in which a producer of goods certifies that the manufacturing has been completed and the goods are now at the disposal of the buyer.

certificate of origin

(customs) A document attesting to the country of origin of goods. A certificate of origin is often required by the customs authorities of a country as part of the entry process. Such certificates are usually obtained through an official or quasi official organization in the country of origin such as a consular office or local chamber of commerce. A certificate of origin may be required even though the commercial invoice contains the information.

Certificate of Origin Form A. A document required by customs in the United States and other developed countries to prove eligibility of merchandise under duty-free import programs such as the Generalized System of Preferences and the Caribbean Basin Initiative.

certificate of weight

(shipping) A document stating the weight of a shipment.

certification; legalization

Official certification of the authenticity of signatures or documents in connection with letter of credits, such as certificates or origin, commercial invoices, etc. by chambers of commerce, consulates and similar recognized government authorities.

Certified Trade Fair Program

(trade event) The U.S. Department of Commerce Certified Trade Fair Program is designed to encourage private organizations to recruit new-to-market and new-to-export U.S. firms to exhibit in trade fairs overseas. To receive certification, the organization must demonstrate: (1) the fair is a leading international trade event for an industry and (2) the fair organizer is capable of recruiting U.S. exhibitors and assisting them with freight forwarding, customs clearance, exhibit design and setup, public relations, and overall show promotion. The show organizer must agree to assist new-to-export exhibitors as well as small businesses interested in exporting.

In addition to the services the organizer provides, the Department of Commerce will:

(1) Assign a Washington coordinator.

(2) Operate a business information office, which provides meeting space, translators, hospitality, and assistance from U.S. exhibitors and foreign customers.

(3) Help contact buyers, agents, distributors, and other business leads and provide marketing assistance.

(4) Provide a press release on certification.

Contact the U.S. Department of Commerce, 14th St. at Constitution Ave. NW, Washington, DC 20230 USA; Tel: [1] (202) 482-2000.

See new-to-market; new-to-export.

Certified Trade Missions Program

(U.S.) (Former name: state/industry organized, government approved (S/IOGA)). The U.S. Department of Commerce, through its Certified Trade Missions Program, offers guidance and assistance to federal, state and local development agencies, chambers of commerce, industry trade associations, and other export-oriented groups that are interested in becoming more actively involved in export promotion. Certified Trade Missions open doors to government and business leaders in promising export markets around the world.

Once the sponsoring organization has selected the countries to be considered, proposed an itinerary, and outlined its mission goals and objectives, the

Department of Commerce coordinates the mission itinerary with its commercial staff at U.S. embassies and consulates overseas. These posts help to arrange the mission's activities to make the most productive use of each member's time at each stop on the itinerary. Some missions also include informational or technical seminars specifically designed to exhibit and promote sales of sophisticated products, technology, or services in targeted markets. Address: Certified Trade Missions, U.S. Department of Commerce, 14th St. and Constitution Ave. NW, Room H2116, Washington, DC 20230 USA; Tel: [1] (202) 482-4908; Fax: [1] (202) 482-0115.

cession of goods

(law) A surrender of goods. A relinquishment of a debtor's property to creditors when the debtor cannot pay his or her debts.

C&F

See cost and freight; Incoterms.

chaebol

(Korea) Korean conglomerates which are characterized by strong family control, authoritarian management, and centralized decision making. Chaebol dominate the Korean economy, growing out of the takeover of the Japanese monopoly of the Korean economy following World War II. Korean government tax breaks and financial incentives emphasizing industrial reconstruction and exports provided continuing support to the growth of Chaebols during the 1970s and 1980s. In 1988, the output of the 30 largest chaebol represented almost 95% of Korea's gross national product.

chargeable weight

(shipping) The weight of a shipment used in determining air or ocean freight charges. The chargeable weight may be the dimensional weight or on container shipments the gross weight of the shipment less the tare weight of the container.

chargé d'affaires

(diplomacy) A subordinate diplomat who takes charge in the absence of the ambassador.

charges advanced

See advancement of charges.

charges collect

(shipping) The total transportation charges which may include pickup and/or delivery charges which are entered on the ocean or air waybill to be collected from the consignee. Equivalent terms are "freight collect" or "charges forward."

charter

(law) (a) An instrument issued by a government to the governed people, a specific part of the people, a corporation, a colony, or a dependency confirming or conferring described rights, liberties, or powers. (b) A legislative act that creates a business corporation or that creates and defines a corporate franchise.

(shipping) (a) A **charter party** or **charter agreement** is a lease or agreement to hire an airplane, vessel, or other means of conveyance to transport goods on a designated voyage to one or more locations. (b) A **gross charter** is a charter agreement by which the shipowner furnishes personnel and equipment and incurs other expenses, such as port costs. (c) A **bareboat charter** is a charter agreement under which an individual or legal entity charters a vessel without a crew, assumes full possession and control of the vessel, and is generally invested with temporary ownership powers.

chartered bank

(Canada) Financial institution licensed by the Canadian Parliament under the Bank Act to operate as a bank.

chartered ship

(shipping) A ship leased by its owner or agent for a stated time, voyage or voyages.

charter party bill of lading

(shipping) A bill of lading issued by a charter party. Charter party bills of lading are not acceptable by banks under letters of credit unless they are specifically authorized in the credit. *See* bill of lading.

charter party contract

(shipping) Contract according to which the precisely designated freight room of a ship or the whole ship is leased by the owner to a charterer for a specific period, specific voyage or voyages. If a ship is chartered without crew this is a bare boat charter. The freight documents issued by the current charterer or his authorized party are called charter party bills of lading.

charter service

(shipping) The temporary hiring of an aircraft, usually on a trip basis, for the movement of cargo or passengers.

chassis

(shipping) A special trailer or undercarriage on which containers are moved over the road. Chassis comes in skeletal types, parallel frame, perimeter frame and goose neck types, among others.

chattel
(law) An item of personal property.

chattel lien
(law) A lien on chattel in favor of a person who has expended labor, skill, or materials on the chattel or has furnished storage for it at the request of the owner, an agent, or a party who legally possesses it.

chattel paper
(law) A writing or a group of writings that constitute a security interest in, or a lease of, specific goods for a monetary obligation.

check digit number
(shipping) A single digit of an air waybill number used to insure that the air waybill number is correctly entered into a computer system.

chemical/biological weapons
(U.S.) The Department of Commerce maintains foreign policy export controls on certain chemical precursors useful in chemical warfare. Through the Australia Group (AG), the United States cooperates with other nations in controlling chemical weapons proliferation. The AG has developed a Core List of nine chemicals (not to be confused with the Coordinating Committee on Multilateral Export Controls (CoCom) "Core List") considered essential to the development of chemical weapons. The AG also developed a Warning List which identifies 41 precursors which are useful for chemical weapons development. The AG also provides the forum in which the member countries share information concerning the activities of non-member countries where the proliferation of these weapons is of concern, including entities that are seeking chemical precursors and related items.

The United States controls all 50 chemical precursors designated by the AG as useful in chemical weapons production. The nine core list chemicals are controlled worldwide, except to the members of the AG and NATO. The remaining 41 chemicals are controlled to selected countries.

The U.S. also maintains unilateral controls on certain biological organisms and requires an individual validated license to all destinations except Canada. U.S. Department of Commerce regulations are designed in the form of a "negative" list. The list identifies those organisms that have been determined to be of no or minimal level of hazard. Any organism that is not included on the list is controlled. The U.S. Department of Commerce requires individual validated licenses for the export of Class 2, 3, and 4 organisms to all destinations except Canada. (The higher the class, the greater the

toxicity.) License applications are referred to the U.S. State Department for review and recommendation. Approval or denial is determined by analysis of the application and intelligence input. *See* Australia Group.

chill a sale
(law) Combining or conspiring (of buyers or bidders) to suppress competition at a sale, in order to acquire property at less than fair value.

China green line
The China green line describes the level of technology below which a Coordinating Committee on Multilateral Export Controls (CoCom) member country can unilaterally approve an export license application requiring only notification to CoCom in Paris. This level of technology is individually defined in notes to the Core List. The China green line is a substantially higher level of technology than the CoCom AEN level. *See* Coordinating Committee on Multilateral Export Controls; core list.

chose in action
See thing in action.

CIF
See cost, insurance, freight; Incoterms.

CIFCI
See cost, insurance, freight, commission and interest; Incoterms.

CIM
(shipping) An internationally standardized freight document issued in rail transport. CIM stands for "Convention Internationale concernant le transport des Marchandises par chemin de fer." The agreement has been in force since January 1, 1965, and constitutes the legal basis for the conclusion of freight contracts in international rail goods transport using one freight document.

city bank
(Japan) A major Japanese commercial bank, located in a city, dealing with corporations and major accounts (as compared to a local bank).

city terminal service
(shipping) A service provided by some airlines to accept shipments at the terminals of their cartage agents or other designated intown terminals or to deliver shipments to these terminals at lower rates than those charged for the door-to-door pickup and delivery service.

Civil Aeronautics Board (CAB)
(U.S.) A U.S. Federal agency created by Congress in 1938 to promote the development of the U.S. air

C

transport system, to award air routes, and to regulate passenger fares and cargo rates. Legislation passed by the U.S. Congress in 1978 terminated the CAB, effective January 1, 1985. Many of the CAB functions such as certificates, air carrier fitness, consumer protection, international rates and services were transferred to the U.S. Department of Transportation (DOT). *See* U.S. Department of Transportation.

civil law
(law) A body of law created by statutes and other enactments of legislatures and by rules and regulations adopted to give effect to those statutes and enactments. *See also* common law.

claim
(shipping) A demand made upon a transportation line for payment on account of a loss sustained through its negligence.
(insurance) A demand made upon an insurance company for payment on account of an insured loss.

claim tracer
(shipping) A request for an advice concerning the status of a claim.

classification
(general) The categorization of merchandise.
(shipping) The assignment of a category to a specific cargo for the purpose of applying class rates, together with governing rules and regulations.
(U.S. Customs) The categorization of merchandise according to the Harmonized Tariff Schedule of the United States (HTS or HTSUS). Classification affects the duty status of imported merchandise.
Classification and valuation of imported merchandise must be provided by commercial importers when an entry is filed. In addition, classification under the statistical suffixes of the tariff schedules must also be furnished even though this information is not pertinent to duitable status. Accordingly, classification is initially the responsibility of an importer, customs broker or other person preparing the entry papers. *See* Harmonized Tariff Schedule of the United States. *See also* valuation.

class or kind (of merchandise)
(customs) A term used in defining the scope of an antidumping investigation. Included in the "class or kind" of merchandize is merchandise sold in the home market which is "such or similar" to the petitioned product. "Such or similar" merchandise is that merchandise which is identical to or like the petitioned product in physical characteristics. *See* dumping.

claused bill of lading
(shipping) Notations on bills of lading which specify deficient condition(s) of the goods and/or the packaging. *See* bill of lading.

clean bill of exchange
(banking) A bill of exchange having no other documents, such as a bill of lading affixed to it.

clean bill of lading
(shipping) A bill of lading receipted by the carrier for goods received in "apparent good order and condition," without damages or other irregularities, and without the notation "Shippers Load and Count."

clean collection
(banking) A collection in which the demand for payment (such as a draft) is presented without additional documents. *See* bill of exchange.

clean draft
(banking) A sight or time draft which has no other documents attached to it. This is to be distinguished from documentary draft. *See* bill of exchange.

clean letter of credit
(banking) A letter of credit against which the beneficiary of the credit may draw a bill of exchange without presentation of documents. *See* letter of credit.

clean on board bill of lading
(shipping) A document evidencing cargo laden aboard a vessel with no exceptions as to cargo condition or quantity.

clearance
(customs) The completion of customs entry formalities resulting in the release of goods from customs custody to the importer.

close corporation
See closely held corporation.

closed conference
(shipping) A shipping conference that reserves the right to refuse membership to applying carriers. *See* conference. *See also* carrier.

closed-end transaction
(finance) A credit transaction that has a fixed amount and time for repayment.

closely held corporation
(law) A corporation with a small number of shareholders, who usually directly operate the corporation and have limited liability. A maximum number of shareholders is usually fixed by law. The mini-

mum capitalization for a closely held corporation is less than that for a public corporation, and fewer formalities are required for managing it. The requirements for closely held corporations vary among jurisdictions. *See* corporation.

coastal trade
(shipping) Trade between ports of one nation.

CoCom
See Coordinating Committee on Multilateral Export Controls.

Code of Federal Regulations (CFR)
(U.S. law) A compilation of the administrative rules adopted and followed by departments and agencies of the United States federal government. Copies of the CFR are available at major public libraries in the United States and for purchase from the Superintendent of Documents, U.S. Government Printing Office, P.O. Box 371954, Pittsburgh PA 15250-7954; http://www.access.gpo.gov/su_docs; to receive catalog, contact U.S. FAX Watch: (202) 512-1716.

codes of conduct
International instruments that indicate standards of behavior by nation states or multi-national corporations deemed desirable by the international community. Several codes of conduct were negotiated during the Tokyo Round of the General Agreement on Tariffs and Trade (GATT) that liberalized and harmonized domestic measures that might impede trade.
The United Nations has also encouraged the negotiation of several "voluntary" codes of conduct, including one that seeks to specify the rights and obligations of trans-national corporations and of governments.

coin silver
Coin or "German" silver is an alloy of silver that is 800/1000 pure. An article of coin or German silver is often marked "800."

collar
(banking) An agreement to put upper and lower (cap and floor) limits on an interest rate which will be adhered to even if the market rate lies outside this range.

collect charges
(shipping) The transportation practice under which the receiver of the goods pays charges.

collecting bank
(banking) The bank that acts as agent for the seller and seller's bank in collecting payment or a time draft from the buyer to be forwarded to the remitting bank (usually the seller's bank).

collection
(general) The presentation for payment of an obligation and the payment thereof.
(banking) The receipt of money for presentation of a draft or check for payment at the bank on which it was drawn, or presentation of any item for deposit at the place at which it is payable.

collection endorsement
See endorsement.

collection papers
(banking) All documents (invoices, bills of lading, etc.) submitted to a buyer for the purpose of receiving payment for a shipment.
See documents against payment; documents against acceptance.

collections system
(U.S. Customs) A part of U.S. Customs' Automated Commercial System, controls and accounts for the billions of dollars in payments collected by Customs each year and the millions in refunds processed each year. Daily statements are prepared for the automated brokers who select this service. The Collections System permits electronic payments of the related duties and taxes through the Automated Clearinghouse capability. Automated collections also meets the needs of the importing community through acceptance of electronic funds transfers for deferred tax bills and receipt of electronic payments from lockbox operations for Customs bills and fees. *See* Automated Commercial System.

collective mark
(law) A trademark or service mark that a cooperative, association, or other collective group uses in commerce. A mark used to indicate membership in a union, association, or other organization.

collect on delivery (COD)
(shipping) A transportation service under which the purchase price of goods is collected by the carrier from the receiver at the time of delivery, and subsequently, payment is transmitted by the carrier to the shipper. Carriers charge a nominal fee for this service. As the term COD implies payment is due upon delivery. There are no credit provisions in COD service. Also called Cash On Delivery.

colon
The currency of:
Costa Rica, 1¢=100 centimos;
El Salvadore, 1¢=100 centavos.

colorable imitation

(law) A mark that is so similar to another registered trademark or service mark that it may be considered as calculated to deceive an ordinary person.

colorable transaction

(law) A transaction that in appearance does not correspond to the actual transaction and that is usually intended to conceal or deceive.

column 1 rates

(U.S. Customs) The Harmonized Tariff Schedules of the United States (HTS) is an organized listing of goods and their import duty rates which is used as the basis of classifying products for entry to the United States. Column 1 duty rates in the HTS are low and apply to imports from countries that have achieved Most Favored Nation (MFN) trading status with the United States. *See* Harmonized Tariff Schedule of the United States; column 2 rates.

column 2 rates

(U.S. Customs) The Harmonized Tariff Schedules of the United States (HTS) is an organized listing of goods and their import duty rates which is used as the basis of classifying products for entry to the United States. Column 2 duty rates in the HTS apply to imports from countries that do not have Most Favored Nation (MFN) trading status with the United States. *See* Harmonized Tariff Schedule of the United States; column 1 rates.

combi aircraft

See combination aircraft.

combination aircraft

(shipping) An aircraft capable of transporting both passengers and cargo on the same flight. Such a plane will generally carry unitized cargo loads on the upper deck of the aircraft forward of the passenger compartment. Some cargo is carried on virtually all scheduled passenger flights in the belly pits below the passenger cabin.

combination in restraint of trade

(law) An understanding or agreement between two or more individuals or legal entities to do the following: (1) restrict competition; (2) monopolize trade; (3) control production, distribution, and price; and (4) otherwise interfere with freedom of trade.

combined bill of lading

(shipping) A bill of lading covering a shipment of goods by more than one mode of transportation. *See* bill of lading.

combined transport

(shipping) Consignment sent by means of various modes of transport, such as by rail and by ocean.

combined transport bill of lading

(shipping) A bill of lading covering a shipment of goods by more than one mode of transportation. *See* bill of lading.

comity

(law) Courtesy, respect, and good will. Government agencies or courts in one jurisdiction, for example, may agree out of comity to give effect to court judgments or arbitration awards of other jurisdictions.

command economy

(economics) An economic system where resources and decisions about production are controlled by a central government authority.

Commanditaire Vennootschap (C.V.)

(Netherlands) Designation for a limited partnership in which at least one of the partners has general personal liability and at least one of the other partners has limited liability.

Commerce Business Daily

(publication) A daily newspaper published by the U.S. Department of Commerce which lists government procurement invitations and contract awards, including foreign business opportunities and foreign government procurements. Available from: U.S. Department of Commerce, 14th St. at Constitution Ave., Washington, DC 20230 USA; Tel: [1] (202) 482-0633; http://www.doc.gov.

Commerce Control List (CCL)

(U.S.) A list of all items—commodities, software, and technical data—subject to U.S. Bureau of Export Administration export controls. Incorporates not only the national security controlled items agreed to by the Coordinating Committee on Multilateral Export Controls (CoCom) (the "core" list), but also items controlled for foreign policy and other reasons. The list adopts a totally new method of categorizing commodities and is divided into 10 general categories: (1) materials, (2) materials processing, (3) electronics, (4) computers, (5) telecommunications and cryptography, (6) sensors, (7) avionics and navigation, (8) marine technology, (9) propulsion systems and transportation equipment, and (10) miscellaneous. Replaced the former Commodity Control List as of September 1, 1991. Address: Bureau of Export Administration, Office of Public Affairs, Room 3897, 14th Street and Constitution Avenue NW, Washington, DC 20226 USA;

Tel: [1] (202) 482-2721; http://www.bxa.doc.gov; *see also* export control classification number.

Commercial Activity Report (CAR)

(U.S.) An assessment of a country's political, economic, and business activities, and its market potential and strategies, with an eye to increasing U.S. export sales. The CAR is prepared annually by the economic and commercial sections of U.S. embassies, covering over 100 countries where the Department of Commerce is not represented. Available as individual reports from the Department of Commerce, 14th St. & Constitution Ave. NW, Washington, DC 20230; Tel: (202) 482-2867; or on the National Trade Data Bank, U.S. Department of Commerce, Office of Business Analysis, HCHB Room 4885, Washington, DC 20230; Tel: (202) 482-1986; http://www.stat-usa.gov; For individual reports, call your district Department of Commerce office.

commercial bank

(banking) A bank that specializes in accepting demand deposits (deposits that can be withdrawn on demand by the depositor) and granting loans.

commercial bill of exchange

See bill of exchange.

commercial credit

(banking) A letter of credit used to facilitate a sale of goods by insuring that the seller will be paid once the seller has complied with the terms of credit that the buyer obtains. A letter of credit is usually issued by a bank (the issuer) on the request of its client (the buyer) to assure the seller that the buyer will pay for the goods sold. *See* letter of credit.

commercial frustration

(law) A legal theory that implies a condition or term into a contract, if no express provision was made, to excuse the parties when performance becomes impossible because an event occurs that the contracting parties could not have reasonably foreseen or controlled. Commercial frustration may arise, for example, if a seller's shipment is lost in a shipwreck or if a manufacturer cannot obtain raw materials because war has broken out in the country supplying them. *See* force majeure.

commercial impracticability

(law) A legal theory that implies a condition or term into a contract, if no express provision was made, to excuse either party when performance becomes impossible in practice because of the occurrence of a contingency, the nonoccurrence of which was a basic assumption for making the contract. A

manufacturer, for example, who contracts to sell goods at a specific price in reliance on a subcontractor's bid to provide certain components at a low price may claim commercial impracticability if the subcontractor defaults and the manufacturer can only procure comparable components at a much higher price.

Commercial Information Management System (CIMS)

(U.S.) CIMS is a trade-related application using National Trade Data Bank CD-ROMs to disseminate market research and international economic data to U.S. & Foreign Commercial Service (US&FCS) domestic offices and overseas posts. The system includes data on American and foreign traders and supports local collection and update of information on business contacts. Not available to the public.

commercial invoice

(general) A document identifying the seller and buyer of goods or services, identifying numbers such as invoice number, date, shipping date, mode of transport, delivery and payment terms, and a complete listing and description of the goods or services being sold including prices, discounts and quantities.

(customs) A commercial invoice is often used by governments to determine the true (transaction) value of goods for the assessment of customs duties and also to prepare consular documentation. Governments using the commercial invoice to control imports often specify its form, content, number of copies, language to be used, and other characteristics.

(U.S. Customs) U.S. Customs requires that a commercial invoice provide the following information: (1) The port of entry, (2) If merchandise is sold or agreed to be sold, the time, place and names of buyer and seller; if consigned, the time and origin of shipment, and names of shipper and receiver, (3) Detailed description of the merchandise, including the name by which each item is known, the grade or quality, and the marks, numbers, and symbols under which sold by the seller or manufacturer to the trade in the country of exportation, together with the marks and numbers of the packages in which the merchandise is packed, (4) The quantities in weights and measures, (5) If sold or agreed to be sold, the purchase price of each item in the currency of the sale, (6) If consigned, the value for each item, in the currency in which the transactions are usually made or, in the absence of such value, the price in such cur-

C

rency that the manufacturer, seller, shipper, or owner would have received, or was willing to receive, for such merchandise if sold in the ordinary course of trade and in the usual wholesale quantities in the country of exportation, (7) The kind of currency, (8) All charges upon the merchandise, itemized by name and amount including freight, insurance, commission, cases, containers, coverings, and cost of packing; and, if not included above, all charges, costs, and expenses incurred in bringing the merchandise from alongside the carrier at the first U.S. port of entry. The cost of packing, cases, containers, and inland freight to the port of exportation need not be itemized by amount if included in the invoice price and so identified. Where the required information does not appear on the invoice as originally prepared, it shall be shown on an attachment to the invoice, (9) All rebates, drawbacks, and bounties, separately itemized, allowed upon the exportation of the merchandise, (10) The country of origin, and (11) All goods or services furnished for the production of the merchandise not included in the invoice price. The invoice and all attachments must be in the English language.

commercial letter of credit

(banking) An instrument by which a bank lends its credit to a customer to enable him to finance the purchase of goods. Addressed to the seller, it authorizes him to draw drafts on the bank under the terms stated in the letter. *See* letter of credit.

Commercial News USA (CNUSA)

(publication) A U.S. & Foreign Commercial Service fee-based magazine, published 10 times per year. CNUSA provides exposure for U.S. products and services through an illustrated catalog and electronic bulletin boards. The catalog is distributed through U.S. embassies and consulates to business readers in 140 countries. Copies are provided to international visitors at trade events around the world. The CNUSA program covers about 30 industry categories and focuses on products that have been on the U.S. market for no longer than three years. To be eligible, products must be at least 51 percent U.S. parts and 51 percent U.S. labor. The service helps U.S. firms identify potential export markets and make contacts leading to representation, distributorships, joint venture or licensing agreements, or direct sales. To order Commercial News USA, contact: Associated Business Publishers International, 317 Madison Avenue, New York NY, 10017-5391 USA; Tel: [1] (212) 490-3999; Fax: [1] (212) 986-7864; http://www.cnewsusa.com.

commercial officers

(diplomacy) Embassy officials who assist businesses through arranging appointments with local business and government officials, providing counsel on local trade regulations, laws, and customs; identifying importers, buyers, agents, distributors, and joint venture partners; and other business assistance. *See* economic officers.

commercial paper

(banking/law) Negotiable instruments used in commerce. Examples of commercial paper are bills of exchange, promissory notes, and bank checks. *See* negotiable instrument; bill of exchange.

commercial set

(law) The primary documents for a shipment of goods. A commercial set usually includes, for example, an invoice, bill of lading, bill of exchange, and certificate of insurance.

commercial treaty

An agreement between two or more countries setting forth the conditions under which business between the countries may be transacted. May outline tariff privileges, terms on which property may be owned, the manner in which claims may be settled, etc.

commingling

(U.S. Customs) The packing or mingling of various articles subject to different rates of duty in such a way that the quantity or value of each class of articles cannot readily be ascertained by Customs without the physical segregation of the shipment or the contents of any package thereof. Commingled articles are subject to the highest rate of duty applicable to any part of the commingled lot, unless the consignee or his agent segregates the articles under Customs supervision.

commission

(general) The amount paid to an agent, which may be an individual, a broker, or a financial institution, for consummating a transaction involving sale or purchase of assets or services.

(banking) Agents and brokers are usually compensated by being allowed to retain a certain percentage of the premiums they produce, known as a commission.

Committee on Foreign Investment in the United States (CFIUS)

(U.S) Created in 1975 to provide guidance on arrangements with foreign governments for advance consultations on prospective major foreign governmental investments in the United States, and to consider proposals for new legislation or regulation relating to forcign investment.

The authority of the Committee was amended by Section 5021 (the Exon-Florio provision) of the Omnibus Trade and Competitiveness Act of 1988 (Section 721 of the Defense Production Act), which gives the President authority to review mergers, acquisitions, and takeovers of U.S. companies by foreign interests and to prohibit, suspend, or seek divesture in the courts of investments that may lead to actions that threaten to impair the national security.

By Executive Order in December 1988, the U.S. Treasury has authority to implement the Exon-Florio provision. CFIUS has eight members: Treasury (the chair), State, Defense, Commerce, the Council of Economic Advisors, the U.S. Trade Representative, the Attorney General, and the Office of Management and Budget.

The Assistant Secretary for Trade Development serves as Commerce's representative to CFIUS. The Commerce working group includes the Bureau of Export Administration, the Economics and Statistics Administration, the Technology Administration, and the Office of the General Counsel. Address: Committee on Foreign Investment in the United States, 1440 New York Avenue NW, Room 4209, Washington, DC 20220 USA; Tel: [1] (202) 622-1860.

commodity

Broadly defined, any article exchanged in trade, but most commonly used to refer to raw materials, including such minerals as tin, copper and manganese, and bulk-produced agricultural products such as coffee, tea and rubber.

commodity code

(shipping) A system for identifying a given commodity by a number in order to establish its commodity rate in freight transport. *See* Harmonized System.

commodity control list

See Commerce Control List.

Commodity Credit Corporation

(U.S.) A U.S. government corporation controlled by the Department of Agriculture which provides financing and stability to the marketing and exporting of agricultural commodities. Address: Commodity Credit Corporation, USDA, 1400 Independence Avenue, SW, Stop 0581, Washington, DC 20250-0581 USA; Tel: [1] (703) 305-1386.

commodity rate

(shipping) The rate (charges) applicable to shipping a specific commodity between certain specified points.

common agricultural policy (CAP)

(EC) A set of regulations by which members states of the European Community (EC) seek to merge their individual agricultural programs into a unified effort to promote regional agricultural development, raise standards of living for the farm population, stabilize agricultural markets, increase agricultural productivity, and establish methods of dealing with food supply security. Two of the principal elements of the CAP are the variable levy (an import duty amounting to the difference between EC target farm prices and the lowest available market prices of imported agricultural commodities) and export restitutions, or subsidies, to promote exports of farm goods that cannot be sold within the EC at the target prices.

common carrier

See carrier.

common external tariff (CXT)

(customs) A uniform tariff rate adopted by a customs union or common market such as the European Community, to imports from countries outside the union. For example, the European Common Market is based on the principle of a free internal trade area with a common external tariff (sometimes referred to in French as the Tarif Exterieur Commun—TEC) applied to products imported from non-member countries. "Free trade areas" do not necessarily have common external tariffs.

common law

(law) The body of law derived from usages, customs, and judicial decisions, as distinguished from statutes. *See* civil law; stare decisis.

common market

(economics) A common market (as opposed to a free trade area) has a common external tariff and may allow for labor mobility and common economic policies among the participating nations. The European Community is the most notable example of a common market.

Common Monetary Agreement

A regional economic alliance of South Africa, Lesotho, and Swaziland under which member states apply uniform exchange control regulations to ensure monetary order in the region. Funds are freely transferable among the three countries, and

Lesotho and Swaziland have free access to South African capital markets. Lesotho also uses the South African currency, the rand. The CMA was formed in 1986 as a result of the renegotiation of the Rand Monetary Agreement (RMA) which was originally formed in 1974 by the same member countries.

common point
(shipping) A point (location) serviced by two or more transportation lines.

common standard level of effective protection
The minimum shared standards between the U.S. and Coordinating Committee on Multilateral Export Controls (CoCom) members for requiring export licenses. *See* Coordinating Committee on Multilateral Export Controls.

common tariff
(shipping) A tariff published by or for the account of two or more transportation lines as issuing carriers. *See* tariff.

commonwealth
A free association of sovereign independent states that has no charter, treaty, or constitution. The association promotes cooperation, consultation, and mutual assistance among members. The British Commonwealth, the most notable example, included 50 states at the beginning of 1991.

Commonwealth of Independent States (CIS)
An association of 11 republics of the former Soviet Union established in December 1991. The members include: Russia, Ukraine, Belarus (formerly Byelorussia), Moldova (formerly Moldavia), Armenia, Azerbaijan, Uzbekistan, Turkmenistan, Tajikistan, Kazakhstan, and Kirgizstan (formerly Kirghiziya). Georgia is presently an "observer"; the Baltic states did not join.

Communications Satellite Corporation
(U.S.) COMSAT was established in 1963 under provision of the Communications Satellite Act of 1962. The legislation directed that COMSAT establish the world's first commercial international satellite communications system. The Act also stipulated that the company operate as a shareholder-owned "for-profit" corporation. COMSAT represents the U.S. in the International Telecommunications Satellite Organization. Address: COMSAT, 6560 Rock Spring Drive, Bethesda, MD 20817 USA; Tel: [1] (301) 214-3000; Fax: [1] (301) 214-7100; http://www.comsat.com.

Compagnie (Cie.)
(France, Luxembourg) General designation for a business organization.

Company (Co.)
(South Africa, United States) General designation for a business organization.

comparative advantage
(economics) A central concept in international trade theory which holds that a country or a region should specialize in the production and export of those goods and services that it can produce relatively more efficiently than other goods and services, and import those goods and services in which it has a comparative disadvantage. This theory was first propounded by David Ricardo in 1817 as a basis for increasing the economic welfare of a population through international trade. The comparative advantage theory normally favors specialized production in a country based on intensive utilization of those factors of production in which the country is relatively well endowed (such as raw materials, fertile land or skilled labor); and perhaps also the accumulation of physical capital and the pace of research.

compensatory trade
(economics) A form of countertrade where any combination of goods and services are bartered. *See* countertrade.

competitive rate
(shipping) Rate established by a transportation line to meet competition of another transportation line.

complementary imports
(economics) Imports of raw materials or products which a country itself does not possess or produce.

composite theoretical performance
(U.S.) Computer hardware export license requirements are evaluated according to composite theoretical performance (CTP), which replaced the former processing data rate (PDR) parameter. CTP is measured in million theoretical operations per second (MTOPS). CTP was developed by the U.S. as a new parameter, and was adopted by the Coordinating Committee on Multilateral Export Controls (CoCom) during the Core List negotiations, because PDR was not applicable to certain modern computer architectures such as vector processors, massively parallel processors, and array processors. CTP is designed to measure all of these architectures, as well as signal processing equipment. *See* Coordinating Committee on Multilateral Export Controls.

composition with creditors

(law) An agreement between an insolvent debtor and one or more creditors under which the creditors consent to accept less than the total amount of their claims in order to secure immediate payment. Creditors will usually prefer a composition if a debtor threatens to declare bankruptcy, because otherwise the creditors are likely to incur costs in making a legal claim against the debtor in a bankruptcy proceeding, payment of debts will be delayed during the proceeding, and the amount paid to each creditor will depend on the judicial decision in that proceeding.

compound rate of duty

(customs) A combination of both a specific rate of duty and an ad valorem rate of duty. For example: 0.7 cents per pound plus 10 per cent ad valorem. *See also* duty; ad valorem; specific rate of duty.

compradore

An intermediary, agent or advisor in a foreign country employed by a domestic individual or company to facilitate transactions with local individuals or businesses in the foreign country.

compressed gases

(shipping) Items requiring storage and handling under pressure in compressed gas cylinders. (UN CLASS 2.) Examples are acetylene and chlorine. Hazards/precautions are: container may explode in heat or fire; contact with liquid may cause frostbite; may be flammable, poisonous, explosive, irritating, corrosive or suffocating; may be EXTREMELY HAZARDOUS.

COMPRO

(information system) An on-line trade data retrieval system maintained by the International Trade Administration within the U.S. Department of Commerce. The system is exclusively for use within the federal government trade community (ITA, USTR, ITC, and other executive branch agencies). COMPRO includes:

(1) U.S. foreign trade data (detailed U.S. merchandise trade statistics compiled by Census);

(2) UN trade data (trade statistics of 170 countries;

(3) International Monetary Fund and World Bank databases (international finance, direction of trade, and developing country debt). COMPRO also maintains gateways to LABSTAT, a product of the Bureau of Labor Statistics.

computed value

(U.S. Customs) Generally, the Customs value of all merchandise exported to the United States is the transaction value for the goods. If the transaction value cannot be used, then certain secondary bases are considered. The secondary bases of value, listed in order of precedence for use, are:

(1) Transaction value of identical merchandise, (2) Transaction value of similar merchandise, (3) Deductive value, and (4) Computed value. The order of precedence of the last two values can be reversed if the importer so requests.

Computed value consists of the sum of the following items:

(1) Materials, fabrication, and other processing used in producing the imported merchandise, (2) Profit and general expenses, (3) Any assist, if not included in items 1 and 2, (4) Packaging costs. *See* valuation; transaction value; identical merchandise; similar merchandise; assist; deductive value.

concealed damage

(shipping) Damage to the contents of a package which is in good order externally. *See also* inherent vice.

concealed loss

(shipping) Loss from a package bearing concealed damage. *See also* inherent vice.

concord

(law) An agreement between two parties that states the terms of a settlement of a right of action for a breach or wrongdoing that one of the parties has against the other. A buyer who has paid for goods but has not received them, for example, may agree to forgo the right to sue the seller for breach if the seller agrees to return the money paid. *See* accord and satisfaction.

conditional endorsement

See endorsement.

conditions of carriage

See contract of carriage.

conference

(shipping) A group of ocean freight carriers banding together, voluntarily, for the purpose of limiting and regulating competition among themselves. It may establish uniform tariff freight charges and terms and conditions of service. Conference establishment in the United States requires Federal Maritime Commission approval. Conferences in the United States are exempt from anti-trust regulation. *See* open conference; closed conference.

conference line

(shipping) Ocean shipping companies whose ships travel according to firmly established schedules along fixed routes. Uniform transport rates are established between the shipping lines. Such agreements are usually called conferences. The conference lines are therefore the shipping routes agreed by the conferences. *See* conference; open conference; closed conference.

Conference on Security and Cooperation in Europe

An economic and defense alliance whose members include all recognized countries of Europe, Canada, the USA, and the former republics of the USSR. Included are: Albania, Armenia, Austria, Azerbaijan, Belgium, Bulgaria, Byelarus, Canada, Cyprus, Czech Republic, Denmark, Estonia, Finland, France, Germany, Greece, the Holy See, Hungary, Iceland, Ireland, Italy, Kazakhstan, Kyrgyzstan, Latvia, Liechtenstein, Lithuania, Luxembourg, Malta, Moldova, Monaco, Netherlands, Norway, Poland, Portugal, Romania, Russia, San Marino, Slovakia, Spain, Sweden, Switzerland, Tajikistan, Turkey, Turkmenistan, Ukraine, the United Kingdom, the United States, Uzbekistan and Yugoslavia. Note: The Federal Republic of Yugoslavia (Serbia & Montenegro) was suspended in July 1992. Address: Conference on Security and Cooperation in Europe, Thunovská 12, Malá Strana, 110 00 Prague 1, Czech Republic; Tel: [420] (2) 311-9793; Fax: [420] (2) 311-6215.

conference rate

(shipping) Rates arrived at by conference of carriers applicable to transportation—generally water transportation. *See* conference.

confirmation

(law) A contract or written memorandum that ratifies, renders valid, and makes binding an agreement that was difficult to prove, invalid, or otherwise unenforceable. Parties who orally agree to a sale of goods, for example, may formalize that agreement by signing a written confirmation that contains all of the oral terms. *See* contract.

confirmed letter of credit

(banking) A letter of credit which contains a guarantee on the part of both the issuing and advising banks of payment to the seller so long as the seller's documentation is in order and the terms of the letter of credit are met.

Confirmation is only added to irrevocable letters of credit, usually available with the advising bank. If confirmation of the letter of credit is desired, the applicant must state this expressly in his/her letter of credit application. The confirming bank assumes

the credit risk of the issuing bank as well as the political and transfer risks of the purchaser's country. If a letter of credit does not contain a confirmation request by the issuing bank, in certain circumstances the possibility exists of confirming the letter of credit "by silent confirmation," i.e. without the issuing bank's knowledge. Without confirmation of the letter of credit, the advising bank will forward the letter of credit to the beneficiary without taking on its own commitment. *See* letter of credit.

confirming

A financial service in which an independent company confirms an export order in the seller's country and makes payment for the goods in the currency of that country. Among the items eligible for confirmation are the goods; inland, air, and ocean transportation costs; forwarding fees; custom brokerage fees; and duties. Confirming permits the entire export transaction from plant to end user to be fully coordinated and paid for.

confirming bank

(banking) In letter of credit transactions, the bank that assumes responsibility to the seller (usually exporter) for payment from the issuing bank (buyer's bank) so long as the terms and conditions of the letter of credit have been met by the seller/exporter. *See* letter of credit.

conflict of laws

(law) Differences between the laws of different countries or other jurisdictions that become significant in determining which law will apply when individuals or legal entities have acquired rights, incurred obligations, suffered injuries or damages, or made contracts in two or more jurisdictions. The rules that courts apply to resolve conflicts of laws vary among countries. In addition, different rules apply depending on the subject matter of a controversy—that is, whether a controversy involves property or personal rights. *See* governing law clause; lex loci actus; lex loci solutionis.

connecting carrier

(shipping) A carrier which has a direct physical connection with another carrier or forms a connecting link between two or more carriers.

consideration

(law) The price or other motivation that induces a party to make a contract. A buyer may agree, for example, to pay a sum of money or to furnish certain products as consideration for receiving the seller's goods. A contracting party may also promise to forgo a legal right, such as a right to sue for breach of contract, as consideration for the other party's promise to pay damages that resulted from the breach.

consignee
(shipping) The person or firm named in a freight contract to whom goods have been shipped or turned over for care. *See also* consignor.

consignee marks
(shipping) A symbol placed on packages for export, generally consisting of a square, triangle, diamond, circle, cross, etc., with designed letters and/or numbers for the purpose of identification.

consignment
(shipping) Shipment of one or more pieces of property, accepted by a carrier for one shipper at one time, receipted for in one lot, and moving on one bill of lading.
(commerce) Delivery of merchandise from an exporter (the consignor) to an agent (the consignee) under agreement that the agent sell the merchandise for the account of the exporter. The consignor retains title to the goods until sold. The consignee sells the goods for commission and remits the net proceeds to the consignor.

consignment contract
(law) An agreement by a seller (consignor) to deliver goods to an individual or legal entity (consignee) who will pay the seller for any goods sold, less a commission, and will return goods not sold. *See* consignment.

consignor
(shipping) The individual, company or entity that ships goods, or gives goods to another for care. The consignor is usually the exporter or his agent. *See also* consignee; consignment.

consolidated container
(shipping) A shipping container containing cargo from a number of shippers for delivery to a number of different consignees.

consolidation
(shipping) The combining of less than truckload (LTL) shipments of cargo from a number of shippers at a centrally located point of origin by a freight consolidator, and transporting them as a single shipment to a destination point. Consolidation of cargo often results in reduced shipping rates.

consolidator
(shipping) A company that provides consolidation services. Freight forwarders perform the functions of a consolidator. *See* consolidation.

consolidator's bill of lading
(shipping) A bill of lading issued by a consolidating freight forwarder to a shipper. *See also* bill of lading; house air waybill.

constructed value
(U.S. Customs) In customs valuation, a means of determining fair or foreign market value when sales of such or similar merchandise do not exist or, for various reasons, cannot be used for comparison purposes. The "constructed value" consists of the cost of materials and fabrication or other processing employed in producing the merchandise, general expenses of not less than 10 percent of material and fabrication costs, and profit of not less than 8 percent of the sum of the production costs and general expenses. To this amount is added the cost of packing for exportation. *See* valuation; transaction value.

constructive total loss
(insurance) An insurance loss where the expense of recovering or repairing the insured goods would exceed their value after this expenditure had been incurred.
In the adjustment of constructive total losses, the value of any remaining salvage abandoned to underwriters may, by agreement, be taken into consideration, with payment to the assured upon a net basis. Otherwise, underwriters pay full insured value and may then dispose of the salvage for their own account, provided they have elected to accept abandonment.
If the loss was due to sea peril, a "master's protest" (also called "captain's protest) will usually be required. This certifies the fact that unusually heavy weather or other exceptional circumstance was encountered during the voyage and is extended to confirm the loss of the shipment in question. In claims for total loss, it is especially necessary that a full set of insurance certificates and bills of lading be submitted to the insurance company representative. *See* abandonment; captain's protest.

consular declaration
A formal statement, made in a country of export by the consul of an importing country, describing goods to be shipped to the importing country. *See* consular invoice.

consular invoice
(customs) An invoice covering a shipment of goods certified (usually in triplicate) by the consul of the country for which the merchandise is destined. This invoice is used by customs officials of the country of entry to verify the value, quantity, and nature of the merchandise imported. *See also* commercial invoice.

C

consular officers
(diplomacy) Embassy officials of a country who extend to its citizens and their property abroad the protection of their home government. They maintain lists of local attorneys, act as liaison with police and other officials and have the authority to notarize documents.

consular visa
(travel/customs) Any one of several official endorsements by a consul of a country. A consular visa can be issued for travel, consular invoices, certificates of origin, shipping documents and other legal documents.

consulate
(diplomacy) The offices representing the commercial interests of the citizens of one country in another country.

consumer goods
(economics) Any goods produced to satisfy the needs of individuals rather than those produced for the manufacturing or production of other goods. Examples of consumer goods are food, clothing and entertainment products. *See also* capital goods.

consumption entry
(U.S. Customs) (a) A U.S. Customs entry where the importer pays applicable duty and merchandise is released from customs custody at a U.S. port, foreign trade zone or from a customs bonded warehouse. (b) The formal U.S. Customs process for entering commercial shipments of goods into the Customs territory of the United States. A "formal entry."

The entry of goods is a two-part process consisting of (1) filing the documents necessary to determine whether merchandise may be released from Customs custody, and (2) filing the documents which contain information for duty assessment and statistical purposes. In certain instances, such as the entry of merchandise subject to quotas, all documents must be filed and accepted by Customs prior to the release of goods. *See* entry.

container
(shipping) A single rigid, sealed, reusable metal "box" in which merchandise is shipped by vessel, truck, or rail.

All containers will have construction fittings, or fastenings able to withstand, without permanent distortion, all stresses that may be applied in normal service use of continuous transportation.

Standard lengths include 10, 20, 30, and 40 feet (40 foot lengths are generally able to hold about 40,000 pounds). Containers of 45 and 48 feet are also used, as well as containers for shipment by air. Container types include: standard, high cube, hardtop, open top, flat, platform, ventilated, insulated, refrigerated, bulk.

container freight charge
(shipping) Charge made for the packing or unpacking of cargo into or from ocean freight containers.

container freight station
(shipping) A facility used by ocean carriers to load/unload cargo to and from containers. Most less than container load lots of cargo are either packed into or devanned at a container freight station.

containerization
(shipping) The practice or technique of using a boxlike device (container) in which a number of packages are stored, protected, and handled as a single unit in transit. Advantages of containerization include: less handling of cargo, more protection against pilferage, less exposure to the elements, and reduced cost of shipping.

(air freight) Container descriptions have been broadened to include a unitized load on a carrier-owned pallet, loaded by shippers, and unloaded by receivers at places other than on airline premises, and restrained and contoured so as to permit proper positioning and tiedown aboard the aircraft.

container load
(shipping) A shipment of cargo that in either volume or weight is sufficient to fill any one of many standard containers.

container number
(shipping) An up to seven-digit number (six plus a check digit) used to identify the size and type of container; usually preceded by a four-letter alpha (letter) code prefix designating container ownership.

container on flatcar
(shipping) A container without wheels put on railcars for transport.

container part load
(shipping) A shipment of cargo that in either volume or weight is not sufficient to fill any one of many standard containers.

container vessel
(shipping) An ocean going vessel designed specifically to easily handle the loading, stowage and off-loading of ocean freight containers. Containers may be stowed either below deck or on deck.

container yard
(shipping) The area adjacent to the vessel berth where containers are delivered to and received from the vessel, and delivered to and received from inland carriers.

contango

(banking/finance/foreign exchange) The amount (generally a percentage) a buyer pays a seller to delay transfer of a stock, security or foreign exchange to the next or any future day. The opposite of backwardation.

contingency insurance

(insurance) Also called difference in conditions insurance. Insurance which protects the interests of the insured in the event another party's insurance fails or falls short. Commonly used in both import and export situations:

Example 1: Exporting
There are several countries whose laws require that marine insurance on shipments to those countries be placed with local insurance companies. This has the effect of requiring the importer to furnish the insurance. The quality and extent of coverage of this insurance, however, may be in question. If the exporter feels that he has insurable interest he can still protect himself by the purchase of contingency or difference in conditions insurance which protects his own interests in the event the importer's insurance fails or falls short. While the cost of this is naturally less than the cost of primary insurance, it must be borne by the exporter.

Example 2: Importing
A domestic buyer on C.I.F. (Cost, Insurance, Freight) terms must rely upon foreign underwriters, since the insurance will have been placed by the seller in the country of origin. Once again, the quality and extent of coverage of this insurance may be in question. If the importer feels that he has insurable interest he can still protect himself by the purchase of "contingency" or "difference in conditions" insurance which protects his own interests in the event the exporter's insurance fails or falls short. Note: By purchasing on FOB, C & F or similar terms, the domestic importer can control his own insurance. He will then be able to deal with his own underwriters in case of loss or in case of demand for general average security. *See* insurable interest.

contra; contra account

(banking) An account with an offsetting credit or debit entry. In accounting, a contra account is generally the right-hand or credit side of a balance sheet in which the liabilities appear.

contraband

(customs) Any product which a nation has deemed to be unsuitable to produce, possess or transport. Any product that a country has deemed to be unsuitable for entry into that country. Contraband is subject to interdiction, possible forfeiture and possible destruction by customs authorities. Examples of contraband are, narcotic drugs (most countries), alcohol (certain Islamic countries), seditious literature (many countries), sexually oriented goods and literature (many countries).

contract

(law) An agreement made between two or more parties who promise to perform or not to perform specified acts, which agreement creates for each party a legal duty and the right to seek a remedy for breach of that duty.

(a) A **constructive or implied contract** is an agreement that is implied by law from the circumstances of a business dealing and in accordance with the common understanding between reasonable persons in order to carry out the intent of the parties and do justice between them. (b) An **express contract** is an oral or written agreement the terms of which are explicitly declared when the contract is made. (c) An **executory contract** is one that has not been performed.

contract carrier

(shipping) Any person not a common carrier who under special and individual contracts or agreements, transports passengers or property for compensation. *See also* carrier.

contracting parties

(law) Two or more individuals, companies or groups who are signatories to an agrement or contract.

contract manufacturing

(a) An agreement whereby a company agrees to manufacture a product to the specifications of another company or individual. This can be on an exclusive or non-exclusive sales basis. (b) An agreement by two companies to manufacture separate components of a product and jointly manufacture and sell the finished product in their respective markets.

contract of carriage

(shipping) The contract between the shipper (consignor) and carrier (shipping firm) for the transport of freight, including the terms and conditions of carriage and costs to the shipper. These conditions are printed on the bill of lading or air waybill and include such items as limits of liability, claims limitations, indemnity and dimensional weight rules. *See* bill of lading.

conventional arms transfer

The transfer of non-nuclear weapons, aircraft, equipment, and military services from supplier states to recipient states.

(U.S.) U.S. arms are transferred by grants as in the U.S. Military Assistance Program (MAP); by private commercial sales; and by government-to-government sales under Foreign Military Sales (FMS). MAP provides defense articles and defense services to eligible foreign governments on a grant basis. FMS provides credits and loan repayment guarantees to enable eligible foreign governments to purchase defense articles and defense services.

Convention on Contracts for the International Sale of Goods

(law) A United Nations convention which establishes uniform legal rules governing formation of international sales contracts and the rights and obligations of the buyer and seller. The CISG applies automatically to all contracts for the sale of goods between traders from two different countries that have both ratified the CISG, unless the parties to the contract expressly exclude all or part of the CISG or expressly stipulate a law other than the CISG. The CISG became the law of the United States in January 1988.

Convention on International Trade in Endangered Species of Wild Fauna and Flora (CITES)

An international convention that controls and/or prohibits trade in endangered and threatened species of fauna and flora. Over 100 nations participate in the treaty that took effect in May 1977. The United States is a signatory to the treaty.

convertibility

(banking/foreign exchange) Ease of exchanging one currency for that of another nation or for gold.

convertible currency

(foreign exchange) Currency that can be easily exchanged, bought and sold for other currencies.

coordinated movement

(shipping) The extending of freight transportation systems to intermediate and smaller size communities through the use of interline agreements and the use of combined services of truck/air, helicopters, regional, and commuter airlines. In many cases such traffic moves under a joint freight rate. The success of such combined service hinges on preplanning on the part of the carriers, and often on the part of shippers, with regard to production and distribution schedules.

Coordinating Committee on Multilateral Export Controls

An informal organization established in 1951 by NATO member countries that cooperatively restricts strategic exports (products and technical data) to controlled countries. To date, CoCom consists of NATO countries plus Japan, minus Iceland.

CoCom controls three lists: (1) the international industrial list (synonymous with the "dual-use" or "core" list), (2) the international munitions list, and (3) the atomic energy list. The 17 CoCom members are: Australia, Belgium, Canada, Denmark, France, Germany, Greece, Italy, Japan, Luxembourg, the Netherlands, Norway, Portugal, Spain, Turkey, the United Kingdom and the United States.

CoCom controls exports at three levels, depending on the item and the proposed destination. (1) At the highest or "general exception" level, unanimous approval by CoCom members is necessary. (2) At the next level, "favorable consideration," there is a presumption of approval; the export may be made if no CoCom members objects within 30 days of submission to CoCom. (3) At the lowest level, "national discretion" (also called "administrative exception"), a member nation may approve the export on its own, but CoCom must be notified after the fact. *See* core list.

copyright

(law) An intangible right granted by law to the creator of a literary, musical, or artistic production to prevent any other person from copying, publishing, and selling those works. A copyright owner holds the sole and exclusive privilege to copy, publish, and sell the copyrighted work for the period specified by law. In general, copyright protection is available only after the work is fixed in a tangible medium, such as on paper, tape, canvas, or other materials, from which the work can be seen, reproduced, or otherwise communicated. It is not available to protect an idea, concept, procedure, process, system, operation method, principle, or discovery, but only the work as presented in a tangible medium. The works that can be copyrighted, the requirements for claiming a copyright, the extent of enforcement, and the time during which a copyright is effective varies from country to country. In the United States, for example, a copyright remains effective until 50 years after the death of the creator. In an effort to standardize copyright protection worldwide, many countries have become members of several international conventions on copyrights, including the Berne Convention for the Protection of Literary and Artistic Works, the Universal Copyright Convention, the UNESCO Treaty, the Convention for Protection of Producers of Phonograms against Unauthorized Duplication of Their Phonograms, and the International Convention for the Protection of Performers, Producers of Phonograms and Broadcasting Organizations. *See* Berne Convention for the Protection of Literary and Artistic Works; Universal Copyright Convention.

cordoba

The currency of Nicaragua. 1C$=100 centavos.

core inflation

(economics) The basic level of inflation over a period of time (e.g., a decade) as opposed to temporary fluctuations in the rate.

core list

A categorization and listing of export controlled strategic products by the Coordinating Committee on Multilateral Export Controls (CoCom). East-West controls are based largely on CoCom's core list, which replaced the old industrial list effective September 1991. The core list includes items in ten categories: (1) materials, (2) materials processing, (3) electronics, (4) computers, (5) telecommunications and cryptography, (6) sensors, (7) avionics and navigation, (8) marine technology, (9) propulsion systems and transportation equipment, and (10) miscellaneous. *See* Coordinating Committee on Multilateral Export Controls.

corporate dumping

The practice of exporting banned or out-of-date products from a domestic market to another national market where they are not banned or where regulations are more lax than in the domestic market. Out-of-date pharmaceuticals, for example, might be shipped from the U.S. to an Asian country that does not impose the same restrictions on the product.

corporation

(law) An association or entity created by persons under the authority of the laws of a particular jurisdiction. A corporation is treated as distinct from the persons (referred to as shareholders) who created it, and therefore the shareholders enjoy limited liability and the corporation has certain legal rights, such as the right to own property, enter contracts, and bring suit, similar to those given to individuals. *See* person.

correspondent bank

(banking) A bank that acts as a depository, for another bank, accepting deposits and collecting items

(such as drafts) on a reciprocal basis. Correspondent banks are often in different countries.

corrosives

(shipping) Items include materials that cause destruction to human tissue and corrode metal (i.e. steel) upon contact. (UN CLASS 8.) Examples are sodium hydroxide, hydrochloric acid, alkaline liquid. Hazards/precautions are: contact causes burns to skin and eyes; may be harmful if breathed; fire may produce poisonous fumes; may react violently with water; may ignite combustibles; and explosive gasses may accumulate.

Cost and Freight (...named port of destination) (CFR)

(Incoterms 2000) An international trade term of sale in which, for the quoted price, the seller/exporter/manufacturer clears the goods for export and is responsible for delivering the goods past the ship's rail at the port of shipment (not destination). The seller is also responsible for paying for the costs associated with transport of the goods to the named port of destination. However, once the goods pass the ship's rail at the port of shipment, the buyer assumes responsibility for risk of loss or damage as well as any additional transport costs.

The Cost and Freight term is used only for ocean or inland waterway transport.

The "named port of destination" in Cost and Freight and all "C" Incoterms 2000 is domestic to the buyer.

The Cost and Freight term is commonly used in the sale of oversize and overweight cargo that will not fit into an ocean freight container or exceeds weight limitations of such containers. The term is also used for LCL (less than container load) cargo and for the shipment of goods by rail in boxcars to the ocean carrier.

See Guide to Incoterms 2000 Appendix.

Cost, Insurance, Freight, Commission, and Interest (CIFCI)

(trade term) The same as CIF (cost, insurance and freight), plus commission and interest.

Cost, Insurance and Freight (...named port of destination) (CIF)

(Incoterms 2000) An international trade term of sale in which, for the quoted price, the seller/exporter/manufacturer clears the goods for export and is responsible for delivering the goods past the ship's rail at the port of shipment (not destination). The seller is responsible for paying for the costs associated with transport of the goods to the named port of destination. However, once the goods pass

C

the ship's rail at the port of shipment, the buyer assumes responsibility for risk of loss or damage as well as any additional transport costs.

The seller is also responsible for procuring and paying for marine insurance in the buyer's name for the shipment.

The Cost and Freight term is used only for ocean or inland waterway transport.

The "named port of destination" in Cost and Freight and all "C" Incoterms 2000 is domestic to the buyer.

See Guide to Incoterms 2000 Appendix.

cost of goods sold

(economics/accounting) The purchase price of goods sold during a specified period, including transportation costs.

cost of production

(economics) The sum of the cost of materials, fabrication and/or other processing employed in producing the merchandise sold in a home market or to another country together with appropriate allocations of general administrative and selling expenses. COP is based on the producer's actual experience and does not include any mandatory minimum general expense or profit as in "constructed value." *See* valuation; constructed value.

cost plus

A pricing method whereby the purchaser agrees to pay the vendor an amount determined by the costs incurred by the vendor to produce the goods or services purchased, plus a fixed percentage of that cost for profit.

costs of manufacture (COM)

(U.S. Customs) In the context of dumping investigations, the costs of manufacture, COM, is equal to the sum of the materials, labor and both direct and indirect factory overhead expenses required to produce the merchandise under investigation. *See* dumping.

cottage industry

(economics) An industry dependent upon a labor force that works out of their own homes and often with their own equipment.

Council of Economic Advisers

(U.S. government) A three-member executive office of the president which analyzes the U.S. economy, advises the president on economic developments, appraises programs and policies, and recommends policies for economic growth to the president. Address: Council of Economic Advisers, Old Executive Office Building, 17th St. & Pennsylvania Ave. NW, Washington, DC 20502 USA; Tel: [1] (202) 395-5084; http://www.whitehouse.gov/WH/EOP/CEA/html/CEA.html, (case-sensitive).

Council of Europe

A regional alliance established in May 1949 to encourage unity and social and economic growth among members, which currently include: Austria, Belgium, Bulgaria, Cyprus, Denmark, Finland, France, Germany, Greece, Hungary, Iceland, Ireland, Italy, Liechtenstein, Luxembourg, Malta, the Netherlands, Norway, Poland Portugal, San Marino, Spain, Sweden, Switzerland, Turkey, and the United Kingdom. Address: The Council of Europe, Point 1, F67075 Strasbourg Cedex, France. Tel: [33] (3) 88-41-20-00; Fax: [33] (3) 88-41-27-81; http://www.coe.fr/index.asp.

Council on Security and Cooperation in Europe

See Conference on Security and Cooperation in Europe.

counteroffer

(law) A reply to an offer that adds to, limits, or modifies materially the terms of the offer. A seller, for example, who accepts a buyer's offer, but informs the buyer that the goods will be of a different color has made a counteroffer. *See* acceptance; offer.

counterpurchase

See countertrade.

countertrade

An umbrella term for several sorts of trade in which the seller is required to accept goods or other instruments or trade, in partial or whole payment for its products.

Countertrade transactions include barter, buy-back or compensation, counterpurchase, offset requirements, swap, switch, or triangular trade, evidence or clearing accounts.

The main types are:

(a) **Counterpurchase** (one of the most common forms of countertrade), where an exporter agrees to purchase a quantity of unrelated goods or services from a country in exchange for and in approximate value to the goods he has sold.

(b) **Offset**, where the exporter agrees to use goods and services from the buyer's country in the product being sold. Offsets may be direct or indirect, depending on whether the goods and services are integral parts of the product. In a **direct offset**, a U.S. manufacturer selling a product in a country uses a component that is made in the purchasing country. In an **indirect offset**, the exporter would buy products made in the purchasing country that are peripheral to the manufacture of its product.

(c) **Compensation** or **buy-back**, where exporters of heavy equipment, technology, or even entire facilities agree to purchase a certain percentage of the output of the new facility once it is in production.

(d) **Barter**, which is a simple swap of one good for another. Two parties directly exchange goods deemed to be of approximately equivalent value without any flow of money taking place.

(e) **Switch** trading, is a more complicated form of barter, that involves a chain of buyers and sellers in different markets. A switch arrangement permits the sale of unpaid balances in a **clearing account** to be sold to a third party, usually at a discount, that may be used for producing goods in the country holding the balance.

(f) **Swap**, where products from different locations are traded to save transportation costs. For example, Russian oil may be "swapped" for oil from a Latin American producer, so the Russian oil can be shipped to a country in South Asia, while the Latin American oil is shipped to Cuba.

(g) **Reverse countertrade** where an importer (a U.S. buyer of machine tools from Poland, for example) is required to export goods equivalent in value to a specified percentage of the value of the imported goods—an obligation that can be sold to an exporter in a third country.

(h) **Clearing** agreements between two countries, which is an agreement to purchase specific amounts of each other's products over a specified period of time, using a designated "clearing currency" in the transactions.

countervailing duties

(customs) Special duties imposed on imports to offset the benefits of subsidies to producers or exporters in the exporting country.

(WTO) The World Trade Organization (WTO) "Agreement on Subsidies and Countervailing Measures" permits the use of such duties if the importing country can prove that the subsidy would cause injury to domestic industry.

(U.S.) The Executive Branch of the U.S. government has been legally empowered since the 1890s to impose countervailing duties in amounts equal to any "bounties" or "grants" reflected in products imported into the United States. Under U.S. law and WTO rules a wide range of practices are recognized as constituting subsidies that may be offset

through the imposition of countervailing duties. The Trade Agreements Act of 1979, through amendments to the Tariff Act of 1930 (both U.S. laws) established rigorous procedures and deadlines for determining the existence of subsidies in response to petitions filed by interested parties such as domestic producers of competitive products and their workers. In all cases involving subsidized products from countries recognized by the United States as signatories to the Agreement on Subsidies and Countervailing Duties, or countries which have assumed obligations substantially equivalent to those under the Agreement, U.S. law requires that countervailing duties may be imposed only after the U.S. International Trade Commission has determined that the imports are causing or threatening to cause material injury to an industry in the United States.

Countervailing duties in the U.S. can only be imposed after the International Trade Commission has determined that the imports are causing or threatening to cause material injury to a U.S. industry.

See dumping; General Agreement on Tariffs and Trade; International Trade Commission.

country desk officers

(U.S. government) Country-specific export trade specialists working at the U.S. Department of Commerce in Washington, DC. Country desk officers provide assistance to U.S. exporters on a country specific, rather than commodity specific basis. Their responsibility is to remain current on any issues that would affect U.S. exporters and travelers in the specific country. For information call the United States Department of Commerce, Tel: [1] (202) 482-2000, or the Trade Information Center, Tel: [1] (800) USA-TRADE. *See* U.S. Department of Commerce.

country groups

(U.S. export control) The U.S. Bureau of Export Administration of the U.S. Commerce Department separates countries into seven country groups designated by the symbols: Q, S, T, V, W, Y, Z. *See* export control classification number; Bureau of Export Administration.

country marketing plan

(U.S.) An analysis of a country's business and economic climate, giving emphasis to marketing and trade issues. Usually prepared by the U.S. embassy in the subject country and published by the U.S. Department of Commerce, International Trade Administration. Also available on CD-ROM in the National Trade Data Bank, and available from the U.S. Department of Commerce, 14th Street and

Constitution Ave., Washington, DC 20230 USA; Tel: [1] (202) 482-2000.

country of departure
(shipping) The country from which a ship or shipment has or is scheduled to depart.

country of destination
(shipping) The country that is the ultimate destination for a ship or shipment of goods.

country of dispatch
(shipping) The country from which cargo was shipped.

country of exportation
(shipping) Usually, but not necessarily, the country in which merchandise was manufactured or produced and from which it was first exported. For example, merchandise made in Switzerland and shipped to the United States through Frankfurt, Germany, has as the country of exportation Switzerland.

country of export destination
The country where the goods are to be consumed, further processed, or manufactured, as known to the shipper at the time of exportation. If the shipper does not know the country of ultimate destination, the shipment is credited for statistical purposes to the last country to which the shipper knows that the merchandise will be shipped in the same form as when exported.

country of origin
The country where merchandise was grown, mined, or manufactured.
(U.S. Customs) In instances where the country of origin cannot be determined, transactions are credited to the country of shipment. Certain foreign trade reports show country subcodes to indicate special tariff treatment afforded some imported articles. *See* certificate of origin.

country risk
(economics) The financial risks of a transaction which relate to the political, economic or social instability of a country.

courier
(shipping) (a) An attendant who accompanies a shipment (generally of documents). (b) A company that provides full transportation service, without an accompanying attendant, offering door-to-door air service for time-sensitive documents or small packages on a same-day or next-day basis. Examples are DHL, FedEx (Federal Express) and UPS (United Parcel Service).

courtage
(banking) A European term for brokerage fee.

cover; coverage
See insurance coverage.

cover note
(insurance) Often also called "broker's cover note." Document issued by insurance companies or insurance brokers in lieu of insurance policies or insurance certificates which serves as proof of usual insurance notification and represents cover approval. Cover notes may be accepted under letters of credit only when they are expressly permitted.

credit arrangements
A series of programs under which service providers (such as ocean and air carriers, trucking companies, customs brokers and freight forwarders) extend credit to shippers and consignees for the payment of charges.

creditor nation
(economics) A nation that is owed more foreign currency obligations that it owes other nations. *See also* debtor nation.

credit risk insurance
(insurance) Insurance designed to cover risks of nonpayment for delivered goods.

critical circumstances
(U.S. Customs) A determination made by the Assistant Secretary for Import Administration as to whether there is a reasonable basis to believe or suspect that there is a history of dumping in the United States or elsewhere of the merchandise under consideration, or that the importer knew or should have known that the exporter was selling this merchandise at less than fair value, and there have been massive imports of this merchandise over a relatively short period. This determination is made if an allegation of critical circumstances is received from the petitioner. *See* dumping.

cross-currency exchange risk
(banking/foreign exchange) The exchange risk inherent in carrying out foreign exchange transactions in two or more currencies.

crossed check
(banking) A check that bears on its face two parallel transverse lines and that cannot be presented for cash. A bank that accepts the check may pay the proceeds only to another bank, which will credit the money to the account of the payee of the check. A crossed check may also include the words "and company." A specially crossed check contains in

the crossing lines the name of the bank that will honor the check.

cross rate
(foreign exchange) Exchange rate parities which are not quoted against the dollar.

cruzeiro real
The currency of Brazil. 1Cr$=100 centavos.

cubic capacity
(shipping) The carrying capacity of a container according to measurement in cubic feet, cubic centimeters or cubic meters.

cubic foot
(measurement) A unit of volume measurement equal to 1,728 cubic inches.

currency
(banking/foreign exchange) Name given to the material form of a country's payment medium, for example, "Swiss francs, divided into 100 centimes."

currency adjustment factor
(shipping) A surcharge on freight charges by a carrier to offset foreign currency fluctuations.

currency area
See currency zone.

currency basket
(banking/foreign exchange) A means of establishing value for a composite unit consisting of the currencies of designated nations. Each currency is represented in proportion to its value in relation to the total. The European Currency Unit, for example, is a weighted average of the currencies of the European Community member nations, used as a unit of value in transactions among businesses in the member countries. *See* European Currency Unit.

currency snake
See snake system.

currency swap
(banking/foreign exchange) System whereby an institution with funds in one currency converts them into another and enters into a forward exchange contract to recover the currency borrowed.

currency (term) of insurance
(insurance) A statement of insurance coverage expressed either in time, or for transit from two physical points. For example: one year commencing on a specific date and time, or, from point a to point b. Formerly, the marine insurance policy covered only from the time goods were actually loaded on board an ocean vessel at the port of shipment until they were "discharged and safely landed" at the port of destination. This was later extended by adding the words "including transit by craft, raft and/or lighter to and from the vessel."

More recently, insurance coverage has included risks to a shipment of goods from the time the goods leave the warehouse for commencement of transit and continue during ordinary course of transit until delivered to final warehouse (warehouse-to-warehouse coverage) at destination, or until the expiration of 15 days (30 if destination is outside the limits of the port), whichever shall first occur. In the case of delay in excess of the time limit specified, if it arises from circumstances beyond his control, the assured is "held covered" if he gives prompt notice and pays additional premium. *See also* all risk; Marine Extension Clause 1943 & 1952.

currency translation
(accounting/foreign exchange) The recording in accounts of assets (or liabilities) in once currency when they are actually in another. No actual exchange of funds takes place. The World Bank, for example, translates all their assets and liabilities into U.S. dollar amounts, regardless of the actual currency in which they are denominated.

currency zone
(banking/foreign exchange) Area of validity in spatial terms of a currency; normally coincides with the national frontiers of a country because it is defined by the monetary order. A **supranational currency zone** arises when different currencies are connected either through convertibility or fixed exchange rates. Examples are the Franc zone and the Sterling zone.

current account
(economics) That portion of a country's balance of payments that records current (as opposed to capital) transactions, including visible trade (exports and imports), invisible trade (income and expenditures for services), profits earned from foreign operations, interest and transfer payments. *See* balance of payments.

current balance
(economics) The value of all exports (goods plus services) less all imports of a country over a specific period of time, equal to the sum of the trade (visible) and invisible balances plus net receipts of interest, profits and dividends from abroad. *See* balance of payments.

custody bill of lading
(shipping) A bill of lading issued by American warehouses as a receipt for goods stored. *See* bill of lading.

C

customer automation
(shipping) The use of carrier automation equipment on the customer's premises that aids in the processing of shipments, i.e., airbill preparations, invoicing, weighing, and tracing.

custom house
(customs) The government office where duties, tolls, or taxes placed on imports or exports are paid and vessels entered or cleared.

customized sales survey
(U.S.) A fee-based International Trade Administration service that provides firms with key marketing, pricing, and foreign representation information about their specific products. Overseas staff conduct on-site interviews to provide data in nine marketing areas about the product, such as sales potential in the market, comparable products, distribution channels, going price, competitive factors, and qualified purchasers. Address: Product Manager, Customized Sales Survey, 14th and Constitution Avenue, Room 1517, Washington, DC 20230 USA; Tel: [1] (202) 482-3334; Fax: [1] (202) 482-0973.

customs
(a) A government authority designated to regulate flow of goods to/from a country and to collect duties levied by a country on imports and exports. The term also applies to the procedures involved in such collection. (b) The United States Customs Service. *See* United States Customs Service. (c) Taxes imposed by a government on the import or export of products or services. *See also* tariff.

customs bond
See bond, surety.

customs bonded warehouse
(customs) A federal warehouse where goods remain until duty has been collected from the importer. Goods under bond are also kept here. *See* surety; bond; in bond; bonded warehouse.

customs broker
(U.S. Customs) An individual or firm licensed by the U.S. Customs Service to act for importers in handling the sequence of custom formalities and other details critical to the legal and speedy exporting and importing of goods.

customs classification
(customs) The particular category in a tariff nomenclature in which a product is classified for tariff purposes; or, the procedure for determining the appropriate tariff category in a country's nomenclature system used for the classification, coding and description of internation-

ally traded goods. *See* Harmonized System; Harmonized Tariff Schedule of the United States.

Customs Cooperation Council (CCC)
An intergovernmental organization created in 1953 and headquartered in Brussels, through which customs officials of participating countries seek to simplify, standardize, and conciliate customs procedures. The Council has sponsored a standardized product classification, a set of definitions of commodities for customs purposes, a standardized definition of value and a number of recommendations designed to facilitate customs procedures. *See* Harmonized System.

Customs Cooperation Council Nomenclature
A customs tariff system formerly used by many countries, including most European nations but not the United States. It has been superseded by the Harmonized System Nomenclature to which most major trading nations, including the U.S., adhere. *See* Harmonized System; Harmonized Tariff Schedule of the United States.

customs court
(U.S. Customs) A U.S. Customs Service court based in New York, NY, consisting of three 3-party divisions to which importers may appeal or protest classification and valuation decisions and certain other actions taken by the U.S. Customs Service.

customs declaration
(U.S. Customs) An oral or written statement attesting to the correctness of description, quantity, value, etc., of merchandise offered for importation into the United States. *See* entry.

customs duty
(customs) A tax levied and collected by custom officials in discharging the tariff regulations on imports. *See also* tariff.

customs harmonization
(customs) International efforts to increase the uniformity of customs nomenclatures and procedures in cooperating countries. The Customs Cooperation Council has developed an up-to-date and internationally accepted "Harmonized Commodity Coding and Description System" for classifying goods for customs, statistical, and other purposes. *See* Customs Cooperation Council; Harmonized System; Harmonized Tariff Schedule of the United States.

customshouse broker
See customs broker.

customs import value
(U.S. Customs) U.S. Customs Service appraisal value of merchandise. Methodologically, the Cus-

toms value is similar to Free Alongside Ship (FAS) value since it is based on the value of the product in the foreign country of origin, and excludes charges incurred in bringing the merchandise to the United States (import duties, ocean freight, insurance, and so forth); but it differs in that the U.S. Customs Service, not the importer or exporter, has the final authority to determine the value of the good. *See* valuation.

Customs Information Exchange
A clearing house of information for U.S. Customs Service officers. *See* United States Customs Service.

customs invoice
(customs) An invoice made out on a special form prescribed by the customs authorities of the importing country. Used only in a few countries. *See also* commercial invoice.

customs tariff
(customs) A schedule of charges assessed by government on imported or exported goods. *See* Harmonized System; Harmonized Tariff Schedule of the United States.

customs territory
The geographic territory upon which a soverign nation imposes its import and export regulations and duties. Certain territorial possessions and special economic zones (such as foreign trade zones) are often considered outside the customs territory of a nation.
(U.S. Customs) The customs territory of the United States consists of the 50 states, the District of Columbia, and Puerto Rico. Foreign trade zones are not considered customs territory of the United States. *See* United States Customs Service; foreign trade zone.

customs union
(customs) An agreement by two or more trading countries to dissolve trade restrictions such as tariffs and quotas among themselves, and to develop a common external policy or trade (e.g., trade agreement).

D

D/A
See documents against acceptance.

dalasi
The currency of Gambia. 1D=100 butut.

damages
(law) (a) A loss or harm to a person or his or her property. (b) An award given to a person (usually as a result of a court action) as compensation for a loss.

dangerous goods
(air transport) Articles or substances which are capable of posing a significant risk to health, safety, or property when transported by air and which are classified according to the most current editions of the International Civil Aviation Organization (ICAO) Technical Instructions for the Safe Transport of Dangerous Goods by Air and the IATA (International Air Transport Association) Dangerous Goods Regulations. Dangerous goods may be transported domestically and internationally by air. *See* hazardous materials.

dangerous when wet
(shipping) These items include flammable solids that are reactive with water. (UN CLASS 4.) Examples are: magnesium; aluminum phosphide; lithium hydride; calcium carbide. Hazards are: may ignite in presence of moisture; contact with water produces flammable gas; may re-ignite after fire is extinguished; contact may cause burns to skin and eyes; skin contact may be poisonous; inhalation or vapors may be harmful. Precautions are: prohibit flames or smoking in area.

date draft
(banking) A draft which matures a specified number of days after the date it is issued, without regard to the date of acceptance.
See acceptance; bill of exchange.

dating
The practice of granting extended credit terms by the seller to induce buyers to receive goods in advance of required delivery dates.

deadweight
(shipping) The maximum carrying capacity of a ship, expressed in tons, of cargo, stores, provisions and bunker fuel. Deadweight is used interchangeably with deadweight tonnage and deadweight car-

D

rying capacity. A vessel's capacity for cargo is less than its total deadweight tonnage.

deadweight cargo
(shipping) Cargo of such weight and volume that a long ton (2,240 pounds) is stowed in an area of less than 70 cubic feet.

dealer
An individual or firm who acts as a principal in the sale of merchandise.

debt-for-export swap; debt-for products swap
(banking/trade) Swap whereby a bank arranges to export a variety of domestic products and commodities to offset part of its outstanding claims in the country.

debt-for-nature swap
(banking/trade) Swap arranged by private conservation group to use the proceeds of debt conversions to finance conservation projects relating to park land or tropical forests.

debtor nation
(economics) A nation that is owed less foreign currency obligations that it owes other nations. *See also* creditor nation.

deck cargo
(shipping) Cargo shipped on the deck of a vessel rather than in holds below deck. Cargo shipped on deck is more likely to be adversely affected by heat, cold, rain, seawater and movement of the ship. Some shippers require that their cargo not be shipped on deck. On the other hand, certain dangerous cargo, such as explosives are required to be shipped on deck.

declaration
(insurance) A method of reporting shipments to an insurance company under an open insurance policy. This "short form" calls for the name of the vessel and sailing date, points of shipment and destination, nature of commodity, description of units comprising the shipment, the amount of insurance desired and the number of the open policy under which the declaration is made. The declaration forms are prepared by the assured and are forwarded daily, weekly, or as shipments are made. The forms are forwarded to the insurance agent or broker for transmission to the insurance company. When full information is not available at the time a declaration is made, a provisional report may be sent in. The "provisional" is closed when value is finally known. The premium is billed monthly in accordance with the schedule of rates provided by the policy. The declaration is generally not used in cases where evidence of insurance must be supplied to a customer, to banks or to other third parties in order to permit collection of claims abroad. This calls for a special marine policy, occasionally referred to as a certificate. Declarations, therefore, are usually used for import shipments, not export shipments. *See* open policy; special marine policy; bordereau.

declared value for carriage
(shipping/insurance) The value of goods declared to the carrier by the shipper for the purposes of determining charges, or of establishing the limit of the carrier's liability for loss, damage, or delay. *See* valuation charges.

declared value for customs
(U.S. Customs) The selling price of a shipment or the replacement cost if the shipment is not for resale. The amount must be equal to or greater than the declared value. *See* valuation.

deductible average
(insurance) The deductible amount that is subtracted from each covered average loss whereby the assured always bears part of the loss. *See also* average; particular average; general average; with average; free of particular average.

deductive value
(U.S. Customs) In valuation of merchandise for customs purposes, deductive value is the resale price of imported merchandise in the United States with deductions for certain items. Generally, the deductive value is calculated by starting with a unit price and making certain additions to and deductions from that price.

Unit Price: One of three prices constitutes the unit price in deductive value. The price used depends on *when* and in *what condition* the merchandise concerned is sold in the United States.

(1) *Time and Condition*: The merchandise is sold in the condition as imported at or about the date of importation of the merchandise being appraised. *Price*: The price used is the unit price at which the greatest aggregate quantity of the merchandise concerned is sold at or about the date of importation.

(2) *Time and Condition*: The merchandise concerned is sold in the condition as imported but not sold at or about the date of importation of the merchandise being appraised. *Price*: The price used is the unit price at which the greatest aggregate quantity of the merchandise concerned is sold after the date of importation of the merchandise being ap-

praised, but before the close of the 90th day after the date of importation.

(3) *Time and Condition*: The merchandise concerned is not sold in the condition as imported and not sold before the close of the 90th day after the date of importation of the merchandise being appraised. *Price*: The price used is the unit price at which the greatest aggregate quantity of the merchandise being appraised, after further processing, is sold before the 180th day after the date of the importation.

The third price is also known as the "further processing price" or "superdeductive."

Additions: Packing costs for the merchandise concerned are added to the price used for deductive value, provided these costs have not otherwise been included. These costs are added regardless of whether the importer or the buyer incurs the cost.

Deductions: Certain items are not part of the deductive value and must be deducted from the unit price. These items include:

(1) Commissions or profits and general expense,

(2) Transportation and insurance costs,

(3) Customs duties and federal taxes,

(4) Value of further processing.

If an assist is involved in a sale, that sale cannot be used in determining deductive value.

See valuation; transaction value; identical merchandise; similar merchandise; computed value.

defense memoranda of understanding (MOU)

(U.S.) Defense cooperation agreements between the U.S. and allied nations. MOUs are signed by the U.S. Department of Defense (DOD) with allied nations and are related to research, development, or production of defense equipment or reciprocal procurement of defense items.

Defense Technology Security Administration (DTSA)

(U.S. government) DTSA is the Department of Defense (DOD) organization which reviews applications for the export of items that are subject to the dual-use license controls of the U.S. Commerce Department. DTSA is located in the Office of the Secretary of Defense, and administers DOD technology security policy so that the U.S. is not technologically surprised on the battlefield. Address: Defense Threat Reduction Agency, 45045 Aviation Drive, Dulles VA 20166-7517 USA; Tel: [1] (703) 810-4326; http://www.dtra.mil.

Defense Trade Controls (DTC)

(U.S.) DTC (formerly the Office of Munitions Control, OMC) at the U.S. Department of State ad-

ministers licenses for the export of items that are exclusively, or primarily, of munitions significance. These items are listed in the International Traffic in Arms Regulations (ITAR) and the U.S. Munitions List. In circumstances in which an item may be considered either dual-use or subject to the ITAR, the State Department has the option to assert jurisdiction. In some cases, decisions about jurisdiction are made after an item has been subject to a dual-use license application sent to the Commerce Department. Commerce is never involved in State's process, unless there are matters involving dual-use or issues involving jurisdiction. Address: Defense Trade Controls, Room 228 SA/6, Department of State, Washington, DC 20522-0602 USA; Tel: [1] (703) 875-6644; http://www.prndt.org.

Defense Trade Working Group

(U.S.) A committee of officials from the U.S. Departments of Commerce, Defense, State and the United States Trade Representative (USTR) was established in 1990 to coordinate agency policies and resources in areas concerned with defense expenditures. The group works with industry to identify ways to target industry needs and increase the success of industry export efforts by minimizing government impediments, streamlining procedures, and improving the availability of market information. The DTWG includes three subgroups: (1) The **Defense Export Market Opportunity Subgroup**, chaired by the U.S. Department of Commerce, which helps implement Administration defense export policy and enhances U.S. government support for U.S. defense exporters; (2) The **European Defense Cooperation Subgroup**, chaired by the U.S. Department of State, which coordinates interagency input to U.S.-NATO International Staff for the NATO Council on National Armaments Directors (CNAD) study on defense trade; and (3) The **Technology Transfer/Third Country Reexport Subgroup**, chaired by the U.S. Department of Defense, which works with industry to define a more proactive technology transfer regime that could be implemented within the limits of U.S. national security and industrial competitiveness interests.

deferred air freight

(shipping) Air freight of a less time sensitive nature, with delivery provided over a period of days.

deferred payment letter of credit

(banking) A letter of credit which enables the buyer to take possession of the title documents and the goods by agreeing to pay the issuing bank at a fixed time in the future. *See* letter of credit.

delay clause

(insurance) An insurance policy clause which excludes claims for loss of market and for loss, damage or deterioration arising from delay. This exclusion appears in almost every marine cargo insurance policy.

Insurance underwriters are exceedingly reluctant to assume any liability for loss of market, which is generally considered a "trade loss" and uninsurable. A market loss, furthermore, is an indirect or consequential damage. It is not a "physical loss or damage." *See* special marine policy.

del credere risk

(law) Risk that a counterparty is either unable or unwilling to fulfill his payment obligations.

Delivered At Frontier (...named place) (DAF)

(Incoterms 2000) An international trade term of sale in which, for the quoted price, the seller/exporter/manufacturer clears the goods for export and is responsible for making them available to the buyer at the named point and place at the frontier, not unloaded, and not cleared for import.

In the DAF term, naming the precise point, place, and time of availability at the frontier is very important as the buyer must make arrangements to unload and secure the goods in a timely manner.

Frontier can mean any frontier including the frontier of export.

The DAF term is valid for any mode of shipment, so long as the final shipment to the named place at the frontier is by land.

The seller is not responsible for procuring and paying for insurance cover.

See Guide to Incoterms 2000 Appendix.

Delivered Duty Paid (...named place of destination) (DDP)

(Incoterms 2000) An international trade term of sale in which, for the quoted price, the seller/exporter/manufacturer clears the goods for export and is responsible for making them available to the buyer at the named place of destination, cleared for import, but not unloaded from the transport vehicle.

The seller, therefore, assumes all responsibilities for delivering the goods to the named place of destination, including all responsibility for import clearance, duties, and other costs payable upon import. The DDP term can be used for any mode of transport.

The DDP term is used when the named place of destination (point of delivery) is other than the seaport or airport.

See Guide to Incoterms 2000 Appendix.

Delivered Duty Unpaid (...named place of destination) (DDU)

(Incoterms 2000) An international trade term of sale in which, for the quoted price, the seller/exporter/manufacturer clears the goods for export and is responsible for making them available to the buyer at the named place of destination, not cleared for import.

The seller, therefore, assumes all responsibilities for delivering the goods to the named place of destination, but the buyer assumes all responsibility for import clearance, duties, administrative costs, and any other costs upon import as well as transport to the final destination.

The DDU term can be used for any mode of transport. However, if the seller and buyer desire that delivery should take place on board a sea vessel or on a quay (wharf), the DES or DEQ terms are recommended.

The DDU term is used when the named place of destination (point of delivery) is other than the seaport or airport.

See Guide to Incoterms 2000 Appendix.

Delivered Ex Quay (...named port of destination) (DEQ)

(Incoterms 2000) An international trade term of sale in which, for the quoted price, the seller/exporter/manufacturer clears the goods for export and is responsible for making them available to the buyer on the quay (warf) at the named port of destination, not cleared for import.

The buyer, therefore, assumes all responsibilities for import clearance, duties, and other costs upon import as well as transport to the final destination. (This is new for Incoterms 2000.)

The DEQ term is used only for shipments of goods arriving at the port of destination by ocean or by inland waterway.

See Guide to Incoterms 2000 Appendix.

Delivered Ex Ship (...named port of destination) (DES)

(Incoterms 2000) An international trade term of sale in which, for the quoted price, the seller/exporter/manufacturer clears the goods for export and is responsible for making them available to the buyer on board the ship at the named port of destination, not cleared for import.

The seller is thus responsible for all costs of getting the goods to the named port of destination prior to unloading.

The DES term is used only for shipments of goods by ocean or inland waterway or by multimodal

transport where the final delivery is made on a vessel at the named port of destination.
See Guide to Incoterms 2000 Appendix.

delivery
(shipping/law) The act of transferring physical possession, such as the transfer of property from consignor to carrier, one carrier to another, or carrier to consignee.

delivery carrier
(shipping) The carrier (transport company) whose responsibility is to place a shipment at the disposal of the consignee at the address stated on the bill of lading. *See* carrier; bill of lading.

delivery instructions
(shipping) Specific delivery instructions for the freight forwarder or carrier (transport company) stating exactly where the goods are to be delivered, the deadline, and the name, address, and telephone number of the person to contact if delivery problems are encountered. *See also* delivery order.

delivery order
(shipping) (a) A document from the consignee, shipper, or owner of freight ordering a terminal operator, carrier, or warehouseman to deliver freight to another party. (b) An order from a steamship company to the terminal superintendent for the release of goods to a consignee following payment of freight charges. (c) Order to deliver specified packages out of a combined consignment covered by one single bill of lading.

delta
(general/statistics) An increment of a variable.
(finance/foreign exchange) Measure of the relationship between an option price and the underlying futures contract or stock price.
The delta ratio indicates by how many units the premium on an option changes for a one unit change in the value of the underlying instrument. An at-the-money option has a delta of about 0.5. The deeper the option is in-the-money, the closer the delta gets to 1 and the deeper the option is out-of-the-money, the more the delta approaches 0.

delta hedging
(banking/foreign exchange) A method used by options writers to hedge risk exposure of written options by purchase or sale of the underlying instrument in proportion to the delta. Example: the writer of a call option with a delta of 0.5 would have to buy half the amount of the instrument underlying the option (e.g., US$), which he might eventually be forced to deliver upon expiry of the option.

demand
(banking/law) (a) A request for the payment of a debt or other amount due. (b) A demand clause is a term in a note by which the note holder can compel full payment if the maker of the note fails to meet an installment.

demise
(law) A lease of property. A demise charter is a bareboat charter. *See* bareboat charter.

demurrage
(shipping) (a) The detention of a freight car or ship by the shipper beyond time permitted (grace period) for loading or unloading, (b) The extra charges a shipper pays for detaining a freight car or ship beyond time permitted for loading or unloading. Used interchangeably with detention. Detention applies to equipment. Demurrage applies to cargo. *See* detention.

denar
The currency of Macedonia. 1 denar=100 deni.

density
(shipping) (a) The weight of an article or container per cubic foot. (b) The ratio of mass to bulk or volume.

Department of Agriculture (DOA)
See United States Department of Agriculture.

Department of Commerce (DOC)
See United States Department of Commerce.

Department of Defense (DOD)
See United States Department of Defense.

Department of Energy (DOE)
See United States Department of Energy.

Department of Labor (DOL)
See United States Department of Labor.

Department of State
See United States Department of State.

Department of the Interior (DOI)
See United States Department of the Interior.

Department of the Treasury
See United States Department of the Treasury.

Department of Transportation (DOT)
See United States Department of Transportation.

deposit dealings
(banking) Money market operations.

deposit money
(banking) Also known as bank or giro money. Bank, giro and postal giro account credit balances which can be converted at any time into notes and coinage, but which are normally used for cash-less payment transactions.

D

deposit of estimated duties
(U.S. Customs) This refers to antidumping duties which must be deposited upon entry of merchandise into the United States which is the subject of an antidumping duty order for each manufacturer, producer or exporter equal to the amount by which the foreign market value exceeds the United States price of the merchandise. *See* antidumping duties; dumping.

depreciation
(economics/accounting) (a) The charges against earnings to write-off the purchase price of an asset over its useful life. (b) The decline in the value of a property or asset.
(foreign exchange) The decline in value of one currency in relation to another currency.

deputy chief of mission (DCM)
(diplomacy) Position second-in-command to ambassador in an embassy. The DCM is responsible for managing the daily operations of all departments in an embassy. Also serves as acting ambassador during the absence of the ambassador.

destination
(shipping) The place to which a shipment is consigned.

detention
(shipping) (a) Holding a carrier's driver and/or trailer beyond a certain stated period of "free time," often resulting in the assessment of detention charges. (b) The delay in clearing goods through customs resulting in storage and other charges. *See* demurrage.

detention charges
(shipping) Charges assessed by a carrier against the consignor or consignee as compensation for holding a carrier's driver and/or trailer beyond a certain stated period of "free time." Detention is an accessorial service and charge. *See also* demurrage.

detention insurance
(insurance) Insurance coverage to pay for the costs resulting in the storage or maintenance of goods delayed in the clearance of customs at a foreign port.

devaluation
(economics) The lowering of the value of a national currency in terms of the currency of another nation. Devaluation tends to reduce domestic demand for imports in a country by raising their prices in terms of the devalued currency and to raise foreign demand for the country's exports by reducing their prices in terms of foreign currencies. Devaluation can therefore help to correct a balance of payments deficit and sometimes provide a short-term basis for economic adjustment of a national economy.
In a fixed exchange rate situation, devaluation occurs as the result of an administrative action taken by a government to reduce the value of its domestic currency in terms of gold or foreign monies.
In a free exchange rate situation, devaluation occurs as a result of the action of the foreign exchange market where the value of the domestic currency drops by market forces against a specific unit of foreign currency.

devanning
(shipping) The unloading of cargo from a container. Also called stripping.

developed countries
(economics) A term used to distinguish the more industrialized nations—including all Organization for Economic Cooperation and Development (OECD) member countries as well as the Soviet Union and most of the socialist countries of Eastern Europe—from "developing"—or less developed countries. The developed countries are sometimes collectively designated as the "North," because most of them are in the Northern Hemisphere. *See also* developing countries.

developing countries
(economics) A broad range of countries that generally lack a high degree of industrialization, infrastructure and other capital investment, sophisticated technology, widespread literacy, and advanced living standards among their populations as a whole. The developing countries are sometimes collectively designated as the "South," because a large number of them are in the Southern Hemisphere. All of the countries of Africa (except South Africa), Asia and Oceania (except Australia, Japan and New Zealand), Latin America, and the Middle East are generally considered "developing countries" as are a few European countries (Cyprus, Malta, Turkey and countries of the former Yugoslavia, for example). Some experts differentiate four sub-categories of developing countries as having different economic needs and interests: (1) A few relatively wealthy Organization of Petroleum Exporting Countries (OPEC) countries— sometimes referred to as oil exporting developing countries—share a particular interest in a financially sound international economy and open capital markets; (2) Newly Industrializing Countries (NIC's) have a growing stake in an open international trading system; (3) A number of middle income countries—principally commodity exporters—have shown a

particular interest in commodity stabilization schemes; and (4) More than 30 very poor countries ("least developed countries") are predominantly agricultural, have sharply limited development prospects during the near future, and tend to be heavily dependent on official development assistance.

difference in conditions insurance
See contingency insurance.

differential
(shipping) An amount added to or deducted from a shipping base rate between two established points to make a rate to or from some other points or via another route.

dimensional weight
(shipping) Dimensional weight refers to density, i.e., weight per cubic foot of a shipment of cargo. The weight of a shipment per cubic foot is one of its most important transportation characteristics. Some commodities, such as machinery, have a relatively high density. Others, like hats, have a relatively low density. Hence, the **dimensional weight rule** was developed as a practice applicable to low density shipments under which the transportation charges are based on a cubic dimensional weight rather than upon actual weight. Examples: one pound for each 194 cubic inches of the shipment in the case of most domestic air freight, one pound for each 266 cubic inches of cut flowers or nursery stock shipments, and one pound for each 194 cubic inches of most international shipments.

dinar
The currency of:
Algeria, 1DA=100 centimes;
Bahrain, 1BD=1,000 fils;
Bosnia-Herzegovina, (no symbol available, no subcurrency);
Croatia, HrD (no subcurrency in use);
Iraq, 1ID=1,000 fils;
Jordan, 1JD=1,000 fils;
Kuwait, 1 KD=1,000 fils;
Libya, 1LD=100 dirhams;
Tunisia, 1D=1,000 fils;
Yugoslavia, Yun (no subcurrency in use).

direct (foreign) investment
(economics) Investment that is made to acquire a lasting interest in an enterprise operating in an economy other than that of the investor.
(U.S.) In the United States, direct investment is defined for statistical purposes as the ownership or control, directly or indirectly, by one person of 10 percent of more of the voting securities of an incorporated business enterprise, or an equivalent interest in an unincorporated business enterprise. Direct investment transactions are not limited to transactions in voting securities. The percentage ownership of voting securities is used to determine if direct investment exists, but once it is determined that it does, all parent-affiliate transactions, including those not involving voting securities, are recorded under direct investment. *See* affiliate; affiliated foreign group; foreign direct investment in the United States.

dirham
The currency of:
Morocco, 1DH=100 centimes;
United Arab Emirates, 1Dh (or 1UD)=1,000 fils.

dirty floating
See floating.

discharge
(shipping) The unloading of passengers or cargo from a vessel, vehicle or aircraft.

disclosure meeting
(U.S.) An informal meeting at which the International Trade Administration (ITA) discloses to parties the proceeding methodology used in determining the results of an antidumping investigation or administrative review. *See* dumping.

discounting
(general) The sale at less than original price value of a commodity or monetary instrument, often for immediate payment.
(banking/letters of credit) The beneficiary under a usance/term letter of credit has the possibility of discounting his claim for immediate payment. The bank credits the beneficiary with the value of the documents, less the discount, but on an unconfirmed credit, reserves the right of recourse. (*See* recourse.) In the case of a confirmed letter of credit the discount would be without recourse.

discount/markdown
(foreign exchange) In foreign exchange, refers to a situation where currency can be bought more cheaply at a future date than for immediate delivery. For example, if US$1 buys FF4 for delivery now, while it buys FF5 for delivery twelve months hence, then the franc is said to be at a discount against the U.S. dollar.

discount rate
(banking) (a) Annualized rate of discount applied to debt securities issued below par (e.g., U.S. Treasury bills). (b) Rate at which a central bank (Fed-

eral Reserve System in the U.S.) (re)discounts certain bills for financial institutions.

discrepancies
(banking/letters of credit) The non-compliance of documents with the terms and conditions of a letter of credit. Information (or missing information or missing documents/papers, etc.) in the documents submitted under a letter of credit, which: (1) is not consistent with its terms and conditions; (2) is inconsistent with other documents submitted; (3) does not meet the requirements of the Uniform Customs and Practice for Documentary Credits (UCPDC).

If the documents show discrepancies of any kind, the issuing bank is no longer obliged to pay and, in the case of a confirmed letter of credit, neither is the confirming bank (strict documentary compliance). *See* letter of credit; Uniform Customs and Practice for Documentary Credits.

discrimination
(shipping) The granting of preferential rates or other privileges to some shippers or receivers which are not accorded to others under practically the same conditions. In the U.S., laws regulating common carriers prohibit discrimination.

dishonor
(banking) The refusal of the maker of a promissory note to pay upon presentation of the note.

dismissal of petition
(U.S.) A determination made by the U.S. Office of Administration that an antidumping petition does not properly allege the basis on which antidumping duties may be imposed, does not contain information deemed reasonably available to the petitioner supporting the allegations, or is not filed by an appropriate interested party. *See* dumping.

dispatch
(shipping) (a) An amount paid by a vessel's operator to a charter if loading or unloading is completed in less time than stipulated in the charter agreement. (b) The release of a container to an interline carrier.

displacement of vessel
(shipping) The weight of the quantity of water displaced by a vessel without stores, bunker fuel or cargo. Displacement "loaded" is the weight of the vessel, plus cargo and stores.

disposable income
(economics) Personal income minus income taxes and other taxes paid by an individual, the balance being available for consumption or savings.

dispute settlement
(general) Resolution of a conflict, usually through a compromise between opposing claims, sometimes facilitated through the efforts of an intermediary such as an arbiter.

distrain
(law) The detention or seizure of the property of an individual or legal entity to secure that party's performance of a particular act. A court may order that property be distrained, for example, to ensure that an individual or legal entity will appear or be represented before the court at a hearing.

distribution license
(U.S.) A license that allows the holder to make multiple exports of authorized commodities to foreign consignees who are approved in advance by the U.S. Bureau of Export Administration. The procedure also authorizes approved foreign consignees to reexport among themselves and to certain approved countries. *See* Bureau of Export Administration.

distribution service
(shipping) A service under which an airline accepts one shipment from one shipper and, after transporting it as a single shipment, separates it into a number of parts at destination and distributes them to many receivers. *See* assembly service.

distributor
An agent who sells directly for a supplier and maintains an inventory of the supplier's products.

District Export Councils
(U.S.) A voluntary auxiliary of the United States and Foreign Commercial Service (US&FCS) district offices to support export expansion activities. There are 51 DECs with 1800 members which help with workshops and also provide counseling to less experienced exporters. *See* United States and Foreign Commercial Service.

diversion
(shipping) (a) Any change in the billing of a shipment after it has been received by the carrier at point of origin and prior to delivery at destination. (b) The diverting of a shipment of goods from the original port of destination to another port due to circumstances such as a storm at sea, breakdown of the vessel or other factors generally out of the control of the shipping line. *See also* reconsignment.

diversionary dumping
(customs) The sale of foreign products to a third country market at less than fair value where the product is further processed and shipped to another country. *See* dumping.

dobra
The currency of Sao Tomé and Principe. 1Db=100 centimos.

dock
(shipping) (a) Loading or unloading platform at an industrial location or carrier terminal. (b) The space or waterway between two piers or wharves for receiving a ship.

dock examination
(U.S. Customs) A U.S. Customs examination during which a container is opened for a thorough inspection, as opposed to a tailgate examination, which requires only a visual inspection at the exit gate. It may be necessary to devan the container in order for customs to make its inspection.

dock receipt
(shipping) A receipt issued by a warehouse supervisor or port officer certifying that goods have been received by the shipping company. The dock receipt is used to transfer accountability when an export item is moved by the domestic carrier to the port of embarkation and left with the international carrier for movement to its final destination.

documentary collection
(banking) A method of effecting payment for goods whereby the seller/exporter ships goods to the buyer, but instructs his bank to collect a certain sum from the buyer/importer in exchange for the transfer of title, shipping and other documentation enabling the buyer/importer to take possession of the goods. The two types of documentary collection are:
(a) **Documents against Payment (D/P)** where the bank releases the documents to the buyer/importer only against a cash payment in a prescribed currency; and
(b) **Documents against Acceptance (D/A)** where the bank releases the documents to the buyer/importer against acceptance of a bill of exchange (draft) guaranteeing payment at a later date.
In documentary collections, banks act in a fiduciary capacity and make every effort to ensure that payment is received, but are liable only for the correct execution of the collection instructions, and do not make any commitment to pay the seller/exporter themselves.
Documentary collections are subject to the Uniform Rules of Collections, Brochure No. 322, revised 1978, of the International Chamber of Commerce (ICC) in Paris.
See Uniform Rules for Collections; International Chamber of Commerce.

documentary credit;
documentary letter of credit
(banking) The formal terminology for letter of credit. *See* letter of credit.

documentary instructions
(banking) The formal list and description of documents (primarily shipping documents) a buyer requires of the seller, especially in a documentary letter of credit. *See* documentation; letter of credit.

documentation
(general) All or any of the financial and commercial documents relating to a transaction.
Documents in an international trade transaction may include: commercial invoice, consular invoice, customs invoice, certificate of origin, bill of lading, inspection certificates, bills of exchange and others.
(banking) The documents required for a letter of credit or documentary collection (documents against payment or documents against acceptance) transaction. *See* letter of credit; documentary collection.
(customs) The documents required by the customs authority of a country to effect entry of merchandise into the country. *See* entry.
(shipping) The function of receiving, matching, reviewing, and preparing all the paperwork necessary to effect the shipment of cargo. This includes bills of lading, dock receipts, export declarations, manifests, etc.

documents against acceptance (D/A)
See documentary collection.

documents against payment (D/P)
See documentary collection.

dollar
The currency of:
American Samoa (uses U.S. dollar)
Anguilla, 1EC$=100 cents;
Antigua and Barbuda, 1EC$=100 cents;
Australia, 1$A=100 cents;
Bahamas, 1B$=100 cents;
Barbados, 1Bds$=100 cents;
Belize, 1Bz$=100 cents;
Bermuda, 1Ber$=100 cents;
British Virgin Islands (uses U.S. dollar);
Brunei, 1B$=100 cents;
Canada, 1Can$=100 cents;
Cayman Islands, 1CI$=100 cents;
Dominica, 1EC$-100 cents;
Fiji, 1F$=100 cents;
Grenada, 1EC$=100 cents;
Guam (uses U.S. dollar);
Guyana, 1G$=100 cents;

D

Hong Kong, 1HK$=100 cents;
Jamaica, 1J$=100 cents;
Kiribati (uses Australian dollar);
Liberia, 1$=100 cents;
Montserrat, 1EC$=100 cents;
Nauru (uses Australian dollar);
New Zealand, 1$NZ=100 cents;
Puerto Rico (uses U.S. dollar);
St. Christopher, 1EC$=100 cents;
St. Kitts-Nevis, 1EC$=100 cents;
St. Lucia, 1EC$=100 cents;
St. Vincent and the Grenadines, 1EC$=100 cents;
Singapore, 1S$=100 cents;
Solomon Islands, 1SI$=100 cents;
Taiwan, 1NT$=100 cents;
Trinidad and Tobago, 1TT$=100 cents;
Turks and Caicos Islands (uses U.S. dollar);
Tuvalu (uses Australian dollar);
United States, 1US$=100 cents;
Virgin Islands, U.S. & British (uses U.S. dollar);
Zimbabwe, 1Z$=100 cents.

dolly
(shipping) A piece of equipment with wheels used to move containers, pallets or freight with or without the aid of a tractor.

domestic exports
(U.S.) Exports of commodities which are grown, produced, or manufactured in the United States, and commodities of foreign origin which have been changed in the United States, including U.S. foreign trade zones, from the form in which they were imported, or which have been enhanced in value by further manufacture in the United States.

domestic international sales corporation (DISC)
(U.S.) A special U.S. corporation authorized by the U.S. Revenue Act of 1971, as amended by the Tax Reform Act of 1984, to borrow from the U.S. Treasury at the average one-year Treasury bill interest rate to the extent of income tax liable on 94 percent of its annual corporate income. To qualify, the corporation must derive 95 percent of its income from U.S. exports; also, at least 95 percent of its gross assets, such as working capital, inventories, building and equipment, must be export-related. Such a corporation can buy and sell independently, or can operate as a subsidiary of another corporation. It can maintain sales and service facilities outside the United States to promote and market its goods. DISCs can now provide a tax deferral on up to $10 million of exports so long as the funds remain in export-related investments.

domicile
(banking) The place where a draft or acceptance is made payable. *See* bill of exchange.

dong
The currency of Vietnam. 1D=100 xu.

door-to-door
(shipping) Shipping service from shipper's door to consignee's door. Originating carrier spots (places) empty container at shipper's facility at carrier's expense for loading by and at expense of shipper. The delivering carrier spots the loaded container at consignee's facility at carrier's expense for unloading by and at expense of consignee.

double-column tariff
(customs) An import tariff schedule listing two rates. The rates in one column are for products imported from preferred trading partner countries, while the rates in the second column are for products imported from non-preferred trading countries. *See* column 1 rates; column 2 rates; Harmonized Tariff Schedules of the United States.

downstream dumping
(customs) The sale of products by a manufacturer below cost to a secondary producer in its domestic market where the product is then further processed and shipped to another country. *See* dumping.

D/P
See documents against payment.

drachma
The currency of Greece. 1Dr=100 lepta.

draft; draft bill of exchange
See bill of exchange.

draft or draught
(shipping) The vertical distance between the waterline and the bottom of the keel of a vessel. The draft of a vessel determines the minimum depth of water in a channel or waterway required for the vessel to travel safely. *See also* plimsoll mark.

drawback—refund of duties
(U.S. Customs) The refund of all or part of customs duties, or domestic tax paid on imported merchandise which was subsequently either manufactured into a different article or reexported.

The purpose of drawback is to enable a domestic manufacturer to compete in foreign markets without the handicap of including in his costs, and consequently in his sales price, the duty paid on imported raw materials or merchandise used in the subsequent manufacture of the exported goods.
There are several types of drawback:

(a) **Direct identification drawback** provides a refund of duties paid on imported merchandise that is partially or totally used in the manufacture of an exported article. Identification of the imported merchandise from import to export is required by proper record-keeping procedures. The imported merchandise must be used in the manufacturing process and exported within 5 years from date of importation of merchandise.

(b) **Substitution drawback** provides for a refund of duties paid on designated imported merchandise upon exportation of articles manufactured or produced with use of substituted domestic or imported merchandise that is of the same kind or quality as the designated imported merchandise. Same kind and quality means merchandise that is interchangeable in a specific manufacturing process. The imported materials must be used in a manufacturing process within 3 years after receipt by manufacturer, the domestic material of same kind and quality as imported materials must be used in manufacturing process within 3 years of receipt of the imported material and the exported products must be manufactured within 3 years after receipt of imported material by manufacturer, and exported within 5 years of date of importation of designated material.

(c) **Rejected merchandise drawback** is a 99 percent refund of duties paid on imported merchandise found not to conform to sample or specification, or shipped without the consent of the consignee, if returned to Customs custody within 90 days of its original Customs release (unless an extension is granted) for examination and exportation under Customs supervision.

Questions regarding the legal aspects of drawback should be addressed to: Chief, Drawback Section, Office of Trade Operations, U.S. Customs Service, 1301 Constitution Avenue NW, Washington, DC 20229 USA; Tel: [1] (202) 927-0300; Fax: [1] (202) 927-1096.

drawback system
(U.S. Customs) A part of U.S. Customs' Automated Commercial System, provides the means for processing and tracking of drawback claims. *See* Automated Commercial System; drawback.

drawee
(banking) The individual or firm on whom a draft is drawn and who owes the indicated amount. In a documentary collection, the drawee is the buyer. *See* drawer; bill of exchange.

drawer
(banking) The individual or firm that issues or signs a draft and thus stands to receive payment of the indicated amount from the drawee. In a documentary collection, the drawer is the seller. *See* drawee; bill of exchange.

dray
(shipping) A vehicle used to haul cargo or goods.

drayage
(shipping) The charge made for hauling freight or carts, drays or trucks.

droit moral
(law) Moral right doctrine, which is a European legal theory that gives artists certain rights with respect to their works, including to create, disclose, and publish a work; to withdraw it from publication; to be identified as its creator; and to prevent alteration of it without permission.

dropoff
(shipping) The delivery of a shipment by a shipper to a carrier for transportation.

dropoff charge
(shipping) A charge made by a transportation company for delivery of a container.

drop shipment
(shipping) A shipment of goods from a manufacturer directly to a dealer or consumer, avoiding shipment to the wholesaler (drop shipper). The wholesaler, however, is compensated for taking the order.

dry-bulk container
(shipping) A container designed to carry any of a number of free-flowing dry solids such as grain or sand.

dry-cargo container
(shipping) Any shipping container designed to transport goods other than liquids.

dry cargo/ freight
(shipping) Cargo which does not require temperature control.

dual exchange rate
(foreign exchange) The existence of two or more exchange rates for a single currency.

dual pricing
The selling of identical products in different markets for different prices. This often reflects dumping practices. *See* dumping.

dumping
(customs) The sale of a commodity in a foreign market at less than fair value, usually considered to

be a price lower than that at which it is sold within the exporting country or to third countries.

"Fair value" can also be the constructed value of the merchandise, which includes cost of production plus a mandatory 8 percent profit margin.

Dumping is generally recognized as an unfair trade practice because it can disrupt markets and injure producers of competitive products in an importing country.

(a) With **price-price dumping**, the foreign producer can use its sales in the high-priced market (usually the home market) to subsidize its sales in the low-priced export market. The price difference is often due to protection in the high-priced market.

(b) **Price-cost dumping** indicates that the foreign supplier has a special advantage. Sustained sales below cost are normally possible only if the sales are somehow subsidized.

(c) **Diversionary dumping** is the sale of foreign products to a third country at less than fair value where the product is further processed and shipped to another country.

(d) **Downstream dumping** is the sale of products below cost to a secondary producer in the original producer's domestic market who then further processes the product and ships it to a foreign country.

(U.S.) The U.S. Antidumping Law of 1921, as amended, considered dumping as constituting "sales at less than fair value," combined with injury, the likelihood of injury, or the prevention of the establishment of a competitive industry in the United States. The Trade Act of 1974 added a "cost of production" provision, which required that dumping determinations ignore sales in the home market of the exporting country or in third country markets at prices that are too low to "permit recovery of all costs within a reasonable period of time in the normal course of trade." The Trade Agreements Act of 1979 repealed the 1921 act, but reenacted most of its substance in Title VII of the Tariff Act of 1930.

See countervailing duties; antidumping duties; constructed value; dumping margin; fair value.

dumping margin

(customs) The amount by which imported merchandise is sold in a country below the home market or third country price or the constructed value (that is, at less than its "fair value"). For example, if the U.S. "purchase price" of an imported article is $200 and the fair value is $220, the dumping margin is $20. This margin is expressed as a percentage of the import country price. In this example, the margin is 10 percent. *See* dumping; fair value.

dunnage

(shipping) Material placed around cargo to prevent damage or breakage by preventing movement. The material is normally furnished by the shipper and its weight is charged for in the rating of the shipment.

durable goods

(economics) Any product which is not consumed through use. Examples are automobiles, furniture, computers and machinery.

dutiable list

(customs) Items listed in a country's tariff schedule for which it charges import duty.

See Harmonized System; Harmonized Tariff Schedule of the United States.

duty

(customs) A tax levied by a government on the import, export or consumption of goods. Usually a tax imposed on imports by the customs authority of a country. Duties are generally based on the value of the goods (ad valorem duties), some other factors such as weight or quantity (specific duties), or a combination of value and other factors (compound duties).

See ad valorem; specific rate of duty; compound rate of duty.

(U.S. Customs) All goods imported into the United States are subject to duty or duty-free entry in accordance with their classification under the applicable items in the Harmonized Tariff Schedule of the United States (HTS or HTSUS). An annotated, loose-leaf edition of the HTS may be purchased from the Superintendent of Documents, U.S. Government Printing Office, Washington, DC 20402 USA; Tel: [1] (202) 512-1800.

Note that duty rates are subject to the classification of goods by Customs. Articles that appear to be similar may have significantly different rates of duty. *See* classification.

Note also that the actual duty paid is also determined by how Customs values the merchandise. *See* Harmonized Tariff Schedule, valuation.

duty drawback

See drawback.

E

easement

(law) A right to use another person's property. A property owner who, to enter and exit the property, is given a right to cross another person's adjoining property holds an easement. The right to use an easement is a servitude against the property burdened. *See* servitude.

Eastern Europe Business Information Center (EEBIC)

(U.S. government) A Department of Commerce facility that was opened in January 1990 to provide information on trade and investment opportunities in Eastern Europe. Address: Eastern Europe Business Information Center, U.S. Department of Commerce, Room 2325, Washington, DC 20230 USA; Tel: [1] (202) 482-2645; Fax: [1] (202) 482-4473; http://www.mac.doc.gov/eebic/ceebic.html.

East-South trade

(economics) Trade between developing countries (South) with non-market economies (East).

East-West trade

(economics) Trade between countries with developed market economies (West) and countries with non-market economies (East).

Economic Bulletin Board (EBB)

(U.S.) A personal computer-based economic bulletin board operated by the U.S. Department of Commerce in Washington, DC. The EBB is an online source for trade leads and statistical releases from the Bureau of Economic Analysis, the Census Bureau, the Office of Administration, the Bureau of Labor Statistics, the Federal Reserve Board, the Department of the Treasury, and other Federal agencies.

The EBB may be reached 24 hours each day, 7 days a week at [1] (202) 482-3870 (300/1200/2400 bps) with PC communication switches set to no parity, 8 bit words and 1 stop bit. The 9600 bps service uses US Robotics Dual Standard HST/V.32 modems and can be reached by dialing [1] (202) 482-2584. Information may be obtained by calling (202) 482-1986 (M-F, 8:30 am - 4:30 pm, EST).

The EBB also operates a fax service for receiving trade leads and the latest trade and economic information. No subscription fees are required for this service, although there is a per-minute charge. Dial

(900) RUN-A-FAX from your fax machine; call or write EBB for more information on this service. Address: Office of Business Analysis, U.S. Department of Commerce, HCHB Room 4885, Washington, DC 20230 USA; Tel: [1] (202) 482-1986; Fax: [1] (202) 482-2164.

Economic Community of West African States (ECOWAS)

Established in May 1975 by the Treaty of Lagos, the ECOWAS brought together 16 West African countries in an economic association aimed at creating a full customs union (not yet achieved). Members include: Benin, Burkina Faso, Cape Verde, Cote d'Ivoire, Gambia, Ghana, Guinea, Guinea-Bissau, Liberia, Mali, Mauritania, Niger, Nigeria, Senegal, Sierra Leone, and Togo.

economic officers

(U.S.) Embassy officials who analyze and report on macroeconomic trends and trade policies and their implications for U.S. policies and programs. Economic officers represent U.S. interests and arrange and participate in economic and commercial negotiations. *See* commercial officers; foreign service.

economy of scale

(economics) The decrease in unit cost as a result of increasing production so that fixed costs may be spread out over a greater number of units produced.

ecu or ECU

See European Currency Unit.

Edge Act corporations

(banking) Banks that are subsidiaries either to bank holding companies or other banks established to engage in foreign business transactions.

EDIFACT

See Electronic Data Interchange for Administration, Commerce, and Transportation.

effective exchange rate

(banking/foreign exchange) Any spot exchange rate actually paid or received by the public, including any taxes or subsidies on the exchange transaction as well as any applicable banking commissions.

Electronic Data Interchange for Administration, Commerce, and Transportation (EDIFACT)

(U.S. Customs) EDIFACT is an international syntax used in the interchange of electronic data. The U.S. Customs Service uses EDIFACT to interchange data with the importing trade community.

E

electronic funds transfer (EFT)
(banking) System of transferring funds from one account to another by electronic impulses rather than transfer of paper (such as a check).

embargo
A prohibition upon exports or imports, either with respect to specific products or specific countries. Historically, embargoes have been ordered most frequently in time of war, but they may also be applied for political, economic or sanitary purposes. Embargoes imposed against an individual country by the United Nations—or a group of nations—in an effort to influence its conduct or its policies are sometimes called "sanctions." *See also* sanctions.

emphyteusis
(law) A tenant's right to enjoy property owned by another individual or legal entity for a lengthy time and for rent as if the tenant owned it. The tenant may, and is usually expected to, improve the property. The tenant may also demise, assign, or otherwise transfer his or her interest in the property, but the tenant must preserve the property from destruction.

enabling clause
(WTO) A part of the World Trade Organization (WTO) framework which permits developed country members to give more favorable treatment to developing countries and special treatment to the least developed countries, notwithstanding most-favored-nation provisions.

endorsement
(banking/law) (In U.K., indorsement) The act of a person who is the holder of a negotiable instrument in signing his or her name on the back of that instrument, thereby transferring title or ownership. An endorsement may be made in favor of another individual or legal entity, resulting in a transfer of the property to that other individual or legal entity.
(a) An **endorsement in blank** is the writing of only the endorser's name on the negotiable instrument without designating another person to whom the endorsement is made, and with the implied understanding that the instrument is payable to the bearer.
(b) A **collection endorsement** is one that restricts payment of the endorsed instrument to purposes of deposit or collection.
(c) A **conditional endorsement** is one that limits the time at which the instrument can be paid or further transferred or that requires the occurrence of an event before the instrument is payable.

(d) A **restrictive endorsement** is one that directs a specific payment of the instrument, such as for deposit or collection only, and that precludes any other transfer of it.

Enhanced Proliferation Control Initiative (EPCI)
(U.S.) A series of measures to tighten export controls on goods and technologies useful in the production of chemical and missile weapons systems. EPCI allows the U.S. Department of Commerce greater authority to deny exports of low-level goods and technologies to nations of proliferation concern. *See* U.S. Department of Commerce.

en route
(shipping) In transit (referring to goods, passengers or vessel).

Enterprise for the Americas Initiative (EAI)
The EAI, which was launched in June 1990, is intended to develop a new economic relationship of the U.S. with Latin America. The EAI has trade investment, debt, and environment aspects. With regard to trade, the EAI involves an effort to move towards free trade agreements with markets in Latin America and the Caribbean, particularly with groups of countries that have associated for purposes of trade liberalization.
To begin the process of creating a hemispheric free trade system, the U.S. seeks to enter into "framework" agreements on trade and investment with interested countries or groups of countries. These agreements set up intergovernmental councils to discuss and, where appropriate, to negotiate the removal of trade and investment barriers.

entrepôt
(shipping) An intermediary storage facility where goods are kept temporarily for distribution within a country or for reexport.

entrepôt trade
The import and export of goods without the further processing of the goods. Usually refers to a country, locale or business that buys and sells (imports and exports) as a middleman.

entry
(customs) A statement of the kinds, quantities and values of goods imported together with duties due, if any, and declared before a customs officer or other designated officer.
(U.S. Customs) The process of, and documentation required for securing the release of imported merchandise from Customs.

See also: entry for consumption; entry for warehouse; mail entry; entry documents.

entry documents

(customs) The documents required to secure the release of imported merchandise.

(U.S Customs) Within five working days of the date of arrival of a shipment at a U.S. port of entry, entry documents must be filed at a location specified by the district/area director, unless an extension is granted. These documents consist of:

(1) Entry Manifest, Customs Form 7533; or Application and Special Permit for Immediate Delivery, Customs Form 3461, or other form of merchandise release required by the district director.

(2) Evidence of right to make entry.

(3) Commercial invoice or a pro-forma invoice when the commercial invoice cannot be produced.

(4) Packing lists if appropriate.

(5) Other documents necessary to determine merchandise admissibility.

If the goods are to be released from Customs custody on entry documents, an entry summary for consumption must be filed and estimated duties deposited at the port of entry within 10 working days of the time the goods are entered and released. *See* entry.

entry for consumption

(U.S. Customs) The process of effecting entry of goods into the United States for use in the United States. The entry of merchandise is a two-part process consisting of: (1) filing the documents necessary to determine whether merchandise may be released from Customs custody and (2) filing the documents which contain information for duty assessment and statistical purposes. In certain instances, such as the entry of merchandise subject to quotas, all documents must be filed and accepted by Customs prior to the release of the goods. *See* entry; entry documents.

entry for warehouse

(U.S. Customs) A type of U.S. Customs entry where the release of goods (and payment of duty) is postponed by having them placed in a Customs bonded warehouse, where they may remain for up to five years from the date of importation. At any time during that period the goods may be reexported without the payment of duty, or they may be withdrawn for consumption upon the payment of duty at the rate of duty in effect on the date of withdrawal. If the goods are destroyed under Customs' supervision, no duty is payable. *See* entry; customs bonded warehouse; entry for consumption.

entry summary selectivity system

(U.S. Customs) A part of U.S. Customs' Automated Commercial System, provides an automated review of entry data to determine whether team or routine review of entry is required. Selectivity criteria include an assessment of risk by importer, tariff number, country of origin, manufacturer, and value. Summaries with Census warnings, as well as quota, antidumping and countervailing duty entry summaries are selected for team review. A random sample of routine review summaries is also automatically selected for team review. *See* Automated Commercial System.

Environmental Protection Agency (EPA)

(U.S. government) An independent agency in the executive branch whose mandate is to control and abate pollution in the areas of air, water, solid waste, pesticides, radiation, and toxic substances. This is achieved through a combination of research, monitoring, standard setting and enforcement activities. Address: Environmental Protection Agency, 401 M St. SW, Washington, DC 20460 USA; Tel: [1] (202) 260-4700; http://www.epa.gov.

equalization

(shipping) A monetary allowance to the customer for picking up or delivering cargo to/from a point which is not the origin/destination shown on the bill of lading. Example, when the bill of lading destination indicates "San Francisco" and cargo is discharged in "Oakland," if the customer picks up the cargo in Oakland, he is allowed the difference in cost between the Oakland pickup to the customer's place of business and the projected actual cost if pick up had been made in San Francisco and drayed to the customer's place of business in San Francisco. This provision is covered by tariff publication.

equitable assignment

(law) An assignment that does not meet statutory requirements but that a court may nevertheless recognize and enforce in equity, that is, to do justice between the parties. If parties make an oral assignment that by statute must be in writing to be enforced, for example, a court may still enforce it as an equitable assignment, particularly if one party has acted in reliance on the assignment and would be harmed if it were not enforced. *See* assignment.

errors & omissions excepted (E&OE)

(shipping) A notation adjacent to a signature on a document signifying that the signor is disclaiming responsibility for typographical errors or unintentional omissions.

escape clause
A provision in a bilateral or multilateral commercial agreement permitting a signatory nation to suspend tariff or other concessions (temporarily violate their obligations) when imports threaten serious harm to the producers of competitive domestic goods.
(U.S.) Section 201 of the U.S. Trade Act of 1974 requires the U.S. International Trade Commission to investigate complaints formally known as "petitions" filed by domestic industries or workers claiming that they have been injured or are threatened with injury as a consequence of rapidly rising imports, and to complete any such investigation within six months. Section 203 of the Act provides that if the Commission finds that a domestic industry has been seriously injured or threatened with serious injury, it may recommend that the President grant relief to the industry in the form of adjustment assistance or temporary import restrictions in the form of tariffs, quotas, or tariff quotas. The President must then take action pursuant to the Commission's recommendations within 60 days, but he may accept, modify or reject them, according to his assessment of the national interest. The Congress can, through majority vote in both the Senate and the House of Representatives within 90 legislative days, override a Presidential decision not to implement the Commission's recommendations. The law permits the President to impose import restrictions for an initial period of five years and to extend them for a maximum additional period of three years. *See* adjustment assistance.

escudo
The currency of:
Cape Verde, 1C.V.Esc=100 centavos;
Portugal, 1Esc=100 centavos.

estimated time of arrival (ETA)
(shipping) The expected date and time of arrival of a shipment, passenger or vessel at a port, airport or terminal.

estimated time of departure (ETD)
(shipping) The estimated date and time of departure of a shipment, passenger or vessel from a port, airport or terminal.

EUR 1
(shipping) Goods transport certificate and proof of preference for export in countries and regions associated with the European Community (EC) and European Economic Area (EEA) through free trade agreements, association or preferential agreements, as long as the goods concerned are included in the tariffs preferences.

Euro
The currency of the European Union.

Eurobond
(finance) A bond issued in a currency other than that of the market or markets in which it is sold. The issue is handled by an international syndicate.

Eurobond market
(finance) Euromarket for international long-term bonds (Eurobonds).

Eurocard
(banking) A European credit card developed by the West German banking system that is accepted in most western European countries.

Eurocheque
(banking) A credit card (in the form of a check) for purchasing goods in several western European countries.

Eurocredit market
(finance) Euromarket for medium-term credits.

Eurocurrency
(banking) A currency deposit held outside the country which issued the currency.

Eurodollars
(banking) U.S. dollar-denominated deposits in banks and other financial institutions outside of the United States. Originating from, but not limited to, the large quantity of U.S. dollar deposits held in western Europe.

Euromarket
(finance) An international capital market on which deposits and claims are traded in currencies outside the sovereign territory of the states in question. Euromoney markets exist in the major financial hubs of western Europe but are focused on London and Luxembourg. Exists alongside the national money markets.

European Bank for Reconstruction and Development (EBRD)
(banking) The EBRD provides assistance through direct loans. The loans are designed to facilitate the development of market-oriented economies and to promote private and entrepreneurial initiatives. EBRD began financing operations in June 1991. Address: European Bank for Reconstruction and Development, One Exchange Square, London EC2A 2JN, UK; Tel: [44] (171) 338-6000; Telex: 8812161; Fax: [44] (171) 338-6100;http://www.ebrd.com.

European Coal and Steel Community

See European Community.

European Commission

One of the five major institutions of the European Community (EC), the Commission is responsible for ensuring the implementation of the Treaty of Rome and EC rules and obligations; submission of proposals to the Council of Ministers; execution of the Council's decisions; reconciliation of disagreements among Council members; administration of EC policies, such as the Common Agricultural Policy and coal and steel policies; taking necessary legal action against firms or member governments; and representing the EC in trade negotiations with non-member countries. Address: European Commission, 200 rue de la Loi, 1049 Brussels, Belgium; Tel: [32] (2) 299-11-11; Telex: 21877; Fax: [32] (2) 295-01-38. *See* European Community; Treaty of Rome; common agricultural policy.

European Committee for Electrotechnical Standardization (CENELEC)

CENELEC is a non-profit international organization under Belgian law. CENELEC seeks to harmonize electrotechnical standards published by the national member organizations and to remove technical barriers to trade that may be caused by differences in standards. CENELEC members include: Austria, Belgium, Denmark, Finland, France, Germany, Greece, Iceland, Ireland, Italy, Luxembourg, Netherlands, Norway, Portugal, Spain, Sweden, Switzerland, and the United Kingdom. Address: CENELEC (Comite European Normalization Electrotechnical), rue de Stassart 35, B-1050 Brussels, Belgium; Tel: [32] (2) 519-68-71; Fax: [32] (2) 519-6819; http://www.cenelec.be.

The National Institute of Standards and Technology of the United States Department of Commerce operates an EC Hotline which provides information on directives and draft CEN and CENELEC standards. Tel: (301) 921-4164.

European Committee for Standardization (CEN)

The CEN (Comité European de Normalisation), is an association of the national standards organizations of 18 countries of the European Community (EC) and of the European Free Trade Association (EFTA). CEN membership is open to the national standards organization of any European country which is, or is capable of becoming, a member of the EC or EFTA. CEN develops voluntary standards in building, machine tools, information technology, and in all sectors excluding the electrical

ones covered by the European Committee for Electrotechnical Standardization. CEN is involved in accreditation of laboratories and certification bodies as well as quality assurance. Address: CEN (Comite European de Normalisation), rue de Stassart 36, B-1050 Brussels, Belgium; Tel: [32] (2) 519-68-11; Fax: [32] (2) 519-6819.

The National Institute of Standards and Technology of the United States Department of Commerce operates an EC Hotline which provides information on directives and draft CEN and CENELEC standards. Tel: [1] (301) 921-4164.

European Community (EC)

A popular term for the European Communities that resulted from the 1967 "Treaty of Fusion" that merged the secretariat (the "Commission") and the intergovernmental executive body (the "Council") of the older European Economic Community (EEC) with those of the European Coal and Steel Community (ECSC) and the European Atomic Energy Community ("EURATOM"), which was established to develop nuclear fuel and power for civilian purposes.

The EC is a regional organization created in 1958 at the Treaty of Rome which provided for the gradual elimination of intraregional customs duties and other internal trade barriers, the establishment of a common external tariff against other countries, the gradual adoption of other integrating measures, including a Common Agricultural Policy and guarantees of free movement of labor and capital.

The original 6 members were Belgium, France, West Germany, Italy, Luxembourg, and the Netherlands. Denmark, Ireland, and the United Kingdom became members in 1973, Greece acceded in 1981, and Spain and Portugal in 1986.

The term European Community is used to refer to three separate regional organizations consisting of the European Coal and Steel Community (ECSC), the European Atomic Energy Community (EURATOM), and the European Economic Community. These have been served since 1967 by common institutions—the EC Commission, the EC Council, the European Parliament, and the Court of Justice of the European Communities. The present 12 member states of the EC are also members of the ECSC and EURATOM.

The three European Communities operate under separate treaties: the European Coal and Steel Community (ECSC), the European Atomic Energy Community (EURATOM), and the European Economic Community (EEC).

The Council meets several times a year at the Foreign Minister level, and occasionally at the Heads of State level. Technical experts from Community capitals meet regularly to deal with specialized issues in such areas as agriculture, transportation or trade policy.

Due to the existence of three separate entities, the expression "European Communities"—abbreviated "EC"—is used to refer to the three Communities in legal documents and official designations, i.e., the Commission of the European Communities. However, since the three Communities function as a single political institution, use of the expression "European Community"—also abbreviated "EC"—has become common usage except for legal texts. Address: European Community, 62 rue Belliard; 1040 Brussels, Belgium; Tel: [32] (2) 233-21-11; Fax: [32] (2) 231-10-74.

European Conference of Postal and Telecommunications Administrations (CEPT)

Founded in 1959 to strengthen relations between postal and telecommunications administrations and to improve their technical services. Address: Norwegian Post and Telecommunications Authority, P.O. Box 447 Sentrum, N-0104 Oslo, Norway; Tel: [47] 22-82-48-80; Fax: [47] 22-82-48-90.

European Currency Unit (ecu or ECU)

(foreign exchange) The ecu is a "basket" of specified amounts of each European Community (EC) currency. Amounts are determined according to the economic size of each EC member, and are revised every five years. The value of the ecu is determined by using the current exchange rate of each member currency. All the member states' currencies participate in the ecu basket. The ecu is the Community's accounting unit and is a popular private financial instrument. *See* currency basket.

European Economic Area (EEA)

The European Economic Area, EEA, joins the member nations of the European Community (EC) and the European Free Trade Association (EFTA). The EEA would comprise 19 nations, nearly 380 million people, and approximately 40 percent of world trade. The EEA is considered a major step towards eventually encompassing all 19 countries in the European Community. *See* European Community; European Free Trade Association.

European Economic Community

See European Community.

European Free Trade Association (EFTA)

A regional trade organization established in 1960 by the Stockholm Convention, as an alternative to the Common Market. EFTA was designed to provide a free trade area for industrial products among member countries. Unlike the European Community (EC) however, EFTA members did not set up a common external tariff and did not include agricultural trade.

The EFTA is headquartered in Geneva, and comprises Austria, Iceland, Norway, Sweden, and Switzerland. Finland is an Associate Member. Denmark and the United Kingdom were formerly members, but they withdrew from EFTA when they joined the European Community in 1973. Portugal, also a former member, withdrew from EFTA in 1986 when it joined the EC.

EFTA member countries have gradually eliminated tariffs on manufactured goods originating and traded within EFTA. Agricultural products, for the most part, are not included on the EFTA schedule for internal tariff reductions. Each member country maintains its own external tariff schedule and each has concluded a trade agreement with the European Community that provides for the mutual elimination of tariffs for most manufactured goods except for a few sensitive products. As a result, the European Community and EFTA form a de facto free trade area. *See* European Economic Area; European Community.

European Investment Bank (EIB)

(banking) The EIB is an independent public institution set up by the Treaty of Rome to contribute to balanced and steady development in the European Community. The EIB provides loans and guarantees to companies and public institutions to finance regional development, structural development, and achieve cross-border objectives. The EIB has emphasized regional development and energy, with Italy, Greece, and Ireland receiving major support. Address: European Investment Bank, 100 blvd. Konrad Adenauer, L-2950 Luxembourg; Tel: [352] 43 79 31 22; Fax: [352] 43 79 31 89; http://www.eib.org.

European Monetary System (EMS)

(banking/foreign exchange) The monetary system of the European Community (EC) member states which aims to create a zone of currency stability as the forerunner of a single currency.

The goal of the EMS is to move Europe toward closer economic integration and avoid the disruptions in trade that can result from fluctuations in currency exchange rates. The EMS member countries deposit gold and dollar reserves with the European Monetary Cooperation Fund in exchange for the issuance of European Currency Units (ECU).

France, West Germany, Belgium, Luxembourg, The Netherlands, Ireland, and Denmark all plan to prevent their currencies from rising or falling in value against each other any more than 2.5 percent. Italy will keep its lira from fluctuating against the other currencies by more than 6 percent.

Established in 1979; all EC members except Greece and the United Kingdom participate in the exchange rate mechanism of the EMS.

See European Currency Unit; European Monetary Union; European Community.

European Monetary Union (EMU)

(banking/foreign exchange) Created on January 1, 1979. Under the EMU, currencies of member nations would rise together, rather than fluctuating separately. Founding members were Germany and France, but the expectation is that all nine Common Market members will join, with invitations going out to non-Common Market countries as well. *See* European Monetary System.

European option

(banking/foreign exchange) An option containing a provision to the effect that it can only be exercised on the expiry or maturity date. *See also* American option; option.

European Organization for Testing and Certification (EOTC)

The EOTC was created in October 1990 by the European Community Commission under a memorandum of agreement with the European Committee for Standardization/European Committee for Electrotechnical Standardization (CEN/CENELEC) and the European Free Trade Association countries. The EOTC promotes mutual recognition of tests, test and certification procedures, and quality systems within the European private sector for product areas or characteristics not covered by European Community legislative requirements.

European Patent Convention (EPC)

An agreement between European nations to centralize and standardize patent law and procedure. The EPC, which took effect in 1977, established a single "European patent" through application to the European Patent Office in Munich. Once granted, the patent matures into a bundle of individual patents—one in each member country. Address: European Patent Office, Erhardtstrasse 27, 80331

Munich, Germany; Tel: [49] (89) 2399-0; Fax: [49] (89) 2399-4465.

European Patent Office

See European Patent Convention.

European (style) option

See European option.

European Telecommunications Standards Institute (ETSI)

ETSI was established in March 1988 in response to the inability of the Council of European Post and Telecommunications Administration (CEPT) to keep up with the schedule of work on common European standards and specifications agreed to in the 1984 Memorandum of Understanding between CEPT and the European Community (EC). ETSI has a contractual relationship with the EC to pursue standards development for telecommunications equipment and services, and it cooperates with other European standards bodies such as the European Committee for Standardization/European Committee for Electrotechnical Standardization (CEN/CENELEC). ETSI membership includes the telecommunications administrations that constitute the CEPT as well as manufacturers, service providers, and users. Address: European Telecommunications Standards Institute (ETSI), F-06921 Sophia Antipolis Cedex, France; Tel: [33] (9) 294-4200; Fax: [33] (9) 365-4716; http://www.etsi.org.

evidence of right to make entry

(U.S. Customs) Goods may be entered into the Customs territory of the United States only by the owner, purchaser, or a licensed customs broker acting on behalf of the owner or purchaser. Customs requires evidence of right to make entry as part of the entry documentation.

When the goods are consigned "to order," the bill of lading properly endorsed by the consignor may serve as evidence of the right to make entry. An air waybill may be used for merchandise arriving by air.

In most instances, entry is made by a person or firm certified by the carrier bringing the goods to the port of entry and is considered the "owner" of the goods for customs purposes. For example, a customs broker with a valid power of attorney signed by the owner of a shipment may present documents to customs as evidence of right to make entry. The document issued by the carrier is known as a "carrier's certificate." In certain circumstances, entry may be made by means of a duplicate bill of lading or a shipping receipt. *See* entry.

E

ex ... (named point of origin)
(trade term) A term of sale where the price quoted applies only at the point of origin and the seller agrees to place the goods at the disposal of the buyer at the specified place on the date or within the period fixed. All other charges are for the account of the buyer. For a more complete definition, *see* ex works. *See also* Incoterms.

exception rates
(shipping) Rates set at a certain percentage above the general commodity rates because they apply to commodities that require special handling, such as live animals, human remains, or automotive vehicles.

excess valuation
See declared value.

exchange control(s)
(foreign exchange) The rationing of foreign currencies, bank drafts, and other monetary instruments for settling international financial obligations by countries seeking to ameliorate acute balance of payments difficulties. When such measures are imposed, importers must apply for prior authorization from the government to obtain the foreign currency required to bring in designated amounts and types of goods. Since such measures have the effect of restricting imports, they are considered non-tariff barriers to trade. *See* balance of trade.

exchange rate
(foreign exchange) The price of one currency expressed in terms of another, i.e., the number of units of one currency that may be exchanged for one unit of another currency. For example, $/SFr = 1.50, means that one US dollar costs 1.50 Swiss francs.
(a) In a system of **free exchange rates**, the actual exchange rate is determined by supply and demand on the foreign exchange market.
(b) In a system of **fixed exchange rates**, the exchange rate is tied to a reference (e.g., gold, US$, etc.).
Influences on exchange rates include differences between interest rates and other asset yields between countries; investor expectations about future changes in a currency's value; investors' views on the overall quantity of assets in circulation; arbitrage; and central bank exchange rate support. *See also* floating.

excise tax
A selective tax—sometimes called a consumption tax—on certain goods produced within or imported into a country. An example is a tax on the import of crude oil, or a tax on certain luxury goods.

exclusive agency
See agency.

exclusive economic zone (EEZ)
(international law) EEZ refers to the rights of coastal states to control the living and nonliving resources of the sea for 200 miles off their coasts while allowing freedom of navigation to other states beyond 12 miles, as agreed at the sixth session of the Third U.N. Conference on the Law of the Sea (UNCLOS). The EEZ also gives the coastal states the responsibility for managing the conservation of all natural resources within the 200-mile limit.

exculpatory clause
(law) A contract clause by which a party is released from liability for wrongful acts committed by the other party. A seller may agree to release a buyer, for example, from liability for all or specified defects in the design, packaging, or manufacture of a product.

ex dock
(trade term) A term of sale where the buyer takes title to the goods only when they are unloaded on his/her dock. *See* ex works; Incoterms.

execution
(law) (a) A signature on a document. (b) A legal process for enforcing a judgment for damages, usually by seizure and sale of the debtor's personal property. If a court awards damages in a breach of contract action, for example, but the breaching party has failed to remit such sum, the party awarded damages may request the court to order seizure and sale of the breaching party's inventory or property to the extent necessary to satisfy the award.

exercise price
See strike price.

ex factory
(trade term) A term of sale where the buyer takes title to the goods when they leave the vendor's dock. *See* ex works; Incoterms.

EXIM Bank
See Export-Import Bank of the United States.

ex parte
(law) By one party or side only. An application ex parte, for example, is a request that is made by only one of the parties involved in a legal action. A hearing ex parte is a court proceeding at which the persons present represent only one side of the controversy. *See* letter of credit.

expiration date
(banking) In letter of credit transaction, the final date the seller (beneficiary of the credit) may

present documents and draw a draft under the terms of the letter of credit. Also called expiry date. *See* letter of credit.

expiry day
(banking/foreign exchange) In foreign exchange options business, the last day on which an option can be exercised.

explosives
(shipping) (UN CLASS 1.) EXPLOSIVE A: Items are capable of exploding with a small spark, shock, or flame and spreading the explosion hazard to other packages. EXPLOSIVE B: Items are very rapidly combustible. EXPLOSIVE C: Items are a low hazard but may explode under high heat when many are tightly packed together. Examples are: A—dynamite; B—propellants or flares; C—common fireworks. Hazards/precautions: no flares, smoking, flames, or sparks in the hazard area; may explode if dropped, heated or sparked.

export
To ship an item away from a country for sale to another country.

Export Administration Act (EAA)
(U.S. law) Authorizes the President to control exports of U.S. goods and technology to all foreign destinations, as necessary for the purpose of national security, foreign policy, and short supply.
As the basic export administration statute, the EAA is the first big revision of export control law since enactment of the Export Control Act of 1949. The EAA is not permanent legislation; it must be reauthorized—usually every three years. There have been reauthorizations of the EAA in 1982, 1985 (the Export Administration Amendments Act), and 1988 (Omnibus Amendments of 1988) which have changed provisions of the basic Act. The Export Administration Act of 1990 was pocket vetoed by the President, charging that provisions involved micro management.

Export Administration Regulations (EAR)
(U.S. law) Provides specific instructions on the use and types of export licenses required and the types of commodities and technical data under export control.

Export Administration Review Board (EARB)
(U.S. government) A U.S. cabinet-level export licensing dispute resolution group. The EARB was originally established in June 1970 under Executive Order 11533. Under Executive Order 12755 of March 1991, EARB membership includes the Departments of Commerce (as chair), State, Defense,

and Energy, the Arms Control and Disarmament Agency and, as non-voting members, the Joint Chiefs of Staff and the Central Intelligence Agency. The EARB is the final review body to resolve differences among agency views on the granting of an export license. Preceding EARB review are: (1) Operating Committees, and (2) the Advisory Committee on Export Policy. National Security Directive #53 requires escalation of disputes regarding an export license to the Advisory Committee on Export Policy (ACEP) not later than 100 days from the filing date of the applicant's application. Any cases not resolved at the ACEP level must be escalated to the EARB within 35 days of the date of the ACEP meeting. Cases not resolved by the EARB must be escalated to the President for resolution. Address: Export Administration Review Board, 14th and Constitution Avenue NW, Herbert Hoover Building, Room 2639, Washington, DC 20230 USA; Tel: [1] (202) 482-5863.

export broker
An individual or firm that brings together buyers and sellers for a fee but does not take part in actual sales transactions.

export commodity classification number
See export control classification number.

Export Contact List Service (ECLS)
(U.S.) A U.S. International Trade Administration (ITA) service that provides mailing lists of prospective overseas customers from ITA's file of foreign firms (the Foreign Traders Index). The ECLS identifies manufacturers, distributors, retailers, service firms, and government agencies. A summary of the information on the company includes contact information, product and service interests, and other data. *See* Foreign Traders Index.

export control
(U.S. Customs) To exercise control over exports for statistical and strategic purposes, Customs enforces export control laws for the U.S. Department of Commerce and other Federal agencies. *See* United States Customs Service.

Export Control Automated Support System (ECASS)
(U.S.) ECASS was implemented by the U.S. Department of Commerce in 1985 to automate a paper-based system. The system currently provides:
(1) electronic submission of export application forms directly by exporters;
(2) optical character recognition of applications submitted on paper;

(3) paperless workstations for all licensing officers to review the application, route it to other officers, branches, or external agencies, and to enter their final action along with riders and conditions;

(4) automated audit of all export licenses issued; and

(5) real time management reporting on Licensing Officer workloads, average processing times, counts and times by license type, destination country, commodity code, and other data. The U.S. Department of Commerce's Bureau of Export Administration is expanding ECASS to include export enforcement activities.

See United States Department of Commerce; Bureau of Export Administration.

export control classification number (ECCN)

(U.S.) Every product has an export control classification number (formerly export commodity classification number) within the Commerce Control List. The ECCN consists of a five character number that identifies categories, product groups, strategic level of control, and country groups. *See* Commerce Control List.

export credit agencies (ECAs)

Government agencies or programs providing government loans, guarantees or insurance to finance exports. In the U.S., the Export/Import Bank is the government's general purpose credit agency, while the Commodity Credit Corporation is the export credit agency for agricultural exports. *See* Export-Import Bank; Commodity Credit Corporation.

Export Credit Enhanced Leverage Program (EXCEL)

The EXCEL program was developed in 1990 by the World Bank in conjunction with a working group of the International Union of Credit and Investment Insurers (the Berne Union). The objective of EXCEL is to provide export credits at consensus rates for private sector borrowers in highly indebted countries, which would previously have been too great a risk for most agencies to cover.

export credit insurance

(insurance) Special insurance coverage for exporters to protect against commercial and political risks of making an international sale. Export credit insurance is available from insurance underwriters as well as from government agencies. *See* export credit agencies.

export declaration

(U.S.) A document required by the U.S. Department of Treasury for the export of goods from the United States. Also known as the Shipper's Export Declaration (SED), this form includes complete particulars on an individual export shipment and is required by the U.S. Department of Commerce to control exports and act as a source document for export statistics. *See* shipper's export declaration.

Export Development Corporation (EDC)

(Canada) Canada's official export credit agency, responsible for providing export credit insurance, loans, guarantees, and other financial services to promote Canadian export trade. Address: Export Development Corporation, 151 O'Connor Street, Ottawa, ON K1A 1K3, Canada; Tel: [1] (613) 598-2500; Fax: [1] (613) 598-6697;http://www.edc.ca.

Export Development Office (EDO)

(U.S. government) Export Development Offices (EDOs) in seven cities (Tokyo, Sydney, Seoul, Milan, London, Mexico City, and Sao Paulo) provide services to U.S. exporters, including market research to identify specific marketing opportunities and products with the greatest sales potential; and to organize export promotion events. EDOs are staffed by U.S. and Foreign Commercial Service officers. When not in use for trade exhibitions, EDOs with exhibit and conference facilities are made available to individual firms or associations. *See* U.S. and Foreign Commercial Service.

export draft

(banking) An unconditional order that is drawn by an exporting seller and that directs an importing buyer to pay the amount stated on the order to the seller or the seller's bank.

(a) A **sight export draft** is one that is payable when presented. (b) A **time export draft or usance** is one that is payable at a specified future date. *See* bill of exchange.

export duty

(customs) A tax imposed on exports of some nations. *See* duty; tariff.

Export Enhancement Program (EEP)

(U.S.) A U.S. Department of Agriculture program that assists exporters who are shipping U.S. agricultural products to countries that subsidize agricultural products. For information, contact the U.S. Department of Agriculture, Foreign Agriculture Service, Washington, DC 20250; Tel: (202) 720-7115.

exporter

An individual or company that transports goods or merchandise from one country to another in the course of trade.

exporter identification number (EIN)

(U.S.) An identification number required on the Shipper's Export Declaration for all export shipments. U.S. corporations may use their federal Employer Identification Number issued by the IRS. Individuals and companies that are not incorporated may use the Social Security number of the exporter. *See* shipper's export declaration.

exporters sales price (ESP)

(U.S.) A statutory term used to refer to the United States sales prices of merchandise which is sold or likely to be sold in the United States, before or after the time of importation, by or for the account of the exporter. Certain statutory adjustments are made to permit a meaningful comparison with the foreign market value of such or similar merchandise, e.g., import duties, United States selling and administrative expenses, and freight are deducted from the United States price.

Export Hotline

(U.S.) A 24 hour fax retrieval system for information on international trade. Supported by the U.S. Department of Commerce and underwritten by international companies such as AT&T and UPS, the hotline provides a menu listing 78 countries and 50 industries to help business people find new markets for their products and services. Hotline and Directory are free; to list company costs $35. For brochure, call: [1] (617) 248-9393.

Export-Import Bank of Japan (JEXIM)

(Japan) Japan's official provider of export credits. About 10 percent of JEXIM's business is providing export credits. The bank's main role is to disburse about half the funds available under the trade surplus recycling program (the Nakasone facility). Address: Export-Import Bank of Japan, 4-1, Otemachi 1-chome, Chiyoda-ku, Tokyo 100, Japan; Tel: [81] (3) 3287-9101; Telex: 23728; Fax: [81] (3) 3287-9539; hhtp://www.japanexim,go.jp.

Export-Import Bank of the United States (Eximbank)

(U.S.) A public corporation created by executive order of the President in 1934 and given a statutory basis in 1945. The Bank makes guarantees and insures loans to help finance U.S. exports, particularly for equipment to be used in capital improvement projects. The Bank also provides short-term insurance for both commercial and political risks, either directly or in cooperation with U.S. commercial banks.

Eximbank offers four major export finance support programs: loans, guarantees, working capital guarantees, and insurance. Eximbank undertakes some of the risk associated with financing the production and sale of American-made goods; provides financing to overseas customers for American goods when lenders are not prepared to finance the transactions; and enhances a U.S. exporter's ability to match foreign government subsidies by helping lenders meet lower rates, or by giving financing incentives directly to foreign buyers. The Export-Import Bank will consider aiding in the export financing of U.S. goods and services when there is a reasonable assurance of repayment. Eximbank is not to compete with private financing, but to supplement it when adequate funds are not available in the private sector. Address: Export-Import Bank of the United States, 811 Vermont Avenue NW, Washington, DC 20571 USA; Tel: [1] (202) 565-3946.

Export Legal Assistance Network (ELAN)

(U.S.) A nationwide group of attorneys with experience in international trade who provide free initial consultations to small businesses on export-related matters. This service is available through the U.S. Small Business Administration (SBA). For the address and phone number of your nearest Small Business Administration District Office, call [1] (800) U-ASK-SBA. Address: National Coordinator Judd Kessler, Porter, Wright, Morris, & Arthur, 1667 K Street NW, Suite 1100, Washington, DC 20006-1605 USA; Tel: [1] (202) 778-3080; Fax: [1] (202) 778-3063; http://www.fita.org/elan/.

export license

A document prepared by a government authority, granting the right to export a specified quantity of a commodity to a specified country. This document may be required in some countries for most or all exports and in other countries only under special circumstances.

(U.S.) A document issued by the U.S. government authorizing the export of commodities for which written export authorization is required by law. For more information on export licensing in general, call Exporter Assistance at: (202) 482-4811. Address: Bureau of Export Administration, U.S. Department of Commerce, 14th St. and Constitution Ave. NW, Washington, DC 20230 USA; Tel: [1] (202) 482-2721; Fax: [1] (202) 482-2387.

Export License and Information Network (ELAIN)

(U.S.) ELAIN is a Bureau of Export Administration 24-hour on-line service which allows exporters to submit license applications. Contact: Bureau of Export Administration, 14th and Constitution Ave. NW, Washington, DC 20230; Tel: [1] (202) 482-2721; http://elain.com.

Export License Voice Information System (ELVIS)

(U.S.) A U.S. Bureau of Export Administration 24-hour on-line service which allows exporters to obtain recorded information on such topics as commodity classifications, emergency handling procedures, and seminars as well as to order information. Tel: [1] (202) 482-4811.

export management company

A private firm that serves as the export department for several manufacturers, soliciting and transacting export business on behalf of its clients in return for a commission, salary, or retainer plus commission.

export merchant

A company that buys products directly from manufacturers, then packages and marks the merchandise for resale under its own name.

export processing zone (EPZ)

Industrial parks designated by a government to provide tax and other incentives to export firms.

export quotas

Specific restrictions or ceilings imposed by an exporting country on the value or volume of certain exports, designed to protect domestic producers and consumers from temporary shortages of the materials or goods affected, or to bolster their prices in world markets. Some International Commodity Agreements explicitly indicate when producers should apply such restraints. Export quotas are also often applied in orderly marketing agreements and voluntary restraint agreements, and to promote domestic processing of raw materials in countries that produce them. *See* international commodity agreement; orderly marketing agreements; voluntary restraint agreements.

export restraint agreements

See voluntary restraint agreements.

export restraints

Quantitative restrictions imposed by exporting countries to limit exports to specified foreign markets, usually pursuant to a formal or informal agreement concluded at the request of the importing countries. *See* voluntary restraint agreements.

export revolving line of credit (ERLC)

(U.S.) Financial assistance provided by the U.S. Small Business Administration (SBA) to exporters of U.S. products. The ERLC guarantees loans to U.S. firms to help bridge the working capital gap between the time inventory and production costs are disbursed until payment is received from a foreign buyer. SBA guarantees 85 percent of the ERLC subject to a $750,000 guarantee limit. The ERLC is granted on the likelihood of a company satisfactorily completing its export transaction. The guarantee covers default by the exporter, but does not cover default by a foreign buyer; failure on the buyer's side is expected to be covered by letters of credit or export credit insurance.

Under the SBA's ERLC program, any number of withdrawals and repayments can be made as long as the dollar limit on the line of credit is not exceeded and disbursements are made within the stated maturity period (not more than 18 months). Proceeds can be used only to finance labor and materials needed for manufacturing, to purchase inventory to meet an export order, and to penetrate or develop foreign markets. Examples of eligible expenses for developing foreign markets include professional export marketing advice or services, foreign business travel, and trade show participation. Under the ERLC program, funds may not be used to purchase fixed assets. Contact: Small Business Administration, 409 Third Street SW, Washington, DC 20416 USA; Tel: [1] (202) 606-4000; http://www.sba.com. *See also* letter of credit.

export service

(shipping) Shipping lines, airlines and freight forwarders perform at the request of shippers, many services relating to the transfer, storage, and documentation of freight destined for export. The same is true of imports. Some carriers have a tariff on such traffic which sets forth a rate covering the air transportation, from airport of origin to seaport and all relevant transfer and documentation procedures. On freight arriving in the United States, via an ocean vessel and having a subsequent movement by air, some airlines have similar tariff program known as "Import Service."

export statistics

(U.S.) Export statistics measure the total physical quantity or value of merchandise (except for shipments to U.S. military forces overseas) moving out of the United States to foreign countries, whether such merchandise is exported from within the U.S. Customs territory or from a U.S. Customs bonded warehouse or a U.S. Foreign Trade Zone.

export subsidies
Government payments, economic inducements or other financially quantifiable benefits provided to domestic producers or exporters contingent on the export of their goods or services.

(WTO) The World Trade Organization (WTO) recognizes that subsidies in general, and especially export subsidies, distort normal commercial activities and hinder the achievement of WTO objectives. An Agreement on Subsidies and Countervailing Measures rules on export subsidies and provides for an outright prohibition of export subsidies by developed countries for manufactured and semi-manufactured products. Under certain conditions, the Agreement allows developing countries to use export subsidies on manufactured and semi-manufactured products, and on primary products as well, provided that the subsidies do not result in more than an equitable share of world exports of the product for the country. *See also* subsidy.

Export Trade Certificate of Review
(U.S.) A certification of partial immunity from U.S. antitrust laws that can be granted based on the Export Trading Company Act legislation by the U.S. Department of Commerce with Department of Justice concurrence. Any prospective or present U.S.-based exporter with antitrust concerns may apply for certification by the International Trade Administration, Mr. Morton Schnabel, Director, Office of Export Trading Company Affairs, Room 1104 Washington, DC 20230 USA; Tel: [1] (202) 482-5131. *See also* Export Trading Company Act.

export trading company
A corporation or other business unit organized and operated principally for the purpose of exporting goods and services, or of providing export related services to other companies. An ETC can be owned by foreigners and can import, barter, and arrange sales between third countries, as well as export.

(U.S.) The Export Trading Company Act of 1982 exempts authorized trading companies from certain provisions of U.S. anti-trust laws. *See* Export Trading Company Act.

Export Trading Company Act
(U.S. law) The Export Trading Company Act of 1982: initiates the Export Trade Certificate of Review program that provides antitrust preclearance for export activities; permits bankers' banks and bank holding companies to invest in Export Trad-

ing Companies; and establishes a Contact Facilitation Service within the U.S. Department of Commerce designed to facilitate contact between firms that produce exportable goods and services and firms that provide export trade services.

express agency
See agency.

ex quay
See delivered ex quay; Incoterms.

ex ship
See delivered ex ship; Incoterms.

external value
(economics/foreign exchange) The purchasing power of a currency abroad, converted using the exchange rate.

extradition
The surrender by one country of an alleged criminal to the authorities of the country that has jurisdiction to try the charge. Extradition usually occurs under the provisions of a treaty between the two countries.

ex warehouse
See ex works; Incoterms.

Ex Works (...named place) (EXW)
(Incoterms 2000) An international trade term of sale in which, for the quoted price, the seller/exporter/manufacturer merely makes the goods available to the buyer at the seller's "named place" of business. This trade term places the greatest responsibility on the buyer and minimum obligations on the seller.

The seller does not clear the goods for export and does not load the goods onto a truck or other transport vehicle at the named place of departure. The parties to the transaction, however, may stipulate that the seller be responsible for the costs and risks of loading the goods onto a transport vehicle. Such a stipulation must be made within the contract of sale. If the buyer cannot handle export formalities the Ex Works term should not be used. In such a case Free Carrier (FCA) is recommended.

The Ex Works term is often used when making an initial quotation for the sale of goods. It represents the cost of the goods without any other costs included. *See* Guide to Incoterms 2000 Appendix.

F

facilitation

Any of a number of programs designed to expedite the flow of international commerce through modernizing and simplifying customs procedures, duty collection, and other procedures to which international cargo and passengers are subject. Examples of progress in facilitation include the elimination of certain export declaration requirements, more expeditious release of cargo from customs, and clearance of cargo at point of origin.

facsimile (fax)

(a) An office machine used to transmit a copy of a document (including graphic images) via telephone lines. (b) The physical paper output of a fax machine which is a copy of the document transmitted. Facsimile use has grown significantly in the past few years. Note that in some countries some facsimile documents are not considered legal documents.

factor

(a) An agent who receives merchandise under a consignment or bailment contract, who sells it for the principal or in the factor's own name, and who is paid a commission for each sale. (b) A firm, such as a finance company, that purchases another company's receivables at a discount and processes and collects the remaining account balances.

factorage

The commission or other compensation paid to a factor.

factoring

The discounting of an account receivable in order to receive immediate payment. In international trade factoring is the discounting of a foreign account receivable that does not involve a draft. The exporter transfers title to its foreign accounts receivable to a factoring house (an organization that specializes in the financing of accounts receivable) for cash at a discount from the face value. Factoring is often done without recourse to the exporter. Factoring of foreign accounts receivable is less common than with domestic receivables.

factoring houses

Certain companies which purchase domestic or foreign accounts receivables (e.g., the as yet unpaid invoices to domestic and foreign buyers) at a discounted price, usually about two to four percent less than their face value. *See* factor; factoring.

factor's lien

The right of a factor to retain the principal's merchandise until the factor receives full compensation from the principal.

fair value

(U.S. Customs) The reference against which U.S. purchase prices of imported merchandise are compared during an antidumping investigation. Generally expressed as the weighted average of the exporter's domestic market prices, or prices of exports to third countries during the period of investigation.

In some cases fair value is the constructed value. Constructed value is used if there are no, or virtually no, home market or third country sales, or if the number of such sales made at prices below the cost of production is so great that remaining sales above the cost of production provide an inadequate basis for comparison. *See* dumping; constructed value.

F.A.K.

(shipping) Freight all kinds. Usually refers to consolidated cargo.

family corporation

See closely held corporation.

FAS

See free alongside ship; Incoterms.

fast track

(U.S.) Fast track procedures for approval of trade agreements were included by the U.S. Congress in trade legislation in 1974, in 1979, and again in the 1988 Trade Act. Fast track provides two guarantees essential to the successful negotiation of trade agreements: (1) a vote on implementing legislation within a fixed period of time, and (2) a vote, yes or no, with no amendments to that legislation.

Provisions in the Omnibus Trade and Competitiveness Act of 1988 include that the foreign country request negotiation of an Free Trade Agreement (FTA) and that the President give the Congress a 60-legislative-day notice of intent to negotiate an FTA. During the 60-legislative-day period, either committee can disapprove fast track authority by a majority vote. Disapproval would likely end the possibility of FTA negotiations. The 60-legislative-days can translate into five to ten months of calendar time, depending on the Congressional schedule.

Formal negotiations would begin following this 60-day Congressional consideration period.

fathom

(measurement) A unit of length equal to six feet. Used primarily to measure the depth of water.

fax

See facsimile.

Federal Aviation Administration (FAA)

(U.S.) Created under the Federal Aviation Act of 1958 as the Federal Aviation Agency and charged with the responsibility of promulgating operational standards and procedures for all classes of aviation in the United States. With the creation of the cabinet level Department of Transportation in 1966, FAA became a unit within the new Department and received the new designation Federal Aviation Administration. The FAA Administrator, however, continues to be a presidential appointee and the FAA remains a separate entity with most of its former functions. In the field of air cargo FAA promulgates certain stress standards which must be met in the tiedown of cargo in flight. For information: Federal Aviation Administration, 800 Independence Avenue, #1010, Washington, DC 20591 USA; Tel: [1] (202) 267-3484; http://www.faa.gov.

federally chartered bank

(U.S. banking) In the United States, a bank that has been chartered by the comptroller of currency, that belongs to the Federal Reserve System and meets the requirements for a national bank as defined under the National Bank Act. In the U.S. only federally and state chartered banks and other authorized institutions may receive deposits.

Federal Maritime Commission (FMC)

(U.S.) The U.S. federal agency responsible for overseeing rates and practices of ocean carriers who handle cargo to or from U.S. ports. Address: Federal Maritime Commission, 800 North Capitol St. NW, Washington, DC 20573-0001 USA; Tel: [1] (202) 523-5911; http://www.fmc.gov.

Federal Reserve System

(U.S. banking) The central banking system of the U.S. It has twelve Federal Reserve Banks divided up by geographical regions. The Board of Governors supervises the operations of the regional banks and coordinates monetary policy through its Federal Open Market Committee.

Federal Trade Commission (FTC)

(U.S.) Plays a key role in ensuring that consumers are protected against unfair methods of competition in the market place. Address: Federal Trade Commission, Pennsylvania Avenue and 6th Street NW, Washington, DC 20580 USA; Tel: [1] (202) 326-2222; http://www.ftc.gov.

feeder vessel

(shipping) A vessel used to connect with a line vessel to service a port which is not served directly by the line vessel. *See* line haul vessel.

FEU

(shipping) Forty foot equivalent units. Two 20 ft. containers equal one FEU.

fieri facias writ

(law) A judicial order issued to "cause to be done," which generally orders an officer of law or another authorized person to satisfy a judgment by seizure and sale of a debtor's property. *See* execution.

final determination

(U.S.) In antidumping investigations a final determination is made after the investigation of sales at "less than fair value" and the receipt of comments from interested parties. This determination usually is made within 75 days after the date a preliminary determination is made. However, if the preliminary determination was affirmative, the exporters who account for a significant proportion of the merchandise under consideration may request, in writing, a postponement of this determination. If the preliminary determination was negative, the petitioner may likewise request a postponement. In neither case can this postponement be more than 135 days after the date of the preliminary determination. If the final determination is affirmative and follows a negative preliminary determination, the matter is referred to the International Trade Commission (ITC) for a determination of the injury caused or threatened by the sales at less than fair value. (Had the preliminary determination been affirmative, the ITC would have begun its investigation at that time.) Not later than 45 days after the date the International Trade Administration makes an affirmative final determination, in a case where the preliminary determination also was affirmative, the International Trade Commission must render its decision on injury. Where the preliminary determination was negative, the ITC must render a decision not later than 75 days after the affirmative final determination. A negative final determination by the Assistant Secretary for Import Administration terminates an antidumping investigation. *See* dumping; International Trade Commission.

financial instrument

(banking/finance) A document which has monetary value, or is evidence of a financial transaction. Examples of financial instruments are: checks, bonds, stock certificates, bills of exchange, promissory notes and bills of lading.

financial market

(banking/finance) Market for the exchange of capital and credit in an economy. It is divided into money markets, and capital market(s).

Financial Times (of London)

(publication) Considered by professionals as one of the best English-language newspapers for business and financial news.

Fines, Penalties, and Forfeitures System (FPFS)

(U.S. Customs) A part of the U.S. Customs' Automated Commercial System, is used to assess, control, and process penalties resulting from violations of law or Customs regulations. FPFS provides retrieval of case information for monitoring case status. *See* Automated Commercial System.

fire insurance

(insurance) Marine insurance coverage that includes both direct fire damage and also consequential damage, as by smoke or steam, and loss resulting from efforts to extinguish a fire. Includes explosion caused by fire.

first world countries

(economics) Western, industrialized, non-communist countries.

five dragons

See five tigers; five dragons.

Five-K Countries (5(k) Countries)

Those countries as defined under Section 5(k) of the U.S. Export Administration Amendments Act of 1985. Such countries are eligible for the same treatment as Coordinating Committee on Multilateral Export Controls (CoCom) countries in relation to export control requirements if those countries maintain comparable export control programs. *See* Coordinating Committee on Multilateral Export Controls.

five tigers; five dragons

Terms used to describe the emerging economies of Hong Kong, Singapore, South Korea, Taiwan and Thailand.

fixed charges

(general) Charges which do not vary with an increase in production or sales volume.

(shipping) Charges which do not vary with an increase or decrease in traffic.

fixed exchange

(foreign exchange) (a) An administratively fixed exchange rate. With rate fixed exchange rates, no rate fluctuations are possible. (b) A concept within the European Monetary System, where all members except Britain maintain fixed exchange rates between their currencies, promoting monetary stability in Europe and throughout the world. *See also* European Monetary System.

fixed exchange rate

See exchange rate; fixed exchange.

fixing

(foreign exchange) Establishing of the official exchange rate of a domestic currency against other negotiable currencies.

flag

(shipping) A reference to the country of registry of a vessel. A vessel flying the flag of the country of its registry.

flag of convenience

(shipping) The national flag flown by a ship that is registered in a country other than that of its owners (e.g., to escape taxes and high domestic wages).

flammable

(shipping) Any substance capable of catching fire. *See* flammable liquid; flammable solid.

flammable liquid

(shipping) Liquids with a flash point less than 100°F. (UN CLASS 3) Examples are ether, acetone, gasoline, toluene and pentane. Hazards/precautions are: no flares, smoking, flames, or sparks in the hazard area; vapors are an explosion hazard; can be poisonous; check labels; if it is poisonous, it can cause death when inhaled, swallowed or touched.

flammable solid

(shipping) Any solid material which, under certain conditions, might cause fires or which can be ignited readily and burns vigorously. (UN CLASS 4) Examples are: calcium resinate; potassium, sodium amide. Hazards/

precautions are: may ignite when exposed to air or moisture, may re-ignite after extinguishing; fires may produce irritation or poisonous gases; contact may cause burns to skin or eyes.

flight of capital

(banking/finance) The movement of capital, which has usually been converted into a liquid asset, from one place to another to avoid loss or to increase gain.

floating

(foreign exchange) (a) **Clean floating**: Free determination of exchange rates without intervention on the part of the central bank. Correspondingly, exchange rates are determined by supply and demand on the foreign exchange market. (b) **Dirty floating**: Monetary policy which in principle recognizes floating exchange rates, but which tries to influence the exchange rate level through more or less frequent interventions. *See* floating currency.

floating currency

(banking/foreign exchange) One whose value in terms of foreign currency is not kept stable (on the basis of the par value or a fixed relationship to some other currency) but instead is allowed, without a multiplicity of exchange rates, to be determined (entirely or to some degree) by market forces. Even where a currency is floating, the authorities may influence its movements by official intervention; if such intervention is absent or minor, the expression "clean float" is sometimes used. *See* floating.

floor

(banking/finance) With cash investments, where the rate of interest is subject to adjustment to the market rate, a so-called floor can be agreed upon, i.e. for a premium, a minimum interest rate is stipulated and remains valid even if the market interest rate is lower.

florin

The currency of Aruba. 1F=100 cents.

flotsam

(shipping) Floating debris or wreckage of a ship or a ship's cargo. *See also* jetsam.

FOB

(trade term) *See* Free On Board, Guide to Incoterms 2000 Appendix.

FOB Airport

(trade term) An incorrect use of the trade term Free On Board. *See* Free on Board, Guide to Incoterms 2000 Appendix.

FOB Destination, Freight Collect

(trade term) An incorrect use of the trade term Free On Board. *See* Free on Board, Guide to Incoterms 2000 Appendix.

FOB Destination, Freight Prepaid

(trade term) An incorrect use of the trade term Free On Board. *See* Free on Board, Guide to Incoterms 2000 Appendix.

FOB Origin, Freight Collect

(trade term) An incorrect use of the trade term Free On Board. *See* Free on Board, Guide to Incoterms 2000 Appendix.

FOB Origin, Freight Prepaid and Charged

(trade term) An incorrect use of the trade term Free On Board. *See* Free on Board, Guide to Incoterms 2000 Appendix.

Food and Agricultural Organization (FAO)

A specialized agency of the United Nations established in 1945 to combat hunger and malnutrition. The FAO serves as a coordinating body between government representatives, scientific groups, and non-governmental organizations to carry out development programs relating to food and agriculture. Address: Food and Agriculture Organization, Via delle Terme di Caracalla, 00100 Rome, Italy; Tel: [39] 065-2251; Telex: 610181; Fax: [39] 065-225-5155; http://www.fao.org.

Food and Drug Administration (FDA)

U.S. governmental agency which enforces the Federal Food Drug and Cosmetic Act, the Fair Packaging and Labeling Act, and sections of the Public Health Service Act. Address: Food and Drug Administration, Public Relations, 5600 Fishers Lane, Rockwell, MD, 20857; Tel: [1] (301) 827-7130; http://www.fda.gov.

FOR

(trade term) Abbreviation for "free on rail" used in connection with transportation by rail, indicating that the price covers the goods loaded on the railcar. *See* Free On Board (Incoterm 2000); Guide to Incoterms 2000 Appendix.

force majeure

(shipping) Any condition or set of circumstances, such as earthquakes, floods, or war, beyond the carrier's control that prevents the carrier from performing fulfillment of their obligations.

F

force majeure clause
(law/insurance/shipping) A contract clause, which usually excuses a party who breaches the contract because that party's performance is prevented by the occurrence of an event that is beyond the party's reasonable control. A force majeure clause may excuse performance on the occurrence of such events as natural disasters, labor strikes, bankruptcy, or failure of subcontractors to perform. If a force majeure clause is not expressly included in a contract, a legal action may be brought on the basis that such a clause should be implied under the doctrine of commercial frustration or commercial impracticability. *See* commercial frustration; commercial impracticability.

foreign affiliate
See affiliate.

foreign affiliate of a foreign parent
(U.S.) Any member of an affiliated foreign group owning a U.S. affiliate that is not a foreign parent of the U.S. affiliate. *See* affiliate.

Foreign Agricultural Service (FAS)
(U.S.) An agency of the U.S. Department of Agriculture (USDA). FAS maintains a global network of agricultural officers as well as a Washington-based staff to analyze and disseminate information on world agriculture and trade, develop and expand export markets, and represent the agricultural trade policy interests of U.S. producers in multilateral forums. FAS also administers USDA's export credit and concessional sales programs. Address: Information Staff, Foreign Agriculture Service, Department of Agriculture, Washington, DC 20250 USA; Tel: [1] (202) 720-7115; http://www.fas.usda.gov.

Foreign Assets Control (FAC)
(U.S.) An agency of the U.S. Treasury Department that administers sanctions programs involving specific countries and restricts the involvement of U.S. persons in third country strategic exports. Address: Office of Foreign Assets Control, Department of Treasury, 1500 Pennsylvania Avenue NW, Washington, DC 20220 USA; Tel: [1] (202) 622-2480; Fax-on-demand: [1] (202) 622-0077 to request licensing; http://www.treas.gov/ofac.

Foreign Assistance Act of 1991
(U.S.) This Act replaced the Support for East European Democracy (SEED) Act. The Foreign Assistance Act allows support to 26 countries, including all East European nations and most of the former Soviet republics.

foreign availability
(U.S.) The U.S. Bureau of Export Administration conducts reviews to determine the foreign availability of selected commodities or technology subject to U.S. export control. The reviews use four criteria to determine foreign availability: comparable quality, availability-in-fact, foreign source, and adequacy of available quantities that would render continuation of the U.S. control ineffective in meeting its intended purpose. A positive determination of foreign availability means that a non-U.S. origin item of comparable quality may be obtained by one or more proscribed countries in quantities sufficient to satisfy their needs so that U.S. exports of such item would not make a significant contribution to the military potential of such countries. A positive determination may result in the decontrol of a U.S. product that has been under export control, or the approval of an export license. However, the control may be maintained if the President invokes the national security override provision.

Beginning with the 1977 amendments to the Export Administration Act, the Congress directed that products with foreign availability be identified and decontrolled unless essential to national security. In January 1983, a program to assess the foreign availability of specific products was established within the Office of Export Administration, now the Bureau of Export Administration, or BXA. Further, 1985 amendments to the Act directed that an Office of Foreign Availability be created. *See* Bureau of Export Administration.

foreign bills
(banking) Bills of exchange or drafts drawn on a foreign party and denominated in foreign currency. *See* bill of exchange.

foreign bond
(banking/finance) An international bond denominated in the currency of the country where it is issued.

Foreign Buyer Program
See International Buyer Program.

foreign commerce
(trade) Trade between individuals or legal entities in different countries.

Foreign Corrupt Practices Act (FCPA)
(U.S. law) The FCPA makes it unlawful for any United States citizen or firm (or any person who acts on behalf of a U.S. citizen or firm) to offer, pay,

transfer, promise to pay or transfer, or authorize a payment, transfer, or promise of money or anything of value to any foreign appointed or elected government official, foreign political party, or candidate for a foreign political office for a corrupt purpose, (that is, to influence a discretionary act or decision of the official) and for the purpose of obtaining or retaining business.

It is also unlawful for a U.S. business owner to make such an offer, promise, payment, or transfer to any person if the U.S. business owner knows, or has reason to know, that the person will offer, give, or promise directly or indirectly all or any part of the payment to a foreign government official, political party, or candidate. For purposes of the FCPA, the term knowledge means *actual knowledge*—the business owner in fact knew that the offer, payment, or transfer was included in the transaction—and *implied knowledge*—the business owner should have known from the facts and circumstances of a transaction that the agent paid a bribe, but failed to carry out a reasonable investigation into the transaction.

The provisions of the FCPA do not prohibit payments made to facilitate a routine government action. A facilitating payment is one made in connection with an action that a foreign official must perform as part of the job. In comparison, a corrupt payment is made to influence an official's discretionary decision. For example, payments are not generally considered corrupt if made to cover an official's overtime required to expedite the processing of export documentation for a legal shipment of merchandise, or to cover the expense of additional crew to handle a shipment.

Any person may request the Department of Justice to issue a statement of opinion on whether specific proposed business conduct would be considered a violation of the FCPA. The opinion procedure is detailed in 28 C.F.R. Part 77. If the Department of Justice issues an opinion stating that certain conduct conforms with current enforcement policy, conduct in accordance with that opinion is presumed to comply with FCPA provisions. Contact: United States Department of Justice, Washington, DC.

Foreign Credit Insurance Association

(U.S.) An agency established in 1961 to offer insurance covering political and commercial risks on U.S. export receivables in partnership with the Export-Import Bank (Eximbank) of the United States. The FCIA was founded in 1961 as a partnership of the Eximbank and a group of private insurance companies. Eximbank is responsible for the political risk and may underwrite or reinsure the commercial risk. The FCIA acts as an agent responsible for the marketing and daily administration of the program. Address: F.C.I.A. Management Co., Inc., 40 Rector St., 11th Floor, New York, NY 10006 USA; Tel: [1] (212) 306-5084. *See* Export-Import Bank of the United States.

foreign currency

(banking) The currency of any foreign country which is the authorized medium of circulation and the basis for record keeping in that country. Foreign currency is traded in by banks either by the actual handling of currency or checks, or by establishing balances in foreign currency with banks in those countries.

foreign currency account

(banking) An account maintained in a foreign bank in the currency of the country in which the bank is located. Foreign currency accounts are also maintained by banks in the United States for depositors. When such accounts are kept, they usually represent that portion of the carrying bank's foreign currency account that is in excess of its contractual requirements.

foreign direct investment in the United States (FDIUS)

(foreign investment) Foreign direct investment in the United States is the ownership or control, directly or indirectly, by a single foreign person (an individual, or related group of individuals, company, or government) of 10 percent or more of the voting securities of an incorporated U.S. business enterprise or an equivalent interest in an unincorporated U.S. business enterprise, including real property. Such a business is referred to as a U.S. affiliate of a foreign direct investor. *See* Committee on Foreign Investment in the United States; foreign person; portfolio investment; affiliate; United States Affiliate.

foreign draft

(banking) A draft drawn by an individual (drawer) or bank in one country on another individual (drawee) or bank in another country. *See* bill of exchange.

Foreign Economic Trends

(publication) Reports prepared by U.S. embassies abroad to describe foreign country economic and commercial trends and trade and investment climates. The reports describe current economic conditions; provide updates on the principal factors influencing development and the possible impacts on American exports; review newly announced foreign government policies as well as consumption, investment, and foreign debt trends. Available from: Superintendent of Documents, U.S. Government Printing Office, Washington, DC 20402 USA; Tel: [1] (202) 512-1800.

foreign exchange
(banking/foreign exchange) Current or liquid claims payable in foreign currency and in a foreign country (bank balances, checks, bills of exchange). Not to be confused with foreign bank notes and coin, which are not included in this definition. *See also* bank notes.

foreign exchange auctions
(foreign exchange) Auctions of foreign currency, as used in some developing countries, whereby the price obtained for the foreign currency at the auction is the rate of exchange applied till the next auction.

foreign exchange contract
(foreign exchange) A contract for the sale or purchase of foreign exchange specifying an exchange rate and delivery date.

foreign exchange control
(foreign exchange) Governmental control and supervision of: transactions within the country involving its currency, foreign exchange for imports and exports, capital movements of any currency or monetary instruments into and out of the country, and expenditures of currency by its own citizens traveling abroad.

foreign exchange desk
(Federal Reserve Bank) The foreign exchange trading desk at the New York Federal Reserve Bank. The desk undertakes operations in the exchange markets for the account of the Federal Open Market Committee, as agent for the U.S. Treasury and as agent for foreign central banks.

foreign exchange holdings
(foreign exchange) Holdings of current or liquid foreign exchange claims denominated in the currency of another country.

foreign exchange market
(foreign exchange) (a) The worldwide system of contacts, either by telephone, teleprinter or in writing, which take place between non-bank foreign exchange dealers and foreign exchange traders at banks as well as foreign exchange traders amongst themselves, where the monies of different countries are bought and sold. (b) Wherever foreign exchange rates are determined.

foreign exchange rate
(foreign exchange) The price of one currency in terms of another.

foreign exchange trader
(foreign exchange) An individual engaged in the business of buying and selling foreign exchange on his own account or as an employee of a bank or other business authorized to deal in foreign exchange.

foreign exchange trading
(foreign exchange) Buying and selling of foreign exchange, holding of currency positions, foreign exchange arbitrage, and foreign exchange speculation on the foreign exchange market.

foreign exchange transactions
(foreign exchange) The purchase or sale of one currency with another. Foreign exchange rates refer to the number of units of one currency needed to purchase one unit of another, or the value of one currency in terms of another.

foreign exports
(U.S.) The U.S. export of foreign merchandise (re-exports), consisting of commodities of foreign origin which have entered the United States for consumption or into Customs bonded warehouses or U.S. Foreign Trade Zones, and which, at the time of exportation, are in substantially the same condition as when imported. *See* reexport.

foreign flag
(shipping) A reference to a carrier not registered in a country, but which flies that country's flag. The term applies to both air and sea transportation.

foreign freight forwarder
See freight forwarder.

foreign income
(economics-U.S.) Income earned by Americans from work performed in another country. Under the Tax Reform Act of 1976, the amount of annual income that can be excluded from taxable income by Americans working abroad was reduced from $20,000 (in some cases from $25,000) to $15,000. Foreign employees of U.S. charitable organizations are able to exclude $20,000 each year.

foreign investment
(banking) The purchase of assets from abroad.

foreign investments

(economics) The flow of foreign capital into U.S. business enterprises in which foreign residents have significant control.

Foreign Labor Trends

(publication) Published by U.S. Department of Labor, provides an overview of the labor sector of a country's economy. Includes information on labor standards, conditions of employment, human resource development and labor relations. Can be purchased from: Superintendent of Documents, U.S. Government Printing Office, Washington, DC 20402 USA; Tel: [1] (202) 512-1800.

foreign market value

The price at which merchandise is sold, or offered for sale, in the principal markets of the country from which it is exported.

(U.S.) In U.S. dumping investigations, if information on foreign home market sales is not available, the foreign market value is based on prices of exports to third countries or constructed value. Adjustments for quantities sold, circumstances of sales, and differences in the merchandise can be made to those prices to ensure a proper comparison with the prices of goods exported to the United States. *See* dumping; constructive value.

foreign military sales (FMS)

See conventional arms transfer.

foreign-owned affiliate in the U.S.

(U.S.) A business in the United States in which there is sufficient foreign investment to be classified as direct foreign investment. To determine fully the foreign owners of a U.S. affiliate, three entities must be identified: the foreign parent, the ultimate beneficial owner, and the foreign parent group. All these entities are "persons" in the broad sense: thus, they may be individuals; business enterprises; governments; religious, charitable, and other nonprofit organizations; estates and trusts; or associated groups.

A U.S. affiliate may have an ultimate beneficial owner (UBO) that is not the immediate foreign parent; moreover, the affiliate may have several ownership chains above it, if it is owned at least 10 percent by more than one foreign person. In such cases, the affiliate may have more than one foreign parent, UBO, and/or foreign parent group.

See also United States Affiliate; foreign parent group; person; ultimate beneficial owner; affiliate; foreign parent.

foreign parent

(U.S.) The first foreign person or entity outside the United States in an affiliate's ownership chain that has direct investment in the affiliate. The foreign parent consists only of the first person or entity outside the United States in the affiliate's ownership chain; all other affiliated foreign persons are excluded.

foreign parent group (FPG)

(U.S.) Consists of: (a) the foreign parent, (b) any foreign person or entity, proceeding up the foreign parent's ownership chain, that owns more than 50 percent of the party below it, up to and including the ultimate beneficial owner (UBO), and (c) any foreign person or entity, proceeding down the ownership chain(s) of each of these members, that is owned more than 50 percent by the party above it. A particular U.S. affiliate may have several ownership chains above it, if it is owned at least 10 percent by more than one foreign party. In such cases, the affiliate may have more than one foreign parent, UBO, and/or foreign parent group. See also United States Affiliate; affiliate; ultimate beneficial owner.

foreign person

(U.S.) A foreign person is any person resident outside the United States or subject to the jurisdiction of a country other than the United States. "Person" is any individual, branch, partnership, association, associated group, estate, trust, corporation, or other organization (whether or not organized under the laws of any state), and any government (including a foreign government, the U.S. government, a state or local government, and any agency, corporation, financial institution, or other entity or instrumentality thereof, including a government sponsored agency.)

foreign policy controls

(U.S.) U.S. export controls that are distinct from national security controls (such as the Coordinating Committee in Multilateral Export Controls or other international agreements) and are imposed to further U.S. foreign policy. The controls are typically imposed in response to developments in a country or countries—such as considerations regarding terrorism and human rights—or to developments involving a type or types of commodities and their related technical data. Foreign policy controls expire annually, unless extended.

F

F

foreign remittances
(banking) The transfer of any monetary instrument across national boundaries.

foreign sales agent
An individual or firm that serves as the foreign representative of a domestic supplier and seeks sales abroad for the supplier.

Foreign Service (U.S.)
(U.S. diplomacy) The Foreign Service supports the President of the United States and the Secretary of State in pursuing America's foreign policy objectives. Foreign service functions include: representing U.S. interests; operating U.S. overseas missions; assisting Americans abroad; public diplomacy and reporting; and communicating and negotiating political, economic, consular, administrative, cultural, and commercial affairs. The Foreign Service comprises officers from the Departments of State, Commerce, and Agriculture and the United States Information Service. *See* commercial officers; economic officers.

Foreign Service Institute
(U.S. government) The FSI was founded in 1946 to train U.S. foreign and civil service officials. Training courses cover administrative, consular, economic, commercial, and political work; foreign languages; and diplomatic life overseas. Address: Foreign Service Institute, National Foreign Affairs Training Center, 4000 Arlington Blvd., Arlington, VA 22204-1500 USA; Tel: [1] (703) 302-6729.

foreign status merchandise
(U.S. foreign trade zones) Imported merchandise which has not been released from U.S. Customs custody. Also refers to domestically-produced merchandise which has been exported and later reimported into the U.S.
See foreign trade zone; Foreign Trade Zone Board; Foreign Trade Zone Act; grantee; operator; zone user; subzone.

Foreign Traders Index (FTI)
(publication) The foreign traders index is the U.S. and Foreign Commercial Service (US&FCS) headquarters compilation of overseas contact files, intended for use by domestic U.S. businesses. The FTI includes background information on foreign companies, address, contact person, sales figures, size of company, and products by SIC code. Contact: U.S. and Foreign Commercial Service, International Trade Administration, U.S. Department of Commerce, Washington, DC 20230; Tel: [1] (202)

482-5777; Fax: (202) 482-5013; http://www.customs.ustreas.gov.

foreign trade zone (FTZ)
FTZs (or free zones, free ports, or bonded warehouses) are special commercial and industrial areas in or near ports of entry where foreign and domestic merchandise, including raw materials, components, and finished goods, may be brought in without being subject to payment of customs duties. Merchandise brought into these zones may be stored, sold, exhibited, repacked, assembled, sorted, graded, cleaned, or otherwise manipulated prior to reexport or entry into the national customs territory.

(U.S.) FTZs are restricted-access sites in or near ports of entry, which are licensed by the Foreign-Trade Zones Board and operated under the supervision of the U.S. Customs Service. Zones are operated under public utility principles to create and maintain employment by encouraging operations in the U.S. which might otherwise have been carried on abroad.

Subzones are a special-purpose type of ancillary zone authorized by the Board for companies unable to operate effectively at public zone sites. Subzones may be approved when it can be demonstrated that the activity to be performed there will result in significant public benefit and is in the public interest.

A **Foreign Trade Zones Board**, created by the Foreign Trade Zones Act of 1934, reviews and approves applications to establish, operate, and maintain foreign trade zones.

See free trade area; grantee; operator; zone user, subzones; free trade agreement.

Location of and general information on U.S. Foreign Trade Zones may be obtained from Foreign Trade Zones Board, Department of Commerce, Washington, DC 20230 USA; Tel: [1] (202) 482-2862; Fax: [1] (202) 482-0002.

Questions relating to legal aspects of Customs Service responsibilities in regard to FTZs should be addressed to Chief, Entry Rulings Branch, U.S. Customs Service, 1301 Constitution Avenue NW, Washington, DC 20229 USA; Tel: [1] (202) 482-7040.

Questions relating to operational aspects of such responsibilities should be addressed to the appropriate district/area director of U.S. Customs.

The Foreign Trade Zones Manual, for grantees, operators, users, Customs brokers, may be purchased from the Superintendent of Documents, U.S. Government Printing Office, Washington, DC 20402;

Tel: [1] (202) 512-1800. When ordering, refer to GPO stock No. 048-002-00111-7 and Customs publication No. 559.

Additional information may be obtained from the National Association of Foreign Trade Zones, 1000 Connecticut Ave. NW, Suite 1001, Washington, DC 20036; Tel: [1] (202) 331-1950; Fax: [1] (202) 331-1994.

Foreign Trade Zone Act (FTZA)
(U.S. law) The principal statute governing foreign trade zones, is the Foreign Trade Zones Act of 1934 (FTZA), which has been codified in the United States Code as Title 19, Sections 81a through 81u. The FTZA has been periodically amended. The FTZA generally covers how and where zones are established, how they are administered and what may and may not be done in them. *See* foreign trade zone; Foreign Trade Zone Board.

Foreign Trade Zones Board
(U.S. Customs) The administrative group responsible for the establishment, maintenance and administration of foreign trade zones in the United States under the Foreign Trade Zone Act. The Foreign Trade Zones Board consists of the U.S. Secretary of Commerce who is chairman and executive officer of the Board, the Secretary of the Treasury, and the Secretary of the Army. Address: Foreign Trade Zone Board, Department of Commerce, Room 3716, Washington, DC 20230 USA; Tel: [1] (202) 482-2862; Fax: [1] (202) 482-0002; http://www.ita.doc.gov/import_admin/records/fgzpage/. *See* foreign trade zone.

foreign trade zone entry
(U.S. Customs) The transfer of goods into a foreign trade zone. *See* foreign trade zone; entry.

forex
Abbreviation for foreign exchange. *See* foreign exchange.

forfaiting
(trade/finance) The selling, at a discount, of medium to longer term accounts receivable or promissory notes of a foreign buyer (including those arising out of a letter of credit transaction) for immediate payment. These instruments may also carry the guarantee of the foreign government. Forfaiting emerged after the Second World War to expedite finance transactions between Eastern and Western European countries. More recently, it has become popular in Asian and Third world countries. Both U.S. and European forfaiting houses, which purchase the instruments at a discount from

the exporters, are active in the U.S. market. *See also* factoring.

forint
The currency of Hungary. 1Ft=100 fillér.

Form A
See Certificate of Origin Form A.

forward contract
(trade/finance) Purchase or sale of a specific quantity of a commodity, security, currency or other financial instrument at a predetermined rate with delivery and settlement at a specified future date.

forwarder
See freight forwarder.

forwarder's bill of lading
(shipping) A bill of lading issued by a forwarding agent. *See* bill of lading.

forward foreign exchange
(foreign exchange) An agreement to purchase foreign exchange (currency) at a future date at a predetermined rate of exchange. Forward foreign exchange contracts are often purchased by international buyers of goods who wish to hedge against foreign exchange fluctuations between the time the contract is negotiated and the time payment is to be made.

forwarding agent's bill of lading
(shipping) A bill of lading issued by a forwarding agent. *See* bill of lading.

forwarding agent's receipt
(shipping) Receipt issued by a forwarding agent for goods received.

forward market
(foreign exchange) The market for the purchase and sale of forward foreign exchange. Forward dates are usually one, three, six or twelve months in the future. *See* forward foreign exchange.

forward operations
(foreign exchange) Foreign exchange transactions, on which the fulfillment of the mutual delivery obligations is made on a date later than the second business day after the transaction was concluded.

forward rate
(foreign exchange) A contractually agreed upon exchange rate for a forward foreign exchange contract.

forward rate agreements
(banking) With forward rate agreements (also known as future rate agreements) two counterparties can hedge themselves against future interest rate changes. They agree upon an interest rate for a future period within a spe-

cific currency segment, which is valid for a pre-determined amount. In contrast to futures, FRA's are not standardized and are not traded on exchanges but are used in interbank trading.

FOT

See free on rail; free on truck; Incoterms.

foul bill of lading

(shipping) A receipt for goods issued by a carrier with an indication that the goods were damaged or short in quantity when received. *See* bill of lading.

four tigers; four dragons

A term used to describe the emerging economies of Hong Kong, Singapore, South Korea and Taiwan.

fractional currency

(banking) Any currency that is smaller than a standard money unit (e.g., any coin worth less than $1).

framework agreement

(a) (GATT/WTO): The Tokyo Round of the GATT called for consideration to be given "to improvements in the international framework for the conduct of world trade." Four separate agreements make up what is known as the "framework agreement." They concern: (1) differential and more favorable treatment for, and reciprocity and fuller participation by, developing countries in the international framework for trade; (2) trade measures taken for balance of payments purposes; (3) safeguard actions for development purposes; and (4) an understanding on notification, consultation, dispute settlement, and surveillance in the GATT.

(b) Under the umbrella of the Enterprise for the Americas Initiative the United States and interested Western hemisphere countries are negotiating bilateral "framework agreements" which establish agreed upon stages for eliminating counter-productive barriers to trade and investment. They also provide a forum for bilateral dispute settlement.

Generally, bilateral framework agreements contain similar objectives. They are based on a statement of agreed principles regarding the benefits of open trade and investment, increased importance of services to economies, the need for adequate intellectual property rights protection, the importance of observing and promoting internationally-recognized worker rights, and the desirability of resolving trade and investment problems expeditiously. The parties establish a Council on Trade and Investment to monitor trade and investment relations, hold consultations on specific trade and investment matters of interest to both sides, and work toward removing impediments to trade and investment flows. Framework agreements do not bind signatories to implement specific trade liberalization measures. *See* General Agreement on Tariffs and Trade.

franc

The currency for:

Andorra (uses French franc);
Belgium, 1BF=100 centimes;
Benin, 1 CFAF=100 centimes;
Burkina Faso, 1CFAF=100 centimes;
Burundi, 1 FBu=100 centimes;
Cameroon, 1 CFAF=100 centimes;
Central African Republic, 1CFAF=100 centimes;
Chad, 1 CFAF=100 centimes;
Comoros, 1CF=100 centimes;
Congo, 1 CFAF=100 centimes;
Djibouti, 1DF=100 centimes;
Equatorial Guinea, 1CFAF=100 centimes;
France, 1F=100 centimes;
French Guiana, 1F=100 centimes;
French Pacific Islands, 1CFPF=100 centimes;
Gabon, 1CFAF=100 centimes;
Guadeloupe, 1F=100 centimes;
Guinea, 1GFr=100 centimes;
Ivory Coast, 1CFAF=100 centimes;
Liechtenstein (uses Swiss franc);
Luxembourg, 1LuxF=100 centimes;
Madagascar, 1FMG=100 centimes;
Mali, 1CFAF=100 centimes;
Martinique, 1F=100 centimes;
Monaco (uses French franc);
Niger, 1CFAF=100 centimes;
Reunion Island, 1F=100 centimes;
Rwanda, 1RF=100 centimes;
St. Pierre, 1F=100 centimes;
Senegal, 1CFAF=100 centimes;
Switzerland, 1SwF=100 centimes;
Togo, 1 CFAF=100 centimes.

franco

(trade term) Free from duties, transportation charges and other levies. Used also as delivery condition, e.g., franco ... (named place of delivery), which means that the seller must bear all transportation charges and duties up to the named place. *See also* Incoterms.

fraud

(law) An intentional deception or false representation made to induce another person to act in reliance on that representation with the result that the person incurs damages. A buyer acts fraudulently, for example, by promising to pay for goods on delivery even though the buyer does not have the funds needed, accepting the goods as satisfactory, but not paying for them.

Free Alongside Ship (...named port of shipment) (FAS)

(Incoterms 2000) An international trade term of sale in which, for the quoted price, the seller/exporter/manufacturer clears the goods for export and then places them alongside the vessel at the "named port of shipment." (The seller's clearing the goods for export is new to Incoterms 2000.)

The parties to the transaction, however, may stipulate in their contract of sale that the buyer will clear the goods for export.

The Free Alongside Ship term is used only for ocean or inland waterway transport.

The "named place" in Free Alongside Ship and all "F" Incoterms 2000 is domestic to the seller.

The Free Alongside Ship term is commonly used in the sale of bulk commodity cargo such as oil, grains, and ore.

See Guide to Incoterms 2000 Appendix.

free-astray

(shipping) A shipment miscarried or unloaded at the wrong station is billed and forwarded to the correct station, free of charges, on account of being astray, hence the term free astray.

Free Carrier (...named place) (FCA)

(Incoterms 2000) An international trade term of sale in which, for the quoted price, the seller/exporter/manufacturer clears the goods for export and then delivers them to the carrier specified by the buyer at the named place.

If the named place is the seller's place of business, the seller is responsible for loading the goods onto the transport vehicle. If the named place is any other location, such as the loading dock of the carrier, the seller is not responsible for loading the goods onto the transport vehicle.

The Free Carrier term may be used for any mode of transport, including multimodal.

The "named place" in Free Carrier and all "F" Incoterms 2000 is domestic to the seller.

"Carrier" has a specific and somewhat expanded meaning. A carrier can be a shipping line, an airline, a trucking firm, or a railway. The carrier can also be an individual or firm who undertakes to procure carriage by any of the above methods of transport including multimodal. Therefore, a person, such as a freight forwarder, can act as a "carrier"

under this term. In such a case, the buyer names the carrier or the individual who is to receive the goods. The Free Carrier term is often used when making an initial quotation for the sale of goods.

See Guide to Incoterms 2000 Appendix.

free domicile

(shipping) A term used in international transportation where the shipper pays all transportation charges and any applicable duties and/or taxes. *See* Incoterms.

free exchange rate

See exchange rate; floating.

free in

(shipping) A pricing term indicating that the loading charges are for the account of the supplier.

free in and out (FIO)

(shipping) A pricing term indicating that the charterer of a vessel is responsible for the cost of loading and unloading goods from the vessel.

free list

(customs) A statement, prepared by the customs department of a country, of items that are not liable to the payment of duties.

freely negotiable

(banking) When a letter of credit is stated as "freely negotiable," the beneficiary of the letter of credit has the right to present his documents at a bank of his choice for negotiation. *See* letter of credit.

free market

(economics) Describes the unrestricted movement of items in and out from the market, unhampered by the existence of tariffs or other trade barriers.

free of capture and seizure (F.C.&S.)

(insurance) An insurance policy provision stating that the policy does not cover warlike operations or its consequences, whether before or after the actual declaration of war. Currently, most open policies omit war perils from its insuring conditions and in all cases will include a F.C.&S. clause. War coverage is customarily furnished in conjunction with an open cargo policy and is written under a separate, distinct policy-the War Risk Only Policy. *See* war risk; all risk; special marine policy.

free of particular average (FPA)

(insurance) A clause in an insurance policy that provides that in addition to total losses, partial losses resulting from perils of the sea are recoverable, but only in the event that the carrying vessel has stranded, sunk, burnt, been on fire or been in collision. *See also* average; particular average; general average; with average; deductible average.

Free On Board
(...named port of shipment) (FOB)

(Incoterms 2000) An international trade term of sale in which, for the quoted price, the seller/exporter/manufacturer clears the goods for export and is responsible for the costs and risks of delivering the goods past the ship's rail at the named port of shipment.

The Free On Board term is used only for ocean or inland waterway transport.

The "named place" in Free On Board and all "F" Incoterms 2000 is domestic to the seller.

The Free On Board term is commonly used in the sale of bulk commodity cargo such as oil, grains, and ore where passing the ship's rail is important. However, it is also commonly used in shipping container loads of other goods.

The key document in FOB transactions is the "On Board Bill of Lading."

Sellers and buyers often confuse the Free On Board term with Free Carrier. Free On Board (FOB) does not mean loading the goods onto a truck at the seller's place of business. Free On Board is used only in reference to delivering the goods past a ship's rail in ocean or inland waterway transport. Free Carrier, on the other hand, is applicable to all modes of transport.

See Guide to Incoterms 2000 Appendix.

free on rail; free on truck (FOR/FOT)

(trade terms) These terms are synonymous, since the word "truck" relates to the railway wagons. The terms should only be used when the goods are to be carried by rail. *See* free carrier; Incoterms.

free out

(shipping) A pricing term indicating that unloading charges are for the account of the receiver.

free port

An area, such as a port city, into which imported merchandise may legally be moved without payment of duties. *See also* foreign trade zone.

free time

(shipping) The time allowed shippers or receivers to load or unload cars before demurrage, detention, or storage charges accrue. *See* demurrage; detention.

free trade

(economics) A theoretical concept that assumes international trade unhampered by government measures such as tariffs or non-tariff barriers. The objective of trade liberalization is to achieve "freer trade" rather than "free trade," it being generally recognized among trade policy officials that some restrictions on trade are likely to remain in effect for the foreseeable future.

free trade agreement (FTA)

An FTA is an arrangement which establishes unimpeded exchange and flow of goods and services between trading partners regardless of national borders. An FTA does not (as opposed to a common market) address labor mobility across borders or other common policies such as taxes. Member countries of a free trade area apply their individual tariff rates to countries outside the free trade area.

free trade area

A group of two or more countries that have eliminated tariff and most non-tariff barriers affecting trade among themselves, while each participating country applies its own independent schedule of tariffs to imports from countries that are not members. A free trade area allows member countries to maintain individually separate tariff schedules for external countries; members of a customs union employ a common external tariff. The best known example is the European Free Trade Association (EFTA) and the free trade area for manufactured goods that has been created through the trade agreements that have been concluded between the European Community and the individual EFTA countries. The World Trade Organization (WTO) spells out the meaning of a free trade area and specifies the applicability of other WTO provisions to free trade areas. *See* European Community; European Free Trade Association; common market.

free trade zone

See foreign trade zone; free zone.

free zone

An area within a country (a seaport, airport, warehouse or any designated area) regarded as being outside its customs territory. Importers may therefore bring goods of foreign origin into such an area without paying customs duties and taxes, pending their eventual processing, transshipment or re-exportation. Free zones are also known as "free ports," "free warehouses," and "foreign trade zones."

freight

(shipping) All merchandise, goods, products, or commodities shipped by rail, air, road, or water, other than baggage, express mail, or regular mail.

freight bill

(shipping) (a) **Destination freight bill**—A bill rendered by a transportation line to consignee, giving a description of the freight, the name of shipper, point or origin, weight and amount of charges (if not prepaid).

(b) **Prepaid freight bill**—A bill rendered by a transportation line to shipper, giving a description of the freight, the names of consignee and destination, weight and amount of charges.

freight carriage ... and insurance paid to

See cost, insurance, freight; Incoterms.

freight carriage ... paid to

See carriage paid to; Incoterms 2000.

freight charge

(shipping) The charge assessed for transporting freight.

freight claim

(shipping) A demand upon a carrier for the payment of overcharge or loss or damage sustained by shipper or consignee.

freighter

(shipping) A ship or airplane used primarily to carry freight.

freight forwarder

(shipping) A person engaged in the business of assembling, collection, consolidating, shipping and distributing less-than-carload or less-than-truckload freight. Also, a person acting as agent in the trans-shipping of freight to or from foreign countries and the clearing of freight through customs, including full preparation of documents, arranging for shipping, warehousing, delivery and export clearance.

full set

All the originals of a particular document (usually the bill of lading). The number of originals is usually indicated on the document itself.

fundamental analysis

(economics) Analysis of basic economic data in a market (supply and demand), in order to be able to make assertions as to the future price trend of a traded commodity. Fundamental exchange rate analysis is based on the economic and business cycle data of the country in question and leads to longer-term exchange rate forecasts.

fungibles

(law) Goods that are identical with other goods of the same nature. A merchant who is unable to deliver a specific load of grain, for example, may negotiate to replace that grain with fungibles, that is another load of grain of the same nature and quality.

future exchange contract

See futures contract.

futures contract

(finance/foreign exchange) A contract for the future delivery of a specified commodity, currency or security on a specific date at a rate determined in the present. Standardized forward contracts are officially traded on an exchange (Chicago Board of Trade (CBOT), London International Financial Futures Exchange (LIFFE), Commodity Exchange Inc. (COMEX), New York Mercantile Exchange (NYMEX)). The contract is valid for a specific amount of a commodity or a fixed amount of a financial instrument.

future trading

The sale or purchase of a commodity, currency or security for future delivery.

G

gamma
(statistics/banking/foreign exchange) The rate of change of an option's delta with respect to a marginal change in the price of the underlying instrument.

gang
(shipping) A group of usually four to six stevedores with a supervisor who are assigned to the loading or unloading of a portion of a vessel.

gangway
(shipping) (a) The opening through which a ship is boarded, (b) Either of the sides of the upper deck of a ship.

gantry crane
(shipping) A specialized machine for the raising or lowering of cargo mounted on a structure spanning an open space on a ship. The hoisting device travels back and forth along the spanning structure from port to starboard, while the spanning structure itself is often mounted on a set of rails which enables it to move from fore to aft.

gateway
(general) A major airport or seaport.
(customs) The port where customs clearance takes place.
(shipping) A point at which freight moving from one territory to another is interchanged between transportation lines.

GATT
See General Agreement on Tariffs and Trade.

geisha bond
(finance/banking) Bond issued on the Japanese market in currencies other than yen. Yen-denominated bonds are known as Samurai bonds.

general agency
See agency.

General Agreement on Tariffs and Trade (GATT)
[*The General Agreement on Tariffs and Trade has been superseded by the World Trade Organization (WTO). The following listing remains for historical purposes. See World Trade Organization (WTO).*]
Both a multilateral trade agreement aimed at expanding international trade and the organization which oversees the agreement. The main goals of GATT are to liberalize world trade and place it on a secure basis thereby contributing to economic growth and development and the welfare of the world's people. GATT is the only multilateral instrument that lays down agreed rules for international trade, and the organization is the principal international body concerned with negotiating the reduction of trade barriers and with international trade relations.

One hundred and seventeen countries accounting for approximately 90 percent of world trade are Contracting Parties to GATT, while some other countries apply GATT rules on a de facto basis. Approximately 2/3 of GATT's membership consists of developing countries.

The GATT was signed in 1948 by 23 nations as a response to the trade conflicts which contributed to the outbreak of World War II. Originally looked upon as an interim agreement, it has become recognized as the key institution concerned with international trade negotiations. An important element which contributed to GATT's importance early on came with the United States' refusal to ratify the Havana Charter of 1948, which would have created an International Trade Organization (ITO) as a Specialized Agency of the United Nations system, similar to the International Monetary Fund and the World Bank. The Interim Commission of the ITO (ICITO), which was established to facilitate the creation of the ITO, subsequently became the GATT Secretariat. One result of the recent Uruguay Round was the decision to replace the GATT Secretariat with a Multilateral Trading Organization (MTO), which will have more authority to enforce free trade rules, as through the assessment of trade penalties. In December, 1993, agreements were reached at the conclusion of the Uruguay Round to revise the framework of GATT. Member nations will sign the agreement in April, 1994, and it will go into effect July 1, 1995.

The purpose of the GATT organization, headquartered in Geneva, is to provide a forum for discussion of world trade issues that allows for the disciplined resolution of trade disputes, based on the founding principles of GATT which include nondiscrimination, national treatment, transparency, and most-favored-nations (MFN) treatment. International negotiations known as "Rounds" are conducted to lower tariffs and other barriers to trade, and a consultative mechanism that may be invoked by governments seeking to protect their trade interests.

A few of the fundamental principles and aims of GATT:

(1) **Trade without discrimination**—The first principle embodied in the famous "most-favored nation" clause is that trade must be conducted on the basis of non-discrimination. No country is to give special trading advantages to another or to discriminate against it; all are on an equal basis and all share the benefits of any moves towards lower trade barriers.

(2) **Protection through tariffs**—Ensures that if protection to a domestic industry is given, it should be extended through the customs tariff, and not through other commercial measures.

(3) **A stable basis for trade**—Provided partly by the binding of the tariff levels negotiated among contracting parties. These bound items are listed, for each country, in tariff schedules which form an integral part of the General Agreement.

(4) **Promoting fair competition**—Concerns over dumping and subsidies are addressed by the "Anti-dumping Code" which provides rules under which governments may respond to dumping in their domestic market by overseas competitors, and rules for the application of "countervailing" duties which can be imposed to negate the effects of export subsidies.

(5) **Quantitative restrictions on imports**—A basic provision of GATT is a general prohibition of quantitative restrictions (import quotas). The main exception to the general rule against these restrictions allows their use in balance-of-payments difficulties under Article XII.

(6) **The "waiver" and the possible emergency action**—Waiver procedures allow a country to seek release from particular GATT obligations, when its economic or trade circumstances so warrant. The "safeguards" rule of GATT (Article XIX) permits members, under carefully defined circumstances, to impose import restrictions or suspend tariff concessions on products which are being imported in such increased quantities and under such conditions that they cause serious injury to competing domestic producers.

(7) **Regional trading arrangements**—Regional trade groupings, as an exception to the general most-favored-nations treatment, are permitted in the form of a customs union or free trade area. Article XXIV recognizes the value of such agreements, which foster free trade by abolishing or reducing barriers against imports from countries in a particular region.

(8) **Settling trade disputes**—Consultation, conciliation, and dispute settlement are fundamental aspects of GATT's work. Countries can petition GATT for a fair settlement of cases in which they feel their rights under the General Agreement are being withheld or compromised by other members. Bilateral consultations are emphasized, but if necessary, unresolved cases go before a GATT panel of experts.

(U.S.) For the United States, the GATT came into existence as an executive agreement, which, under the U.S. Constitution does not require Senate ratification.

See also rounds; Tokyo Round; Uruguay Round; multilateral trade negotiations; rollback; standstill; safeguards; special and different treatment.

See also World Trade Organization (WTO).

general average

(shipping) A loss that affects all cargo interests on board a vessel as well as the ship herself. These include the owner of the hull and the owners of all the cargoes aboard for their respective values plus the owner or charterer who stands to earn a specific income from freight charges for the voyage.

A general average loss may occur whether goods are insured or not. It is one that results from an intentional sacrifice (or expenditure) incurred by the master of a vessel in time of danger for the benefit of both ship and cargo. The classic example of this is jettison to lighten a stranded vessel. From the most ancient times, the maritime laws of all trading nations have held that such a sacrifice shall be borne by all for whose benefit the sacrifice was made, and not alone by the owner of the cargo thrown overboard.

The principles of general average have been refined over the years, and they have inevitably come to reflect the increasing complexity of present day commerce. A vessel owner may and does declare his vessel under general average whenever, for the common good in time of danger an intentional sacrifice of ship or cargo has been made, or an extraordinary expenditure has been incurred. In actual practice, general averages result mainly from strandings, fires, collisions and from engaging salvage assistance or putting into a port of refuge following a machinery breakdown or other peril.

As the name implies, general average claims affect all the interests which stand to suffer a financial loss if a particular voyage is not successfully completed.

(insurance) Insurance coverage for a general average loss.

See also average; particular average; with average; free of particular average; deductible average.

G

general cargo rate
(shipping) The rate a carrier charges for the shipment of cargo which does not have a special class rate or commodity rate.

general cargo vessels
(shipping) A vessel designed to handle break-bulk cargo such as bags, cartons, cases, crates and drums, either individually or in unitized or palletized loads. *See* breakbulk vessel.

general commodity rate
(shipping) A freight rate applicable to all commodities except those for which specific rates have been filed. Such rates are based on weight and distance and are published for each pair of ports or cities a carrier serves.

general exception
The Coordinating Committee for Multilateral Export Controls (CoCom) controls exports at three levels, depending on the item and the proposed destination. At the highest or "general exception" level, unanimous approval by CoCom members is necessary. *See* Coordinating Committee on Multilateral Export Controls.

general imports
(U.S. Customs) The total physical arrivals of merchandise from foreign countries, whether such merchandise enters consumption channels immediately or is entered into bonded warehouses or Foreign Trade Zones under U.S. Customs custody.

Generalized System of Preferences (GSP)
A program providing for free rates of duty for merchandise from beneficiary developing independent countries and territories to encourage their economic growth.

GSP is one element of a coordinated effort by the industrial trading nations to bring developing countries more fully into the international trading system.

The GSP reflects international agreement, negotiated at the United Nations Conference on Trade and Development II (UNCTAD-II) in New Delhi in 1968, that a temporary and non-reciprocal grant of preferences by developed countries to developing countries would be equitable and, in the long term, mutually beneficial.

(U.S.) The U.S. GSP scheme is a system of nonreciprocal tariff preferences for the benefit of these countries. The U.S. conducts annual GSP reviews to consider petitions requesting modification of product coverage and/or country eligibility. United States GSP law requires that a beneficiary country's laws and practices relating to market access, intellectual property rights protection, investment, export practices, and workers rights be considered in all GSP decisions.

The GSP eligibility list includes a wide range of products classifiable under approximately 3,000 different subheadings in the Harmonized Tariff Schedule of the United States (HTS or HTSUS). These items are identified either by an "A" or "A*" in the "Special" column 1 of the tariff schedule. Note that the eligible countries and eligible items change from time-to-time over the life of the program.

Eligible merchandise will be entitled to duty-free treatment provided the following conditions are met: (1) The merchandise must be destined for the United States without contingency for diversion at the time of exportation from the beneficiary developing country. (2) The UNCTAD (United Nations Conference on Trade and Development) Certificate of Origin Form A must be properly prepared, signed by the exporter and either be filed with the customs entry or furnished before liquidation or other final action on the entry if requested to do so by Customs. (3) The merchandise must be imported directly into the United States from the beneficiary country. (4) The cost or value of materials produced in the beneficiary developing country and/or the direct cost of processing performed there must represent at least 35 percent of the appraised value of the goods.

See Certificate of Origin Form A; Harmonized Tariff Schedule of the United States.

general liability
(law) Unlimited responsibility for an obligation, such as payment of the debts of a business. *See* joint and several liability; limited liability.

general license (GL)
(U.S.) [Obsolete as of January 1997; information provided for historical reference only.] Licenses, authorized in the past by the U.S. Bureau of Export Administration, that permitted the export of nonstrategic goods to specified countries without the need for a validated license. No prior written authorization was required and no individual license was issued for these categories

There were over twenty different types of general licenses, each represented by a symbol. These licenses included:

(a) General license BAGGAGE
(b) General license CREW
(c) General license GATS
(d) General license GCG

(e) General license G-COCOM

(f) General license GCT

(g) General license G-DEST

(h) General license GFW

(i) General license GIFT

(j) General license GIT

(k) General license GLR

(l) General license GLV

(m) General license G-NNR

(n) General license GTDA

(o) General license GTDR

(p) General license G-TEMP

(q) General license GTF-U.S.

(r) General license GUS

(s) General license PLANE STORES

(t) General license RCS

(u) General license SAFEGUARDS

(v) General license SHIP STORES

Contact: Bureau of Export Administration, Office of Public Affairs, Room 3895, Fourteenth Street and Constitution Avenue NW, Washington, DC 20230 USA; Tel: [1] (202) 482-2721; http://www.bxa.doc.gov.

general order (GO)

(U.S. Customs/shipping) Merchandise not entered within 5 working days after arrival of the carrier and then stored at the risk and expense of the importer. *See* general order warehouse.

general order warehouse

(U.S. Customs) A customs bonded warehouse to which customs sends goods (at the owner's expense and risk) which have not been claimed within five days of arrival.

general partnership

(law) A partnership in which all of the partners have joint and several liability for the partnership obligations. *See* joint and several liability.

general tariff

A tariff that applies to countries that do not enjoy either preferential or most-favored-nation tariff treatment. Where the general tariff rate differs from the most-favored-nation rate, the general tariff rate is usually the higher rate.

"German" silver

"German," or coin silver is an alloy of silver that is 800/1000 pure. An article of German or coin silver is often marked "800".

Gesellschaft mit beschrankter Haftung (GmbH)

(Austria, Germany, Switzerland) Designation for a private limited liability corporation with limited liability to shareholders.

giro

See deposit money.

global bond

(banking/finance) A bond that can be traded immediately in any United States capital market and in the Euromarket.

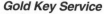

global quota

(customs) A quota on the total imports of a product from all countries.

gnomes of Zurich

(banking) Those financial and banking people of Zurich, Switzerland, involved in foreign exchange speculation. The term was coined by Great Britain's Labor ministers during the 1964 sterling crisis.

godown

(Chinese) A warehouse where goods are stored.

gold exchange standard

(banking/foreign exchange) An international monetary agreement according to which money consists of fiat national currencies that can be converted into gold at established price ratios.

gold fixing

(banking/commodity markets) In London, Paris and Zurich, at 10:30 a.m. and again at 3:30 p.m., gold specialists or bank officials specializing in gold bullion activity determine the price for the metal.

Gold Key Service

(U.S.) An International Trade Administration, U.S. Department of Commerce service that provides customized information for U.S. firms visiting a country—market orientation briefings, market research, introductions to potential business partners, an interpreter for meetings, assistance in developing a market strategy, and help in putting together a follow-up plan. Trade specialists design an agenda of meetings, screen and select the right companies, arrange meetings with key people, and go with U.S. representatives to ensure that no unforeseen difficulties occur. For further information, in the U.S. call [1] (800) USA-TRADE to find the nearest district office of the Department of Commerce International Trade Administration.

gold reserves

(banking/foreign exchange) Gold, retained by a nation's monetary agency, forming the backing of currency that the nation has issued.

gold standard

(economics) A monetary agreement whereby all national currencies are backed 100 percent by gold and the gold is utilized for payments of foreign activity.

gold tranche position in International Monetary Fund

(banking) Represents the amount that a member country can draw in foreign currencies virtually automatically from the International Monetary fund if such borrowings are needed to finance a balance-of-payments deficit.

(U.S.) In the case of the U.S., the gold tranche itself is determined by the U.S. quota paid in gold minus the holdings of dollars by the fund in excess of the dollar portion of the U.S. quota. Transactions of the fund in a member country's currency are transactions in monetary reserves. When the fund sells dollars to other countries to enable them to finance their international payments, the net position of the United States in the fund is improved. An improvement in the net position in the gold tranche is similar to an increase in the reserve assets of the United States. On the other hand, when the United States buys other currencies from the fund, or when other countries use dollars to meet obligations to the fund, the net position of the United States in the fund is reduced.

gondola car

(shipping) An open railway car with sides and ends, used principally for hauling coal, sand, etc.

goods

(law) (a) Merchandise, supplies, raw materials, and completed products. (b) All things that are movable and are designated as sold to a particular buyer. (c) **Durable goods** are ones that last a relatively long time and that are not dissipated or depleted when used generally, such as machinery and tools. (d) **Consumer goods** are ones that are purchased primarily for the buyer's personal, family, or household use. (e) **Hard goods** are consumer durable goods, such as appliances. (f) **Soft goods** are consumer goods that are not durable, such as clothing.

gourde

The currency of Haiti. 1G=100 centimes.

governing law clause

(law) A contract clause by which the parties agree that their contract should be interpreted in accordance with the law of a designated jurisdiction. A court may decide not to follow the choice made by the parties, because the parties cannot deprive a court of jurisdiction, but courts will often agree to apply the law that the parties have specified.

Government Printing Office

See Superintendent of Documents.

government procurement policies and practices

The means and mechanisms through which official government agencies purchase goods and services. Government procurement policies and practices may be considered to be non-tariff barriers to trade, involving the discriminatory purchase by official government agencies of goods and services from domestic suppliers, despite their higher prices or inferior quality as compared with competitive goods that could be imported.

(U.S.) The United States pressed for an international agreement during the Tokyo Round (of the General Agreement on Tariffs and Trade, GATT) to ensure that government purchase of goods entering into international trade should be based on specific published regulations that prescribe open procedures for submitting bids, as had been the traditional practice in the United States. Most governments had traditionally awarded such contracts on the basis of bids solicited from selected domestic suppliers, or through private negotiations with suppliers that involved little, if any, competition. Other countries, including the United States, gave domestic suppliers a specified preferential margin, as compared with foreign suppliers. The Government Procurement Code negotiated during the Tokyo Round sought to reduce, if not eliminate, the "Buy National" bias underlying such practices by improving transparency and equity in national procurement practices and by ensuring effective recourse to dispute settlement procedures. The Code became effective Jan. 1, 1981.

See General Agreement on Tariffs and Trade; Tokyo Round, World Trade Organization (WTO).

graduation

The presumption that individual developing countries are capable of assuming greater responsibilities and obligations in the international community—within the WTO or the World Bank, for example—as their economies advance, as through industrialization, export development, and rising living standards. In this sense, graduation implies that donor countries may remove the more advanced developing countries from eligibility for all or some products under the Generalized System of Preferences. Within the World Bank, graduation moves a country from dependence on concessional grants to non-concessional loans from international financial institutions and private banks.

grandfather clause
(law) A contract clause in a legal document granting a formal exemption to a rule or law based on previously existing conditions or circumstances.
(WTO) A World Trade Organization (WTO) provision that allows the original contracting parties to exempt from general WTO obligations mandatory domestic legislation which is inconsistent with WTO provisions, but which existed before the WTO/GATT was signed. Newer members may also "grandfather" domestic legislation if that is agreed to in negotiating the terms of accession.

grantee
(U.S. foreign trade zones) A public or private corporation to which the privilege of establishing, operating or maintaining a foreign trade zone has been given. *See* foreign trade zone; Foreign Trade Zone Board; Foreign Trade Zone Act; operator; zone user; subzones.

green card
(U.S. immigration) An identity card (visa) issued by the U.S. Immigration and Naturalization Service entitling a foreign national to enter and reside in the United States as a permanent resident.

green line
See China green line.

grey list
(U.S.) A list of disreputable end users in nations of concern for missile proliferation from the U.S. intelligence community. Licensing officials in the U.S. Departments of Commerce and State use this list as a cross-reference when reviewing export license applications for commodities listed in the Missile Technology Control Regime (MTCR) Equipment and Technology Annex.

grid
(foreign exchange) Fixed margin within which exchange rates are allowed to fluctuate.

gross
(general) 12 dozen or 144 articles.
(finance) The total amount before any deductions have been made.

gross domestic product (GDP)
(economics) A measure of the market value of all goods and services produced within the boundaries of a nation, regardless of asset ownership. Unlike gross national product, GDP excludes receipts from that nation's business operations in foreign countries, as well as the share of reinvested earning in foreign affiliates of domestic corporations. *See also* gross national product.

gross national product (GNP)
(economics) A measure of the market value of all goods and services produced by the labor and property of a nation. Includes receipts from that nation's business operation in foreign countries, as well as the share of reinvested earnings in foreign affiliates of domestic corporations. *See also* gross domestic product.

gross weight
(shipping) The full weight of a shipment, including goods and packaging. *See also* tare weight.

Group of Five (G-5)
Similar to the Group of Seven (G-7), with the exception of Canada and Italy.

Group of Seven (G-7)
Group comprising the major industrialized nations in economic terms, which in view of the global economic importance of the member states have made it their objective to coordinate their respective domestic economic policies. The coordination of economic, exchange rate and monetary policy aims is achieved both at government, central bank and also on other institutionalized levels. Member states are the USA, France, Great Britain, Germany, Japan, Canada, and Italy.

Group of Ten (G-10)
A group of originally 10 countries (following Switzerland's accession, 11) comprising Belgium, Germany, France, Great Britain, Italy, Japan, Canada, Holland, Sweden and the United States, who within the framework of the General Arrangements to Borrow (GAB) have decided to put the equivalent of 17 billion in Special Drawing Rights (SDRs) in their various currencies at the International Monetary Fund's (IMF) disposal for granting loans. The Group of Ten plays an important role in discussions concerning international monetary policy. The Group of Ten is also called the Paris Club.

Group of Fifteen (G-15)
The G-15, established in 1990, consists of relatively prosperous or large developing countries. The G-15 discusses the benefits of mutual coopera-

tion in improving their international economic positions. Members include: Algeria, Argentina, Brazil, Egypt, India, Indonesia, Jamaica, Malaysia (a very active member), Mexico, Nigeria, Peru, Senegal, Venezuela, Yugoslavia, and Zimbabwe.

Group of Twenty-Four (G-24)
A grouping of finance ministers from 24 developing country members of the International Monetary Fund. The Group, representing eight countries from each of the African, Asian, and Latin American country groupings in the Group of 77, was formed in 1971 to counterbalance the influence of the Group of Ten.

Group of Seventy-Seven (G-77)
A grouping of developing countries which had its origins in the early 1960s. This numerical designation persists, although membership had increased to more than 120 countries. The G-77 functions as a caucus for the developing countries on economic matters in many forums including the United Nations.

gross ton
(measure) A unit of mass or weight measure equal to 2,240 pounds.

gross tonnage
(shipping) The capacity of a vessel (not cargo) expressed in vessel tons. It is determined by dividing by 100 the contents, in cubic feet, of the vessels closed-in spaces. (A vessel ton is 100 cubic feet.) The register of a vessel states both gross and net tonnage.

gross weight
(shipping) The entire weight of a shipment, including containers and packaging materials.

GSP
See Generalized System of Preferences.

guarani
The currency of Paraguay. 1G=100 centesimos.

guarantor
(law) An individual or legal entity that makes a guaranty, by which the guarantor agrees to be held liable for another's debt or performance. *See* guaranty.

guaranty
(law) A contract by which one person (the guarantor) agrees to pay another's debt or to perform another's obligation only if that other individual or legal entity fails to pay or perform. A guaranty is usually a separate contract from the principal agreement, and therefore the guarantor is second-

arily liable to the third person. *See* guarantor; surety.

guilder
The currency of:
Netherlands, 1G (or 1f)=100 cents;
Netherlands Antilles, 1 CFls (or 1Ant.f)=100 cents;
Suriname, 1G (or 1Sur.f)=100 cents.

Gulf Cooperation Council (GCC)
The six member countries (Saudi Arabia, Kuwait, the United Arab Emirates, Bahrain, Qatar, and Oman) of the Gulf Cooperation Council (GCC) control half the proven oil reserves outside the Soviet Union, and account for about 40 percent of all the oil moving in international trade. The GCC was created in 1981, largely in response to the outbreak of the Iran-Iraq war. In creating the GCC, the members tried to maintain the balance of power in the Gulf by strengthening multilateral cooperation in security and economic matters. As regards trade, the GCC is only a policy-coordinating forum; the Council cannot impose policies on the members. GCC headquarters are in Riyadh, Saudi Arabia. The presidency of the GCC rotates yearly among the rulers of the member countries. Address: Gulf Cooperation Council, PO Box 7153, Riyadh 11462, Saudi Arabia; Tel: [966] (1) 482-7777; Telex: (1) 403635; Fax: [966] (1) 482-9089.

hallmark

An impression made on gold and silverware introduced in the beginning of the fourteenth century in England to identify the quality of the metal used.

harbor fees

(shipping) Charges assessed to users for use of a harbor, used generally for maintenance of the harbor. *See* users fees.

harbor master

(shipping) An officer who attends to the berthing, etc. of ships in a harbor.

hard loan

(banking) A foreign loan that must be paid in hard money.

hard money (currency)

(general) (a) Currency of a nation having stability in the country and abroad. Refers to currency that is accepted internationally and freely convertible. (b) Coins, in contrast with paper currency, or soft money.

(finance) Describes a situation in which interest rates are high and loans are difficult to arrange. synonymous with dear money.

Harmonized System (HS)

A multipurpose international goods classification system designed to be used by manufacturers, transporters, exporters, importers, customs, statisticians, and others in classifying goods moving in international trade under a single commodity code.

Developed under the auspices of the Customs Cooperation Council (CCC), an international Customs organization in Brussels, this code is a hierarchically structured product nomenclature containing approximately 5,000 headings and subheadings describing the articles moving in international trade. It is organized into 99 chapters arranged in 22 sections with the sections generally covering an industry (e.g., Section XI, Textiles and Textile Articles) and the chapters covering the various materials and products of the industry (e.g., Chapter 50—Silk; Chapter 55—Man-made Staple Fibers; Chapter 57—Carpets). The basic code contains 4-digit headings and 6-digit subheadings.

(U.S.) The United States has added digits for tariff and statistical purposes. In the United States, duty rates are in the 8-digit level; statistical suffixes at the 10-digit level. The Harmonized System (HS) supplanted the U.S. Tariff Schedule (TSUSA) in January 1989.

For the United States, the HS numbers are the numbers that are entered on the actual export and import documents. Any other commodity code classification number (SIC, SITC, end-use, etc.) are just rearrangements and transformations of the original HS numbers.

See also Harmonized Tariff Schedule of the United States.

Harmonized Tariff Schedule of the United States (HTS or HTSUS)

(U.S.) An organized listing of goods and their duty rates which is used by U.S. Customs as the basis for classifying imported products and therefore establishing the duty to be charged and providing the U.S. Census with statistical information about imports and exports. The categorization of product listings in the HTSUS is based on the international Harmonized Commodity Description and Coding System developed under the auspices of the Customs Cooperation Council (Harmonized System, HS).

Familiarity with the organization of the HTSUS facilitates the classification process. The tariff schedule is divided into various sections and chapters dealing separately with merchandise in broad product categories. These categories, for example, separately cover animal products, vegetable products, products of various basic materials such as wood, textiles, plastics, rubber, and steel and other metal products in various stages of manufacture. Other sections encompass chemicals, machinery and electrical equipment, and other specified or nonenumerated products. The last section, Section XXII, covers certain exceptions from duty and special statutory exceptions.

In Sections I through XXI, products are classifiable (1) under items or descriptions which name them, known as an eo nomine provision; (2) under provisions of general description; (3) under provisions which identify them by component material; or (4) under provisions which encompass merchandise in accordance with its actual or principal use. When two or more provisions seem to cover the same merchandise, the prevailing provision is determined in accordance with the legal notes and the General Rules of Interpretation for the tariff schedule. Also applicable are tariff classification principles contained in administrative precedents or in the case law of the U.S. Court of International Trade (formerly the U.S. Customs Court) or the

U.S.Court of Appeals for the Federal Circuit Court (formerly the U.S. Court of Customs and Patent Appeals).

The Harmonized Tariff Schedules of the United States also contain two rates of duty for each commodity listed. Column 1 duty rates are low and apply to imports from countries that have achieved Most Favored Nation (MFN) trading status with the United States. Column 2 duty rates apply to imports from countries that do not have Most Favored Nation (MFN) trading status with the United States. *See also* classification; Harmonized System.

Harter Act

(shipping) Legislation protecting a ship's owner against claims for damage resulting from the behavior of the vessel's crew, provided the ship left port in a seaworthy condition, properly manned and equipped.

hatch

(shipping) The opening in the deck of a vessel which gives access to the cargo hold.

haulage

(shipping) The local transport of goods. Also the charge(s) made for hauling freight on carts, drays or trucks. Also called cartage or drayage.

Hawley-Smoot Act

See Smoot-Hawley Tariff Act of 1930.

hazardous materials

(shipping) (U.S.) A hazardous material is a substance or material which has been determined by the U.S. Secretary of Transportation to be capable of posing an unreasonable risk to health, safety, and property when transported in commerce and which has been so designated. Title 49, Code of Federal Regulations (U.S.) Transportation—Parts 100-199, govern the transportation of hazardous materials. Hazardous materials may be transported domestically, but they may be classified as Dangerous Goods when transported internationally by air. *See also* restricted article; dangerous goods.

heavy lift

(shipping) Articles too heavy to be lifted by a ship's tackle.

heavy lift charge

(shipping) A charge made for lifting (onloading or offloading) articles too heavy to be lifted by a ship's tackle. Usually requiring the use of heavy lift equipment at a port.

heavy lift vessel

(shipping) A vessel with heavy lift cranes and other equipment designed to be self-sustaining in the handling of heavy cargo.

hedge

To offset. Also, a security that has offsetting qualities. Thus one attempts to "hedge" against inflation by the purchase of securities whose values should respond to inflationary developments. Securities having these qualities are "inflation hedges." *See* hedging; delta hedging.

hedge ratio

(finance/foreign exchange) The amount of an underlying instrument or the number of options which are needed to hedge a covered option. The hedge ratio is determined by the size of the delta. *See* delta; delta hedging.

hedging

(finance/foreign exchange) A type of economic insurance used by dealers in commodities, foreign exchange and securities, manufacturers, and other producers to prevent loss due to price fluctuations. Hedging consists of counterbalancing a present sale or purchase by a purchase or sale of a similar commodity or of a different commodity, usually for delivery at some future date. The desired result is that the profit or loss on a current sale or purchase be offset by the loss or profit on the future purchase or sale. *See also* arbitrage; delta hedging.

high density

(shipping) The compression of flat or standard bales of cotton to high density of approximately 32 pounds. This compression usually applies to cotton exported or shipped coast to coast.

hitchment

(shipping) The marrying of two or more portions of one shipment that originate at different geographical locations, moving under one bill of lading, from one shipper to one consignee. Authority for this service must be granted by tariff publication.

hold

(shipping) The space below deck in a vessel used to carry cargo.

holder in due course

(law) An individual or legal entity (holder) who possesses a negotiable instrument, document of title, or similar document, and who took possession for value, in good faith, and without notice of any other individual's or legal entity's claim or defense against the instrument or document. A buyer, for example, who receives title to goods after remitting the contract price to the seller is a holder in due course, provided the buyer has no notice of any lien or other claim against the goods. A holder in due course is generally protected from the claims of third parties against the item transferred, and thus the only recourse of a third party is against the person that transferred the title, instrument, or other item to the holder in due course.

hold for pickup

(shipping) Freight to be held at the carrier's destination location for pickup by the recipient.

hold harmless contract

(law) An agreement by which one party accepts responsibility for all damages and other liability that arise from a transaction, relieving the other party of any such liability. A commercial tenant, for example, may agree to hold a landlord harmless for all liabilities that could arise from injuries to customers who enter the premises. A guarantor may agree to guaranty a person's debt only if that person agrees to hold the guarantor harmless from all damages that may arise if the person fails to pay the debt. A hold harmless contract provides complete indemnity. *See* guaranty; indemnity; surety.

honor

(banking) To pay or to accept a draft complying with the terms of credit. *See* bill of exchange.

horizontal export trading company

An export trading company which exports a range of similar or identical products supplied by a number of manufacturers or other producers. Webb-Pomerene Organizations, trade-grouped organized export trading companies, and an export trading company formed by an association of agricultural cooperatives are prime examples of horizontally organized export trading companies.

house air waybill (HAWB)

(shipping) A bill of lading issued by a freight forwarder for consolidated air freight shipments. In documentary letter of credit transactions HAWBs are treated exactly the same as conventional air waybills, provided they indicate that the issuer itself assumes the liability as carrier or is acting as the agent of a named carrier, or if the credit expressly permits the acceptance of a HAWB. *See* air waybill; bill of lading.

house-to-house

(shipping) A term usually used to indicate a container yard to container yard (CY/CY) shipment.

hub and spoke routing

(shipping) Aircraft routing service pattern that feeds traffic from many cities into a central hub designed to connect with other flights to final destinations. The system maximizes operating flexibility by connecting many markets through a central hub with fewer flights than would be required to connect each pair of cities in an extensive system.

hull

(shipping) The outer shell of a vessel usually made of steel.

hump

(shipping) That part of a rail track which is elevated so that when a car is pushed up on "the hump" and uncoupled it runs down on the other side by gravity.

hundredweight pricing

(shipping) Special pricing for multiple-piece shipments traveling to one destination which are rated on the total weight of the shipment (usually over 100 pounds) as opposed to rating on a per package basis.

H

I

identical merchandise

(U.S. Customs) In establishing the customs value of merchandise exported to the United States, identical merchandise is merchandise that is: (1) Identical in all respects to the merchandise being appraised, (2) Produced in the same country as the merchandise being appraised, and (3) Produced by the same person as the merchandise being appraised.

If merchandise meeting all these criteria cannot be found, then identical merchandise is merchandise satisfying the first two criteria but produced by a different person than the producer of merchandise being appraised.

Note: Merchandise can be identical to the merchandise being appraised and still show minor differences in appearance.

Exclusion: Identical merchandise does not include merchandise that incorporates or reflects engineering, development, artwork, design work, and plans and sketches provided free or at reduced cost by the buyer and undertaken in the United States.

See valuation; transaction value; computed value; similar merchandise.

immediate delivery

(U.S. Customs) An alternate U.S. Customs entry procedure which provides for immediate release of a shipment in certain cases. Application must be made to Customs for a Special Permit for Immediate Delivery on Customs Form 3461 prior to the arrival of the merchandise. If the application is approved, the shipment is released expeditiously following arrival. An entry summary must then be filed in proper form and estimated duties deposited within 10 working days of release. *See* entry.

immediate transportation entry

(U.S. Customs) A form of U.S. Customs entry which allows imported merchandise to be forwarded from the port of original entry to another final destination for customs clearance. Merchandise travels in bond, without appraisal, from the original port of entry to the final destination, where it is then inspected by customs. *See* entry.

immigration

The entry of foreign nationals into a country for the purpose of establishing permanent residence. *See also* green card.

implied agency

See agency.

implied conditions

(insurance) Certain implied conditions are not written into marine insurance policies, but they are so basic to understanding between underwriter and assured that the law gives them much the same effect as if written. Thus, it is implied: (1) that the assured will exercise the utmost good faith in disclosing to his underwriter all facts material to the risk when applying for insurance; (2) that the generally established usages of trade applicable to the insured subject matter are followed; and (3) that the assured shall not contribute to loss through willful fault or negligence. *See* special marine policy.

implied volatility

See volatility.

implied warranties

(insurance) Legal decisions have established two important implied warranties in marine insurance policies, that of legality of the venture and that of seaworthiness. The latter is of little concern today since insurance policies commonly waive the warranty of seaworthiness by stating that seaworthiness is admitted as between the assured and the insurer. The insurer is not at liberty, however, to waive the implied warranty of legality. Such a waiver would be against public policy and the law of the land. *See* special marine policy.

import

(a) To receive goods and services from abroad. (b) An imported item.

import credit

(banking) A commercial letter of credit issued for the purpose of financing the importation of goods. *See* letter of credit.

import duty

(customs) Any tax on items imported. *See also* tariff; Harmonized Tariff Schedule of the United States.

importer

The individual, firm or legal entity that brings articles of trade from a foreign source into a domestic market in the course of trade.

importer number
(U.S. Customs) An identification number assigned by the U.S. Customs Service to each importer, used to track entries and other transactions.

Importers Manual USA
(publication) A reference book detailing specific requirements for importing 99 different product groups into the United States, plus extensive sections on banking, letters of credit, foreign exchange, packing, shipping, insurance, and U.S. Customs Entry. Published by World Trade Press, 1450 Grant Ave., Novato, CA 94945 USA; Tel: [1] (415) 898-1124; Fax: [1] (415) 898-1080; http://www.worldtradepress.com.

import license
(customs) A document required and issued by some national governments authorizing the importation of goods.

import quota
(customs) A protective ruling establishing limits on the quantity of a particular product that can be imported. Quotas are a means of restricting imports by the issuance of licenses to importers, assigning each a quota, after determination of the total amount of any commodity which is to be imported during a period. Import licenses may also specify the country from which the importer must purchase the goods. *See* quota; tariff quotas.

import quota auctioning
(customs) The process of auctioning the right to import specified quantities of quota-restricted goods.

import relief
Any of several measures imposed by a government to temporarily restrict imports of a product or commodity to protect domestic producers from competition.

import restrictions
Any one of a series of tariff and non-tariff barriers imposed by an importing nation to control the volume of goods coming into the country from other countries. May include the imposition of tariffs or import quotas, restrictions on the amount of foreign currency available to cover imports, a requirement for import deposits, the imposition of import surcharges, or the prohibition of various categories of imports. *See* tariff; non-tariff barriers.

imports
Commodities of foreign origin as well as goods of domestic origin returned to the producing country with no change in condition, or after having been processed and/or assembled in other countries.

(U.S.) For statistical purposes, imports to the U.S. are classified by type of transaction:
(a) Merchandise entered for immediate consumption. ("duty free" merchandise and merchandise on which duty is paid on arrival);
(b) Merchandise withdrawn for consumption from U.S. Customs bonded warehouses, and U.S. Foreign Trade Zones;
(c) Merchandise entered into U.S. Customs bonded warehouses and U.S. Foreign Trade Zones from foreign countries.

import sensitive producers
Domestic producers whose economic viability is threatened by competition (quality, price or service) from imported products.

import service
See export service.

imports for consumption
(U.S. Customs) The total of merchandise that has physically cleared through U.S. Customs either entering domestic consumption channels immediately or entering after withdrawal for consumption from bonded warehouses under U.S. Customs custody or from U.S. Foreign Trade Zones. Many countries use the term "special imports" to designate statistics compiled on this basis. *See also* consumption entry.

imports of goods and services (U.S.)
(economics) Represent the sum of all payments for merchandise imports, military expenditures, transportation and travel costs, other private and U.S. government services, and income and service payments to foreign parent companies by their affiliates operating in the United States. By far the largest component of this category is merchandise imports, which includes all goods bought or otherwise transferred from a foreign country to the United States.

import substitution
A strategy which emphasizes the replacement of imports with domestically produced goods, rather than the production of goods for export, to encourage the development of domestic industry.

impost
A tax, usually an import duty. *See also* tariff.

impound
(law/customs) (a) To seize or hold. (b) To place in protective custody by order of a court (e.g., impounded property, impounded records).

in bond

(U.S. Customs) A procedure under which goods are transported or warehoused under customs supervision until they are either formally entered into the customs territory of the United States and duties paid, or until they are exported from the United States.

The procedure is so named because the cargo moves under the carrier's bond (financial liability assured by the carrier) from the gateway sea port or airport and remains "in bond" until customs releases the cargo at the inland customs point.

This procedure is used in several ways:

(1) To postpone the payment of import duties on high duty merchandise, (such as alcoholic beverages), until they are needed,

(2) To hold goods that may or may not meet a requirement of customs until a determination is made and the importer decides to enter the goods or re-export them,

(3) To effect the transport of goods originating in one foreign country through the United States for export to a third country without having to pay customs duties.

See also temporary importation under bond.

in bond goods

See in bond.

in bond shipment

(customs) An import or export shipment which has not been cleared by U.S. Customs officials. *See* in bond.

in-bond system

(U.S. Customs) A part of U.S. Customs' Automated Commercial System, controls merchandise from the point of unloading at the port of entry or exportation. The system works with the input of departures (from the port of unlading), arrivals, and closures (accountability of arrivals). *See* Automated Commercial System; in bond.

incentive

(economics) A motivational force that stimulates people to greater activity or increased efficiency.

Inchmaree Clause

(insurance) An insurance policy extension to cover loss resulting from a latent defect of the carrying vessel's hull or machinery which is not discoverable by due diligence. (So-called for a celebrated legal decision involving a vessel of that name.) Latent defect is not, by law, recoverable from the vessel owner, and the Inchmaree Clause thus plugs a gap that would otherwise exist in complete insurance protection. Loss resulting from errors of navigation or management of the vessel by the master or the crew, and for which the vessel owner is likewise relieved of liability by law, is also covered by the Inchmaree Clause. *See* special marine policy.

income

(economics) Money or its equivalent, earned or accrued, arising from the sale of goods or services.

Incorporated (Inc.)

(South Africa) Designation for a private limited liability corporation with limited liability to shareholders but with joint and several liability to the directors.

(United States) Designation for a corporation with limited liability to shareholders.

Incoterms

A codification of international rules for the uniform interpretation of common contract clauses in export/import transactions involving goods. Developed and issued by the International Chamber of Commerce (ICC) in Paris. The version which is currently valid is from 2000. The thirteen Incoterms 2000 are:

(1) Ex Works (EXW),
(2) Free Carrier (FCA),
(3) Free Alongside Ship (FAS),
(4) Free On Board FOB),
(5) Cost and Freight CFR),
(6) Cost, Insurance and Freight (CIF),
(7) Carriage Paid To (CPT),
(8) Carriage and Insurance Paid To (CIP),
(9) Delivered At Frontier (DAF),
(10) Delivered Ex Ship (DES),
(11) Delivered Ex Quay (DEQ),
(12) Delivered Duty Unpaid (DDU), and
(13) Delivered Duty Paid (DDP).

Refer to individual listings for definitions of these terms. Also refer to the Appendix Guide to Incoterms 2000. For a book fully describing responsibilities of the seller and the buyer in each term, contact: International Chamber of Commerce (ICC), 38, Cours Albert 1er, 75008 Paris, France; Tel: [33] (1) 49-53-28-28; Fax: [33] (1) 49-53-29-42; http:www.iccwbo.org; In U.S. contact: ICC Publishing, Inc., 156 Fifth Avenue, New York, NY 10010 USA; Tel: [1] (212) 206-1150; Fax: [1] (212) 633-6025.

indemnify

(insurance/law) To compensate for actual loss sustained. Many insurance policies and all bonds promise to "indemnify" the insureds. Under such a contract, there can be no recovery until the insured has actually suffered a loss, at which time he or she is entitled to be compensated for the damage that has occurred (i.e. to be restored to the same financial position enjoyed before the loss).

indemnity

(insurance/law) An agreement to reimburse another individual or legal entity who incurs a loss that is covered by the agreement. An indemnity against loss may be partial or whole. A buyer may obtain indemnity insurance, for example, to insure against damage to or destruction of goods that may occur after title has passed to the buyer.

(finance) A bond protecting the insured against losses from others failing to fulfill their obligations.

(investments) An option to buy or sell a specific quantity of a stock at a state price within a given time period.

(law) An act of legislation, granting exemption from prosecution to certain people.

independent action

(shipping) The right of a conference member to depart from the common freight rates, terms or conditions of the conference without the need for prior approval of the conference. *See* conference.

indexed currency borrowings

(banking/finance) Borrowings in a foreign currency where the rate of interest is linked to an agreed scale.

indexed currency option note

(banking/finance) Note denominated and paying interest in one currency but whose redemption value is linked to an exchange rate for another currency. Also called Heaven and Hell Bond.

individual validated license

(U.S.) Written approval by the U.S. Department of Commerce granting permission, which is valid for 2 years, for the export of a specified quantity of products or technical data to a single recipient. Individual validated licenses also are required, under certain circumstances, as authorization for re export of U.S.-origin commodities to new destinations abroad. *See* United States Department of Commerce.

indorsement

See endorsement.

industrial list

The Coordinating Committee for Multilateral Export Controls (CoCom) industrial list contains dual-use items whose export are controlled for strategic reasons. *See* Coordinating Committee for Multilateral Export Controls.

industrial policy

(economics) Encompasses traditional government policies intended to provide a favorable economic climate for the development of industry in general or specific industrial sectors. Instruments of industrial policy may include tax incentives to promote investments or exports, direct or indirect subsidies, special financing arrangements, protection against foreign competition, worker training programs, regional development programs, assistance for research and development, and measures to help small business firms. Historically, the term industrial policy has been associated with some degree of centralized economic planning or indicative planning, but this connotation is not always intended by its contemporary advocates.

Industry Consultations Program

(U.S.) An advisory committee structure created by the Trade Act of 1974, expanded by the Trade Agreements Act of 1979, and amended by the Omnibus Trade and Competitiveness Act of 1988. Jointly sponsored by the U.S. Department of Commerce and the U.S. Trade Representative, the program includes over 500 industry executives who provide advice and information to the U.S. government on trade policy matters. The advisors focus on objectives and bargaining positions for multilateral trade negotiations, bilateral trade negotiations, and other trade-related matters. Members of the committees are appointed by the Secretary of Commerce and the U.S. Trade Representative.

The present structure consists of 17 Industry Sector Advisory Committees (ISACs), 3 Industry Functional Advisory Committees (IFACs), a Committee of Chairs, and an Industry Policy Advisory Committee (IPAC). The focus of the 3 Functional Advisory Committees are: (1) Customs Matters, (2) Standards, and (3) Intellectual Property Rights.

The focus of the 17 Industry Sector Advisory Committees are: (1) Aerospace Equipment, (2) Capital Goods, (3) Chemicals and Allied Products, (4) Consumer Goods, (5) Electronics and Instrumentation, (6) Energy, (7) Ferrous Ores and Metals, (8) Footwear, Leather, and Leather Products, (9) Building Products and Other Materials, (10) Lumber and Wood Products, (11) Nonferrous Ores and Metals, (12) Paper and Paper Products, (13) Services, (14) Small and Minority Business, (15) Textiles and Apparel, (16) Transportation, Construction, and Agricultural Equipment, (17) Wholesaling and Retailing.

See Advisory Committee on Trade Policy and Negotiations.

Industry Functional Advisory Committee

See Industry Consultations Program.

Industry Policy Advisory Committee

See Industry Consultations Program.

Industry Sector Advisory Committee

See Industry Consultations Program.

Industry Subsector Analysis

(U.S.) Overseas market research for a given industry subsector (such as cardiological equipment for the medical equipment industry) that presents basic information about a foreign market such as market size, the competitive environment, primary end users, best prospect products, and market access information. Available as individual reports from the U.S. Department of Commerce, or on the National Trade Data Bank, U.S. Dept. of Commerce, Office of Business Analysis, HCHB Room 4885, Washington, DC 20230 USA; Tel: [1] (202) 482-1986. For individual reports, call your district Department of Commerce office.

infant industry argument

(economics) The view that "temporary protection" for a new industry or firm in a particular country through tariff and non-tariff barriers to imports can help it to become established and eventually competitive in world markets. Historically, new industries that are soundly based and efficiently operated have experienced declining costs as output expands and production experience is acquired. However, industries that have been established and operated with heavy dependence on direct or indirect government subsidies have sometimes found it difficult to relinquish that support. The rationale underlying the Generalized System of Preferences is comparable to that of the infant industry argument. *See* Generalized System of Preferences.

inflammable

See flammable.

inflammable liquids

See flammable liquids.

inflation

(economics) Loss of purchasing power of money, caused by growth of the amount of money in circulation which, if the supply of goods stays the same or only increases at a slower rate, leads to an increase in prices.

in-flight survey (IFS)

(U.S.) A survey of U.S. and foreign travelers departing the U.S. as a means of obtaining data on visitor characteristics, travel patterns and spending habits, and for supplying data on the U.S. international travel dollar accounts as well as to meet balance of payments estimation needs. The IFS covers about 70 percent of U.S. carriers and 35 percent of foreign carriers, who voluntarily choose to participate. Sample results are expanded to universe estimates to account for non response of passengers on each sampled flight, for coverage of all flights on each major airline route, and for all international routes. The basis for the expansion is the number of passengers departing the United States, obtained from the Immigration and Naturalization Service.

informal entry

(U.S. Customs) A simplified import entry procedure accepted at the option of Customs for any noncommercial shipment (baggage) and any commercial shipment not over $1,000 in value. *See* entry.

infrastructure

(economics) The basic structure of a nation's economy, including transportation, communications, and other public services, on which the economic activity relies.

inherent vice

(shipping/insurance) Damage to goods which one can foresee is bound to occur during any normal transit, and which arises solely because of the nature or condition of the goods shipped. Such damage is said to arise from "inherent vice" which may be defined as an internal cause rather than an external cause of damage. An example of damage from inherent vice is deterioration of imperfectly cured skins.

Exclusion of insurance coverage for inherent vice is implied in every cargo policy. This type of exclusion is reinforced by the words "from any external cause" in the "all risks" coverage. The word "risk" itself implies that only fortuitous losses are intended to be covered. Insurance protects against hazards, not certainties.

initial margin

(finance/foreign exchange) The amount of margin which has to be deposited with the clearing house both by the buyer and the seller through the respective broker and/or bank in order to establish a position in a futures contract.

initial negotiating right (INR)

(WTO) A right held by a World Trade Organization (WTO) country to seek compensation for an impairment of a given bound tariff rate by another WTO country. INRs stem from past negotiating concessions and allow the INR holder to seek compensation for an impairment of tariff concessions regardless of its status as a supplier of the product in question. *See* World Trade Organization (WTO).

injury

(U.S.) A finding by the U.S. International Trade Commission that imports are causing, or are likely to cause, harm to a U.S. industry. An injury determination is the basis for a Section 201 case. It is also a requirement in all antidumping and most countervailing duty cases, in conjunction with Commerce Department determinations on dumping and subsidization. *See* dumping; countervailing duty; Section 201.

inland bill of lading

(shipping) A bill of lading used in transporting goods overland to the exporter's international carrier. Although a through bill of lading can sometimes be used, it is usually necessary to prepare both an inland bill of lading and an ocean bill of lading for export shipments. *See* bill of lading.

inland carrier

(shipping) A transportation line which hauls import/export traffic between ports and inland points.

in personam

(law) Against the person. In personam jurisdiction, for example, is a court's authority in a legal action to subject a person to its order or judgment.

in rem

(law) Against the thing. In rem jurisdiction, for example, is a court's authority in a legal action to determine title to, or affect interests in, property of the parties.

insolvency

See bankruptcy.

inspection certificate

A document confirming that goods have been inspected for conformity to a set of industry, customer, government or carrier specifications prior to shipment. Inspection certificates are generally obtained from independent, neutral testing organizations.

instrument

(law) Any written document that gives formal expression to a legal agreement or act. *See also* financial instrument.

insurable interest

(insurance) The financial interest of an individual or business in property, even if that individual is not the owner of the property.

A typical case of insurable interest is where title to goods has passed from the seller to the buyer, but where the seller has yet to receive payment, and still has exposure for loss.

Example 1: When a seller sells on FOB inland point terms, he transfers the title to the buyer before the commencement of the ocean voyage. In this case the obligation to place marine and war risk insurance rests, strictly speaking, with the buyer. However, it is customary in many trades for the seller on FOB terms (or similar terms), to obtain insurance, as well as ocean freight space, for account of the buyer.

This is, in effect, an agency relationship. It can be provided for by a policy clause reading: "to cover all shipments made by or to the assured for their own account as principals, or as agents for others and in which they have an insurable interest, or for the account of others from which written instructions to insure them have been received prior to any known or reported loss, damage or accident prior to sailing of vessel."

Example 2: The seller on FOB or other terms, under which the title passes to the buyer at some inland point of departure, will have a financial interest in the goods until payment has been received. This situation arises when the terms of payment call for sight draft against documents, or for acceptance at 30-60-90 days sight, or for open account. Under such circumstances, the seller will be well advised to place his own insurance to protect himself in the event that the loss or damage to the shipment impairs the buyer's desire to make payment as originally contemplated. For example, the buyer may be uninsured, or the buyer's coverage may be inadequate because of under-insurance or restricted conditions. The buyer's insurance company may be less liberal in loss adjustments than would the insurer of the seller or, because of currency restrictions, a foreign company may be hampered in its ability to transmit funds. *See* contingency insurance.

insurance

(general) A method whereby those concerned about some form of hazard contribute to a common fund usually an insurance company, out of which losses sustained by the contributors are paid.

(law) A contractual relationship that exists when one party (the insurer), for a consideration (the premium), agrees to reimburse another party (the insured) for loss to a specified subject (the risk) caused by designated contingencies (hazards or perils), or to pay in behalf of the insured all reasonable sums for which he may be liable to a third party (the claimant).

insurance broker

(insurance) An individual or firm who represents buyers of insurance and deals with insurance companies or their agents in arranging for insurance coverage for the buyer.

An insurance agent represents a single insurance company whereas an insurance broker is free to obtain insurance coverage from any insurance company.

insurance certificate

(insurance) A document indicating the type and amount of insurance coverage in force on a particular shipment. Used to assure the consignee that insurance is provided to cover loss of or damage to the cargo while in transit.

In some cases a shipper may issue a document that certifies that a shipment has been insured under a given open policy, and that the certificate represents and takes the place of such open policy, the provisions of which are controlling.

Because of the objections that an instrument of this kind did not constitute a "policy" within the requirements of letters of credit, it has become the practice to use a special marine policy. A special marine policy makes no reference to an open policy and stands on its own feet as an obligation of the underwriting company.

See special marine policy; declaration; bordereau; open policy.

insurance company

(insurance) An organization chartered under state or provincial laws to act as an insurer. In the United States, insurance companies are usually classified as fire and marine, life, casualty, and surety companies and may write only the kinds of insurance for which they are specifically authorized by their charters.

insurance coverage

(insurance) The total amount of insurance that is carried.

insurance document

See insurance certificate.

insurance policy

(insurance) Broadly, the entire written contract of insurance. More specifically, it is the basic written or printed document, as well as the coverage forms and endorsement added to it.

insurance premium

(insurance) The amount paid to an insurance company for coverage under an insurance policy.

insured

(insurance) The person(s) protected under an insurance contract (policy).

insured value

(insurance) The combined value of merchandise, inland freight, ocean freight, cost of packaging, freight forwarding charges, consular fees, and insurance cost, for which insurance is obtained.

insurer

(insurance) The party to the insurance contract who promises to indemnify losses or provide service; the insurance company.

integrated cargo service

(shipping) A blend of all segments of the cargo system providing the combined services of carrier, forwarder, handlers and agents.

integrated carriers

(shipping) Carriers that have both air and ground fleets; or other combinations, such as sea, rail, and truck. Since they usually handle large volumes, they are often less expensive and offer more diverse services than regular carriers.

intellectual property

(law) An original work that can be copyrighted, patented, or registered as a trademark or service mark. Ownership conferring the right to possess, use, or dispose of products created by human ingenuity, including patents, trademarks and copyrights. *See* copyright; patent; service mark; trademark.

intellectual property rights

(law) The ownership of the right to possess or otherwise use or dispose of products created by human ingenuity. See copyright; patent; service mark; trademark.

intended

(shipping) A reference which may appear on marine/ocean bills of lading, non-negotiable sea waybills and multimodal transport documents where the carrier reserves the right to change the port of loading, the ship or the port of discharge. Examples: "intended port of shipment Hamburg," "intended ocean vessel MV Swissahoi," "intended port of discharge Hong Kong."

inter absentee
(law) Among absent parties. An inter absentee contract, for example, is made between parties who do not meet face-to-face.

Interagency Group on Countertrade
(U.S.) Established in December 1988 under Executive Order 12661, reviews policy and negotiates agreements with other countries on countertrade and offsets. The IGC operates at the Assistant Secretary level, with the Department of Commerce as chair. Membership includes 11 other agencies: the Departments of Agriculture, Defense, Energy, Justice, Labor, State, Treasury, the Agency for International Development, the Federal Emergency Management Agency, the U.S. Trade Representative, and the Office of Management and Budget. Contact: Assistant Secretary of Trade Development, Office for Counter Trade, U.S. Department of Commerce, 14th Street and Constitution Ave. NW, Washington, DC 20230 USA; Tel: [1] (202) 482-1461. *See* countertrade; offsets.

Inter-American Development Bank
A regional financial institution established in 1959 to advance the economic and social development of 27 Latin American member countries. Address: Inter-American Development Bank, 1300 New York Avenue NW, Washington, DC 20577; Tel: [1] (202) 623-1000; http://www.iadb.org.

interbank dealings
(banking) Dealings between the banks.

interbank offered rate (IBOR)
(banking/finance) Rate of interest offered by banks for their loans to the most creditworthy banks for a large loan, for a specific period and in a specific currency. The best known one is the London Interbank Offered Rate (LIBOR), but they also exist for Abu Dhabi (ADIBOR), Amsterdam (AIBOR), Bahrein (BIBOR), Brussels (BRIBOR), Hong Kong (HIBOR) or (HKIBOR), Kuwait (KIBOR), Luxembourg (LUXIBOR), Madrid (MIBOR), Paris (PIBOR) (occasionally known as taux interbancaire offert à Paris - TIOP), Saudi Arabia (SAIBOR), Singapore (SIBOR), 6 month SDRs (SDRIBOR), Zurich (ZIBOR) and other financial centers.

interchange agreement
(shipping) An agreement which fixes specific accountability for use and maintenance of carrier-owned equipment. It formalizes terms and conditions under which equipment will be leased, in order to protect the carrier's financial and legal interest in the operation of the leased equipment.

interchange point
(shipping) A location where one carrier delivers freight to another carrier.

Interessantelskab (I/S)
(Denmark, Norway) Designation for a general partnership, in which all partners have joint and several liability.

interest arbitrage
(banking) The attempt to make a profit out of differing interest rates for various maturities and/or various instruments. *See* arbitrage.

interline shipping
(shipping) The movement of a single shipment of freight via two or more carriers. *See* intermodal; coordinated movement; intermodal compatibility.

interlocutory
(law) Temporary or interim. An interlocutory injunction, for example, may be granted pending trial as a temporary restraint against a party before final judgment is rendered.

intermediate consignee
A bank, forwarding agent, or other intermediary (if any) which acts in a foreign country as an agent for the exporter, the purchaser, or the ultimate consignee, for the purpose of effecting delivery of the export to the ultimate consignee.

intermodal transport
(shipping) The coordinated transport of freight, especially in connection with relatively long-haul movements using any combination of freight forwarders, piggyback, containerization, air-freight, ocean freight, assemblers, motor carriers.

intermodal compatibility
(shipping) The capability which enables a shipment to be transferred from one form of transport to another, as from airplane to highway truck, to railway freight car, to ocean vessel.

International Air Transport Association (IATA)
A trade association serving airlines, passengers, shippers, travel agents, and governments. Address: International Air Transport Association, 800 Place Victoria, P.O. Box 113, Montreal, Quebec   H4Z 1M1 Canada; Tel: [1] (514) 874-0202; Fax: [1] (514) 874-9632; http://www.iata.org.

International Anticounterfeiting Coalition

A non-profit organization located in Washington, DC that seeks to advance intellectual property rights protection on a worldwide basis by promoting laws, regulations, and directives designed to render theft of intellectual property rights unattractive and unprofitable. Address: International Anticounterfeiting Coalition, 1001 Pennsylvaia Ave. NW, 6th Floor, Washington, DC 20004 USA; Tel: [1] (202) 223-5728; Fax: [1] (202) 872-5848; http://www.iacc.org.

International Atomic Energy Agency (IAEA)

The primary international organization that enforces a system of safeguards to ensure that non-nuclear weapons states do not divert shipments of sensitive equipment from peaceful applications to the production of nuclear weapons. Before a supplier state of nuclear materials or equipment may approve an export to a non-nuclear weapons NPT (Nuclear Non-Proliferation Treaty) signatory state, it must receive assurances that the recipient will place the material under IAEA safeguards. Subsequent to shipment, the recipient state must allow IAEA officials to verify the legitimate end use of the exported materials or equipment.

IAEA, established in July 1957, gives advice and technical assistance to developing countries on nuclear power development, nuclear safety, radioactive waste management, and related efforts. Safeguards are the technical means applied by the IAEA to verify that nuclear equipment or materials are used exclusively for peaceful purposes. Address: International Atomic Energy Agency, Vienna International Centre, Wagramerstrasse 5, Postfach 100, A-1400 Vienna, Austria; Tel: [43] (1) 23-600; Telex: 112645 ATOMA; Fax: [43] (1) 23-4564; http://www.iaea.org.

International Atomic Energy List

One of three lists maintained by the Coordinating Committee on Multilateral Export Controls (Co-Com). The IAEL, comprised strictly of nuclear-related items that are also of commercial value, consists of: materials, facilities, nuclear-related equipment, and software. *See* Coordinating Committee on Multilateral Export Controls.

International Bank for Reconstruction and Development (The World Bank)

(banking) The International Bank for Reconstruction and Finance (IBRF) was proposed at Bretton Woods on July 1944, commencing operation in June 1946. Originally established to help countries reconstruct their economies after World War II. IBRD, commonly referred to as the World Bank, now assists developing member countries by lending to government agencies, or by guaranteeing private loans for such projects as agricultural modernization or infrastructural development. Address: International Bank for Reconstruction and Development, 1818 H Street NW, Washington, DC 20433 USA; Tel: [1] (202) 477-1234. *See also* International Monetary Fund; World Bank; World Bank Group; http://www.worldbank.org.

international banking facility (IBF)

(U.S.) One of four categories of foreign banking in the United States. An IBF is a set of asset and liability accounts that is segregated and limited to financing international trade.

International Buyer Program

(U.S.) (Formerly Foreign Buyer Program) A joint industry-U.S. International Trade Administration program to assist exporters in meeting qualified foreign purchasers for their product or service at trade shows held in the United States. ITA selects leading U.S. trade shows in industries with high export potential. Each show selected for the FBP receives promotion through overseas mailings, U.S. embassy and regional commercial newsletters, and other promotional techniques. ITA trade specialists counsel participating U.S. exhibitors. Contact: International Buyer Program, International Trade Administration, Department of Commerce, Washington, DC 20230 USA; Tel: [1] (202) 482-0481; http://www.ita.doc.gov/uscs/uscsibp.html.

International Center for Settlement of Investment Disputes (ICSID)

(banking) A separate organization of the World Bank which encourages greater flows of investment capital by providing facilities for the conciliation and arbitration of disputes between governments and foreign investors. The ICSID also conducts and publishes research in foreign-investment law. Address: International Centre for Settlement of Investment Disputes, 1818 H Street NW, Washington, DC 20433 USA; Tel: [1] (202) 477-1234; Fax: [1] (202) 477-1269.

International Chamber of Commerce (ICC)

A non-governmental organization serving as a policy advocate for world business. Members in 110 countries comprise tens of thousands of companies and business organizations. The ICC aims to facilitate world trade, investment, and an international free market economy through consultation with other inter-governmental organizations.

The ICC was founded in Atlantic City in 1919. It now encompasses associations and companies from all branches of industry. As an institution of international economic self-administration, it operates through expert commissions, sub-committees and working groups to address questions which are of importance for the international business community. These include, for example, contract and delivery clauses (Incoterms); standardization of means of payment, (Uniform Rules for Collection, Uniform Customs and Practice for Documentary Credits, Uniform Rules for Demand Guarantees); arbitral jurisdiction (Rules of Conciliation and Arbitration); questions relating to such issues as competition, foreign investments, and transportation.

The ICC also offers various services to the business community such as the ATA Carnet system. The ICC publishes many books and references which are valuable to the international trade community. Address: International Chamber of Commerce, 38 Cours Albert 1er, 75008 Paris, France; Tel: (1) 49-53-28-28; Fax: (1) 49-53-29-42; http://www.uscib.org; For U.S. representative, contact: U.S. Council for International Business, 1212 Avenue of the Americas, New York, NY 10036; Tel: (212) 354-4480, or, for ICC publications in the U.S. contact ICC Publishing, Inc., 156 Fifth Avenue, New York, NY 10010 USA; Tel: [1] (212) 206-1150; Fax: [1] (212) 633-6025. Refer to the Appendix for a list of ICC publications.

International Cocoa Agreement

See international commodity agreement.

International Coffee Agreement

See international commodity agreement.

international commodity agreement

An international understanding, usually reflected in a legal instrument, relating to trade in a particular basic commodity, and based on terms negotiated and accepted by most of the countries that export and import commercially significant quantities of the commodity. Some commodity agreements (such as exists for coffee, cocoa, natural rubber, sugar, and tin) center on economic provisions intended to defend a price range for the commodity through the use of buffer stocks or export quotas or both. Other commodity agreements (such as existing agreements for jute and jute products, olive oil, and wheat) promote cooperation among producers and consumers through improved consultation, ex-

change of information, research and development, and export promotion.

International Communications Satellite Organization (Intelsat)

The organization formed under a multilateral agreement which owns, maintains, and operates the global satellite system used by over 100 participating countries. COMSAT is the United States' representative to and participant in Intelsat. Address: International Communications Satellite Organization (Intelsat), 3400 International Drive NW, Washington, DC 20008-3098 USA; Tel: [1] (202) 944-6800; Fax: [1] (202) 944-7898; http://www.intelsat.int.

International Congress Office (ICO)

A U.S. Travel and Tourism Administration office that persuades international associations to select the U.S. as venues for their meetings. The ICO operates out of the American Embassy in Paris. Address: International Congress Office, Embassy of the United States, 2 Avenue Gabriel, 75382 Paris Cedex 08, Paris, France; Tel: [33] (1) 42-96-12-02.

International Dairy Agreement

See international commodity agreement.

International Development Association (IDA)

An affiliate of the World Bank Group that was created in 1959 to lend money to developing countries at no interest and for a long repayment period. By providing development assistance through soft loans, IDA meets the needs of many developing countries that cannot afford development loans at ordinary rates of interest and in the time span of conventional loans. Address: International Development Association, World Bank, 1818 H Street NW, Room E1227, Washington, DC 20433 USA; Tel: [1] (202) 712-4310; Fax:[1] (202) 477-6391.

International Development Cooperation Agency (IDCA)

The U.S. coordinating body of all aspects of U.S. economic assistance and cooperation with lesser developed countries. The IDCA consists of three parts: Agency for International Development (AID), Trade and Development Program (TDP) and the Overseas Private Investment Corporation (OPIC). The Administrator of AID currently serves as the Acting Director of IDCA. Address: International Development Cooperation Agency, 320 21st St. NW, Washington, DC 20523-0001 USA; Tel: [1] (202) 647-1850.

International Electrotechnical Commission (IEC)

The IEC was established in 1906 to deal with questions related to international standardization in the electrical and electronic engineering fields. The members of the IEC are the national committees, one for each country, which are required to be as representative as possible of all electrical interests in the country concerned: manufacturers, users, governmental authorities, teaching, and professional bodies. They are composed of representatives of the various organizations which deal with questions of electrical standardization at the national level. Most of them are recognized and supported by their governments. Address: International Electrotechnical Commission, 3 rue de Varembé, PO Box 131, 1211 Geneva 20, Switzerland; Tel: [41] (22) 34-01-50; http://www.iec.ch.

International Emergency Economic Powers Act (IEEPA)

(U.S. law) The IEEPA was enacted in 1977 to extend emergency powers previously granted to the President by the Trading with the Enemy Act of 1917 (which still authorized the President to exercise extraordinary powers when the United States is at war). IEEPA enables the President, after declaring that a national emergency exists because of a threat from a source outside the United States, to investigate, regulate, compel or prohibit virtually any economic transaction involving property in which a foreign country or national has an interest.

International Energy Agency (IEA)

The IEA was founded in 1974 as a forum for energy cooperation among 21 member nations. The IEA helps participating countries prepare to reduce the economic risks of oil supply disruptions and to reduce dependence on oil through coordinated and cooperative research efforts. Headquarters address: International Energy Agency, 9 rue de la Federation, 75739 Paris Cedex 15, France; Tel: [33] (1) 40 57 65 51. U.S. office: International Energy Agency, 2001 L St. NW, Suite 700, Washington, DC 20036 USA; Tel: [1] (202) 785-6323; http://www.iea.org.

International Finance Corporation (IFC)

The IFC was established in 1956 as a member of the World Bank Group. The IFC promotes capital flow into private investment in developing countries. *See* World Bank Group.

International Frequency Registration Board (IFRB)

An organizational entity under the International Telecommunication Union (ITU). Located in Geneva, IFRB is composed of five full-time elected officials with a rotating chairmanship. IFRB maintains the International Frequency Register, monitors and analyzes all ITU records of frequency use around the world, and makes determinations as to whether or not certain systems are in compliance with the Radio Regulations. *See* International Telecommunications Union.

international investment

See foreign direct investment in the U.S.

International Jute Agreement

See international commodity agreement.

International Labor Organization (ILO)

The ILO, set up in 1919, became a specialized agency of the United Nations in 1946. The ILO seeks to promote improved working and living conditions by establishing standards that reduce social injustice. Address: International Labor Organization, 4, rue des Morillons, CH-1211, Geneva 22, Switzerland; Tel: [41] (22) 799-6111; Telex: 415647 ILO CH; Fax: [41] (22) 798-8685; http://www.ilo.org.

International Maritime Organization (IMO)

The International Maritime Organization, IMO, was established as a specialized agency of the United Nations in 1948. The IMO facilitates cooperation on technical matters affecting merchant shipping and traffic. It publishes "Guidelines for Packing and Securing Cargoes in Containers for Transport by Land or Sea" (Container Packing Guidelines). Address: International Maritime Organization, 4 Albert Embankment, London SE1 7SR, England; Tel: [44] (71) 735-7611; Telex: 23588; Fax: [44] (71) 587-3210: http://www.imo.org.

International Maritime Satellite Organization (IMSO or INMARSAT)

An international partnership of signatories from 62 nations. The partnership provides mobile satellite capacity to its signatories, who, in turn, use the capacity to provide worldwide mobile satellite services to their maritime, aeronautical and landmobile customers—including shipping, cruise, fishing, research and offshore exploration industries, and airlines. INMARSAT began service in 1976. COMSAT is the U.S. signatory to INMARSAT. Address: International Maritime Satellite Organization, 90 City Road, London EC1Y 1AX,

UK; Tel: [44] (171) 728 1777 1; Telex: 297201 INMSATG; Fax: [44] (171) 728-1746; http://www.imso.org.

International Market Insights (IMI)

(U.S.) Reports prepared by staff at American embassies and consulates covering developments in a single country that are of interest to traders and investors. Topics may include: new laws, policies and procedures, new trade regulations, and marketplace changes. Available from the National Trade Data Bank CD-ROM, online via the Economic Bulletin Board, or as individual reports from the Department of Commerce. For address information, *see* National Trade Data Bank; Economic Bulletin Board; United States Department of Commerce.

international market research

See Industry Subsector Analysis.

International Monetary Fund (IMF)

(banking/finance/foreign exchange) An international financial institution proposed at the 1944 Bretton Woods Conference and established in 1946 that seeks to stabilize the international monetary system as a sound basis for the orderly expansion of international trade. Specifically, among other things, the Fund monitors exchange rate policies of member countries, lends them foreign exchange resources to support their adjustment policies when they experience balance of payments difficulties, and provides them financial assistance through a special "compensatory financing facility" when they experience temporary shortfalls in commodity export earnings. Membership in the fund is a prerequisite to membership in the International Bank for Reconstruction and Development.

Address: International Monetary Fund, 700 19th Street NW, Washington, DC 20431 USA; Tel: [1] (202) 623-7430; Fax: [1] (202) 623-4661; http://www.imf.org.

See Bretton-Woods Agreement; International Bank for Reconstruction and Development; World Bank Group.

International Munitions List (IML)

The IML is one of three lists controlled by the 17-member Coordinating Committee on Multilateral Export Controls (CoCom). The IML contains 23 categories and is similar in coverage, but less restrictive, than the U.S. Munitions List (USML). *See* Coordinating Committee on Multilateral Export Controls, United States Munitions List.

International Olive Oil Agreement

See international commodity agreement.

International Organization for Standardization.

See International Standards Organization.

International POW WOW

(U.S.) An annual trade fair, coordinated by the Travel Industry Association of America (TIA) to promote foreign tourism to the United States, which brings together over 1,200 international buyers (tour operators and wholesalers) from 55 countries. The buyers are chosen through international selection criteria and purchase packages which they sell to their respective travel retailers.

Each non-U.S. country has a chairman and the chairman has a selection committee. Each country has a quota of buyers they can send to either the U.S. or the European POW WOW. If a buyer wants to go and hasn't already been selected, they can try contacting the selection committee via the chairman. One way to find out who this is, would be to contact the Travel Industry Association of America (see address below.) U.S. sellers do not need to go through such a process. However, to have a booth at the European POW WOW they must be TIA members. They do not have to be TIA members to participate in the U.S. POW WOW. Organizer: Travel Industry Association of America, 1100 New York Ave. NW, Suite 450, Washington, DC 20005-3934 USA; Tel: [1] (202) 408-8422; Fax: [1] (202) 408-1255. The TIA coordinates the POW WOW with the U.S. Travel and Tourism Administration of the U.S. Department of Commerce, Tel: [1] (202) 482-0137; http://www.tia.org.

International Rubber Agreement (IRA)

An international agreement among natural rubber exporting and importing nations whose purpose is to stabilize the price of rubber through import quotas, thereby protecting rubber exporting countries in the developing world from the effects of extreme price fluctuations. *See* international commodity agreement.

International Standards Organization (ISO)

The ISO, established in 1947, is a worldwide federation of national bodies, representing approximately 90 member countries. The scope of the International Standards Organization covers standardization in all fields except electrical and electronic engineering standards, which are the responsibility of the International Electrotechnical Commission (IEC). Together, the ISO and IEC form the specialized system for worldwide standardization—the world's largest non-governmental system for voluntary industrial and technical collaboration at the international level.

The result of ISO technical work is published in the form of International Standards. There are, for example, ISO standards for the quality grading of steel; for testing the strength of woven textiles; for storage of citrus fruits; for magnetic codes on credit cards; for automobile safety belts; and for ensuring the quality and performance of such diverse products as surgical implants, ski bindings, wire ropes, and photographic lenses.

ISO 9000 is a new series of voluntary international quality standards. Its formal name is ISO 9000 Series of Standards. Adoption of ISO standards has become a virtual prerequisite for doing business internationally. Address: International Standards Organization, 1 rue de Varembé, PO Box 56, CH-1211 Geneva 20, Switzerland; Tel: [41] (22) 749-0111; Fax: [41] (22) 733-3430. In the United States contact: International Organization for Standards, The American National Standards Institute, 11 West 42nd St., New York, NY 10036 USA; Tel: [1] (212) 642-4900; http://www.iso.ch.

International Sugar Agreement

See international commodity agreement.

International Telecommunications Satellite Organization (INTELSAT)

Created in 1964 under a multilateral agreement, INTELSAT is a nonprofit cooperative of (presently) 116 countries that jointly own and operate a global communications satellite system serving the world. The system is used primarily for international communications, and by many countries for domestic communications. In 1991, the INTELSAT system comprised a network of 16 satellites in geosynchronous orbit over the Atlantic, Indian, and Pacific Ocean regions, with service to about 1,500 international and domestic earth station antennas.

International Telecommunications Union

A specialized agency of the United Nations with responsibilities for developing operational procedures and technical standards for the use of the radio frequency spectrum, the satellite orbit, and for the international public telephone and telegraph network. There are over 160 member nations of the ITU. The Radio Regulations that result from ITU conferences have treaty status and provide the principal guidelines for world telecommunications. In the case

of the U.S., they are the framework for development of the U.S. national frequency allocations and regulations. The ITU has four permanent organs: the General Secretariat, the International Frequency Registration Board (IFRB), the International Radio Consultative Committee (CCIR), and the International Telegraph and Telephone and Consultative Committee (ITCC). Address: International Telecommunications Union, Place des Nations, CH-1211 Geneva 20, Switzerland; Tel: [41] (22) 730-5111; Fax: [41] (22) 733-7256; http://www.itu.int.

International Tin Agreement

See international commodity agreement.

International Trade Administration (ITA)

(U.S.) The trade unit of the U.S. Department of Commerce, ITA was established in 1980 to carry out the U.S. government's nonagricultural foreign trade activities and support the policy negotiations of the U.S. Trade Representative. It encourages and promotes U.S. exports of manufactured goods, administers U.S. statutes and agreements dealing with foreign trade, and advises on U.S. international trade and commercial policy. An important arm of the ITA is the United States and Foreign Commercial Service. Address: International Trade Administration, 14th Street and Constitution Avenue NW, Washington, DC 20230 USA; Tel: [1] (202) 482-2867. *See also* United States Department of Commerce; United States and Foreign Commercial Service; United States Trade Representative.

International Trade Commission (ITC)

(U.S.) An independent U.S. government fact-finding agency with six commissioners who review and make recommendations concerning countervailing duty and antidumping petitions submitted by U.S. industries seeking relief from imports that benefit unfair trade practices. Known as the U.S. Tariff Commission before its mandate was broadened by the Trade Act of 1974. Address: U.S. Department of Commerce, International Trade Commission, 500 E. Street SW, Washington, DC 20436 USA; Tel: [1] (202) 205-2000; http://www.usitc.gov. *See* dumping; countervailing duty.

International Traffic in Arms Regulations

(U.S.) Regulations administered in the United States by the U.S. State Department to control the export of weapons and munitions.

International Union for the Protection of Literary and Artistic Works

See Berne Convention; World Intellectual Property Organization.

International Wheat Agreement

See international commodity agreement.

interstate carrier

(shipping-U.S.) A common carrier whose business extends beyond the boundaries of one state. *See* carrier; common carrier.

interstate commerce

(U.S.) Trade between or among several states of the United States. A seller that uses a telephone or facsimile across state lines in its transactions, or transports goods by rail or interstate roads is using interstate commerce.

Interstate Commerce Act of 1887

(U.S. law) Federal legislation regulating the practices, rates, and rules of transportation for carriers engaged in handling interstate shipments or the movement for a fee of people across state lines.

intervention

(banking/foreign exchange) Efforts by central banks and national governments to influence the exchange rates for its currency. Intervention is usually done in one of two ways: (1) The purchase of large amounts of a currency in order to bolster the price, or (2) The sale of large amounts of a currency to lower the price of the currency. Central banks can also raise interest rates in order to attract capital into the country or lower interest rates to discourage the flow of capital into the country.

intervention currency

(banking/foreign exchange) The foreign currency a country uses to ensure by means of official exchange transactions that the permitted exchange rate margins are observed. Intervention usually takes the form of purchases and sales of foreign currency by the central bank or exchange equalization fund in domestic dealings with commercial banks.

in-the-money

(foreign exchange) An option is in-the-money in the following cases: (1) Call option: market price is greater than the strike price; and (2) Put option: market price less than the strike price. For European options, replace the market price by the forward price of the underlying instrument on the expiry date of the option. *See also* call option; put option; strike price; European option; out-of-the-money.

intrinsic value

(banking/finance/foreign exchange) The difference between the strike price of an option and the forward price of the underlying security up to maturity, as long as the option is in-the-money. The premium of an option is made up of the time value and the intrinsic value.

in trust (goods/documents)

(banking) In documentary collections, when a bank releases documents to the importer/buyer to allow him to inspect them prior to payment.

investment climate statements

(U.S.) Reports prepared occasionally by the commercial sections of U.S. embassies for the U.S. and Foreign Commercial Service, covering 67 individual countries. The ICSs provide statistics and analysis of policies and issues effecting the climate for direct investment in the individual country. *See* United States and Foreign Commercial Service.

investment performance requirements

(foreign investment) Special conditions imposed on direct foreign investment by recipient governments, sometimes requiring commitments to export a certain percentage of the output, to purchase given supplies locally, or to ensure the employment of a specified percentage of local labor and management.

invisible balance

See invisible trade balance.

invisible barriers to trade

Government regulations that do not directly restrict trade, but indirectly impede free trade by imposing excessive or obscure requirements on goods sold within a country, especially imported goods. These regulations are often known to business owners within the country, because they may be required to comply with them, but are often not known by foreign businesses seeking to export their products, and therefore such regulations are "invisible." Examples include labelling requirements, sanitary standards, and size or measurement standards.

invisibles; invisible trade

(economics) Non-merchandise items such as freight, insurance, and financial services that are included in a country's balance of payments accounts (in the "current" account), even though they are not recorded as physically visible exports and imports. *See* balance of trade.

invisible trade balance

(economics) As contrasted with the import and export of goods—the trade balance created by the import and export of services, including consulting and advisory services, transportation services, income and expenditure on travel services, insurances, licenses, earnings and interest income from international capital movements. *See* balance of trade.

invoice

A document identifying the seller and buyer of goods or services, identifying numbers such as invoice number, date, shipping date, mode of transport, delivery and payment terms, and a complete listing and description of the goods or services being sold including prices, discounts and quantities. *See* commercial invoice.

inward foreign manifest (IFM)

(U.S. Customs) A U.S. Customs mandated document requiring the complete listing by bill of lading numbers of an arriving ship's freight being imported into the United States.

ipso jure

(law) By operation of law. Contract terms that are implied by a court from the conduct of the parties, for example, are enforceable ipso jure.

irrevocable letter of credit

(banking) A letter of credit which cannot be amended or canceled without prior mutual consent of all parties to the credit. Such a letter of credit guarantees payment by the bank to the seller/exporter so long as all the terms and conditions of the credit have been met.

Documentary letters of credit issued subject to the Uniform Customs and Practice for Documentary Credits (UCPDC) Publication No. 500 are deemed to be irrevocable unless expressly marked as revocable. *See* letter of credit.

irritating material

(shipping) Items capable of causing discomfort such as tearing, choking, vomiting and skin irritation. (UN CLASS 6.) Examples are tear gas and riot control agents. Hazards/precautions are: may cause difficulty in breathing; may burn but do not ignite readily; exposure in enclosed areas may be harmful; may cause tearing of the eyes, choking, nausea or skin irritation.

ISO 9000

A new series of voluntary international quality standards. Its formal name is ISO 9000 Series of Standards. Adoption of ISO standards has become a virtual prerequisite for doing business internationally. *See* International Standards Organization. *See also* American National Standards Institute.

issuance

(banking) The establishment of a letter of credit by the issuing bank (buyer's bank) based on the buyer's application and credit relationship with the bank. *See* letter of credit; advice; amendment.

issuance date of the documents

(shipping) Unless otherwise stipulated in a transport document, the date of issuance is deemed to be the date of shipment or loading on board of the goods.

(banking) Unless prohibited by the documentary letter of credit, documents bearing a date of issuance prior to that of the letter of credit are acceptable.

issuing bank

(banking) The buyer's bank which establishes a letter of credit at the request of the buyer, in favor of the beneficiary (seller/exporter). Also called the buyer's bank or the opening bank. *See also* advising bank; negotiating bank.

J

Japan Corporate Program

(U.S.) The Japan Corporate Program was initiated by the U.S. Department of Commerce to help increase U.S. exports to Japan. The program was initiated in January 1991, following selection of 20 companies to participate in a five-year pilot project to improve U.S. knowledge of, and access to, the Japanese market. As part of the five-year commitment to the program, the companies arrange four visits a year to Japan, including two by their chief executives; publish their product literature in Japanese; participate in at least one trade promotion event in Japan each year; and modify products to enhance consumer acceptance and promote sales in Japan. The U.S. Department of Commerce supports the 20 firms with market data, arranges introductory meetings with prospective Japanese buyers, and recommends market development strategies. Address: Japan Corporate Program, Office of Export Promotion Coordination, Room 2001A, Department of Commerce, 14th and Constitution Ave. NW, Washington, DC 20230 USA; Tel: [1] (202) 482-4792; Fax: [1] (202) 482-1999.

Japan Development Bank (JDB)

(Japan) The Japan Development Bank was founded in 1951 to aid in developing and diversifying the Japanese economy. The JDB is a non-profit organization owned entirely by the Japanese Government. U.S. companies may participate in JDB funding activity under the Bank's Loan Division in the International Department. The International Department disburses loans to foreign companies under two primary loan programs: Promotion of Foreign Direct Investment in Japan and Facilities for Import Products. The other loan programs of JDB are also available to foreign-owned companies under the principle of equal treatment of clients regardless of nationality. Address: Japan Development Bank, 9-1, 1-chome, Otemachi , Chiyoda-ku, Tokyo 100-0004, Japan; Tel: [81] (3) 3244-1770; Fax: [81] (3) 3245-1938; Telex: 24343.

Japan Export Information Center (JEIC)

(U.S.) Provides information on doing business in Japan, market entry alternatives, market information and research, product standards and testing requirements, tariffs and non-tariff barriers. The Center maintains a commercial library and partici-

pates in private- and government-sponsored seminars on doing business in Japan. JEIC is operated by the International Trade Administration of the U.S. Department of Commerce, 14th Street and Constitution Ave. NW, Washington, DC 20230 USA; Tel: [1] (202) 482-2425 and [1] (202) 482-4524; Fax: [1] (202) 482-0469;

Japan External Trade Organization (JETRO)

(Japan) Although legally under the aegis of the Ministry of International Trade and Industry (MITI), JETRO administers the export programs of the Japanese Government independently. The MITI subsidizes about 60 percent of JETRO's total annual expenditures and, technically, has final decision-making authority over JETRO management and programs. Originally established to help Japanese firms export, JETRO also assists American companies seeking to export to Japan and promotes Japanese direct investment in the United States and U.S. direct investment in Japan. JETRO offices in the U.S. have excellent trade libraries open to the public. There are seven branches throughout the U.S. Headquarters are in Tokyo: Japan External Trade Organization, 2-5 Toranomon, 2-chome, Minato-ku, Tokyo 105, Japan; Tel: [81] (3) 3582-5522; New York branch Tel: [1] (212) 997-0400; San Francisco branch Tel: [1] (415) 392-1333; Fax: (415) 788-6927; http://www.jetro.go.jp.

Japan International Cooperation Agency (JICA)

Established in August 1974 to administer the bilateral grant portion of Japan's Official Development Assistance (ODA). JICA covers both: (1) grant aid cooperation (offered without the obligation of repayment) and (2) technical cooperation (offering trainees, experts, equipment, project-type technical cooperation, and development studies). Address: Japan International Cooperation Agency, Shinjuku Mitsui Bldg., 1-1, Nishi Shinjuku 2-chome, Shinjuku-ku, Tokyo 103; Tel: [81] (3) 3346-5311; http://www.jica.go.jp.

jetsam

(shipping) Articles from a ship or ship's cargo which are thrown overboard, usually to lighten the load in times of emergency or distress and that sinks or is washed ashore. *See also* flotsam.

jettison

(shipping) To unload or throw overboard at sea a part of a ship's paraphernalia or cargo to lighten the ship in time of emergency.

joint agent
(shipping) A person having authority to transact business for two or more transportation lines.

joint and several guarantee
See aval.

joint and several liability
(law) Liability for damages imposed on two or more individuals or legal entities who are responsible together and individually, allowing the party harmed to seek full remedy against all or any number of the wrongdoers. The availability of joint and several liability varies among countries, and some jurisdictions have placed limitations on the amount of damages for which a single person can be held liable when multiple parties could be responsible.

Joint Committee for Investment & Trade (JCIT)
(U.S./Mexico) The JCIT, was established in October 1990 to demonstrate U.S. and Mexican commitment to greater economic cooperation. The Committee identifies trade and investment opportunities and coordinates trade promotion events. For marketing and trade information, contact the 24 hour Flash Fax number: [1] (202) 482-4464; For questions not addressed in the flash fax menu, contact: Office of Mexico, Department of Commerce, 14th Street and Constitution Ave. NW, Room 3022, Washington, DC 20230 USA; Tel: [1] (202) 482-0300.

joint rate
(shipping) A single through-rate on cargo moving via two or more carriers.

joint stock company
(law) An unincorporated business association with ownership interests represented by shares of stock. These companies have characteristics of both corporations and partnerships. They are created under authority of law and are treated differently from jurisdiction to jurisdiction. *See* corporation; partnership.

joint venture
(law) (a) A combination of two or more individuals or legal entities who undertake together a transaction for mutual gain or to engage in a commercial enterprise together with mutual sharing of profits and losses. (b) A form of business partnership involving joint management and the sharing of risks and profits as between enterprises based in different countries. If joint ownership of capital is involved, the partnership is known as an equity joint venture.

jurat
(law) A statement signed by a person authorized to take oaths certifying to the authenticity of a document or affidavit. *See* authentication; notary public.

juridical person
See person, as defined by law.

juristic act
(law) Action intended to, and capable of having, a legal effect, such as the creation, termination, or modification of a legal right. Signing a power of attorney, for example, is a juristic act because it gives legal authority to an agent.

juristic person
See person, as defined by law.

just in time
(economics/manufacturing) The principle of production and inventory control that prescribes precise controls for the movement of raw materials, component parts and work-in-progress. Goods arrive when needed (just in time) for production for use rather than becoming expensive inventory that occupies costly warehouse space.

Kabushiki Kaisha (KK)
(Japan) Designation for a joint stock company with limited personal liability to shareholders.

karbovanet
The currency of Ukraine. The abbreviation is Uak. No subcurrency is in use.

keelage
(shipping) The charges paid by a ship entering or remaining in certain ports.

Keidanren
(Japan) Keidanren (the Japanese Federation of Economic Organizations) was established in 1946 as a private, non-profit economic organization representing virtually all branches of economic activity in Japan. Address: Japan Federation of Economic Organizations (Keidanren), 9-4, Otemachi 1-chome, Chiyoda-ku, Tokyo 100, Japan; Tel: [81] (3) 3279-1444; Fax: [81] (3) 5255-6250; http://www.keidanren.or.jp.

keiretsu
(Japan) Keiretsu refers to the horizontally and vertically linked industrial structure of post-war Japan. The horizontally linked groups include a broad range of industries linked via banks and general trading firms. There are eight major industrial groups, sometimes referred to as "Kigyo Shudan": Mitsubishi, Mitsui, Sumitomo, Fuyo, DKB, Sanwa, Tokai, and IBJ. The vertically linked groups (such as Toyota, Matshushita, and Sony) are centered around parent companies, with subsidiaries frequently serving as suppliers, distributors, and retail outlets. Common characteristics among the groups include crossholding of company shares, intra-group financing, joint investment, mutual appointment of officers, and other joint business activities. The keiretsu system emphasizes mutual cooperation and protects affiliates from mergers and acquisitions. Ties within groups became looser after the oil shocks of the 1970s as a result of decreasing dependence on banks for capital.

key currency
(foreign exchange) A major currency in the global economy. Small countries, which are highly dependent on exports, orientate their exchange rate to major currencies in the global economy, the so-called key currencies. Key currencies include the U.S. dollar, the British pound sterling, the German mark, the Swiss franc, the French franc, the Dutch gilder, the Japanese yen and the Canadian dollar.

kilogram
(measure) A unit of mass or weight measure equal to 2.2046 lbs. Abbreviated as k, K, KS, kg, KG, kgs, or KGS.

kilo ton (metric ton)
(measure) A unit of mass or weight measure equal to 2,204.6 pounds.

kina
The currency of Papua New Guinea. 1K=1 toea.

kind or quality
See drawback—refund of duties.

kip
The currency of Laos. 1K=100 at.

kiwi bond
(banking/finance) Bond issued in New Zealand dollars on the New Zealand market by non New Zealand borrowers.

knocked down (K.D.)
An article taken apart and folded or telescoped in such a manner as to reduce its bulk at least 66 2/3 percent from its normal shipping cubage when set up or assembled.

knot
(measure) A unit of measurement of speed of a vessel in water or an airplane in air equal to one nautical mile (6082.66 feet) per hour.

known loss
(shipping/insurance) A loss discovered before or at the time of delivery of a shipment.

Kokusai Denshin Denwa
(Japan) The Kokusai Denshin Denwa Company, KDD, was established in 1953 but traces its history back to 1871 and the establishment of its predecessor organizations. For more than a century, the company was Japan's sole supplier of international telecommunications services and today remains Japan's leading international carrier. KDD is Japan's signatory to INTELSAT and INMARSAT.

Kommanditgesellschaft (KG)
(Austria, Germany, Switzerland) Designation for a limited partnership in which at least one of the partners has general liability and at least one of the other partners has limited liability.

Kommanditselskab (K/S)
(Denmark) Designation for a limited partnership in which at least one of the partners has general liabil-

ity and at least one of the other partners has limited liability.

koruna
The currency of the Czech and the Slovak Republics. 1Kcs=100 halers.

krona
The currency of:
Iceland, 1IKr=100 aurar;
Sweden, 1SKr=100 öre.

krone
The currency of:
Denmark, 1DKr=100 öre;
Norway, 1NKr=100 öre;
Greenland (*see* Denmark).

kroon
The currency of Estonia. 1Eek=100 senti.

kwacha
The currency of:
Malawi, 1MK=100 tambala;
Zambia, 1K=100 ngwee.

kwanza
The currency of Angola. 1Kz=100 lwei.

kyat
The currency of Myanmar (Burma). 1K=100 pyas.

L

laissez-faire
(economics) A term used to describe minimal governmental involvement in an economy, allowing market forces and individuals to make their own decisions, with little or no regulation.

landbridge
(shipping) The movement of containers from a foreign country by vessel, transiting a country by rail or truck, and then being loaded aboard another vessel for delivery to a second foreign country. An example would be a container from Shanghai which arrives in the U.S. at Tacoma, Washington and is carried by rail to New Jersey where it is shipped by ocean to London (water-rail-water operation).

landed price (named location)
See Incoterms.

Lanham Act of 1947
(U.S. law) Federal legislation governing trademarks and other symbols for identifying goods sold in interstate commerce. As amended, it allows a manufacturer to protect his brand or trademark in the United States by having it recorded on a government register in the U.S. Patent Office. Also provides for the legal right to register any distinctive mark.

lash
See lighter aboard ship.

lat
The currency of Latvia. 1LvL=100 sintim.

Latin American Free Trade Association (LAFTA)
See Latin American Integration Association.

Latin American Integration Association (LAIA)
(regional trade alliance) LAIA was created by the 1980 Montevideo Treaty as a replacement to the Latin American Free Trade Association (LAFTA). LAFTA was rejected because members felt its rules governing integration trends were too rigid. LAIA, an association involving Argentina, Bolivia, Brazil, Chile, Colombia, Ecuador, Mexico, Paraguay, Peru, Uruguay, and Venezuela, since has declined as a major Latin American integration effort in favor of regional efforts, such as Mercosur. *See* Mercosur.

lay order
(customs) The period during which imported merchandise may remain at the place of unlading without some action being taken for its disposition, i.e., beyond the 5-day General Order period. *See* general order.

League of Arab States
See Arab League.

least developed countries (LDC's)
(economics) Some 36 of the world's poorest countries. considered by the United Nations to be the least developed of the less developed countries. Most of them are small in terms of area and population, and some are land-locked or small island countries. They are generally characterized by low: per capita incomes, literacy levels, and medical standards; subsistence agriculture; and a lack of exploitable minerals and competitive industries. Many suffer from aridity, floods, hurricanes, and excessive animal and plant pests, and most are situated in the zone 10 to 30 degrees north latitude. These countries have little prospect of rapid economic development in the foreseeable future and are likely to remain heavily dependent upon official development assistance for many years. Most are in Africa, but a few, such as Bangladesh, Afghanistan, Laos, and Nepal, are in Asia. Haiti is the only country in the Western Hemisphere classified by the United Nations as "least developed." *See* developing countries; less developed country.

legal entity
(law) Any individual, proprietorship, partnership, corporation, association, or other organization that has, in the eyes of the law, the capacity to make a contract or an agreement, and the abilities to assume an obligation and to discharge an indebtedness. A legal entity is a responsible being in the eyes of the law and can be sued for damages if the performance of a contract or agreement is not met. *See also* person.

legal person
See person; legal entity.

legal tender
(banking/currency/law) Any money that is recognized as being lawful for use by a debtor to pay a creditor, who must accept same in the discharge of a debt unless the contract between the parties specifically states that another type of money is to be used.

lek
The currency of Albania. 1L=100 qintars.

lempira
The currency of Honduras. 1L=100 centavos.

lender of last resort
(banking) One of the functions and a major raison d'être of a modern central bank; whereby the bank has to provide liquid assets to the banking system when the existing liquid assets of the banking system threaten to deplete.

leone
The currency of Sierra Leone. 1Le=100 cents.

less developed country (LDC)
(economics) A country showing: (1) a poverty level of income, (2) a high rate of population increase, (3) a substantial portion of its workers employed in agriculture, (4) a low proportion of adult literacy, (5) high unemployment, and (6) a significant reliance on a few items for export.
Terms such as third world, poor, developing nations, and underdeveloped have also been used to describe less developed countries.

lesser developed country (LLDC)
(economics) The classification LLDC was developed by the United Nations to give some guidance to donor agencies and countries about an equitable allocation of foreign assistance. The criteria for designating a country an LLDC, originally adopted by the UN Committee for Development Planning in 1971, have been modified several times. Criteria have included low: per capita income, literacy, and manufacturing share of the country's total gross domestic product. There is continuing concern that the criteria should be more robust and less subject to the possibility of easy fluctuation of a country between less developed and least developed status.

less than container load (LCL)
(shipping) A shipment of cargo that does not fill a container and is merged with cargo for more than one consignee or from more than one shipper. A container may be packed with LCL cargo at a container freight station for LCL delivery.

less than truckload (LTL)
(shipping) A shipment weighing less than the weight required for the application of the truckload rate.

letter of assignment
A document with which the assignor assigns rights to a third party. *See* assignment.

letter of credit (L/C)
(banking) Formal term: Documentary credit or documentary letter of credit.

A letter of credit is a document issued by a bank stating its commitment to pay someone (supplier/exporter/seller) a stated amount of money on behalf of a buyer (importer) so long as the seller meets very specific terms and conditions. Letters of credit are more formally called documentary letters of credit because the banks handling the transaction deal in documents as opposed to goods.

The terms and conditions listed in the credit all involve presentation of specific documents within a stated period of time, hence the formal name—documentary credits.

The documents the buyer requires in the credit may vary, but at a minimum include an invoice and a bill of lading. Other documents the buyer may specify are certificate of origin, consular invoice, insurance certificate, inspection certificate and others.

Letters of credit are the most common method of making international payments, because the risks of the transaction are shared by both the buyer and the supplier.

Documentary letters of credit are subject to the Uniform Customs and Practice for Documentary Credits (UCPDC), Brochure No. 500, of the International Chamber of Commerce (ICC) in Paris. *See* Uniform Customs and Practice.

Basic Letters of Credit

There are two basic forms of a letter of credit: the Revocable Credit and the Irrevocable Credit. There are also two types of irrevocable credit: the Irrevocable Credit not Confirmed, and the Irrevocable Confirmed Credit. Each type of credit has advantages and disadvantages for the buyer and for the seller. Also note that the more the banks assume risk by guaranteeing payment, the more they will charge for providing the service.

(a) **Revocable credit**—This credit can be changed or canceled by the buyer without prior notice to the supplier. Because it offers little security to the seller, revocable credits are generally unacceptable and are rarely used.

(b) **Irrevocable credit**—The irrevocable credit is one which the issuing bank commits itself irrevocably to honor, provided the beneficiary complies with all stipulated conditions. This credit cannot be changed or canceled without the consent of both the buyer and the seller. As a result, this type of credit is the most widely used in international trade. Irrevocable credits are more expensive because of the issuing bank's added liability in guaranteeing the credit. There are two types of irrevocable credits:

(1) **The Irrevocable credit not confirmed (Unconfirmed credit).** This means that the buyer's bank which issues the credit is the only party responsible for payment to the supplier, and the supplier's bank is obliged to pay the supplier only after receiving payment from the buyer's bank. The supplier's bank merely acts on behalf of the issuing bank and therefore incurs no risk.

(2) **The Irrevocable, confirmed credit.** In a confirmed credit, the advising bank adds its guarantee to pay the supplier to that of the issuing bank. If the issuing bank fails to make payment, the advising bank will pay. If a supplier is unfamiliar with the buyer's bank which issues the letter of credit, he may insist on an irrevocable confirmed credit. These credits may be used when trade is conducted in a high risk area where there are fears of outbreak of war or social, political, or financial instability. Confirmed credits may also be used by the supplier to enlist the aid of a local bank to extend financing to enable him to fill the order. A confirmed credit costs more because the bank has added liability.

Special Letters of Credit

There are numerous special letters of credit designed to meet specific needs of buyers, suppliers, and intermediaries. Special letters of credit usually involve increased participation by banks, so financing and service charges are higher than those for basic letters of credit. The following is a brief description of some special letters of credit.

(a) **Standby letter of credit**—This credit is primarily a payment or performance guarantee. It is used primarily in the United States because U.S. banks are prevented by law from giving certain guarantees. Standby credits are often called non-performing letters of credit because they are only used as a backup payment method if the collection on a primary payment method is past due.

Standby letters of credit can be used, for example, to guarantee the following types of payment and performance:

- repayment of loans,
- fulfillment by subcontractors,
- securing the payment for goods delivered by third parties.

The beneficiary to a standby letter of credit can draw from it on demand, so the buyer assumes added risk.

(b) **Revolving letter of credit**—This credit is a commitment on the part of the issuing bank to restore the credit to the original amount after it has been used or drawn down. The number of times it can be utilized and the period of validity is stated in the credit. The credit can be cumulative or noncumulative. Cumulative means that unutilized sums can be added to the next installment, whereas noncumulative means that partial amounts not utilized in time expire.

(c) **Deferred payment letter of credit**—In this credit the buyer takes delivery of the shipped goods by accepting the documents and agreeing to pay the bank after a fixed period of time. This credit gives the buyer a grace period for payment.

(d) **Red clause letter of credit**—This is used to provide the supplier with some funds prior to shipment to finance production of the goods. The credit may be advanced in part or in full, and the buyer's bank finances the advance payment. The buyer, in essence, extends financing to the seller and incurs ultimate risk for all advanced credits.

(e) **Transferable Letter of Credit**—This credit allows the supplier to transfer all or part of the proceeds of the letter of credit to a second beneficiary, usually the ultimate supplier of the goods. This is a common financing tactic for middlemen and is used extensively in the Far East.

(f) **Back-to-Back Letter of Credit**—This is a new credit opened on the basis of an already existing, nontransferable credit. It is used by traders to make payment to the ultimate supplier. A trader receives a letter of credit from the buyer and then opens another letter of credit in favor of the supplier. The first letter of credit is used as collateral for the second credit. The second credit makes price adjustments from which come the trader's profit. *See* Guide to Letters of Credit Appendix.

letter of indemnity (LOI)

(shipping) A document which serves to protect the carrier/owner financially against possible repercussions in connection with the release of goods without presentation of an original bill of lading. A letter of indemnity (usually as an indemnity for missing bill of lading) is used in cases in which the goods arrive at the port of destination before the original bills of lading. The issuance of the letter of indemnity allows the purchaser to take immediate delivery of the goods, thus saving himself time, additional demurrage, storage expenses, insurance costs, etc.

letter of intent

(law) A document, such as a written memorandum, that describes the preliminary understanding between parties who intend to make a contract or join together in another action, such as a joint venture or a corporate merger.

leu

The currency of Romania. 1L=100 bani.

lev

The currency of Bulgaria. 1Lv=100 stotinki.

leverage

(finance/foreign exchange) In options terminology, this expresses the disproportionately large change in the premium in terms of the relative price movement of the underlying instrument.

lex loci actus

(law) A legal rule to apply the law of the place where a wrongful act occurred. A court may apply this law in a legal action if the parties have not expressly agreed to the law that will govern their contract and if the laws of more than one jurisdiction could apply. If a buyer and seller, for example, are located in different countries and the buyer breaches the contract, under the rule of lex loci actus the court will apply the law of the buyer's country in interpreting the contract. This rule is usually applied when the wrongful act has a greater effect in the jurisdiction where it occurred than in any other jurisdiction. *See* conflict of laws; nexus; lex loci solutionis.

lex loci solutionis

(law) A legal rule to apply the law of the place where payment is to be made or a contract is to be performed. A country may apply this law in a legal action if the parties have not expressly agreed to the law that will govern their contract and if the laws of more than one jurisdiction could apply. If a buyer and seller, for example, are located in different countries and the buyer breaches the contract, under the law of lex loci solutionis the court will apply the law of the seller's country, which is where payment is to be made. This rule is usually applied when performance of the contract has a greater effect in the jurisdiction where it is to occur than in any other jurisdiction. *See* conflict of laws; nexus; lex loci actus.

liberal

(economics) When referring to trade policy, "liberal" usually means relatively free of import controls or restraints and/or a preference for reducing existing barriers to trade, often contrasted with the protectionist preference for retaining or raising selected barriers to imports.

LIBID

See London Interbank Bid Rate.

LIBOR

See London Interbank Offered Rate.

L

licensing agreement
(law) A contract whereby the holder of a trademark, patent, or copyright transfers a limited right to use a process, sell or manufacture an article, or furnish specialized services covered by the trademark, patent or copyright to another firm.

life-cycle processing
(economics/accounting) An accounting approach in which a company sets product prices based on recovering costs over the life cycle of the product.

(U.S.) In antidumping cases, U.S. authorities dispute the validity of this approach because projections of future yield improvements cannot be verified at the time of dumping calculations. *See* dumping.

lift van
(shipping) A wooden or metal container used for packing household goods and personal effects. A lift van must be at least 100 cubic feet and be suitable for lifting by mechanical device.

lighter
(shipping) An open or covered barge towed by a tugboat and used mainly in harbors and inland waterways for the transport of cargo. Lighters are used in situations where shallow water prevents the ocean going vessel from coming close to shore.

lighter aboard ship (LASH)
(shipping) A floatable large container (lighter) used in the combined ocean and inland waterway transport of goods. Lighters are transported on specially constructed ships.

lighterage
(shipping) (a) The loading or unloading of a ship by means of a lighter. (b) Charges assessed for lighter service.

lilangeni
The currency of Swaziland. 1L=100 cents. The plural of lilangeni is emalangeni (E).

LIMEAN
(banking/finance) The calculated average of the London Interbank Bid Rate (LIBID) and the London Interbank Offered Rate (LIBOR).

See London Interbank Bid Rate; London Interbank Offered Rate.

Limitada (Ltda.)
(Brazil, Portugal) Designation for a private limited liability corporation with limited liability to shareholders. *See* Sociedad por Quota.

limitation period
(law) A maximum period set by statute within which a legal action can be brought or a right enforced. A statute may prohibit, for example, any individual or legal entity from bringing an action for breach of contract more than one year after the breach occurred.

Limited (Ltd.)
(United Kingdom) Designation for a private limited liability corporation with limited liability to shareholders. (South Africa, United States) Designation for a public corporation with limited liability to shareholders.

limited appointment
(diplomacy) Limited appointees to the U.S. & Foreign Commercial Service (or to other foreign services) are persons from the private sector or from the federal government who are non-career officers assigned overseas for a limited time.

limited liability
(law) Restricted liability for the obligations of a business. Liability may be limited, for example, to the amount of a partner's or shareholder's contribution to the capital of partnership or corporation.

limited partnership
(law) A partnership in which at least one partner has general liability and at least one of the other partners has limited liability.

Limitée (Ltée.)
(Canada) Designation for a public corporation with limited liability to shareholders.

line haul
(shipping) The direct movement of freight between two major ports by a single ship.

line haul vessel
(shipping) A vessel which is on a regularly defined schedule.

liner
(shipping) A vessel carrying passengers and cargo that operates on a route with a fixed schedule.

line release system
(U.S. Customs) A part of the U.S. Customs' Automated Commercial System, is designed for the release and tracking of shipments through the use of personal computers and bar code technology. To qualify for line release, a commodity must have a history of invoice accuracy, and be selected by local Customs districts on the basis of high volume. To release the merchandise, Customs reads the bar code into a personal computer, verifies that the bar code matches the invoice data, and enters the quan-

tity. The cargo release is transmitted to the Automated Commercial System, which establishes an entry and the requirement for an entry summary, and provides the Automated Broker Interface system participants with release information. *See* Automated Commercial System.

liner terms
(shipping) Conditions under which a shipping company will transport goods, including the amount payable for carriage of the goods (freight) and the cost both for loading and discharge of the vessel.

liquidated damages
(law) A sum of money that a contracting party agrees to pay to the other party for breaching an agreement, particularly important in a contract in which damages for breach may be difficult to assess. A manufacturer, for example, that agrees to develop, produce, and sell unique products to a buyer may insist on a contract clause for liquidated damages in the event that the buyer rejects the goods without justifiable reason because the market for resale of the unique goods will be so limited that damages will be difficult to assess.

liquidation
(U.S. Customs) The final review of a U.S. Customs entry, and determination of the rate of duty and amount of duty by Customs. Liquidation is accomplished by Customs posting a notice on a public bulletin board at the customshouse. An importer may receive an advance notice on Customs Form 4333A "Courtesy Notice" stating when and in what amount duty will be liquidated. This form is not the liquidation, and protest rights do not accrue until the notice is posted. Time limits for protesting do not start to run until the date of posting, and a protest cannot be filed before liquidation is posted.

The Customs Service may determine that an entry cannot be liquidated as entered for one reason or another. For example, the tariff classification may not be correct or may not be acceptable because it is not consistent with an established and uniform classification practice. If the change required by this determination results in a rate of duty more favorable to an importer, the entry is liquidated accordingly and a refund of the applicable amount of the deposited duties is authorized. On the other hand, a change may be necessary which imposes a higher rate of duty. For example, a claim for an exemption from duty under a duty-free provision or under a conditional exemption may be found to be insufficient for lack of the required supporting documentation. In this situation, the importer will be

given an advance notice of the proposed duty rate advancement and an opportunity to validate the claim for a free rate or more favorable rate of duty. If the importer does not respond to the notice or if the response is found to be without merit, duty is liquidated in accordance with the entry as corrected and the importer is billed for the additional duty. The port or district may find that the importer's response raises issues of such complexity that resolution by a Customs Headquarters decision through the internal advise procedure is warranted. Internal advice from Customs Headquarters may be requested by the local Customs officers on their own initiative or in response to a request by the importer. Public Law 95-410 (Customs Procedural Reform and Simplification Act of 1978) requires that all liquidations be performed within one year from the date of consumption entry or final withdrawal on a warehouse entry. Three one-year extensions are permitted. *See* protest; entry; classification; valuation.

liquidation system
(U.S. Customs) A part of U.S. Customs' Automated Commercial System, closes the file on each entry and establishes a batch filing number which is essential for recovering an entry for review or enforcement purposes. An entry liquidation is a final review of the entry. Public Law 95-410 (Customs Procedural Reform and Simplification Act of 1978) requires that all liquidations be performed within one year from the date of consumption entry or final withdrawal on a warehouse entry. Three one-year extensions are permitted. *See* liquidation; Automated Commercial System.

liquidity
(economics) (a) A company's ability to meet its obligations at all times. (b) The availability of liquid funds in an economy. (c) The possibility of being able to carry out financial transactions without influencing the market.

lira
The currency of:
Italy, 1L=100 centesimi;
Malta, 1£M (or 1 LM)=100 cents;
San Marino (uses Italian lira);
Turkey, 1T£=100 kurus;
Vatican, 1VLit=100 centesimi.

litas
The currency of Lithuania. 1Lit=100 centai.

Lloyds (of London)
(insurance) An association of English insurance underwriters, the oldest of its kind in the world. Not in

itself an insurance company. The Corporation of Lloyds also provides a daily newspaper.

Lloyd's Registry

(shipping) An organization maintained for the surveying and classifying of ships so that insurance underwriters and other interested parties may know the quality and condition of the vessels offered by insurance or employment.

loading

(shipping) The physical placing of cargo into carrier's container, or onto a vessel.

locus

(law) A place. The locus of arbitration, for example, is the place where arbitration proceedings are held.

logistics

The process of planning, implementing and controlling the flow of personnel, materials and information from the point of origin to the point of destination at the required time and in the desired condition.

(shipping) The process of planning and controlling the flow of raw materials, work in progress or finished products from the point of origin to the point of destination (either to a factory for further processing, to a warehouse for storage or to the marketplace for sale) at the required time and in the desired condition.

Lombard rate

(banking/finance-Germany) The interest rate applied to loans backed by collateral in the form of movable, easily-sold assets (goods or securities). Particularly used with reference to the German Bundesbank, which normally maintains its Lombard rate at about 1/2 percent above its discount rate.

Lomé Convention

A 1975 agreement between the European Community (EC) and 62 African, Caribbean, and Pacific (ACP) states (mostly former colonies of the EC members). The agreement covers some aid provisions as well as trade and tariff preferences for the ACP countries when shipping to the EC. The Lome Convention grew out of the 1958 Treaty of Rome's "association" with the 18 African colonies/countries that had ties with Belgium and France.

London Interbank Bid Rate (LIBID)

(banking/finance) The bid in a quotation representing the interest rate at which U.S. dollar deposits are retraded in London. *See* London Interbank Offered Rate; LIMEAN.

London Interbank Offered Rate (LIBOR)

(banking/finance) The interest rate at which banks in London are prepared to lend funds to first-class banks. It is used to determine the interest rate payable on most Eurocredits. *See* London Interbank Bid Rate; LIMEAN.

London Metal Exchange

(banking/finance) A commodity exchange whose members, approximately 110 in number, deal in copper, lead, zinc, and tin. Address: London Metal Exchange, Plantation House, Fenchurch St., London EC3M 3AP, UK; http://www.lme.co.uk.

long of exchange

(banking/foreign exchange) When a trader in foreign currency holds foreign bills in an amount exceeding the bills of his or her own that have been sold and remain outstanding, the trader is long of exchange.

longshoreman

(shipping) A laborer who loads and unloads ships at a seaport. *See also* stevedore; gang.

long ton

(measure) A unit of mass or weight measurement equal to 2,240 pounds. A short ton is 2,000 pounds.

loss of specie

(insurance) A loss when goods arrive so damaged as to cease to be a thing of the kind insured. Examples of "loss of specie" are cement arriving as rock, or textiles as rags. *See also* total loss.

loti

The currency of Lesotho. 1L=100 lisente. Plural of loti is maloti (M).

lot labels

(shipping) Labels attached to each piece of multiple lot shipment for identification purposes.

lower deck containers

(shipping) Carrier owned containers specially designed as an integral part of the aircraft to fit in the cargo compartments (lower deck) of a wide body aircraft.

M

Maastricht

The popular name for the European treaty for economic union. Named for the Dutch city in which it was signed. *See* European Community.

Maatschappij (Mij.)

(Netherlands) Designation for a combination of two or more persons who enter into a joint arrangement to conduct certain business activities.

macroeconomics

(economics) (a) The study of statistics (e.g., total consumption, total employment) of the economy as a whole rather than as single economic units. (b) Synonymous with aggregate economics. *See also* microeconomics.

mail entry

(U.S. Customs) A means of shipping and entering goods into the Customs Territory of the United States. Mail entry has several advantages as well as several limitations.

(1) Duties on parcels valued at US$1,200 or less are collected by the letter carrier delivering the parcel to the addressee.

(2) No formal entry paperwork is required on duty-free merchandise not exceeding US$1,200 in value.

(3) There is no need to clear shipments personally if under US$1,200 in value.

Joint Customs and postal regulations provide that all international parcel post packages must have a Customs declaration securely attached giving an accurate description and the value of the contents. This declaration is obtained at post offices. Commercial shipments must also be accompanied by a commercial invoice enclosed in the parcel bearing the declaration.

Parcels and packages not labeled or endorsed properly and found to contain merchandise subject to duty or taxes are subject to forfeiture.

If the value of a mail importation exceeds US$1,250, the addressee is notified to prepare and file a formal Customs entry (consumption entry) for it at the nearest Customs port.

A mail entry limit of US$250 has been set for a number of articles classified in sub-chapters III and IV, chapter 99, of the Harmonized Tariff Schedule of the U.S. as an exception to the above US$1,250 limit. Items on this list include billfolds, feathers,

flowers, footwear, fur, gloves, handbags, headwear, leather, luggage, millinery, pillows, plastics, skins, rubber, textiles, toys, games, sports equipment and trimmings.

Unaccompanied shipments of made-to-measure suits from Hong Kong require a formal entry regardless of value.

See entry; consumption entry.

mala fide

(law) In bad faith. A seller's representation that goods are usable for a particular purpose when in fact the seller knows that the goods are not is a representation made mala fide.

manifest

(shipping) A document giving the description of a ship's cargo or the contents of a car or truck.

Manufactured Imports Promotion Organization (MIPRO)

(Japan) A non-profit organization, established in 1978 by the joint efforts of the Japanese Government and the private sector to promote imports of foreign manufactured products by hosting exhibitions and providing a wide range of market information. MIPRO's activities are broadly classified into three categories: (1) holding imported product trade exhibitions for buyers and the general public; (2) disseminating information regarding imported products and the Japanese market; and (3) promoting sales of foreign products to Japanese consumers to promote recognition of the quality of imported goods. Address: Manufactured Imports Promotion Organization, 1-3, Higashi Ikebukuro 3-chome, Toshima-ku, Tokyo 170, Japan; Tel: [81] (3) 3988-2791; Fax: [81] (3) 3988-1629.

maquiladora

(Mexico) A program which allows foreign manufacturers to ship components into Mexico duty-free for assembly and subsequent reexport. Industry established under the maquiladora program is Mexico's second largest source of foreign revenue (following oil exports).

In December 1989, the Mexican government liberalized the maquiladora program to make it a more attractive and dynamic sector of the economy. As a result, maquiladora operations may import, duty and import license free, products not directly involved in production, but that support production, including computers and other administrative materials and transportation equipment.

The maquiladora program may decline in importance over time as provisions of the North American Free Trade Agreement take effect. *See* North American Free Trade Agreement.

margin
(general) The difference between the cost of sold items and the total net sales income.
(finance) The difference between the market value of collateral pledged to secure a loan and the face value of the loan itself.
(investments—U.S.) The amount paid by the customer when he or she uses a broker credit to buy a security under Federal Reserve regulations, the initial margin required in past decades has ranged from 50 to 100 percent of the purchase price.
(finance) The spread between bid and asked rates
(foreign exchange) The good faith deposit which the writer of an option or the buyer of a forward or futures contract has to put up to cover the risk of adverse price movements.

marginal cost
(economics) The increase in the total cost of production that results from manufacturing one more unit output.

marine cargo insurance
(insurance) Broadly, insurance covering loss of, or damage to, goods at sea. Marine insurance typically compensates the owner of merchandise for losses in excess of those which can be legally recovered from the carrier that are sustained from fire, shipwreck, piracy, and various other causes. *See* special marine policy; all risk.

Marine Extension Clause 1943 & 1952
(insurance) An insurance extension which broadens warehouse-to-warehouse insurance coverage by eliminating the requirement that ordinary course of transit be maintained as well as the 15- or 30-day time limit at destination. Moreover, continuation of coverage is provided when certain conditions necessitate discharge of goods from vessel at a port other than the original destination. The most recent form of Marine Extension Clause was developed in 1952. It too provides for extensions as does the 1943 version, and adds that the assured will act with reasonable dispatch. The Warehouse-to-Warehouse Clause is now found in practically all open cargo policies. *See also* warehouse-to-warehouse.

marine insurance
See marine cargo insurance.

marine protection and indemnity insurance
(insurance) Insurance against legal liability of the insured for loss, damage, or expense arising out of or incident to the ownership, operation, chartering, maintenance, use, repair, or construction of any vessel, craft, or instrumentality in use in ocean or inland waterways, including liability of the insured for personal injury or death, and for loss of or damage to the property of another person.

maritime
Business pertaining to commerce or navigation transacted upon the sea or in seaports in such matters as the court of admiralty have jurisdiction over, concurrently with the courts of common law.

mark
The currency of Germany. 1DM=100 pfennig.

market access
(economics) The openness of a national market to foreign products. Market access reflects a government's willingness to permit imports to compete relatively unimpeded with similar domestically produced goods.

Market Access Program (MAP)
(U.S.) A U.S. government program authorized by the U.S. Food, Agriculture, Conservation, and Trade Act of 1990 and administered by the U.S. Department of Agriculture's Foreign Agricultural Service. Under the MPP, surplus stocks or funds from the Commodity Credit Corporation are used to partially reimburse agricultural organizations conducting specific foreign market development projects for eligible products in specified countries. Proposals for MPP programs are developed by trade organizations and private firms. Activities financed by the programs vary from commodity to commodity, and include activities such as market research, construction of a three-story wood demonstration building, construction of a model feed mill, and consumer promotion activities. (MPP is similar to the Targeted Export Assistance (TEA) program which was repealed by the 1990 Farm Bill.) Contact: U.S. Department of Agriculture, Foreign Agriculture Service, Marketing Operations Staff, 1400 Independence Ave., Washington, DC 20250 USA; Tel: [1] (202) 720-4327; Fax: [1] (202) 720-9361; http://www.fas.usda.gov/mos/programs/mapprog.html.

market disruption
(economics) The situation created when a surge of imports in a given product area causes sales of domestically produced goods in a particular country to decline to such an extent that the domestic producers and their employees suffer major economic hardship.

market economy
(economics) An economic system where resources are allocated and production of products determined by market forces rather than by government decree.

Market-Oriented Cooperation Plan
(U.S./Japan) A U.S. Japan trade agreement aimed at improving long-term business relations between Japan's automotive manufacturers and U.S. auto parts suppliers.

Market-Oriented Sector-Selective
(U.S./Japan) Bilateral trade discussions between the U.S. and Japan begun in January 1985 in an effort to remove many trade barriers at once in a given sector. MOSS talks have focused on five sectors: (1) telecommunications, (2) medical equipment and pharmaceuticals, (3) electronics, (4) forest products, and (5) auto parts. Overall, the talks focus high-level attention on reducing certain market obstacles opening communication channels to resolve follow-up disputes.

market price
(economics) (a) The price established in the market where buyers and sellers meet to buy and sell similar products. (b) The price determined by factors of supply and demand rather than by decisions made by management.

marking: country of origin
The physical markings on a product that indicate the country of origin where the article was produced.
(U.S. Customs) U.S. Customs laws require each imported article produced abroad to be marked in a conspicuous place as legibly, indelibly, and permanently as the nature of the article permits, with the English name of the country of origin, to indicate to the ultimate purchaser in the United States the name of the country in which the article was manufactured or produced. Articles which are otherwise specifically exempted from individual marking are an exception to this rule. *See* United States Customs Service.

markka
The currency of Finland. 1Fmk=100 pennia.

marks
(shipping) Information placed on outer surface of shipping containers or packages such as address labels, identifying numbers, box specifications, caution, or directional warnings.

markup
See premium.

master's protest
See captain's protest.

matador bond
(banking/finance) Bond issued on the Spanish market, denominated in currencies other than the peseta.

Matchmaker Program
(U.S.) Matchmaker trade delegations are organized and led by the U.S. International Trade Administration to help new-to-export and new-to-market firms meet prescreened prospects who are interested in their products or services in overseas markets. Matchmaker delegations usually target two major country markets in two countries and limit trips to a week or less. This approach is designed to permit U.S. firms to interview a maximum number of prospective overseas business partners with a minimum of time away from their home office. The program includes U.S. embassy support, briefings on market requirements and business practices, and interpreters' services. Matchmaker events, based on specific product themes and end-users, are scheduled for a limited number of countries each year. Contact: International Trade Administration, Department of Commerce, 14th and Constitution Ave. NW, Room 2012, Washington, DC 20230 USA; Tel: [1] (202) 482-2000. *See* new-to-export; new-to-market.

material contract terms
(law) Terms that are necessary to the agreement. Clauses that describe the goods, fix the price, and set the delivery date are examples of material contract terms.

mate's receipt
(shipping) A declaration issued by an officer of a vessel in the name of the shipping company stating that certain goods have been received on board his vessel. A mate's receipt is not a title document. Used as an interim document until the bill of lading is issued.

measurement cargo
(shipping) A cargo on which the transportation charge is assessed on the basis of measurement.

measurement ton
(shipping) Also known as a cargo or freight ton. A space measurement usually 40 cubic feet or one cubic meter. The cargo is assessed a certain rate for every 40 cubic feet of space it occupies.

medium of exchange
(economics) Any commodity (commonly money) which is widely accepted in payment for goods and

M

services and in settlement of debts, and is accepted without reference to the standing of the person who offers it in payment.

memorandum bill of lading
(shipping) The duplicate copy of a bill of lading. *See* bill of lading.

memorandum of understanding (MOU)
(general) An informal record, document or instrument that serves as the basis of a future contact.
(U.S.) A very detailed document devised by executive branch agencies of the government in areas such as aviation and fisheries that serve as agreements between nations.

memorandum tariff
(shipping) Publications which contain rule and rate information extracted from official tariffs. Memorandum tariffs are published by many carriers and are available from these carriers upon request. *See* tariff.

mercantilism
(economics) A prominent economic philosophy in the 16th and 17th centuries that equated the accumulation and possession of gold and other international monetary assets, such as foreign currency reserves, with national wealth. Although this point of view is generally discredited among 20th century economists and trade policy experts, some contemporary politicians still favor policies designed to create trade "surpluses," such as import substitution and tariff protection for domestic industries, as essential to national economic strength.

merchandise trade balance
See balance of payments.

merchant bank
(banking) A term used in Great Britain for an organization that underwrites securities for corporations, advises such clients on mergers, and is involved in the ownership of commercial ventures.

merchant's credit
(banking) A letter of credit issued by the buyer himself. Contains no commitment whatever on the part of a bank. *See* letter of credit.

merchant's haulage
(shipping) The inland move from or to a port that has all arrangements made by the cargo interests (seller/exporter).

Mercosur
(regional trade alliance) Mercosur (Spanish; Mercosul in Portuguese) or Southern Common Market, is comprised of Argentina, Brazil, Paraguay, and Uru-

guay. Mercosur is scheduled to enter into force in December 1994 for Argentina and Brazil and to enter into force in December 1995 for Paraguay and Uruguay. Mercosur, modeled similarly to the European Community's Treaty of Rome, will establish a common external tariff and eliminate barriers to trade in services. Chile has not sought entry to Mercosur, but does have an agreement with Argentina which will provide for some similar benefits.

merry-go-round
(banking/finance/foreign exchange) The circulation of money through various sources, ending up where it started. For instance the German Central Bank recycles excess capital by selling U.S. dollars to banks under a repurchase agreement and the banks place the U.S. dollars in the Euromarket. As the financial institutions could run up a U.S. dollar debt on the Euromarket, the Central Bank must buy back the U.S. dollars and sell domestic currency to avoid an excessive increase in the mark.

meter
(measure) A unit of linear measure equal to 39.37 inches (approximately). *See* Weights and Measures in the Appendix.

metical
The currency of Mozambique. 1Mt=100 centavos.

metric system
(measurement) A decimal system of weights and measures based on the meter of approximately 39.37 inches and the kilogram of approximately 2.2046 pounds. *See* Weights and Measures in the Appendix.

metric ton
(measure) A unit of mass or weight measure equal to 2,204.6 pounds or 1,000 kilograms preferably called kiloton.

microbridge
(shipping) A landbridge movement in which cargo originating/destined to an inland point is railed or trucked to/from the water port for a shipment to/from a foreign country. Carrier is responsible for cargo and costs from origin to destination.

microeconomics
(economics) The examination of the economic behavior of individual units in the economy, such as households or corporations. *See also* macroeconomics.

Military Critical Technologies List
(U.S.) A document listing technologies that the U.S. Defense Department considers to have current or future utility in military systems. The MCTL de-

scribes arrays of design and manufacturing know-how; keystone manufacturing, inspection, and test equipment; and goods accompanied by sophisticated operation, application, and maintenance know-how. Military justification for each entry is included in a classified version of the list. *See* United States Department of Defense.

minibridge
(shipping) Movement of cargo from a port over water, then over land to a port on an opposite coast.

minimum bill of lading
(shipping) Ocean bills of lading are known as minimum because they contain a clause which specifies the least charge that the carrier will make for the issuance of a lading. The charge may be a definite sum, or the current charge per ton or for any specified quantity of cargo. *See* bill of lading.

minimum charge
(shipping) The lowest rate applicable on each type of cargo service no matter how small the shipment.

Ministry of Foreign Economic Relations and Trade (MOFERT)
Renamed Ministry of Foreign Economic Trade and Economic Cooperation. *See* Ministry of Foreign Economic Trade and Economic Cooperation.

Ministry of Foreign Economic Trade and Economic Cooperation
(China) The People's Republic of China (PRC) Ministry of Foreign Economic Trade and Economic Cooperation implements national trade policies through administrative actions, drafting laws and issuing foreign trade regulations. It does not engage in foreign trade transactions but facilitates the foreign trading corporations (FTCs) which do. Address: Ministry of Foreign Trade & Economic Cooperation (MOFTEC), 2 Dongchangan Ave., Beijing 100731, CHINA; Tel: [86] (10) 670 81526; Fax: [86] (10) 670 81513; http://www.moftec.gov.cn.

Ministry of International Trade and Industry (MITI)
(Japan) MITI occupies a central position in Japan's "economic bureaucracy" and is regarded as one of the three most powerful and prestigious ministries of the central government (along with the Ministry of Finance and the Ministry of Foreign Affairs). In formulating and implementing Japan's trade and industrial policies, MITI is responsible for funding most of Japan's export promotion programs (although operation of these programs is left to JETRO). The Ministry also supervises the export fi-

nancing programs of Japan's Export-Import Bank, operates several types of export insurance programs, supports research organizations, and facilitates various types of overseas technical and cooperation training programs. Lately, MITI has assumed a role in encouraging imports of foreign products into Japan. Address: Ministry of International Trade and Industry, 3-1, Kasumiguseki 1-chome, Chiyoda-ku, Tokyo 100, Japan; Tel: [81] (3) 3501-1511; http://www.miti.go.jp.

Ministry of Posts and Telecommunications (MPT)
(Japan) MPT is Japan's telecommunications regulatory agency. The Ministry is authorized to adjust supply and demand among service providers to ensure that there is not excessive competition in a given market. To do so, MPT issues "administrative guidance" to the industry and recommends "unification" when there appears to be excessive competition in a given market.

mitigation of damages
(law/insurance) A legal doctrine that charges a party who suffers contract damages with a duty to use reasonable diligence and ordinary care in attempting to minimize damages or avoid aggravating the injury. If a seller of oranges, for example, is entitled to prepayment before shipment and the buyer fails to pay, the seller should make a reasonable attempt to sell the oranges to another buyer before they spoil so as to mitigate the seller's damages. The seller may then recover from the breaching buyer the difference between the contract price and the price at which the oranges were sold to the other buyer.

The concept also applies to insurance where the insured has the responsibility to minimize damages to an insured cargo shipment.

mixed credit
(banking) The combining of concessional (liberal) and market-rate export credit as an export promotion mechanism.

monetary instrument
See financial instrument.

monetary system
(banking) The authority of the state in matters of establishing monetary policy, including determining the monetary unit, the monetary authorities, and the ways in which money is issued and the way the money supply is controlled.

M

money

(banking) Any denomination of coin or paper currency of legal tender that passes freely as a medium of exchange; anything that is accepted in exchange for other things (e.g., precious metals). Major characteristics of money include easy recognition, uniformity in quality, easy divisibility, and a relatively high value within a small area.

money creation

(banking) The increase in money supply by the central or commercial banks.

money market

(banking/finance) The market for short-term financial instruments, such as certificates of deposit, commercial paper, banker's acceptances, Treasury bills, discount notes and others. These instruments are all liquid and tend to be safe. *See* capital market, financial market.

money market operations

(banking) Comprises the acceptance and re-lending of deposits (*see* time deposits) on the money market.

money supply

(economics/banking) The amount of domestic cash and deposit money available in an economy.

moor

(shipping) To secure a vessel to an anchor, buoy or pier.

moorage

(shipping) Charges assessed for mooring a vessel to a pier or wharf.

Most Favored Nation (MFN)

A non-discriminatory trade policy commitment on the part of one country to extend to another country the lowest tariff rates it applies to any other country. (WTO) All contracting parties to the World Trade Organization (WTO) undertake to apply such treatment to one another under Article I of the treaty.

Under MFN principles, when a country agrees to cut tariffs on a particular product imported from one country, the tariff reduction automatically applies to imports of this product from any other country eligible for most-favored nation treatment. This principle of nondiscriminatory treatment of imports appeared in numerous bilateral trade agreements prior to establishment of the WTO. A country is under no obligation to extend MFN treatment to another country unless both are bilateral contracting parties of the World Trade Organization or MFN treatment is specified in a bilateral agreement.

(U.S.) The most favored nation principle was a feature of U.S. trade policy as early as 1778. Since 1923 the United States has incorporated an "unconditional" Most Favored Nation clause in its trade agreements, binding the contracting governments to confer upon each other all the most favorable trade concessions that either may grant to any other country subsequent to the signing of the agreement. The United States now applies this provision to its trade with all of its trading partners except for those specifically excluded by law. *See also* Harmonized Tariff Schedule of the United States.

motor carrier's terminal

(shipping) The place where loaded or empty shipping containers are received or delivered by a motor carrier and where the motor carrier maintains an equipment pool.

motor vehicle

(shipping) Any vehicle, machine, tractor, trailer or semi-trailer propelled or drawn by mechanical power and used upon the highways in the transportation of passengers or property.

multicurrency clause

(banking) a clause in a loan agreement stating that more than one currency may be used in paying or redeeming the loan.

Multi-Fiber Arrangement, textiles (MFA)

(WTO) An international compact under the World Trade Organization (WTO) that allows an importing signatory country to apply quantitative restrictions on textiles imports when it considers them necessary to prevent market disruption.

The MFA provides a framework for regulating international trade in textiles and apparel with the objectives of achieving "orderly marketing" of such products, and of avoiding "market disruption" in importing countries. It provides a basis on which major importers, such as the United States and the European Community, may negotiate bilateral agreements or, if necessary, impose restraints on imports from low-wage producing countries. It provides, among other things, standards for determining market disruption, minimum levels of import restraints, and annual growth of imports.

The MFA provides that such restrictions should not reduce imports to levels below those attained during the preceding year. Bilateral agreements usually allow for import growth tied to anticipated greater demand.

Since an importing country may impose such quotas unilaterally to restrict rapidly rising textiles imports, many important textiles-exporting countries consider it advantageous to enter into bilateral agreements with the principal textiles-importing countries.

The MFA went into effect on Jan. 1, 1974, was renewed in December 1977, in December 1981, and again in July 1986. It succeeded the Long-term Agreement on International Trade in Cotton Textiles ("The LTA"), which had been in effect since 1962. Whereas the LTA applied only to cotton textiles, the MFA now applies to wool, man-made (synthetic) fiber, silk blend and other vegetable fiber textiles and apparel. Note: The MFA will eventually be phased out as a result of the Uruguay Round of the General Agreement on Tariffs and Trade. *See also* quotas; bilateral trade agreement; Uruguay Round; General Agreement on Tariffs and Trade.

multilateral agreement

An international compact involving three or more parties. For example, the World Trade Organization (WTO), has been seeking to promote trade liberalization through multilateral negotiations. *See also* bilateral trade agreement.

Multilateral Investment Fund

Under the Enterprise for the Americas Initiative, the fund complements the Inter-American Development Bank. The fund provides program and project grants to advance specific, market-oriented investment policy initiatives and reforms, and encourages domestic and foreign investment in Latin America and the Caribbean. Contact: InterAmerican Development Bank, 1300 New York Avenue NW, Washington, DC 20577 USA; Tel: [1] (202) 623-1000.

Multilateral Investment Guarantee Agency (MIGA)

A part of the World Bank Group. MIGA encourages equity investment and other direct investment flows to developing countries through the mitigation of noncommercial investment barriers. The agency offers investors guarantees against noncommercial risks; advises developing member governments on the design and implementation of policies, programs, and procedures related to foreign investments; and sponsors a dialogue between the international business community and host governments on investment issues. Address: Multilateral Investment Guarantee Agency, World Bank, 1818 H Street NW, Washington, DC 20433 USA; Tel: [1] (202) 473-6168; http://www.miga.org.

multilateral trade negotiations

(GATT/WTO) A term describing the multilateral rounds of negotiations held under the auspices of the General Agreement on Tariffs and Trade (GATT) and World Trade Organization (WTO) since 1947. Each Round represented a discrete and lengthy series of interacting bargaining sessions among the participating Contracting Parties in search of mutually beneficial agreements looking toward the reduction of barriers to world trade. The agreements ultimately reached at the conclusion of each Round became new commitments and thus amounted to an important step in the evolution of the world trading system. *See* General Agreement on Tariffs and Trade; rounds; Tokyo Round; Uruguay Round, World Trade Organization (WTO).

multimodal transport

(shipping) Shipping which includes at least two modes of transport, such as shipping by rail and by sea.

multinational corporation

(economics) A corporation having subsidiaries in more than one country.

mutatis mutandis

(law) Meaning changing what needs to be changed; used when cases are nearly the same except for minor details. A statute that governs one type of transaction, for example, may also be applied to another transaction with minor exceptions, in which event the statute applies mutatis mutandis. A country may apply its trademark law mutatis mutandis to service marks, in which event the same law will apply except for changes to account for such details as the use of the mark to distinguish services instead of goods.

M

N

Naamloze Vennotschap (N.V.)
(Belgium, Netherlands) Designation for a joint stock company with limited personal liability to shareholders.

NAFTA
See North American Free Trade Agreement.

naira
The currency of Nigeria. 1N=100 kobo.

named insured
(insurance) Any person or firm or corporation or any of its members, specially designated by name as insured(s) in a policy, as distinguished from others who, although unnamed, are protected under some circumstances.

National Association of Export Companies
A non-profit organization established in 1965 to act as the information provider, support clearinghouse forum, and advocate for those involved in exporting and servicing exporters. Provides networking opportunities, counseling, publications, seminars, etc. Address: National Association of Export Companies, PO Box 1330, Murray Hill Station, New York, NY 10156 USA; Tel: [1] (212) 725-3311; Fax: [1] (212) 725-3312; http://www.nexco.org.

National Association of State Development Agencies (NASDA)
NASDA was formed in 1946 to provide a forum for directors of state economic development agencies to exchange information, compare programs, and deal with issues of mutual interest. NASDA's organization includes International Trade and Foreign Investment components. Trade activities include maintenance of a State Export Program Database. Address: NASDA, 750 First Street NE, Suite 710, Washington, DC 20002 USA; Tel: [1] (202) 898-1302; Fax: [1] (202) 898-1312; http://www.nasda.com.

National Customs Brokers and Freight Forwarders Association of America
A non-profit organization founded in 1897 which serves as the trade organization of customs brokers and international freight forwarders in the U.S. Through ongoing communications with industry trade publications and the general media, the Association projects the industry's interests and objectives. Membership includes brokers and freight forwarders in 32 affiliated associations located at major ports throughout the U.S. Address: National Customs Brokers and Freight Forwarders Association of America, One World Trade Center, Suite 1153, New York, NY 10048 USA; Tel: [1] (212) 432-0050.

nationalization
(economics) Takeover by the government, with or without compensation, of a public or private activity.

national security controls
(U.S.) National security controls restrict exports of U.S. goods and technology which would make a significant contribution to the military potential of another country and thus be detrimental to national security.

National Security Directive #53
(U.S.) NSD-53 deals with the export licensing process and sets specified time periods for resolving disputes on both national security and foreign policy export license applications. Under NSD-53, exports controlled on both of these grounds are subject to explicit timetables for interagency dispute resolution at the Sub-Cabinet level by the Advisory Committee on Export Policy (ACEP), and at the cabinet level by the Export Administration Review Board (EARB). The Directive requires escalation to the ACEP not later than 100 days from the filing date of the applicant's application, and if the disagreement cannot be resolved by the ACEP, for review and resolution by the EARB within 35 days of the date of the ACEP meeting. Cases not resolved by the EARB must be escalated to the President for resolution. The new procedures also permit an agency to refer a case at any stage of the dispute resolution process to the NSC for a 30 day policy review. *See* National Security Directives.

National Security Directives (NSD)
(U.S.) NSDs provide policy or procedural guidance and are signed by the President. In 1989, the President reorganized the national security council committee process (separate from the Export Administration Review Board (EARB)). As reorganized, under the National Security Council (NSC), there are committees for Coordinating Committee for Multilateral Export Controls (CoCom), terrorism, nonproliferation, etc. NSDs were known as National Security Decision Directives, NSDDs, before President Bush's reorganization. NSD-1 reorganized the process; NSD-10 established the

committees; NSD-53 deals with export licensing. The scope of coverage and the players are about the same under the NSD and NSDD processes.

National Security Override (NSO)

(U.S.) In some cases of U.S. export law, despite a finding of foreign availability of a controlled commodity, control is maintained over exporting the commodity because it is deemed a national security sensitive item. The term national security override is used to describe this circumstance.

The term has also been used in other contexts. For example, under a November 16, 1990 directive, the President instructed the interagency control groups to move as many dual use items from the U.S. State Department's International Munitions List to the Commerce Department's Commerce Control List. In some circumstances, a national security override is applied to prevent transfer of a particular item.

See also International Munitions List; Commerce Control List.

National Tourism Policy Act

(U.S. law) Legislation passed in 1981 that created the U.S. Travel and Tourism Administration and required the establishment of the Tourism Policy Council and the Travel and Tourism Advisory Board.

National Trade Data Bank (NTDB)

(CD-ROM publication/web database) The NTDB is an electronic data base available on CD-ROM and on the World Wide Web (fee based) which contains international economic and export promotion information supplied by 15 U.S. governmental agencies. Data are updated monthly and are presented in one of three standard formats: text, time series, or matrix. The NTDB contains data from the Departments of Agriculture (Foreign Agricultural Service), Commerce (Bureau of the Census, Bureau of Economic Analysis, Office of Administration, and National Institute for Standards and Technology), Energy, Labor (Bureau of Labor Statistics), the Central Intelligence Agency, Eximbank, Federal Reserve System, U.S. International Trade Commission, Overseas Private Investment Corporation, Small Business Administration, the U.S. Trade Representative, and the University of Massachusetts (MISER data on state origins of exports). Source: U.S. Department of Commerce, Office of Business Analysis, HCHB Room 4885, Washington, DC 20230 USA; Tel: [1] (202) 482-1986. www.stat-usa.gov.

National Trade Estimates Report

(U.S.) An annual report by the United States Trade Representative (USTR) that identifies significant foreign barriers to and distortions of trade. Contact: Office of the United States Trade Representative, Executive Office of the President, 600 17th Street NW, Washington, DC 20508 USA; Tel: [1] (202) 395-3350; http://www.ustr.gov.

national treatment

National treatment affords individuals and firms of foreign countries the same competitive opportunities, including market access, as are available to domestic parties.

natural advantage

(economics) Economic theory that states that a country has a competitive advantage in the production of certain products as a result of access to natural resources, transportation or climatic conditions.

near-bank

(banking-Canada) A financial institution, excluding standard commercial bank, such as savings bank, credit union, etc.

negligence

(law) Failure to do that which an ordinary, reasonable, prudent person would do, or the doing of some act that an ordinary, prudent person would not do. Reference is made of the situation, circumstances, and awareness of the parties involved.

negotiable

(general) Anything that can be sold or transferred to another for money or as payments of a debt. In international trade, usually refers to the transferability of a title document—such as a negotiable bill of lading.

(investments) Refers to a security, title to which is transferable by delivery.

See negotiable instrument.

negotiable bill of lading

(shipping) Bill of lading transferred by endorsement. There are three possibilities: (1) to XY & Co. or their order; (2) to the order of XY & Co.; and (3) to order, without the name of the party. In the latter case the bill remains to the order of the shipper until he endorses it.

These types of bills of lading are usually endorsed on the reverse. The opposite of a negotiable bill of lading is the straight bill of lading *See* bill of lading; endorsement.

negotiable instrument

(law/banking/shipping) A written document (instrument) that can be transferred merely by en-

N

dorsement (signing) or delivery. Checks, bills of exchange, bills of lading and warehouse receipts (if marked negotiable), and promissory notes are examples of negotiable instruments.

(U.S.) The Uniform Negotiable Instruments Act states: "An instrument, to be negotiable, must conform to the following requirements: (1) it must be in writing and signed by the maker or drawer; (2) it must contain an unconditional promise or order to pay a certain sum in money; (3) it must be payable on demand, or at a fixed or determinable future time; (4) it must be payable to order or to bearer; and (5) where the instrument is addressed to a drawee, he must be named or otherwise indicated therein with reasonable certainty."

negotiable warehouse receipt

(shipping) A certificate issued by an approved warehouse that guarantees the existence and the grade of a commodity held in store. *See* negotiable instrument.

negotiating bank

(banking) In a letter of credit transaction, the bank that (1) receives and examines the seller's documents for adherence to the terms and conditions of the letter of credit, (2) gives value to the seller, so long as the terms of the credit have been met, and (3) forwards them to the issuing bank (the buyer's or importer's bank). Depending upon the type of credit, the negotiating bank will either credit or pay the seller/exporter immediately under the terms of the letter of credit, or credit or pay the exporter once it has received payment from the issuing bank. *See* advising bank; issuing bank.

negotiation

(banking) (a) The action by which a negotiable instrument is circulated (bought and sold) from one holder to another. (b) In letter of credit transactions, (1) the examination of the seller's documentation by the negotiating bank to determine if they comply with the terms and conditions of the letter of credit and (2) the giving of value for draft(s) and/or document(s) by the bank authorized to negotiate. Mere examination of the documents without giving value does not constitute a negotiation. *See* letter of credit.

negotiation credit

(banking) A documentary letter of credit available by negotiation. *See* letter of credit.

NES

See not elsewhere specified.

nested

(shipping) Packed one within another.

net cash

Payment for goods sold usually within a short period of time with no deduction allowed from the invoice price.

net export of goods and services

(economics) The excess of exports of goods and services (domestic output sold abroad, and the production abroad credit to U.S.-owned resources) over imports (U.S. purchases of foreign output, domestic production credit to foreign-owned resources, and net private cash remittances to creditors abroad).

net foreign investment

(economics/foreign investment) The net change in a nation's foreign assets and liabilities, including the monetary gold stocks, arising out of current trade, income on foreign investment, and cash gifts and contributions. It measures the excess of: (1) exports over imports, (2) income on U.S. public and private investment abroad over payments on foreign investment in the U.S., and (3) cash gifts and contributions of the U.S. (public and private) to foreigners over cash gifts and contributions received from abroad.

Net foreign investment may also be viewed as the acquisition of foreign assets by that country's residents, less the acquisition of that country's assets by foreign residents.

net income

(economics) The remains from earnings after all costs, expenses and allowances for depreciation and probable loss have been deducted.

net loss

(economics) The excess of expenses and losses during a specified period over revenues and gains in the same time frame.

net national product

(economics) Gross national product minus capital consumption (depreciation). The market value of the net output of goods and services produced by the nation's economy.

net price

Price after all discounts, rebates, etc., have been allowed.

net ton (N.T.)

(measure) A unit of mass or weight measurement equal to 2,000 pounds. Also called short ton (S.T.).

net tonnage

(shipping) A vessel's gross tonnage minus deductions for space occupied by accommodations for crew, machinery for navigation, the engine room, and fuel. A vessel's net tonnage represents the space available for the accommodation of passengers and the stowage of cargo.

net weight
(general) The weight of goods without packaging. (shipping) The weight of merchandise without the shipper container. Also the weight of the contents of a freight car.

neutral air waybill
(shipping) A standard air waybill without identification of issuing carrier. *See* air waybill; bill of lading.

neutral body
(shipping) A regulatory entity operating within the framework of a shipping conference, established by the member carriers to act as a self-policing force to ferret out malpractices and other tariff violations. The neutral body has authority to scrutinize all documents kept by the carriers and the carriers' personnel with right of entry to all areas of the carrier's facilities including desks, briefcases, etc. Violations found are reported to the membership with significant penalties being assessed. Repeated offenses are subject to escalating penalty amounts. Revenue from penalties are used to support the cost of the neutral body activity. *See* carrier; conference.

newly industrializing countries (NICs)
(economics) Relatively advanced developing countries whose industrial production and exports have grown rapidly in recent years. Examples include Brazil, Hong Kong, Korea, Mexico, Singapore, and Taiwan. The term was originated by the Organization for Economic Cooperation and Development (OECD).

new-to-export (NTE)
(U.S.) As defined by the United States Department of Commerce, a new-to-export action is one that results from documented assistance to a company that assists the client's first verifiable export sale. Either the company has not exported to any destination during the past 24 months or prior exports have resulted from unsolicited orders or were received through a U.S.-based intermediary. *See* United States Department of Commerce.

new-to-market (NTM)
(U.S.) As defined by the U.S. Department of Commerce, a reportable new-to-market export action is one that results from documented assistance to an exporter that facilitates a verifiable sale in a new foreign market. Either the company has not exported to that market during the past 24 months or previous exports to that market have resulted from unsolicited orders or were received through a U.S. based intermediary. *See* United States Department of Commerce.

nexus
(law) A party's connection with, or presence in, a place that is sufficient enough that it would be fair to subject the party to the jurisdiction of the court or government located there.

ngultrum
The currency of Bhutan. 1Nu=100 chetrum.

Nippon Telegraph and Telephone Corporation (NTT)
(Japan) NTT is Japan's largest telecommunications enterprise and was converted from a public corporation to a private enterprise in April 1985. Although competition has been allowed, the Japanese Government still owns the majority of NTT stock and postponement of a decision in NTT divestiture is an issue of considerable importance to market access by foreign companies. NTT was established in 1952. Address: Nippon Telegraph and Telephone Corporation, 1-6, Uchisaiwai-cho 1-chome, Chiyoda-ku, Tokyo 100, Japan; Tel: [81] (3) 3509-5111; http://www.ntt.co.jp.

non-market economy
(economics) A national economy or a country in which the government seeks to determine economic activity largely through a mechanism of central planning, as formerly in the Soviet Union, in contrast to a market economy that depends heavily upon market forces to allocate productive resources. In a "non-market" economy, production targets, prices, costs, investment allocations, raw materials, labor, international trade, and most other economic aggregates are manipulated within a national economic plan drawn up by a central planning authority, and hence the public sector makes the major decisions affecting demand and supply within the national economy.

non-negotiable
(law) Not transferable from one person to another. Usually refers to the transferability of a title document (e.g., non-negotiable bill of lading). Possession of a non-negotiable title document alone does not entitle the holder to receive the goods named therein (e.g., non-negotiable sea waybill, air waybill, forwarder's receipt, etc.). *See also* negotiable; negotiable instrument.

nonperforming assets
(banking) Assets which have no financial return.

N

nonperforming debt
(banking) A debt which has no financial return (i.e. no interest is paid on it).

nonperforming loan; nonaccruing loan
(banking) Loan where payment of interest has been delayed for more than 90 days.

nonstructural container
(shipping) A unit load device composed of a bottomless rigid shell used in combination with a pallet and net assembly. Note: The expression "nonstructural container" is also used to refer to the shell part of a device.

non-tariff barriers or measures
(economics) Any number of import quotas or other quantitative restrictions, non-automatic import licensing, customs surcharges or other fees and charges, customs procedures, export subsidies, unreasonable standards or standards-setting procedures, government procurement restrictions, inadequate intellectual property protection and investment restrictions which deny or make market access excessively difficult for goods or services of foreign origin.
(GATT) Participants in the Tokyo Round of the General Agreement on Tariffs and Trade attempted to address these barriers through the negotiations of a number of GATT codes, open for signature to all GATT members. Seven codes were negotiated during the Tokyo Round, covering customs valuations, import licensing, subsidies and countervailing duties, antidumping duties, standards, government procurement and trade in civil aircraft. Although the Tokyo Round codes had alleviated some of the problems caused by non-tariff measures, overall use of NTMs has increased since conclusion of the Tokyo Round.
See also import restrictions; non-tariff barriers; Tokyo Round; General Agreement on Tariffs and Trade, World Trade Organization.

non-vessel operating common carrier
(shipping) A carrier issuing bills of lading for carriage of goods on vessels which he neither operates nor owns.
(U.S.) A "carrier" defined by maritime law offering an international cargo transport service through the use of underlying carriers and under their own rate structure in accordance with tariffs filed with the Federal Maritime Commission in Washington, DC. The rates filed are required only to port-to-port portion. Specific authority for the NVOCC is given in the code of Federal Regulations, Title 46, Chapter IV, Federal Maritime Commission Sub-Part B, entitled "Regulations Affecting Maritime Carriers and Related Activities." General Order 4, Amendment i, Section 510.2 (d) states:
"The term 'non-vessel operating common carrier by water' means a person who holds himself out by the establishment and maintenance of tariffs, by advertisement, solicitation, or otherwise, to provide transportation for hire by water in interstate commerce as defined in the Act, and in commerce from the United States as defined in paragraph (b) of the section; assumes responsibility or has liability imposed by law for safe transportation of shipments; and arranges in his own name with underlying water carriers for the performance of such transportation whether or not owning or controlling the means by which such transportation is affected."

Nordic Council
(regional alliance) The Nordic Council, established in 1952, supports cooperation among Nordic countries in communications, cultural, economic, environmental, fiscal, legal and social areas. Members include: Denmark, Finland, Iceland, Norway and Sweden. Address: Nordic Council, Tyrgatan 7, PO Box 19506, 10432 Stockholm, Sweden; Tel: (8) 453-47-00; Fax: (8) 411-75-36.

North American Free Trade Agreement (NAFTA)
A free trade agreement that comprises Canada, the U.S. and Mexico. The objectives of the Agreement are to eliminate barriers to trade, promote conditions of fair competition, increase investment opportunities, provide protection for intellectual property rights and establish procedures for the resolution of disputes.
NAFTA eliminates all tariffs on goods originating in Canada, Mexico and the United States over a transition period. Rules of origin are necessary to define which goods are eligible for preferential tariff treatment.
NAFTA contains special provisions for market access, customs administration, automotive goods, textiles and apparel, energy and petrochemicals, agriculture, sanitary and phytosanitary measures, technical standards, emergency action, antidumping and countervailing duty matters, government procurement, trade in services, land transportation, telecommunications, investment, financial services, intellectual property, temporary entry for business persons, dispute settlement, administration of law and the environment.
NAFTA will produce a market exceeding 360 million consumers and a combined output of more

than $6 trillion—20 percent larger than the European Community. The agreement took effect January 1, 1994.

There are a large number of resources available for more information on NAFTA. The Mexico and Canada country desks of the U.S. Department of Commerce offer an automated information system called Flash Fax with a wide range of information on NAFTA available 24 hours a day. Documents are sent free of charge to caller's fax machine within 30 minutes. For Mexico, call (202) 482-4464, and for Canada, call (202) 482-3101. A booklet called "Questions/Answers about U.S.-Mexico and North American Free Trade," and a bibliography of recent information on NAFTA is available from: U.S. Department of Commerce, Office of Mexico, 14th St. and Constitution Ave. NW, Washington, DC 20230 USA; Tel: [1] (202) 482-0621. The entire text of NAFTA is available from the U.S. Government Printing Office, Washington, DC 20402-9325 USA; Tel: [1] (202) 512-1800. Ask for stock number 041-001-00407-6; or on the National Trade Data Bank on CD-ROM, Tel: [1] (202) 482-1986.

North-South trade

(economics) Trade between developed countries (North) and developing countries (South). *See* developed countries; developing countries.

no show

(shipping) Freight that has been booked to a ship, but has not physically arrived in time to be loaded to that ship.

nostro account

(banking) "Our" account. An account maintained by a bank with a bank in a foreign country. Nostro accounts are kept in foreign currencies of the country which the monies are held, with the equivalent dollar value listed in another column for accounting purposes.

notary public

(law-U.S.) A person commissioned by a state for a stipulated period (with the privilege of renewal) to administer certain oaths and to attest and certify documents, thus authorizing him or her to take affidavits and depositions. A notary is also authorized to "protect" negotiable instruments for nonpayment or nonacceptance.

The role of a notary public varies from country to country. In some countries they take on many of the responsibilities which in the U.S. an attorney would assume, while in other countries they do not exist at all.

not elsewhere specified (N.E.S.)

(shipping) The abbreviation N.E.S. often appears in air freight tariffs. For example: "advertising matter, N.E.S.," "printed matter, N.E.S.," indicating that the rate stated in the tariff applies to all commodities within the commodity group except those appearing under their own rate. The abbreviation N.E.S., as used in air freight tariffs, is comparable to the abbreviation N.O.I.B.N. (not otherwise indexed by number) and N.O.S. (not otherwise specified) which appear in tariffs published by the surface modes.

notify address

(shipping) Address mentioned in the transport document (bill of lading or an air waybill), to which the carrier is to give notice when goods are due to arrive.

notify party

(shipping) Name and address of a party in the transport document (bill of lading or air waybill), usually the buyer or his agent, to be notified by the shipping company of the arrival of a shipment.

Nuclear Energy Agency (NEA)

Promotes the safe and effective use of nuclear energy through the exchange of information among technical experts, the sharing of analytical studies, and undertaking joint research and development projects by member countries. Headquarters are in Paris, France. Address: Nuclear Energy Agency, Le Seine-Saint Germain, 12 blvd. des Iles, 92130 Issy-les-Moulineaux, France; Tel: [33] (1) 45-24-82-00; Fax: [33] (1) 45-24-11-10; http://www.nea.fr.

Nuclear Non-Proliferation Act

(U.S. law) Among other actions, this Act made the U.S. Energy Department responsible for approving arrangements for nuclear exports and transfers. Each arrangement requires U.S. State Department concurrence, as well as consultations with the Arms Control and Disarmament Agency, the Nuclear Regulatory Commission, and the Departments of Defense and Commerce.

Nuclear Non-Proliferation Treaty

The NPT became effective in 1970 and was intended to limit the number of states with nuclear weapons to five: the U.S., the Soviet Union, Britain, France, and China. In doing so, the NPT attempts to: (1) prevent nuclear weapons sales by not assisting other nations with nuclear weapons development; (2) halt the nuclear weapons development programs of non-nuclear weapons states; and (3) promote nuclear disarmament and the peaceful use of nuclear technologies and materials. Over 140 states have pledged not to acquire nuclear weapons and to accept the safeguards of the International Atomic Energy Agency over all their nuclear materials. The treaty, however, is not of indefinite duration. One of the provisions of the treaty was to convene a conference 25 years after entry to decide whether the treaty would continue indefinitely or be extended for a specified time.

Nuclear Referral List

See Nuclear Regulatory Commission.

Nuclear Regulatory Commission (NRC)

(U.S.) The NRC regulates the transfer of nuclear facilities, materials and parts with uniquely nuclear applications (such as items associated with nuclear reactors). The U.S. Department of Energy regulates the transfer of information relating to nuclear technology. The U.S. State Department controls defense articles and services, such as nuclear weapons design and test equipment. The U.S. Department of Commerce controls a range of dual-use items with potential nuclear application. Validated licensing controls are in effect for commodities and technical data identified to be useful in the design, development, production or use of nuclear weapons or nuclear explosive purposes. These commodities compose the "Nuclear Referral List" (NRL). Any item under national security-based licensing requirements and intended for a nuclear-related end-use/end-user is also subject to review. In addition, any commodity that will be used in a sensitive nuclear activity is also subject to validated licensing controls. License applications for U.S. export of NRL items as well as applications that may involve possible nuclear uses are reviewed by the U.S. Department of Commerce in consultation with the Department of Energy. When either Department believes that the application requires further review, the application is referred to the Subgroup on Nuclear Export Coordination (SNEC). The SNEC is comprised of representatives from State, Defense, ACDA, and the NRC. *See* Nuclear Suppliers Group; Zangger Committee.

Nuclear Suppliers Group

An organization of nuclear supplier nations which coordinates exports of nuclear materials and equipment with the International Atomic Energy Agency (IAEA) inspectorate regime. The reason for creating the NSG was to allow member states some flexibility (which they do not enjoy in the Zangger Committee) in controlling items to non-nuclear weapons states.

The NSG's independence from the Nuclear Non-Proliferation Treaty (NPT) enables NSG to enlist the cooperation of supplier states that are not signatories to the NPT and thus not involved in the nuclear export control activities of the Zangger Committee. The NSG's control list is more comprehensive than the Zangger Committee's "trigger list"; it requires the imposition of safeguards on exports of nuclear technology in addition to nuclear materials and equipment.

See Nuclear Non-Proliferation Treaty; Zangger Committee; Nuclear Regulatory Commission.

O

ocean bill of lading (B/L)

(shipping) A receipt for the cargo and a contract for transportation between a shipper and the ocean carrier. It may also be used as an instrument of ownership (negotiable bill of lading) which can be bought, sold, or traded while the goods are in transit. To be used in this manner, it must be a negotiable "Order" Bill-of-Lading.

(a) A **clean bill of lading** is issued when the shipment is received in good order. If damaged or a shortage is noted, a clean bill of lading will not be issued.

(b) An **on board bill of lading** certifies that the cargo has been placed aboard the named vessel and is signed by the master of the vessel or his representative. In letter of credit transactions, an on board bill of lading is usually necessary for the shipper to obtain payment from the bank. When all bills of lading are processed, a ship's manifest is prepared by the steamship line. This summarizes all cargo aboard the vessel by port of loading and discharge.

(c) An **inland bill of lading** (a waybill on rail or the "pro forma" bill of lading in trucking) is used to document the transportation of the goods between the port and the point of origin or destination. It should contain information such as marks, numbers, steamship line, and similar information to match with a dock receipt.

See also bill of lading.

Offene Handelsgesellschaft (OHG)

(Austria) Designation for a general partnership, in which all partners have joint and several liability.

offer

(law) A proposal that is made to a certain individual or legal entity to enter into a contract, that is definite in its terms, and that indicates the offeror's intent to be bound by an acceptance. For example, an order delivered to a seller to buy a product on certain terms is an offer, but an advertisement sent to many potential buyers is not. *See* acceptance; counteroffer.

Office of Export Licensing (OEL)

(U.S.) Under the Bureau of Export Administration, the OEL administers export licenses. Address: Office of Export Licensing, U.S. Department of Commerce, 14th and Pennsylvania NW, Washington, DC

20230 USA; Tel: [1] (202) 482-0436; http://www.bxa.doc.gov. *See* Bureau of Export Administration; Export Licensing Voice Information System.

Office of Management and Budget (OMB)

(U.S.) An executive office of the President which evaluates, formulates and coordinates management procedures and program objectives within and among federal departments and agencies. It also controls the administration of the federal budget. Address: Office of Management and Budget, New Executive Office Building, 726 Jackson Place NW, Washington, DC 20503 USA; Tel: [1] (202) 395-3080; http://www.ombwatch.org.

Office of Munitions Control

See Defense Trade Controls.

official development assistance

(U.S.) Financial flows to developing countries and multilateral institutions provided by official agencies of national, state, or local governments. Each transaction must be:

(1) administered with the promotion of the economic development and welfare of developing countries as its main objective; and

(2) concessional in character and contain a grant element of at least 25 percent.

offset(s)

(general) In non-defense trade, governments sometimes impose offset requirements on foreign exporters, as a condition for approval of major sales agreements in an effort to either reduce the adverse trade impact of a major sale or to gain specified industrial benefits for the importing country. In these circumstances, offset requirements generally take one of two forms. In one formulation, an exporter may be required to purchase a specified amount of locally-produced goods or services from the importing country. For example, a commercial aircraft manufacturer seeking sales to an airline in another country might be required to purchase products as different from airplanes as canned hams. In other instances, an exporter might be required to establish manufacturing facilities in the importing country or to secure a specified percentage of the components used in manufacturing his product from established local manufacturers. *See* countertrade.

(defense related–U.S.) In trade of defense items, "offsets" are industrial compensation practices mandated by many foreign governments when purchasing U.S. defense systems. Types of offsets include mandatory coproduction, subcontractor production, technology transfer, countertrade, and foreign investment. Countries require offsets for a variety of reasons: to ease (or "offset") the burden of large defense purchases on their economies, to increase domestic employment, to obtain desired technology, or to promote targeted industrial sectors. *See* countertrade.

offshore

(banking) Refers to financial operations transacted outside the country in question.

offshore bank

(banking) Bank located outside the country in question.

offshore banking center

(banking) Financial center where many of the financial institutions have little connection with that country's financial system. Usually established for purposes of tax avoidance. Examples are the Cayman Islands, where many of the corporations are engaged in business in the U.S. and Europe, and London, where many of the financial institutions are engaged in Eurodollar trading.

offshore banking unit (OBU)

(banking) Department within a bank that, in certain countries (e.g., Bahrain), is permitted to engage in specific transactions (usually Euromarket business) that ordinary domestic banks are not allowed to do.

old-to-market (OTM)

(U.S.) A committed to export, experienced, larger-scale firm. A significant portion of manufacturing capability may be foreign sourced. Export sales volume is often in excess of 15 percent of total sales.

on board

(shipping) Notation on a bill of lading indicating that the goods have been loaded on board or shipped on a named ship. In the case of received for shipment bills of lading, the following four parties are authorized to add this "on board" notation: (1) the carrier, (2) the carrier's agent, (3) the master of the ship, and (4) the master's agent. *See* ocean bill of lading; bill of lading; negotiable bill of lading.

on deck

(shipping) Notation on a bill of lading which indicates that the goods have been loaded on the deck of the ship. In letter of credit transactions documents with an "on deck" notation will only be accepted if expressly authorized in the credit. *See* ocean bill of lading.

on deck bill of lading

(shipping) Bill of lading containing the notation that goods have been placed on deck.
See ocean bill of lading; bill of lading.

on their face

(banking) In letter of credit and other documentary operations banks must examine documents with reasonable care to ascertain whether or not they appear, on their face, to be in compliance with the terms or conditions of the documentary letter of credit. *See* letter of credit; documentary collection.

open account

Credit extended that is not supported by a note, mortgage, or other formal written evidence of indebtedness (e.g., merchandise for which a buyer is billed later). Because this method poses an obvious risk to the supplier, it is essential that the buyer's integrity be unquestionable.

open conference

(shipping) A shipping conference in which there are no restrictions upon membership other than ability and willingness to serve the trade. U.S. law requires all conferences serving the U.S. to be open. *See* conference; closed conference.

open economy

(economics) An economy free of trade restrictions.

open-end contract

(law) An agreement by which the buyer may purchase goods from a seller for a certain time without changes in the price or the contract terms.

open policy

(insurance) An insurance contract (policy) which remains in force until cancelled and under which individual successive shipments are reported or declared and automatically covered on or after the inception date. The open policy saves time and expense for all concerned, whether underwriter, agent or assured.

The shipper gains many advantages from the use of an open policy.

(1) He or she has automatic protection (up to the maximum limits stated in the policy) from the time shipments leave the warehouse at the place named in the policy for the commencement of transit. The policyholder warrants that shipments will be declared as soon as practicable, but unintentional failure to report will not void the insurance, since the goods are "held covered," subject to policy conditions. In effect, this is errors and omissions coverage, and it forestalls the possibility that, because of the press of business, goods may commence transit without being insured.

(2) The open policy provides a convenient way to report shipments. It also relieves the shipper from

the necessity of arranging individual placings of insurance for each shipment.

(3) Under an open policy the shipper has prior knowledge of the rate of premium that will be charged and thus can be certain of the cost. This in turn facilitates his quoting a landed sales price.

(4) The use of the open policy creates a business relationship that may exist over a long period of time. This permits the insurer to learn the special requirements of its assureds and so to provide them with individualized protection, tailor-made to fit the specific situation. This may be an important factor in the case of loss adjustments at out-of-the-way ports around the world, or in overcoming problems peculiar to a given commodity.

Some letter of credit transactions require evidence of an individual "policy" covering the specified shipment. In such cases it has become the practice to use a special marine policy.

See bordereau; declaration; special marine policy.

operating committees

(U.S.) There are four operating committees (OCs), which are the first step in resolving interagency disputes over the disposition of export license applications. The operating committees are: (1) the State Department's Subgroup on Nuclear Export Coordination (SNEC), (2) the State Department's working group on Missile Technology, (3) the State Department's working group on Chemical and Biological Warfare, and (4) the Department of Commerce's operating committee on all other dual-use items. Operating committees must make recommendations within 90 days of the date of the filing of an export license application. Operating committees generally meet a couple of times per month. *See* United States Department of Commerce; United States Department of State.

Operation Exodus

(U.S.) A U.S. Customs Service export enforcement program that was developed in 1981 to help stem the flow of the illegal export of U.S.-sourced arms and technology to the Soviet bloc and other prohibited destinations. *See* United States Customs Service.

operator

(U.S. foreign trade zones) A corporation, partnership or person that operates a foreign trade zone under the terms of an agreement with a foreign trade zone grantee. If there is no operator agreement and the grantee operates his own zone, the grantee is considered the operator for Customs Regulations purposes. *See* foreign trade zone; Foreign Trade Zone Board; Foreign Trade Zone Act; grantee; zone user; subzones.

option

(general) (a) A right to take up an offer. (b) The right to choose from several different possibilities. (c) A privilege to buy or sell, receive, or deliver property, given in accordance with the terms stated, with a consideration for price. This privilege may or may not be exercised at the option holder's discretion. Failure to exercise the option leads to forfeiture of the option.

(securities) A contract giving the holder the right to buy or sell a stated number of shares of a particular security at a fixed price within a predetermined period.

(foreign exchange) The contractually agreed upon right to buy (call option) or sell (put option) a specific amount of an underlying instrument at a predetermined price on a specific date (European option) or up to a future date (American option).

See call option; put option; American option; European option.

order

(law/banking/shipping) A request to deliver, sell, receive, or purchase goods or services.

order bill

(law) A bill of lading that states that goods are consigned to the order of the person named in the bill. *See* bill of lading; ocean bill of lading.

orderly marketing agreements

International agreements negotiated between two or more governments, in which the trading partners agree to restrain the growth of trade (limit exports) in specified "sensitive" products, usually through the imposition of import quotas. Orderly Marketing Agreements are intended to ensure that future trade increases will not disrupt, threaten or impair competitive industries or their workers in importing countries.

order notify

(shipping) A bill of lading term to provide for surrender of the original bill of lading before freight is surrendered; usually handled through a bank. *See* letter of credit; bill of lading; ocean bill of lading; documentary collection.

Organization for Economic Cooperation and Development (OECD)

The OECD is the primary forum for the discussion of common economic and social issues confronting the U.S., Canada, Western Europe, Japan, Australia, and New Zealand. It was founded in 1960 as the successor to the Organization for European Economic Cooperation which oversaw European participation in the Marshall Plan. The OECD's fundamental objective is "to achieve the highest sustainable economic growth and employment and a rising standard of living in member countries while maintaining financial stability and thus contribute to the world economy." Members currently include: Australia, Austria, Belgium-Luxembourg, Canada, Denmark, Finland, France, Germany, Greece, Iceland, Ireland, Italy, Japan, the Netherlands, New Zealand, Norway, Portugal, Spain, Sweden, Switzerland, Turkey, the United Kingdom, and the United States. Address: Organization for Economic Cooperation and Development, 2 rue Andre Pascal, F-75775 Paris Cedex 16, France; Tel: [33] (1) 45-24-82-00; Fax: [33] (1) 45-24-85-00; http://www.oecd.org.

Organization of African Unity (OAU)
The OAU was founded in May 1963 with 32 African countries as original members; it had 51 members in 1990. The Organization aims to further African unity and solidarity, to coordinate political, economic, cultural, scientific, and defense policies; and to eliminate colonialism in Africa. Address: Organization of African Unity, PO Box 3243, Addis Ababa, Ethiopia; Tel: [251] (1) 517700; Telex: OAU 21046; Fax: [251] (1) 513036; http://www.oau-oua.org.

Organization of American States (OAS)
The OAS is a regional organization established in April 1948 which promotes Latin American economic and social development. Members include the United States, Mexico, and most Central American, South American, and Caribbean nations. Members include: Antigua and Barbuda, Argentina, the Bahamas, Barbados, Belize, Bolivia, Brazil, Canada, Chile, Colombia, Costa Rica, Cuba (participation suspended), Dominica, Dominican Republic, Ecuador, El Salvador, Grenada, Guatemala, Guyana, Haiti, Honduras, Jamaica, Mexico, Nicaragua, Panama, Paraguay, Peru, St. Christopher-Nevis, St. Lucia, St. Vincent and the Grenadines, Suriname, Trinidad and Tobago, the United States, Uruguay, and Venezuela. Address: Organization of American States, 17th Street and Constitution Avenue NW, Washington, DC 20006; Tel: [1] (202) 458-6046; http://www.oas.org.

Organization of Arab Petroleum Exporting Countries (OAPEC)
OAPEC was established in 1968 to safeguard the interests of its members and to provide a forum for cooperation in the petroleum industry. Approximately 25% of the annual world petroleum production is from the member states of OAPEC. OAPEC members include: Algeria, Bahrain, Egypt, Iraq, Kuwait, Libya, Qatar, Saudi Arabia, Syria, and the United Arab Emirates. Address: Organization of Arab Petroleum Exporting Countries, PO Box 108, Maglis Al Shaab, Cairo 11516, Egypt; Tel: [20] (2) 354-2660; Fax: [20] (2) 354-2601. Note: OAPEC moved to Cairo from Kuwait in 1990 as a result of the Gulf War.

Organization of Petroleum Exporting Countries (OPEC)
An association of the world's oil-producing countries, formed in 1960. The chief purpose of OPEC is to coordinate oil production and pricing policies of its members: Algeria, Ecuador, Gabon, Indonesia, Iran, Iraq, Kuwait, Libya, Nigeria, Qatar, Saudi Arabia, the United Arab Emirates, and Venezuela. Address: Organization of Petroleum Exporting Countries, Obere-Donaustrasse 93, A-1020 Vienna, Austria; Tel: [43] (1) 21-1120; Fax: [43] (1) 26-4320; http://www.opec.org.

Organization of the Islamic Conference (OIC)
The OIC, established in May 1971, promotes cooperation in cultural, economic, scientific and social areas among Islamic nations. Headquarters are located in Jeddah, Saudi Arabia. Members include: Afghanistan, Algeria, Bahrain, Bangladesh, Benin, Brunei, Burkina Faso, Cameroon, Chad, Comoros, Cyprus, Djibouti, Egypt, Gabon, the Gambia, Guinea, Guinea-Bissau, Indonesia, Iran, Iraq, Jordan, Kuwait, Lebanon, Libya, Malaysia, Maldives, Mali, Mauritania, Morocco, Niger, Nigeria, Oman, Pakistan, Qatar, Saudi Arabia, Senegal, Sierra Leone, Somalia, Sudan, Syria, Tunisia, Turkey, Uganda, the United Arab Emirates, and Yemen. Address: Organization of the Islamic Conference, Kilo 6, Mecca Rd., PO Box 178, Jeddah 21411, Saudi Arabia; Tel: [966] (2) 680-0800; Fax: [966] (2) 687-3568; http://www.oic-un.org.

original documents
(banking/letters of credit) Unless otherwise stated in the letter of credit, the requirement for an original document may also be satisfied by the presentation of documents produced or appearing to have been produced:

(1) reprographically,

(2) by automated or computerized systems, or

(3) as carbon copies,

and marked as "originals" and where necessary appearing to be signed. *See* letter of credit.

ORM (other regulated material)
See hazardous materials; restricted articles; ORM; ORM-A, B, C, D, E.

ORM-A
(shipping) Material with an anesthetic, irritating, noxious, toxic or other properties that can cause discomfort to persons in the event of leakage. Examples are trichloroethylene, 1,1,1-trichloroethane, dry ice, chloroform, carbon tetrachloride.

ORM-B
(shipping) Material specifically named or capable of causing significant corrosion damage from leakage. Examples are lead chloride, quicklime, metallic mercury, barium oxide.

ORM-C
(shipping) Material specifically named and with characteristics which make it unsuitable for shipment unless properly packaged. Examples are bleaching powder, lithium batteries (for disposal), magnetized materials, sawdust, asbestos.

ORM-D
(shipping) Material such as consumer commodities which present a limited hazard due to form, quantity and packaging. They must be materials for which exceptions are provided. Examples are chemical consumer commodities (e.g., hair spray and shaving lotion) and small arm ammunition (reclassified because of packaging).

ORM-E
(shipping) Material that is not included in any other hazard class, but is regulated as ORM. Examples are hazardous waste and hazardous substances.

other regulated materials
See ORM.

ouguiya
The currency of Mauritania. 1UM=5 khoums.

out-of-the-money
(foreign exchange) An option is out-of-the-money in the following cases:
(1) Call option: market price less than the strike price.
(2) Put option: market price greater than the strike price.
For European options, replace the market price by the forward price of the underlying instrument on the expiry date of the option. *See also* call option; put option; option; in-the-money.

output contract
(law) An agreement by which one party agrees to sell his or her entire production to the other, who agrees to purchase it.

outright
(foreign exchange) A forward purchase or sale of foreign exchange which is not offset by a corresponding spot transaction, i.e. which has not been contracted through swaps. *See* foreign exchange.

outward swap
(foreign exchange) Spot purchase of foreign exchange and forward resale of the same currency against domestic currency. *See* foreign exchange.

overland common point (OCP)
(shipping) A special rate concession made by shipping lines, rail carriers, and truckers serving the U.S. West Coast for export and import traffic intended to benefit midwest shippers and importers by equalizing rates to and from other coastal areas, and offering these Midwest companies a comparable alternative. The steamship companies lower their rates and their inland carriers pick up the terminal charges, which consist of handling charges, wharfage charges, and carloading or unloading charges. OCP rates apply to cargo shipped from or consigned to the states of North Dakota, South Dakota, Nebraska, Colorado, New Mexico and all states east thereof. OCP rates in Canada apply to the provinces of Manitoba, Ontario and Quebec.

overnight
(foreign exchange) Swap from settlement date until the following business day, i.e., one day or three days over the weekend. *See* foreign exchange.

Overseas Business Reports (OBR)
A series of publications by the U.S. Department of Commerce providing basic background data on the major trading countries of the world. Each report is a marketing study which provides updated export and economic outlooks, industrial trends, trade regulations, distribution and sales channels, transportation, and credit situation in individual countries. Source: Superintendent of Documents, U.S. Government Printing Office, Washington, DC 20402; Tel: [1] (202) 512-1800.

Overseas Private Investment Corporation
(U.S.) OPIC is a self-sustaining U.S. agency, under the International Development Cooperation Agency, whose purpose is to promote economic growth in developing countries by encouraging U.S. private investment in those nations. The Corporation assists American investors in three princi-

pal ways: (1) financing investment projects through direct loans and/or guaranties; (2) insuring investment projects against a broad range of political risks; and (3) providing a variety of investor services including investor counseling, country and regional information kits, computer-assisted project and investor matching, and investment missions. OPIC does not support projects that will result in the loss of domestic jobs or have a negative impact on the host country's environment or worker's rights. Address: Overseas Private Investment Corporation, 1100 New York Ave. NW, Washington, DC 20527 USA; Tel: [1] (202) 336-8799; http://www.opic.gov. *See* International Development Cooperation Agency.

over the counter (OTC)
(finance) Securities trading which takes place outside the normal exchanges. In contrast to normal exchanges, it is not tied to a central set-up in any one place but is conducted mainly by telephone and telex between traders, brokers and customers.

over the counter small package service
See small package service.

oxidizing material
(shipping) These items are chemically reactive and will provide both heat and oxygen to support a fire. (UN CLASS 5.) Examples are calcium permanganate, calcium hypochlorite, barium perchlorate, hydrogen peroxide and ammonium nitrate. Hazards/precautions are: may ignite combustibles (wood, paper, etc.); reaction with fuels may be violent; fires may produce poisonous fumes; vapors and dusts may be irritating; contact may burn skin and eyes; and peroxides may explode from heat or contamination.

P

pa'anga
The currency of Tonga. 1T$=100 seniti.

Pacific Rim
Refers to countries and economies bordering the Pacific ocean. Pacific Rim is an informal, flexible term which generally has been regarded as a reference to East Asia, Canada, and the United States. At a minimum, the Pacific Rim includes Canada, Japan, the People's Republic of China, Taiwan, and the United States. It may also include Australia, Brunei, Cambodia, Hong Kong/Macau, Indonesia, Laos, North Korea, South Korea, Malaysia, New Zealand, the Pacific Islands, the Philippines, Russia (or the Commonwealth of Independent States), Singapore, Thailand, and Vietnam. As an evolutionary term, usage sometimes includes Mexico, the countries of Central America, and the Pacific coast countries of South America.

packing credit
(banking) A monetary advance granted by a bank in connection with shipments of storable goods guaranteed by the assignment of the payment expected later on under a documentary letter of credit.

packing list
(shipping) A document prepared by the shipper listing the kinds and quantities of merchandise in a particular shipment. A copy is usually sent to the consignee to assist in checking the shipment when received. Also referred to as a bill of parcels.

pallet
(shipping, general) A platform with or without sides, on which a number of packages or pieces may be loaded to facilitate handling. Most carriers offer container discounts for palletized loads.

(air freight) A platform with a flat metal framed undersurface on which goods are assembled and secured by nets and straps. *See also* aircraft pallet.

Palletization results in more efficient use of space and better cargo handling, particularly when used as part of mechanized loading systems.

palletizing
(shipping) The loading and securing of a number of sacks, bags, boxes or drums on a pallet base.

pallet loader

(shipping) A device employing one or more vertical lift platforms for the mechanical loading or unloading of palletized freight at planeside.

pallet transporter

(shipping) A vehicle for the movement of loaded pallets between the aircraft and the freight terminal or truck dock.

parcel post air freight

(shipping) An airline service through which a shipper can consolidate a number of parcel post packages (with destination postage affixed by the shipper) for shipment as air freight to the postmaster at another city for subsequent delivery within local postal zones or beyond.

parent bank

(banking) A bank in a major industrial country that sets up a subsidiary in a developing country.

par exchange rate

(foreign exchange) The free market price of one country's money in terms of the currency of another.

pari passu

(law) On an equal basis without preference. Creditors who receive payment pari passu, for example, are paid in proportion to their interests without regard to whether any of the claims would have taken priority over others.

Paris Club

Under the International Monetary Fund's (IMF) General Agreements to Borrow (GAB), established in 1962, 10 of the wealthiest industrial members of the IMF agreed to lend funds to the IMF, up to specified amounts "when supplementary resources are needed." The finance ministers of these countries comprise the Paris Club (also called the Group of 10).

The Paris Club has become a popular designation for meetings between representatives of a developing country that wishes to renegotiate its "official" debt (normally excluding debts owed by and to the private sector without official guarantees) and representatives of the relevant creditor governments and international institutions. These meetings usually occur at the request of a debtor country that wishes to consolidate all or part of its debt service payments falling due over a specified period. Meetings are traditionally chaired by a senior official of the French Treasury Department. Comparable meetings occasionally take place in London and in New York for countries that wish to renegotiate re-

payment terms for their debts to private banks. These meetings are sometimes called "creditor clubs." *See* International Monetary Fund; Group of Ten.

Paris Convention

The Paris Convention for the Protection of Industrial Property, first adopted in 1883, is the major international agreement providing basic rights for protecting industrial property. It covers patents, industrial designs, service marks, trade names, indications of source, and unfair competition. The U.S. ratified this treaty in 1903. The treaty provides two fundamental rights:

(1) The **principle of national treatment** provides that nationals of any signatory nation shall enjoy in all other countries of the union the advantages that each nation's laws grant to its own nationals.

(2) The **right of priority** enables any resident or national of a member country to, first, file a patent application in any member country and, thereafter, to file a patent application for the same invention in any of the other member countries within 12 months of the original filing and receive benefit of the original filing date.

See patent; trademark; copyright; World Intellectual Property Organization; Patent Cooperation Treaty.

Paris Union

See World Intellectual Property Organization.

parity

(general) Equality in amount or value. For example, if the price for goods sold in two different markets is the same, the price is in parity.

(foreign exchange) Exchange relationship of a currency to a legally binding reference, i.e., to a specific amount of gold, to Special Drawing Rights (SDRs) or to other currencies. *See also* special drawing right(s).

(foreign exchange/official parity) Predetermined exchange rate relationship between two currencies.

par of exchange

(foreign exchange) The market price of money in one national currency that is exchanged at the official rate for a specific amount in another national currency, or another commodity of value (gold, silver, etc.).

parol

(law) Oral expression. A parol contract, for example, is one that is verbal only and that has not be put into writing by the parties.

particular average

(insurance) An insurance loss that affects specific interests only. There are two kinds of particular average losses: the total loss of a part of the goods, and the arrival of goods at destination in a damaged condition.

In the first situation, it is necessary to determine how much of the total amount insured is applicable to the missing item. In homogeneous or fungible cargo—that is, cargo which is capable of mutual substitution, like oil or coal—it is frequently a matter of simple arithmetic. The value of the unit of measurement of the cargo is found by dividing the amount of insurance by the total number of units in the shipment. This value multiplied by the number of missing units gives the value of the loss.

Where a normal or trade loss is to be expected, as in cargo subject to leakage, slackage or loss of moisture during the voyage, the method of calculation is slightly different. The value of the insurance is divided by the number of units in the "expected outturn," that is, the expected arrived quantity rather than the shipped quantity. This can be determined either by the normal percentage of trade loss for similar shipments or by examinations of sound arrived cargo forming part of the shipment in question. While this method will produce a somewhat higher insured value per unit, it naturally requires the normal or trade loss to be deducted in calculating the actual shortage sustained.

See also average; general average; with average; free of particular average; deductible average; trade loss.

parties to the credit

(banking) At least the following three parties are involved in a documentary letter of credit transaction:
(1) Applicant (buyer/importer),
(2) Issuing bank (buyers bank), and
(3) Beneficiary (seller/exporter).
As a rule, however, the issuing bank will entrust a correspondent bank with the task of advising and authenticating the credit and, if applicable, with payment, acceptance or negotiation. The issuing bank may also request the advising bank to add its confirmation.
See letter of credit; confirmation; issuing bank; advising bank.

partnership

(law) An unincorporated business owned and operated by two or more persons (partners), who may have general or limited liability in accordance with the partnership agreement. Note: The definition of status of partnership varies from country to country, and is not recognized as a business entity in some countries. See general partnership; limited partnership.

par value

(foreign exchange) The official fixed exchange rate between two currencies or between a currency and a specific weight of gold or a basket of currencies. *See* foreign exchange.

pataca

The currency of Macao. 1P=100 avos.

patent

(law) A grant by law to an inventor of a device of the right to exclude other persons from making, using, or selling the device. The patent holder has the right to license to another person the right to make, use, or sell the device. A patent is available only for devices that embody a new idea or principle and that involve a discovery. Patent protection varies from country to country, and may not be available in some jurisdictions. A country that is a member the Paris Convention for the Protection of Industrial Property may recognize patents held in other jurisdictions. *See* copyright; service mark; trademark; Paris Convention; World Intellectual Property Organization.

Patent Cooperation Treaty (PCT)

The PCT, is a worldwide convention, open to any Paris Convention country. The PCT entered into force in 1978. Unlike the Paris Convention, which addresses substantive intellectual property rights, the PCT addresses procedural requirements, aiming to simplify the filing, searching, and publication of international patent applications. *See* Paris Convention.

payable in exchange

(foreign exchange) The requirement that a negotiable instrument be paid in the funds of the place from which it was originally issued.

payee

(banking) The person or organization to whom a check or draft or note is made payable. The payee's name follows the expression "pay to the order of." *See also* payer; negotiable; negotiable instrument.

payer

(banking) The party primarily responsible for the payment of the amount owed as evidenced by a given negotiable instrument. *See also* payee; negotiable; negotiable instrument.

payments surplus

(economics) The excess of the value of a nation's exports over its imports. *See also* balance of trade.

penalties

(customs) The charges assessed or action taken by customs in response to a violation of a customs-enforced regulation or law.

perfect competition

(economics) A description for an industry or market unit consisting of a large number of purchasers and sellers all involved in the buying and selling of a homogeneous good, with awareness of prices and volume, no discrimination in buying and selling, and a mobility of resources.

performance

(law) The proper fulfillment of a contract or obligation.

performance bond

(insurance) A bond which guarantees proper fulfillment of the terms of a contract. In practice, the beneficiary of the bond (usually the buyer of services and/or goods), will claim financial restitution under the bond if the principal (supplier of the services and/or goods) fails to comply with the terms and conditions of the contract. *See* bond; surety.

peril point

(economics) A hypothetical limit beyond which a reduction in tariff protection would cause serious injury to a domestic industry.

(U.S.) U.S. legislation in 1949 that extended the Trade Agreements Act of 1934 required the Tariff Commission to establish such "peril points" for U.S. industries, and for the President to submit specific reasons to Congress if and when any U.S. tariff was reduced below those levels. This requirement, which was an important constraint on U.S. negotiating positions in early General Agreement on Tariffs and Trade (GATT) tariff-cutting Rounds, was eliminated by the Trade Expansion Act of 1962.

perils of the sea

(insurance) Marine insurance coverage that includes unusual action of wind and waves (often described as "stress of weather" or "heavy weather"), stranding, lightning, collision and damage by sea water when caused by insured perils such as opening of the seams of the vessel by stranding or collision. *See also* special marine policy; all risk.

perishable freight

(shipping) Freight subject to decay or deterioration.

person

(law) An individual or legal entity recognized under law as having legal rights and obligations. In the United States, for example, corporations and part-nerships are examples of legal entities that are recognized as persons under the law. In countries that allow the formation of limited and unlimited liability companies, those companies are recognized as persons under the law.

personal income

(economics) National income less various kinds of income not actually received by individuals, non-profit institutions, and so on (e.g., undistributed corporate profits, corporate taxes, employer contributions for social insurance), plus certain receipts that do not arise from production (i.e., transfer payments and government interest).

peseta

The currency of:
Andorra (uses Spanish peseta);
Spain, 1Pts=100 centimos.

peso

The currency of:
Argentina, 1$a=100 centavos;
Chile, 1Ch$=100 centavos;
Columbia, 1Col$=100 centavos;
Cuba, 1$=100 centavos;
Dominican Republic, 1RD$=100 centavos;
Guinea-Bissau, 1PG=100 centavos;
Mexico, 1Mex$=100 centavos;
Philippines, 1P=100 centavos;
Uruguay, 1UR$=100 centesimos.

petrodollars

(foreign investment/banking) Huge sums of money from oil-producing nations other than the United States or Great Britain. These funds are initially converted into Eurocurrency and deposited with international banks to be used for future investment and for paying debts. These banks traditionally set limits on the sum they will accept from any one country.

phytosanitary inspection certificate

(U.S.) A certificate, issued by the U.S. Department of Agriculture to satisfy import regulations of foreign countries, indicating that a U.S. export shipment has been inspected and is free from harmful pests and plant diseases.

pickup and delivery service

(shipping) An optional service for the surface transport of shipments from shipper's door to originating carrier's terminal and from the terminal of destination to receiver's door. Pickup service, at an additional charge, is provided upon shipper's request. In air cargo shipments delivery service is provided automatically by the air carrier at an additional charge unless the shipper requests otherwise. PU&D service is provided between all airports and all local points of such airports. For service beyond the terminal area *See* truck/air service.

pickup order
(shipping) An order from a broker (working as the agent of a consignee) to a carrier to pick up freight at a location.

pier-to-pier
(shipping) Shipment of cargo by carrier from origin pier to discharge pier. Applies to container yard (CY) cargo. Drayage to/from pier is borne by customer.

piggyback
(shipping) The transportation of truck trailers and containers on specially equipped railroad flat-cars.

pilferage
(shipping/insurance) The loss of goods due to steady theft in small amounts.

pilot
(shipping) A person whose office or occupation is to steer ships, particularly along a coast, or into and out of a harbor.

pips
(foreign exchange) In foreign exchange dealing, the last decimal places of a price quotation are called pips for purposes of simplicity (1/100th of 1 percent or 0.0001 of a unit). In futures trading the smallest possible price fluctuation upwards or downwards (1 pip) is called a tick.

plimsoll mark
(shipping) The depth to which a vessel may safely load is identified by a horizontal line painted on the outside of the ship. This "plimsoll mark" must remain above the surface of the water. Named after English shipping reformer Samuel Plimsoll. *See also* draft or draught.

point of origin
(shipping) The location at which a shipment is received by a transportation line from the shipper.

point-to-point; door-to-door
(shipping) Designates service and rates for shipments in door-to-door service. Originating carrier spots (places) empty container at shipper's facility at carrier's expense for loading by and at expense of shipper, the delivering carrier spots the loaded container at consignee's facility at carrier's expense for unloading by and at expense of consignee. *See also* demurrage; detention.

poisonous material
(shipping) Items that are extremely toxic to man and animals. (UN CLASS 6.) Examples are cyanogen gas, lead cyanide and parathion. Hazards/precautions are: may cause death quickly if breathed, swallowed or touched; may be flammable, explosive, corrosive or irritating; may be EXTREMELY HAZARDOUS. Look for the "Skull and Crossbones" on the label; degree of hazard key words: poison, danger, warning, highly toxic, moderately toxic, least toxic; and read the label carefully for storage and safety information.

political risk
(economics) Extraordinary measures of foreign countries and political events abroad which make it impossible for a debtor to comply with a contract or which lead to the loss, confiscation of or damage to goods belonging to the exporter, e.g., war, revolution, annexation, civil war, which can have detrimental effect upon the exporter. An exporter may be able to cover this risk by utilizing a confirmed letter of credit or by applying for cover from export credit agencies.

port
(shipping) (a) A harbor or haven where ships may anchor and discharge or receive cargo. (b) The left side of a ship when one is facing the bow.

port charge
(shipping) A charge made for services performed at ports.

portfolio investment
(foreign investment) In general, any foreign investment that is not direct investment is considered portfolio investment. Foreign portfolio investment includes the purchase of voting securities (stocks) at less than a 10 percent level, bonds, trade finance, and government lending or borrowing, excluding transactions in official reserves.

port of discharge
(shipping) The port at which a shipment is off-loaded by a transportation line, not to be confused with destination which may be a point further inland.

port of embarkation
See port of export.

port of entry
(shipping/customs) A port at which foreign goods are admitted into the receiving country. Ports of entry are officially designated by the importing country's government.

(U.S. Customs) Any place designated by act of U.S. Congress, executive order of the President of the United States, or order of the U.S. Secretary of the Treasury, at which a U.S. Customs officer is assigned with authority to accept entries of merchandise, to collect duties, and to enforce the various provisions of the U.S. Customs laws.

port of export

(shipping) The port, airport or customs point from which an export shipment leaves a country for a voyage to a foreign country.

port-of-origin air cargo clearance

(shipping) For the convenience of exporters moving goods by air from inland U.S. cities, certain U.S. Customs formalities can now be handled at the originating airport city. This avoids delaying such procedures until the export reaches a gateway point sometimes hundreds of miles from the exporter's business.

postdated check

(banking) A check bearing a date that has not yet arrived. Such a check cannot be paid by a bank before the date shown and must be returned to the maker or to the person attempting to use it. If presented on or after the date shown, the same check will be honored if the account contains sufficient funds.

post-shipment verifications (PSV)

(U.S.) An inspection to determine that an exported strategic commodity is being used for the purposes for which its export was licensed. Firms or individuals representing the end user, intermediate consignees, or the purchaser may be subject to inquiries pertaining to the post-shipment verification. As part of the PSV process, the Bureau of Export Administration (BXA) forwards a cable to the U.S. embassy or consulate in the respective geographical location to conduct an on-site inspection to ensure that the commodity is physically present and used as stated in the application. Post-shipment verifications are usually conducted six-to-eight months subsequent to export of the commodity. *See* Bureau of Export Administration.

pound

The currency for:
Cyprus, 1£C=100 cents;
Egypt, 1LE (or 1E£)=100 piasters=1,000 milliemes;
Falkland Islands, 1£F=100 pence;
Ireland, (pound or punt), 1RE=100 pence;
Lebanon, 1LL (or 1L£) =100 piasters;

St. Helena (uses U.K. pound);
Syria, 1S£=100 piasters;
United Kingdom, 1£=100 pence.

power of attorney

(law) A written legal document by which one person (principal) authorizes another person (agent) to perform stated acts on the principal's behalf. For example: to enter into contracts, to sign documents, to sign checks, and spend money, etc.

A principal may execute a **special power of attorney** authorizing an agent to sign a specific contract or a **general power of attorney** authorizing the agent to sign all contracts for the principal.

(U.S. Customs) Importers often give a limited power of attorney to their customs broker to conduct business with U.S. Customs on their behalf.

Tip: When you set up a power of attorney, make sure that it is broad enough in its language to cover the types of situations likely to arise, but not so broad that it gives more power to that individual than you intend. Power of attorney falls under "agency" law, which varies from country to country. Before giving someone power of attorney in a foreign country, be sure you understand what the local legal ramifications are. *See* agent; agency.

POW WOW

See International POW WOW.

pre-advice

(banking/letters of credit) At the request of an applicant to a letter of credit, the issuing bank may give a pre-advice of issuance and/or amendment of the letter of credit. A pre-advice is usually marked with a reference such as "Full details to follow." Unless otherwise stated, the pre-advice irrevocably commits the issuing bank to issue/amend the credit in a manner consistent with said pre-advice. *See* letter of credit; advice; advising bank; issuing bank; amendment.

preferences

(law) A creditor's right to be paid before other creditors of the same debtor. A creditor who holds a secured note, for example, generally has preference over one who holds an unsecured note.

Preferential Trade Agreement for Eastern and Southern Africa

PTA was founded in 1981 in order to improve commercial and economic cooperation in Eastern and Southern Africa; transform the structure of national economies in the region; promote regional trade; support inter-country cooperation, cooperation in agricultural development, and improvement of transport links. Accomplishments include: tariff reductions, multilateral trade, common travellers checks, a federation of chambers of commerce, a federation of commercial banks, and a commercial Arbitration board. The PTA Trade and Development Bank is in Burundi. Current goals include monetary harmonization and the establishment of a commodity futures market and stock exchange.

The PTA's members are: Burundi, Comoros, Djibouti, Ethiopia, Kenya, Lesotho, Malawi, Mauritius, Rwanda, Somalia, Swaziland, Tanzania, Uganda, Zambia, and Zimbabwe. Address: Preferential Trade Area for Eastern and Southern Africa, PO Box 30051, Lotti House, Cairo Rd., Lusaka, Zambia; Tel: [260] (1) 229725; Telex: 40127; Fax: [260] (1) 225107.

pre-license checks (PLC)

(U.S.) Pre-license checks are conducted to determine that a request for a license to export a controlled commodity represents a legitimate order. Firms or individuals representing the licensee (the applicant), a consignee, the purchaser, an intermediate consignee, or the end user may be subject to inquiries pertaining to the pre-license check. As part of the process, the Bureau of Export Administration (BXA) forwards a cable to the U.S. embassy or consulate in the respective geographical location to conduct an inspection or meet with company representatives to conduct inquiries on BXA's behalf. *See* Bureau of Export Administration.

preliminary determination

(U.S.) The determination announcing the results of a dumping investigation conducted within 160 days (or, in extraordinarily complicated cases, 210 days) after a petition is filed or an investigation is self-initiated by the International Trade Administration (ITA). If it is determined that there is a reasonable basis to believe or suspect that the merchandise under consideration is being sold or is likely to be sold at less than fair value, liquidation of all affected entries is suspended, and the matter is referred to the International Trade Commission. "Preliminary determination" also refers to the decision by the ITC where there is a reasonable indication that an industry in the United States is materially injured, or threatened with material injury, or the establishment of an industry in the United States is materially retarded by reason of the imports of the merchandise which is the subject of the petition. The ITC must make its decision within 45 days after the date on which the petition is filed or an investigation is self-initiated by the International Trade Administration. If this determination is negative, the investigation is terminated. *See* dumping; International Trade Administration; fair value.

premium

(general) The amount above a regular price, paid as an incentive to do something. For example, a buyer might pay a premium for quick delivery. Opposite of discount.

(insurance) The amount paid to an insurance company for coverage under an insurance policy.

(foreign exchange) (a) Premium, markup (forward premium) or contango of a forward rate against the spot rate. (b) The price at which an option sells.

prepaid

(shipping) (a) A notation on a shipping document indicating that shipping charges have already been paid by the shipper or his agent to the carrier. (b) Also, that shipping charges are to be paid by the consignee or his agent prior to release of the shipment.

prepaid charges

(shipping) The transportation trade practice under which the shipper pays transportation charges.

prescription period

See limitation period.

President's Export Council (PEC)

(U.S.) Advises the President on government policies and programs that affect U.S. trade performance; promotes export expansion; and provides a forum for discussing and resolving trade-related problems among the business, industrial, agricultural, labor, and government sectors.

The Council was established by Executive Order of the President in 1973 and was originally composed only of business executives. The Council was reconstituted in 1979 to include leaders of the labor and agricultural communities, Congress, and the Executive branch.

Twenty-eight private sector members serve "at the pleasure of the President" with no set term of office. Other members include five U.S. Senators and five Members of the House, the Secretaries of Agriculture, Commerce, Labor, State, and Treasury, the Chairman of the Export-Import Bank, and the U.S. Trade Representative. The Council reports to the President through the Secretary of Commerce.

price support

(economics) Subsidy or financial aid offered to specific growers, producers, or distributors, in accordance with governmental regulations to keep market prices from dropping below a certain minimum level.

pricing (of a loan)
(banking/finance) Fixing the cost of a loan, i.e., the interest rate and any other charges, such as front end fees.

prima facie
(law) A presumption of fact as true unless contradicted by other evidence. For example, unless an agreement assigning contract rights clearly states that outstanding interest payments are retained by the assignor, the right to collect such payments is deemed transferred prima facie to the assignee.

principal
(law) An individual or legal entity who authorizes another party (agent) to act on the principal's behalf. *See* agency; agent; power of attorney.

priority air freight
(shipping) Reserved air freight or air express service wherein shipments have a priority after mail and the small package services. Any size or weight allowed within air freight service limits is acceptable. Advanced reservations are permitted for movement on a given flight and in some cases a partial refund is paid the shipper if the shipment is not moved on the flight specified.

priority foreign countries
See Special 301.

priority logistics management
(shipping) The application of the just in time transportation theory. *See* just in time.

priority watchlist
See Special 301.

private corporation
(law) (a) A business corporation with shares that are not traded among the general public. (b) A corporation that is established by individuals to conduct business or other activities and that does not perform government functions. *See* corporation; close corporation; public corporation.

Private Export Funding Corporation
(U.S.) PEFCO works with the Export-Import Bank in using private capital to finance U.S. exports. PEFCO acts as a supplemental lender to traditional commercial banking sources by making loans to public and private borrowers located outside of the United States who require medium and/or longer-term financing of their purchases of U.S. goods and services. *See* Export-Import Bank of the United States.

Private Limited (Pte. Ltd.)
(India, Rhodesia, Singapore) Designation for a private limited liability corporation with limited liability to shareholders.

private limited liability corporation
See closely held corporation.

procurement and lead time
The time required by the buyer to select a supplier and to place and obtain a commitment for specific quantities of material at specified times.

product groups
(U.S.) Commodity groupings used for export control purposes. *See* export control classification number.

productivity
(economics) A measurement of the efficiency of production. A ratio of output to input (e.g., 10 units per man-hour).

profit, gross
(economics/accounting) (gross profit/gross margin) Net sales less cost of goods sold (before consideration of selling and administrative expenses). Gross profit is expressed in dollar figures; gross margin is expressed as a percentage of net sales.
(U.S. Customs) For the purposes of constructed value in an antidumping duty investigation or review, the profit used is the profit normally earned by a producer, from the country of export, of the same or similar product as that under investigation. By statute, the amount of profit shall not be less than 8 percent of the sum of general expenses and cost. *See* dumping; countervailing duty.

pro forma
When coupled with the title of another document (pro forma invoice, pro forma manifest), it means an informal document presented in advance of the arrival or preparation of the required document in order to satisfy a requirement, usually a customs requirement.

pro forma invoice
An invoice provided by a supplier prior to a sale or shipment of merchandise, informing the buyer of the kinds and quantities of goods to be sent, their value, and important specifications (weight, size, and similar characteristics). A pro forma invoice is used: (1) as a preliminary invoice together with a quotation; (2) for customs purposes in connection with shipments of samples, advertising material, etc.
(U.S. Customs) An invoice provided by the importer in lieu of a commercial invoice when a commercial invoice is not available at the time of

merchandise entry. In such cases the importer must present a bond to Customs guaranteeing production of the required commercial invoice not later than 120 days from the date of entry. If the invoice is needed by Customs for statistical purposes, it must generally be produced within 50 days from the date the entry summary is required to be filed.

If the required commercial invoice is not presented to Customs before the expiration of the 120-day period, the importer incurs a liability under his bond for failure to file.

See also invoice; commercial invoice; entry; bond.

project license
(U.S.) A license which authorizes large-scale exports of a wide variety of commodities and technical data for specified activities. Those activities can include capital expansion, maintenance, repair or operating supplies, or the supply of materials to be used in the production of other commodities for sale. *See* Bureau of Export Administration.

promissory note
(banking) (a) Any written promise to pay. (b) A negotiable instrument that is evidence of a debt contracted by a borrower from a creditor, known as a lender of funds. If the instrument does not have all the qualities of a negotiable instrument, it cannot legally be transferred. *See* negotiable instrument.

promoter of corporation
(law) Individual or entity that organizes a corporation.

promotional rate
(shipping) A rate applying to traffic under special conditions and usually confined to movement between a limited number of cities. Early rates on fresh farm produce which helped develop increased air freight volumes from the West Coast to eastern cities are examples of promotional rates. *See* special rates.

proof of delivery
(shipping) Information provided to payor containing name of person who signed for the package with the date and time of delivery.

Proprietary Limited (Pty. Ltd.)
(Australia, South Africa) Designation for a private limited liability corporation with limited liability to shareholders.

proprietor
(law) A person who has an exclusive right or interest in property or in a business.

proprietorship
(law) A business owned by one person. The individual owner has all the rights to profits from the business as well as all the liabilities and losses. Synonymous with "individual proprietorship."

protectionism
(economics) The deliberate use or encouragement of restrictions on imports to enable relatively inefficient domestic producers to compete successfully with foreign producers.

protective order
(U.S. Customs) With regard to antidumping cases, a term for the order under which most business proprietary information is made available to an attorney or other representative of a party to the proceeding. *See* dumping.

protective service
(shipping) Many airlines offer a protective service where shippers can arrange to have their shipments under carrier surveillance at each stage of transit from origin to destination. This service can be extended to pickup and delivery. Shippers can also arrange for armed guard protection. There is usually an extra charge for various levels of protective service. *See* signature service.

protective tariff
(customs/economics) A duty or tax imposed on imported products for the purpose of making them more expensive in comparison to domestic products, thereby giving the domestic products a price advantage. *See* tariff.

protest
(U.S. Customs) The means by which an importer, consignee, or other designated party may challenge decisions, (usually regarding the duitable status of imported goods) made by a District Director of Customs. The importer files a protest and an application for further review on Customs Form 19 within 90 days after liquidation. If the Customs Service denies a protest, an importer has the right to litigate the matter by filing a summons with the U.S. Court of International Trade within 180 days after denial of the protest. The rules of the court and other applicable statutes and precedents determine the course of Customs litigation.

While the Customs ascertainment of duitable status is final for most purposes at the time of liquidation, a liquidation is not final until any protest which has been filed against it has been decided. Similarly, the administrative decision issued on a protest is not final until any litigation filed against it has become final.

Entries must be liquidated within one year of the date of entry unless the liquidation needs to be extended for another one-ycar period not to exceed a total of four years from the date of entry. The Customs Service will suspend liquidation of an entry when required by statute or court order. A suspension will remain in effect until the issue is resolved. Notifications of extensions and suspensions are given to importers, surety companies and customs brokers who are parties to the transaction. *See* entry; liquidation.

(banking) Legal procedure noting the refusal of the drawee to accept a bill of exchange (protest for non-acceptance) or to pay it (protest for non-payment). Essential in order to preserve the right of recourse on the endorser.

protest system

(U.S. Customs) A part of U.S. Customs' Automated Commercial System, tracks protests from the date they are received through final action. *See* Automated Commercial System.

protocol

(diplomacy) (a) A preliminary document or memorandum signed by diplomatic or commercial negotiators which is used as a basis for final negotiations, agreements conventions or treaties. (b) The etiquette and ranking of diplomatic personnel.

(U.S.) U.S. diplomatic ranking is as follows: (1) Ambassadors-at-large have a higher rank than a regular Ambassador and are higher ranked on protocol than, say, the head of the C.I.A.; (2) The Deputy Chief of Mission, almost always a career officer, has the personal rank of Minister which is one rank down from Ambassador; (3) The rank of Minister-Counselor is just a little step below Minister; (4) The Chargé d'Affaires may either be acting, or indefinite, and is regarded as the acting Ambassador when the Ambassador is out of the country or when, for political reasons, an Ambassador is not appointed to a country; (5) An Attaché may be either fairly high or fairly low; in terms of rank an Attaché can be anything; a Military Attaché is of at least medium rank, but the military hold no diplomatic rank; (6) A consulate is not a diplomatic mission, nor is it autonomous; it is established by an international organization (such as U.S. Mission to the European Communities (USEC) or NATO) or is used for reasons of diplomatic snobbery or pique.

Protocol of Provisional Application

(GATT/WTO) A legal device that enabled the original contracting parties to accept General Agreement on Tariffs and Trade (GATT) obligations and benefits, despite the fact that some of their existing domestic legislation at that time discriminated

against imports in a manner that was inconsistent with certain GATT provisions. Although meant to be "temporary," the Protocol has remained in effect; and countries that signed the PPA in 1947 continue to invoke it to defend certain practices that are otherwise inconsistent with their GATT/WTO obligations. Countries that acceded to the GATT/WTO after 1947 have also done so under the terms of the Protocol. *See* General Agreement on Tariffs and Trade, World Trade Organization (WTO).

publication

(law) (a) Offering or distributing information or materials to the public generally. (b) Communicating defamatory information to a third person.

public corporation

(law) (a) A business corporation with shares traded among the general public, such as through a stock exchange. (b) A corporation created by a government to administer its operations. *See* corporation; close corporation; private corporation.

Public Limited Company (PLC)

(United Kingdom) Designation for a public corporation with limited liability to shareholders.

published rate

(shipping) The charges for a particular class of cargo as published in a carrier's tariff.

pula

The currency of Botswana. 1P=100 thebe.

purchase order

A purchaser's written offer to a supplier formally stating all terms and conditions of a proposed transaction.

purchase price

(U.S. Customs) A statutory term used in dumping investigations to refer to the United States sales price of merchandise which is sold or likely to be sold prior to the date of importation, by the producer or reseller of the merchandise for exportation to the United States. Certain statutory adjustments (e.g., import duties, commissions, freight) are made, if appropriate, to permit a meaningful comparison with the foreign market value of such or similar merchandise. *See* dumping.

purchaser

(U.S.) Within the context of export controls, the purchaser is that person abroad who has entered into the export transaction with the applicant to purchase the commodities or technical data for delivery to the ultimate consignee.

purchasing agent
(law) An agent who purchases goods in his/her own country on behalf of foreign buyers such as government agencies and private businesses. *See* agent; agency.

pure market economy
(economics) A competitive economic system of numerous buyers and sellers, where prices are determined by the free interaction of supply and demand.

put
(banking/finance) A right to redeem a debt instrument before maturity at par under specific circumstances outlined in the original agreement. *See* option; put option; call; call option.

put option
(banking/finance) A contract which entitles one party, at his option, to sell a specified amount of a commodity, security or foreign exchange to another party, at the price fixed in the contract, during the life of the contract. *See* option; call option; American Option; European Option.

quadrilateral meetings
Meetings involving trade ministers from the U.S., the European Community, Canada, and Japan to discuss trade policy matters.

quantitative restrictions (QRs)
(customs) Explicit limits, or quotas, on the physical amounts of particular commodities that can be imported or exported during a specified time period, usually measured by volume but sometimes by value. The quota may be applied on a "selective" basis, with varying limits set according to the country of origin, or on a quantitative global basis that only specifies the total limit and thus tends to benefit more efficient suppliers. Quotas are frequently ministered through a system of licensing.

(WTO) The World Trade Organization (WTO) generally prohibits the use of quantitative restrictions, except under conditions specified by other WTO articles.

See quotas; General Agreement on Tariffs and Trade (GATT) , World Trade Organization (WTO).

quarantine
(shipping) (a) The term during which an arriving ship or airplane, including its passengers, crew and cargo, suspected of carrying a contagious disease, is held in isolation to prevent the possible spread of the disease. (b) The place where a ship, airplane, individual or cargo is detained during quarantine.

quay
(shipping) A structure built for the purpose of mooring a vessel. Also called a pier.

quetzal
The currency of Guatemala. 1Q=100 centavos.

queue
(a) A line or group of people waiting for service, such as a line of people waiting in a teller line at a bank. (b) Paperwork in a stack waiting for processing. (c) Items on a waiting list waiting for processing or repair.

quid pro quo
(law/business) "Something for something" (Latin). A mutual consideration; securing an advantage or receiving a concession in return for a similar favor.

quota
(customs) A limitation on the quantity of goods that may be imported into a country from all countries or from specific countries during a set period of time.
(a) **Absolute quotas** permit a limited number of units of specified merchandise to be entered or withdrawn for consumption in a country during specified periods.
(b) **Tariff-rate quotas** permit a specified quantity of merchandise to be entered or withdrawn in a country at a reduced rate during a specified period.
(U.S. Customs) In the United States, quotas are established by Presidential Proclamations, Executive Orders, or other legislation. *See also* quantitative restrictions; quota system; visa.

quota system
(U.S. Customs) A part of the U.S. Customs' Service Automated Commercial System, controls quota levels (quantities authorized) and quantities entered against those levels. Visas control exports from the country of origin. Visa authorizations are received from other countries and quantities entered against those visas are transmitted back to them. Control of visas and quotas simplify reconciliation of other countries' exports and U.S. imports.
See Automated Commercial System; visa.

quotation
(foreign exchange) The price quotation of a currency can be made either directly or indirectly. (a) The **direct quotation** gives the equivalent of a certain amount of foreign currency (normally in units of 100 or 1) in domestic currency. (b) In an **indirect price quotation** (less common) the domestic currency is valued in units of foreign currency.

R

radioactive materials
(shipping) Degree of hazard will vary depending on type and quantity of material. (UN CLASS 7.) Examples are thorium 232, carbon 14 and radium 226. Hazards/precautions are: avoid touching broken or damaged radioactive items; persons handling damaged items must wear rubber or plastic gloves; damaged items will be monitored and safely packaged under the surveillance of the radiological monitor; and persons having come in direct contact with damaged or broken radioactive items must move away from the spill site (but stay in the area) to be monitored and decontaminated.

rail waybill
(shipping) Freight document that indicates goods have been received for shipment by rail. A duplicate is given to the shipper as a receipt for acceptance of the goods (also called duplicate waybill). *See* bill of lading.

rand
The currency of:
Namibia, 1R=100 cents.
South Africa, 1R=100 cents;

rate of exchange
(banking/foreign exchange) The amount of funds of one nation that can be bought, at a specific date, for a sum of currency of another country. Rates fluctuate often because of economic, political and other forces. *See* foreign exchange.

realignment
(foreign exchange) Simultaneous and mutually coordinated re- and devaluation of the currencies of several countries. The concept was first used in 1971 for the exchange rate corrections made in a number of countries within the framework of the Smithsonian Agreement. Since then, it has mainly been used to describe the exchange rate corrections within the European Monetary System.

real rights
(law) Rights in real estate or in items attached to real estate.

reasonable person standard
(law) A legal test that is used to determine whether a person is liable for damages. It is based on a comparison of the person's conduct with the actions or

conduct expected of a reasonable person of the same characteristics in similar circumstances.

receipt
(law) Any written acknowledgment of value received.

received for shipment bill of lading
(shipping) A bill of lading which confirms the receipt of goods by the carrier, but not their actual loading on board. *See* bill of lading.

(banking/letters of credit) A received for shipment bill of lading can be accepted under letters of credit only if this is expressly permitted in the letter of credit, or if the credit stipulates a document covering multimodal transport. Otherwise, "received for shipment" bills of lading must show an additional "On board" notation in order to be accepted as an ocean bill of lading. *See* bill of lading; ocean bill of lading.

receiving papers
(shipping) Paperwork that accompanies a shipment when it is brought to the dock. Usual information listed is name and address of shipper, number of pieces, commodity, weight, consignee, booking number and any special requirements, such as label cargo or temperature control.

reciprocal defense procurement memoranda of understanding
(NATO/USA) Reciprocal memoranda of understanding (MOU) are broad bilateral umbrella MOUs that seek to reduce trade barriers on defense procurement. They usually call for the waiver of "buy national" restrictions, customs and duties to allow the contractors of the signatories to participate, on a competitive basis, in the defense procurement of the other country. These agreements were designed in the late 1970's to promote rationalization, standardization, and interoperability of defense equipment within NATO. At that time, the MOUs were also intended to reduce the large defense trade advantage the United States possessed over the European allies. The first agreements were signed in 1978. *See* memorandum of understanding.

reciprocal trade agreement
(trade) An international agreement between two or more countries to establish mutual trade concessions that are expected to be of equal value.

reciprocity
(general) The mutual exchange of priviledges or benefits. Also called "mutuality of benefits," "quid pro quo," and "equivalence of advantages."

(international trade) The practice by which governments extend similar concessions to each other, as when one government lowers its tariffs or other barriers (non-tariff barriers) impeding its imports in exchange for equivalent concessions from a trading partner on barriers affecting its exports (a "balance of concessions"). Reciprocity has traditionally been a principal objective of negotiators in the World Trade Organization (WTO) "Rounds."

In practice, this principle applies only in negotiations between developed countries. Because of the frequently wide disparity in their economic capacities and potential, the relationship between developed and developing countries is generally not one of equivalence.

The concept of "relative reciprocity" has emerged to characterize the practice by developed countries to seek less than full reciprocity from developing countries in trade negotiations.

reconsignment
(shipping) A change in the name of the consignor or consignee; a change in the place of delivery; a change in the destination point; or relinquishment of shipment at point of origin.

recourse
(banking) Right of claim against the joint and several guarantors (e.g., endorsers, drawers) of a bill of exchange or cheque. *See* protest; bill of exchange.

red clause (letter of credit)
(banking) A special clause included in a documentary letter of credit which allows the seller to obtain an advance on an unsecured basis from the correspondent bank to finance the manufacture or purchase of goods to be delivered under the documentary letter of credit. Liability is assumed by the issuing bank rather than the corresponding bank. It is called red clause because red ink used to be used to draw attention to the clause. *See* letter of credit.

redeliver
(U.S. Customs) A demand by the U.S. Customs Service to return previously released merchandise to Customs custody for reexamination, reexport or destruction.

reefer container
(shipping) A controlled temperature shipping container (usually refrigerated).

reexport
(general) The export of imported goods without added value.

(U.S.) For U.S. export control purposes: the shipment of U.S. origin products from one foreign destination to another.

For U.S. statistical reporting purposes: exports of foreign-origin merchandise which have previously entered the United States for consumption or into Customs bonded warehouses for U.S. Foreign Trade Zones.

R

refund

(shipping) An amount returned to the consignor or consignee as a result of the carrier having collected charges in excess of the originally agreed upon, or legally applicable, charges.

(customs) Refund of import duties. *See* drawback.

reimbursing bank

(banking) The bank named in a documentary credit (letter of credit) from which the paying, accepting or negotiating bank may request cover after receipt of the documents in compliance with the documentary credit. The reimbursing bank is often, but not always, the issuing bank. If the reimbursing bank is not the issuing bank, it does not have a commitment to pay unless it has confirmed the reimbursement instruction. The issuing bank is not released from its commitment to pay through the nomination of a reimbursing bank. If cover from the reimbursing bank should not arrive in time, the issuing bank is obliged to pay (also any accrued interest on arrears).

rejected merchandise drawback

See drawback.

relative reciprocity

See reciprocity.

relay

(shipping) A shipment that is transferred to its ultimate destination port after having been shipped to an intermediate point.

relief from liability

(U.S. Customs) In cases where articles imported under temporary importation under bond (TIB), relief from liability under bond may be obtained in any case in which the articles are destroyed under Customs supervision, in lieu of exportation, within the original bond period. However, in the case of articles imported solely for testing or experimentation, destruction need not be under Customs supervision where articles are destroyed during the course of experiments or tests during the bond period or any lawful extension, but satisfactory proof of destruction shall be furnished to the district or port director with whom the customs entry was filed. *See* temporary importation under bond; drawback; in bond.

remittance

(banking) Funds forwarded from one person to another as payment for bought items or services.

remittance following collection

(shipping) In instances when the shipper has performed services incident to the transportation of goods a carrier will collect payment for these services from the receiver and remit such payment to the shipper. Carriers charge nominal fees for this service.

remitter

(banking) In a documentary collection, an alternate name given to the seller who forwards documents to the buyer through banks. *See* documentary collection.

remitting

(banking) Paying, as in remitting a payment; also canceling, as in remitting a debt.

remitting bank

(banking) In a documentary collection, a bank which acts as an intermediary, forwarding the remitter's documents to, and payments from the collecting bank. *See* documentary collection.

renminbi (RMB)

(People's Republic of China) Literally "people's currency." The official currency of China, issued by the Central Bank of China. As of January 1, 1994, China's dual currency system of RMB and FEC (Foreign Exchange Certificate) was united in a step toward making the RMB more freely convertible and bringing its exchange rate closer to market value.

replevin

(law) A legal action for recovering property brought by the owner or party entitled to repossess the property against a party who has wrongfully kept it. A seller that furnishes products to a sales representative on consignment, for example, may sue for replevin if the sales representative wrongfully retains products not sold at the end of the term of the consignment agreement.

request for quotation (RFQ)

A negotiating approach whereby the buyer asks for a price quotation from a potential seller/suppler for specific quantities of goods (or services) to specifications the buyer establishes in the request for quotation letter.

requirement contract

(law) An agreement by which a seller promises to supply all of the specified goods or services that a buyer needs over a certain time and at a fixed price, and the buyer agrees to purchase such goods or services exclusively from the seller during that time.

rescind

(law) To cancel a contract. A contract may, for example, give one party a right to rescind if the other party fails to perform within a reasonable time.

rescission

See rescind.

reserved freight space

(shipping) A service by some airlines enabling shippers to reserve freight space on designated flights. *See* priority air freight.

residual restrictions

(GATT/WTO) Quantitative restrictions that have been maintained by governments before they became contracting parties to the General Agreement on Tariffs and Trade (GATT) and the World Trade Organization (WTO) and, hence, permissible under the GATT/WTO "grandfather clause." Most of the residual restrictions still in effect are maintained by developed countries against the imports of agricultural products. *See* grandfather clause; General Agreement on Tariffs and Trade, World Trade Organization (WTO).

restitution

(law) A legal remedy for a breach of contract by which the parties are restored to their original positions before the contract was made or the breach occurred. Damages are distinguished from restitution in that damages compensate for a party who has suffered a loss. If a buyer, for example, partially pays for merchandise in advance and the seller delivers merchandise that fails to meet the buyer's specifications, the buyer may file a legal action seeking restitution, that is, a return of the advance payment to the buyer and of the goods to the seller. Alternatively, the buyer may accept the goods and may sue for damages in the amount by which the worth of the goods is less than the original contract price.

restricted articles

(shipping) An airline term meaning a hazardous material as defined by Title 49, Code of Federal Regulations (U.S.) and Air Transport Restricted Articles Circular 6-D. Restricted articles may be transported domestically and be classified dangerous goods when transported internationally by air. *See* dangerous goods; hazardous material.

restricted letter of credit

(banking) A letter of credit, the negotiation of which is restricted to a bank specially mentioned. *See* letter of credit.

restrictive business practices

(economics) Actions in the private sector, such as collusion among the largest suppliers, designed to restrict competition so as to keep prices relatively high.

restrictive endorsement

See endorsement.

retaliation

Action taken by a country to restrain its imports from a country that has increased a tariff or imposed other measures that adversely affect its exports.

(WTO) The World Trade Organization, in certain circumstances, permits retaliation, although this has very rarely been practiced. The value of trade affected by such retaliatory measures should in theory, approximately equal the value affected by the initial import restriction.

retaliatory duty

See retaliation.

returned without action

(U.S.) For export control purposes, the return of an export license application without action because the application is incomplete, additional information is required, or the product is eligible for a general license. *See* Bureau of Export Administration; general license.

revaluation

(economics) The increase of the value (restoration) of a nation's currency (that had once been devalued) in terms of the currency of another nation.

reverse preferences

Tariff advantages once offered by developing countries to imports from certain developed countries that granted them preferences. Reverse preferences characterized trading arrangements between the European Community and some developing countries prior to the advent of the Generalized System of Preferences (GSP) and the signing of the Lome Convention.

reverse swap

(banking/trade) A swap which offsets the interest rate or currency exposure on an existing swap. It can be written with the original counterparty or with a new counterparty. In either case, it is typically executed to realize capital gains.

Revised American Foreign Trade Definitions

A set of foreign trade terms which are considered obsolete, but still sometimes used in domestic U.S. trade. The most widely accepted international trade terms are Incoterms 2000. *See* Incoterms 2000.

revocable letter of credit

(banking) A letter of credit which can be cancelled or altered by the drawee (buyer) after it has been issued by the drawee's bank. Due to the low level of security of this type of credit, they are extremely rare in practice. *See* letter of credit.

revocation of antidumping duty order & termination of suspended investigation

(U.S. Customs) An antidumping duty order may be revoked or a suspended investigation may be terminated upon application from a party to the proceeding. Ordinarily the application is considered only if there have been no sales at less than fair value for at least the two most recent years. However, the Department of Commerce may on its own initiative revoke an antidumping duty order or terminate a suspended investigation if there have not been sales at less than fair value for a period of 3 years. *See* dumping.

revolving letter of credit

(banking) A letter of credit which is automatically restored to its full amount after the completion of each documentary exchange.

The number of utilizations and the period of time within which these must take place are specified in the documentary letter of credit. The revolving letter of credit is used when a purchaser wishes to have certain partial quantities of the ordered goods delivered at specified intervals (multiple delivery contract) and when multiple documents are presented for this purpose. Such credit may be cumulative or non-cumulative. *See* letter of credit.

rial

The currency of:
Iran, 1Rl=100 dinars;
Oman, 1RO=1,000 baiza;
Yemen, 1YR=100 fils.

riel

The currency of Kampuchea. 1CR=100 sen.

ringgit

The currency of Malaysia. 1M$=100 sen.

risk position

(banking/finance/foreign exchange) An asset or liability, which is exposed to fluctuations in value through changes in exchange rates or interest rates.

riyal

The currency of:
Qatar, 1QR=100 dirhams;
Saudi Arabia, 1SR=100 halala.

road waybill

(shipping) Transport document that indicates goods have been received for shipment by road haulage carrier. *See* bill of lading.

rollback

(GATT) Refers to an agreement among Uruguay Round participants to dismantle all trade-restrictive or distorting measures that are inconsistent with the provisions of the General Agreement on Tariffs and Trade (GATT). Measures subject to rollback would be phased out or brought into conformity within an agreed timeframe, no later than by the formal completion of the negotiations. The rollback agreement is accompanied by a commitment to "standstill" on existing trade-restrictive measures. Rollback is also used as a reference to the imposition of quantitative restrictions at levels less than those occurring in the present.

See standstill; General Agreement on Tariffs and Trade; rounds; Tokyo Round; Uruguay Round.

roll-on, roll-off (RoRo)

(shipping) A broad category of ships designed to load and discharge cargo which rolls on wheels. Broadly interpreted, this may include train ships, trailer ships, auto, truck and trailer ferries, and ships designed to carry military vehicles.

rollover

(finance/foreign exchange) (a) Extension of a maturing financial instrument, such as a loan or certificate of deposit. (b) Extension of a maturing foreign exchange operation through the conclusion of a swap agreement (e.g., tom/next swap). (c) Variability of an interest rate according to the appropriate, currently prevailing rates on the Euromarket (normally LIBOR) for a medium-term loan.

rollover credit

(banking) Any line of credit that can be borrowed against up to a stated credit limit and into which repayments go for crediting. *See* letter of credit.

rouble

The currency of Russia and throughout the Commonwealth of Independent States. 1R=100 kopecks.

rounds (of trade negotiations)

(GATT/WTO) Cycles of multilateral trade negotiations under the General Agreement on Tariffs and Trade (GATT) and the successor World Trade Organization (WTO), culminating in simultaneous agreements among participating countries to reduce tariff and non-tariff trade barriers.

1st Round: 1947, Geneva (creation of the GATT);

2nd Round: 1949, Annecy, France (tariff reduction);

3rd Round: 1951, Torquay, England (accession & tariff reduction);

4th Round: 1956, Geneva (accession and tariff reduction);

5th Round: 1960-62, Geneva ("Dillon" Round; revision of GATT; addition of more countries);

6th Round: 1964-67, Geneva ("Kennedy" Round);

7th Round: 1973-79, Geneva ("Tokyo" Round);
8th Round: 1986-93, Geneva ("Uruguay" Round).
See General Agreement on Tariffs and Trade; Tokyo
Round; Uruguay Round, World Trade Organization.

route

(shipping) (a) The course or direction that a shipment moves. (b) To designate the course or direction a shipment shall move.

royalty

(law) Compensation for the use of a person's property
based on an agreed percentage of the income arising
from its use (e.g., to an author on sale of his book, to a
manufacturer for use of his machinery in the factory
of another person, to a composer or performer, etc.). A
royalty is a payment, lease or similar right, while a residual payment is often made on properties that have
not been patented or are not patentable.

rufiyaa

The currency of Maldives. 1Rf=100 larees.

rulings on imports

(U.S. Customs) An exporter, importer, or other interested party may get advance information on any matter affecting the dutiable status of merchandise by
writing the District Director of Customs where the
merchandise will be entered, or to the Regional Commissioner of Customs, New York Region, New York,
NY 10048 USA, or to the U.S. Customs Service, Office of Regulations and Rulings, Washington, DC
20229 USA. Detailed information on the procedures
applicable to decisions on prospective importations is
given in 19 Code of Federal Regulations part 177.
Tip: Do not depend on a small "trial" or "test" import shipments since there is no guarantee that the
next shipment will receive the same tariff treatment. Small importations may slip by, particularly
if they are processed under informal procedures
which apply to small shipments or in circumstances
warranting application of a flat rate.

rupee

The currency of:
India, 1Re=100 paise;
Mauritius, 1MauRe=100 cents;
Nepal, 1NRe=100 paise;
Pakistan, 1PRe=100 paisas;
Seychelles, 1Re=100 cents;
Sri Lanka, 1R=100 cents.

rupiah

The currency of Indonesia. 1Rp=100 sen.

safeguards

(WTO) The World Trade Organization (WTO) permits two forms of multilateral safeguards: (1) a
country's right to impose temporary import controls or other trade restrictions to prevent commercial injury to domestic industry, and (2) the
corresponding right of exporters not to be deprived
arbitrarily of access to markets.
Article XIX permits a country whose domestic industries or workers are adversely affected by increased imports to withdraw or modify concessions
the country had earlier granted, to impose, for a
limited period, new import restrictions if the country can establish that a product is "being imported
in such increased quantities as to cause or threaten
serious injury to domestic producers," and to keep
such restrictions in effect for such time as may be
necessary to prevent or remedy such injury. *See*
General Agreement on Tariffs and Trade, World
Trade Organization.

said to contain (s.t.c.); said to weigh (s.t.w.); shipper's load and count

(shipping) Clauses in transport documents which
exclude liability of the carrier for the consistency of
the description of the goods or the weight of the
goods actually loaded, e.g., goods in containers.
This provides protection to the carrier against
claims by the consignee.

sales agreement

(law) A written document by which a seller agrees
to convey property to a buyer for a stipulated price
under specified conditions. *See also* contract.

sales representative

An agent who distributes, represents, services, or
sells goods on behalf of sellers. *See also* agent;
agency.

sales tax

A tax placed by a state or municipality on items at
the time of their purchase. It may be a tax on the
sale of an item every time it changes hands (value
added tax, VAT), or only upon its transfer of ownership at one specific time.
In the case of a VAT, the sales of manufacturers are
taxed when the items are considered to be completed goods; the sales of wholesalers are taxed
when their goods are sold to retailers; and retail

sales are taxed when the goods are purchased by consumers. *See* value added tax.

salvage

(insurance) (a) Compensation paid for the rescue of a ship, its cargo or passengers from a loss at sea, (b) The act of saving a ship or its cargo from possible loss, (c) Property saved from a wreck or fire.

salvage loss

(insurance) A method of insurance adjustment where the underwriter pays the difference between the amount of insurance and the net proceeds of the sale of damaged goods. It is sometimes incorrectly assumed that when damaged goods are sold to determine the extent of loss, the underwriter is obligated to pay the difference between the amount of insurance and the net proceeds of the sale. The salvage loss method is regularly used only if goods are justifiably sold short of destination.

samurai bond

(banking/finance) Bond issued on the Japanese market in yen outside Japan.

sanction

(economics) An embargo imposed against an individual country by the United Nations—or a group of nations—in an effort to influence its conduct or its policies. *See also* embargo.

sanitary certificate

A document attesting to the absence of disease or pests in a shipment of animal or plant products, especially foodstuffs. *See* phytosanitary inspection certificate.

Saudi Arabian Standards Organization

(Saudi Arabia) SASO was established in April 1972 as the sole Saudi Arabian government organization to promulgate standards and measurements in the kingdom. Primarily, SASO promulgates standards for electrical equipment and some food products. Some of these standards have been adopted by the Gulf Cooperation Council. *See also* International Standards Organization.

schilling

The currency of:
Austria, 1S=100 groschen.

SDR

See special drawing rights.

seal

(law) A mark or sign that is used to witness and authenticate the signing of an instrument, contract, or other document. A corporation, for example, uses a seal to authenticate its contracts and records of its corporate acts.

(shipping) A small metal strip and lead fastener used for fastening or locking the doors of a container, which is usually numbered and which provides proof that a container has not been opened since the seal was applied.

sea waybill

(banking) A transport document which is not a document of title/negotiable document. The sea waybill indicates the "on board" loading of the goods and can be used in cases where no ocean bill of lading, i.e. no document of title is required. For receipt of the goods, presentation of the sea waybill by the consignee named therein is not required, which can speed up processing at the port of destination. *See* bill of lading; ocean bill of lading.

seaworthiness

(shipping) The fitness or safety of a vessel for its intended use.

Section 201

(U.S.) Section 201, the "escape clause" provision of the Trade Act of 1974, permits temporary import relief, not to exceed a maximum of eight years, to a domestic industry which is seriously injured, or threatened with serious injury, due to increased imports. Import relief, granted at the President's discretion, generally takes the form of increased tariffs or quantitative restrictions. To be eligible for section 201 relief, the International Trade Commission (ITC) must determine that: (1) the industry has been seriously injured or threatened to be injured and (2) imports have been a substantial cause (not less than any other cause) of that injury. Industries need not prove that an unfair trade practice exists, as is necessary under the antidumping and countervailing duty laws. However, under section 201, a greater degree of injury—"serious" injury— must be found to exist, and imports must be a "substantial" cause (defined as not less than any other cause) of that injury.

If the ITC finding is affirmative, the President's remedy may be a tariff increase, quantitative restrictions, or orderly marketing agreements. At the conclusion of any relief action, the Commission must report on the effectiveness of the relief action in facilitating the positive adjustment of the domestic industry to import competition. If the decision is made not to grant relief, the President must provide an explanation to the Congress. *See* escape clause; unfair trade advantage; orderly marketing agreements; adjustment assistance; International Trade

S

Administration. *See also* quantitative restrictions; International Trade Commission.

Section 232

(U.S.) Under Section 232 of the Trade Expansion Act of 1962, as amended, the U.S. Department of Commerce determines whether articles are being imported into the U.S. in quantities or circumstances that threaten national security. Based on the investigation report, the President can adjust imports of the article(s) in question.

The U.S. Department of Commerce must report on the effects these imports have on national security and make recommendations for action or inaction within 270 days after starting an investigation. Within 90 days of the report, the President decides whether to take action to adjust imports on the basis of national security. The President must notify Congress of his decision within 30 days.

Section 301

(U.S.) Under Section 301 of the Trade Act of 1974, firms can complain about a foreign country's trade policies or practices that are harmful to U.S. commerce. The section empowers the United States Trade Representative (USTR) to investigate the allegations and to negotiate the removal of any trade barriers. The section requires that the World Trade Organization (WTO) dispute resolution process be invoked where applicable and, if negotiations fail, to retaliate within 180 days from the date that discovery of a trade agreement violation took place.

This provision enables the President to withdraw concessions or restrict imports from countries that discriminate against U.S. exports, subsidize their own exports to the United States, or engage in other unjustifiable or unreasonable practices that burden or discriminate against U.S. trade. *See* Super 301; Special 301.

Section 337

(U.S.) Section 337 of the Tariff Act of 1930 requires investigations of unfair practices in import trade. Under this authority, the International Trade Commission (ITA) applies U.S. statutory and common law of unfair competition to the importation of products into the United States and their sale. Section 337 prohibits unfair competition and unfair importing practices and sales of products in the U.S., when these threaten to: (1) destroy or substantially injure a domestic industry, (2) prevent the establishment of such an industry, or (3) restrain or monopolize U.S. trade and commerce. Section 337 also prohibits infringement of U.S. patents, copyrights or registered trademarks.

secured

(law/banking) Guaranteed as to payment by the pledge of something valuable.

security

(general) Property pledged as collateral.
(investments) Stocks and bonds placed by a debtor with a creditor, with authority to sell for the creditor's account if the debt is not paid.
(law) (a) Any evidence of debt or right to a property. (b) An individual who agrees to make good the failure of another to pay.

seizure

(law) The act of taking possession of property.

self-insurance

(insurance) A system whereby a firm or individual, by setting aside an amount of monies, provides for the occurrence of losses that would ordinarily be covered under an insurance program. The monies that would normally be used for premium payments are added to this special fund for payment of losses incurred.

seller's market

Exists when goods cannot easily be secured and when the economic forces of business tend to cause goods to be priced at the vendor's estimate of value.

selling, general and administrative (expenses)

(U.S. Customs) In establishing valuation of an import shipment, the sum of:
(1) General and administrative expenses (such as: salaries of non-sales personnel, rent, heat, and light);
(2) Direct selling expenses (that is, expenses that can be directly tied to the sale of a specific unit, such as: credit, warranty, and advertising expenses); and
(3) Indirect selling expenses (that is, expenses which cannot be directly tied to the sale of a specific unit but which are proportionally allocated to all units sold during a certain period, such as: telephone, interest, and postal charges).
See valuation.

selling rate

(banking/foreign exchange) Rate at which a bank is willing to sell foreign exchange or to lend money.

Semiconductor Trade Arrangement

The U.S.-Japan Semiconductor Trade Arrangement is a bilateral agreement which came into effect on August 1, 1991, replacing the prior 1986 Semiconductor Trade Arrangement. The new Arrangement contains provisions to: (1) increase foreign access to the Japanese semiconductor market; and (2) deter dumping of semiconductors by Japanese suppliers into the U.S. market, as well as in third country markets. In evaluating market access improvement, both governments agreed to pay particular attention to market share. The expectation of a 20 percent foreign market share by the end of 1992 is included in the Arrangement. The Arrangement explicitly states, however, that the 20 percent figure is not a guarantee, a ceiling, or a floor on the foreign market share.

senior commercial officer (SCO)
(U.S. diplomacy) The SCO is the senior U.S. and Foreign Commercial Officer at an embassy and reports in-country to the Ambassador. At major posts, this position carries the title of Commercial Counselor; in key posts, Minister Counselor. Usually reporting to the SCO are a Commercial Attaché and Commercial Officers. The latter are sometimes assigned to subordinate posts throughout the country.

sequestration
See attachment.

service a loan
(banking) To pay interest due on a loan.

service commitments
(shipping) Pickup and/or delivery commitments agreed to by carrier and shipper.

service mark
(law) A mark used in sales or advertising to identify a service offered by an individual or legal entity and to distinguish that service from services offered by others. A service mark is distinguished from a trademark in that the former identifies services, while the later identifies goods. Protection for service marks varies from country to country, and may not be available in some jurisdictions. Service marks are often, but not necessarily, regulated by the same laws that govern trademarks. A country that is a member the Paris Convention for the Protection of Industrial Property may recognize service marks held in other jurisdictions. *See* trademark; patent; Paris Convention; World Intellectual Property Organization.

services
(economics) Economic activities—such as transportation, banking, insurance, tourism, space launching telecommunications, advertising, entertainment, data processing, consulting and the licensing of intellectual property—that are usually of an intangible character and often consumed as they are produced. Service industries have become increasingly important since the 1920s. Services now account for more than two-thirds of the economic activity of the United States and about 25 percent of world trade.

servitude
(law) A charge against or burden on property that benefits a person with an interest in another property. An owner of property may grant another person, for example, a right to travel over that property to reach adjoining land, in which case the owner has created a servitude against the property. *See* easement.

settlement date
(banking) The date on which payment for a transaction must be made.

severability clause
(law) A contract term that provides that each portion of the agreement is independent of the others, allowing a court to invalidate a clause of the contract without voiding the entire agreement.

shared foreign sales corporation
(U.S.) A foreign sales corporation consisting of more than one and less than 25 unrelated exporters. *See* foreign sales corporation.

shekel
The currency of Israel. 1IS=100 agorot.

shilling
The currency of:
Kenya, 1KSh=100 cents;
Somalia, 1 SoSh=100 cents;
Tanzania, 1 TSh=100 cents;
Uganda, 1USh=100 cents.

shipment
(shipping) Except as otherwise provided, cargo tendered by one shipper, on one bill of lading, from one point of departure, for one consignee, to one destination, at one time, via a single port of discharge.

shipment record
(shipping) A repository of information for each shipment that reflects all activity throughout each step of the shipment life cycle.

shipped on deck
(shipping) Annotation in a bill of lading stating that the goods have been shipped on the deck of a ship. *See* bill of lading.

shipper
(shipping) The company or person who ships cargo to the consignee.

S

shipper's export declaration

(shipping) Form required for all U.S. export shipments by mail valued at more than $500 and for non-mail shipments with declared value greater than $2,500. Also required for shipments requiring a U.S. Department of Commerce validated export license or U.S. Department of State license regardless of value of goods. Prepared by a shipper indicating the value, weight, destination, and other basic information about the shipment. The shipper's export declaration is used to control exports and compile trade statistics.

shipper's letter of instruction

(shipping) A form used by a shipper to authorize a carrier to issue a bill of lading or an air waybill on the shipper's behalf. The form contains all details of shipment and authorizes the carrier to sign the bill of lading in the name of the shipper. *See* bill of lading.

shipper's load and count

(shipping) A clause in, or notation on, a transport document noting that the contents of a container were loaded and counted by the shipper and not checked or verified by the carrier. Such a notation provides protection to the carrier against claims by the consignee.

shipping instructions

(shipping) Information supplied by the shipper/exporter providing detailed instructions pertaining to the shipment (e.g., shipper, consignee, bill-to party, commodity, pieces, weight, cube, etc.).

shipping order

(shipping) Instructions of shipper to carrier for forwarding of goods; usually the triplicate copy of the bill of lading.

shipping weight

(shipping) The total weight usually expressed in kilograms of shipments, including the weight of moisture content, wrappings, crates, boxes, and containers (other than cargo vans and similar substantial outer containers).

ship's manifest

(shipping) A list, signed by the captain of a ship, of the individual shipments constituting the ship's cargo. *See* manifest.

ship's papers

(shipping) The documents a ship must carry to meet the safety, health, immigration, commercial and customs requirements of a port of call or of international law.

ship's stores

(shipping) The food, medical supplies, spare parts and other provisions carried for the day-to-day running of a vessel.

shogun bond

(finance) Non-resident bond issues denominated in foreign currencies on the Tokyo market. Started June 1985.

shortage

(shipping) A deficiency in quantity shipped.

short form bill of lading

(shipping) A bill of lading on which the detailed conditions of transportation are not listed in full. A deviation from a regular bill of lading (long form) since it only refers to the contract terms but fails to include them. *See* bill of lading.

short of exchange

(banking/foreign exchange) The position of a foreign exchange trader who has sold more foreign bills than the quantity of bills he or she has in possession to cover sales.

short supply

(U.S.) Commodities in short supply may be subject to export controls to protect the domestic economy from the excessive drain of scarce materials and to reduce the serious inflationary impact of satisfying foreign demand. Two commodities which the U.S. controls for short supply purposes are crude oil and unprocessed western red cedar.

short ton

(measure) A unit of mass or weight measurement equal to 2,000 pounds. A long ton is 2,240 pounds.

short weight

(shipping) Notation of a shipment's weight as less than that noted on the original bill of lading, indicating loss during shipment.

sight draft

(banking) A financial instrument payable upon presentation or demand. A bill of exchange may be made payable, for example, at sight or after sight, which means it is payable upon presentation or demand, or within a particular period after demand is made. *See* bill of exchange.

signature service

(shipping) A service designed to provide continuous responsibility for the custody of shipments in transit, so named because a signature is required from each person handling the shipment at each stage of its transit from origin to destination.

silent confirmation

(banking/letters of credit) In addition to the commitment of the issuing bank of a letter of credit, the advising bank can, by silent confirmation, enter into its own, independent commitment to pay or accept. In contrast to the confirmed letter of credit, in this case there is no confirmation instruction given by the issuing bank. Silent confirmations are thus purely agreements between the beneficiary and the "silently confirming" bank. In order to enforce its claim, the "silently confirming" bank requires the assignment of all the rights of the beneficiary under the letter of credit. *See* letter of credit.

similar merchandise

(U.S. Customs) For purposes of establishing the customs value of imported merchandise, similar merchandise is merchandise that is:

(1) Produced in the same country and by the same person as the merchandise being appraised,

(2) Like merchandise being appraised in characteristics and component materials,

(3) Commercially interchangeable with the merchandise being appraised.

If merchandise meeting all these criteria cannot be found, then similar merchandise is merchandise having the same country of production, like characteristics and component materials, and commercially interchangeability, but produced by a different person.

In determining whether goods are similar, some of the factors to be considered are the quality of the goods, their reputation, and existence of a trademark.

Exclusion: Similar merchandise does not include merchandise that incorporates or reflects engineering, development, artwork, design work, and plans and sketches provided free or at reduced cost by the buyer and undertaken in the United States.

See valuation; transaction value; computed value; identical merchandise.

Single European Act

The SEA, which entered into force in July 1987, provided the legal and procedural support for achievement of the single European Market by 1992. The SEA revised the European Economic Community (EEC) Treaty and, where not already provided for in the Treaty, majority decisions were introduced for numerous votes facing the Council of Ministers, particularly those affecting establishment of the single European Market and the European financial common market. The role of the European Parliament was strengthened; decisions on fiscal matters remained subject to unanimity.

Single Internal Market Information Service

SIMIS, run by the the the European Community Affairs Office under the United States International Trade Administration (ITA), is a clearinghouse for information on European Community activities. Contact: European Community Affairs Office, United States Department of Commerce, 14th and Constitution Ave. NW, Room 3036, Washington, DC 20230 USA; Tel: [1] (202) 482-5276.

SITC

See standard international trade classification.

sling

(shipping) A contrivance into which freight is placed to be hoisted into or out of a ship.

slip

(shipping) A vessel's berth between two piers.

Small Business Administration (SBA)

(U.S. government) An independent government organizations which acts as an advocate to small business, providing aid, counseling, assistance and protection. The SBA's Office of International Trade plans, develops and implements programs to encourage small business participation in international trade. The Office also coordinates the Administrations' International Trade Program with the Departments of Commerce and Agriculture, the Export-Import Bank of the United States, the Agency for International Development, and with other Federal and State agencies with private organizations concerned with international trade. Address: Small Business Administration, 1110 Vermont Ave. NW, 9th Floor, Washington, DC 20416 USA; Tel: [1] (202) 606-4000; http://www.sba.gov.

small package service

(shipping) A specialized service to guarantee the delivery of small parcels within specified express time limits, e.g., same day or next day. This traffic is subject to size and weight limitations. Air carriers that also transport passengers often accept these packages at airport ticket counters with delivery at destination baggage claim area. Many carriers provide door-to-door service on a 24-hour basis.

Smoot Hawley Tariff Act of 1930

(U.S.) The Tariff Act of 1930, also commonly known as the Smoot Hawley Tariff, was protectionist legislation that raised tariff rates on most articles

S

imported by the United States, triggering comparable tariff increases by U.S. trading partners.

smuggling

(customs) Conveying goods or persons, without permission, across the borders of a country or other political entities (e.g., cigarette smuggling across state lines).

snake system

(banking/foreign exchange) An international agreement between Belgium, The Netherlands, Luxembourg, Denmark, Sweden, Norway, and West Germany, linking the currencies of these countries together in an exchange system. The signatories have agreed to limit fluctuations in exchange rates among their currencies to 2.25 percent above or below set median rates. The snake was designed to be the first stage in forming a uniform Common Market currency. Members maintain fairly even exchange rates among themselves by buying or selling their currencies when the rates threaten to drop or rise beyond the 2.25 percent limits specified.

Sociedad Anónima (S.A.)

(Latin America, Mexico, Spain) Designation for a joint stock company with limited personal liability to shareholders.

Sociedad a Responsabilidad Limitada (S.R.L.)

(Latin America, Mexico, Spain) Designation for a private limited liability corporation with limited liability to shareholders.

Sociedad por Quota (S.Q.)

(Portugal) Designation for a private limited liability corporation with limited liability to shareholders. *See* Limitada.

Società a Garanzia Limitata (S.G.L.)

(Switzerland) Designation for a private limited liability corporation with limited liability to shareholders.

Società Cooperativa a Responsabilità (SCaRL)

(Italy, Switzerland) Designation for an incorporated association with limited liability for its members, unless its articles provide otherwise.

Società in Accomandita Semplice (S.A.S.)

(Italy) Designation for a limited partnership in which at least one of the partners has general liability and at least one of the other partners has limited liability.

Società per Azioni (S.p.A.)

(Italy) Designation for a joint stock company with limited personal liability to shareholders.

Société (Sté.)

(France, Luxembourg, Switzerland) General designation for a corporation, partnership, or association.

Société Anonyme (S.A.)

(Belgium, France, Luxembourg, Switzerland) Designation for a joint stock company with limited personal liability to shareholders.

Société à Responsabilité Limitée (S.R.L.)

(France, Luxembourg, Switzerland) Designation for a private limited liability corporation with limited liability to shareholders.

Société Cooperative (Sté. Cve.)

(Belgium, Switzerland) Designation for an incorporated association with limited liability for its members, unless its articles provide otherwise.

Société de Personnes à Responsabilité Limitée (S.P.R.L.)

(Belgium) Designation for a private limited liability company with limited liability to shareholders.

Société en Commandité par Actions (S.C.)

(France, Luxembourg) Designation for a limited partnership in which the partners have limited liability.

Société en Commandité Simple (S.C.S.)

(France, Luxembourg) Designation for a limited partnership in which at least one of the partners has general personal liability and at least one of the other partners has limited liability.

Société en Nom Collectif (S.N.C.)

(France, Luxembourg) Designation for a general partnership, in which all partners have joint and several liability.

soft clause

(banking) Clauses in a documentary letter of credit which make it impossible for the beneficiary (seller) to meet the conditions of the documentary letter of credit on his own and independently of the purchaser.
Example: "The goods must be accepted prior to shipment by a representative of the purchaser." The name of the representative is made known via an amendment in the documentary letter of credit at a later stage when it is either too late or very inconvenient to follow through on the requirement. It is not recommended for exporters to agree to this type of request.

soft currency
(banking/foreign exchange) The funds of a country that are controlled by exchange procedures, thereby having limited convertibility into gold and other currencies.

soft loan
(general) A loan made with easy or generous terms such as low or no interest and long payback.
(banking) This term refers to the no-interest loans granted to developing countries by the International Development Association. Such a "soft loan" carries no interest (although there is a small annual service charge), is payable in 50 years, and has an amortization rate of 1% repayable annually for the 10 years following an initial 10-year grace period, followed by 3% repayable annually for the remaining 30 years.

sogo bank
(banking/finance) Regional finance institutions in Japan, dealing chiefly with smaller enterprises.

sol
The currency of Peru. 1S=100 centavos.

Southern Africa Development Community (SADC)
A regional economic pact comprising Angola, Botswana, Lesotho, Malawi, Mozambique, Namibia, Swaziland, Tanzania, Zambia, and Zimbabwe. Note: The Southern Africa Development Coordinating Conference (SADCC) became the Southern Africa Development Community (SADC) in August, 1992, when the 10 member countries signed a treaty to establish it and replace the SADCC. The SADC placed binding obligations on member countries with the aim of promoting economic integration towards a fully developed common market. Address: Southern Africa Development Community, Private Bag 0095, Gaborone, Botswana; Tel: [267] (31) 351863; Fax: [267] (31) 372848; http:www.saep.org/sadc.

Southern Africa Development Coordination Conference
Note: The Southern Africa Development Coordinating Conference (SADCC) became the Southern Africa Development Community (SADC) in August, 1992, when the 10 member countries signed a treaty to establish it and replace the SADCC. *See* Southern Africa Development Community.

Southern African Customs Union
SACU, established in 1910, includes Botswana, Lesotho, Namibia, South Africa, and Swaziland. SACU provides for the free exchange of goods within the area, a common external tariff, and a sharing of custom revenues. External tariffs, excise duties, and several rebate and refund provisions are the same for all SACU members. SACU's revenues are apportioned among its members according to a set formula. These funds constitute a significant contribution to each member's government revenues.

Southern Common Market
See Mercosur.

southern cone
The southern cone consists of Argentina, Brazil, Chile, Paraguay, and Uruguay. With the exception of Chile, these countries also comprise the Southern Common Market.

sovereign credit
(finance) A borrowing guaranteed by the government of a sovereign state.

sovereign risk
(finance) The risk to a lendor that the government of a sovereign state may default on its financial obligations.

sovereignty
The rights of a nation to self determination over all that transpires within its boundaries, especially concerning the rights of its people, immigration policy, business dealings, and jurisdiction over airspace, land and maritime matters.

space arbitrage
See arbitrage, space.

Special 301
(U.S.) The Special 301 statute requires the United States Trade Representative (USTR) to review annually the condition of intellectual property protection among U.S. trading partners. Submissions are accepted from industry after which the USTR, weighing all relevant information, makes a determination as to whether a country presents excessive barriers to trade with the United States by virtue of its inadequate protection of intellectual property. If the USTR makes a positive determination, a country may be named to the list of: (1) Priority Foreign Countries (the most egregious), (2) the Priority Watch List, or (3) the Watch List. *See* Section 301; Super 301.

special agency
See agency.

Special American Business Internship Training Program
(U.S. government agency) SABIT, formerly the Soviet-American Business Internship Training Pro-

gram, is a program in which American companies give managers from the Confederation of Independent States (CIS) an opportunity to work in a U.S. corporate setting for up to six months. CIS business managers are referred by the U.S. Department of Commerce to sponsoring U.S. companies, which make the final selection of their interns. The SABIT program matches U.S. corporate sponsors with CIS business executives from the same industries. The CIS provides transportation; the companies provide living expenses and training in management techniques (production, distribution, marketing, accounting, wholesaling, and publishing). SABIT is funded by the U.S. Agency for International Development. Contact: U.S. Department of Commerce, SABIT, Room 3413, 14th and Constitution NW, Washington, DC 20230 USA; Tel: [1] (202) 482-0073; Fax: [1] (202) 482-2443.

special and differential treatment

(GATT/WTO) The principle, enunciated in the Tokyo Declaration, that the Tokyo Round of the General Agreement on Tariffs and Trade (GATT) negotiations should seek to accord particular benefits to the exports of developing countries, consistent with their trade, financial, and development needs. Among proposals for special or differential treatment are reduction or elimination of tariffs applied to exports of developing countries under the Generalized System of Preferences (GSP), expansion of product and country coverage of the GSP, accelerated implementation of tariff cuts agreed to in the Tokyo Round for developing country exports, substantial reduction or elimination of tariff escalation, special provisions for developing country exports in any new codes of conduct covering nontariff measures, assurance that any new multilateral safeguard system will contain special provisions for developing country exports, and the principle that developed countries will expect less than full reciprocity for trade concessions they grant developing countries.

See General Agreement on Tariffs and Trade; Generalized System of Preferences, World Trade Organization.

special drawing right(s) (SDR)

(banking) Reserve assets of the member states of the International Monetary Fund, (IMF) (Bretton-Woods system), for which they can draw an amount of SDRs proportional to their predetermined quota in the IMF. The value of an SDR is based on a currency basket (the last realignment

was in January 1991: $=40%, DM=21%, Yen=17%, GB£ = 11%, FF=11%.) Some countries define the parity of their currencies in SDRs.

(banking/foreign exchange) The amount by which each member state of the IMF is permitted to have its international checking account with the International Monetary Fund go negative before the nation must ask for additional loans.

SDRs were established at the Rio de Janeiro conference of 1967. SDRs are available to governments through the Fund and may be used in transactions between the Fund and member governments.

IMF member countries have agreed to regard SDRs as complementary to gold and reserve currencies in settling their international accounts. The unit value of an SDR reflects the foreign exchange value of a "basket" of currencies of several major trading countries (the U.S. dollar, the German mark, the French franc, the Japanese yen, and the British pound). The SDR has become the unit of account used by the IMF and several national currencies are pegged to it. Some commercial banks accept deposits denominated in SDR's (although they are unofficial and not the same units transacted among governments and the fund). *See* International Monetary Fund.

special marine policy

(insurance) An insurance policy which is issued to cover a single shipment. The special marine policy form calls for the name of the vessel and sailing date, points of shipment and destination, nature of commodity, description of units comprising the shipment, and the amount of insurance desired. In addition, it calls for the marks and numbers of the shipment, the name of the party to whom loss shall be payable (usually the assured "or orders" thus making the instrument negotiable upon endorsement by the assured), and the applicable policy provisions. Some of these provisions are standard clauses and are incorporated by reference only, while others are specific and apply to the individual shipment in question.

A special marine policy is usually utilized on export shipments when the sale is financed through a bank by letter of credit and evidence of insurance is a part of the required documentation.

The special marine policy is generally prepared in four or more copies. The original (and duplicate if necessary) is negotiable and is forwarded with the shipping documents to the consignee. The remaining documents serve as office copies for the assured and for the insurance company.

The terms "special marine policy" and "certificate" are often used interchangeably. The practical effect of the two is the same, but a word as to their difference will be of interest.

In former years the use of "certificate" was customary. This, as the name implies, certifies that a shipment has been insured under a given open policy, and that the certificate represents and takes the place of such open policy, the provisions of which are controlling.

Because of the objections that an instrument of this kind did not constitute a "policy" within the requirements of letters of credit, it has become the practice to use a special marine policy. This makes no reference to an open policy and stands on its own feet as an obligation of the underwriting company.

In some cases, exporters insure through freight forwarders when arranging for forwarding, warehousing, documentation, ocean freight space and the other requirements of overseas trade. While this method may have the merit of simplicity, it should be emphasized that there are definite advantages in having one's own policy and that this need not entail burdensome clerical detail.

See open policy; declaration; bordereau.

special rates
(shipping) Rates that apply to cargo traffic under special conditions and usually at a limited number of cities. Examples of such rates are container rates, exception ratings, surface-air rates, and import rates.

specific commodity rate
(shipping) Rate applicable to certain classes of commodities, usually commodities moving in volume shipments. Hence, specific commodity rates are usually lower than the general commodity rate between the same pair of cities.

specific rate of duty
(customs) A specified amount of duty per unit of weight or other quantity. For example 5.9 cents per pound, or 8 cents per dozen. *See also* ad valorem; compound rate of duty.

spot
See spot operations.

spot cash
(banking) Immediate cash payment in a transaction, as opposed to payment at some future time.

spot exchange
(foreign exchange) The purchase and sale of foreign exchange for delivery and payment at the time of the transaction.

spot exchange rate
(foreign exchange) The price of one currency expressed in terms of another currency at a given moment in time.

spot market
(foreign exchange) The market (or exchange) for a commodity or foreign exchange available for immediate delivery (usually one or two days after the transaction date).

spot/next
(foreign exchange) Swap transaction, the spot side of which has the normal spot value date while the forward side becomes due one business day later.

spot operations
(foreign exchange) Foreign exchange dealing in which settlement of the mutual delivery commitments is made at the latest two days (normally on the second business day) after the transaction was carried out.

spot price
A price quotation for immediate sale and delivery of a commodity or currency.

spot rate
The rate for purchase or sale of a commodity for immediate delivery.

spotting
(shipping) The placing of a container where required to be loaded or unloaded.

spot trading
See spot market; spot operations.

squaring (positions)
(finance/foreign exchange) Covering an open position (securities, foreign exchange or commodities) by means of corresponding contra business.

standard industrial classification (SIC)
(U.S.) The classification standard underlying all establishment-based U.S. economic statistics classified by industry.

standard international trade classification (SITC)
One of a number of numerical commodity codes developed by the United Nations and used solely by international organizations for reporting international trade. The SITC has been revised several times; the current version is Revision 3. *See also* Harmonized System.

standard of living
(economics) The level of material affluence of a nation as measured by per capita output.

standards
As defined by the Multilateral Trade Negotiations "Agreement on Technical Barriers to Trade" (Standards Code), a standard is a technical specification contained in a document that lays down characteristics of a product such as levels of quality, performance, safety, or dimensions. Standards may include, or deal exclusively with, terminology, symbols, testing and test methods, packaging, marking, or labeling requirements as they apply to a product. *See* International Standards Organization; American National Standards Institute.

standby commitment
(banking) A bank commitment to loan money up to a specified amount for a specific period, to be used only in a certain contingency.

standby letter of credit
(banking) The standby letter of credit is very similar in nature to a guarantee. The beneficiary can claim payment in the event that the principal does not comply with its obligations to the beneficiary. Payment can usually be realized against presentation of a sight draft and written statement that the principal has failed to fulfill his obligations.
With this instrument the following payments and performances, among others, can be supported:
(1) repay funds borrowed or advanced,
(2) fulfill subcontracts, and
(3) undertake payment of invoices made on open account. *See* letter of credit.

standing to sue
(law) A party's interest in a controversy that is sufficient to allow the party to request a judicial resolution. A buyer who suffers damages because of the seller's breach of contract, for example, has standing to sue, but a friend of the buyer who was not a party to the contract and who has not suffered damages from the breach has no standing to sue.

standstill
(GATT) Standstill refers to a commitment of the General Agreement on Tariffs and Trade (GATT) contracting parties not to impose new trade-restrictive measures during the Uruguay Round negotiations. *See* rollback; General Agreement on Tariffs and Trade; Uruguay Round.

starboard
(shipping) The right side of a ship when one is facing the bow.

stare decisis
(law) A legal doctrine under which courts, in resolving current disputes, follow cases decided previously. This doctrine is followed in countries that adhere to common law principles. *See* common law.

State Export Program Database
(U.S.) The SEPD is a trade lead system maintained by the National Association of State Development Agencies (NASDA). The SEPD includes information on state operated trade lead systems. *See* National Association of State Development Agencies.

state/industry-organized, government approved (S/IOGA)
The name of this program has recently been changed to Certified Trade Missions Program. *See* Certified Trade Missions Program.

state trading enterprises
Entities established by governments to import, export and/or produce certain products. Examples include: government-operated import/export monopolies and marketing boards, or private companies that receive special or exclusive privileges from their governments to engage in trading activities.

state trading nations
(economics) Countries such as the former Soviet Union, the People's Republic of China, and nations of Eastern Europe that rely heavily on government entities, instead of the private sector, to conduct trade with other countries. Some of these countries, (e.g., Cuba) have long been Contracting Parties to the General Agreement on Tariffs and Trade (GATT) and now the World Trade Organization (WTO), whereas others (e.g., Poland, Hungary, and Romania), became Contracting Parties later under special Protocols of Accession. The different terms and conditions under which these countries acceded to GATT and the WTO were designed in each case to ensure steady expansion of the country's trade with other GATT/WTO countries taking into account the relative insignificance of tariffs on imports into state trading nations.

statute of frauds
(U.S. law) A law that requires designated documents to be written in order to be enforced by a court. Contracting parties, for example, may orally agree to transfer ownership of land, but a court may not enforce that contract, and may not award damages for breach, unless the contract is written.

steamship indemnity

(shipping) An indemnity received by an ocean carrier issued by a bank indemnifying him for any loss incurred for release of goods to the buyer without presentation of the original bill of lading.

sterling

(a) The money of Great Britain. (b) An article made from sterling silver. Sterling silver is an alloy of silver that is 925/1000 pure. An article of sterling silver is generally marked "925".

stern

(shipping) The rear part of a ship, boat or airplane.

stevedore

(shipping) A person having charge of the loading and unloading of ships in port. *See also* longshoreman; gang.

stop loss order

(foreign exchange) An order to buy (on a short position) or to sell (on a long position) foreign exchange if the rate rises above or falls below a specific limit. As soon as the rate reaches the prescribed limit, the order will be carried out at the next rate. Depending on the market situation, this rate can differ considerably from the limit rate.

storage

(shipping) The keeping of goods in a warehouse.

storage demurrage

(shipping) A charge made on property remaining on the dock past the prescribed "free-time period." *See* demurrage.

storage in transit

(shipping) The stopping of freight traffic at a point located between the point of origin and destination to be stored and reforwarded at a later date.

store-door delivery

(shipping) The movement of goods to the consignee's place of business, customarily applied to movement by truck.

stores

See ship's stores.

stowage

(shipping) The arranging and packing of cargo in a vessel for shipment.

stowage instructions

(shipping) Specific instructions given by the shipper or his agent concerning the way in which cargo is to be stowed. For example, a shipper may require that his shipment be placed below deck if it may be damaged by exposure to the elements above deck,
or midships if it may be damaged by the greater movement of the vessel in fore and aft sections.

stowplan or stowage plan

(shipping) A diagram showing how cargo or containers have been placed on a vessel.

straight bill of lading

(shipping) A nonnegotiable bill of lading that designates a consignee who is to receive the goods and that obligates the carrier to deliver the goods to that consignee only. A straight bill of lading cannot be transferred by endorsement. *See* bill of lading; negotiable instrument; ocean bill of lading.

strategic level of controls

(U.S.) Commodity groupings used for export control purposes. *See* export control classification number.

strike clause

(insurance) An insurance clause included in policies to cover against losses as a result of strikes.

strike price

(finance/foreign exchange) Price at which the option buyer obtains the right to purchase (call option) or sell (put option) the underlying security or currency.

strikes, riots and civil commotion

(insurance) An insurance policy endorsement, usually referred to as S.R.&C.C. (strikes, riots and civil commotion) coverage, which extends the insurance policy to cover damage, theft, pilferage, breakage or destruction of the insured property directly caused by strikers, locked-out workmen or persons taking part in labor disturbances, riots or civil commotions.

Destruction of and damage to property caused by vandalism, sabotage and malicious acts of person(s) regardless of (political/ideological/terroristic) intent be it accidental or otherwise is also held covered under S.R.&C.C. unless so excluded in the F.C.&S. (free of capture and seizure) warranty in the policy.

The S.R.&C.C. endorsement excludes coverage for any damage or deterioration as a result of delay or loss of market, change in temperature/humidity, loss resulting from hostilities or warlike operations, absence/shortage/withholding power, fuel, labor during a strike (riot or civil commotion) or weapons of war that employ atomic or nuclear fusion/fission.

In order to eliminate the war cover from the marine policy it became customary to add a "free of capture and seizure" clause, stating that the policy did

S

not cover warlike operations or its consequences, whether before or after the actual declaration of war. Currently, most open policies omit war perils from its insuring conditions and in all cases will include a F.C.&S. clause. War coverage is customarily furnished in conjunction with an open cargo policy and is written under a separate, distinct policy-the War Risk Only Policy.

See war risk; war risk insurance; open policy.

striking price; exercise price
See strike price.

stripping
(shipping) The unloading of cargo from a container. Also called devanning.

Structural Impediments Initiative (SII)
(U.S./Japan) The SII was started in July 1989 to identify and solve structural problems that restrict bringing two-way trade between the U.S. and Japan into better balance.

Both the U.S. and Japanese governments chose issues of concern in the other's economy as impediments to trade and current account imbalances. The areas which the U.S. government chose included: (1) Japanese savings and investment patterns, (2) land use, (3) distribution, (4) keiretsu, (5) exclusionary business practices, and (6) pricing. Areas which the Japanese Government chose included: (1) U.S. savings and investment patterns, (2) corporate investment patterns and supply capacity, (3) corporate behavior, (4) government regulation, (5) research and development, (6) export promotion, and g) workforce education and training.

In a June 1990 report, the U.S. and Japan agreed to seven meetings in the following three years to review progress, discuss problems, and produce annual joint reports.

stuffing
(shipping) The loading of cargo into a container.

subrogation
(insurance) The right of the insurer, upon payment of a loss, to the benefit of any rights against third parties that may be held by the assured himself. This usually involves recoveries from carriers that handled the shipment.

subsidiary
(law) Any organization more than 50 percent of whose voting stock is owned by another firm.

subsidy
(economics) A bounty, grant or economic advantage paid by a government to producers of goods for the manufacture, production, or export of an ar-

ticle, often to strengthen their competitive position. Export subsidies are contingent on exports; domestic subsidies are conferred on production without reference to exports.

The subsidy may be direct (a cash grant), or indirect, low-interest export credits guaranteed by a government agency, for example), or take a less direct form (R&D support, tax breaks, loans on preferential terms, and provision of raw materials at below-market prices).

(WTO) The payment of subsidies by a national government to export producers in a major trade issue. *See* World Trade Organization.

subzone
(U.S. foreign trade zones) A special purpose foreign trade zone established as part of a foreign trade zone project for a limited purpose that cannot be accommodated within an existing zone. Subzones are often established to serve the needs of a specific company and may be located within an existing facility of the company. *See* foreign trade zone; Foreign Trade Zone Board; Foreign Trade Zone Act; operator; grantee; zone user.

sucre
The currency of Ecuador. 1S/=100 centavos.

sue and labor
(insurance) The responsibility of the assured to act to keep his insured loss at a minimum. The sue and labor clause of the open cargo policy reads essentially as follows:

"In case of any loss or misfortune it shall be lawful and necessary to and for the assured, his or their factors, servants and assigns to sue, labor, and travel, for, in and about the defense, safeguard and recovery of the goods and merchandise or any part thereof ... to the charges whereof this company will contribute according to the rate and quantity of the sum herein insured."

Reasonable charges incurred for this purpose are generally collectible under the insurance policy. For example, when a shipment of canned goods arrives with some leaking cans in each of several cartons, the leaking cans must be taken out if rusting and label damage are to be minimized. The expense insured in this operation may be recovered under the insurance policy.

summary investigation
(U.S.) A 20-day investigation conducted immediately following filing of an antidumping petition to ascertain if the petition contains sufficient information with respect to sales at "less than fair value" and the injury or threat of material injury to a do-

mestic industry caused by the alleged sales at "less than fair value" to warrant the initiation of an anti-dumping investigation. *See* dumping.

summit conference
(diplomacy) An international meeting at which heads of government are the chief negotiators, major world powers are represented, and the meeting serves substantive rather than ceremonial purposes. The term first came into use in reference to the Geneva Big Four Conference of 1955.

Super 301
(U.S.) This provision was enacted due to U.S. Congressional concern that the regular Section 301 procedures narrowly limit U.S. attention to the market access problems of individual sectors or companies. Super 301 sets procedures to identify and address within three years certain "priority," systemic trade restriction policies of other nations. Super 301 authority expired May 30, 1990. *See* Section 301; Special 301.

superdeductive
See deductive value.

superficies
(law) A right to build on the surface of real property. A landowner may transfer a superficies right, for example, to a developer who agrees to build on the property in exchange for an annual rent to the landowner.

Superintendent of Documents
(U.S.) Official supplier of U.S. government documents, publications, books, etc. Government Periodicals and Subscription Services is a catalog of products and prices. Address: Superintendent of Documents, U.S. Government Printing Office, Washington, DC 20402 USA; Tel: [1] (202) 512-1800.

supply access
(economics/customs) Assurances that importing countries will, in the future, have fair and equitable access at reasonable prices to supplies of raw materials and other essential imports. Such assurances should include explicit constraints against the use of the export embargo as an instrument of foreign policy.

surcharge
(shipping) A charge above the usual or customary charge.

surety
(insurance) A bond, guaranty, or other security that protects a person, corporation, or other legal entity in cases of another's default in the payment of a given obligation, improper performance of a given contract, malfeasance of office, and others.

(law) A surety is usually a party to the contract with the principal debtor and the third person, making the surety equally liable with the debtor. In contrast, a guarantor is usually not a party to the contract between the debtor and the third person.

(U.S. Customs) Surety Bond—U.S. Customs entries must be accompanied by evidence that a bond is posted with Customs to cover any potential duties, taxes, and penalties which may accrue. Bonds may be secured through a resident U.S. surety company, but may be posted in the form of United States money or certain United States government obligations. In the event that a customs broker is employed for the purpose of making entry, the broker may permit the use of his bond to provide the required coverage. *See* bond; guaranty.

survey
(shipping) To examine the condition of a vessel for purposes of establishing seaworthiness and/or value.

(insurance) To inspect goods as to their condition, weight and/or value in order to establish the extent of an insured loss.

survey report
Report of an expert, issued by an independent party. *See* inspection certificate.

sushi bond
(banking/finance) Eurodollar bonds issued by Japanese corporations on the Japanese market for Japanese investors.

suspension of investigation
(U.S.) A decision to suspend an antidumping investigation if the exporters who account for substantially all of the imported merchandise agree to stop exports to the U.S. or agree to revise their prices promptly to eliminate any dumping margin. An investigation may be suspended at any time before a final determination is made. No agreement to suspend an investigation may be made unless effective monitoring of the agreement is practicable and is determined to be in the public interest. *See* dumping.

suspension of liquidation
(U.S. Customs) When a preliminary determination of dumping or subsidization, or final determination after a negative preliminary determination is affirmative, there is a provision for suspension of liquidation of all entries of merchandise subject to the determination which are entered, or withdrawn from warehouse, for consumption, on or after the date of the publication of the notice in the Federal Register. Customs is directed to require a cash deposit, or the posting of a bond or other security, for

each entry affected equal to the estimated amount of the subsidy or the amount by which the fair value exceeds the U.S. price. When an administrative review is completed, Customs is directed to collect the final subsidy rate or amount by which the foreign market value exceeds the U.S. price, and to require for each entry thereafter a cash deposit equal to the newly determined subsidy rate or margin of dumping. *See* liquidation; dumping.

swap (transaction)
(banking/finance/foreign exchange) A spot purchase of foreign exchange (currency swaps), fixed or floating rate funds (interest rate swaps) or assets (asset swaps) with simultaneous forward sale or vice versa.

Pase financiero is an Argentinian system, related to the swap system, whereby persons or institutions making capital investments are given an "exchange guarantee," which guarantees that the funds can be reexchanged at a predetermined exchange rate on a specific date. The French government is recommending the term *crédit croisé* but it is fighting a losing battle.

(foreign exchange) Sale of one currency against another currency at a specific maturity and the simultaneous repurchase from the same counterparty at a different maturity. Normally, one of the maturity dates will be that of spot operations.
See also countertrade.

switch arrangements
A form of countertrade in which the seller sells on credit and then transfers the credit to a third party. *See* countertrade.

System for Tracking Export License Applications (STELA)
(U.S.) STELA is a U.S. Department of Commerce, Bureau of Export Administration (BXA) computer-generated voice unit that interfaces with the BXA database: ECASS (Export Control Automated Support System). STELA enables a caller to check on an export license by making a telephone call to [1] (202) 482-2752. *See* Bureau of Export Administration.

T

table of denial orders
(U.S.) A list of individuals and firms which have been disbarred from shipping or receiving U.S. goods or technology. Firms and individuals on the list may be disbarred with respect to either controlled commodities or general destination (across-the-board) exports.

taka
The currency of Bangladesh. 1Tk=100 paise.

tala
The currency of Western Samoa. 1WS$=100 sene.

tare or tare weight
(shipping) The weight of a container and/or packing materials, but without the goods being shipped. The gross weight of a shipment less the net weight of the goods being shipped.

tariff
(general) A comprehensive list or "schedule" of merchandise with applicable rates to be paid or charged for each listed article.

(shipping) A schedule of shipping rates charged, together with governing rules and regulations. A tariff sets forth a contract of carriage for the shipper, the consignee, and the carrier. Individual carriers also publish their own tariffs covering special services. International tariffs containing freight rates of the U.S. international carriers are published by the U.S. flag carriers.

(customs) A schedule of duties or taxes assessed by a government on goods as they enter (or leave) a country. Tariffs may be imposed to protect domestic industries from imported goods and/or to generate revenue. Types include ad valorem, specific, variable, or compound. In the United States, the imposition of tariffs is made on imported goods only.

Tariffs raise the prices of imported goods, thus making them less competitive within the market of the importing country. Tariffs are much less important measures of protection than they used to be.
See ad valorem; specific rate of duty; variable rate of duty; compound rate of duty.

tariff anomaly
(customs) A tariff anomaly exists when the tariff on raw materials or semi-manufactured goods is higher than the tariff on the finished product.

tariff escalation

(customs) A situation in which tariffs on manufactured goods are relatively high, tariffs on semi-processed goods are moderate, and tariffs on raw materials are nonexistent or very low.

tariff quotas

(customs) Application of a higher tariff rate to imported goods after a specified quantity of the item has entered the country at a lower prevailing rate. *See* quota.

tariff schedule

(customs) A comprehensive list of the goods which a country may import and the import duties applicable to each product. *See* Harmonized System; Harmonized Tariff Schedule of the United States.

Tariff Schedule of the United States

See Harmonized Tariff Schedule of the United States.

tariff trade barriers

See trade barriers.

tariff war

When one nation increases the tariffs on goods imported from, or exported to another country, and that country then follows by raising tariffs itself in a retaliatory manner.

tau

(foreign exchange) The price change of a foreign exchange option for a 1 percent change in the implied volatility.

tax haven

(trade) A nation offering low tax rates and other incentives for individuals and businesses of other countries.

Tax Information Exchange Agreement

An agreement concluded between the U.S. and a beneficiary country designated pursuant to the Caribbean Basin Economic Recovery Act of 1983. This agreement generally involves an expanded version of the standard exchange of information article usually included in a bilateral income tax treaty. The U.S. has similar agreements with most major trading partners. Like the standard tax treaty exchange of information article, a TIEA imposes on the agreeing countries a mutual and reciprocal obligation to exchange information relating to the enforcement of their respective tax laws.

Technical Advisory Committee(s)

(U.S.) Voluntary groups of industry and government representatives who provide guidance and expertise to the U.S. Department of Commerce on technical and export control matters, including evaluation of technical issues; worldwide availability, use and production of technology; and licensing procedures related to specific industries. TACs have been set up for: (1) materials, (2) biotechnology, (3) computer systems, (4) electronics (formerly "semiconductors"), (5) sensors (formerly "electronic instrumentation"), (6) materials processing equipment (formerly "automated manufacturing equipment"), (7) military critical technologies, (8) telecommunications equipment, and (9) transportation and related equipment. *See* United States Department of Commerce.

technical analysis

(economics/foreign exchange) The analysis of past price and volume trends–often with the help of chart analysis–in a market, in order to be able to make forecasts about the future price developments of the commodity being traded. Technical exchange rate analysis is often used in professional dealing for short-term foreign exchange rate forecasts.

technical barrier to trade

A specification which sets forth stringent standards a product must meet (such as levels of quality, performance, safety, or dimensions) in order to be imported. A technical barrier to trade has the effect of adding to the cost of an imported article, thereby making it less competitive in the marketplace when compared to domestically produced articles.

technical data

Information of any kind that can be used, or adapted for use, in the design, production, manufacture, utilization, or reconstruction of articles or materials. All software is technical data. Technical data can be either "tangible" or "intangible." Models, prototypes, blueprints or operating manuals (even if stored on recording media) are examples of tangible technical data. Intangible technical data consists of technical services, such as training, oral advice, information, guidance and consulting.

technology transfer

The transfer of knowledge generated and developed in one place to another, where is it is used to achieve some practical end. Technology may be transferred in many ways: by giving it away (technical journals, conferences, emigration of technical experts, technical assistance programs); by industrial espionage; or by sale (patents, blueprints, industrial processes, and the activities of multinational corporations).

T

temperature controlled ground handling

(air freight) Many of the commodities moving in air freight must be protected against sudden changes in temperatures. The temperature of a jet freighter's cabin is ideal to maintain perishables in peak condition; but the increase in the shipment of perishables by air required new strides in ground handling to protect cargoes from spoilage induced by marked differences in temperatures often encountered on the ground at points of origin and destination. To meet these needs the airlines have, at some cities, special equipment and facilities ranging from heated vans to temperature controlled holding rooms in which 100,000 pounds of perishables can be held at one time.

temporary importation under bond (TIB)

(U.S. Customs) Temporary admission into the United States under a conditional bond for articles not imported for sale or for sale on approval.

Certain classes of goods may be admitted into the United States without the payment of duty, under bond, for their exportation within one year from the date of importation when they are not imported for sale, or for sale on approval. Generally, the amount of the bond is double the estimated duties. The one-year period for exportation may, upon application to the district or port director of Customs, be extended for one or more further periods which, when added to the initial one year, shall not exceed a total of three years. There is an exception in the case of automobiles or any parts thereof which are subject to a total period of six months which may not be extended.

Merchandise entered under TIB must be exported before expiration of the bond period, or any extension, to avoid assessment of liquidated damages in the amount of the bond.

Classes of goods which may be entered under a TIB include a wide range of merchandise. Some examples are: (1) merchandise to be repaired or altered; (2) wearing apparel for use as samples; (3) articles imported by illustrators or photographers for use solely as models; (4) samples for use in taking orders; (5) articles solely for examination with a view to reproduction; (6) articles intended solely for testing; (7) automobiles and other motor vehicles, boats, balloons, racing shells etc. and the usual equipment of the forgoing, imported by non-residents for the purposes of taking part in races; (8) locomotives and railway equipment for use in clearing obstructions; (9) containers for holding merchandise; (10) articles of special design for temporary use in connection with the manufacture of articles for export; (11) animals brought into the United States for the purposes of breeding; (12) theatrical scenery, properties and costumes; (13) works of fine art brought in by lecturers; (14) automobiles, other motor vehicles, and parts thereof brought in for show purposes.

Relief from Liability. Relief from liability under bond may be obtained in any case in which the articles are destroyed under Customs supervision, in lieu of exportation, within the original bond period. However, in the case of articles imported solely for testing or experimentation, destruction need not be under Customs supervision where articles are destroyed during the course of experiments or tests during the bond period or any lawful extension, but satisfactory proof of destruction shall be furnished to the district or port director with whom the customs entry was filed. *See* ATA Carnet; bond; in bond.

tender

(shipping) A small vessel which serves a larger vessel in a port for the purpose of supplying provisions and carrying passengers from ship to shore.

(law) (a) An offer or proposal to purchase a specified quantity of a commodity for a specified price. (b) An offer of money in satisfaction of a debt or obligation.

tenor

(law/banking) The period between the formation of a debt and the date of expected payment.

terminal

(shipping) An area at the end of a rail, ship, air or truck line which serves as a loading, unloading and transfer point for cargo or passengers, and often includes storage facilities, management offices and repair facilities.

terminal charge

(shipping) A charge made for services performed at terminals (e.g., storage, drayage).

terms of trade

(economics) The volume of exports that can be traded for a given volume of imports. Changes in the terms of trade are generally measured by comparing changes in the ratio of export prices to import prices. The terms of trade are considered to have improved when a given volume of exports can be exchanged for a larger volume of imports.

theta

(statistics/foreign exchange) A ratio expressing the price change of an option (i.e. the change in the premium) over a period of time (per time unit). Mathematically, this corresponds to the 1st derivative of the option premium according to the time factor.

thing in action
(law) A right to bring a legal action to recover personal property, money, damages, or a debt. A seller, for example, who has a right to recover payment for goods and who is not in possession of the buyer's payment has a thing in action, that is, a right to procure payment by lawsuit.

Third Country Meat Directive
A regulation by which the European Community (EC) controls meat imports based on sanitary requirements. The TCMD requires individual inspection and certification by EC veterinarians of meat plants wishing to export to the EC. *See* European Community.

third-party beneficiary
(law) An individual or legal entity that benefits from, but is not a contracting party of, a contract between two or more other individuals or legal entities. A bank, for example, that loans a business owner funds to purchase specific property is a third-party beneficiary to the sales contract between the business owner and seller.

third party documents
(banking) In letter of credit operations, documents which indicate a party other than the beneficiary of the credit as the consignor of the goods. Banks accept third party transport documents. *See* transport documents; letter of credit.

third world countries
(economics) Developing countries, especially in Asia, Africa and Latin America, but excluding communist countries and industrial non-communist countries.

through bill of lading
(shipping) A single bill of lading covering receipt of the cargo at the point of origin for delivery to the ultimate consignee, using two or more modes of transportation. *See* bill of lading; ocean bill of lading.

through rate
(shipping) A shipping rate applicable from point of origin to destination. A through rate may be either a joint rate or a combination of two or more rates.

tick
See pips.

tied aid credit
The practice of providing grants and/or concessional loans, either alone or combined with export credits, linked to procurement from the donor country.

tied loan
(banking) A loan made by a government agency that requires a foreign borrower to spend the proceeds in the lender's country.

time arbitrage
See arbitrage, time.

time definite delivery
(shipping) The range of service performance standards offered by air freight carriers which permit the customer to select a specific time frame for delivery based on requirements for service and economy. These service standards provide door-to-door (pickup and delivery) schedule patterns based on same day, next day, second or third day delivery needs.

time deposits
(banking) Funds invested in a bank for a pre-determined time and at a specific interest rate. For large amounts, conditions can be freely negotiable (maturity, interest rate).

time draft
(banking) A financial instrument that is payable at a future fixed or determinable date. *See* bill of exchange.

time value
(finance) The value of an option if the intrinsic value is zero. It merely reflects possible price fluctuations of the underlying instrument, so that at a later point in time the option could achieve an intrinsic value.

Tokyo Round
(GATT) The seventh round of multilateral negotiations concerning the General Agreement on Tariffs and Trade (GATT). Begun in 1973, it concluded November 1979, with agreements covering the following: (1) an improved legal framework for the conduct of world trade (which includes preferential tariff and non-tariff treatment in favor of, and among, developing countries as a permanent legal feature of the world trading system); (2) non-tariff measures (subsidies and countervailing measures; technical barriers to trade; government procurement; customs valuation; import licensing procedures; a revision of the 1967 GATT anti-dumping code); (3) bovine meat; (4) dairy products; (5) tropical products; and (6) an agreement on free trade in civil aircraft.

Participating countries (99) also agreed to reduce tariffs on thousands of industrial and agricultural products. These cuts were gradually implemented over a period of eight years ending January 1, 1987. The total value of trade affected by Tokyo Round most-favored-nation (MFN) tariff reductions, and by bindings of prevailing tariff rates, amounted to more than US$300 billion, measured on MFN imports in 1981. As a result of these cuts, the weighted average (the average tariff measured against actual trade flows) on manufactured products in the world's nine major industrial markets declined 7.0 to 4.7 percent, representing a 34 percent reduction of customs collection. This can be contrasted with the average tariff of around 40 percent at the time of GATT's establishment in the late 1940's. Since the tariff-cutting formula adopted by most industrialized countries resulted in the largest reductions generally being made in the highest duties, the customs duties of different countries were brought closer together or "harmonized."

See also General Agreement on Tariffs and Trade; rounds; Uruguay Round; World Trade Organization.

tolar

The currency of Slovenia. 1SiT=100 stotinev.

tom/next

(foreign exchange) Swap transaction where the spot side becomes due on the business day following the day on which the contract was concluded and where the forward side becomes due on the day after, i.e. on the normal spot value date.

ton

(measure) A unit of mass or weight equal to 1.1016 metric tons, 2,240 pounds, or 1,016.06 kilograms.

ton mile

(shipping) The transport of one ton of cargo for one mile. Used most often in air cargo services.

to order

(law/banking/shipping) A term on a financial instrument or title document indicating that it is negotiable and transferable. For example, on a bill of lading "to order" means that it is negotiable and transferable by the person or entity whose name appears on the document.

total cost of distribution

(shipping) The sum total of all the costs incurred in the distribution of goods. The total cost of distribution includes such items as: (1) Transportation charges, (2) Inventory carrying costs, (3) Warehousing expenses, (4) Packaging, (5) Insurance, (6) Product obsolescence while en route or in storage, and (7) Pilferage.

total loss

(insurance) An actual total loss occurs when the goods are destroyed, when the assured is irretrievably deprived of their possession or when they arrive so damaged as to cease to be a thing of the kind insured. Examples of this last, which is spoken of as a "loss of specie," are cement arriving as rock or textiles as rags. Disasters likely to give rise to total loss include fire, sinking or stranding of the vessel, collision and loss overboard in the course of loading or discharge.

tracer

(shipping) (a) A request upon a transportation line to trace a shipment for the purpose of expediting its movement or establishing delivery;

(general/banking) (b) A request for an answer to a communication, or for advice concerning the status of a subject.

tracking; tracing

(shipping) A carrier's system of recording movement intervals of shipments from origin to destination.

tractor

(shipping) A vehicle designed and used primarily for drawing other vehicles and not so constructed as to carry a load other than part of the weight of the vehicle and load so drawn.

Trade Act of 1974

(U.S. law) Legislation enacted late in 1974 and signed into law in January 1975, granting the President broad authority to enter into international agreements to reduce import barriers. Major purposes were to: (1) stimulate U.S. economic growth and to maintain and enlarge foreign markets for the products of U.S. agriculture, industry, mining and commerce; (2) strengthen economic relations with other countries through open and non-discriminatory trading practices; (3) protect American industry and workers against unfair or injurious import competition; and (4) provide "adjustment assistance" to industries, workers and communities injured or threatened by increased imports. The Act allowed the President to extend tariff preferences to certain imports from developing countries and set conditions under which Most-Favored-Nation Treatment could be extended to non-market economy countries and provided negotiating authority for the Tokyo Round of multilateral trade negotiations. *See* trade adjustment assistance; most favored nation; Tokyo Round.

trade adjustment assistance (TAA)

(U.S.) TAA for firms and workers is authorized by the 1974 Trade Act. TAA for firms is administered by the U.S. Department of Commerce; TAA for workers is administered by the U.S. Department of Labor.

Eligible firms must show that increased imports of articles like or directly competitive with those produced by the firm contributed importantly to declines in its sales and/or production and to the separation or threat of separation of a significant portion of the firm's workers. These firms receive help through Trade Adjustment Assistance Centers (TAACs), primarily in implementing adjustment strategies in production, marketing, and management.

Eligible workers must be associated with a firm whose sales or production have decreased absolutely due to increases in like or directly competitive imported products resulting in total or partial separation of the employee and the decline in the firm's sales or production. Assistance includes training, job search and relocation allowances, plus reemployment services for workers adversely affected by the increased imports.

See United States Department of Commerce; United States Department of Labor.

Trade Adjustment Assistance Centers

(U.S.) TAACs are nonprofit, nongovernment organizations established to help firms qualify for and receive assistance in adjusting to import competition. TAACs are funded by the U.S. Department of Commerce as a primary source of technical assistance to certified firms. *See* trade adjustment assistance; United States Department of Commerce.

Trade Agreements Act of 1979

(U.S.) Legislation authorizing the U.S. to implement trade agreements dealing with non-tariff barriers negotiated during the Tokyo Round of the General Agreement on Tariffs and Trade (GATT), including agreements that required changes in existing U.S. laws, and certain concessions that had not been explicitly authorized by the Trade Act of 1974. The Act incorporated into U.S. law the Tokyo Round (GATT) agreements on dumping, customs valuation, import licensing procedures, government procurement practices, product standards, civil aircraft, meat and dairy products, and liquor duties. The Act also extended the President's authority to negotiate trade agreements with foreign countries to reduce or eliminate non-tariff barriers to trade. *See* General Agreement on Tariffs and Trade; Tokyo Round.

Trade and Development Program (TDP)

(U.S.) The TDP started within the Agency for International Development but was spun off as an independent agency in 1981. TDP offers tied aid and resembles Japan's tied aid funding. The program provides project planning funding only for projects that are priorities of the host country and present a good opportunity for sales of U.S. goods and services. *See* International Development Cooperation Agency.

trade balance

See current balance; balance of payments.

trade barriers

Any one or group of tariff or non-tariff barriers to trade often classified into eight general categories: (1) import policies (tariffs and other import charges, quantitative restrictions, import licensing, and customs barriers); (2) standards, testing, labeling, and certification; (3) government procurement; (4) export subsidies; (5) lack of intellectual property protection; (6) service barriers; (7) investment barriers; and (8) other barriers (e.g., barriers encompassing more than one category or barriers affecting a single sector). *See* technical barrier to trade; tariff; quota.

trade concordance

Trade concordance refers to the matching of Harmonized System (HS) codes to larger statistical definitions, such as the Standard Industrial Classification (SIC) code and the Standard International Trade Classification (SITC) system. The U.S. Bureau of the Census, the United Nations, as well as individual U.S. Federal and private organizations, maintain trade concordances for the purpose of relating trade and production data. *See* Harmonized System.

trade deficit

(economics) A nation's excess of imports over exports over a period of time.

trade event

A promotional activity that may include a demonstration of products or services and brings together in one viewing area the principals in the purchase and sale of the products or services. As a generic term, trade events may include trade fairs, trade missions, trade shows, catalog shows, matchmaker events, foreign buyer missions, and similar functions.

Trade Expansion Act of 1962

(U.S. law) The Act provided authority for U.S. participation in the Kennedy Round of the General Agreement on Tariffs and Trade (GATT). The leg-

T

islation granted the President general authority to negotiate, on a reciprocal basis, reductions of up to 50 percent in U.S. tariffs. The Act explicitly eliminated the "Peril Point" provision that had limited U.S. negotiating positions in earlier GATT Rounds, and instead called on the Tariff Commission, the U.S. International Trade Commission, and other federal agencies to provide information regarding the probable economic effects of specific tariff concessions. This Act superseded the Trade Agreements Act of 1934, as amended. *See* General Agreement on Tariffs and Trade; peril point.

trade fair

A stage-setting event in which firms of several nationalities present their products or services to prospective customers in a pre-formatted setting (usually a booth of a certain size which is located adjacent to other potential suppliers). A distinguishing factor between trade fairs and trade shows is size. A trade fair is generally viewed as having a larger number of participants than other trade events, or as an event bringing together related industries.

Trade Fair Certification Program

(U.S.) The U.S. Department of Commerce Trade Fair Certification program was started in 1983 to promote selected privately organized trade shows. The program helps private sector organizations in mounting certified international fairs. The Department of Commerce assistance includes promoting the fair among foreign customers and helping exhibitors to make commercial contacts. *See* United States Department of Commerce.

Trade Information Center

(U.S.) A U.S. government one-stop source for information on Federal programs to assist U.S. exporters; Tel: [1] (800) USA-TRADE, [1] (800) 872-8723). Address: Trade Information Center, U.S. Department of Commerce, 14th St. and Constitution Ave. NW, Washington, DC 20230 USA.

trade loss

(insurance) The ordinary and unavoidable loss of weight caused by evaporation as in ore shipments. May also include shortages due to other causes which are considered normal and unavoidable. These losses are generally uninsurable.

trademark

(law) A distinctive identification of a manufactured product or of a service taking the form of a name, logo, motto, and so on; a trademarked brand has legal protection and only the owner can use the mark.

A trademark is distinguished from a servicemark in that the former identifies products while the later identifies services.

Trademark protection varies from country to country, and may not be available in some jurisdictions. If trademark protection is available under the laws of a particular country, a trademark may usually be registered only if it is distinguishable from other registered trademarks and if it contains a name, brand, label, signature, word, letter, numeral, device, or any combination of these items. A country that is a member the Paris Convention for the Protection of Industrial Property may recognize trademarks held in other jurisdictions.

(U.S.) Organizations that file an application at the U.S. Patent Office and use the brand for five years may be granted a trademark. A firm may lose a trademark that has become generic. Generic names are those which consumers use to identify the product, rather than to specify a particular brand (e.g., escalator, aspirin and nylon).

See copyright; service mark; patent; World Intellectual Property Organization; Patent Cooperation Treaty.

trade mission

Generically, a trade mission is composed of individuals who are taken as a group to meet with prospective customers overseas. Missions visit specific individuals or places with no specific stage setting other than appointments. Appointments are made with government and/or commercial customers, or with individuals who may be a stepping stone to customers.

(U.S.) International Trade Administration (ITA) trade missions are scheduled in selected countries to help participants find local agents, representatives, and distributors, to make direct sales, or to conduct market assessments. Some missions include technical seminars to support sales of sophisticated products and technology in specific markets. ITA missions include planning and publicity, appointments with qualified contacts and with government officials, market briefings and background information on contacts, as well as logistical support and interpreter service. Trade missions also are frequently organized by other Federal, State, or local agencies.

trade name

(law) The name under which an organization conducts business, or by which the business or its goods and services are identified. It may or may not be registered as a trademark.

Trade Negotiations Committee

(GATT) The steering group which managed the General Agreement on Tariffs and Trade (GATT) Uruguay Round negotiations. The TNC was comprised of all countries participating in the Uruguay Round negotiations (that is, it is not limited simply to members of the GATT). The TNC functioned at the non-ministerial level. *See* General Agreement on Tariffs and Trade; rounds; Uruguay Round.

tradeoffs

(shipping) Interaction between related activities such as the offsetting of higher costs in one area with reduced costs or other benefits in another. In air freight, for example, the classic "tradeoff" is one of time (quick delivery) versus money (greater expense).

Trade Opportunities Program

(U.S.) An International Trade Administration service which provides sales leads from overseas firms seeking to buy or represent U.S. products and services. Through overseas channels, U.S. foreign commercial officers gather leads and details, including specifications, quantities, end use, and delivery deadlines. TOP leads are telexed to Washington and listed on the Commerce Department's Economic Bulletin Board and redistributed by the private sector. Contact Economic Bulletin Board office at Tel: [1] (202) 482-1986; Fax: [1] (900) 786-2329.

Trade Policy Committee (TPC)

(U.S.) A cabinet-level, interagency trade committee established by the Trade Expansion Act of 1962 (chaired by the U.S. Trade Representative) to provide broad guidance on trade issues. Members include the Secretaries of Commerce, State, Treasury, Agriculture, and Labor. The Committee was renewed by an Executive Order at the end of the Carter Administration. Toward the end of the first Reagan Administration, with much dissension over Japan policy between the TPC, the Senior Interagency Group (chaired by Treasury), and the other groups, the White House created the Economic Policy Council (EPC) in 1985 as a single forum to reduce tensions. *See* Economic Policy Council.

Trade Policy Review Mechanism

The TPRM was created at the General Agreement on Tariffs and Trade (GATT) Uruguay Round midterm ministerial meeting in Montreal. Under the TPRM, the trade policies of any GATT contracting party were subject to regularly scheduled review by the GATT Council. Reviews led to recommendations on ways to improve a contracting party's trade

policies. *See* General Agreements on Tariffs and Trade; Uruguay Round.

Trade Promotion Coordinating Committee

(U.S.) The President established the TPCC in May 1990 to unify and streamline the government's decentralized approach to export promotion. TPCC members include Departments of Commerce (as chair), State, Treasury, Agriculture, Defense, Energy, and Transportation, the Office of Management and Budget, the U.S. Trade Representative, the Council of Economic Advisers, Eximbank, the Overseas Private Investment Corporation, the U.S. Information Agency, the Agency for International Development, the Trade and Development Program, and the Small Business Administration. The TPCC chair office is at the U.S. Department of Commerce. 19 agencies are on the committee. The Trade Information Center was created as one of the main missions of the TPCC. The TPCC is not a body which would be contacted by the general public. If you have questions about what they do, or how it works, call [1] (800) USA-TRADE.

trade-related aspects of intellectual property rights (TRIPs)

(WTO) TRIPs refers to intellectual property rights objectives in the General Agreement on Tariffs and Trade (GATT) Uruguay Round and the successor World Trade Organization (WTO). These objectives include achieving a comprehensive agreement that would include: (1) substantive standards of protection for all areas of intellectual property (patents, trademarks, copyrights, etc.); (2) effective enforcement measures (both at the border and internally); and (3) effective dispute settlement provisions. *See* Uruguay Round, World Trade Organization.

trade show

A trade show is a stage-setting event in which firms present their products or services to prospective customers in a pre-formatted setting (usually a booth of a certain size which is located adjacent to other potential suppliers). The firms are generally in the same industry but not necessarily of the same nationality. A distinguishing factor between trade fairs and trade shows is size. A trade show is generally viewed as a smaller assembly of participants.

trade surplus

(economics) A nation's excess of exports over imports over a period of time.

T

Trade Tariff Act of 1930

(U.S. law) U.S. statutes originally enacted in 1930 and amended periodically that impose duties payable for the importation of articles into the United States and that contain schedules of the duties for specific merchandise. The Act is found at 19 United States Code, sections 1202, et seq.

trade terms

(a) The terms of a sale. The setting of responsibilities of the buyer and seller in a sale, including: sale price, responsibility for shipping, insurance and customs duties. (b) One of the several recognized sets of definitions of trade terms. The most widely used trade terms are Incoterms 2000, which are published by the International Chamber of Commerce, which have replaced the now obsolete Revised American Foreign Trade Definitions. *See* Incoterms; International Chamber of Commerce.

trade-weighted revaluation rate

(foreign exchange) The change in value of a currency is ascertained in terms of an index against a basket of currencies. The make-up of the currencies in the basket and their weighting are determined according to the percentage of exports of the country whose currency is to be valued with its trading partners.

trailer

(shipping) A vehicle without motor power designed to be drawn by another vehicle and so constructed that no part of its weight rests upon the towing vehicle.

tramp line

(shipping) A transportation line operating tramp steamers.

tramp steamer

(shipping) A steamship which does not operate under any regular schedule from one port to another, but calls at any port where cargo may be obtained.

transaction value

(general) The price actually paid or payable for merchandise.

(U.S. Customs) U.S. Customs officers are required by law to determine the value of imported merchandise. Valuation is necessary for statistical purposes as well as to determine the amount of import duty which must be paid if the duty rate is stated as a percentage of value (ad valorem duty).

The transaction value of imported merchandise is the price actually paid or payable for the merchandise when sold for exportation to the United States, plus amounts for the following items if not included in the price:

(1) The packing costs incurred by the buyer.

(2) Any selling commission incurred by the buyer,

(3) The value of any assist,

(4) Any royalty or license fee that the buyer is required to pay as a condition of the sale, and

(5) The proceeds, accruing to the seller, of any subsequent resale, disposal, or use of the imported merchandise.

The amounts for the above items are added only to the extent that each is not included in the price actually paid or payable and information is available to establish the accuracy of the amount. If sufficient information is not available, then the transaction value cannot be determined and the next basis of value, in order of precedence, must be considered for appraisement.

If the transaction value cannot be used, then certain secondary bases are considered. The secondary bases of value, listed in order of precedence for use, are:

(1) Transaction value of identical merchandise,

(2) Transaction value of similar merchandise,

(3) Deductive value, and

(4) Computed value.

The order of precedence of the last two values can be reversed if the importer so requests.

See valuation; identical merchandise; similar merchandise; computed value; deductive value; assist.

transferable letter of credit

(banking) A letter of credit where the beneficiary specified in the credit has the option of instructing his bank to transfer the credit fully or in part to another beneficiary.

A letter of credit can only be transferred if it is expressly designated as "transferable" by the issuing bank. This type of letter of credit enables intermediaries (first beneficiaries) to offer security in the form of a letter of credit to their suppliers (second beneficiaries). *See* letter of credit.

transfer of technology

The movement of modem or scientific methods of production or distribution from one enterprise, institution or country to another, as through foreign investment, international trade licensing of patent rights, technical assistance or training.

transfer pricing

(law/customs) The overpricing of imports and/or underpricing of exports between affiliated companies in different countries for the purpose of transferring profits, revenues or monies out of a country in order to evade taxes.

transfer risk
(banking) Currency measures of foreign governments which make it impossible for the debtor to allocate and transfer foreign exchange abroad. Transfer risks can be covered through use of bank guarantees, confirmed letters of credits, export credit agencies, etc.

transfers (mail, wire, cable)
(banking) Transfers are the remittance of money by a bank to be paid to a party in another town or city. If the instruction to pay such funds is transmitted by regular mail, the term "mail transfer" is used. Wire transfer is used to designate a transfer of funds from one point to another by wire or telegraph. Cable transfer is used to designate a transfer of funds to a city or town located outside the United States by cable. Commissions or fees are charged for all typed of transfers. When transfers are made by wire or cable, the cost of transmitting the instructions to pay by wire or cable is charged to the remitter in addition to the commission.

Transit Air Cargo Manifest
(shipping-U.S.) Procedures under which air cargo imports move through a gateway city to the city of final U.S. Customs destination for the collection of duty and other import processing, thereby expediting shipment movements, reducing gateway congestion, and saving expense for importers, the U.S. Customs Service, and the airlines.

transit zone
(shipping) A port of entry in a coastal country that is established as a storage and distribution center for the convenience of a neighboring country lacking adequate port facilities or access to the sea. A zone is administered so that goods in transit to and from the neighboring country are not subject to the customs duties, import controls or many of the entry and exit formalities of the host country. A transit zone is a more limited facility then a free trade zone or a free port.

transmittal letter
(shipping) A list of the particulars of a shipment and a record of the documents being transmitted together with instructions for disposition of documents. Any special instructions are also included.

transparency
The extent to which laws, regulations, agreements, and practices affecting international trade are open, clear, measurable, and verifiable.
(GATT/WTO) Some of the codes of conduct negotiated during the Tokyo Round of the General Agreement on Tariff and Trade sought to increase the transparency of non-tariff barriers that impede trade. *See* General Agreement on Tariff and Trade, World Trade Organization.

Transparency International
A non-profit, non-governmental organization dedicated to counter corrupt international business and government practices. The organization's stated concerns include: 1) humanitarian, as corruption undermines and distorts development and leads to increasing levels of human rights abuse, 2) democratic, as corruption undermines democracies and in particular the achievements of many developing countries and countries in transition, 3) ethical, as corruption undermines a society's integrity, and 4) practical, as corruption distorts the operations of markets and deprives ordinary people of the benefits which should flow from them. The organization is headquartered in Germany and has chapter offices around the world. Transparency International; Otto-Suhr-Allee 97/99; 10585 Berlin; Germany; Tel: [49] (30) 343 8200; Fax: [49] (30) 3470 3912; E-mail: ti@transparency.org; http://www.transparency.org.

transportation and exportation entry
(U.S. Customs) Customs entry used when merchandise arrives in the U.S. and is destined for a foreign country. Under a transportation and exportation entry, merchandise may be transported in bond through U.S. territory. For example, a transportation and exportation entry would be used for merchandise destined for Canada, arriving in Seattle, from Japan. *See* entry; in bond.

transport documents
(shipping) All types of documents evidencing acceptance, receipt and shipment of goods. Examples: bill of lading; ocean bill of lading; air waybill; rail waybill; dock receipt; etc.

trans-ship
(shipping) To transfer goods from one transportation line to another, or from one ship to another of different ownership.

Travel Advisories
(U.S.) Reports by the U.S. Department of State to inform traveling U.S. citizens of conditions abroad which may affect them adversely. Travel advisories are generally about physical dangers, unexpected arrests or detention, serious health hazards, and other conditions abroad with serious consequences for traveling U.S. citizens. Travel advisories are available at any of the U.S. passport agencies, field offices of the U.S. Department of Commerce and

T

U.S. Embassies and consulates abroad. They are also available at the Bureau of Consular Affairs, Room 4811, N.S., U.S. Department of State, Washington, DC 20520 USA; Tel: [1] (202) 647-5225; http://travel.state.gov.

traveler

(U.S.) A traveler is a person who stays for a period of less than 1 year in a country of which he or she is not a resident. Military and other government personnel and their dependents stationed outside their country of residence are not considered travelers, regardless of the length of their stay abroad; they are considered to have remained within the economy of their home country. The definition of travelers also excludes owners or employees of business enterprises who temporarily work abroad in order to further the enterprise's business, but intend to return to their country of residence within a reasonable period of time.

traveler's checks

(banking) A form of check especially designed for travelers, including persons on vacation and business trips. These checks are usually preprinted in denominations of $10, $20, $50, and $100, and can be cashed and used to purchase goods and services in places of business that accept them.

traveler's letter of credit

(banking) A letter of credit issued by a bank to a customer preparing for an extended trip. The customer pays for the letter of credit, which is issued for a specified period of time in the amount purchased. The bank furnishes a list of correspondent banks or its own foreign branches at which drafts drawn against the letter of credit will be honored. *See* letter of credit.

Travel Industry Association of America (TIA)

Organizer of the International POW WOW. Address: Travel Industry Association of America, 2 Lafayette Center, 1100 New York Ave. NW, Suite 450, Washington, DC 20005-3934 USA; Tel: [1] (202) 408-8422; Fax: [1] (202) 408-1255; http://www.tia.org. *See* International POW WOW.

travel mission

See trade mission.

Treaty of Fusion

See European Community.

Treaty of Rome

The 1957 Treaty of Rome was intended to create a single market for the European Community, with free movement of goods, persons, services, and capital. Article 30 of the Treaty prohibited not only quantitative restrictions on imports but also all measures having an equivalent effect. *See* European Community.

triangular trade

(trade) Trade between three countries, in which an attempt is made to create a favorable balance for each.

trigger price mechanism

(U.S.) System for monitoring imported goods (particularly steel) to identify imports that are possibly being "dumped" in the United States or subsidized by the governments of exporting countries. The minimum price under this system is based on the estimated landed cost at a U.S. port of entry of the product produced by the world's most efficient producers.

Imported products entering the United States below that price may "trigger" formal anti-dumping investigations by the Department of Commerce and the U.S. International Trade Commission. The TPM was first used to protect the U.S. steel industry and was in effect between early 1978 and March 1980. It was reinstated in October 1980 and suspended for all products except for stainless steel wire in January 1982. *See* dumping.

tri-temp

(shipping) A container that can maintain three exact temperature zones in difference compartments simultaneously.

tropical products

Traditionally, agricultural goods of export interest to developing countries in the tropical zones of Africa, Latin America, and East Asia (coffee, tea, spices, bananas, and tropical hardwoods).

truck/air service

(shipping) The surface movement of air freight to and from airports and origin and destination points beyond the terminal area of pickup and delivery service. A directory listing cities served is available through your local airline office.

trust bank (shintaku ginko)

(banking-Japan) Japanese bank involved in both lending and money management.

trust receipt

(banking) A declaration by a client to a bank that ownership in goods released by the bank are retained by the bank, and that the client has received the goods in trust only.

Release of merchandise by a bank to a buyer in which the bank retains title to the merchandise. The buyer, who obtains the goods for manufacturing or sales purposes, is obligated to maintain the goods (or the proceeds from their sale) distinct from the remainder of his/her assets and to hold them ready for repossession by the bank.

Trust receipts are used under letters of credit or collections so that the buyer may receive the goods before paying the issuing bank or collecting bank. *See* documentary collection; letter of credit.

tugrik

The currency of Mongolia. 1Tug=100 mongos.

turnkey

A method of construction whereby the contractor assumes total responsibility from design through completion of the project (and then hands over the "key" to the owner).

turnkey contract

An agreement under which a builder agrees to complete a facility so that it is ready for use when delivered to the other contracting party. A contractor may agree, for example, to build a fully equipped and operational factory under a turnkey contract. The responsibility of the contractor ends when he hands the completed installation over to the client.

two-tier market

(foreign exchange) An exchange rate regime which normally insulates a country from the balance of payments effects of capital flows while it maintains a stable exchange rate for current account transactions. Capital transactions are normally required to pass through a "financial" market while current transactions go through an "official" market, though other arrangements are possible. Examples are found in Belgium and the United Kingdom, though France and Italy have experimented with such systems.

tying arrangement

(law) A condition that a seller imposes on a buyer, requiring that if the buyer desires to purchase one product (tying product), the buyer must also agree to purchase another product (tied product), which the buyer may or may not want. The laws of some countries prohibit certain tying arrangements.

ultimate beneficial owner (UBO)

(U.S.) The UBO of a U.S. affiliate is that person, proceeding up the affiliate's ownership chain beginning with and including the foreign parent, that is not owned more than 50 percent by another person. The UBO consists of only the ultimate owner, other affiliated persons are excluded. If the foreign parent is not owned more than 50 percent by another person, the foreign parent and the UBO are the same. A UBO, unlike a foreign parent, may be a U.S. person.

ultimate consignee

(shipping) The person who is the true party in interest, receiving goods for the designated end-use.

ultimo day

(finance/foreign exchange) The last business day or last stock trading day of a month.

ultra vires

(law) An act performed without authority to do so. If a contract provision, for example, requires both parties to approve an assignment of the contract but one party agrees to an assignment without obtaining the other's consent, the assignment is ultra vires.

unclean bill of lading

See claused bill of lading; bill of lading; ocean bill of lading.

unconfirmed

(banking) A documentary letter of credit where the advising bank makes no commitment to pay, accept or negotiate. *See* letter of credit; silent confirmation.

unconscionable

(law) Unfair or oppressive. A contract with unconscionable terms, for example, favors one party over the other to such an extent that it is unjust, and if the oppressed party made the contract under duress or without meaningful negotiation as to the terms, a court may refuse to enforce it against that party.

underdeveloped country

(economics) A nation in which per capita real income is proportionately low when contrasted with the per capita real income of nations where industry flourishes. *See also* less developed countries; least developed country; lesser developed country.

unfair trade practice

(general) Unusual government support to firms—such as export subsidies to certain anti-competitive practices by firms themselves—such as dumping, boycotts or discriminatory shipping arrangements— that result in competitive advantages for the benefiting firms in international trade.

(U.S.) Any act, policy, or practice of a foreign government that: (1) violates, is inconsistent with, or otherwise denies benefits to the U.S. under any trade agreement to which the United States is a party; (2) is unjustifiable, unreasonable, or discriminatory and burdens or restricts United States commerce; or (3) is otherwise inconsistent with a favorable Section 301 determination by the U.S. Trade Representative. *See* Section 301; dumping.

Uniform Commercial Code

(U.S. law) A set of statutes purporting to provide some consistency among states' commercial laws. It includes uniform laws dealing with bills of lading, negotiable instruments, sales, stock transfers, trust receipts, and warehouse receipts.

Uniform Customs and Practice (UCP)

(banking) Full name: Uniform Customs and Practice for Documentary Credits (UCPDC). The internationally recognized codification of rules unifying banking practice regarding documentary credits (letters of credit).

The UCPDC was developed by a working group attached to the International Chamber of Commerce (ICC) in Paris, France. It is revised and updated from time to time and the current valid version as of January 1, 1994 is ICC Publication 500 which is the 1993 edition.

It is highly recommended that all documentary credits (letters of credit) specify that they are subject to the UCPDC. *See* letter of credit; International Chamber of Commerce; and the Appendix for a listing of ICC publications that relate to the UCPDC.

Uniform Rules for Collections (URC)

(banking) The internationally recognized codification of rules unifying banking practice regarding collection operations for drafts, their payment or non-payment, protest and for documentary collections, (documents against payment, D/P, and documents against acceptance, D/A).

The URC was developed by a working group attached to the International Chamber of Commerce (ICC) in Paris, France. It is revised and updated from time to time and the current valid version as of January 1, 1994 is ICC Publication 322.

See documentary collection; International Chamber of Commerce; and the Appendix for a listing of ICC publications that relate to the URC.

United Nations Conference on Trade and Development (UNCTAD)

UNCTAD was set up in December 1964 as a permanent organ of the UN General Assembly. UNCTAD promotes international trade and seeks to increase trade between developing countries and countries with different social and economic systems. UNCTAD also examines problems of economic development within the context of principles and policies of international trade and seeks to harmonize trade, development, and regional economic policies. The Conference was first convened (UNCTAD-1) in Geneva in 1964.

United Nations Industrial Development Organization (UNIDO)

Established in 1967, under the UN Secretariat, UNIDO serves as a specialized agency to foster industrial development in lesser developed countries through offering technical assistance in the form of expert services, supplying equipment and/or training. Address: United Nations Industrial Development Organization, PO Box 300, 1400 Vienna, Austria; Tel: [43] (1) 21-13-10; Telex: 135612; Fax: [43] (1) 23-21-56; http:..www.unido.org.

United States Affiliate

(U.S. foreign investment) A U.S. business enterprise in which there is foreign direct investment—that is, in which a single foreign person owns or controls, directly or indirectly, 10 percent or more of its voting securities if the enterprise is incorporated or an equivalent interest if the enterprise is unincorporated. The affiliate is called a U.S. affiliate to denote that the affiliate is located in the U.S. (although it is owned by a foreign person). *See* foreign person; affiliate.

United States and Foreign Commercial Service (US&FCS)

(U.S.) An agency of the U.S. Department of Commerce that helps U.S. firms compete more effectively in the global marketplace. The US&FCS has a network of trade specialists in 68 U.S. cities and 66 countries worldwide. US&FCS offices provide information on foreign markets, agent/distributor location services, trade leads, and counseling on business opportunities, trade barriers and prospects abroad. Address: United States and Foreign Commercial Service, International Trade Administration, Department of Commerce, Room 3802,

Washington, DC 20230 USA; Tel: [1] (202) 482-5777; Fax: (202) 482-5013.

United States-Canada Free Trade Agreement (FTA)

The provisions of the US/Canada Free Trade Agreement were adopted by the US with the enactment of the FTA Implementation Act of 1988. The FTA not only reduced tariffs on imported merchandise between Canada and the U.S., but opened up new areas of trade in investment services, agriculture, and business travel. In order to be eligible for FTA treatment, goods must not enter the commerce of a third country, or, if shipped through a third country, must remain under customs control.

Several publications about the United States-Canada Free Trade Agreement are available from: the National Technical Information Service (NTIS), 5285 Port Royal Road, Springfield, VA 22161; Tel: [1] (703) 487-4650; Revenue Canada, 875 Heron Rd., Ottawa, ON K1A 0L8, Canada; Tel: [1] (613) 993-0534; http://www.ntis.gov.

Other sources of information about the agreement can be obtained from the Office of Canada, U.S. Department of Commerce, 14th St. and Constitution Ave. NW, Washington, DC 20230 USA; Tel: [1] (202) 482-3101 and from the Office of North American Affairs, Office of the United States Trade Representative (USTR), Room 501, 600 17th St. NW, Washington, DC 20506 USA; Tel: [1] (202) 395-3412.

United States Code (USC)

(U.S. law) A set of volumes containing the official compilation of U.S. law. A new edition of the USC is printed every six years with supplemental volumes issued every year. The USC is found in larger public libraries and is available for purchase from the Superintendent of Documents, U.S. Government Printing Office, Washington, DC 20402 USA; Tel: (202) 512-1800. There are also local offices of the U.S. Government Printing Office in major U.S. cities.

United States Customs House Guide

(publication) A 2,200 page reference for importing to the United States. Profiles of U.S. and Canadian ports, tariff schedules, customs regulations plus service directories. Publisher: Global Trade Publishing Group, 401 North Broad Street, Philadelphia, PA 19108 USA; In the U.S. Tel: [1] (800) 777-8074.

United States Customs Service

(U.S. Customs) U.S. governmental agency, whose major responsibility is to administer the Tariff Act of 1930, as amended. Primary duties include the assessment and collection of all duties, taxes and fees on imported merchandise, and the enforcement of customs and related laws and treaties. As a major enforcement organization, the Customs Service combats smuggling and fraud on the revenue and enforces the regulations of numerous other federal agencies at ports of entry and along the land and sea borders of the U.S.

The customs territory of the United States consists of the 50 states, the District of Columbia, and Puerto Rico. The Customs Service, an agency under the Department of Treasury, has its headquarters in Washington, DC and is headed by a Commissioner of Customs. The field organization consists of seven geographical regions further divided into districts with ports of entry within each district. These organizational elements are headed respectively by regional commissioners, district directors (or area directors in the case of the New York Region), and port directors. The Customs Service is also responsible for administering the customs laws of the Virgin Islands of the United States.

Address: U.S. Customs Service Headquarters, 1301 Constitution Avenue NW, Washington, DC 20229 USA; Tel: [1] (202) 927-1000; http://www.customs.ustreas.gov.

U.S. Customs regional and district offices are in Boston, Massachusetts; New York, NY; Miami, Florida; New Orleans, Louisiana; Houston, Texas; Los Angeles, California; and Chicago, Illinois.

The U.S. Customs Service also has offices in Austria, Belgium, Canada, France, Hong Kong, Italy, Japan, Korea, Mexico, The Netherlands, Panama, Singapore, Thailand, The United Kingdom, Uruguay, and Germany. These offices are a part of the U.S. Embassy complex in each country.

United States Department of Agriculture (DOA)

(U.S. government) An executive department which serves as the principal adviser to the president on agricultural policy. The Department works to improve and maintain farm income, implement nutrition programs and develop and expand markets abroad for U.S. agricultural products. It is also charged with inspecting and grading food products for safe consumption. Organizations within the Department of Agriculture include: Agricultural Marketing Service, Agricultural Stabilization and

Conservation Service, Animal and Plant Inspection Service, the Commodity Credit Corporation, the Extension Service, the Farmers Home Administration, Federal Grain Inspection Service, the Food and Inspection Service, the Food Safety and Inspection Service, the Foreign Agricultural Service, Forest Service, Rural Electrification Administration, Soil Conservation Service. Address: United States Department of Agriculture, 14th St. and Independence Ave. SW, Washington, DC 20250 USA; Tel: [1] (202) 720-2791; http://www.usda.gov. Foreign Agricultural Service; Tel: [1] (202) 720-7115.

United States Department of Commerce (DOC)

(U.S. government) An executive department which encourages and promotes the United States' economic growth, international trade, and technological advancement. The Department provides a wide variety of programs to increase American competitiveness in the world economy and to assist business. The DOC also: works to prevent unfair foreign trade competition, provides social and economic statistics and analyses, supports the increased use of scientific engineering and technological development, grants patents and registers trademarks, and provides assistance to promote domestic economic development. Organizations within the DOC include the Bureau of Export Administration, Tel: [1] (202) 482-2000; the Census Bureau, Tel: [1] (301) 763-7662; the Economic Development Administration, Tel: [1] (202) 482-2000; the International Trade Administration, Tel: [1] (202) 482-2000; the Minority Business Development Agency, Tel: [1] (202) 482-2000; the National Institute of Standards and Technology, Tel: [1] (301) 975-2000; the National Oceanic and Atmospheric Administration, Tel: [1] (301) 443-8910; the Patent and Trademark Office, Tel: [1] (703) 305-8341 (Public Affairs) or [1] (800) 786-9199; the Technology Administration, Tel: [1] (202) 482-2100; and the U.S. Travel and Tourism Administration, Tel: [1] (202) 482-0137. Address: United States Department of Commerce, 14th Street & Constitution Ave. NW, Washington, DC 20230 USA; Tel: [1] (202) 482-2000; http://www.doc.gov. *See also* Bureau of Export Administration; International Trade Administration.

United States Department of Defense

(U.S. government) A civilian executive department providing the military forces needed to deter war and protect the security of the U.S. There are three departments within the Department of Defense: the Air Force, Army, and Navy. Address: United States Department of Defense, The Pentagon, Washington, DC 20301 USA; Tel: [1] (703) 697-5737; http://www.defenselink.mil.

United States Department of Energy (DOE)

(U.S. government) An executive department created in 1977 to consolidate all major Federal energy functions into one department. The principal programmatic missions are energy programs, weapons and waste clean-up programs, and science and technology programs. Organizations under the department include the Economic Regulatory Administration, the Energy Information Administration, and the Federal Energy Regulatory Commission. Address: United States Department of Energy, 1000 Independence Ave. SW, Washington, DC 20585 USA; Tel: [1] (202) 586-5806; http://www.doe.gov.

United States Department of Labor (DOL)

(U.S. government) An executive department which promotes and develops the welfare of U.S. wage earners, improves working conditions, and advances opportunities for profitable employment. The DOL keeps track of changes in employment, prices, and other national economic measures. Organizations under the Department include the Bureau of Labor Statistics, the Employment and Training Administration, the Employment Standards Administration, Labor-Management Standards, the Mine Safety and Health Administration, Occupational Safety and Health, and the Pension and Welfare Benefits Administration. Address: United States Department of Labor, 200 Constitution Ave. NW, Washington, DC 20210 USA; Tel: [1] (202) 219-6666; http://www.dol.gov.

United States Department of State

(U.S. government) An executive department which directs U.S. foreign relations and negotiates treaties and agreements with foreign nations. Activities of the State Department are coordinated with foreign activities of other U.S. departments and agencies. Organizations within the Department include the Bureau of Consular Affairs, the Bureau of Economic and Business Affairs, the Bureau of Intelligence and Research, the Bureau of International Organization Affairs, and the Bureau of Oceans. Address: United States Department of State, 2201 C St. NW, Washington, DC 20520 USA; Tel: [1] (202) 647-4000; http://www.state.gov.

United States Department of the Interior (DOI)

(U.S. government) An executive department that has responsibility for most U.S. federal government owned public lands and natural resources; the principal U.S. conservation agency. The office of Territorial and International Affairs oversees activities pertaining to U.S. territorial lands and the Freely Associated States and coordinates the international affairs of the Department. Organizations under the DOI include: the Bureau of Indian Affairs, the Bureau of Land Management, the Bureau of Mines, the Bureau of Reclamation, the Minerals Management Service, the National Park Service, the U.S. Fish and Wildlife Service, and the U.S. Geological Survey. Address: United States Department of the Interior, 1849 C St. NW, Washington, DC 20240 USA; Tel: [1] (202) 208-3171; http://www.doi.gov.

United States Department of the Treasury

(U.S. government) An executive department which performs four basic functions: formulating and recommending economic, financial, tax and fiscal policies; serving as financial agent for the U.S. government; enforcing the law; and manufacturing coins and currency. The International Affairs unit is responsible for Department activities in international monetary affairs, trade and investment policy, international debt strategy, and U.S. participation in international financial institutions. The Under Secretary of the International Affairs unit acts as the U.S. Group of Seven (G-7) Deputy. Organizations within the Department include the Bureau of Alcohol, Tobacco and Firearms; the Bureau of Engraving and Printing; the Comptroller of the Currency; the Internal Revenue Service; the Office of Thrift Supervision; the U.S. Customs Service; the U.S. Mint; the U.S. Secret Service. Address: United States Department of the Treasury, 1500 Pennsylvania Ave. NW, Washington, DC 20220 USA; Tel: [1] (202) 622-2000; http://www.ustreas.gov. *See also* Group of Seven (G-7); United States Customs Service; Bureau of Alcohol, Tobacco and Firearms.

United States Department of Transportation (DOT)

(U.S. government) An executive department of the U.S. government established by the Department of Transportation Act of 1966 (80 Stat 931) for the purpose of developing national transportation policies. Organizations within the Department of Transportation include the Federal Aviation Administration, the Federal Highway Administration, the Federal Railroad Administration, the Federal Transit Administration, the Maritime Administration, the National Highway Traffic Safety Administration, the Research and Special Programs Administration, the St. Lawrence Seaway Development Corporation, and the U.S. Coast Guard. Address: United States Department of Transportation, 400 7th Street SW, Washington, DC 20590 USA; Tel: [1] (202) 366-4000; http://www.dot.gov.

United States Foreign Trade Definitions

An obsolete standard of trade terms, although they are sometimes specified in U.S. domestic contracts. The international standard of trade terms is Incoterms 2000. *See* Incoterms 2000.

United States Information Agency (USIA)

(U.S. government) Responsible for the U.S. government overseas information and cultural programs, including Voice of America. Conducts a wide variety of communication activities—academic and cultural exchanges to press, radio, television and library programs abroad—in order to strengthen foreign understanding of American society, obtain greater support of U.S. policies, and increase understanding between the U.S. and other countries. Overseas, the USIA is known as the U.S. Information Service (USIS). Address: United States Information Agency, 301 Fourth Street SW, Washington, DC 20547 USA; Tel: [1] (202) 619-4700; http://www.usia.gov.

United States International Trade Commission

(U.S. government) Formerly the U.S. Tariff Commission, which was created in 1916 by an Act of Congress. Its mandate was broadened and its name changed by the Trade Act of 1974. It is an independent fact-finding agency of the U.S. government that studies the effects of tariffs and other restraints to trade on the U.S. economy. It conducts public hearings to assist in determining whether particular U.S. industries are injured or threatened with injury by dumping, export subsidies in other countries, or rapidly rising imports. It also studies the probable economic impact on specific U.S. industries of proposed reductions in U.S. tariffs and non-tariff barriers to imports. Its six members are appointed by the President with the advice and consent of the U.S. Senate for nine-year terms (six-year terms prior to 1974). Address: International Trade Commission, 500 E Street SW, Washington, DC 20436 USA; Tel: [1] (202) 205-2511.

U

United States-Japan Semiconductor Trade Arrangement

See Semiconductor Trade Arrangement.

United States Munitions List

(U.S.) The USML identifies those items or categories of items considered to be defense articles and defense services subject to export control. The USML is similar in coverage to the International Munitions List (IML), but is more restrictive in two ways. First, the USML currently contains some dual-use items that are controlled for national security and foreign policy reasons (such as space-related or encryption-related equipment). Second, the USML contains some nuclear-related items. Under Presidential directive, most dual-use items are to be transferred from the USML to the Commerce Department's dual-use list. The Department of State, with the concurrence of Defense, designates which articles will be controlled under the USML. Items on the Munitions List face a stricter control regime and lack the safeguards to protect commercial competitiveness that apply to dual-use items. *See* International Munitions List; United States Department of State.

United States price

(U.S.) In the context of dumping investigations, this term refers to the price at which goods are sold in the U.S. compared to their foreign market value. The comparisons are used in the process of determining whether imported merchandise is sold at less than fair value. *See* dumping.

United States Trade and Development Agency

(U.S. government) An independent agency within the executive branch. Its mandate is to promote economic development in, and simultaneously export U.S. goods and services to, developing and middle-income countries. The Agency conducts feasibility studies and orientation visits, and provides trade-related training to assist U.S. firms in becoming involved in developing projects with substantial U.S. export potential. It also coordinates government-to-government technical assistance. Address: United States Trade and Development Agency, Room 309, State Annex 16, Washington, DC 20523-1602 USA; Tel: [1] (703) 875-4357.

United States Trade Representative

(U.S. government) A cabinet-level official with the rank of Ambassador who is the principal adviser to the President on international trade policy, and has responsibility for setting and administering overall trade policy. The U.S. Trade Representative is concerned with the expansion of U.S. exports; U.S. participation in the World Trade Organization (WTO), commodity issues; East-West and North-South trade; and direct investment related to trade. As Chairman of the U.S. Trade Policy Committee he is also the primary official responsible for U.S. participation in all international trade negotiations. Prior to the Trade Agreements Act of 1979, which created the Office of the U.S. Trade Representative, the comparable official was known as the President's Special Representative for Trade Negotiations (STR), a position first established by the Trade Expansion Act of 1962. Address: United States Trade Representative, 600 17th St. NW, Room 522, Washington, DC 20508 USA; Tel: [1] (202) 395-3204.

unitization

(shipping) The practice or technique of consolidating many small pieces of freight into a single unit for easier handling.

unit load

(shipping) The strapping or banding together of a number of individual cartons, packages, sacks, drums or other cargo, often on a pallet, in order to create a single unit.

unit load device

(shipping) Term commonly used when referring to containers and pallets.

universal agency

See agency.

Universal Copyright Convention

An international agreement that was concluded to afford copyright protection to literary and artistic works in all countries that voluntarily agree to be bound by the Convention terms. *See* copyright; trademark; service mark.

unloading

(shipping) The physical removal of cargo from carrier's container.

unrestricted letter of credit

(banking) A letter of credit which may be negotiated through any bank of the beneficiary's choice. *See* letter of credit.

Uruguay Round

(GATT) The eighth round of multilateral trade negotiations concerning the General Agreement on Tariffs and Trade (GATT). The Uruguay Round (so named because meetings began in Punta del Este, Uruguay in 1987) concluded in December, 1993 after seven years of talks with 117 member nations. The major goals of the Uruguay Round were to reduce barriers to trade in goods; to strengthen the role of GATT and improve the multilateral trading system; to increase the responsiveness of GATT to the evolving international economic environment; to encourage cooperation in strengthening the inter-relationship between trade and other economic policies affecting growth and development; and the establishment of a multilateral framework of principles and rules for trade in services, including the elaboration of possible disciplines for individual service sectors.

Key provisions of the Uruguay Round agreements were: a reduction of import tariffs, with an overall cut of more than 33 percent of global tariffs; a gradual reduction of 36 percent of government subsidies for farmers; a phasing-out of import protection for textile producers in industrialized countries allowing more open markets for entry of cheaper products from Third World countries; stricter anti-dumping rules; greater global protection of intellectual property rights, including patents and copyrighted goods such as films and music. Although agriculture and other industries were brought under GATT for the first time, certain industries (such as the entertainment industry) were, in the end, excluded from the Round negotiations in order for negotiators to reach a final agreement. Particularly disappointing to many was the lack of progress in opening access to the trade of financial services, such as banking, accounting, and insurance. Most aspects of the agreement went into effect July 1, 1995.

Agreements reached at the Uruguay Round covered:

(1) **Market Access for Goods**—Tariffs to be reduced by an average of one-third, with the U.S. and other major industrial nations eliminating tariffs altogether on some products, by one-half on others, while cutting tariffs much less in the rest of the world.

(2) **Agriculture**—Strengthened long-term rules for agricultural trade and assures reduction of specific policies that distort agricultural trade. Addressed export subsidies, domestic subsidies, and market access. Agricultural export subsidies and some farm subsidies made subject to multilateral disciplines, and to be bound and reduced. Many non-tariff measures, including quotas to be converted to low tariffs over time.

(3) **Textiles and Clothing**—The Multi-Fiber Arrangement (MFA), a system of quotas that limits imports of textiles and apparel to the U.S. and other developed countries, to be phased out over a 10

year period. The quotas will eventually be replaced by tariffs.

(4) **Safeguards**—Provided incentives for countries to use GATT safeguard rules when import-related, serious injury problems occur.

(5) **Antidumping**—Revised the 1979 Antidumping Code, by improving provisions to define, deter, and discourage the use of dumping practices. Disputes between GATT members to be settled by binding dispute settlement.

(6) **Subsidies and Countervailing Measures**—Established clearer rules and stronger disciplines in the subsidies area while also making certain subsidies non-actionable.

(7) **Trade-related Investment Measures** (TRIMs)—Limited the ability of countries to favor domestically owned factories at the expense of foreign-owned ones. Prohibits local content and trade balancing requirements. Established a 5 to 7-year transition period for developing and least-developed countries.

(8) **Import Licensing Procedures**—More precisely defined automatic and non-automatic licensing. Signatories that adopt new procedures to notify the Import Licensing Committee within 60 days and provide information about it.

(9) **Customs Valuation**—Amendments to the Customs Valuation Code to help stem fraud, retain established minimum values, and encourage developing countries to study areas of concern in customs valuation.

(10) **Preshipment Inspection**—Regulated activities of Preshipment Inspection companies and reduced impediments to international trade resulting from the use of such companies, particularly in developing countries where they may supplement or replace national customs services.

(11) **Rules of Origin**—A program to be implemented to harmonize rules for determination of the origin of goods. Established a GATT Committee on Rules of Origin and a Customs Cooperation Council Technical Committee on Rules of Origin.

(12) **Technical Barriers to Trade**—Updated and improved rules respecting standards, technical regulations and conformity assessment procedures.

(13) **Sanitary and Phytosanitary Measures**—Established rules for the development of measures which are taken to protect human, animal or plant life or health in food safety or agriculture. Included quarantine procedures, food processing measures, meat inspection rules, procedures for approval of food additives or use of pesticides.

U

(14) **Services**—The General Agreement on Trade in Services (GATS) was the first multilateral, legally enforceable agreement covering trade investment in the service sectors. Principal elements included most-favored-nation treatment, national treatment, market access, transparency, and the free flow of payments and transfers.

(15) **Trade-Related Intellectual Property Rights** (TRIPs)—Established improved standards for the protection of a full range of property rights and the enforcement of those standards both internally and at the border. Covered: copyrights, patents, trademarks, industrial designs, trade secrets, integrated circuits, and geographical indications. Provided for a 20-year term of protection for most of these rights.

(16) **Dispute Settlement**—The Dispute Settlement Understanding (DSU) created new procedures for settlement of disputes arising under any of the Uruguay Round agreements.

(17) **World Trade Organization** (WTO)—Established a new organization available only to countries that were contracting parties to the GATT and that agreed and adhered to all of the Uruguay Round agreements. Encompassed and extended the then current GATT structure. The intention was for the new WTO to have a stature similar to that of the Bretton Woods financial institutions, the World Bank, and the International Monetary Fund.

(18) **GATT Articles**—Updated articles relating to balance-of-payment reform, state trading enterprises, regional trading arrangements, and waivers of obligation.

(19) **Trade Policy Review Mechanism**—Provided for regular examination of national trade policies and other economic policies bearing on international trading.

(20) **Ministerial Decisions and Declaration**—Stated the views and objectives of the Uruguay Round participants on a number of issues relating to the operation of the global trading system.

(21) **Government Procurement**—A new Agreement on Government Procurement replaced the existing agreement. Included procurement of services and construction and some coverage of subcentral governments and government-owned utilities.

See also General Agreement on Tariffs and Trade; rounds; Tokyo Round, World Trade Organization

U.S. ...
See United States ....

usance letter of credit

(banking) A documentary letter of credit which is not available by sight payment and which is therefore available against:
(1) acceptance of a term bill of exchange,
(2) or in certain usages by deferred payment. *See* letter of credit.

users fees

(U.S. Customs) Assessments collected by the U.S. Customs Service as part of the entry process to help defray various costs involved in the importation of goods to the United States.

(a) The **harbor maintenance fee** is an ad valorem fee assessed on cargo imports and admissions into foreign trade zones. The fee is 0.125 percent of the value of the cargo and is paid quarterly, except for imports which are paid at the time of entry. Customs deposits the harbor maintenance fee collections into the Harbor Maintenance Trust Fund. The funds are made available, subject to appropriation, to the Army Corps of Engineers for the improvement and maintenance of U.S. ports and harbors.

(b) The **merchandise processing fee** sets a fee schedule for formal entries (generally, those valued over US$1,250) at a minimum of US$21 per entry and a maximum of US$400 per entry, with an ad valorem rate of 0.17 percent. The fee for informal entries (those valued at under US$1,250) is US$2 for automated entries, US$5 for manual entries not prepared by Customs, and US$8 for manual entries prepared by Customs.

usuance

(banking) The time allowed for payment of an international obligation. A usuance credit is a credit available against time drafts. *See* letter of credit; usance letter of credit.

U

validated export license

(U.S.) A document issued by the U.S. government authorizing the export of commodities for which written export authorization is required by law. For more information on export licensing in general, call Exporter Assistance at: [1] (202) 482-4811. Address: Bureau of Export Administration, U.S. Department of Commerce, 14th St. and Constitution Ave. NW, Washington, DC 20230 USA; Tel: [1] (202) 482-2721; Fax: [1] (202) 482-2387.

validity

(banking) The time period for which a letter of credit is valid. After receiving notice of a letter of credit opened in his behalf, the seller/exporter/beneficiary must meet all the requirements of the letter of credit within the period of validity. *See* letter of credit.

valuation

The fixing of value to anything.

(customs) The appraisal of the worth of imported goods by customs officials for the purpose of determining the amount of duty payable in the importing country. The WTO Customs Valuation Code obligates governments that sign it to use the "transaction value" of imported goods—or the price actually paid or payable for them—as the principal basis for valuing the goods for customs purposes.

(U.S. Customs) U.S. Customs officers are required by law to determine the value of imported merchandise. Valuation is necessary for statistical purposes as well as to determine the amount of import duty which must be paid if the duty rate is stated as a percentage of value (ad valorem duty).

Generally, the Customs value of all merchandise exported to the United States is the transaction value for the goods. The transaction value of imported merchandise is the price actually paid or payable for the merchandise when sold for exportation to the United States, plus amounts for the following items if not included in the price:

(1) The packing costs incurred by the buyer.

(2) Any selling commission incurred by the buyer,

(3) The value of any assist,

(4) Any royalty or license fee that the buyer is required to pay as a condition of the sale, and

(5) The proceeds, accruing to the seller, of any subsequent resale, disposal, or use of the imported merchandise.

The amounts for the above items are added only to the extent that each is not included in the price actually paid or payable and information is available to establish the accuracy of the amount. If sufficient information is not available, then the transaction value cannot be determined and the next basis of value, in order of precedence, must be considered for appraisement. The secondary bases of value, listed in order of precedence for use, are:

(1) Transaction value of identical merchandise,

(2) Transaction value of similar merchandise,

(3) Deductive value, and

(4) Computed value.

The order of precedence of the last two values can be reversed if the importer so requests.

See transaction value; deductive value; computed value.

valuation charges

(shipping) Transportation charges assessed shippers who declare a value of goods higher than the value of carriers' limits of liability. *See* declared value for carriage.

valuation clause

(insurance) A clause in an insurance policy stating the value of the policy. A valuation clause commonly in use reads:

"valued premium included at amount of invoice, including all charges in the invoice and including prepaid and/or advanced and/or guaranteed freight, if any, plus _____%." (This is usually 10% on exports.)

value added

(economics) That part of the value of produced goods developed in a company. It is determined by subtracting from sales the costs of materials and supplies, energy costs, contract work, and so on, and it includes labor expenses, administrative and sales costs, and other operating profits. *See also* value-added tax.

value added counseling

Valued added (export) counseling is defined as assessing a company's current international business operations and assisting a client in one or more of the following: (1) identifying and selecting the most viable markets; (2) developing an export market strategy; (3) implementing the export market strategy; and (4) increasing market presence.

value-added tax (VAT)

(taxation) An indirect tax on consumption that is assessed on the increased value of goods at each discrete point in the chain of production and distribution, from the raw material stage to final consumption. The tax on processors or merchants is levied on the amount by which they increase the value of items they purchase and resell.

value date
(banking) Fixing of a value date for accounting purposes on banking operations, i.e. the date on which the interest accrual for the respective accounting entry begins or ends.

variable rate of duty
(customs) A tariff subject to alterations as world market prices change, the alterations are designed to assure that the import price after payment of the duty will equal a predetermined "gate" price.

vatu
The currency of Vanuatu. 1VT=100 centimes.

vega
(statistics/foreign exchange) The price change of a foreign exchange option for a 1 percent change in the implied volatility.

vendor
A company or individual that supplies goods or services.

Vennootschap onder firma
(Netherlands) Designation for a general partnership, in which all partners have joint and several liability.

vertical export trading company
An export trading company that integrates a range of functions taking products from suppliers to consumers.

vessel ton
(shipping/measurement) A unit of measurement in the shipping industry assuming that 100 cubic feet of cargo equals one ton.

visa
(general) A certificate or stamp placed in a passport by a foreign government's embassy, consular office or other representative. It permits the holder to either visit (tourist visa) conduct business in (business visa), work (work permit or visa) in, or immigrate (residency or immigration visa) to the issuing country for a specified time.
(customs) A license issued by the government of an exporting country for the export to a specific importing country of a certain quantity of a quota controlled commodity (such as textiles) subject to a voluntary export restriction or a voluntary restraint agreement.

visa waiver
A program of selected countries to eliminate their visa requirement on a test basis.

vis major
(law) A major force or disturbance, usually a natural cause, that a person cannot prevent despite exercise of due care. Floods and labor strikes are examples of vis major events.

void ab initio
(law) Invalid from the time of initiation. A contract, for example, that violates law or public policy is void ab initio, that is, it is invalid when it is made.

voidable contract
(law) An agreement that is valid but that one party may declare invalid because of a defect or illegality in making it. A contract that is entered into in reliance on a fraudulent misrepresentation, for example, will be enforced against the party that committed the fraud, but the party harmed by the misrepresentation may elect to void the contract.

void contract
(law) An agreement that has no legal effect and that cannot be ratified or otherwise made effective. A contract that requires the performance of an illegal act, for example, is void and cannot become effective.

volatility
(foreign exchange) The measure of the relative deviation of a price from the mean.

volume rate
(shipping) A rate applicable in connection with a specified volume of freight.

voluntary export restriction
An understanding between trading partners in which the exporting nation, in order to reduce trade friction, agrees to limit its exports of a particular good. Also called voluntary restraint agreement. *See* voluntary restraint agreements.

voluntary restraint agreements (VRA's)
Informal bilateral or multilateral arrangements through which exporters voluntarily restrain certain exports, usually through export quotas to avoid economic dislocation in an importing country and to avert the possible imposition of mandatory import restrictions.

These arrangements do not involve an obligation on the part of the importing country to provide "compensation" to the exporting country, as would be the case if the importing country unilaterally imposed equivalent restraints on imports. *See* voluntary export restriction; quota; visa.

W

war clause
(insurance) An insurance clause included in policies to cover against losses as a result of war. *See* war risk.

warehouse receipt
(shipping) An instrument (document) listing the goods or commodities deposited in a warehouse. It is a receipt for the commodities listed, and for which the warehouse is the bailee. Warehouse receipts may be either non-negotiable or negotiable.

warehouse-to-warehouse
(insurance) Insurance coverage of risks to a shipment of goods from the time the goods leave the warehouse for commencement of transit and continue during ordinary course of transit until delivered to final warehouse at destination, or until the expiration of 15 days (30 if destination is outside the limits of the port), whichever shall first occur. In the case of delay in excess of the time limit specified, if it arises from circumstances beyond his control, the assured is "held covered" if he gives prompt notice and pays additional premium. *See* Marine Extension Clause 1943 & 1952; currency (term) of insurance.

warehouse, U.S. Customs bonded
(U.S. Customs) A federal warehouse where goods remain until duty has been collected from the importer. Goods under bond are also kept here. *See* surety; bond; in bond.

warranty
(law) A promise by a contracting party that the other party can rely on certain facts or representations as being true. A seller, for example, may warrant that certain products will meet a list of specifications furnished by the buyer.

war risk
(insurance) The risk to a vessel, its cargo and passengers by aggressive actions of a hostile nation or group. *See* war risk insurance.

war risk insurance
(insurance) Insurance coverage against war risks as outlined in detail in some dozen rather specific paragraphs of an insurance policy. The policy conditions must be read for complete understanding. In general, they cover risks of capture and seizure, destruction or damage by warlike operations in prose-

cution of hostilities, civil wars and insurrections or in the application of sanctions under international agreements. Delay or loss of market is excluded. Loss or expense arising from detainments, nationalization of the government to or from which the goods are insured or seizure under quarantine or customs regulations is also excluded.

War risk insurance generally attaches as goods are first loaded on board a vessel at the port of shipment, and it ceases to attach as goods are landed at the intended port of discharge or on expiry of 15 days from arrival of the overseas vessel whichever first occurs. It includes transshipment and intermediate overland transit to an on-carrying overseas vessel, if any, but in no case for more than 15 days counting from midnight of the day of arrival of the overseas vessel at the intended port of discharge. If in transshipment, the 15-day period is exceeded, the insurance re-attaches as the interest is loaded on the on-carrying vessel. In case the voyage is terminated and the goods are discharged at a port or place other than the original port of discharge, such port or place shall be deemed the intended port of discharge.

The war risk policy is subject to 48 hours cancellation by either party. However, it cannot be cancelled on shipments upon which insurance has already attached. Since the cancellation provision is used at times for changing the conditions of insurance the current coverage should be studied for exact understanding of the war risk policy.

War risk insurance is routinely obtained for protection against mines and other implements of war from former wars.

Warsaw Convention
(shipping) Formal name: The Convention for the Unification of Certain Rules Relating to International Carriage by Air, signed in Warsaw in 1929. An international multilateral treaty which regulates, in a uniform manner, the conditions of international transportation by air. Among other things it establishes the international liability of air carriers and establishes the monetary limits for loss, damage, and delay.

Watch List
See Special 301.

waybill
(shipping) A document prepared by a transportation line at the point of a shipment, showing the point or origin, destination, route, consignor, consignee, description of shipment and amount charged for the transportation service, and forwarded with the shipment, or direct by mail, to the

agent at the transfer point or waybill destination. *See* bill of lading; air waybill; ocean bill of lading.

Webb-Pomerene Act of 1918

(U.S. law) Federal legislation exempting exporters' associations from the antitrust regulations.

Webb-Pomerene Association

(U.S.) Associations engaged in exporting that combine the products of similar producers for overseas sales. These associations have partial exemption from U.S. anti-trust laws but may not engage in import, domestic or third country trade, or combine to export services.

weight break

(shipping) Levels at which the freight rate per 100 pounds decreases because of substantial increases in the weight of the shipment. Examples of levels at which weight breaks occur (in pounds) are 100, 500, 1,000, 3,000, 5,000 and 10,000.

weights and measures

See Weights and Measures in the Appendix for a complete listing.

weight ton

(measurement) (a) Short ton = 2,000 pounds, (b) Long ton = 2,240 pounds, (c) Metric ton = 2,204.68 pounds.

West Africa Economic Community

A regional alliance CEAO (French for Communauté Economique de l'Afrique), created in 1974, includes: Benin, Burkina Faso, Cote d'Ivoire, Mali, Mauritania, Niger, and Senegal. (Togo has observer status). The CEAO operates as a free trade area for agricultural products and raw materials and as a preferential trading area for approved industrial products, with a regional cooperation tax (TCR) replacing import duties and encouraging trade among member states. In order to ensure that benefits of the regional grouping flow to all members, especially the least developed ones (Mali, Mauritania, Niger, and Burkina Faso), the CEAO has established a fund to provide financial services and guarantees to development lenders in both public and private sectors for projects in member states. In addition, CEAO has the long-term objective of creating a customs union with extensive harmonization of fiscal policies between member states, though no concrete achievements in this direction have been recorded. Address: Communauté économique de l'Afrique de l'ouest (CEAO), rue Agostino Neto, 01 BP 643, Ouagadougou 01, Burkina Faso; Tel: 30-61-87; Telex: 5212.

West African Economic and Monetary Union

A regional alliance, WAMU (French: Union Monetaire Ouest Africaine, UMOA) was created by treaty signed in May 1962. WAMU comprises seven French-speaking African countries: Benin, Burkina Faso, Cote d'Ivoire, Mali, Niger, Senegal, and Togo. Within WAMU, these countries share a common currency (CFA Franc) freely convertible into the French Franc at a fixed parity, and a common Central Bank (BCEAO) responsible for the conduct of the Union's monetary and credit policies. There is also a common regional development bank, the Headquarters Address: 01 B.P. 543, Ouagafdougou 01, Burkina Faso; Tel: [226] 31-88-73; Fax: [226] 31-88-72 .

wharfage

(shipping) (a) A charge assessed by a pier or dock owner for handling incoming or outgoing cargo, (b) The charge made for docking vessels at a wharf.

with average (WA)

(insurance) Insurance coverage which gives the assured protection for partial damage by sea perils, if the partial damage amounts to 3% (or other percentage as specified) or more of the value of the whole shipment or of a shipping package. If the vessel has stranded, sunk, been on fire or in collision, the percentage requirement is waived and losses from sea perils are recoverable in full.

Additional named perils may be added to the WA Clause. Theft, pilferage, nondelivery, fresh water damage, sweat damage, breakage and leakage are often covered. The combination of perils needed by a particular assured will naturally depend upon the commodity being shipped and the trade involved.

In its standard form a typical with average clause may read:

Subject to particular average if amounting to 3%, unless general or the vessel and/or craft is stranded, sunk, burnt, on fire and/or in collision, each package separately insured or on the whole."

The "all risk" clause is a logical extension of the broader forms of "With Average" coverage. This clause reads:

To cover against all risks of physical loss or damage from any external cause irrespective of percentage, but excluding, nevertheless, the risk of war, strikes, riots, seizure, detention and other risks excluded by the F.C.&S. (Free of Capture and Seizure) Warranty and the S.R.&C.C. (Strikes, Riots and Civil Commotion) Warranty in this policy, excepting to the extent that such risks are specifically covered by endorsement."

Some types of loss are commonly excluded and others not recoverable, even under the "all risk" clauses.

See also average; particular average; general average; free of particular average; deductible average; all risk; special marine policy.

without reserve

(shipping) A term indicating that a shipper's agent or representative is empowered to make definitive decisions and adjustments abroad without approval of the group or individual represented.

with particular average

(insurance) Insurance covering also the loss of single cases or partial quantities (as opposed to free from particular average, fpa). *See also* average; particular average; deductible average; all risk.

won

The currency of:
North Korea, 1W=100 jun;
South Korea, 1W=100 jeon.

World Administrative Radio Conference

WARC refers to the conference convened regularly by the United Nations' International Telegraphic Union (ITU) to allocate and regulate radio frequencies for the purposes of television and radio broadcasting, telephone data communications, navigation, maritime and aeronautical communication, and satellite broadcasting. *See* International Telecommunications Union.

World Bank

(banking) The International Bank for Reconstruction and Development (IBRD), commonly referred to as the World Bank, is an intergovernmental financial institution located in Washington, DC. Its objectives are to help raise productivity and incomes and reduce poverty in developing countries. It was established in December 1945 on the basis of a plan developed at the Bretton Woods Conference of 1944. The Bank loans financial resources to credit worthy developing countries. It raises most of its funds by selling bonds in the world's major capital markets. Its bonds have, over the years, earned a quality rating enjoyed only by sound governments and leading corporations. Projects supported by the World Bank normally receive high priority within recipient governments and are usually well planned and supervised. The World Bank earns a profit, which is plowed back into its capital. Address: World Bank, 1818 H Street NW, Washington, DC 20433 USA; Tel: [1] (202) 477-1234; Telex: 248423; Fax: [1] (202) 477-6391. *See* International Bank for Reconstruction and Development; World Bank Group.

World Bank Group

(banking) An integrated group of international institutions that provides financial and technical assistance to developing countries. The group includes the International Bank for Reconstruction and Development, the International Development Association, and the International Finance Corporation. Address: World Bank Group, 1818 H Street NW, Washington, DC 20433; Tel: [1] (202) 477-1234; Fax: [1] (202) 477-6391; http://www.worldbank.org.

World Intellectual Property Organization

A specialized agency of the United Nations system of organizations that seeks to promote international cooperation in the protection of intellectual property around the world through cooperation among states, and administers various "Unions," each founded on a multilateral treaty and dealing with the legal and administrative aspects of intellectual property.

WIPO administers the International Union for the Protection of Industrial Property (the "Paris Union"), which was founded in 1883 to reduce discrimination in national patent practices, the International Union for the Protection of Literary and Artistic Works (the "Bern Union"), which was founded in 1886 to provide analogous functions with respect to copyrights, and other treaties, conventions and agreements concerned with intellectual property. Address: World Intellectual Property Organization, 34, chemin des Colombettes, CH-1211 Geneva 20, Switzerland; Tel: [41] (22) 730-9111; Telex: 412912 OMPI CH; Fax: [41] (22) 733-5428; http://www.wipo.int *See also* patent; copyright; service mark; trademark; Patent Cooperation Treaty.

World Meteorological Organization

The WMO facilitates worldwide cooperation in establishing a network for meteorological, hydrological, and geophysical observations, for exchanging meteorological and related information, and for promoting standardization in meteorological measurements. Address: World Meteorological Organization, Case Postale 2300, CH-1211 Geneva 2, Switzerland; Tel: [41] (22) 730-8111; Telex: 414199 OMMCH; Fax: [41] (22) 734-2326 http://www.wmo.ch

World Tourism Organization (WTO)

An intergovernmental technical body dealing with all aspects of tourism. The WTO promotes and develops tourism as a means of contributing to economic development, international understanding, peace, and prosperity. Headquarters address: World Tourism Organization, Calle Capitan Haya 42, E-28020 Madrid, Spain; Tel: [34] (1) 571-0628; Telex: 42188 OMT E; Fax: [34] (1) 571-3733; http://www.world-tourism.org.

world trade clubs / centers

Local or regional based organizations in the United States and around the world of importers, exporters, customs brokers, freight forwarders, attorneys, bankers, manufacturers and shippers.

Each world trade club provides different services and activities, but many provide: information services including data bases and libraries, educational services including seminars and regularly scheduled classes, meeting space, club atmosphere, dining, exhibit facilities, and trade missions. Most major cities in the world have world trade clubs. For a list of world trade clubs internationally contact: World Trade Center Association, One World Trade Center, Suite 7701, New York, NY 10048 USA; Tel: [1] (212) 432-2626; Fax: [1] (212) 488-0064; http://iserve.wtca.org.

World Trade Organization (WTO)

The WTO is the premier international organization seeking to deal with the global rules of trade between nations. Created by the Uruguay Round of trade negotiations (1986-1994) of the GATT (General Agreement on Tariffs and Trade), the WTO was established 1 January 1995, and is comprised of 134 nations with others actively seeking membership.

WTO Objective

The WTO's stated objective is to help trade flow smoothly, freely, fairly and predictably. It does this by administering WTO trade agreements, acting as a forum for international trade negotiations, settling trade disputes, monitoring national trade policies, assisting developing countries in trade policy issues through technical assistance and training programs, and cooperation with other international organizations.

The activities of the WTO are based on the implementation of multilateral trade agreements which have been negotiated and signed by a majority of the world's trading nations, and ratified by their parliments. These agreements are contracts guaranteeing member countries important trade rights. They also bind governments to keep their trade policies within agreed limits to the benefit of the whole.

WTO Structure

The WTO is run by its member governments. Major decisions are made by the membership as a whole, either by ministers (who meet every two years at a ministerial conference) or by officials (who meet regularly in Geneva). Decisions are normally made by consensus.

The ministerial conference can make decisions on all matters under any of the multilateral trade agreements. Day-to-day work in between the ministerial conferences is handled by three bodies: 1) The General Council, 2) The Dispute Settlement Body, and 3) The Trade Policy Review Body. All three are called The General Council, although they meet under different terms of reference.

Three more councils, each handling a different broad area of trade, report to the General Council. These are: 1) The Council for Trade in Goods (Goods Council), 2) The Council for Trade in Services (Services Council), and 3) The Council for Trade-Related Aspects of Intellectual Property (TRIPS Council).

Additional groups report to the General Council. The scope of their coverage is smaller, so they are called "committees." These committees cover such issues as trade and development, the environment, regional trading agreements, investment and competition policy, government procurement, trade facilitation, and others.

Each of the higher level councils has subsidiary bodies. For example, the Goods Council has 11 committees dealing with specific subjects such as agriculture, market access, subsidies, anti-dumping, and others.

The most difficult issues are not resolved in these upper level councils, but rather in much smaller meetings with representatives from as many as 40 countries to as few as two countries.

Successes

The WTO (and its predecessor GATT) has played a major role in the following areas: the reduction of tariffs on manufactured goods and agricultural products, the opening of banking, insurance and telecommunications markets to foreign competition, standards for the protection of intellectual property rights, food safety regulations, and bans on local preferences for government purchasing.

Challenges

With all its successes, the WTO is challenged by disputes by member nations to: 1) tariffs—lower or eliminate tariffs on agricultural, aquiculture and

forest products, scientific, environmental and medical equipment, and chemicals, 2) agricultural subsidies—eliminate government subsidies to
agriculture that set artificially low prices for agricultural products (thus hurting exporters), 3) intellectual property rights—either strengthen
intellectual property rights (primarily proposed by
advanced western nations that are home to major
pharmaceutical companies) or establish exemp-
tions from such rules (primarily proposed by developing nations that desire cheap access to drugs to
treat HIV/AIDS and other health probelms), 4) environment—establish more stringent rules designed to protect the environment, 5) services—
continue to open up such service industries such as
banking, insurance and medical technology, as well
as maintain a tax-free status on Internet commerce,
6) genetically modified food products—give nations more lattitude in their ability to exclude genetically altered food products based on public health
or environmental concerns, 7) labor—open discussions on how international trade affects labor and
possibly to establish international labor standards
in the areas of child labor, health, and safety issues,
and 8) transparency—make the WTO more trans-
parent by eliminating sectretive practices.

World Trade Organization; Centre William Rap-
pard; Rue de Lausanne 154; CH-1211 Geneva 21;
Switzerland; Tel: [41] (22) 739-51-11; http://
www.wto.org. WTO Information and Media Relations Division; Tel: [41] (22) 739-50-07; Fax: [41]
(22) 739-54-58; email: enquiries@wto.org. WTO
Publications; Tel: [41] (22) 739-52-08 / 739-53-08;
Fax: [41] (22) 739-57-92; email: publica-
tions@wto.org.

See also General Agreement on Tariffs and Trade,
Uruguay Round.

World Traders Data Reports

(U.S.) A fee-based service which provides a background report on a specific foreign firm, prepared
by U.S. commercial officers overseas. WTDRs provide information about the type of organization,
year established, relative size, number of employees, general reputation, territory covered, language
preferred, product lines handled, principal owners,
financial references, and trade references. WTDRs
include narrative information about the reliability
of the foreign firm. Cost is $100 per report. Issued
by the ITA. To obtain a World Traders Data Report,
contact the nearest Department of Commerce district office, or call [1] (800) USA-TRADE.

World Wide Web (WWW)

(Internet) The international network of electronic
links that connect personal computers with computer servers. Also referred to as 'the Web'.

writ

(law) A judicial order to a person, often a shcriff,
judge, or another officer of the law, to perform a
specified act or to have the act performed. Writs of
attachment, execution, and replevin are examples
of writs that courts issue to require officials to carry
out court judgments. *See* attachment; execution; replevin.

writer

(foreign exchange) The party which writes an option (also known as the option seller). The writer
undertakes the obligation to carry out the conditions of the options contract according to the choice
of the option buyer during the whole life to maturity of the option. For this he receives a premium
which is paid to him by the buyer of the option.

WTO

See World Trade Organization (WTO).

WWW

See World Wide Web

X-Y-Z

yen
The currency of Japan. 1¥=100 sen.

yuan
The currency of China. 1¥=100 fen.

zaire
The currency of Zaire. 1Z=100 makuta.

Zangger Committee
Examines controls enacted pursuant to the Nuclear Nonproliferation Treaty by refining the list of items requiring nuclear safeguards. The Zangger Committee consists of 23 Nuclear Non-Proliferation Treaty (NPT) nuclear supplier nations and includes all nuclear weapons states except France and China. Through a series of consultations in the early 1970's, the countries of the Zangger Committee compiled a "trigger list" of nuclear materials and equipment. The shipment of any item on the list to a non-nuclear weapons state "triggers" the requirement of International Atomic Energy Agency (IAEA) safeguards. Since the Zangger Committee is associated with the NPT, its members are obligated to treat all non-nuclear weapons parties to the treaty alike. For fear of discrediting the NPT, the Zangger countries cannot target strict nuclear controls toward certain nations with questionable proliferation credentials; the NPT binds them to assist non-nuclear weapons states with peaceful atomic energy projects. *See* International Atomic Energy Agency; Nuclear Non-Proliferation Treaty.

zip code
(shipping) A numerical code, established by the U.S. Postal Service, used for the purpose of routing and to identify delivery zones. Some U.S. carriers apply this code for freight in the same manner.

zloty
The currency of Poland. 1Zl=100 groszy.

zone
(shipping) Any one of a number of sections or districts of the United States or of the world used for the purpose of establishing proper rates for parcels, mail, and pickup and delivery.

zone status
(U.S. foreign trade zones) The legal status of merchandise which has been admitted to a U.S. foreign trade zone, thereby becoming subject to the provisions of the Foreign Trade Zone Act (FTZA). *See* foreign trade zone; Foreign Trade Zone Board; Foreign Trade Zone Act; grantee; operator; zone user; subzones.

zone user
(U.S. foreign trade zones) A corporation, partnership or party that uses a U.S. foreign trade zone for storage, handling, processing, or manufacturing merchandise in zone status, whether foreign or domestic. Usually, the zone user is the party which requests a Customs permit to admit, process or remove zone status merchandise. In subzones, the operator and zone user are usually the same party. Users pay the grantee or operator for services such as rent on facilities, storage, handling, promotion and similar services. *See* foreign trade zone; Foreign Trade Zone Board; Foreign Trade Zone Act; operator; zone user; subzones; zone status.

X
Y
Z

Acronyms and Abbreviations[1]

A

AAA
American Arbitration Association

AAB
Arab-African Bank

AAEI
American Association of Exporters and Importers

AAR
Against All Risks (insurance)

AB
Aktiebolag. company limited by shares. *See* Business Entities Appendix.

ABI
Automated Broker Interface
American Business Initiative

ABTA
Association of British Travel Agents

A/C
Account Current

ACC
Arab Cooperation Council

ACDA
Arms Control and Disarmament Agency

ACE
Agrupamento Complementar de Empresas, *See* Business Entities Appendix.

ACEP
Advisory Committee on Export Policy

ACH
Automated Clearinghouse

ACP
African, Caribbean, and Pacific

ACS
Automated Commercial System

ACTPN
Advisory Committee on Trade Policy and Negotiations

a/d
After date

AD
Aktzionerno Drouzestvo. *See* Business Entities Appendix.

ADB
Asian Development Bank

ADF
African Development Foundation

ADS
Agent Distributor Service

Ad Val (or A.V.)
Ad Valorem

AE
Anonymos Eteria. *See* Business Entities Appendix.

AECA
Arms Export Control Act

AEIE
Agrupamento Europeu de Interêsse Econômico. *See* Business Entities Appendix.

AEN
Administrative Exception Note

AEV
Articles of Extraordinary Value

AFDB
African Development Bank

AFT
Bureau of Alcohol, Tobacco, and Firearms

AG
Aktiengesellschaften. *See* Business Entities Appendix.
Australia Group

AGX
Agriculture Export Connections

AID
Agency for International Development

AIES
Automated Information Exchange System

AIMS
Agriculture Information and Marketing Services

AIT
American Institute in Taiwan

AL
Arab League

AMB
Ambassador

AMF
Airport Mail Facility

AMS
Automated Manifest System

AMU
Arab Maghreb Union

ANSI
American National Standards Institute

A/O
Account Of

AOSIS
Alliance of Small Island States

APAC
Agriculture Policy Advisory Committee
Auto Parts Advisory Committee

APEC
Asian-Pacific Economic Cooperation

APHIS
Animal and Plant Health Inspection Service

---

1. Most acronyms are written in upper case letters without periods (.). However, due to different customs and practice they may be written in uppercase and/or lowercase, and with or without various punctuation. Some examples: Facsimile may be abbreviated as Fax, fax, Fax:, fax., or telefax. Foreign Exchange may be abbreviated as FX or F/X. United States of America may be abbreviated as U.S.A., U.S., USA or US.

A C R O N Y M S

APO
Administrative Protective Order

a.s.
Akciova Spolecnost, *See* Business
    Entities Appendix.

A.S.
Anonim Sirket. *See* Business
    Entities Appendix.

A/S
Aktieselskab. *See* Business
    Entities Appendix.
Aksjeselskap

ASEAN
Association of Southeast Asian
    Nations

ASIC
Application-Specific Integrated
    Circuit

ATA Carnet
"Admission Temporaire-
    Temporary Admission" Carnet

ATI
American Traders Index
Andean Trade Initiative

ATP
Advanced Technology Products

ATPI
Andean Trade Preference
    Initiative

AT&T
American Telephone & Telegraph

AUTOVON
Automatic Voice Network

avdp.
avoirdupois (weight)

A.V. (or Ad Val)
Ad Valorem

B

B.A.
Buenos Aires (Argentina)

B/A
Bill of Adventure

BAF
Bunker Adjustment Factor

BATF
Bureau of Alcohol, Tobacco, and
    Firearms

Bbl
Barrel

B/C
Bill of Credit

B/D
Bank Draft

B./Dft.
Bank Draft

Bd. Ft. (also fbm)
Board Foot

Bdl
Bundle

B/E
Bill of Exchange

BENELUX
Belgium, Netherlands,
    Luxembourg Economic Union

BF
Board Foot

BFP
Bona Fide Purchaser

B.H.
Bill of Health

BHC
Bank Holding Company
British High Commission

Bhd.
Berhad. *See* Business Entities
    Appendix.

BIE
Bureau of International
    Expositions

BIS
Bank for International Settlements

BIT(s)
Bilateral Investment Treaty(ies)

B/L
Bill of Lading

BLEU
Belgium-Luxembourg Economic
    Union

Bls
Bales

B/M
Board measure

B.O.
Bad order

BOP
Balance of Payments

BOT
Balance of Trade

B/P
Bill of Parcels
Bills Payable

B/R
Bills Receivable

BRITE
Basic Research in Industrial
    Technologies in Europe

B.S.
Bill of Sale

BSA
Bilateral Steel Agreement

BSP
Business Sponsored
Between Show Promotion

Bt
Betéti Társaság. *See* Business
    Entities Appendix.

BTN
Brussels Tariff Nomenclature

B/V
Book Value

B.V.B.A.
Besloten Vennootschap met
    Beperkte Aansprakelijkheid.
    See Business Entities Appendix.

BWS
Bank Wire Service
Bretton-Woods System

Bx
Box

BXA
Bureau of Export Administration

C

C
Consulate

C.A.
Compainía Anómima. *See*
Business Entities Appendix.

CAB
Civil Aeronautics Board

CACM
Central American Common
Market

CAD/CAM
Computer Aided Design/
Computer Aided Manufacturing

C.A.F.
Currency Adjustment Factor

CAP
Common Agricultural Policy
Country Action Plan

CAR
Commercial Activity Report

CARICOM
Caribbean Common Market

CASE
Council of American States in
Europe

CBD
Commerce Business Daily

CBERA
Caribbean Basin Economic
Recovery Act

CBI
Caribbean Basin Initiative

Cbm/ (or C.B.M.)
Cubic Meter

CBW
Chemical and Biological
Weapons

CCC
Canadian Commercial
Corporation
Commodity Credit Corporation
Customs Cooperation Council

CCCN
Customs Cooperation Council
Nomenclature

CCL
Commerce Control List.
(Commodity Control List)

C.D.
Carried Down
Certificate of Deposit

CD-R
Compact Disc—Rewritable

CD-ROM
Compact Disc—Read Only
Memory

CDT
Center for Defense Trade

CEA
Council of Economic Advisors

CEAO
West Africa Economic
Community (Communauté
Economique de l' Afrique)

Celsius
centigrade

CEN
European Committee for
Standardization

C. en C.
Compainía en Comandita. *See*
Business Entities Appendix.

C. en C. por A.
Compainía en Comandita por
Acciones. *See* Business Entities
Appendix.

CENELEC
European Committee for
Electrotechnical
Standardization

CEO
Chief Executive Officer

CEPT
European Conference of Postal
and Telecommunications
Administrations

CERN
European Center for Nuclear
Research (Centre Européen de
Recherche Nucléaire)

CET
Common External Tariff

C&F
Cost and Freight

CFIUS
Committee on Foreign Investment
in the U.S.

CFO
Chief Financial Officer

CFR
Code of Federal Regulations
Cost and Freight

CFS
Country Focused Seminar

Cft. (or CuFt.)
Cubic Foot (Feet)

CFTA
Canadian Free Trade Agreement

CG
Consul General, Consulate
General

CHG
Charge d' Affairs

C.I.
Cost and insurance

Cía
Sociedad Colectiva. *See* Business
Entities Appendix.

CIB
Council for International Business

Cie
Compagnie
Offene Handelsgesellschaft. *See*
Business Entities Appendix.

CIF
Cost, Insurance and Freight

C.I.F.& C.
Cost, insurance, freight and
commission.

C.I.F.C.I.
Cost, insurance, freight, collection
and interest.

C.I.F.I.&E.
Cost, insurance, freight, interest,
and exchange.

CIM
Convention Internationale
Concernant le Transport des
Marchandises par Chemin de
Fer (The International
Convention for Transport of
Merchandise by Rail)

CIMS
Commercial Information Management System

CIO
Congress of Industrial Organizations

CIP
Carriage and Insurance Paid To
Commodity Import Program

CIS
Census Interface System
Commonwealth of Independent States

CISG
Convention on Contracts for the International Sale of Goods

CIT
Court of International Trade

CITA
Committee for the Implementation of Textile Agreements

CITES
Convention on International Trade in Endangered Species in Wild Fauna and Flora

C.K.D.
Completely Knocked Down

C.L.
Carload

CL
Containerload

CLS
Company Limited by Shares. *See* Business Entities Appendix.

C. Ltda.
Compainía de Responsabilidad Limitada. *See* Business Entities Appendix.

C.M.
Cubic Meter (capital letters);

cm
cm (small letters) centimeter

CMA
Common Monetary Agreement

CMEA
Council for Mutual Economic Assistance

CMP
Country Marketing Plan

C/N
Circular Note
Credit Note

CNUSA
Commercial News USA

C/O
In Care Of
Carried Over
Cash Order

Co.
Company. *See* Business Entities Appendix.
Offene Handelsgesellschaft. *See* Business Entities Appendix.
S Corporation. *See* Business Entities Appendix.

COCOM
Coordinating Committee on Multilateral Export Controls

C.O.D.
Collect (cash) on delivery

COE
Council of Europe

C.O.F.C.
Container on flatcar

COGSA
Carriage of Goods by Sea Act

COM
Chief of Mission
Cost of Manufacture

COMECON
Council for Mutual Economic Assistance

COMEX
Commodity Exchange Inc. (futures contracts)

COMSAT
Communications Satellite Corporation

Conc'd.
Concluded

Cont'd.
Continued

COO
Chief Operating Officer

COP
Cost of Production

Corp.
Corporation, *See* Business Entities Appendix.
Stock Corporation. *See* Business Entities Appendix.

CPE
Centrally Planned Economy

C. por A.
Companía por Acciones. *See* Sociedad Anónima in Business Entities Appendix.

c.p.t.
Cuideachta Phoibli Theoranta. *See* Business Entities Appendix.

CPT
Carriage Paid To

C.S.C.
Container Service Charge

CSCE
Conference on Security and Cooperation in Europe

CSIS
Center for Strategic and International Studies

CSP
Common Standard Level of Effective Protection

CSS
Cargo Selectivity System
Comparison Shopping Service

CT
Countertrade

CTD
Committee on Trade and Development

CTF
Certified Trade Fair (Certified Event)

CTIS
Center for Trade and Investment Services

CTM
Certified Trade Mission

CTP
Composite Theoretical Performance

Ctr
Container

Cu.
Cubic (measure)

CV
Constructed Value

C.V.
Commanditaire Vennootschap.
See Business Entities Appendix.

CVD
Countervailing Duty

Cwt.
(measure) Hundredweight
(U.S.A. is 100 lbs., United
Kingdom 112 lbs.)

CXT
Common External Tariff

C.Y.
Container Yard.

D

D/A
Documents Against Acceptance

DAF
Delivered at Frontier

D.B.A.
Doing Business As

DCM
Deputy Chief of Mission

D/D
Delivered

DDP
Delivered Duty Paid

DDU
Delivered Duty Unpaid

DEC
District Export Council

DEQ
Delivered Ex Quay

DES
Delivered Ex Ship

DISC
Domestic International Sales
Corporation

DISCO
Defense Industrial Security
Clearing Office

DL
Distribution License

D/O
Delivery Order

DOA
Department of Agriculture

DOC
Department of Commerce (U.S.)

DOD
Department of Defense (U.S.)

DOE
Department of Energy (U.S.)

DOL
Department of Labor (U.S.)

DOT
Department of Transportation

D/P
Documents Against Payment

DPAC
Defense Policy Advisory
Committee

D-RAM
Dynamic Random Access
Memory

DTC
Defense Trade Controls

DSL
Digital Subscriber Line

DTSA
Defense Technology Security
Administration

DTWG
Defense Trade Working Group

E

Ea or ea.
each

EAA
Export Administration Act

EAAA
Export Administration
Amendments Act

EAC
Export Assistance Center

EAEC
European Atomic Energy
Community

EAI
Enterprise for the Americas
Initiative

EAN
Except as otherwise noted

EAR
Export Administration
Regulations

EARB
Export Administration Review
Board

EBB
Economic Bulletin Board

EBRD
European Bank for
Reconstruction and
Development

EC
European Community

ECAs
Export Credit Agencies

ECASS
Export Control Automated
Support System

ECCN
Export Control Classification
Number; formerly: Export
Commodity Classification
Number

ECLS
Export Contact List Service

ECO/COM
Economic/Commercial Section

ECOWAS
Economic Community of West
African States

ECSC
European Coal and Steel
Community

ECU
European Currency Unit

EDC
Export Development Corporation

EDI
Electronic Data Interchange

EDIFACT
Electronic Data Interchange for
Administration, Commerce, and
Transportation

EDO
Export Development Office

ACRONYMS

ACRONYMS

EE
Eterorythmos Eteria. *See* Business Entities Appendix.

EEA
European Economic Area

EEBIC
Eastern Europe Business Information Center

EEC
European Economic Community

EEP
Export Enhancement Program

EEPROM
Electronically Erasable Programmable Read-Only Memory

EEZ
Exclusive Economic Zones

EFT
Electronic Funds Transfer

EFTA
European Free Trade Association

EIB
European Investment Bank

E.I. de R.L.
Empresa Individual de Responsibilidad Limitada. *See* Business Entities Appendix.

EIN
Employer Identification Number
Exporter Identification Number

EIRL
Eestabelecimento Individual de Responsabildade Limitada. *See* Business Entities Appendix.

ELAIN
Electronic License Application and Information Network

ELAN
Export Legal Assistance Network

ELP
Exempted Limited Partnership. *See* Business Entities Appendix.

ELVIS
Export License Voice Information System

EMC
Export Management Company

EMS
European Monetary System

EMU
European Monetary Union

E&OE
Errors and Omissions Excepted

EOTC
European Organization for Testing and Certification

EP
European Parliament

EPA
Environmental Protection Agency

EPC
Economic Policy Council
European Patent Convention

EPCI
Enhanced Proliferation Control Initiative

EPE
Eteria Periorismenis Efthinis. *See* Business Entities Appendix.

EPROM
Erasable Programmable Read-Only Memory

EPS
Export Promotion Services

EPZ
Export Processing Zone

ERLC
Export Revolving Line of Credit

ERM
Exchange Rate Mechanism

ESA
European Space Agency

ESP
Exporter's Sale Price

ESPRIT
European Strategic Program for Research and Development in Information Technologies

ESSS
Entry Summary Selectivity System

ETA
Estimated Time of Arrival

etc.
etcetra

ETC
Export Trading Company

ETD
Estimated Time of Departure

ETSI
European Telecommunications Standards Institute

EU
European Union

EUCLID
European Cooperation for the Long-term in Defense

EURAM
European Research in Advanced Materials

EURATOM
European Atomic Energy Community

EUREKA
European Research Coordination Agency

E.U.R.L.
Entreprise Unipersonnelle à Responsabilité Limitée. *See* Business Entities Appendix.

EXCEL
Export Credit Enhanced Leverage

EXIMBANK
Export-Import Bank of the U.S.A.

EXW
Ex Works

F

F
Fahrenheit

FAA
Federal Aviation Administration
Foreign Assistance Act

FAAS
Foreign Affairs Administrative Support

FAC
Foreign Assets Control

F.A.K.
Freight All Kinds

FAO
Food and Agricultural Organization

FAS
Foreign Agricultural Service
Free Alongside Ship

fax
facsimile (fax machine or fax
letter)

FBIS
Foreign Broadcast Information
Service

fbm (also Bd.Ft.)
Board Foot

FBP
Foreign Buyer Program

FBT
Flatbed Trailer

FCA
Free Carrier

FCIA
Foreign Credit Insurance
Association

FCPA
Foreign Corrupt Practices Act

F.C.&S.
Free of Capture and Seizure
Warranty

FDA
Food and Drug Administration

FDIC
Federal Deposit Insurance
Corporation

FDIUS
Foreign Direct Investment in the
United States

FEMA
Federal Emergency Management
Agency

FET
Foreign Economic Trends

FEU
Forty Foot Equivalent Units

FFP
Food For Progress

FI
Free In

FIO
Free In and Out

F.I.O.S.
Free In, Out and Stow

FIT
Foreign Independent Tour

F.M.C. (or FMC)
Federal Maritime Commission

FMS
Foreign Military Sales

FMV
Foreign Market Value

FO
Free Out

FOB
Free on Board

FOR/FOT
Free on Rail/Free on Truck

FOREX
Foreign Exchange

FPA
Free of Particular Average

FPFS
Fines, Penalties, and Forfeitures
System

FPG
Foreign Parent Group

FR
Flat Rack

FRA
Forward/Future Rate Agreement

FSC
Foreign Sales Corporation

FSI
Foreign Service Institute

FSN
Foreign Service National

FSO
Foreign Service Officer

ft
Foot/Feet (measure)

FTA
Free Trade Agreement
Free Trade Area

FTC
Federal Trade Commission (U.S.)

FTI
Foreign Traders Index

FTO
Foreign Trade Organization

FTZ
Foreign Trade Zone

FTZA
Foreign Trade Zone Act

FTZB
Foreign Trade Zone Board

FTZ-SZ
Foreign Trade Zone-Subzone

F/X
Foreign Exchange

G

G-5
Group of Five

G-7
Group of Seven

G-10
Group of Ten

G-24
Group of Twenty-Four

G-77
Group of Seventy-Seven

G/A
General Average

GAB
General Agreements to Borrow
(Paris Club)

GATS
General License - Aircraft on
Temporary Sojourn

GATT
General Agreement on Tariffs and
Trade

G-BAGGAGE
General License - Baggage

GCC
Gulf Cooperation Council

GCG
General License - Shipments to
Agencies of Cooperating
Governments

G-COCOM
General License - COCOM

G-DEST
General License - Destination

GDP
Gross Domestic Product

GEM
Global Export Manager

ACRONYMS

GFW
General License - Free World

GIT
General License - In Transit Shipments

GL
General License

GLR
General License - Return (Replacement)

GLV
General License - Shipments of Limited Value

GmbH
Gesellschaft mit beschränkter Haftung. *See* Business Entities Appendix.

G-NNR
General License - Non-Naval Reserve

GNP
Gross National Product

GO
General Order

GPO
Government Printing Office (U.S.)

G.R.I.
General Rate Increase

GSP
Generalized System of Preferences

GTDA
General License - Technical Data

GTDR
General License - Technical Data Restricted

G-TEMP
General License - Temporary Export

GTF-U.S.
General License - Goods Imported for Display at U.S. Exhibitions or Trade Fairs

GUS
General License - Shipments to Personnel and Agencies of the U.S. Government

H

H
Height

HAWB
House Air Waybill

HC
High Commission (British)

H/H
House to House

HMHC
Her Majesty's High Commission

H.P.
Horsepower

H/P
House to Pier

HS
Harmonized System

HTS
Harmonized Tariff Schedule

HTSUS
Harmonized Tariff Schedule of the U.S.

HTWG
High Technology Working Group

I

IACC
International Anticounterfeiting Coalition

IAEA
International Atomic Energy Agency

IAEL
International Atomic Energy List

IATA
International Air Transport Association

IBF
International Banking Facility

IBOR
Interbank Offered Rate

IBM
International Business Machines (Company)

IBRD
International Bank for Reconstruction and Development

IC
Import Certificate
Integrated Circuit

ICA
International Cocoa Agreement
International Coffee Agreement
International Commodity Agreement

ICAO
International Civil Aviation Organization

ICC
International Chamber of Commerce (Paris)
Interstate Commerce Commission

ICO
International Congress Office

ICP
Industry Consultations Program

ICS
Investment Climate Statement

ICSID
International Center for the Settlement for Investment Disputes

ICSU
International Council of Scientific Unions

I.D.
Inside Diameter

IDA
International Development Association

IDB
Inter-American Development Bank

IDCA
International Development Cooperation Agency

IEA
International Energy Agency

IEC
International Electrotechnical Commission

ACRONYMS

IEEPA
International Emergency
Economic Powers Act

IEPG
Independent European Program
Group

IESC
International Executive Service
Corps

IFAC
Industry Functional Advisory
Committee

IFAD
International Fund for
Agricultural Development

IFC
International Finance Corporation

IFM
Inward Foreign Manifest

IFRB
International Frequency
Registration Board

IFS
Industry Focused Seminar
In-Flight Survey

IGC
Interagency Group on
Countertrade

IGPAC
Intergovernmental Policy
Advisory Committee

IJA
International Jute Agreement

IL
Industrial List

ILO
International Labor Organization

IMF
International Monetary Fund

IMI
International Market Insight

IML
International Munitions List

IMO
International Maritime
Organization

IMSO
International Maritime Satellite
Organization

In.
Inch

Inc. or Corp.
Incorporated
Corporation
C corporation, *See* Business
Entities Appendix.
Close Corporation, *See* Business
Entities Appendix.
Stock Corporation. *See* Business
Entities Appendix.

info.
Information

INMARSAT
International Maritime Satellite
Organization

INPAC
Investment Policy Advisory
Committee

INR
Initial Negotiating Right

INS
Immigration and Naturalization
Service

INTELSAT
International Telecommunications
Satellite Organization

IOGA
Industry-Organized, Government-
Approved Mission

IPAC
Industry Policy Advisory
Committee

IPO
Initial Public Offering (stock)

IPR
Intellectual Property Rights

IRA
International Rubber Agreement

IRS
Internal Revenue Service

I/S
Interessantelskab

ISA
Industry Sub-Sector Analysis
International Sugar Agreement

ISAC
Industry Sector Advisory
Committee

ISBN
International Standard Book
Number (publishing)

ISC
Intermodal Service Charge

ISDN
Integrated Services Digital
Network

ISO
International Standards
Organization

ITA
International Tin Agreement
International Trade
Administration

ITAR
International Traffic in Arms
Regulations

ITC
International Trade Commission

ITT
International Telephone &
Telegraph

ITU
International Telecommunication
Union

IVL
Individual Validated License

IWC
International Whaling
Commission

J

JCIT
Joint Committee for Investment
and Trade

JDB
Japan Development Bank

JEIC
Japan Export Information Center

JETRO
Japan External Trade
Organization

JEXIM
The Export-Import Bank of Japan

JICA
Japan International Cooperation
Agency

K

K.D.
Knocked Down

KDD
Kokusai Denshin Denwa

K.D.F.
Knocked Down Flat

KEG
Kommandit Erwerbsgesellschaft.
See Business Entities Appendix.

Kft
Korlátolt Felelosségu Társaság.
See Business Entities Appendix.

KG
Kommanditgesellschaft

KGS or Kilo(s)
Kilogram(s)

KK
Kabushiki Kaisha

Kkt
Közkereseti Társaság. See
Business Entities Appendix.

k.s.
Komanditní Spolecnost. See
Business Entities Appendix.

K/S
Kommanditselskab

L

L
Length

LAFTA
Latin American Free Trade
Association

LAIA
Latin American Integration
Association

LASH
Lighter Aboard Ship

Lb (s)
Pound(s) (weight measure)

L/C
Letter of Credit

LCL
Less Than Container Load

Lda.
Sociedade por Quota. See
Business Entities Appendix.

LDC
Least (Less, Lesser) Developed
Country
Limited Duration Companies. See
Business Entities Appendix.

LIBID
London Interbank Bid Rate

LIBOR
London Interbank Offered Rate

LIFFE
London International Financial
Futures Exchange

LIMEAN
London Interbank Mean

LLC
Limited Liability Company. See
Business Entities Appendix.

LLP
Limited Liability Partnership. See
Business Entities Appendix.

L.O.A.
Length Overall

LOI
Letter of Indemnity

L.S.
Lump Sum

L.T.
Long Ton (2,240 Pounds)

Ltd.
Limited
Corporation, See Business Entities
Appendix.
Private Company. See Business
Entities Appendix.

Ltda.
Sociedad de Responsabilidad
Limitada. See Business Entities
Appendix.
Limitada

Ltée.
Corporation, See Business Entities
Appendix.
Limitée

L.T.L.
Less than truckload

M

M
Measurement
Thousand (1,000 units)

max.
Maximum

MBF or MBM
One Thousand Board Feet

MC
Minister Counsellor

MCTL
Militarily Critical Technologies
List

M/D
Month's Date

MD
Managing Director

MDB
Multilateral Development Bank

MFA
Multi-Fiber Arrangement

MFN
Most Favored Nation

MFT
Per Thousand Feet

MHW
Ministry of Health and Welfare

MIF
Multilateral Investment Fund

MIGA
Multilateral Investment Guarantee
Agency

Mij.
Maatschappij

min.
Minimum

MIPRO
Manufactured Imports Promotion
Organization

MITI
Ministry of International Trade
and Industry

MKR
Matchmaker Program

M.O.
Money Order

ACRONYMS

MOCP
Market-Oriented Cooperation
Plan

MOFERT
Ministry of Foreign Economic
Relations and Trade

MOFTEC
Ministry of Foreign Economic
Trade and Economic
Cooperation

MOSS
Market-Oriented, Sector-Selective

MOU
Memorandum of Understanding

MPA
Major Projects Agreement

MPP
Market Promotion Program

MPT
Ministry of Posts and
Telecommunications

MRA
Mutual Recognition Agreement

MT
Marine Terminal

MTAG
Missile Technology Advisory
Group

MTCR
Missile Technology Control
Regime

MTEC
Missile Technology Export
Control Group

MTN
Multilateral Trade Negotiations

MTO
Multilateral Trade Organization

N

N/A
Not Applicable

NAEC
National Association of Export
Companies

NAFTA
North American Free Trade
Agreement

NASDA
National Association of State
Development Agencies

NATO
North Atlantic Treaty
Organization

N.B.
Note Below

NCC
National Chambers of Commerce

NEA
Nuclear Energy Agency

N.E.S.
Not Elsewhere Specified

NICs
Newly Industrializing Countries

NIPA
National Income and Product
Accounts

NMEs
Nonmarket Economies

NNPA
Nuclear Non-Proliferation Act

NNPT
Nuclear Non-Proliferation Treaty

No
Number

N.O.I.B.N.
Not Otherwise Indexed by
Number

N.O.S.
Not Otherwise Specified

NPT
Nuclear Non-Proliferation Treaty

NRC
Nuclear Regulatory Commission

NRL
Nuclear Referral List

NRPB
Natural Resource Based Products

N/S (also NSF)
Not Sufficient Funds

NS
Not Subject To

NSC
National Security Council

NSD
National Security Directive

NSF (also N/S)
Not Sufficient Funds

NSG
Nuclear Suppliers Group

NSO
National Security Override

NT
Net Ton

NTBs
Non-Tariff Barriers

NTDB
National Trade Data Bank

NTE
National Trade Estimates Report
New-To-Export

NTM
New-To-Market

NTMs
Non-Tariff Measures

NTT
Nippon Telegraph and Telephone
Corporation

N.V.
Naamloze Vennootschap. *See*
Business Entities Appendix.

NVOCC
Non-Vessel Operating Common
Carrier

NYMEX
New York Mercantile Exchange

NYSE
New York Stock Exchange

O

OAPEC
Organization of Arab Petroleum
Exporting Countries

OAS
Organization of American States

OAU
Organization of African Unity

O.B.L.
Ocean bill of lading

OBR
Overseas Business Report

OBU
Offshore Banking Unit

ACRONYMS

O/C
Overcharge

OC
Operating Committee

OCP
Overland Common Point

O.D.
Outside Diameter

ODA
Official Development Assistance

OE
Omorythmos Eteria. *See* Business Entities Appendix.

OECD
Organization for Economic Cooperation and Development

OEG
Offene Erwerbsgesellschaft. *See* Business Entities Appendix.

OEL
Office of Export Licensing

OFAC
Office of Foreign Assets Control

OHG
Offene Handelsgesellschaft. *See* Business Entities Appendix.

OIC
Organization of the Islamic Conference

OIEC
Organization for Economic Cooperation

OMA
Orderly Marketing Agreement

OMB
Office of Management and Budget

OMC
Office of Munitions Control

OOD
Drouzestvo s Ogranichena Otgovornost. *See* Business Entities Appendix.

OPEC
Organization of Petroleum Exporting Countries

OPIC
Overseas Private Investment Corporation

ORM
Other Regulated Materials

O/S
Out of Stock

OSHA
Occupational Safety and Health Administration

OT
Open Top

O/T
Overtime

OTC
Over the Counter

OTM
Old-To-Market

OWC
On Wheels Charge

Oy
Osakeyhtiö. *See* Business Entities Appendix.

P

P/A
Power of Attorney

PC
Per Container
Personal Computer

P/C
Prices Current
Petty Cash

PCS
Piece(s)

PCT
Patent Cooperation Treaty

PEC
President's Export Council

PEFCO
Private Export Funding Corporation

P/H
Pier to House

P&I
Principal and Interest

PIP
Post-Initiated Promotion

Pkg(s)
Package(s)

P&L
Profit and Loss

P.L.C.
Public Company. *See* Business Entities Appendix.

PLC
Pre-License Check
Public Limited Company

P/N
Promissory Note

PP
Purchase Price

P.P.
Prepaid (Freight Prepaid)

P/P
Pier to Pier

PPA
Protocol of Provisional Application

P.R.C.
People's Republic of China

PSV
Post-Shipment Verification

p/t
Part-time
Pte. Ltd.
Private Limited

PT
Per Trailer

PT 20
Per 20 Foot Trailer/Container

PT 40
Per 40 Foot Trailer/Container

PTA
Preferential Trade Agreement for Eastern and Southern Africa

PU&D
Pick Up and Delivery

Pvt. Ltd.
Private Company. *See* Business Entities Appendix.

Q

QRs
Quantitative Restrictions

R

R
Rail Ramp

RACE
Research in Advanced
   Communications in Europe

RAM
Random Access Memory

RBPs
Restrictive Business Practices

RCS
Regular Catalog Show

R&D
Research and Development

RFP
Request for Proposal

RFQ
Request for Quotation

ROM
Read Only Memory

RoRo
Roll-on, Roll-off

R.R.
Railroad

Rt
Részvénytársaság. *See* Business
   Entities Appendix.

RWA
Returned Without Action

S

S.A.
Sociedad Anónima. *See* Business
   Entities Appendix.
Sociedade Anónima. *See* Business
   Entities Appendix.
Società per Azioni. *See* Business
   Entities Appendix.
Société Anonyme. *See* Business
   Entities Appendix.
Spólka Akcyjna. *See* Business
   Entities Appendix.

SABIT
Special American Business
   Internship Training Program

SADC
Southern Africa Development
   Community

SACU
Southern African Customs Union

SADCC
Southern Africa Development
   Coordination Conference

S.A. de C.A.
Sociedad Anónima de Capital
   Abierto. *See* Business Entities
   Appendix.

S.A.R.L.
Société à Responsabilité Limitée.
   See Business Entities Appendix.

S.A.S.
Società in Accomandita Semplice.
   See Business Entities Appendix.
Société par Actions Simplifée. *See*
   Business Entities Appendix.

SASO
Saudi Arabian Standards
   Organization

SBA
Small Business Administration

S.C.
Sociedad Colectiva. *See* Business
   Entities Appendix.
Société en Commandite. Société
   Coopérative. *See* Business
   Entities Appendix.

S.C.A.
Sociedad en Comandita por
   Acciones. *See* Business Entities
   Appendix.

SCaRL
Società Cooperativa a
   Responsabilità. *See* Business
   Entities Appendix.

S.C.I.
Sociedad de Capital e Industria.
   See Business Entities Appendix.

SCM
Southern Common Market

SCO
Senior Commercial Officer

S.C. par A.
Société en Commandite par
   Actionss. *See* Business Entities
   Appendix.

SCRL
Sociedade Cooperativa. *See*
   Business Entities Appendix.

S.C.S.
Société en Commandite Simple.
   See Business Entities Appendix.

S&D
Special and Differential Treatment

S. de R.L. (also Ltda.)
Sociedad de Responsabilidad
   Limitada. *See* Business Entities
   Appendix.

Sdn. Bhd.
Sendirian Berhard. *See* Business
   Entities Appendix.

SDRs
Special Drawing Rights (banking)

SEA
Single European Act

SEC
Securities and Exchange
   Commission
Special Equipment Compensation

SED
Shipper's Export Declaration

SEED
Support for East European
   Democracy

SEM
Seminar Mission

S. en C.
Sociedad en Comandita. *See*
   Business Entities Appendix.
Société en Commandite Simple.
   See Business Entities Appendix.

S. en C.S.
Société en Commandite Simple.
   See Business Entities Appendix.

SEPD
State Export Program Database

SFO
Solo Fair (overseas procured)

SFSC
Shared Foreign Sales Corporation

ACRONYMS

SFW
Solo Fair (Washington procured)

SGA
Selling, General, and Administrative (Expenses)

S.G.L.
Società a Garanzia Limitata. *See* Business Entities Appendix.

SIC
Standard Industrial Classification

SII
Structural Impediments Initiative

SIMIS
Single Internal Market Information Service

SIMS
Single Internal Market Service

S/IOGA
State/Industry-Organized, Government-Approved

SITC
Standard International Tariff Classification

SLI
Shipper's Letter of Instruction

SM (or sm)
Service Mark

SMSA
Standard Metropolitan Statistical Area

SNC
Société en Nom Collectif. *See* Business Entities Appendix.

SNEC
Sub-Group on Nuclear Export Coordination

s/o (or S.O.)
Ship's Option, (rate yielding greater revenue; must be charged)

SOD
Shipped on Deck

SOGA
State-Organized, Government-Approved Mission

S.p.A.
Società per Azioni. *See* Business Entities Appendix.

SPAC
Services Policy Advisory Committee

spol. s r.o.
Spolecnost s Rucením Omezenym. *See* Business Entities Appendix.

S.P.R.L.
Société Privée a Reponsabilité Limitéeprivate. *See* Business Entities Appendix.

S.P.R.L.
Société de Personnes à Responsabilité Limitée. *See* Business Entities Appendix.

Sp. z o.o.
Spólka z Ograniczona Odpowied Zialnóscia. *See* Business Entities Appendix.

S.Q.
Sociedad por Quota

S.R.&C.C.
Strikes, Riots and Civil Commotion Warranty (all risk insurance)

S.R.L.
Sociedad de Responsabilidad Limitada. *See* Business Entities Appendix.
Società a Responsabilità Limitata. *See* Business Entities Appendix.
Société à Responsabilité Limitée. *See* Business Entities Appendix.

s.r.o.
Spolecnost s Rucením Omezenym. *See* Business Entities Appendix.

SSA
Sub-Saharan Africa

STA
Semiconductor Trade Agreement

S.T.C.
Said to Contain

Sté.
Société

Ste. Cve.
Société Cooperative. *See* Business Entities Appendix.

STELA
System for Tracking Export License Applications

STEs
State Trading Enterprises

STM
State Trade Mission

S.T.W.
Said to Weigh

S.U.
Set Up

T

T.
Ton of 2,240 lbs

TA
Trade Assistant

TAA
Trade Adjustment Assistance

TAAC
Trade Adjustment Assistance Center

TAC
Technical Advisory Committee

TACM
Transit Air Cargo Manifest

TAPO
Trade Assistance and Planning Office

TCI
Third Country Initiative

TCMD
Third Country Meat Directive

TDO
Table of Denial Orders

TDP
Trade and Development Program

TEC or CXT
Tarif Extérieur Commun (common external tariff)

Tel.
Telephone

Teo.
Steoranta. *See* Business Entities Appendix.

ACRONYMS

TEU
Twenty foot equivalent unit. A forty foot container is equal to two (2) TEU'S.

TFC
Trade Fair Certification

TFO
Trade Fair (Overseas-Recruited)

TFW
Trade Fair (Washington-Recruited)

THC
Terminal Handling Charge

TIA
Travel Industry Association of America

TIB
Temporary Importation under Bond

TIC
Trade Information Center

TIEA
Tax Information Exchange Agreement

TIFTs
Trade and Investment Facilitation Talks

TIMS
Textiles Information Management System

T.L.
Total Loss (shipping)
Truckload

T.L.S.
Türk Limited Sirket. *See* Business Entities Appendix.

T.M.
Traffic Manager

TM
Trademark
Trade Mission

TNC
Trade Negotiations Committee

T.O.F.C.
Trailer (On Wheels) Flat Car

TOP
Trade Opportunities Program

TPC
Trade Policy Committee

TPCC
Trade Promotion Coordinating Committee

TPIS
Trade Policy Information System

TPM
Trigger Price Mechanism

TPRG
Trade Policy Review Group

TPRM
Trade Policy Review Mechanism

TPSC
Trade Policy Staff Committee

TRA
Trade Reference Assistant

TRIMs
Trade-Related Investment Measures

TRIPs
Trade-Related Aspects of Intellectual Property Rights

TRO
Temporary Restraining Order

TS
Trade Specialist

TSB
Textile Surveillance Body

TSUSA
Tariff Schedules of the United States Annotated. Usually referred to as HTSUS or Harmonized Tariff Schedules of the United States

T.T.S.
Telegraphic transfer selling rate

TWEA
Trading With the Enemy Act

U

U.A.E.
United Arab Emirates

UBO
Ultimate Beneficial Owner

UCC
Uniform Commercial Code

UCP
Uniform Customs and Practices

UCPDC
Uniform Customs and Practice for Documentary Credits

U.K.
United Kingdom

ULD
Unit Load Device

UMOA
West African Monetary Union (Union Monétaire Ouest Africaine)

UN
United Nations

UNCDF
United Nations Capital Development Fund

UNCSTD
United Nations Conference on Science and Technology for Development

UNCTAD
United Nations Conference on Trade and Development

UNDP
United Nations Development Program

UNDRO
United Nations Disaster Relief Organization

UNEP
United Nations Environment Program

UNESCO
United Nations Educational, Scientific, and Cultural Organization

UNFPA
United Nations Fund for Population Activities

UNGA
United Nations General Assembly

UNHCR
United Nations High Commissioner for Refugees

UNICEF
United Nations International Children's Emergency Fund

UNIDO
United Nations Industrial
  Development Organization

UNITAR
United Nations Institute for
  Training and Research

UNRISD
United Nations Research Institute
  for Social Development

UNRWA
United Nations Relief and Works
  Agency

URC
Uniform Rules for Collection

U.S. or U.S.A.
United States of America

USC
United States Code

USCS
United States Customs Service

USD (also US$)
United States Dollar

USDA
U.S. Department of Agriculture

USDIA
U.S. Direct Investment Abroad

USEC
U.S. Mission to the European
  Communities

US&FCS
United States and Foreign
  Commercial Service

USGPO
U.S. Government Printing Office

USIA
U.S. Information Agency

USIS
United States Information Service

USITC
United States International Trade
  Commission

U.S.M.C
United States Maritime
  Commission

USML
U.S. Munitions List

USP
United States Price

USSR
Union of Soviet Socialist
  Republics

USTDA
U.S. Trade and Development
  Agency

USTR
United States Trade
  Representative

USTTA
United States Travel and Tourism
  Administration

USUN
U.S. Mission to the United
  Nations

V

VAT
Value-Added Tax

VER
Voluntary Export Restriction

VHF
Very High Frequency

Viz
Namely

VL
Variable Levy

VOA
Voice of America

v.o.s.
Verejná Obchodní Spolecnost. *See*
  Business Entities Appendix.

VP
Vice President

VRA
Voluntary Restraint Agreement

W-X-Y-Z

W
Width

W
Ton of 1000 kilos

w/ (also W/)
With

WA
With Average

WAMU
West African Monetary Union

WARC
World Administrative Radio
  Conference

W/B
Waybill

WFG
Wharfage

WIPO
World Intellectual Property
  Organization

WLL
Sharika That Massouliyyah
  Mahdoodah. *See* Business
  Entities Appendix.

WMO
World Meteorological
  Organization

W/O
Without

W.P.A.
With Particular Average
  (insurance)

WTDR
World Traders Data Report

WTO
World Tourism Organization
World Trade Organization

WWW
World Wide Web

International Dialing Guide

The introductory matter and table in this section provides specific information for dialing direct to over 400 cities in nearly 200 countries and territories around the world. This material has been designed to be useful for anyone, regardless of the country of origin or country of destination of their call.

Countries and territories are listed alphabetically. For each, the country dialing code, the capital city (when applicable), the city (or regional) code, and time zone information is provided. For some countries more than one city, with corresponding city codes and time zones, are listed. The capital city is indicated with a ✪.

HOW TO DIAL INTERNATIONAL CALLS

Direct dialing international calls from most countries has become quite easy in the past decade. The typical international call simply consists of dialing a series of numbers in sequence as follows:

1. The international direct dialing prefix (IDD),
2. The country code,
3. The city code, and
4. The local telephone number.

If you are calling from the United States, the IDD is 011. The IDD differs from country to country. For Brazil it is 00. Some countries do not allow direct dialing for international calls but require them to be placed through the operator. The table on the next page lists IDD prefixes for most countries that allow international direct dialing. You may need to wait for a dial tone after dialing the IDD.

The IDD is followed by the country code (shown in square brackets [ ] in the table starting on page 228), the city code or area code (if there is one) (shown in parentheses ( ) in the table starting on page 228), and the local telephone number. When city codes are not required, a * appears in place of the city code in our table.

If you are calling to other countries or territories that use the same country code as the country you are calling from, you will normally not use the international IDD prefix (the IDD prefix is sometimes called the "international access code"). For example, the United States, Canada, and many Caribbean Islands all use the country code [1], so calls made between countries within this zone will be dialed as regular long-distance calls and not as international calls.

Example: To call Chicago from London, U.K., dial:
010 + [1] + (312) + (local telephone number).
(The U.K. international access code is 010, the country code for the U.S. is [1] and the area code for Chicago is (312).)

Example: To call Sydney, Australia from Denmark, dial:
00 + [61] + (2) + (local telephone number).
(The Denmark international access code is 00, the country code for Australia is [61] and the city code for Sydney is (2).)

Example: To call New Delhi, India from Hong Kong, dial:
001 + [91] + (11) + (local telephone number).

(The Hong Kong international access code is 011, the country code for India is [91], and the city code for New Delhi is (11).

Example: To call Hong Kong from the United States, dial:
011 + [852] + (local telephone number)
(The U.S. international access code is 011, the country code for Hong Kong is [852], and there are no city codes.)

Example: To call Vancouver, British Columbia from the United States, dial:
1 + (604) + (the local number).
(The prefix 1 is used for long-distance calls within Canada, the US, and the Caribbean. (604) is the area code for British Columbia)

Example: To call any point in the Dominican Republic from the United States, dial:
1+ (809) + (local telephone number)

(The prefix 1 is used for long-distance calls within Canada, the US, and the Caribbean and (809) is the area code for the Dominican Republic.)

INTERNATIONAL DIRECT DIALING (IDD) PREFIXES

Algeria	00*
Argentina	00
Australia	0011, (fax calls 0015)
Austria	00, 900 (Vienna)
Bahamas	001
Bahrian	0
Belgium	00
Bolivia	00
Brazil	00
Bulgaria	00
Cameroon	00
Canada	011
Chile	00
China (PRC)	00
Colombia	90
Congo, Democratic Rep. of (formerly Zaire)	00
Costa Rica	00
Cuba	119
Cuba (Guantánamo Bay)	00
Cyprus	00
Czech Republic	00
Denmark	00
Dominican Republic	011
Ecuador	00
Egypt	00
El Salvador	0
Finland	00, 990, 994, 999
France	00
French Antilles	00
Germany	00
Greece	00
Guam	011
Guatemala	00
Guyana	001
Haiti	00
Honduras	00
Hong Kong	001
Hungary	00
Iceland	00
India	00
Indonesia	001, 008
Iran	00
Iraq	00
Ireland	00
Israel	00
Italy	00
Ivory Coast	00
Jamaica	011
Japan	001
Korea, South	001
Korea, North	00
Kuwait	00
Lebanon	00
Liberia	00
Libya	00
Liechtenstein	00
Luxembourg	00
Macau	00
Madagascar	00
Malawi	101
Malaysia	00
Mexico	00
Monaco	00
Morocco	00*
Namibia	09
Netherlands	00
Netherlands Antilles	00
New Zealand	00
Nicaragua	00
Niger	00
Nigeria	009
Norway	00
Pakistan	00
Panama	0
Peru	00
Phillipines	00
Poland	0*0
Portugal	00
Qatar	0
Russia	8*10
Saudi Arabia	00
Senegal	00
Singapore	001
Slovakia	00
Somalia	19
South Africa	09 or 091
Spain	00
Sri Lanka	00
Sweden	00
Switzerland	00
Taiwan	002
Thailand	001 (except to Malaysia 007)
Tunisia	00
Turkey	00
United Arab Emirates	00
United Kingdom	00
United States of America	011
Venezuela	00
Vietnam	00
Yugoslavia	99
Zambia	00
Zimbabwe	00

* Wait for dial tone after dialing these international access codes

DIALING

TIME ZONES

Time differences, that is, how many hours the given city or country is ahead or behind the four major U.S. time zones and Greenwich Mean Time, have been given in the right-hand columns in the following table. All cities in a given country or territory are in one time zone unless a †† symbol appears next to the country name. Find the city you wish to call, and the column which corresponds to the time zone you are calling from. Add or subtract the number shown to your own current time to find the time in that city.

Example: You are calling France from New York. +6 appears in the EST (Eastern Standard Time) column for France, which means France is 6 hours *ahead* of New York. Thus, when it is 9 a.m. Monday in New York, it is 3:00 p.m. Monday in France.

Example: You are calling Japan from San Francisco. +17 appears in the PST (Pacific Standard Time) column for Japan, which means Japan is 17 hours ahead of San Francisco. Thus, when it is 4:00 p.m. Monday in San Francisco, it is 9:00 a.m. Tuesday in Japan.

DAYLIGHT SAVINGS TIME

The time differences given are based on Standard Time, and may require adjustment if either you or the country you are calling is following Daylight Savings Time (DST) at the time you place the call.

Most of the United States is in DST from the first Sunday in April until the last Sunday in October. Many, but not all, countries north of the Tropic of Cancer also use DST during a similar period. DST is not used in most tropical areas. Countries in the southern hemisphere that follow a daylight savings period normally use it from mid-March through mid-October, their summertime.

The dates used for DST vary considerably from country to country and even from year to year. Also, in a few larger countries like the United States, Australia, and Brazil, some regions of the country may follow daylight savings while others do not.

If you are in DST, and the country you are calling is not, *subtract* one hour from the time shown. If you are in Standard Time, and the country you are calling is currently following DST, *add* one hour to the time shown. If you and the country you are calling are both using DST the time difference shown in the table will be correct.

Example: You are calling Japan from San Francisco in June. California follows DST in the summer, while Japan does not. The PST (Pacific Standard Time) column for Japan shows +17. Subtract one hour from this, to find that Japan is 16 hours ahead of San Francisco. Thus, when it is 4:00 p.m. Monday in San Francisco, it is 8:00 a.m. Tuesday in Japan.

FOR FURTHER INFORMATION

Listed information was current as of February 1999. City codes and dialing systems are changing rapidly as the need for more telephone numbers increases worldwide.

For codes not listed here, or for the current time anywhere in the world, call your international operator. In the United States, dial 00 for AT&T information. AT&T publishes an International Dialing Guide that is updated regularly and is free on request.

There are some resources available on the Internet. World time listed by country is at www.isbister.com/worldtime/. World time and dialing codes is at www.whitepages.com.au/time.shtml. Type in from where you are calling and to where you want to dial—time and code will then appear. Local Times Around the World is at http://www.hilink.com.au/times/. A list of International Dialing Codes is at http://kropla.com/dialcode.htm, and the AmeriCom Long Distance Area Decoder at http://www.xmission.com/~americom/aclookup.html will allow you to look up both U.S. and international country codes, city codes, and area codes.

DIALING

International Dialing Codes

Country	Country Code	City/Area Codes	Hours ahead or behind: EST	CST	MST	PST	UTC
Afghanistan	[93]	✪Kabul *	+9½	+10½	+11½	12½	+4½
Albania	[355]	✪Tiranë (42)	+6	+7	+8	+9	+1
Algeria	[213]	✪Algiers (2)	+6	+7	+8	+9	+1
American Samoa	[684]	✪Pago Pago *	-6	-5	-4	-3	-11
Andorra	[376]	✪Andorra la Vella *	+6	+7	+8	+9	+1
Angola	[244]	✪Luanda (2)	+6	+7	+8	+9	+1
Anguilla	[1]	✪ The Valley (264) **	+1	+2	+3	+4	-4
Antigua & Barbuda	[1]	✪St. John's (268) **	+1	+2	+3	+4	-4
Argentina††	[54]	✪Buenos Aires (11) Cordoba (351) Mendoza (361) Rosario (341)	+2	+3	+4	+5	-3
Armenia	[374]	✪Yerevan (2)	+8	+9	+10	+11	+3
Aruba	[297]	✪ Oranjestad (8)**	+1	+2	+3	+4	-4
Australia††	[61]	✪Canberra (2)	+15	+16	+17	+18	+10
		Adelaide (8)	+14½	+15½	+16½	+17½	+9½
		Brisbane (7)	+15	+16	+17	+18	+10
		Melbourne (3)	+15	+16	+17	+18	+10
		Perth (8)	+13	+14	+15	+16	+8
		Sydney (2)	+15	+16	+17	+18	+10
Austria	[43]	✪Vienna (1) Innsbruck (512) Salzburg (662)	+6	+7	+8	+9	+1
Azerbaijan	[994]	✪Baku (12)	+8	+9	+10	+11	+3
Bahamas	[1]	✪Nassau (242) **	0	+1	+2	+3	-5
Bahrain	[973]	✪Manama *	+8	+9	+10	+11	+3
Bangladesh	[880]	✪Dhaka (2) Khulna (41)	+11	+12	+13	+14	+6
Barbados	[1]	✪Bridgetown (246) **	+1	+2	+3	+4	-4
Belarus	[375]	✪Minsk (172)	+7	+8	+9	+10	+2
Belgium	[32]	✪Brussels (2) Antwerp (3) Brugge (50) Ghent (9) Liege (4)	+6	+7	+8	+9	+1
Belize	[501]	✪Belmopan (8)	-1	0	+1	+2	-6
Benin	[229]	✪Porto-Novo *	+6	+7	+8	+9	+1
Bermuda	[1]	✪Hamilton (441)**	+1	+2	+3	+4	-4
Bhutan	[975]	✪Thimphu *	+11	+12	+13	+14	+6

Country	Country Code	City/Area Codes	Hours ahead or behind: EST	CST	MST	PST	UTC
Bolivia	[591]	✪La Paz (2)	+1	+2	+3	+4	-4
		✪Sucre (64)					
		Cochabamba (42)					
		Santa Cruz (3)					
Bosnia & Herzegovina	[387]	✪Sarajevo (71)	+6	+7	+8	+9	+1
Botswana	[267]	✪Gaborone	+7	+8	+9	+10	+2
		Serowe (430)					
Brazil††	[55]	✪Brasilia (61)	+2	+3	+4	+5	-3
		Belém (91)					
		Belo Horizonte (31)					
		Curitiba (41)					
		Manaus (92)					
		Recife (81)					
		Rio de Janeiro (21)					
		Salvador (71)					
		Sao Paulo (11)					
Brunei	[673]	✪Bandar Seri Begawan (2)	+13	+14	+15	+16	+8
Bulgaria	[359]	✪Sofia (2)	+7	+8	+9	+10	+2
		Varna (52)					
Burkina Faso	[226]	✪Ouagadougou *	+5	+6	+7	+8	0
Burundi	[257]	✪Bujumbura (2)	+7	+8	+9	+10	+2
Cambodia	[855]	✪Phnom Penh (23)	+12	+13	+14	+15	+7
Cameroon	[237]	✪Yaoundé *	+6	+7	+8	+9	+1
Canada††	[1]	✪Ottawa, ON (613)	0	+1	+2	+3	-5
		Calgary, AB (403)	-2	-1	0	+1	-7
		Edmonton,AB (403)	-2	-1	0	+1	-7
		Fredericton, NB (506)	+1	+2	+3	+4	-4
		Halifax, NS (902)	+1	+2	+3	+4	-4
		London, ON (519)	0	+1	+2	+3	-5
		Montreal, PQ (514)	0	+1	+2	+3	-5
		Quebec City, PQ (418)	0	+1	+2	+3	-5
		Regina, SK (306)	-1	0	+1	+2	-6
		Saskatoon, SK (306)	-2	-1	0	+1	-7
		St. John's, NF (709)	+1 1/2	+2 1/2	+3 1/2	+4 1/2	-3 1/2
		Toronto, ON Metro (416)	0	+1	+2	+3	-5
		Toronto Vicinity (905)	0	+1	+2	+3	-5
		Vancouver, BC (604)	-3	-2	-1	0	-8
		Victoria, BC (250)	-3	-2	-1	0	-8
		Winnipeg, MB (204)	-1	0	+1	+2	-6
Cape Verde Islands	[238]	✪Praia *	+4	+5	+6	+7	-1

✪ Capital city
* City codes not required in this country
EST = US Eastern Standard Time
MST = US Mountain Standard Time
UTC = Universal Time Coordinated (Greenwich, England)

†† More than one time zone in this country.
** This city code used for entire country or territory.
CST = US Central Standard Time
PST = US Pacific Standard Time

DIALING

Country	Country Code	City/Area Codes	Hours ahead or behind:				
			EST	CST	MST	PST	UTC
Cayman Islands	[1]	✪George Town (345) **	0	+1	+2	+3	-5
Central African Rep.	[236]	✪Bangui (6 digit numbers)	+6	+7	+8	+9	+1
Chad	[235]	✪N'Djamena (51)	+6	+7	+8	+9	+1
Chagos Archipelago	[246]	✪Diego Garcia (9)	+10	+11	+12	+13	+5
Chile	[56]	✪Santiago (2) Concepcion (41) Valparaiso (32)	+1	+2	+3	+4	-4
China, People's Republic	[86]	✪Beijing (10) Guangzhou (20) Harbin (451) Nanjing (25) Nanjing Fujian (596) Shanghai (21) Shenzhen (755) Tianjin (22); Wuhan (27) Xiamen (592); Xian (29)	+13	+14	+15	+16	+8
Colombia	[57]	✪Bogota (1) Barranquilla (58) Cali (2); Medellin (4)	0	+1	+2	+3	-5
Comoros	[269]	✪Moroni*	+8	+9	+10	+11	+3
Congo, Dem. Rep. of	[243]	✪Kinshasa (12)	+6	+7	+8	+9	+1
Congo	[242]	✪Brazzaville *	+6	+7	+8	+9	+1
Cook Islands	[682]	✪Avarua*	-5	-4	-3	-2	-10
Costa Rica	[506]	✪San José *	-1	0	+1	+2	-6
Côte d'Ivoire	[225]	✪Yamoussoukro *	+5	+6	+7	+8	0
Croatia	[385]	✪Zagreb (1); Split (21)	+6	+7	+8	+9	+1
Cuba	[53]	✪Havana (7)	0	+1	+2	+3	-5
Cyprus	[357]	✪Nicosia (2)	+7	+8	+9	+10	+2
Czech Republic	[420]	✪Prague (2)	+6	+7	+8	+9	+1
Denmark	[45]	✪Copenhagen *	+6	+7	+8	+9	+1
Djibouti	[253]	✪Djibouti *	+8	+9	+10	+11	+3
Dominica	[1]	✪Roseau (767) **	+1	+2	+3	+4	-4
Dominican Republic	[1]	✪Santo Domingo (809) **	+1	+2	+3	+4	-4
Ecuador	[593]	✪Quito (2) Guayaquil (4)	0	+1	+2	+3	-5
Egypt	[20]	✪Cairo (2) Alexandria (3) Al Hada (3); Port Said (66)	+7	+8	+9	+10	+2
El Salvador	[503]	✪San Salvador *	-1	0	+1	+2	-6
Equatorial Guinea	[240]	✪Malabo (9)	+6	+7	+8	+9	+1
Estonia	[372]	✪Tallinn (2)	+7	+8	+9	+10	+2
Ethiopia	[251]	✪Addis Ababa (1)	+8	+9	+10	+11	+3

DIALING

Country	Country Code	City/Area Codes	Hours ahead or behind: EST	CST	MST	PST	UTC
Faeroe Islands	[298]	✪Tórshavn *	+5	+6	+7	+8	0
Falkland Islands	[500]	✪Stanley* (all points 5 digits)	+1	+2	+3	+4	-4
Fiji	[679]	✪Suva *	+17	+18	+19	+20	+12
Finland	[358]	✪Helsinki (9)	+7	+8	+9	+10	+2
France	[33]	✪Paris (1) Bordeaux (556) Grenoble (476) Le Havre (235) Lyon (562) Marseille (491) Nantes (240) (251) Nice (493) Rouen (235) Strasbourg (388) Toulouse (5)	+6	+7	+8	+9	+1
French Antilles	[596]	Martinique*	+1	+2	+3	+4	-4
French Guiana	[594]	✪Cayenne *	+2	+3	+4	+5	-3
French Polynesia††	[689]	✪Papeete, Tahiti *	-5	-4	-3	-2	-10
Gabon	[241]	✪Libreville *	+6	+7	+8	+9	+1
Gambia	[220]	✪Banjul *	+5	+6	+7	+8	0
Georgia	[995]	✪Tbilisi (32)	+8	+9	+10	+11	+3
Germany	[49]	✪Berlin (30) Bonn (228); Bremen (421) Cologne (221) Dresden (351) Dusseldorf (211) Essen (201) Frankfurt am Main (69) Frankfurt Oder (335) Freiburg (761) Freiburg Elb (4779) Hamburg (40) Hannover (511) Leipzig (341) Munich (89) Postdam (331) Stuttgart (711) Würzburg (931)	+6	+7	+8	+9	+1
Ghana	[233]	✪Accra (21)	+5	+6	+7	+8	0
Gibraltar	[350]	✪Gibraltar*	+6	+7	+8	+9	+1

✪ Capital city   †† More than one time zone in this country.
* City codes not required in this country   ** This city code used for entire country or territory.
EST = US Eastern Standard Time   CST = US Central Standard Time
MST = US Mountain Standard Time   PST = US Pacific Standard Time
UTC = Universal Time Coordinated (Greenwich, England)

DIALING

Country	Country Code	City/Area Codes	Hours ahead or behind:				
			EST	CST	MST	PST	UTC
Greece	[30]	✪Athens (1) Thessaloniki (31)	+7	+8	+9	+10	+2
Greenland††	[299]	✪Nuuk (Godthaab)*	+2	+3	+4	+5	-3
Grenada	[1]	✪St. George's (473) **	+1	+2	+3	+4	-4
Guadeloupe	[590]	✪Basse-Terre (81)	+1	+2	+3	+4	-4
Guam	[671]	✪Agana *	+15	+16	+17	+18	+10
Guatemala	[502]	✪Guatemala City*	-1	0	+1	+2	-6
Guinea	[224]	✪Conakry (4)	+5	+6	+7	+8	0
Guinea-Bissau	[245]	✪Bissau (all points 6 digits)	+5	+6	+7	+8	0
Guyana	[592]	✪Georgetown (2)	+2	+3	+4	+5	-3
Haiti	[509]	✪Port-au-Prince (all points 6 digits)	0	+1	+2	+3	-5
Honduras	[504]	✪Tegucigalpa (all points 7 digits)	-1	0	+2	+3	-6
Hong Kong	[852]	✪Hong Kong (2 + 7 digits) (9 + 7 digits: mobile phones)	+13	+14	+15	+16	+8
Hungary	[36]	✪Budapest (1)	+6	+7	+8	+9	+1
Iceland	[354]	✪Reykjavik (all points 7 digits)	+5	+6	+7	+8	0
India	[91]	✪New Delhi (11) Ahmadabad (79) Bangalore (80) Calcutta (33) Hyderabad (40) Jaipur (141) Lucknow (522) Madras (44) Mumbai (Bombay) (22)	+10 1/2	+11 1/2	+12 1/2	+13 1/2	+5 1/2
Indonesia††	[62]	✪Jakarta (21)	+12	+13	+14	+15	+7
		Bandung (22)	+12	+13	+14	+15	+7
		Denpasar, Bali (361)	+13	+14	+15	+16	+8
		Medan (61)	+12	+13	+14	+15	+7
		Padang (751)	+12	+13	+14	+15	+7
		Palembang (711)	+12	+13	+14	+15	+7
		Semarang (24)	+12	+13	+14	+15	+7
		Surabaya (31)	+12	+13	+14	+15	+7
		Yogyakarta (274)	+12	+13	+14	+15	+7
Iran	[98]	✪Tehran (21); Mashhad (51) Shiraz (71); Tabriz (41)	+9	+10	+11	+12	+4
Iraq	[964]	✪Baghdad (1) Basrah (40)	+8	+9	+10	+11	+3
Ireland	[353]	✪Dublin (1) Cork (21) Limerick (61); Waterford (51)	+5	+6	+7	+8	0

DIALING

Country	Country Code	City/Area Codes	Hours ahead or behind: EST	CST	MST	PST	UTC
Israel	[972]	✪Jerusalem (2) Tel Aviv (3)	+7	+8	+9	+10	+2
Italy Italy has stopped using city codes. City codes are now incorporated into local numbers, including a zero (0) as a prefix.	[39]	✪Rome (06) Bologna (051) Florence (055) Milan (02) Naples (081) Turin (011) Vatican City (06) Venice (041)	+6	+7	+8	+9	+1
Ivory Coast	[225]	✪Yamoussoukro * ✪Abidjan*	+5	+6	+7	+8	0
Jamaica	[1]	✪Kingston (876) **	0	+1	+2	+3	-5
Japan	[81]	✪Tokyo (3) Fukuoka (92) Hiroshima (82) Kobe (78); Kyoto (75) Nagoya (52) Osaka (66) Sapporo (11) Yokohama (45) Cell phones (090 + 8 digits)	+14	+15	+16	+17	+9
Jordan	[962]	✪Amman (6)	+8	+9	+10	+11	+3
Kazakhstan	[7]	✪Alma-Ata (3272)	+11	+12	+13	+14	+6
Kenya	[254]	✪Nairobi (2) Mombasa (11)	+8	+9	+10	+11	+3
Korea, North	[850]	✪Pyongyang (2)	+14	+15	+16	+17	+9
Korea, South	[82]	✪Seoul (2) Cheju (64) Inchon (32) Pusan (51) Taegu (53)	+14	+15	+16	+17	+9
Kuwait	[965]	✪Kuwait *	+8	+9	+10	+11	+3
Kyrgyzstan	[996]	✪Bishkek (3312+6 digits)	+10	+11	+12	+13	+5
Laos	[856]	✪Vientiane (21) (all other points no city code)	+12	+13	+14	+15	+7
Latvia	[371]	✪Riga (2)	+7	+8	+9	+10	+2
Lebanon	[961]	✪Beirut (1)	+7	+8	+9	+10	+2
Lesotho	[266]	✪Maseru *	+7	+8	+9	+10	+2
Liberia	[231]	✪Monrovia *	+5	+6	+7	+8	0

✪ Capital city
* City codes not required in this country
EST = US Eastern Standard Time
MST = US Mountain Standard Time
UTC = Universal Time Coordinated (Greenwich, England)

†† More than one time zone in this country.
** This city code used for entire country or territory.
CST = US Central Standard Time
PST = US Pacific Standard Time

DIALING

DIALING

Country	Country Code	City/Area Codes	Hours ahead or behind: EST	CST	MST	PST	UTC
Libya	[218]	✪Tripoli (21)	+7	+8	+9	+10	+2
Liechtenstein	[428]	✪Vaduz*	+6	+7	+8	+9	+1
Lithuania	[370]	✪Vilnius (2)	+7	+8	+9	+10	+2
Luxembourg	[352]	✪Luxembourg *	+6	+7	+8	+9	+1
Macau	[853]	✪Macau *	+13	+14	+15	+16	+8
Macedonia	[389]	✪Skopje (91)	+6	+7	+8	+9	+1
Madagascar	[261]	✪Antananarivo (2)	+8	+9	+10	+11	+3
Malawi	[265]	✪Lilongwe * (city codes exist for other cities)	+7	+8	+9	+10	+2
Malaysia	[60]	✪Kuala Lumpur (3) Kotha Bahru (9) Melaka (6); Penang (4)	+13	+14	+15	+16	+8
Maldives	[960]	✪Malé *	+10	+11	+12	+13	+5
Mali	[223]	✪Bamako *	+5	+6	+7	+8	0
Malta	[356]	✪Valletta *	+6	+7	+8	+9	+1
Marshall Islands	[692]	✪Majuro (625) Ebeye (329)	+17	+18	+19	+20	+12
Martinique	[596]	✪Fort-De-France	+1	+2	+3	+4	-4
Mauritania	[222]	✪Nouakchott*	+5	+6	+7	+8	0
Mauritius	[230]	✪Port Louis *	+9	+10	+11	+12	+4
Mexico††	[52]	✪Mexico City (5)	-1	0	+1	+2	-6
		Acapulco (74)	-1	0	+1	+2	-6
		Cuidad Juarez (16)	-1	0	+1	+2	-6
		Durango (18)	-1	0	+1	+2	-6
		Ensenada (667)	-3	-2	-1	0	-8
		Guadalajara (3)	-1	0	+1	+2	-6
		Mazatlan (678)	-2	-1	0	+1	-7
		Mexicali (65)	-3	-2	-1	0	-8
		Monterrey (8)	-1	0	+1	+2	-6
		Nuevo Laredo (87)	-1	0	+1	+2	-6
		Tijuana (66)	-3	-2	-1	0	-8
		Veracruz (29)	-1	0	+1	+2	-6
Midway Islands	[808]		-6	-5	-4	-3	-11
Moldova	[373]	✪Kishinev (2)	+7	+8	+9	+10	+2
Monaco	[377]	✪Monaco *	+6	+7	+8	+9	+1
Mongolia	[976]	✪Ulan Bator (1)	+13	+14	+15	+16	+8
Montenegro & Serbia	[381]	✪Belgrade (11)	+6	+7	+8	+9	+1
Montserrat	[1]	✪Plymouth (664) **	+1	+2	+3	+4	-4
Morocco	[212]	✪Rabat (7 + 6 digits or 77 + 5 digits) Casablanca (2); Fez (5) Marrakech (4); Tangiers (99)	+5	+6	+7	+8	0
Mozambique	[258]	✪Maputo (1)	+7	+8	+9	+10	+2

Country	Country Code	City/Area Codes	Hours ahead or behind:				
			EST	CST	MST	PST	UTC
Myanmar (Burma)	[95]	✪Yangon (1)	+11½	+12½	+13½	+14½	+6½
Namibia	[264]	✪Windhoek (61)	+7	+8	+9	+10	+2
Nepal	[977]	✪Kathmandu (1)	+10¾	+11¾	+12¾	+13¾	+5¾
Netherlands	[31]	✪Amsterdam (20) ✪The Hague (70) Rotterdam (10)	+6	+7	+8	+9	+1
Netherlands Antilles	[599]	✪Willemstad (9) St. Maarten (5)	+1	+2	+3	+4	-4
New Caledonia	[687]	✪Nouméa *	+16	+17	+18	+19	+11
New Zealand	[64]	✪Wellington (4) Auckland (9) Christchurch (3) Telcom Mobile Phones (25) Telecom Pager (26)	+17	+18	+19	+20	+12
Nicaragua	[505]	✪Managua (2)	-1	0	+1	+2	-6
Niger Republic	[227]	✪Niamey *	+6	+7	+8	+9	+1
Nigeria	[234]	✪Abuja (9) ✪Lagos (1) Cell Phones (90)	+6	+7	+8	+9	+1
Northern Mariana Islands	[670]	✪Saipan*	+15	+16	+17	+18	+10
Norway	[47]	✪Oslo *	+6	+7	+8	+9	+1
Oman	[968]	✪Muscat *	+9	+10	+11	+12	+4
Pakistan	[92]	✪Islamabad (51) Karachi (21); Lahore (42)	+10	+11	+12	+13	+5
Palau	[680]	✪Koror*	+14	+15	+16	+17	+9
Panama	[507]	✪Panama City*	0	+1	+2	+3	-5
Papua New Guinea	[675]	✪Port Moresby *	+15	+16	+17	+18	+10
Paraguay	[595]	✪Asuncion (21)	+1	+2	+3	+4	-4
Peru	[51]	✪Lima (1)	0	+1	+2	+3	-5
Philippines	[63]	✪Manila (2) Cebu (32) Davao (82)	+13	+14	+15	+16	+8
Poland	[48]	✪Warsaw (22) Gdansk (58); Kraków (12) Lodz (42); Poznan (61) Mobile Phones (0*601) and (0*602)	+6	+7	+8	+9	+1

✪ Capital city
* City codes not required in this country
EST = US Eastern Standard Time
MST = US Mountain Standard Time
UTC = Universal Time Coordinated (Greenwich, England)

†† More than one time zone in this country.
** This city code used for entire country or territory.
CST = US Central Standard Time
PST = US Pacific Standard Time

DIALING

Country	Country Code	City/Area Codes	Hours ahead or behind:				
			EST	CST	MST	PST	UTC
Portugal	[351]	✪Lisbon (1)	+6	+7	+8	+9	+1
		Porto (2)					
		Faro (89)					
Puerto Rico	[1]	✪San Juan (787) **	+1	+2	+3	+4	-4
Qatar	[974]	✪Doha *	+8	+9	+10	+11	+3
Reunion Island	[262]	✪St. Denis*	+9	+10	+11	+12	+4
Romania	[40]	✪Bucharest (1)	+7	+8	+9	+10	+2
Russia††	[7]	✪Moscow (095)	+8	+9	+10	+11	+3
		Metro Moscow (096)	+8	+9	+10	+11	+3
		St. Petersburg (812)					
Rwanda	[250]	✪Kigali *	+7	+8	+9	+10	+2
St. Kitts & Nevis	[1]	✪Basseterre (869) **	+1	+2	+3	+4	-4
St. Lucia	[1]	✪Castries (758) **	+1	+2	+3	+4	-4
St. Vincents & the Grenadines	[1]	✪Kingstown (809) **	+1	+2	+3	+4	-4
San Marino	[378]	✪San Marino*	+6	+7	+8	+9	+1
São Tomé & Principe	[239]	✪São Tomé*	+5	+6	+7	+8	0
Saudi Arabia	[966]	✪Riyadh (1)	+8	+9	+10	+11	+3
		Jeddah (2)					
		Makkah (Mecca) (2)					
Senegal	[221]	✪Dakar *	+5	+6	+7	+8	0
Seychelles	[248]	✪Victoria	+9	+10	+11	+12	+4
Sierra Leone	[232]	✪Freetown (22)	+5	+6	+7	+8	0
Singapore	[65]	✪Singapore *	+13	+14	+15	+16	+8
Slovakia	[421]	✪Bratislava (7)	+6	+7	+8	+9	+1
Slovenia	[386]	✪Ljubljana (61)	+6	+7	+8	+9	+1
Solomon Islands	[677]	✪Honiara*	+16	+17	+18	+19	+11
Somalia	[252]	✪Mogadishu (1)	+8	+9	+10	+11	+3
South Africa	[27]	✪Cape Town (21)	+7	+8	+9	+10	+2
		✪Pretoria (12)					
		Bloemfontein (51)					
		Durban (31)					
		Johannesburg (11)					
Spain	[34]	✪Madrid (91)	+6	+7	+8	+9	+1
Spain has stopped using city codes. City codes are now incorporated into local numbers which you must dial even when in the city.		Barcelona (93) Bilbao (94) Cordoba (957) Ibiza (971) Malaga ((95) Seville (95) Valencia (96) Zaragoza (976)					
Sri Lanka	[94]	✪Colombo (1)	+10½	+11½	+12½	+13½	+5½
Sudan	[249]	✪Khartoum (11)	+7	+8	+9	+10	+2

Country	Country Code	City/Area Codes	Hours ahead or behind:				
			EST	CST	MST	PST	UTC
Suriname	[597]	✪Paramaribo*	+2	+3	+4	+5	-3
Swaziland	[268]	✪Mbabane * ✪Lobamba*	+7	+8	+9	+10	+2
Sweden	[46]	✪Stockholm (8) Goteberg (31); Malmö (40)	+6	+7	+8	+9	+1
Switzerland	[41]	✪Bern (31) Basel (61) Geneva (22) Lucerne (41); Zurich (1)	+6	+7	+8	+9	+1
Syria	[963]	✪Damascus (11)	+7	+8	+9	+10	+2
Taiwan All old one-digit Taiwan city codes now have a prefix of 2.	[886]	✪Taipei (22) Kaohsiung (27) Taichung (24)	+13	+14	+15	+16	+8
Tajikistan	[7]	✪Dushanbe (3772)	+10	+11	+12	+13	+5
Tanzania	[255]	✪Dar es Salaam (51)	+8	+9	+10	+11	+3
Thailand	[66]	✪Bangkok (2)	+12	+13	+14	+15	+7
Togo	[228]	✪Lomé*	+5	+6	+7	+8	0
Tonga	[676]	✪Nukualofa**	-6	-5	-4	-3	-11
Trinidad & Tobago	[1]	✪Port-of-Spain (868)**	+1	+2	+3	+4	-4
Tunisia	[216]	✪Tunis (1)	+6	+7	+8	+9	+1
Turkey	[90]	✪Ankara (312) Istanbul (212), (216)	+7	+8	+9	+10	+2
Turkmenistan	[993]	✪Ashkhabad (12)	+10	+11	+12	+13	+5
Turks & Caicos Islands	[1]	✪Grand Turk (649) **	0	+1	+2	+3	-5
Tuvalu	[688]	✪Funafuti*	+17	+18	+19	+20	+12
Uganda	[256]	✪Kampala (41)	+8	+9	+10	+11	+3
Ukraine	[380]	✪Kiev (44); Odessa (048)	+7	+8	+9	+10	+2
United Arab Emirates	[971]	✪Abu Dhabi (2) Dubai (4)	+9	+10	+11	+12	+4
United Kingdom	[44]	✪London, as of April 2000: (171) becomes (020) and add '7' to begining of telephone # (181) becomes (020) and add '8' to begining of telephone # Belfast (1232) Birmingham (121) Bristol (117) Edinburgh (131) Glasgow (141) Leeds (113); Liverpool (151) Manchester (161) Sheffield (114)	+5	+6	+7	+8	0

D I A L I N G

Country	Country Code	City/Area Codes	Hours ahead or behind: EST	CST	MST	PST	UTC
United States ††	[1]	✪Washington, DC (202)	0	+1	+2	+3	-5
		Atlanta (404)	0	+1	+2	+3	-5
		Baltimore (410)	0	+1	+2	+3	-5
		Boston (617)	0	+1	+2	+3	-5
		Chicago (312) (773)	-1	0	+1	+2	-6
		Dallas (214) (972)	-1	0	+1	+2	-6
		Denver (303)	-2	-1	0	+1	-7
		Detroit (313)	0	+1	+2	+3	-5
		Honolulu (808)	-5	-4	-3	-2	-10
		Houston (713) (281)	0	0	+1	+2	-6
		Los Angeles (213), (310)	-3	-2	-1	0	-8
		Miami (305)	0	+1	+2	+3	-5
		Minneapolis (612)	-1	0	+1	+2	-6
		New York (212), (718)	0	+1	+2	+3	-5
		Philadelphia (215)	0	+1	+2	+3	-5
		Sacramento (916) (530)	-3	-2	-1	0	-8
		Salt Lake City (801)	-2	-1	0	+1	-7
		San Diego (619)	-3	-2	-1	0	-8
		San Francisco (415)	-3	-2	-1	0	-8
		San Jose (408)	-3	-2	-1	0	-8
		Seattle (206)	-3	-2	-1	0	-8
Uruguay	[598]	✪Montevideo (2)	+2	+3	+4	+5	-3
Uzbekistan	[998]	✪Tashkent (712) + 6 digits (71) + 7digits	+10	+11	+12	+13	+5
Vanuatu	[678]	✪Port Vila*	+16	+18	+19	+20	+11
Venezuela	[58]	✪Caracas (2) Maracaibo (61) Valencia (41)	+1	+2	+3	+4	-4
Vietnam	[84]	✪Hanoi (4) Ho Chi Minh City (8)	+12	+13	+14	+15	+7
Virgin Islands, British	[1]	✪Road Town (284) **	+1	+2	+3	+4	-4
Virgin Islands, U.S.	[1]	✪Charlotte Amalie* (340) St. Thomas (340)	+1	+2	+3	+4	-4
Western Samoa	[685]	✪Apia *	-6	-5	-4	-3	-11
Yemen	[967]	✪Sana'a (1)	+8	+9	+10	+11	+3
Yugoslavia	[381]	✪Belgrade (11)	+6	+7	+8	+9	+1
Zaire †† See Congo	[243]	✪Kinshasa (12)	+6	+7	+8	+9	+1
Zambia	[260]	✪Lusaka (1)	+7	+8	+9	+10	+2
Zimbabwe	[263]	✪Harare(4)	+7	+8	+9	+10	+2

✪ Capital city
* City codes not required in this country
EST = US Eastern Standard Time
MST = US Mountain Standard Time
UTC = Universal Time Coordinated (Greenwich, England)

†† More than one time zone in this country.
** This city code used for entire country or territory.
CST = US Central Standard Time
PST = US Pacific Standard Time

North America

Arctic Ocean
Greenland Sea
60°
Iceland
Greenland (Denmark)
Bering Sea
Alaska (U.S.A.)
Beaufort Sea
Baffin Bay
Fairbanks
Anchorage
Nuuk (Godthab)
50°
Gulf of Alaska
Whitehorse
Yellow Knife
Labrador Seaa
Canada
Churchill
Hudson Bay
Goose Bay
40°
Edmonton
Vancouver
Seattle
Calgary
Winnipeg
Quebec
Montreal
Halifax
Portland
Ottawa
North Pacific Ocean
Minneapolis
Toronto
Boston
San Rafael
Salt Lake City
Chicago
Detroit
New York
San Francisco
Denver
Pittsburgh
Washington
North Atlantic Ocean
30°
St. Louis
Los Angeles
United States of America
Raleigh
Tijuana
Phoeni x
Memphis
Atlanta
164°
Hermosillo
Houston
Niihau   Kauai
Oahu   Molokai
Lanai   Maui
Chihuahua
New Orleans
Gulf of Mexico
Miami
Tropic Of Cancer
20°
Kahoolawe   Hawaii
La Paz
Monterrey
20°
Mexico
Hawaii (U.S.A.)
Guadalajara
Mexico City
Merida
Acapulco
Oaxaca
Caribbean Sea
10°
LEGEND
✪ Capital
● Major City

125   250 Kilometers

125   250 Miles

Venezuela
Colombia
100°
90°
80°
110°

M A P S

Map Copyright © 1999 by World Trade Press.
All Rights Reserved.

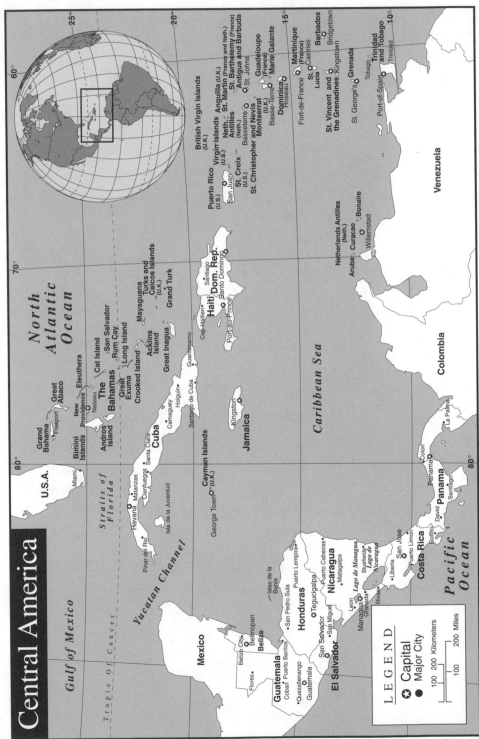

Central America

MAPS

Gulf of Mexico

North Atlantic Ocean

Tropic of Cancer

Straits of Florida

U.S.A.

Miami

Yucatan Channel

Pinar del Rio
Havana
Matanzas
Cienfuegos
Santa Clara
Cuba
Isla de la Juventud
Camaguey
Holguin
Santiago de Cuba

Grand Bahama
Freeport
Great Abaco
Eleuthera
New Providence
Nassau
Bimini Islands
Andros Island
The Bahamas
Cat Island
San Salvador
Rum Cay
Great Exuma
Long Island
Crooked Island
Acklins Island
Great Inagua
Guantanamo

Cayman Islands (U.K.)
George Town

Kingston
Jamaica

Mayaguana
Turks and Caicos Islands (U.K.)
Grand Turk

British Virgin Islands (U.K.)

Puerto Rico (U.S.)
San Juan
Virgin Islands (U.S.)
St. Croix (U.S.)
St. Christopher and Nevis
Montserrat (U.K.)
Basseterre
Basse-Terre
Guadeloupe (France)
Marie Galante
Dominica
Roseau
Fort-de-France
Martinique (France)
St. Lucia
Castries
St. Vincent and the Grenadines
St. George's
Grenada
Barbados
Bridgetown
Kingstown

Anguilla (U.K.)
St. Martin (France and Neth.)
St. Barthélemy (France)
Antigua and Barbuda
St. Johns
Neth. Antilles (Neth.)

Cap-Haïtien
Haiti
Port-au-Prince
Santiago
Dom. Rep.
Santo Domingo

Caribbean Sea

Netherlands Antilles (Neth.)
Aruba
Curaçao
Bonaire
Willemstad

Venezuela

Colombia

Trinidad and Tobago
Port-of-Spain
Tobago
Trinidad

Mexico

Belize City
Belmopan
Belize
Flores
Quezaltenango
Guatemala
Coban
Puerto Barrios
Guatemala
San Pedro Sula
San Salvador
San Miguel
El Salvador
Honduras
Tegucigalpa
Puerto Lempira
Islas de la Bahía
Puerto Cabezas
Nicaragua
Matagalpa
Leon
Managua
Granada
Lago de Managua
Bluefields
Lago de Nicaragua
Rivas
Liberia
San Jose
Costa Rica
Puerto Limón
Golfito
Colon
Panama
Panama
David
Santiago
La Palma
Pacific Ocean

LEGEND
✪ Capital
● Major City

100　200 Kilometers
100　200 Miles

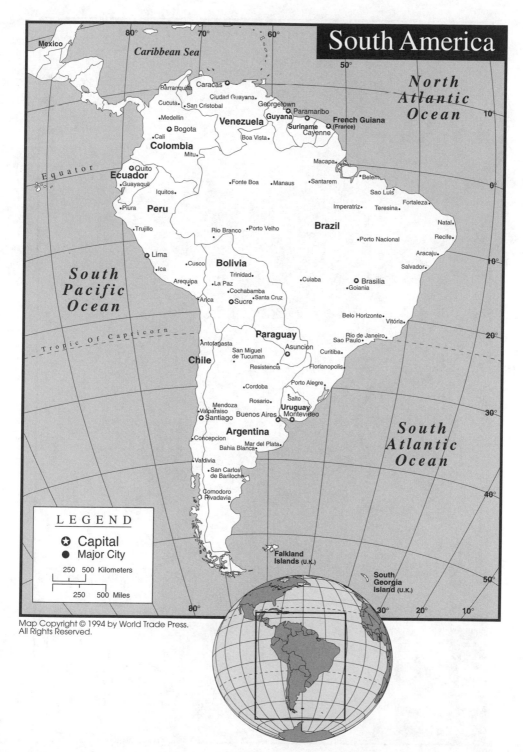

South America

North Atlantic Ocean

Caribbean Sea

Mexico

Barranquilla
Caracas ✪
Ciudad Guayana
Cucuta
San Cristobal
Georgetown
Paramaribo
Medellin
Venezuela
Guyana
Suriname
French Guiana (France)
✪ Bogota
Cayenne
Cali
Boa Vista
Colombia
Mitu
Macapa
✪ Quito
Belem
Ecuador
Guayaquil
Fonte Boa
Manaus
Santarem
Sao Luis
Iquitos
Fortaleza
Imperatriz
Teresina
Piura
Peru
Natal
Trujillo
Rio Branco
Porto Velho
Brazil
Recife
Porto Nacional
Aracaju
Lima
Cusco
Bolivia
Salvador
Ica
Trinidad
Arequipa
La Paz
Cochabamba
Cuiaba
✪ Brasilia
Arica
Santa Cruz
Goiania
✪ Sucre
Belo Horizonte
Vitória
Antofagasta
Paraguay
Rio de Janeiro
Sao Paulo
San Miguel de Tucuman
Asuncion
Curitiba
Chile
Resistencia
Florianopolis
Cordoba
Porto Alegre
Rosario
Salto
Mendoza
Uruguay
Valparaiso
Buenos Aires
Montevideo
✪ Santiago
Argentina
Concepcion
Mar del Plata
Bahia Blanca
Valdivia
San Carlos de Bariloche
Comodoro Rivadavia

Equator

South Pacific Ocean

Tropic Of Capricorn

South Atlantic Ocean

LEGEND

✪ Capital
● Major City

250   500 Kilometers

250   500 Miles

Falkland Islands (U.K.)

South Georgia Island (U.K.)

M A P S

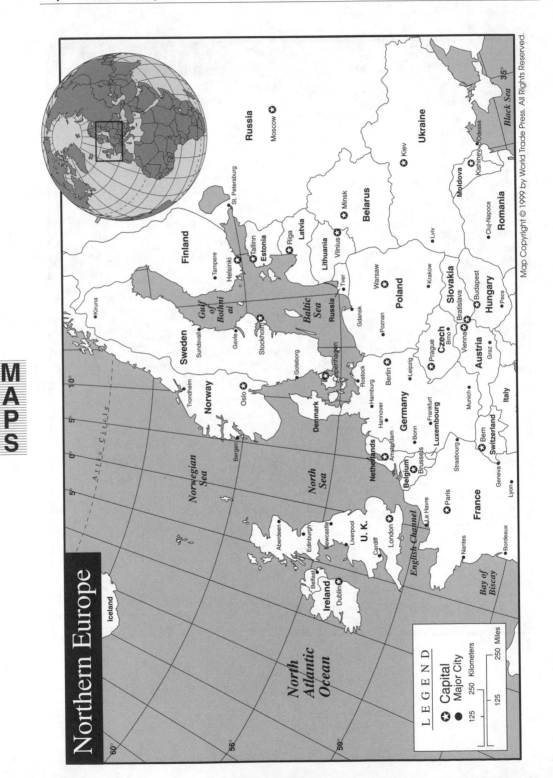

Northern Europe

LEGEND
✪ Capital
● Major City

125   250 Kilometers
125   250 Miles

MAPS

Africa

North Atlantic Ocean

Spain
Italy
Black Sea
Turkey
Iraq
Iran

Tangier
Algiers
Oran · Constantine
Tunis
Rabat
Casablanca
Ghardaia
Tunisia
Mediterranean Sea

Morocco
Marrakech
Tripoli
Banghazi
Alexandria
Cairo
Saudi Arabia

Canary Islands (Spain)

Tindouf
La'youn
Algeria
Libya
Al Jawf
Egypt
Aswan

Western Sahara

Tamanrasset

Mauritania
Nouakchott
Mali
Niger
Faya-Largeau
Port Sudan
Red Sea

Nema
Tombouctou
Agadez
Chad
Lake Chad
Khartoum
Asmera
Eritrea
Djibouti

Burkina Faso
Niamey
Zinder
El Fashir
Sudan
Djibouti
Berbera

Senegal
Dakar
Banjul
Gambia
Guinea Bissau
Ouagadougou
Kano
Maiduguri
N'Djamena
Addis Ababa

Bissau
Guinea
Bamako
Benin
Abuja
Central African Republic
Wau
Ethiopia
Lake Turkana
Somalia

Conakry
Freetown
Togo
Nigeria
Sierra Leon
Ivory Coast
Ghana
Porto Novo
Lagos
Cameroon
Bangui
Juba
Kenya
Mogadishu

Monrovia
Accra
Lome
Liberia
Yamoussoukro
Douala
Malabo
Yaounde
Lake Albert
Uganda
Kisangani
Kampala
Lake Victoria
Nairobi

Equatorial Guinea
Sao Tome
Bata
Libreville
Congo
Rwanda
Kigali
Mombasa

Sao Tome & Principe
Gabon
Zaire
Burundi
Bujumbura
Tanzania
Indian Ocean

Brazzaville
Kananga
Kalemie
Dar es Salaam

Pointe-Noire
Kinshasa
Lake Tanganyika

Cabinda (Angola)
Mbeya

Luanda
Lubumbashi
Kasama
Malawi
Lake Nyasa
Nacala

South Atlantic Ocean

Lobito
Luena
Kitwe
Lilongwe

Namibe
Angola
Zambia
Lusaka
Mahajanga

Lake Kariba
Harare
Mozambique
Antananarivo

Zimbabwe
Beira

Namibia
Windhoek
Botswana
Bulawayo
Madagascar
Toliara

Tropic Of Capricorn

Walvis Bay (South Africa)
Gaborone
Pretoria
Maputo

Luderitz
Johannesburg
Mbabane
Swaziland
Maseru

Lesotho
Durban

South Africa
Cape Town
Port Elizabeth

M A P S

Equator

LEGEND

⍟ Capital
● Major City

500   1000 Kilometers

500   1000 Miles

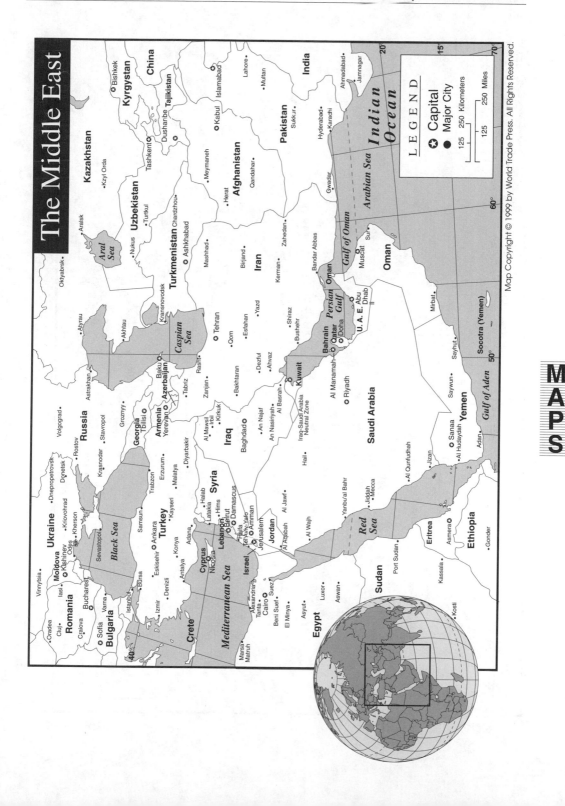

The Middle East

LEGEND

⚙ Capital
● Major City

125   250 Kilometers
125   250 Miles

M A P S

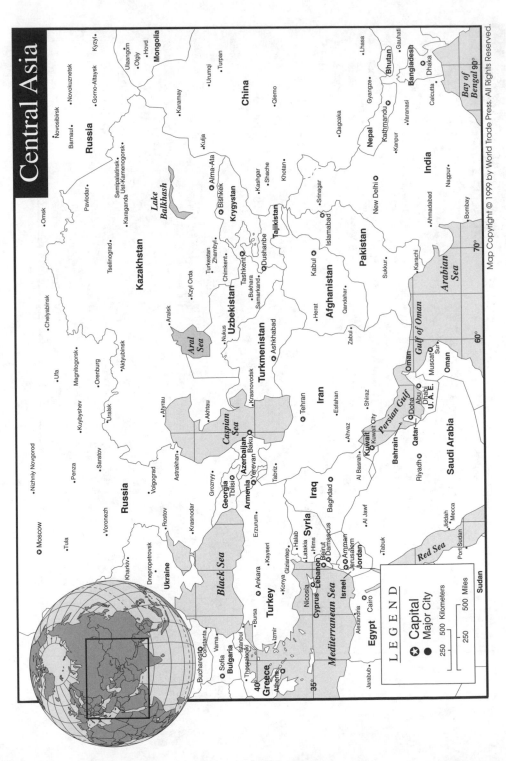

Central Asia

L E G E N D

⊗ Capital

● Major City

250   500 Kilometers

250   500 Miles

East Asia

MAPS

Southeast Asia

LEGEND

✪ Capital
● Major City

250   500 Kilometers
250   500 Miles

M
A
P
S

North Pacific Ocean

Philippine Seaa

South China Sea

Andaman Sea

Bay of Bengal

Indian Ocean

Gulf of Carpentaria

Gulf of Thailand

Tropic of Cancer

Equator

China
Nepal
Bhutan
Bangla-desh
India
Calcutta • Dhaka

Myanmar (Burma)
Mandalay
Rangoon

Thailand
Bangkok
Songkhla

Laos
Vientiane

Vietnam
Hanoi
Ho Chi Minh City

Kampuchea
Phnom Penh

Kunming
Guiyang
Guangzhou (Canton)
Fuzhou
Haikou
Hong Kong
Macau

Taiwan
Taipei
Kaohsiung

Philippines
Manila
Iloilo
Cebu
Davao

Malaysia
Kuala Lumpur
Singapore

Brunei
Bandar Seri Begawan
Sibu

Borneo
Pontianak
Banjarmasin
Balikpapan

Medan
Padang
Telukbetung
Jakarta

Ujungpandang
Majene
Manado
Ternate
Kupang

Papua New Guinea
Port Moresby
Kavieng
Hoskins
Wewak
Daru
Merauke

Jayapura
Kaimana
Bula

Darwin
Wyndham
Daly Waters
Derby
Cairns

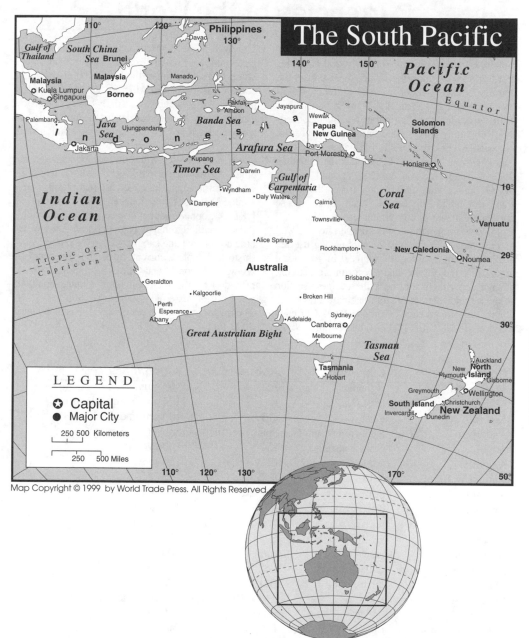

Currencies of the World

The table below lists the names of the currencies and subcurrencies in use in nearly 200 countries and territories around the world. Included are the commonly used symbols for each currency. Countries are listed alphabetically. Many currencies are "soft," meaning they are either legally inconvertible, or simply undesirable because they are not very stable. The currencies most often referred to as "hard" currencies are the U.S. dollar, the Canadian dollar, the Japanese yen, the British pound sterling, the German mark, the French franc, the Swiss franc, the Italian lira, and the Dutch guilder. These currencies are easily convertible world-wide.

Up-to-date information on exchange rates, as well as on changes in the type of currency in use are available from a variety of sources. In your local area, call a major bank and ask for the foreign exchange department, or check the business section of the a major newspaper for a table of foreign exchange. Another source is Thomas Cook Currency Services; In USA Tel: [1] (212) 883-0400.

The Wall Street Journal publishes the most complete table of foreign exchange rates against the dollar ("World Value of the Dollar") in its Monday edition, using Bank of America, Global Trading as its source. It also publishes a daily table of currency trading, with fewer currencies listed, and "Key Currency Cross Rates," which shows the relationships between nine hard currencies.

Other Internet sites with currency information include "Currencies of the World" at URL http://pacific.commerce.ubc.ca/trade/currencies.html; the United Nations "Operational Rates of Exchange" at URL gopher://gopher.undp.org/00/uncurr/exch_rates; "Pacific Exchange Rate Service" at www.pacific.commerce.ubc.ca/xr/; "The Currency Site" (historical tables, current rates and forecasts) at www.oanda.com/; and "Exchange Rates" (rates provided by the International Monetary Fund) at www.imf.org/external/np/tre/sdr/sdr.html.

The information given here is current as of January 2000.

CURRENCY

Country	Currency	Abbreviation	Subcurrency
Afghanistan	afghani	Af	100 puls
Albania	lek	L	100 qintars (quindarka)
Algeria	dinar	DA	100 centimes
Andorra	Andorran peseta (see Spain) or Andorran franc (see France)		
Angola	new kwanza	Kz	100 lwei
Anguilla	dollar	EC$	100 cents
Antigua & Barbuda	dollar	EC$	100 cents
Argentina	peso	A$	100 centavos
Armenia	dram	(n/a)	100 luma
Australia	dollar	A$	100 cents
Austria	schilling	S	100 groschen
Azerbaijan	manat	(n/a)	100 gopik
Bahamas	dollar	B$	100 cents
Bahrain	dinar	BD	1,000 fils
Bangladesh	taka	Tk	100 paisa (sing., poisha)
Barbados	dollar	Bds$	100 cents
Belarus (Byelorussia)	ruble	BR	(n/a)
Belgium	franc	BF	100 centimes
Belize	dollar	BZ$	100 cents
Benin	franc	CFAF	100 centimes
Bermuda	dollar	Bd$	100 cents
Bhutan	ngultrum	Nu	100 chetrum
Bolivia	boliviano	Bs	100 centavos
Bosnia & Herzegovina	B.H. dinar	(n/a)	100 para

Country	Currency	Abbreviation	Subcurrency
Botswana	pula	P	100 thebe
Brazil	real	R$	100 centavos
Brunei	ringitt (or Bruneian Dollar)	B$	100 sen or cents
Bulgaria	leva	Lv	100 stotinki (sing., stotinka)
Burkina Faso	franc	CFAF	100 centimes
Burundi	franc	FBu	100 centimes
Cambodia	new riel	CR	100 sen
Cameroon	franc	CFAF	100 centimes
Canada	dollar	Can$	100 cents
Cape Verde Islands	escudo	C.V.Esc	100 centavos
Cayman Islands	dollar	CI$	100 cents
Central African Rep.	franc	CFAF	100 centimes
Chad	franc	CFAF	100 centimes
Chile	peso	Ch$	100 centavos
China, People's Rep.	yuan renminbi	Y	100 fen = 10 jiao
Colombia	peso	Col$	100 centavos
Comoros	franc	CF	100 centimes
Congo	franc	CFAF	100 centimes
Costa Rica	colon	¢	100 centimos
Côte d'Ivoire	franc	CFAF	100 centimes
Croatia	kuna	HRK	100lipas
Cuba	peso	Cu$	100 centavos
Cyprus	pound	£C	100 cents
Czech Rep.	koruna	Kc	100 haleru
Denmark	krone (pl., kroner)	Dkr	100 øre
Djibouti	franc	DF	100 centimes
Dominica	dollar	EC$	100 cents
Dominican Rep.	peso	RD$	100 centavos
Ecuador	sucre	S/	100 centavos
Egypt	pound	£E	100 piasters = 1,000 milliemes
El Salvador	colon	¢	100 centavos
Equatorial Guinea	ekwele	CFAF	100 centimes
Eritrea	nafka	Nfa	100 cents
Estonia	kroon (pl, krooni)	KR	100 senti
Ethiopia	birr	Br or E$	100 cents
European Union	European Currency Unit (ecu)		100 cents
Falkland Islands	pound	£F	100 pence (sing., penny)
Fiji	dollar	F$	100 cents
Finland	markka	mk	100 pennia (sing., penni)
France	franc	F	100 centimes
French Guiana	French franc (*See* France)		
French Polynesia	franc	CFPF	100 centimes
Gabon	franc	CFAF	100 centimes
Gambia	dalasi	D	100 butut

CURRENCY

Country	Currency	Abbreviation	Subcurrency
Georgia	lari	(n/a)	100 tetri
Germany	deutsche mark	DM	100 pfennig
Ghana	new cedi	¢	100 psewas
Gibraltar	pound	£G	100 pence
Greece	drachma	Dr	100 lepta (sing., lepton)
Greenland	Danish krone (*See* Denmark)		
Grenada	dollar	EC$	100 cents
Guadeloupe	French franc (*See* France)		
Guam	U.S. dollar (*See* United States)		
Guatemala	quetzal	Q	100 centavos
Guinea	syli	FG	10 francs, 1 franc = 100 cent.
Guinea-Bissau	franc	CFAF	100 centimes
Guyana	dollar	G$	100 cents
Haiti	gourde	G	100 centimes
Honduras	lempira	L	100 centavos
Hong Kong	dollar	HK$	100 cents
Hungary	forint	Ft	none
Iceland	króna	IKr	100 aurar (sing., aur)
India	rupee	Rs	100 paise (sing., paisa)
Indonesia	rupiah	Rp	100 sen (not used)
Iran	rial	Rl (p., Rls)	10 rials = 1 toman
Iraq	dinar	ID	1,000 fils
Ireland	pound or punt	Ir£	100 pence (sing., penny)
Israel	new shekel	NIS	100 new agorot (sing., agora)
Italy	lira (pl., lire)	Lit or L	100 centisimi
Jamaica	dollar	J$	100 cents
Japan	yen	¥	100 sen (not used)
Jordan	dinar	JD	1,000 fils
Kazakhstan	tenge	(n/a)	100 tyyn
Kenya	shilling	KSh	100 cents
Kiribati	Australian dollar (*See* Australia)		
Korea, North	won	Wn	100 jun or chon
Korea, South	won	W	100 jeon or chon
Kuwait	dinar	KD	1,000 fils
Kyrgyzstan	som	(n/a)	(n/a)
Laos	new kip	KN	100 at
Latvia	lat	Ls	100 santims
Lebanon	pound or livre	£L	100 piastres
Lesotho	loti (pl., maloti)	L (pl., M)	100 lisente (sing., sente)
Liberia	dollar	$	100 cents
Libya	dinar	LD	1000 dirhams
Liechtenstein	Swiss franc (*See* Switzerland)		
Lithuania	litas (pl., litai)	Lit	100 centu
Luxembourg	franc	LuxF	100 centimes
Macao (Macau)	pataca	P	100 avos
Macedonia	denar	(n/a)	(n/a)
Madagascar	ariary = 5 francs	FMG	1 franc = 100 centimes

Country	Currency	Abbreviation	Subcurrency
Malawi	kwacha	MK	100 tambala
Malaysia	ringgit	RM	100 sen
Maldives	rufiyaa	Rf	100 lari
Mali	franc	CFAF	100 centimes
Malta	lira (pl., liri)	£m	100 cents
Martinique	French franc (*See* France)		
Mauritania	ouguiya	UM	5 khoums
Mauritius	rupee	MauRs	100 cents
Mexico	nuevo peso	Mex$	100 centavos
Moldova	leu (pl., lei)	(n/a)	(n/a)
Monaco	French franc (*See* France)		
Mongolia	tughrik	Tug	100 mongos
Montserrat	dollar	EC$	100 cents
Morocco	dirham	DH	100 centimes
Mozambique	metical	Mt	100 centavos
Myanmar (Burma)	kyat	K	100 pyas
Namibia	dollar	N$	100 cents
Nauru	Australian dollar (*See* Australia)		
Nepal	rupee	NRs	100 paise (sing., paisa)
Netherlands	guilder (gulden)	f.	100 cents
Netherlands Antilles	N.A. guilder	Ant.f. or NAf.	100 cents
New Zealand	dollar	NZ$	100 cents
Nicaragua	gold cordoba	C$	100 centavos
Niger	franc	CFAF	100 centimes
Nigeria	naira	dble-dashed N	100 kobo
Norway	krone (pl., kroner)	NKr	100 øre
Oman	rial	RO	1,000 baizas
Pakistan	rupee	Rs	100 paisa
Panama	balboa	B	100 centesimos
Papua New Guinea	kina	K	100 toeas
Paraguay	guarani	slashed G	100 centimos
Peru	nuevo sol	S/	100 centimos
Philippines	peso	dashed P	100 centavos
Poland	zloty	Z dashed l	100 groszy
Portugal	escudo	Esc	100 centavos
Puerto Rico	U.S. dollar (*See* United States)		
Qatar	riyal	QR	100 dirhams
Reunion Island	French franc (*See* France)		
Romania	leu (pl., lei)	L	100 bani
Russia	ruble	R	100 kopecks
Rwanda	franc	RF	100 centimes
St. Helena	pound	(n/a)	100 pence
St. Kitts and Nevis	dollar	EC$	100 cents
St. Lucia	dollar	EC$	100 cents
St. Pierre	French franc (*See* France)		
St. Vincent & Grenadines	dollar	EC$	100 cents

Country	Currency	Abbreviation	Subcurrency
Samoa (American)	U.S. dollar (*See* United States)		
San Marino	Italian lira (*See* Italy)		
São Tomé & Principe	dobra	Db	100 centimos
Saudi Arabia	riyal	SRls	100 halalat
Senegal	franc	CFAF	100 centimes
Seychelles	rupee	SR	100 cents
Sierra Leone	leone	Le	100 cents
Singapore	dollar	S$	100 cents
Slovakia	koruna	Sk	100 haliers
Slovenia	tolar	SlT	100 stotinov (stotins)
Solomon Islands	dollar	SI$	100 cents
Somalia	shilling	So. Sh.	100 cesntesimi
South Africa	rand	R	100 cents
Spain	peseta	Ptas	100 centimos
Sri Lanka	rupee	SLRs	100 cents
Sudan	pound	(n/a)	100 piasters
Suriname	guilder (gulden)	Sf. or Sur.f.	100 cents
Swaziland	lilangeni (singular)	L (singular)	100 cents
	emalangeni (plural)	E (plural)	
Sweden	krona (pl. kroner)	Sk	100 öre
Switzerland	franc	SwF	100 centimes/rappen
Syria	pound	£S	100 piasters
Taiwan	new dollar	NT$	100 cents
Tajikistan	ruble	(n/a)	(n/a)
Tanzania	shilling	TSh	100 cents
Thailand	baht	Bt or Bht	100 sastangs
Togo	franc	CFAF	100 centimes
Tonga Islands	pa'anga	T$ or PT	100 seniti
Trinidad & Tobago	dollar	TT$	100 cents
Tunisia	dinar	D	1,000 millimes
Turkey	lira	LT	100 kurus
Turkmenistan	manat	(n/a)	100 tenga
Turks & Caicos	U.S. dollar (*See* United States)		
Uganda	shilling	USh	100 cents
Ukraine	Hryvnia	UaK	100 kopiykas
United Arab Emirates	dirham	Dh	100 fils
United Kingdom	pound sterling	£	100 pence
United States	dollar	$	100 cents
Uruguay	peso uraguayo	$U	100 centesimos
Uzbekistan	som	(n/a)	100 tiyin
Venezuela	bolivar	Bs	100 centimos
Vietnam	new dong	D	100 xu or hao
Virgin Islands	U.S. dollar (*See* United States)		
Samoa	tala	WS$	100 sene
Yemen	rial	YRls	100 fils
Yugoslavia	dinar	Din	100 paras
Zambia	kwacha	ZK	100 ngwee
Zimbabwe	dollar	Z$	100 cents

Business Entities Worldwide

The following is a list of the most common business entities worldwide. It is not intended to be exhaustive of all enterprises in the world. Nonprofit enterprises and informal associations have generally not been included, unless they are in common use among traders. Emphasis has been given to private enterprises, as opposed to government or civil enterprises.

The detailed legal requirements for enterprises are numerous, complex, and different from country to country. Moreover, they usually have little meaning within a general definition or comparison of enterprises. The following definitions include some of these details for purposes of giving a general idea of the relative size and complexity of the enterprises, but it is beyond the scope of this work to list and explain every single characteristic, legal nuance, and exception to the exception. For more detailed information, advice should be sought from legal counsel in the relevant country. Another source is the "Martindale-Hubbell International Law Guide." See Resources Appendix for source information.

In many countries, the words "company", "association", and "venture" have special meanings, and therefore the word "enterprise" has been used as a generic term for the concept of a group of persons who join together for purposes of conducting business for profit. Similarly, the word "incorporate" in many countries refers to the procedure for registration of a business, even a partnership; therefore usage of this word has been avoided.

Note: Several definitions are useful at this time:

corporate person
An enterprise whether incorporated or not.

entity
An individual or an enterprise, having an organizational presence separate from the owner, recognized by law as having rights and obligations.

natural person
An individual.

joint liability
Liability for the obligations of an enterprise imposed on two or more owners of an enterprise.

person
An individual or legal entity recognized under law as having legal rights and obligations.

share or stock
An ownership interest in an enterprise. Stock usually refers to an ownership interest evidenced by a formal document issued by the enterprise. Share has a broader meaning in that it can describe a formal interest (such as stock) as well as a less formal interest such as in a partnership. Shares can have different characteristics depending upon the type of enterprise and country of the enterprise. For example: shares can be of equal or unequal value, be voting or non-voting, or can convey limited or unlimited liability for its owner(s).

several liability
Liability for the full obligations of an enterprise imposed on a single owner when other owners who also share responsibility cannot or do not pay.

---

additional liability company
(Russian Federation)
An enterprise with ownership interests divided into "parts" or "shares," formed to conduct business activities, and owned by one or more natural or corporate persons (members) who are jointly and severally liable for enterprise obligations in the percentage of their respective contributions to the enterprise.

agrupamento complementar de empresas
(ACE) (association of business entities) **(Portugal)**
An association of natural or corporate persons in Portugal formed to facilitate and develop the economic activities of the association members for their mutual benefit. Members have unlimited liability for association obligations.

agrupamento Europeu de interêsse econômico
(AEIE) (European economic interest group) **(Portugal)**
An association of natural or corporate persons from different European Community countries, formed to facilitate and develop the economic activities of the association members for their mutual benefit. Members have unlimited liability for association obligations.

Akciova Spolecnost
(a.s.) (joint stock company) **(Czech Republic)**
An enterprise with ownership interests in the form of shares and minimal capitalization of Kc 1,000,000, formed to undertake business activities,

and owned by a single entity or by two or more individuals or entities (shareholders) whose liability for enterprise obligations is limited to the price of the shares.

Aktiebolag
(AB) (company limited by shares)
(Finland, Sweden)
An enterprise with ownership interests in the form of shares and minimum capital of SEK 100,000 (private company) or SEK 500,000 (public company), owned by one or more natural or corporate persons (shareholders) who receive dividends and whose liability for enterprise obligations is limited to the price of the shares.

Aktiengesellschaft
(AG) (corporation limited by shares)
(Germany, Liechtenstein)
An enterprise with ownership interests in the form of shares, owned by one or more natural or corporate persons (shareholders) who receive dividends and whose liability for enterprise obligations is limited to the price of the shares.

Aktiengesellschaften
(AG) (joint stock corporation) **(Austria)**
An enterprise with ownership interests in the form of shares and having minimal capital of ATS 1,000,000, formed for commercial purposes, and owned by natural or corporate persons (stockholders) whose liability for enterprise obligations is limited to the price of the shares.

Aktieselskab
(A/S) (joint stock company) **(Denmark)**
An enterprise with ownership interests in the form of shares and minimum capital of DKK 500,000, formed to conduct business activities, and owned by three or more natural or corporate natural or corporate persons (shareholders) whose liability for enterprise obligations is limited to the price of the shares.

Aktzionerno Drouzestvo
(AD) (public limited company) **(Bulgaria)**
An enterprise with ownership interests in the form of stock, formed to conduct any business, and owned by two or more natural or corporate persons (stockholders) who receive dividends, but whose liability for enterprise obligations is limited to the price of the stock.

anonim sirket
(A.S.) (public company) **(Turkey)**
An enterprise with ownership interests in the form of shares that are traded publicly, formed for any lawful purpose, and owned by five or more natural or corporate persons (shareholders) who receive

dividends but whose liability for enterprise obligations is limited to the price of the shares.

anonymos eteria
(AE) (joint stock company) **(Greece)**
An enterprise with ownership interests in the form of shares which may be traded publicly or privately, formed for any lawful purpose, and owned by one or more natural or corporate persons (shareholders) who receive dividends but who are liable only for the price of the shares.

Anpartsselskaber
(private company) **(Denmark)**
An enterprise with ownership interests in the form of shares and minimum capital of DKK 125,000, owned by one or more natural or corporate persons whose liability for enterprise obligations is limited to the price of the shares.

Anstalt
(establishment) **(Liechtenstein)**
An enterprise in which ownership interests are placed in an undivided fund, usually formed as a holding or investment company, and owned by one or more natural or corporate members who share profits in accordance with contractual provisions in the founding documents.

Ansvarlig Selskap
(unlimited partnership) **(Norway)**
An enterprise with ownership interests stated by contract and formed for commercial purposes by two or more natural or corporate natural or corporate persons who have unlimited and joint liability for enterprise obligations.

Artel
(production cooperative) **(Russian Federation)**
An enterprise with ownership interests combined into a single fund, formed by individuals to produce goods or engage in business activities jointly for their mutual benefit. The owners contribute labor and property to the enterprise, profits are divided in accordance with the labor contributed, and liability for enterprise obligations is stated in the enterprise bylaws.

Associazione in Partecipazione
(participation in association) **(Italy)**
An enterprise with ownership interests determined by contract and formed by a combination of individuals who contribute capital funds and individuals who provide only services. The partners who provide services have unlimited and joint liability for enterprise obligations, while the liability of partners who contribute capital is limited to the amount

of their contribution. Profit-sharing is fixed by the partnership agreement.

Berhad
(Bhd.) (public limited liability company) **(Malaysia)**
An enterprise with ownership interests in the form of shares that arc publicly traded, owned by one or more natural or corporate persons who receive dividends and whose liability for enterprise obligations is limited to the price of the shares.

Besloten Vennootschap met Beperkte Aansprakelijkheid
(B.V.B.A.) (private limited company) **(Belgium, Netherlands)**
An enterprise with ownership interests in the form of shares that are not publicly traded, owned by one or more natural or corporate persons who receive dividends and whose liability for enterprise obligations is limited to the price of the shares.

Betéti Társaság
(Bt) (limited partnership) **(Hungary)**
An enterprise with ownership interests determined by contract and owned by one or more general partners and one or more limited partners. General partners have unlimited and joint liability for enterprise obligations, while limited partners have liability only to the amount of funds they have agreed to invest in the enterprise.

C corporation
(inc. or corp.) **(United States)**
A name derived from United States tax laws to refer to a corporation. *See* corporation.

Chusik-Hosea
(stock companies) **(Korea, Republic of)**
An enterprise with ownership interests in the form of shares, owned by one or more natural or corporate natural or corporate persons who receive dividends and whose liability for enterprise obligations is limited to the price of the shares.

Close Corporation
(Inc.) **(Canada, South Africa, United States)**
An enterprise with ownership interests in the form of shares, formed for purposes of conducting business, and owned by one or more persons (shareholders) who usually restrict the power of the managing directors to operate the enterprise. The shares are usually not traded publicly and the number of shareholders is usually less than 30. In some countries, the owners must be natural persons only, while in other countries corporate or natural persons may own shares in a close corporation.

Closed Company
(private company) **(Brazil)**
A sociedade anonima having shares traded privately. *See* Sociedade Anonima.

closed joint stock company
(Russian Federation)
An enterprise with ownership interests in the form of stock that can be transferred by private sale only, owned by one to fifty natural or corporate persons (stockholders) who receive dividends and whose liability for enterprise obligations is limited to the price of the stock.

Commanditaire Vennootschap
(special partnership) **(Belgium, Netherlands)**
An enterprise with ownership interests determined by written contract, and owned by one or more general partners and one or more special partners. General partners have unlimited and joint liability for enterprise obligations, while special partners have liability only to the amount of capital they have agreed to invest in the company.

Compainía Anómima
(C.A.) (corporation)
(Dominican Republic, Ecuador, Venezuela)
See Sociedad Anónima.

Compainía de Responsabilidad Limitada
(C. Ltda.) (limited liability company) **(Ecuador)**
An enterprise with ownership interests divided in shares of equal value known as participations, formed for any commercial purpose, and owned by at least 3 but no more than 25 members. Liability of each member for enterprise obligations is limited to the amount that the member agrees to invest in the enterprise.

compainía en comandita
(C. en C.) (limited partnership)
(Dominican Republic, Ecuador, Venezuela)
An enterprise with ownership interests in the form of "parts" and formed for commercial purposes by two or more general and limited partners. General partners have unlimited and joint liability for enterprise obligations, while limited partners are liable only to the capital that the partner has agreed to invest in the enterprise.

compainía en comandita por acciones
(C. en C. por A.) (limited partnership with shares)
(Dominican Republic, Ecuador, Venezuela)
A compaiñía en comandita with ownership interests in the form of shares instead of "parts". *See* compaiñía en comandita.

compainía por acciones
(C. por A.) (corporation) **(Dominican Republic)**
See Sociedad Anónima.

Company
(Co.) **(Australia, England, Papua New Guinea)**
An enterprise having ownership interests in the form of shares owned by natural or corporate persons whose liability is limited to the price of the shares. *See* public company; private company.

company limited by guarantee
(Papua New Guinea, South Africa)
An enterprise with ownership interests in the form of shares and owned by members who are liable for enterprise obligations in the amount stated in the formation documents.

Company Limited by Shares
(CLS) **(China)**
An enterprise with ownership interests in the form of shares and having minimum capital of RMB 10,000,000, formed for commercial purposes, and owned by natural or corporate persons (shareholders) whose liability for enterprise obligations is limited to the price of the shares. Shares may be sold privately or offered to the public at large.

Compaõnía en Nombre Colectivo
(Compaõnía) (general partnership)
(Dominican Republic, Ecuador, Venezuela)
An enterprise with ownership interests stated by contract and formed for commercial purposes by two or more natural or corporate persons who have unlimited and joint liability for enterprise obligations.

Corporation
(Inc. or Corp. or Ltd. or Ltée.)
(Bahamas, Canada, United States)
An enterprise with ownership interests in the form of shares, formed to do business for gain, and owned by one or more natural or corporate persons (shareholders) who receive dividends but whose liability for enterprise obligations is limited to the price of the shares.

Cuideachta Phoibli Theoranta
(c.p.t.) **(Ireland)**
See Private Company.

Drouzestvo s Ogranichena Otgovornost
(OOD) (private limited company) **(Bulgaria)**
An enterprise with ownership interests in the form of shares and with minimum capital of 50,000 leva, formed for business purposes, and owned by one or more natural or corporate persons (shareholders) who receive dividends but whose liability for enterprise obligations is limited to the price of the shares. New members may be admitted only by approval of the existing members.

Empresa Individual de Responsibilidad Limitada
(E.I. de R.L.) (individual limited liability company) **(Costa Rica, El Salvador)**
An enterprise with ownership interests stated in the formation documents, formed for any lawful purpose, and owned by a single individual who may withdraw profits and whose liability for enterprise obligations is limited to the enterprise property.

Entreprise Unipersonnelle à Responsabilité Limitée
(E.U.R.L.) (individual limited liability company) **(France)**
A société à responsabilité limitée formed and owned by one person (associé unique) who receives dividends and whose liability for enterprise obligations is limited to the price of the participations. *See* société à responsabilité limitée.

Eshamli Komandit Sirket
(special partnership with shares) **(Turkey)**
An enterprise with ownership interests in the form of shares and formed for commercial purposes by two or more general and special partners. General partners have unlimited and joint liability for enterprise obligations, while special partners are liable only to the funds that the partner has agreed to invest in the enterprise.

estabelecimento individual de responsabildade limitada
(EIRL) (individual limited liability company) **(Portugal)**
An enterprise with ownership interests stated in the formation documents, formed for any lawful purpose, having minimum capital of Esc 400,000 and owned by a single individual who may withdraw profits and whose liability for enterprise obligations is limited to the enterprise property.

eteria periorismenis efthinis
(EPE) (limited liability company) **(Greece)**
An enterprise with ownership interests in the form of shares that are transferred privately and owned by one or more natural or corporate persons (shareholders) whose liability for enterprise obligations is limited to the price of the shares.

eterorythmos eteria
(EE) (limited partnership) **(Greece)**
An enterprise with ownership interests and profit-sharing determined by written contract, formed to undertake business activities, and owned by general and limited partners. Each general partner has unlimited and joint liability for enterprise obligations,

while each limited partner is liable only for the funds that the partner has agreed to invest in the enterprise.

Exempted Limited Partnership

(ELP) **(Bahamas)**
An enterprise that is formed and operated similarly to a limited partnership, but that is exempt from business liccnsee fees and government-imposed taxes for 50 years. General partners have unlimited and joint liability for enterprise obligations, while limited partners incur no liability except for the purchase of their interests.

General Partnership

(Australia, Bahamas, Canada, Channel Islands, China, Cyprus, England, Hong Kong, India, Israel, Russian Federation, South Africa, Turkey, United States, Zimbabwe)
An enterprise with ownership interests and profit-sharing fixed by contract and formed to carry on business for gain by the partners, all of whom have unlimited and joint personal liability for enterprise obligations.

Gesellschaft mit beschränkter Haftung

(GmbH) (limited liability company)
(Austria, Germany, Liechtenstein)
An enterprise with ownership interests in the form of shares that are transferred privately and owned by one or more natural or corporate persons (shareholders) whose liability for enterprise obligations is limited to the price of the shares.

Gomei Kaisha

(partnership corporation) **(Japan)**
An enterprise with ownership interests in the form of shares and formed for commercial purposes by two or more partners.

Goshi Kaisha

(limited partnership corporation) **(Japan)**
An enterprise with ownership interests in the form of shares, owned by one or more general partners and one or more special partners. General partners have unlimited and joint liability for enterprise obligations, while special partners have liability only to the amount of funds they have agreed to invest in the enterprise.

Handelsbolag

(general partnership) **(Sweden)**
An enterprise with ownership interests stated by contract and formed for commercial purposes by two or more natural or corporate persons who have unlimited and joint liability for enterprise obligations.

Hapcha-Hosea

(limited partnership) **(Korea, Republic of)**
An enterprise with ownership interests determined by contract, and owned by one or more general

partners and one or more special partners. General partners have unlimited and joint liability for enterprise obligations, while special partners have liability only to the amount of funds they have agreed to invest in the enterprise.

Hapmyong-Hosea

(partnership) **(Korea, Republic of)**
An enterprise with ownership interests stated by contract and formed for commercial purposes by two or more natural or corporate persons who have unlimited and joint liability for enterprise obligations.

Is Ortakligi

(business partnership) **(Turkey)**
An enterprise with ownership interests stated by contract and formed for commercial purposes by two or more natural or corporate persons who have unlimited and joint liability for enterprise obligations.

Julkinen Osakeyhtiö-oyj

(public limited liability company) **(Finland)**
An enterprise with ownership interests in the form of shares and minimum capital of Fmk 500,000, formed to conduct any business, and owned by one or more natural or corporate persons (shareholders) whose liability for enterprise obligations is limited to the price of the shares.

Kollektif Sirket

(general partnership) **(Turkey)**
An enterprise with ownership interests stated by contract and formed for commercial or other lawful purposes by two or more natural or corporate persons who have unlimited and joint liability for enterprise obligations.

Kollektivgesellschaft

(general partnership) **(Liechtenstein)**
An enterprise with ownership and profit-sharing interests stated by contract and formed for commercial purposes by two or more natural or corporate persons who have unlimited and joint liability for enterprise obligations.

Komandit Sirket

(special partnership) **(Turkey)**
An enterprise with ownership interests determined by contract, and owned by one or more general partners and one or more special partners. General partners have unlimited and joint liability for enterprise obligations, while special partners have liability only to the amount of funds they have agreed to invest in the enterprise.

Komanditní Spolecnost

(k.s.) (limited partnership) **(Czech Republic)**
An enterprise with ownership interests and profit-

sharing determined by written contract, formed to undertake business activities, and owned by general and limited partners. Each general partner has unlimited and joint liability for enterprise obligations, while each limited partner is liable only to the amount of the funds that the partner has agreed to invest in the enterprise.

Komanditno Druzestvo
(limited partnership) (**Bulgaria**)
An enterprise with ownership interests determined by written contract and formed to conclude commercial transactions by two or more individuals who decide to act in concert, but at least one of whom has unlimited liability for enterprise obligations and at least one of whom has liability limited in accordance with the partnership contract.

Kommandit Erwerbsgesellschaft
(KEG) (limited professional association) (**Austria**)
An enterprise with ownership interests determined by contract, formed to provide professional or business services that require special regulatory licenses, and owned by partners who have limited liability for enterprise obligations.

Kommanditbolag
(limited partnership) (**Sweden**)
An enterprise with ownership interests determined by contract, and owned by one or more general partners and one or more limited partners. General partners have unlimited and joint liability for enterprise obligations, while limited partners have liability only to the amount of the funds they have agreed to invest in the enterprise.

Kommanditgesellschaft
(limited partnership)
(**Austria, Germany, Liechtenstein**)
An enterprise with ownership interests determined by contract, formed to carry on trade or production, and owned by two or more partners. At least one partner (Komplementaer) has unlimited liability for enterprise obligations, while at least one other partner (Kommanditist) is liable only to the amount of the funds that the partner has invested in the enterprise.

Kommanditselskap
(limited partnership) (**Norway**)
An enterprise with ownership interests determined by contract, and owned by one or more general partners and one or more limited partners. General partners have unlimited and joint liability for enterprise obligations, while limited partners have liability only to the amount of the funds they have agreed to invest in the enterprise.

korlátolt felelosségu társaság
(Kft) (limited liability company) (**Hungary**)
An enterprise with ownership interests in the form of "parts" and minimum capital of HUF 1,000,000, formed to conduct business for profit, owned by one or more natural or corporate persons who receive dividends and whose liability for enterprise obligations is limited to the price of the parts.

közkereseti társaság
(Kkt) (general partnership) (**Hungary**)
An enterprise with ownership interests stated by contract and formed to conduct business for profit by two or more natural or corporate persons who have unlimited and joint liability for enterprise obligations.

közös vállalat
(joint venture) (**Hungary**)
An enterprise formed for profit from commercial activities by two or more natural or corporate persons who are liable for enterprise obligations in proportion to their respective contributions to the enterprise.

Limited Duration Companies
(LDC) (**Bahamas**)
An enterprise with a limited duration of 30 years or less, formed to allow for automatic termination of the enterprise when the period of existence has elapsed. The formation documents determine whether ownership interests are in the form of shares or otherwise, and liability of the shareholders may be limited or unlimited.

limited liability company
(LLC)
(**China, Russian Federation, United States**)
An enterprise with ownership interests in the form of shares, formed for commercial purposes, and owned by one or more natural or corporate persons (shareholders) but no more than the statutory maximum (usually 50 shareholders). The liability of the shareholders for enterprise obligations is limited to the price of the shares.

limited liability partnership
(LLP) (**United States**)
An enterprise with ownership interests determined by written contract among the partners, all of whom must be professionals licensed or otherwise specially qualified to offer services regulated by law and must be permitted to offer services through a limited liability partnership. The partners remain personally liable for their own obligations, jointly and severally liable for partnership obligations, but have no liability for the actions of other partners.

limited partnership
(Bahamas, Canada, Channel Islands, Cyprus, England, India, Israel, South Africa, United States, Zimbabwe)
An enterprise with ownership interests and profit-sharing fixed by contract among the partners and formed to carry on business for gain by two or more partners. At least one partner has unlimited liability for enterprise obligations, while at least one other partner is liable only to the amount of the funds that the partner has invested in the enterprise, provided that the limited partner contributes no services and takes no part in controlling the day-to-day partnership business.

Maatschap
(partnership) **(Netherlands)**
An enterprise with ownership interests stated by contract and formed to conduct business or to offer services for profit by two or more natural or corporate persons who contribute labor, funds, and property to the enterprise and who have unlimited and joint liability for enterprise obligations. The formation contract may limit a partner's liability to the partner's percentage of contribution to the enterprise.

Naamloze Vennootschap
(N.V.) (public joint stock company)
(Belgium, Netherlands)
An enterprise with ownership interests in the form of shares that are publicly traded, owned by one or more natural or corporate persons who receive dividends and whose liability for enterprise obligations is limited to the price of the shares.

Offene Erwerbsgesellschaft
(OEG) (general professional association) **(Austria)**
An enterprise with ownership interests determined by contract, formed to provide professional or business services that require special regulatory licenses, and owned by partners who have unlimited and joint liability for enterprise obligations.

Offene Handelsgesellschaft
(Co. or Cie.) (general partnership)
(Austria, Germany)
An enterprise with ownership interests determined by contract, formed to carry on a trade or production, and owned by partners who are jointly and severally liable for enterprise obligations.

omorythmos eteria
(OE) (general partnership) **(Greece)**
An enterprise with ownership interests stated by contract and formed for commercial purposes by two or more natural or corporate persons (partners) who have unlimited and joint liability for enterprise actions.

Open Company
(public company) **(Brazil)**
A sociedade anonima having shares traded publicly through a stock exchange or otherwise in an over-the-counter market. *See* Sociedade Anonima.

open joint stock company
(Russian Federation)
An enterprise with ownership interests in the form of stock sold to the public, owned by one or more natural or corporate persons (stockholders) who receive dividends and whose liability for enterprise obligations is limited to the price of the stock.

Ordinary Partnership
(England, Hong Kong, Zimbabwe)
See General Partnership.

Osakeyhtiö
(Oy) (private limited liability company) **(Finland)**
An enterprise with ownership interests in the form of shares and minimum capital of Fmk 50,000, owned by one or more natural or corporate persons whose liability for enterprise obligations is limited to the price of the shares.

osuuskunta
(osuus) (cooperative association) **(Finland)**
An enterprise with ownership and profit-sharing interests determined by contract, formed by five or more members who contribute their property and labor for purposes of carrying on business to their mutual benefit. The liability of the members for enterprise obligations is determined by the formation contract.

Partnership
(England, United States)
An enterprise with ownership interests determined by contract between the owners (partners) who join together for purposes of acting in concert to attain common goals. *See* general partnership, limited partnership, and limited liability partnership.

partnership in commendam
(limited partnership) **(Russian Federation)**
An enterprise with ownership interests and profit-sharing fixed by contract among the partners and formed to carry on business for gain by two or more partners. At least one partner has unlimited liability for enterprise obligations, while at least one other partner is liable only to the amount of the funds that the partner has agreed to invest in the enterprise.

Private Company
(Ltd. or Pvt. Ltd.) **(Australia, Bahamas, Channel Islands, Cyprus, England, Hong Kong, India, Israel, Nigeria, Pakistan, Zimbabwe)**
An enterprise with ownership interests in the form of

shares that are not sold to the public at large, owned by natural or corporate persons (shareholders) who receive dividends but whose liability for enterprise obligations is limited to the price of the shares.

Public Company

(P.L.C.) **(Australia, Bahamas, Channel Islands, Cyprus, England, Hong Kong, India, Israel, Nigeria, Pakistan, Zimbabwe)**
An enterprise having ownership interests in the form of shares that are sold to the public at large and owned by natural or corporate persons (shareholders) who receive dividends but whose liability for enterprise obligations is limited to the price of the shares.

Publikt Aktiebolag-abp

(public limited liability company) **(Finland)**
See Julkinen Osakeyhtiö-oyj.

Részvénytársaság

(Rt) (corporation limited by shares) **(Hungary)**
An enterprise with ownership interests in the form of shares and minimum capital of HUF 10,000,000, owned by one or more natural or corporate persons (shareholders) who receive dividends and whose liability for enterprise obligations is limited to the price of the shares.

S Corporation

(Inc. or Co.) **(United States)**
An enterprise with special tax features, having ownership interests in the form of shares, owned by one to thirty-five natural or corporate persons (shareholders) who receive a share of annual net profits as determined by their respective share percentages, and whose liability for enterprise obligations is limited to the funds they agree to invest in the enterprise.

Sendirian Berhard

(Sdn. Bhd.) (private limited liability company) **(Malaysia)**
An enterprise with ownership interests in the form of shares that are privately traded only, owned by one or more natural or corporate persons who receive dividends and whose liability for enterprise obligations is limited to the price of the shares.

sharika mossahmah

(joint stock company) **(Bahrain, Egypt, Qatar)**
An enterprise with ownership interests in the form of stock or shares, formed for commercial purposes, and owned by natural or corporate persons (stockholders or shareholders) who receive dividends but whose liability for enterprise obligations is limited to the price of the stock or shares.

sharika tadhamun

(general partnership) **(Bahrain, Egypt, Qatar)**
An enterprise with ownership interests stated by contract and formed for commercial purposes by two or more natural or corporate persons (partners) who have unlimited and joint liability for enterprise actions.

sharika tawsiyah baseetah

(limited partnership) **(Bahrain, Egypt, Qatar)**
An enterprise with ownership interests and profit-sharing fixed by contract among the partners and formed to carry on business for gain by two or more partners. At least one partner has unlimited liability for enterprise obligations, while at least one other partner is liable only to the amount of the funds that the partner has agreed to invest in the enterprise.

sharika tawsiyah biel-ash-nam

(partnership limited by shares)
(Bahrain, Egypt, Qatar)
An enterprise with ownership interests in the form of shares and formed for commercial purposes by two or more general and limited partners. General partners have unlimited and joint liability for enterprise actions, while limited partners are liable only to the price of the shares.

sharika that massouliyyah mahdoodah

(WLL) (limited liability company)
(Bahrain, Egypt, Qatar)
An enterprise with ownership interests divided in shares that cannot be sold publicly, formed for any commercial purpose, having limited duration of no more than 25 years, and owned by at least two natural or corporate persons but no more than the number of members permitted by law (usually 50 or fewer). Liability of members for enterprise obligations is limited to the amount stated in the formation documents.

Sociedad Anónima

(S.A.) (stock company)
(Argentina, Bahamas, Bolivia, Chile, Columbia, Costa Rica, Denmark, Dominican Republic, Ecuador, El Salvador, Guatemala, Honduras, Mexico, Paraguay, Peru, Spain, Uruguay)
An enterprise with ownership interests in the form of stock or shares, formed to sell goods or services, and owned by natural or corporate persons (stockholders or shareholders) who receive dividends based on enterprise net profits but whose liability for enterprise obligations is limited to the price of the stock or shares.

Sociedad Anónima de Capital Abierto

(S.A. de C.A.) (public corporation) **(Costa Rica)**
A sociedad anónima registered on the Costa Rican

stock exchange, having at least 50 stockholders none of whom own more than 10 percent of the shares, and with at least 10 percent of its shares transferred annually through the stock exchange. *See* Sociedad Anónima.

Sociedad Colectiva

(S.C. or Cía) (general partnership)

(Argentina, Bolivia, Chile, Columbia, El Salvador, Guatemala, Honduras, Peru, Uruguay)

An enterprise with ownership interests stated by contract and formed for commercial purposes by two or more natural or corporate persons who have unlimited and joint liability for enterprise obligations.

Sociedad Commanditaria

(limited partnership) **(Spain)**

An enterprise with ownership interests determined by contract, and owned by one or more general partners and one or more limited partners. General partners have unlimited and joint liability for enterprise obligations, while limited partners have liability only to the amount of the funds they have agreed to invest in the enterprise.

Sociedad de Capital e Industria

(S.C.I.) (capital and industry partnership)

(Argentina)

An enterprise with ownership interests determined by contract and formed by a combination of individuals who contribute funds and individuals who provide only services. The partners who contribute funds have unlimited liability, while the other partners are not liable personally for enterprise obligations. Profit-sharing is fixed by the partnership agreement.

Sociedad de Responsabilidad Limitada

(S.R.L. or S. de R.L. or Ltda.) (limited liability company)

(Argentina, Bolivia, Brazil, Chile, Columbia, El Salvador, Honduras, Mexico, Spain)

An enterprise with ownership interests divided in shares of equal value known as quotas, formed for any commercial purpose, and owned by no more than the number of members permitted by law (usually 50 or fewer). Liability of members for enterprise obligations is limited to the amount stated in the enterprise contract.

Sociedad en Comandita

(S. en C.) (limited partnership) **(Argentina, Bolivia, Chile, Columbia, El Salvador, Guatemala, Honduras, Mexico, Peru, Uruguay)**

An enterprise with ownership interests stated by contract and formed for commercial purposes by two or more active and silent partners. Active partners have unlimited and joint liability for enterprise obliga-

tions, while silent partners are liable only to the funds that the partner has invested in the enterprise.

Sociedad en Comandita por Acciones

(S.C.A.) (joint stock company) **(Argentina, Columbia, Guatemala, Honduras, Mexico)**

An enterprise having attributes of both a stock company and partnership, with ownership interests in the form of stock, and owned by active and silent partners. Active partners are liable for enterprise obligations and obligations to the same degree as in a general partnership. The liability of each silent partner is limited to the funds that the partner has agreed to invest in the enterprise.

Sociedad en Nombre Colectivo

(general partnership) **(Mexico)**

An enterprise with ownership interests stated by contract and formed for commercial purposes by two or more natural or corporate persons who have unlimited and joint liability for enterprise obligations.

Sociedad Regular Colectiva

(general partnership) **(Spain)**

An enterprise with ownership interests stated by contract and formed for commercial purposes by two or more natural or corporate persons who have unlimited and joint liability for enterprise obligations.

sociedade anónima

(S.A.) (stock company) **(Brazil, Portugal)**

An enterprise with ownership interests in the form of shares, formed for any object or gain not contrary to law or public order, and owned by two or more natural or corporate persons (shareholders) who receive dividends and whose liability for enterprise obligations is limited to the price of the shares.

sociedade cooperativa

(SCRL) (cooperative) **(Portugal)**

An enterprise with ownership interests in the form of shares and minimum capitalization of Esc 50,000, formed for commercial purposes, and owned by ten or more natural or corporate persons (shareholders) who share profits in relation to their labor contributions to the business and whose liability for enterprise obligations may be limited or unlimited as stated in the formation documents.

sociedade em comandita por acções

(partnership with shares) **(Portugal)**

An enterprise with ownership interests in the form of shares and formed for commercial purposes by two or more general and limited partners. General partners have unlimited and joint liability for enterprise actions, while limited partners are liable only to the funds that they have agreed to invest in the enterprise.

sociedade em commandita simple
(limited partnership) **(Portugal)**
An enterprise with ownership interests in the form of "quotas" and formed for commercial purposes by two or more active and silent partners. Active partners have unlimited and joint liability for enterprise actions, while silent partners are liable only to the amount of funds that the partner has invested in the enterprise.

sociedade em nome colectivo
(general partnership) **(Portugal)**
An enterprise with ownership interests stated by contract and formed for commercial purposes by two or more natural or corporate persons who have unlimited and joint liability for enterprise actions.

sociedade por quota
(Lda.) (limited liability companyl) **(Portugal)**
An enterprise with ownership interests in the form of "quotas", formed for any commercial purpose, and owned by no more than the number of members permitted by law (usually 50 or fewer). Liability of members for enterprise obligations is limited to the amount stated in the enterprise contract.

Società a Responsabilità Limitata
(S.R.L.) (limited liability company) **(Italy)**
An enterprise with ownership interests in the form of "quotas", having limits on the transfer of quotas, and owned by one or more natural or corporate persons (quotaholders) whose liability for enterprise obligations is limited to the price of the shares, except that a sole quotaholder that is a corporate entity has unlimited liability for enterprise obligations if the enterprise becomes insolvent.

Società in Accomandita per Azioni
(company with liability limited per share) **(Italy)**
An enterprise with ownership interests in the form of shares, owned by one or more natural or corporate persons (partners) whose liability for enterprise obligations is limited to the price of the shares.

Società in Accomandita Semplice
(unlimited liability share company) **(Italy)**
An enterprise with ownership interests in the form of shares, owned by one or more natural or corporate persons (partners) who have unlimited and joint liability for enterprise obligations.

Società in Nome Collettivo
(general partnership) **(Italy)**
A enterprise with ownership interests stated by contract and formed for commercial purposes by two or more natural or corporate persons (partners) who have unlimited and joint liability for enterprise obligations.

Società per Azioni
(S.A.) (corporation) **(Italy)**
An enterprise with ownership interests in the form of shares and minimum capital of 200,000,000 lire, owned by one or more natural or corporate persons who receive dividends and whose liability for enterprise obligations is limited to the price of the shares, except that a sole shareholder has unlimited liability for enterprise obligations in the event the enterprise becomes insolvent.

Società Semplice
(simple partnership) **(Italy)**
An enterprise with ownership interests stated by written or verbal contract, formed other than for industrial or commercial purposes by two or more individuals who act severally but have unlimited and joint liability for enterprise obligations.

Societate cu Raspundere Limitata
(limited liability company) **(Romania)**
An enterprise with ownership interests in the form of "shares" or "parts", owned by one or more natural or corporate persons whose liability for enterprise obligations is limited to the price of the shares.

Societate in Comandita pe Actiuni
(limited joint stock company) **(Romania)**
An enterprise with ownership interests in the form of shares that are privately traded, owned by one or more natural or corporate persons who receive dividends and whose liability for enterprise obligations is limited to the price of the shares.

Societate in Comandita Simpla
(limited partnership) **(Romania)**
An enterprise with ownership interests determined by contract, and owned by one or more general partners and one or more limited partners. General partners have unlimited and joint liability for enterprise obligations, while limited partners have liability only to the amount of the funds they have agreed to invest in the enterprise.

Societate in Nume Colectiv
(general partnership) **(Romania)**
An enterprise with ownership interests stated by contract and formed for commercial purposes by two or more natural or corporate persons who have unlimited and joint liability for enterprise obligations.

Societate pe Actiuni
(joint stock company) **(Romania)**
An enterprise with ownership interests in the form of shares that are publicly traded, owned by one or more natural or corporate persons who receive dividends and whose liability for enterprise obligations is limited to the price of the shares.

Société à Responsabilité Limitée
(S.A.R.L.) (limited liability company)
(France, Luxembourg, Morocco)
An enterprise with ownership interests in the form of "participations", having a maximum duration of 99 years, and owned by one to fifty natural or corporate persons (associés) who receive dividends and whose liability for enterprise obligations is limited to the price of the participations.

Société Anonyme
(S.A.) (joint stock company) **(Bahamas, Belgium, France, Lebanon, Luxembourg, Morocco)**
An enterprise with ownership interests in the form of shares, formed for any lawful purpose, and owned by natural or corporate persons (shareholders) who receive dividends but who are liable only for the price of the shares.

Société Coopérative
(S.C.) (cooperative company) **(Belgium)**
An enterprise with ownership interests in the form of shares and minimum capitalization of BF 750,000, formed for commercial purposes, and owned by three or more natural or corporate persons (shareholders) who share profits in relation to the amount of business with the enterprise and whose liability for enterprise obligations may be limited or limited as stated in the enterprise formation documents.

Société en Commandite
(S. en C.) (special partnership)
(France, Lebanon, Morocco)
See Société en Commandite Simple.

Société en Commandite par Actions
(S.C. par A.) (special partnership by shares)
(France, Morocco)
An enterprise with ownership interests in the form of shares and formed for commercial purposes by two or more general and limited partners. General partners have unlimited and joint liability for enterprise obligations, while limited partners are liable only to the funds that the partner has agreed to invest in the enterprise.

Société en Commandite Simple
(S. en C.S.) (special partnership)
(France, Lebanon, Morocco)
An enterprise with ownership interests determined by public deed or private written contract, and owned by one or more general partners and one or more special partners. General partners have unlimited and joint liability for enterprise obligations, while special partners have liability only to the amount of the funds they have agreed to invest in the company.

Société en Nom Collectif
(SNC) (general partnership)
(Belgium, France, Lebanon, Morocco)
An enterprise with ownership interests determined by public deed or private written contract, and owned by two or more partners who have unlimited and joint liability for all enterprise obligations.

société en participation
(joint venture) **(France)**
An enterprise formed by written or verbal contract by natural or corporate persons who agree to act in concert for a particular purpose. Partners conduct business in their own names and are personally liable for enterprise obligations.

Société par Actions Simplifée
(S.A.S.) (simplified shares company) **(France)**
An enterprise with ownership interests in the form of shares and minimum capital of FF 250,000, formed by companies for the purpose of conducting business jointly, and owned by two or more corporations (shareholders) that receive dividends and that have liability for enterprise obligations limited to the price of the shares.

Société Privée a Reponsabilité Limitée
(S.P.R.L.) (private limited company) **(Belgium)**
An enterprise with ownership interests in the form of shares and minimum capitalization of BEF 750,000, and owned by two or more members with liability limited to the amount of the funds they agreed to invest in the enterprise.

Spolecnost s Rucením Omezenym
(s.r.o. or spol. s r.o.) (limited liability company)
(Czech Republic)
An enterprise with ownership interests in the form of investments agreed by the members in advance, formed to undertake business activities, and owned by one or more natural or corporate persons, to a maximum of 50. Liability of members for enterprise obligations is limited to the investment amount stated in the founding documents for the enterprise.

spólka akcyjna
(S.A.) (joint stock company) **(Poland)**
An enterprise with ownership interests in the form of shares and minimum capital of Zl 1 billion, owned by one or more natural or corporate persons (shareholders) who receive dividends and whose liability for enterprise obligations is limited to the price of the shares.

spólka cywilna
(civil partnership) **(Poland)**
An enterprise with ownership interests determined by private written or verbal contract, formed for

business purposes but not registered nationally, and owned by two or more partners who have unlimited and joint liability for all enterprise obligations.

spólka jawna
(registered general partnership) **(Poland)**
An enterprise with ownership interests determined by written or verbal contract, formed for commercial purposes and registered nationally, and owned by two or more partners who have unlimited and joint liability for all enterprise obligations.

spólka komandytowa
(limited partnership) **(Poland)**
An enterprise with ownership interests determined by contract, and owned by one or more general partners and one or more special partners. General partners have unlimited and joint liability for enterprise obligations, while special partners have liability only to the amount of funds they have agreed to invest in the enterprise.

spólka z ograniczona odpowied zialnóscia
(Sp. z o.o.) (limited liability company) **(Poland)**
An enterprise with ownership interests in the form of shares that are transferred privately, having minimum capital of Zl 40 million, and owned by one or more natural or corporate persons (shareholders) whose liability for enterprise obligations is limited to the price of the shares.

Stock Corporation
(Inc. or Corp.) **(Philippines)**
An enterprise with ownership interests in the form of shares, owned by one or more natural or corporate persons who receive dividends and whose liability for enterprise obligations is limited to the price of the shares.

Subiratelno Druzestvo
(sudrudzie) (general partnership) **(Bulgaria)**
An enterprise with ownership interests determined by written contract and formed to conclude commercial transactions by two or more individuals who decide to act in concert and who have unlimited and joint liability for enterprise obligations.

Teoranta
(Teo.) **(Ireland)**
See Public Company.

Trading Company
(Brazil)
An enterprise with ownership interests in the form of stocks, formed to manufacture goods for export only, and owned by natural or corporate persons (stockholders) whose liability is limited to the purchase of the shares.

Treuunternehmen
(business trust) **(Liechtenstein)**
An enterprise that has both corporate and trust attributes because a natural or corporate person (trustor) places property into the trust, and the trust property is then invested or otherwise utilized to conduct the business stated in the trust documents. The trust is administered by an trustee on behalf of the trust beneficiaries.

türk limited sirket
(T.L.S.) (limited liability company) **(Turkey)**
An enterprise with ownership interests in the form of shares that are transferred privately only, having minimum capital of TL 10,000, and owned by two to 50 natural or corporate persons (shareholders) whose liability for enterprise obligations is limited to the price of the shares.

Vennootschap Onder Firma
(general partnership) **(Belgium, Netherlands)**
An enterprise with ownership interests stated by contract, registered to conduct business, and formed for commercial purposes by two or more natural or corporate persons who have unlimited and joint liability for enterprise obligations.

Verejná Obchodní Spolecnost
(v.o.s.) (general commercial partnership)
(Czech Republic)
An enterprise with ownership interests and profit-sharing determined by written contract, formed to undertake business activities, and owned by two or more partners who have unlimited and joint liability for enterprise obligations.

Yugen Kaisha
(joint stock corporation) **(Japan)**
An enterprise with ownership interests in the form of shares that are publicly traded, owned by one or more natural or corporate persons who receive dividends and whose liability for enterprise obligations is limited to the price of the shares.

Yuhan-Hosea
(limited companies) **(Korea, Republic of)**
An enterprise with ownership interests in the form of "shares" that are privately transferred, owned by one or more natural or corporate persons whose liability for enterprise obligations is limited to the price of the shares.

Weights and Measures

LINEAR MEASURES

U.S. CUSTOMARY LINEAR MEASURES

Many of these measures are based on those developed in medieval England, when a yard was a measure of King Edward I's waist, a rod was an actual 10-foot pole and a furlong was the width of 32 plowed rows. The mile began with the Romans measuring it as 1,000 paces. The United States is one of the few countries which still uses many of them. Our yard is now officially 3600/3937 of a meter (exactly 0.9144 meter), while a survey foot is 1200/3937 of a meter (approximately 0.3048 meter).

1000 mil	= 1 inch	= 2.54 centimeters
12 inches (in)	= 1 foot (ft)	= 30.48 centimeters
3 feet	= 1 yard (yd)	= 0.9144 meter
5-1/2 yards	= 1 rod (rd), pole, or perch = 16-1/2 ft	= 5.029 meters
40 rods	= 1 furlong (fur) = 220 yds = 660 ft	= 0.201 kilometers
8 furlongs	= 1 statute mile (mi) = 1,760 yds = 5,280 ft	= 1.609 kilometers
3 statute miles	= 1 league* = 5,280 yds = 15,840 ft	= 4.82 kilometers

* A league is an imprecise measure that may range from approximately 2.4 to 4.6 statute miles, but in most English-speaking countries it refers to 3 statute miles.

GUNTER'S OR SURVEYOR'S CHAIN MEASURES

These measures are based on a 17th century British surveyor's tool that was, in fact, a 66-foot long chain composed of 100 links. They fit in with the rod and furlong already in use.

7.92 inches	= 1 link (li)	= 20.12 centimeters
25 links	= 1 rod (rd) = 16-1/2 feet	= 5.029 meters
100 links	= 1 chain (ch) = 4 rods = 66 ft	= 20.11 meters
10 chains	= 1 furlong (fur) = 660 ft	= 0.201 kilometers
80 chains	= 1 statute mile = 320 rods = 5,280 ft	= 1.609 kilometers

NAUTICAL MEASURES

A nautical mile is based on the circumference of the earth, but the precise definition of it has varied considerably through the centuries. Most recently, a nautical mile has meant a minute (1/60) of a degree. The current International Nautical Mile, defined in 1929 and adopted by U.S. in 1954 is slightly shorter than the U.S. Nautical Mile, which is no longer used.

6 feet	= 1 fathom	= 1.82 meters
120 fathoms	= 1 cable = 720 feet	= 219.45 meters
8.44 cables	= 1 International Nautical Mile	= 1.852 kilometers
1.15 statute mi	= 1 Int'l Nautical Mile = 6,076.11549 feet	= 1.852 kilometers

METRIC LINEAR MEASURES

A meter is the length of the path traveled by light in a vacuum during the time interval of 1/299,794,458 second. Originally, it was one 10-millionth of a line running from the equator, through Paris to the North Pole. The metric system is also called SI (Systèm Internationale).

10 millimeters (mm)	= 1 centimeter (cm)	= 0.39 inch
10 centimeters	= 1 decimeter (dm) = 100 millimeters	= 3.94 inches
10 decimeters	= 1 meter (m) = 1000 millimeters	= 39.37 inches
10 meters	= 1 dekameter (dam)	= 32.81 feet
10 dekameters	= 1 hectometer (hm) = 100 meters	= 328.1 feet
10 hectometers	= 1 kilometer (km) = 1000 meters	= 0.62 mile

W & M

AREA MEASURES

Squares and cubes of units are sometimes abbreviated by using "superior" figures. For example, ft^2 means square foot, and m^3 means cubic meter.

U.S. CUSTOMARY AREA MEASURES

144 square inches	$= 1$ sq ft (ft^2)	$= 0.093$ sq meter
9 square feet	$= 1$ sq yd $(yd^2) = 1,296$ sq in	$= 0.836$ sq meter
30-1/4 square yards	$= 1$ sq rd $(rd^2) = 272$-1/4 sq ft	$= 25.29$ square meters
160 square rods	$= 1$ acre $= 4,840$ yd^2 $= 43,560$ ft^2	$= 0.405$ hectare
640 acres	$= 1$ square mile (mi^2)	$= 2.590$ sq kilometers
1 square mile	$= 1$ section (of land)	$= 2.590$ sq kilometers
6 square miles	$= 1$ township* $= 36$ sections $= 36$ square mi.	$= 93.24$ sq kilometers

* 6 square miles is a somewhat imprecise measure of a township, but one which is used for many practical purposes. In actuality, the east and west borders follow the meridians, making the north or south border slightly less than 6 miles long due to the curve of the earth.

METRIC AREA MEASURES

100 square millimeters $(mm^2) = 1$ square centimeter (cm^2)		$= 0.155$ square inch
10,000 square centimeters $= 1$ square meter $(m^2) = 1,000,000$ mm^2		$= 1.19$ square yards
100 square meters	$= 1$ are (a)	$= 119.60$ square yards
100 ares	$= 1$ hectare (ha) $= 10,000$ m^2	$= 2.471$ acres
100 hectares	$= 1$ square kilometer $(km^2) = 1,000,000$ m^2	$= 0.3861$ square miles

CAPACITY MEASURES

The American method of measuring volume is based on an Ancient Egyptian measure, a 12th century British measure and a custom of doubling each measure to find the next. Some measures dropped along the way, so this is no longer apparent. There are two official sets of volume measures in the U.S., wet and dry.

U.S. CUSTOMARY LIQUID MEASURES

The gallon is now officially defined in terms of cubic inches, which, in turn, are defined in terms of the meter. When necessary to distinguish the liquid pint or quart from the dry pint or quart, the word "liquid" or the abbreviation "liq" should be used in combination with the name or abbreviation of the liquid unit.

8 fluid drams	$= 1$ fluid ounce	$= 29.57$ milliliters
4 fluid ounces (oz)	$= 1$ gill	$= 0.118$ liter
4 gills (gi)	$= 1$ pint (pt) $= 28.875$ in^3	$= 0.473$ liter
2 pints	$= 1$ quart (qt) $= 57.75$ in^3	$= 0.946$ liter
4 quarts	$= 1$ gallon (gal) $= 231$ in^3 $= 8$ pts $= 32$ gills	$= 3.785$ liters

U.S. CUSTOMARY DRY MEASURES

The bushel is now officially defined in terms of cubic inches, which, in turn, are defined in terms of the meter. When necessary to distinguish the dry pint or quart from the liquid pint or quart; the word "dry" should be used in combination with the name or abbreviation of the dry unit.

2 dry pints (pt)	$= 1$ dry quart (qt) $= 67.2006$ in^3	$= 1.101$ liters
8 dry quarts	$= 1$ peck (pk) $= 537.605$ in^3 $= 16$ pt	$= 8.81$ liters
4 pecks	$= 1$ bushel (bu)* $= 2,150.42$ in^3 $= 32$ dry qt	$= 35.239$ liters

* This is also called a bushel, struck measure. One bushel, heaped measure is frequently recognized as 1-1/4 bushels, struck measure. More precisely, one bushel, heaped is equal to 1.278 bushels, struck.

APOTHECARIES' FLUID MEASURES

These units were once widely used in the U.S. for pharmaceutical purposes, but have largely been replaced by metric units. These measures are actually the same as those for U.S. customary wet measure (above), with some additional subdivisions.

60 minims (min)	= 1 fluid dram (fl dr) = 0.2256 in^3	= 3.888 grams
8 fluid drams	= 1 fluid ounce (fl oz) = 1.8047 in^3	= 31.103 grams
16 fluid ounces	= 1 pint (pt) = 28.875 in^3 = 128 fl drs	= 0.473 liter
2 pints	= 1 quart (qt) = 57.75 in^3= 32 fl oz = 256 fl drs	= 0.946 liter
4 quarts	= 1 gallon (gal) = 231 in^3 = 128 fl oz = 1,024 fl drs	= 3.785 liters

U.S. COOKING MEASURES

76 drops	= 1 teaspoon = 1-1/3 fl drams	= 4.9288 milliliters
3 teaspoons	= 1 tablespoon = 4 fl drams	= 14.786 milliliters
16 tablespoons	= 1 cup = 8 fl ounces	= 0.2366 liter
2 cups	= 1 pint = 16 fl ounces	= 0.4732 liter
2 pints	= 1 quart = 32 fl ounces	= 0.9463 liter

W & M

BRITISH IMPERIAL LIQUID AND DRY MEASURES

The British changed their definitions of capacity measures slightly in the 19th century, so that British Imperial measures having the same names as U.S. measures are slightly larger than their U.S. counterparts.

British imperial		cubic inches	U.S. equiv.	Metric
60 minims	= 1 fluidram (fl dr)	= 0.216734 in^3	= 0.961 fl dr	= 3.552 milliliters
8 fluidrams	= 1 fluidounce (fl oz)	= 1.7339 in^3	= 0.961 fl oz	= 28.412 milliliters
5 fluidounces	= 1 gill	= 8.669 in^3	= 4.805 fl oz	= 142.066 milliliters
4 gills	= 1 pint	= 34.678 in^3	= 1.201 fl pt	= 0.5683 liters
2 pints	= 1 quart	= 69.355 in^3	= 1.201 fl qt, 1.032 dry qt	
				= 1.136 liters
4 quarts	= 1 gallon	= 277.420 in^3	= 1.201 fl gal	= 4.546 liters
2 gallons	= 1 peck	= 554.84 in^3	= 1.0314 pecks	= 9.087 liters
4 pecks	= 1 bushel	= 2219.36 in^3	= 1.032 bushels	= 36.369 liters

METRIC MEASURES OF CAPACITY

The liter was derived from the kilogram, originally the volume occupied by a kilogram of water. It is now officially defined as a cubic decimeter of pure water, which is nearly the same. This one set of measures is used for all capacity measures.

10 milliliters (ml)	= 1 centiliter (cl)	= 0.338 fluid ounce
10 centiliters	= 1 deciliter (dl) = 100 milliliters	= 0.21 pint
10 deciliters	= 1 liter (l) = 1000 milliliters	= 1.057 quarts
10 liters	= 1 dekaliter (dal)	= 2.6417 gallons
10 dekaliters	= 1 hectoliter (hl) = 100 liters	= 26.417 gallons
10 hectoliters	= 1 kiloliter (kl) = 1,000 liters	= 264.17 gallons

CUBIC MEASURES

U.S. CUSTOMARY CUBIC MEASURES

1,728 cubic inches (in^3)	= 1 cubic foot (ft^3)	= 0.028 cubic meter
27 cubic feet	= 1 cubic yard (yd^3)	= 0.765 cubic meter

METRIC

1,000 cubic millimeters (mm^3)	= 1 cubic centimeter (cm^3)	= 0.061 cubic inch
1,000 cubic centimeters	= 1 cubic decimeter (dm^3)	= 61.023 cubic inches
1,000 cubic decimeters	= 1 cubic meter (m^3) = 1 stere	= 1.307 cubic yards

WEIGHTS

When necessary to distinguish avoirdupois units from troy or apothecaries' units, the word "avoirdupois" or the abbreviation "avdp" should be used in combination with the name or abbreviation of the unit.

AVOIRDUPOIS WEIGHT

This is the weight system in everyday use in the U.S. Historically, it is a rearrangement of the troy system. The word avoirdupois is French, meaning goods of weight. The avoirdupois pound is now officially defined as 0.45359237 kilogram.

27-11/32 grains	= 1 dram (dr)	= 1.1772 grams
16 drams	= 1 ounce (oz) = 437-1/2 grains	= 28.35 grams
16 ounces	= 1 pound (lb) = 256 drams = 7,000 grains	= 0.454 kilogram
100 pounds	= 1 hundredweight (cwt)*	= 45.359 kilograms
112 pounds	= 1 gross or long hundredweight (cwt)*	= 50.802 kilograms
20 hundredweights	= 1 short ton (tn) = 2,000 lbs*	= 0.907 metric ton
20 gross or long hundredweights	= 1 gross or long ton = 2,240 lbs*	= 1.016 metric tons

*When the terms "hundredweight" and "ton" are used unmodified, they are commonly understood to mean the 100-pound hundredweight and the 2,000-pound (short) ton, respectively; these units may be designated "net" or "short" when necessary to distinguish them from the corresponding units in gross of long measure.

TROY WEIGHT

The troy system began in Ancient Egypt and was modified over the years by Europeans. The British used the troy as the official weight system for currency, while the U.S. mint adopted it in America. These units are still used for over-the-counter sales of precious metals, although they have largely fallen into disuse, in favor of the metric system.

24 grains (gr)	= 1 pennyweight (dwt)	= 1.555 grams
20 pennyweights	= 1 ounce troy (oz t) = 480 grains	= 31.103 grams
12 ounces troy	= 1 pound troy (lb t) = 240 dwt = 5,760 gr	= 0.373 kilogram

APOTHECARIES' WEIGHT

While one pound apothecaries' is equivalent to 1 pound troy, the apothecaries' system differs in its subdivisions. These units were once widely used in the United States for pharmaceutical purposes, but have largely been replaced by metric units, although they are still legal standards.

20 grains (gr)	= 1 scruple (s ap)	= 1.296 grams
3 scruples	= 1 dram apothecaries' (dr ap) = 60 gr	= 3.888 grams
8 drams apothecaries	= 1 ounce apothecaries' (oz ap) = 24 s ap = 480 gr	= 31.103 grams
12 ounces apothecaries	= 1 pound apothecaries' (lb ap) = 96 dr ap	= 373.24 grams
	= 288 s ap = 5,760 grains	

METRIC WEIGHT (MASS)

A kilogram was originally defined as the mass of one cubic decimeter of water at the temperature of maximum density, but is now a cylinder of platinum-iridium alloy of the same size.

10 milligrams (mg)	= 1 centigram (cg)	= 0.154 grain
10 centigrams	= 1 decigram (dg) = 100 milligrams	= 1.543 grains
10 decigrams	= 1 gram (g) = 1,000 milligrams	= 0.035 ounce
10 grams	= 1 dekagram (dag)	= 0.353 ounce
10 dekagrams	= 1 hectogram (hg) = 100 grams	= 3.527 ounces
10 hectograms	= 1 kilogram (kg) = 1,000 grams	= 2.2046 pounds
1,000 kilograms	= 1 metric ton (t)	= 1.102 short tons

W
&
M

MISCELLANEOUS UNITS OF MEASURE

acre
A measure of area, used for surveying land. One acre is equal to 160 square rods or 43,560 square feet. The term originally referred to the area of land a yoke of oxen (two oxen) could plow in one day.

agate
A measure used in printing, especially for classified advertising, equivalent to 1/14 inch. An agate line is a space one column wide and 1/14 inch deep (1/14 of a column inch). Originally, a measure of type size of 5-1/2 points. *See also* point.

ampere (Amp)
A unit of electrical current in electrons per second. Equivalent to a flow of one coulomb per second or to the steady current produced by the pressure of one volt applied across a resistance of one ohm. *See also* ohm; volt.

assay ton (AT)
A unit of weight used in assaying. One assay ton is equal to 29.167 grams. The relationship between one assay ton to one milligram is the same as one net ton (2,000 pounds avoirdupois) to one ounce troy. Therefore, the weight in milligrams of precious metal from one assay ton gives the number of troy ounces to the net ton.

bale
An imprecise measure of a large bundle of goods, especially cotton or hay. The weight varies from country to country. In the U.S., the approximate weight of a bale of cotton is 500 pounds, while in Egypt it is approximately 750 pounds.

barrel (bbl)
A measure of volume, which varies according to the commodity, and can also vary from state to state. A barrel can be either a wet or dry volume measure. One barrel is generally between 31 and 42 gallons. One barrel of fermented liquors often means 31 gallons, one barrel of liquid is often 31-1/2 gallons, on barrel of beer is often 36 gallons, one barrel of "proof spirits" is 40 gallons by U.S. federal law, and one barrel of crude oil for statistical purposes is generally 42 gallons. Two common barrel measurements for dry commodities are:
1 barrel, standard for fruits, vegetables, and other dry commodities (except cranberries) = 105 dry quarts = 7,056 in3 = 3.281 bushels, struck measure.
1 barrel, standard, cranberries = 86-45/64 dry quarts = 5,826 in3 = 2.709 bushels, struck measure.

board foot (fbm, BF, bd ft)
A unit of measurement used for lumber. One board foot is 12 inches by 12 inches by 1 inch, or one square foot of lumber one inch thick. Rough lumber is often sold by the board foot.

bolt
A unit of measurement used for fabric. One bolt is 40 yards long.

British thermal unit (Btu)
A unit used to describe heating capacity. One Btu is the amount of energy needed to raise the temperature of one pound of water one degree Fahrenheit. 1 Btu = 252 Calories. *See also* calorie.

caliber
A unit for measuring the diameter of the bore of a gun. In the U.S. and Britain, this has traditionally been expressed in hundredths or thousandths of an inch and written as a decimal fraction (i.e., .22 or .465). It has become more common for caliber to be expressed in millimeters. Naval gun caliber is the number by which one multiplies the bore diameter to find the barrel length.

caliper
A unit used to measure the thickness of paper or board. One caliper is equal to one mil, or 1/1,000 of an inch.

calorie
A measurement of heat used in place of British thermal units (Btu) by countries using the metric system. One small calorie is the amount of energy needed to raise the temperature of one gram of water by one degree Celsius, from 14.5°C to 15.5°C, or 4.1840 joules. One big calorie (kilocalorie) = 1,000 small Calories. *See also* British thermal unit; joule.

carat
A unit for measuring the weight of precious stones. One international carat is 200 milligrams (approximately 3.086 grains). Originally, a carat was the weight of a locust tree seed, about 1/142 of an ounce. *See also* karat.

cord
A unit of volume used for firewood. One cord is a stack of wood that measures 8 feet by 8 feet by 2 feet, or 128 cubic feet. A face cord (or short cord) is a stack of logs measuring 8 feet by 4 feet by whatever the length of the logs happens to be.

cubit
An ancient unit of length based on the length of the forearm, from the elbow to the tip of the middle finger. One cubit is not a precise length, although it is usually figured between 17 and 21 inches, and most often at 18 inches.

decibel

Not an actual unit of measurement, but a comparison between one sound an another to show the level of a sound's energy. 0 decibels is the softest sound audible to the human ear, and 130 decibels is painful to the human ear. The decibel scale is logarithmic, so that a 10 decibel increase doubles the loudness.

displacement ton

A unit used for measuring the weight of water displaced by a ship, in place of weighing the ship itself. One displacement ton is equal to a long ton, or 2,240 pounds. It is calculated by finding the number of cubic feet of water displaced and figuring the weight of the water. Loaded displacement tonnage refers to the displacement tonnage of a ship when it is carrying its usual cargo, fuel and crew load. Light displacement tonnage is the displacement tonnage of an unloaded ship, while the dead weight tonnage is the weight that the ship can carry, or the difference between the loaded displacement and the light displacement tonnage. Different types of ships are more commonly described according to one type of displacement tonnage or another.

ell

A unit of length used for measuring fabric. An English term, an ell is 45 inches, or 1/32 of a bolt. Bolts of fabric are often sold in the United States and England in 45 inch widths. *See also* bolt.

em

A unit of length used in printing. An em is equal to the point size of the type in use, that is, a 6-point em is 6 points wide. An en is equal to one half of an em. Nut is another printer's term for an en.

freight ton (also called measurement ton)

A unit of volume used most often for sea freight. One freight ton is usually equal to 40 cubic feet of merchandise. A freight ton may also refer to a unit of volume for freight that weighs one ton, varying depending on the commodity.

gauge

A measure of shotgun bore diameter. Gauge numbers originally were determined by finding the number of lead balls with a diameter equal to that of the bore that made up a pound (i.e., a 12 gauge shotgun), so that the smaller the gauge number, the bigger the shotgun bore. Today an international agreement assigns millimeter measures to each gauge. *See also* caliber.

great gross

A numerical figure used for counting commercial items. One great gross is a dozen gross, or 1,728 items. *See also* gross.

gross

A numerical figure used for counting commercial items. One gross is a dozen dozen, or 144 items. *See also* great gross.

hand

A unit of length, usually used for measuring horses at withers. One hand is 4 inches or 10.16 cm. It was derived from the width of the hand.

hertz

Measurement unit for the frequency of electromagnetic waves. One hertz is equal to one cycle per second.

hogshead (hhd)

A liquid measurement for a large cask or barrel. One hogshead is 63 U.S. gallons, or 238 liters. A hogshead may also refer to a large cask containing anywhere from 63 to 140 gallons.

horsepower (hp)

A unit used to measure the power of engines. One horsepower is equal to 746 watts or to 2,546.0756 Btu per hour. It was derived from the power needed by a horse to lift 33,000 pounds a distance of 1 foot in 1 minute or to lift 550 pounds 1 foot in 1 second. *See also* British thermal unit, Watt.

joule

A unit of energy. One joule is equal to the amount of work done by a force of one newton when its point of application moves through a distance of one meter in the direction of the force.

karat

A measure of the purity of gold in an alloy. Each karat represents a ratio of 1/24 purity, indicating how many parts out of 24 are pure. 24 karat gold is pure, while 18 karat gold is 3/4 gold and 1/4 alloy. The system was derived from a time when a karat was used to describe 1/24 of a troy pound and 24 karat was one full troy pound.

knot

A rate of travel used to measure a ship's speed, but also used for airplanes and other vehicles. One knot is the rate of one nautical mile (1,852 meters) per hour.

league

A unit of distance. One league is usually estimated at 3 statute miles in English-speaking countries, but it can range anywhere from about 2.4 to 4.6 statute miles. The league was originally a Gaulish unit of distance equal to 1.5 Roman miles.

light-year

A unit of distance used by astronomers. One light year is 5,880,000,000,000 miles, which is the distance light travels in a vacuum in a year at the rate of 186,281.7 miles (299,792 kilometers) per second.

magnum

A unit of volume for liquid, most often for wine. A magnum is not a precise unit, but may refer to 1.5 liters, 2/5 of a gallon or two quarts. It also refers to the bottle itself.

ohm

A unit of electrical resistance which slow the flow of amps. A circuit in which a potential difference of one volt produces a current of one ampere has a resistance of one ohm. *See also* ampere; volt.

parsec

A unit of measure used by astronomers. One parsec is approximately 3.26 light-years or 19.2 trillion miles. The term is derived from a combination of first syllables of parallax and second. A parsec is the distance is a distance having a heliocentric parallax of one second (1/3600 degree). *See also* light-year.

pi (π)

The ratio of the circumference of a circle to its diameter. The value of pi is approximately 3.1416.

pica

A unit of length used in printing to describe the width of a line of type. One pica is usually calculated as 1/6 inch or 12 points. *See also* point.

pipe

A unit of liquid measure, most often used for wine or oil. One pipe is equal to two hogsheads, or 126 gallons. *See also* hogshead.

point

A unit of measurement for the height of type in printing. One point is approximately .013837, 1/72 inch, or 1/12 pica. Used in printing for measuring type size. Originally one point was 1/72 of a French inch. European and American point sizes are slightly different. A point can also a unit of measurement used in printing and binding equal to 1/1,000 of an inch. *See also* pica.

ream

The numerical unit used for measuring pieces of paper. One ream is 20 quires, which is now usually 500 sheets, but can be 480 sheets, and occasionally is 516 sheets of paper.

register tons

A unit of volume, and not weight, used to express the total capacity of a ship, called gross register tonnage, gross tonnage, or gross weight. One register ton is equal to 100 cubic feet. Most often used for passenger ships, but may be applied to other types of ships.

roentgen

An unit to measure radiation exposure produced by X-rays. One roentgen is equal to the amount of radiation produced in one cubic centimeter of dry air at 0°C and standard atmospheric pressure ionization equal to one electrostatic unit of charge.

score

A numerical figure. One score is 20 units.

sound, speed of

A rate of speed, which varies depending on temperature, altitude and the media through which the sound is traveling. In general terms, the "speed of sound" is usually placed at 1,088 feet per second, or about 750 miles per hour at 32°F at sea level.

span

A British unit of length, now little used. One span is equivalent to 9 inches or 22.86 cm. It is derived from the distance between the end of the thumb and the end of the little finger of a spread hand.

square

A unit of square measure used in the building trade. One square is equal to 100 square feet. It often refers to roofing materials.

stone

A unit of weight still in use in the United Kingdom. One stone is equal to 14 pounds avoirdupois, or approximately 6.3 kilograms.

therm

A unit of heat, although it may be defined in different ways. One therm is equal to 100,000 Btu's or to 1,000 large calories. *See also* British thermal unit; calorie.

ton mile

(shipping) The transport of one ton of cargo for one mile. Used most often in air cargo services.

township

A unit of land measurement used in the U.S. One township is almost 36 square miles. The south border is 6 miles long. The east and west borders, also 6 miles long, follow the meridians, making the north border slightly less than 6 miles long.

tun

A unit of liquid measurement, used for wine and other liquids. One tun is equal to two pipes, or four hogsheads, or 252 gallons. In practice a tun may be more than 252 gallons. *See also* hogsheads; pipes.

volt

A measure of electrical potential difference. Volts are the pressure that moves the amps along a wire. Normal household voltage in the U.S. is 120 volts.

watt

A unit of power which is a measure of the amount of work an appliance is capable of. A watt is the power used by a current of one ampere across a potential difference of one volt.

Guide to INCOTERMS 2000

While the terms of sale in international business often sound similar to those commonly used in domestic contracts, they often have different meanings. Confusion over these terms can result in a lost sale or a financial loss on a sale. Thus, it is essential that you understand what terms you are agreeing to before you finalize a contract.

Incoterms 2000[1]

By the 1920s, commercial traders had developed a set of trade terms to describe their rights and liabilities with regard to the sale and transport of goods. These trade terms consisted of short abbreviations for lengthy contract provisions. Unfortunately, there was no uniform interpretation of them in all countries, and therefore misunderstandings often arose in cross-border transactions.

To improve this aspect of international trade, the International Chamber of Commerce (ICC) in Paris developed INCOTERMS (INternational COmmercial TERMS), a set of uniform rules for the interpretation of international commercial terms defining the costs, risks, and obligations of buyers and sellers in international transactions. First published in 1936, these rules have been periodically revised to account for changing modes of transport and document delivery. The current version is Incoterms 2000.

Use of Incoterms

Incoterms are not implied into contracts for the sale of goods. If you desire to use Incoterms, you must specifically include them in your contract. Further, your contract should expressly refer to the rules of interpretation as defined in the latest revision of Incoterms, for example, *Incoterms 2000*, and you should ensure the proper application of the terms by additional contract provisions. Also, Incoterms are not "laws." In case of a dispute, courts and arbitrators will look at: 1) the sales contract, 2) who has possession of the goods, and 3) what payment, if any, has been made. See *International Contracts*, also by World Trade Press.

Illustrated Guide to Incoterms

This guide was designed to give a graphic representation of the buyer's and seller's risks and costs under each Incoterm. The material on each facing page gives a summary of seller and buyer responsibilities.

Incoterms Do . . .

Incoterms 2000 may be included in a sales contract if the parties desire the following:
1. To complete a sale of goods.
2. To indicate each contracting party's costs, risks, and obligations with regard to delivery of the goods as follows:
   a. When is the delivery completed?
   b. How does a party ensure that the other party has met that standard of conduct?
   c. Which party must comply with requisite licenses and government-imposed formalities?
   d. What are the mode and terms of carriage?
   e. What are the delivery terms and what is required as proof of delivery?
   f. When is the risk of loss transferred from the seller to the buyer?
   g. How will transport costs be divided between the parties?
   h. What notices are the parties required to give to each other regarding the transport and transfer of the goods?
3. To establish basic terms of transport and delivery in a short format.

Incoterms Do Not . . .

Incoterms 2000 are not sufficient on their own to express the full intent of the parties. They will not:
1. Apply to contracts for services.
2. Define contractual rights and obligations other than for delivery.
3. Specify details of the transfer, transport, and delivery of the goods.
4. Determine how title to the goods will be transferred.
5. Protect a party from his/her own risk of loss.
6. Cover the goods before or after delivery.
7. Define the remedies for breach of contract.

Tip: Incoterms can be quite useful, but their use has limitations. If you use them incorrectly, your contract may be ambiguous, if not impossible to perform. It is therefore important to understand the scope and purpose of Incoterms—when and why you might use them—before you rely on them to define such important terms as mode of delivery, customs clearance, passage of title, and transfer of risk.

1. INCOTERMS 2000 are Copyright © 1999 by ICC Publishing S.A. All rights reserved. The actual text of INCOTERMS 2000 is contained in ICC publication No. 560. Contact: ICC Publishing, Inc.; 156 Fifth Avenue; New York, New York 10010; Tel: +1 (212) 206-1150. ICC Publishing S.A.; 38 Cours Albert, 1er; 75008 Paris, France; Tel: +[33] (1) 49 53 29 23; e-mail: pub@iccbo.org; www.iccbooks.com.
2. This Illustrated Guide to Incoterms 2000 is © Copyright 2000 by World Trade Press. All Rights Reserved. World Trade Press; 1450 Grant Avenue; Suite 204, Novato, CA 94945 USA; Tel: (415) 898-1124

Organization of Incoterms

Incoterms are grouped into four categories:

1. **The "E" term (EXW)**—The only term where the seller/exporter makes the goods available at his or her own premises to the buyer/importer.
2. **The "F" terms (FCA, FAS and FOB)**—Terms where the seller/exporter is responsible to deliver the goods to a carrier named by the buyer.
3. **The "C" terms (CFR, CIF, CPT and CIP)**—Terms where the seller/exporter/manufacturer is responsible for contracting and paying for carriage of the goods, but not responsible for additional costs or risk of loss or damage to the goods once they have been shipped. C terms evidence "shipment" (as opposed to "arrival") contracts.
4. **The "D" terms (DAF, DES, DEQ, DDU and DDP)**—Terms where the seller/exporter/manufacturer is responsible for all costs and risks associated with bringing the goods to the place of destination. D terms evidence "arrival" contracts.

The following table sets out these categories.

INCOTERMS 2000

Group E Departure	EXW	Ex Works (...named place)
Group F Main Carriage Unpaid	FCA	Free Carrier (...named place)
	FAS	Free Alongside Ship (...named port of shipment)
	FOB	Free On Board (...named port of shipment)
Group C Main Carriage Paid	CFR	Cost and Freight (...named port of destination)
	CIF	Cost, Insurance and Freight (...named port of destination)
	CPT	Carriage Paid To (...named port of destination)
	CIP	Carriage and Insurance Paid To (...named port of destination)
Group D Arrival	DAF	Delivered at Frontier (...named place)
	DES	Delivered Ex Ship (...named port of destination)
	DEQ	Delivered Ex Quay (...named port of destination)
	DDU	Delivered Duty Unpaid (...named port of destination)
	DDP	Delivered Duty Paid (...named port of destination)

Mode of transport

Not all Incoterms are appropriate for all modes of transport. Some terms were designed with sea vessels in mind while others were designed to be applicable to all modes. The following table sets out which terms are appropriate for each mode of transport.

INCOTERMS 2000

All modes of transport including multimodal	EXW	Ex Works (...named place)
	FCA	Free Carrier (...named place)
	CPT	Carriage Paid To (...named port of destination)
	CIP	Carriage and Insurance Paid To (...named port of destination)
	DAF	Delivered at Frontier (...named place)
	DDU	Delivered Duty Unpaid
	DDP	Delivered Duty Paid
Sea and inland waterway transport only	FAS	Free Alongside Ship (...named port of shipment)
	FOB	Free On Board (...named port of shipment)
	CFR	Cost and Freight (...named port of destination)
	CIF	Cost, Insurance and Freight (...named port of destination)
	DES	Delivered Ex Ship (...named port of destination)
	DEQ	Delivered Ex Quay (...named port of destination)

Helpful Definitions

Pre-carriage—The initial transport of goods from the seller's premises to the main port of shipment. Usually by truck, rail or on inland waterways.

Main carriage—The primary transport of goods, generally for the longest part of the journey and generally from one country to another. Usually by sea vessel or by airplane, but can be by truck or rail as well.

On-carriage—Transport from the port of arrival in the country of destination to the buyer's premises. Usually by truck, rail or on inland waterways.

Notes on Incoterms

1. **Underlying Contract**—Incoterms were designed to be used within the context of a written contract for the sale of goods. Incoterms, therefore, refer to the contract of sale, rather than the contract of carriage of the goods. Buyers and sellers should specify that their contract be governed by Incoterms 2000.

2. **EXW and FCA**—If you buy Ex Works or Free Carrier you will need to arrange for the contract of carriage. Also, since the shipper will not receive a bill of lading, using a letter of credit requiring a bill of lading will not be possible.

3. **EDI: Electronic Data Interchange**—It is increasingly common for sellers to prepare and transmit documents electronically. Incoterms provides for EDI so long as buyers and sellers agree on their use in the sales contract.

4. **Insurable Interest**—Note that in many cases either the buyer or the seller is not *obligated* to provide insurance. In a number of cases neither party is obligated to provide insurance. However, both the seller and buyer should be aware that they may have insurable interest in the goods and prudence dictates purchase of insurance coverage.

5. **Customs of the Port or Trade**—Incoterms are an attempt to standardize trade terms for all nations and all trades. However, different ports and different trades have their own customs and practices. It is best if specific customs and practices are specified in the sales contract.

6. **Precise Point of Delivery**—In some cases it may not be possible for the buyer to name the precise point of delivery at contract. However, if the buyer does not do so in a timely manner, it may give the seller the option to make delivery within a range of places that is within the terms of the contract. For example, the original terms of sale may state CFR Port of Rotterdam. The Port of Rotterdam is huge and the buyer may find that a particular point within the port is best and should so state in the sales contract and in the trade term. Also, since the buyer becomes liable for the goods once they arrive, he or she may be responsible for unloading, storage and other charges once the goods have been made available at the place named.

7. **Export and Import Customs Clearance**—It is usually desirable that export customs formalities be handled by the seller and import customs formalities be handled by the buyer. However, some trade terms require that the buyer handle export formalities and others require that the seller handle import formalities. In each case the buyer and seller will have to assume risk from export and import restrictions and prohibitions. In some cases foreign exporters may not be able to obtain import licenses in the country of import. This should be researched before accepting final terms.

8. **Added Wording**—It is possible, and in many cases desirable, that the seller and buyer agree to additional wording to an Incoterm. For example, if the seller agrees to DDP terms, agreeing to pay for customs formalities and import duties, but not for VAT (Value Added Taxes) the term "DDP VAT Unpaid" may be used.

9. **Packing**—It is the responsibility of the seller to provide packaging unless the goods shipped are customarily shipped in bulk (usually commodities such as oil or grain). In most situations it is best if the buyer and seller agree in the sales contract on the type and extent of packing required. However, it may not be possible to know beforehand the type or duration of transport. As a result, it is the responsibility of the seller to provide for safe and appropriate packaging, but only to the extent that the buyer has made the circumstances of the transport known to the seller beforehand.

   If the seller is responsible for packing goods in an ocean or air freight container it is also his responsibility to pack the container properly to withstand shipment.

10. **Inspection**—These are several issues related to inspections: a) the seller is responsible for costs of inspection to make certain the quantity and quality of the shipment is in conformity with the sales contract, b) pre-shipment inspections as required by the export authority are the responsibility of the party responsible for export formalities, c) import inspections as required by the import authority are the responsibility of the party responsible for import formalities, and d) third-party inspections for independent verification of quality and quantity (if required) are generally the responsibility of the buyer. The buyer may require such an inspection and inspection document as a condition of payment.

11. **Passing of Risks and Costs**—The general rule is that risks and costs pass from the seller to the buyer once the buyer has delivered the goods to the point and place named in the trade term.

INCOTERMS

INCOTERMS

EXW
Ex Works (. . . named place)

Seller/ Exporter Premises	Export Documents Formalities	Delivered at named place of: Frontier/Terminal/Quay	Loading Port of Shipment	Onboard Ship's Rail	Onboard Ship's Rail	Discharging Port of Arrival	Delivery at named place of destination: Frontier/Terminal/Quay	Import Documents Formalities	Buyer/ Importer Premises
SELLER'S RISKS								BUYER'S RISKS	
SELLER'S COSTS								BUYER'S COSTS	

EXW, Ex Works (...named place)

In Ex Works, the seller/exporter/manufacturer merely makes the goods available to the buyer at the seller's "named place" of business. This trade term places the greatest responsibility on the buyer and minimum obligations on the seller.

The seller does not clear the goods for export and does not load the goods onto a truck or other transport vehicle at the named place of departure.

The parties to the transaction, however, may stipulate that the seller be responsible for the costs and risks of loading the goods onto a transport vehicle. Such a stipulation must be made within the contract of sale.

If the buyer cannot handle export formalities the Ex Works term should not be used. In such a case Free Carrier (FCA) is recommended.

The Ex Works term is often used when making an initial quotation for the sale of goods. It represents the cost of the goods without any other costs included. Normal payment terms for Ex Works transactions are generally cash in advance and open account.

Examples
EXW Ex Works ABC Factory Paris, France
EXW Ex Works XYZ Printing Plant Singapore

EXW
Ex Works (. . . named place)

Incoterm Category

EXW is the only "E" Incoterm. The "E" Incoterm is where the seller/exporter makes the goods available to the buyer/importer at the seller/exporter's premises/factory/warehouse.

Modes of Transport Covered

All modes of transport including multimodal.

Seller's Responsibilities (summary)

1. **Goods**—Provide the goods, commercial invoice or electronic message, and other documentation as required by the sales contract.

2. **Licenses and Customs Formalities**—Provide the buyer at the buyer's request, risk and cost, every assistance in obtaining any license, authorization or documentation required for export of the goods.

3. **Carriage and Insurance**—The seller has no obligation to provide carriage of goods or insurance.

4. **Delivery**—Make the goods available to the buyer, unloaded, at the named place and on the date stipulated in the sales contract.

5. **Risk Transfer**—Assume all risks to the goods (loss or damage) until they have been made available to the buyer as above in # 4 above.

6. **Costs**—Pay all costs until the goods have been made available to the buyer in accordance with #4 above.

7. **Notice to the Buyer**—Provide sufficient notice to the buyer of the location and time of availability of the goods.

8. **Proof of Delivery, Transport Documents**—

The seller has no obligation to provide the buyer with a proof of delivery or a transport document.

9. **Checking, Packing, Marking**—Pay all costs associated with checking the quality and quantity of the goods to be in conformity with the sales contract. Provide appropriate packing (unless the goods are traditionally delivered unpackaged) as required for the transport of the goods, to the extent that the buyer has made transport circumstances known to the seller prior to the execution of the sales contract. Provide marking appropriate to the packaging.

10. **Other**—Provide the buyer, at the buyer's request, risk and expense, assistance in securing documentation originating in the country of origin or of export as required for export and import. Provide the buyer at the buyer's request information necessary to obtain insurance.

Buyer's Responsibilities (summary)

1. **Payment**—Pay for the goods as provided in the sales contract.

2. **Licenses and Customs Formalities**—Obtain at own risk and cost all export and import licenses and authorizations. Carry out all export and import formalities at own risk and cost.

3. **Carriage and Insurance**—The buyer has no obligation to the seller to provide contract of carriage or insurance.

4. **Taking Delivery**—Take delivery of the goods when they have been made available by the seller in accordance with the terms of the sales

contract.

5. **Risk Transfer**—Assume all risks (loss or damage) from the time the goods have been made available by the seller in accordance with the terms of the sales contract.

6. **Costs**—Pay all costs for carriage and insurance from the time the goods have been made available by the seller in accordance with the terms of the sales contract. Pay all costs resulting from failure to take delivery at the named place and time. Pay all costs relating to export and import including duties, taxes, customs formalities and other charges including transshipment.Reimburse the seller for costs of providing assistance in obtaining export licenses and authorizations.

7. **Notice to Seller**—If, according to the sales contract, the buyer is able to specify a time within a stipulated period, and/or specify a place of taking delivery, to give the seller sufficient notice.

8. **Proof of Delivery**—Provide the seller with evidence of having taken delivery.

9. **Inspection(s)**—Pay for the costs of pre-shipment inspection(s) including inspections required by the country of export.

10. **Other**—Pay and/or reimburse the seller for all costs associated with securing documentation originating in the country of origin or export as required for export and import.

INCOTERMS

FCA
Free Carrier (. . . named place)

Seller/ Exporter Premises	Export Documents Formalities	Delivered at named place of: Frontier/Terminal/Quay	Loading Port of Shipment	Onboard Ship's Rail	Onboard Ship's Rail	Discharging Port of Arrival	Delivery at named place of destination: Frontier/Terminal/Quay	Import Documents Formalities	Buyer/ Importer Premises
SELLER'S RISKS								**BUYER'S RISKS**	
SELLER'S COSTS								**BUYER'S COSTS**	

FCA, Free Carrier (...named place)

In Free Carrier, the seller/exporter/manufacturer clears the goods for export and then delivers them to the carrier specified by the buyer at the named place. If the named place is the seller's place of business, the seller is responsible for loading the goods onto the transport vehicle. If the named place is any other location, such as the loading dock of the carrier, the seller is not responsible for loading the goods onto the transport vehicle.

The Free Carrier term may be used for any mode of transport, including multimodal.

The "named place" in Free Carrier and all "F" terms is domestic to the seller. "Carrier" has a specific and somewhat expanded meaning. A carrier can be a shipping line, an airline, a trucking firm, or a railway. The carrier can also be an individual or firm who undertakes to procure carriage by any of the above methods of transport including multimodal. Therefore, a person, such as a freight forwarder, can act as a "carrier" under this term. In such a case, the buyer names the carrier or the individual who is to receive the goods. The Free Carrier term is often used when making an initial quotation for the sale of goods.

Normal payment terms for Free Carrier transactions are generally cash in advance and open account.

Examples

FCA Free Carrier ABC Shipping Lines Hamburg Germany
FCA Free Carrier XYZ Air Lines SFO (San Francisco International Airport)
FCA Free Carrier AZ Freight Forwarders Tokyo Japan

FCA
Free Carrier (... named place)

Incoterm Category

FCA is an "F" Incoterm where the seller/exporter delivers the goods export cleared to a carrier named by the buyer, but does not bear risk or costs once the goods have been handed over.

Modes of Transport Covered

All modes of transport including multimodal.

Seller's Responsibilities (summary)

1. **Goods**—Provide the goods, commercial invoice or electronic message, and other documentation as required by the sales contract.

2. **Licenses and Customs Formalities**—Obtain at own risk and cost all required export licenses, documentation and authorizations and carry out all export formalities and procedures.

3. **Carriage and Insurance**—The seller has no obligation to provide carriage of goods or insurance. However, if requested by buyer, the seller may contract for carriage on standard industry terms at the buyer's risk and cost. If so, the seller must notify buyer who may chose to decline the contract and notify the seller.

4. **Delivery**—Deliver the goods to the named carrier, freight forwarder or person at the named place and at the time stipulated in the sales contract. Requirements for delivery to the carrier vary depending upon the means of transport and the size of the shipment. In general, delivery is considered complete when the seller either loads the goods onto the vehicle provided, or delivers the goods to the carrier's terminal, unloaded

5. **Risk Transfer**—Assume all risks to the goods (loss or damage) until they have been delivered to the carrier.

6. **Costs**—Pay all costs until the goods have been delivered to the carrier as well as all costs relating to export including duties, taxes and customs formalities.

7. **Notices**—Provide sufficient notice to the buyer that the goods have been delivered to the carrier.

8. **Proof of Delivery, Transport Documents**—Provide the buyer with a proof of delivery (to the carrier) or a transport document, or to assist the buyer in obtaining a transport document.

9. **Checking, Packing, Marking**—Pay all costs associated with checking the quality and quantity of the goods to be in conformity with the sales contract. Provide appropriate packing (unless the goods are traditionally delivered unpackaged) as required for the transport of the goods, to the extent that the buyer has made transport circumstances known to the seller prior to the execution of the sales contract. Provide marking appropriate to the packaging.

10. **Other**—Provide the buyer, at the buyer's request, risk and expense, assistance in securing documentation originating in the country of origin or of export as required for import or transshipment through another country. Provide the buyer at the buyer's request information necessary to obtain insurance.

Buyer's Responsibilities (summary)

1. **Payment**—Pay for the goods as provided in the sales contract.

2. **Licenses and Customs Formalities**—Obtain all import licenses, documentation and authorizations and carry out all import formalities.

3. **Carriage and Insurance**—Provide for contract of carriage from the named place. No obligation to seller for insurance.

4. **Taking Delivery**—Take delivery of the goods as provided in the sales contract.

5. **Risk Transfer**—Assume all risk of loss or damage from the time the goods have been delivered to the carrier as provided in the sales contract.

6. **Costs**—Pay all costs for carriage and insurance from the time the goods have been delivered to the carrier as provided in the sales contract. Pay all costs resulting from failure to take delivery at the named place and time. Pay all costs relating to import formalities including duties, taxes and other charges including transshipment.

7. **Notice to Seller**—Give the seller sufficient notice of the name of the carrier, the time or period for delivery and the place of delivery.

8. **Proof of Delivery, Transport Document**—Accept the seller's proof of delivery or transport document.

9. **Inspection(s)**—Pay for the costs of pre-shipment inspection except inspections required by the country of export.

10. **Other**—Pay all costs associated with securing documentation originating in the country of origin or export as required for import. Reimburse seller for costs in providing documentation or assistance. Give the seller instructions regarding carriage.

INCOTERMS

INCOTERMS

FAS
Free Alongside Ship (. . . named port of shipment)

SELLER →   BUYER →

	Seller/Exporter Premises	Export Documents Formalities	Delivered at named place of: Frontier/Terminal/Quay	Loading Port of Shipment	Onboard Ship's Rail	Onboard Ship's Rail	Discharging Port of Arrival	Delivery at named place of destination: Frontier/Terminal/Quay	Import Documents Formalities	Buyer/Importer Premises
SELLER'S RISKS / BUYER'S RISKS										
SELLER'S COSTS / BUYER'S COSTS										

FAS, Free Alongside Ship (...named port of shipment)

In Free Alongside Ship, the seller/exporter/manufacturer clears the goods for export and then places them alongside the vessel at the "named port of shipment." [The seller's clearing the goods for export is new to Incoterms 2000.]

The parties to the transaction, however, may stipulate in their contract of sale that the buyer will clear the goods for export.

The Free Alongside Ship term is used only for ocean or inland waterway transport.

The "named place" in Free Alongside Ship and all "F" terms is domestic to the seller.

The Free Alongside Ship term is commonly used in the sale of bulk commodity cargo such as oil, grains, and ore.

Normal payment terms for Free Carrier transactions are generally cash in advance and open account, but letters of credit are also used.

Examples
FAS Free Alongside Ship Port Elizabeth South Africa.
FAS Free Alongside Ship Le Havre France

FAS
Free Alongside Ship (. . . named port of shipment)

Incoterm Category

FAS is an "F" Incoterm where the seller/exporter delivers the goods, non-export cleared, alongside a ship, and does not bear risk or costs once the goods have been handed over.

Modes of Transport Covered

Used only for ocean or inland waterway transport.

Seller's Responsibilities (summary)

1. **Goods**—Provide the goods, commercial invoice or electronic message, and other documentation as required by the sales contract.

2. **Licenses and Customs Formalities**—Obtain at own risk and cost any export licenses and authorizations and carry out all export formalities and procedures.

3. **Carriage and Insurance**—The seller has no obligation to the buyer to provide carriage of goods or insurance.

4. **Delivery**—Deliver the goods on the quay alongside the named vessel at the named place and at the time stipulated in the sales contract.

5. **Risk Transfer**—Assume all risks of loss or damage to the goods until they have been delivered to the port at the named place and time as provided in the sales contract.

6. **Costs**—Pay all costs until the goods have been delivered alongside the named vessel and all costs related to export formalities.

7. **Notice to the Buyer**—Provide sufficient notice to the buyer that the goods have been delivered alongside the named vessel.

8. **Proof of Delivery, Transport Documents**—Provide the buyer with a proof of delivery (to the carrier) or a transport document, or to assist the buyer in obtaining a transport document.

9. **Checking, Packing, Marking**—Pay all costs associated with checking the quality and quantity of the goods to be in conformity with the sales contract. Provide appropriate packing (unless the goods are traditionally delivered unpackaged) as required for the transport of the goods, to the extent that the buyer has made transport circumstances known to the seller prior to the execution of the sales contract. Provide marking appropriate to the packaging.

10. **Other**—Provide the buyer at the buyer's request, risk and expense any and all assistance in securing documentation originating in the country of export or of origin required for import and transshipment through another country. Provide the buyer at the buyer's request information necessary to obtain insurance.

Buyer's Responsibilities (summary)

1. **Payment**—Pay for the goods as provided in the sales contract.

2. **Licenses and Customs Formalities**—Obtain at own risk and cost any import licenses and authorizations and carry out all import formalities.

3. **Carriage and Insurance**—Provide for contract of carriage from the named port of shipment. No obligation for insurance.

4. **Taking Delivery**—Take delivery of the goods as provided in the sales contract.

5. **Risk Transfer**—Assume all risk of loss or damage from the time the goods have been delivered alongside the ship as provided in the sales contract.

6. **Costs**—Pay all costs for carriage and insurance from the time the goods have been delivered alongside the vessel in accordance with the terms of the sales contract. Pay all costs resulting from failure of the named ship to arrive on time or to be able to take the goods. Pay all costs relating import formalities including duties, taxes and other charges including transshipment.

7. **Notice to Seller**—Give sufficient notice to the seller of the name of the vessel, the time or period for delivery and the place of delivery.

8. **Proof of Delivery, Transport Document**—Accept the seller's proof of delivery or transport document.

9. **Inspection(s)**—Pay for the costs of pre-shipment inspection except inspections required by the country of export.

10. **Other**—Pay all costs associated with securing documentation originating in the country of origin or export as required for import formalities. Reimburse seller for seller's costs in providing such documentation or assistance. Also, to give the seller instructions regarding contract for carriage.

INCOTERMS

INCOTERMS

FOB
Free On Board (... named port of shipment)

Seller/ Exporter Premises	Export Documents Formalities	Delivered at named place of: Frontier/Terminal/Quay	Loading Port of Shipment	Onboard Ship's Rail	Onboard Ship's Rail	Discharging Port of Arrival	Delivery at named place of destination: Frontier/Terminal/Quay	Import Documents Formalities	Buyer/ Importer Premises
SELLER'S RISKS								**BUYER'S RISKS**	
SELLER'S COSTS								**BUYER'S COSTS**	

FOB, Free On Board (...named port of shipment)

In Free On Board, the seller/exporter/manufacturer clears the goods for export and is responsible for the costs and risks of delivering the goods past the ship's rail at the named port of shipment.

The Free On Board term is used only for ocean or inland waterway transport. The "named place" in Free On Board and all "F" terms is domestic to the seller.

Normal payment terms for Free On Board transactions include cash in advance, open account, and letters of credit.

The Free On Board term is commonly used in the sale of bulk commodity cargo such as oil, grains, and ore where passing the ship's rail is important. However, it is also commonly used in shipping container loads of other goods. The key document in FOB transactions is the "On Board Bill of Lading."

Sellers and buyers often confuse the Free On Board term with Free Carrier. Free On Board (FOB) does not mean loading the goods onto a truck at the seller's place of business. Free On Board is used only in reference to delivering the goods past a ship's rail in ocean or inland waterway transport. Free Carrier, on the other hand, is applicable to all modes of transport.

Examples
FOB Free on Board "Vessel ABC" Buenos Aires Argentina
FOB Free on Board Gdansk Poland

FOB
Free on Board (. . . named port of shipment)

Incoterm Category

FOB is an "F" Incoterm where the seller/exporter is responsible for delivering the goods, export cleared, on board a ship, and does not bear risk or costs afterwards.

Modes of Transport Covered

Used only for ocean or inland waterway transport.

Seller's Responsibilities (summary)

1. **Goods**—Provide the goods, commercial invoice or electronic message, and other documentation as required by the sales contract.
2. **Licenses and Customs Formalities**—Obtain at own risk and cost any export licenses and authorizations and carry out all export formalities and procedures.
3. **Carriage and Insurance**—The seller has no obligation to the buyer to provide carriage of goods or insurance.
4. **Delivery**—Deliver the goods on board the named vessel at the named port and place and at the time stipulated in the sales contract.
5. **Risk Transfer**—Assume all risks of loss or damage to the goods until they have passed the ship's rail on the named vessel as provided in the sales contract.
6. **Costs**—Pay all costs until the goods have passed the ship's rail on the named vessel as well as all costs relating to export including duties, taxes and customs formalities.
7. **Notice to the Buyer**—Provide sufficient notice to the buyer that the goods have been delivered on board the named vessel.
8. **Proof of Delivery, Transport Documents**—Provide the buyer with a proof of delivery or a transport document, or to assist the buyer in obtaining a transport document.
9. **Checking, Packing, Marking**—Pay all costs associated with checking the quality and quantity of the goods to be in conformity with the sales contract. Provide appropriate packing (unless the goods are traditionally delivered unpackaged) as required for the transport of the goods, to the extent that the buyer has made transport circumstances known to the seller prior to the execution of the sales contract. Provide marking appropriate to the packaging.
10. **Other**—Provide the buyer at the buyer's request, risk and expense any and all assistance in securing documentation originating in the country of export or of origin required for import and transshipment through another country. Provide the buyer at the buyer's request information necessary to obtain insurance.

Buyer's Responsibilities (summary)

1. **Payment**—Pay for the goods as provided in the sales contract.
2. **Licenses and Customs Formalities**—Obtain at own risk and cost any import licenses and authorizations and carry out all import formalities.
3. **Carriage and Insurance**—Provide for contract of carriage from the named port of shipment. No obligation for insurance.
4. **Taking Delivery**—Take delivery of the goods as provided in the sales contract.

5. **Risk Transfer**—Assume all risks of loss or damage from the time the goods have passed the ship's rail at the port of shipment.
6. **Costs**—Pay all costs for carriage and insurance from the time the goods have passed the ship's rail at the port of shipment in accordance with the terms of the sales contract. Pay all costs resulting from failure of the named ship to arrive on time or to be able to take the goods. Pay all costs relating to import formalities including duties, taxes and other charges including transshipment.
7. **Notice to Seller**—Give sufficient notice to the seller of the name of the vessel, the time or period for delivery and the place of delivery.
8. **Proof of Delivery, Transport Document**—Accept the seller's proof of delivery or transport document.
9. **Inspection(s)**—Pay for the costs of pre-shipment inspection except inspections required by the country of export.
10. **Other**—Pay all costs associated with securing documentation originating in the country of origin or export as required for import. Reimburse seller for seller's costs in providing such documentation or assistance.

INCOTERMS

INCOTERMS

CFR
Cost and Freight (... named port of destination)

Seller/ Exporter Premises	Export Documents Formalities	Delivered at named place of: Frontier/Terminal/Quay	Loading Port of Shipment	Onboard Ship's Rail		Discharging at Port of Arrival	Delivery at named place of destination: Frontier/Terminal/Quay	Import Documents Formalities	Buyer/ Importer Premises
SELLER'S RISKS								BUYER'S RISKS	
SELLER'S COSTS								BUYER'S COSTS	
				SELLERS INSURABLE INTEREST*					

Cost and Freight (...named port of destination)

In Cost and Freight, the seller/exporter/manufacturer clears the goods for export and is responsible for delivering the goods past the ship's rail at the port of shipment (not destination).

The seller is also responsible for paying for the costs associated with transport of the goods to the named port of destination. However, once the goods pass the ship's rail at the port of shipment, the buyer assumes responsibility for risk of loss or damage as well as any additional transport costs.

The Cost and Freight term is used only for ocean or inland waterway transport. The "named port of destination" in Cost and Freight and all "C" terms is domestic to the buyer.

Normal payment terms for Cost and Freight transactions include cash in advance, open account, and letters of credit.

The Cost and Freight term is commonly used in the sale of oversize and overweight cargo that will not fit into an ocean freight container or exceeds weight limitations of such containers. The term is also used for LCL (less than container load) cargo and for the shipment of goods by rail in boxcars to the ocean carrier.

*Insurance Note

While the seller may not be legally responsible for the goods once they pass the ship's rail in the port of shipment, he may have "insurable interest" during the voyage. Prudence may dictate purchase of additional insurance coverage.

Examples

CIF Cost and Freight Port-au-Prince Haiti
CIF Cost and Freight Bombay India

CFR
Cost and Freight (. . . named port of destination)

Incoterm Category

CFR is a "C" Incoterm where the seller is responsible for contracting and paying for carriage of the goods, but not responsible for additional costs or risk of loss or damage to the goods once they have been shipped. C terms evidence "shipment" (as opposed to "arrival") contracts.

Modes of Transport Covered

Used only for ocean or inland waterway transport.

Seller's Responsibilities (summary)

1. **Goods**—Provide the goods, commercial invoice or electronic message, and other documentation as required by the sales contract.

2. **Licenses and Customs Formalities**—Obtain at own risk and cost any export licenses and authorizations and carry out all export formalities and procedures.

3. **Carriage and Insurance**—Contract for and pay all costs of carriage by sea vessel to the named port of destination. No obligation to provide insurance.

4. **Delivery**—Deliver the goods on board the named vessel at the named port and on the date or within the time period stipulated in the sales contract.

5. **Risk Transfer**—Assume all risks of loss or damage to the goods until they have passed over the ship's rail at the port of shipment.

6. **Costs**—Pay all costs until the goods have been delivered to the named port of shipment and passed over the ship's rail plus costs of loading, carriage to the port of destination and normal un-loading. Also to pay all costs relating to export including duties, taxes and customs formalities.

7. **Notice to the Buyer**—Provide sufficient notice to the buyer that the goods have been delivered on board the named vessel.

8. **Proof of Delivery, Transport Documents**—Provide the buyer with a transport document that will allow the buyer to claim the goods at the destination and (unless otherwise agreed) allow the buyer to sell the goods while in transit through the transfer of the transport document or by notification to the sea carrier.

9. **Checking, Packing, Marking**—Pay all costs associated with checking the quality and quantity of the goods to be in conformity with the sales contract. Provide appropriate packing (unless the goods are traditionally delivered unpackaged) as required for the transport of the goods, to the extent that the buyer has made transport circumstances known to the seller prior to the execution of the sales contract. Provide marking appropriate to the packaging.

10. **Other**—Provide the buyer at the buyer's request, risk and expense any and all assistance in securing documentation originating in the country of export or of origin required for import and transshipment (as necessary). Provide the buyer at the buyer's request information necessary to obtain insurance.

Buyer's Responsibilities (summary)

1. **Payment**—Pay for the goods as provided in the sales contract.

2. **Licenses and Customs Formalities**—Obtain and pay costs of all import licenses and authorizations and carry out all import formalities.

3. **Carriage and Insurance**—No obligation to the seller.

4. **Taking Delivery**—Take delivery of the goods at the port of destination as provided in the sales contract.

5. **Risk Transfer**—Assume all risk of loss or damage from the time the goods have passed over the ship's rail at the port of shipment.

6. **Costs**—Pay all additional costs for the goods once they have passed over the ship's rail at the port of shipment, including unloading, lighterage and wharfage at the port of destination. Pay all costs relating to import formalities including duties, taxes and other charges including transshipment.

7. **Notice to Seller**—If, according to the sales contract, the buyer is able to specify a time for shipping and/or specify a port of destination, to give the seller sufficient notice.

8. **Proof of Delivery, Transport Document**—Accept the seller's transport document so long as it is in conformity with the sales contract.

9. **Inspection(s)**—Pay for the costs of pre-shipment inspection except inspections required by the country of export.

10. **Other**—Pay all costs of securing documentation from the country of origin or export as required for import. Reimburse seller for costs in providing such documentation or assistance.

INCOTERMS

INCOTERMS

CIF
Cost, Insurance and Freight (... named port of destination)

Seller/ Exporter Premises	Export Documents Formalities	Delivered at named place of: Frontier/Terminal/Quay	Loading Port of Shipment	Onboard Ship's Rail	Onboard Ship's Rail	Discharging Port of Arrival	Delivery at named place of destination: Frontier/Terminal/Quay	Import Documents Formalities	Buyer/ Importer Premises
SELLER'S RISKS								**BUYER'S RISKS**	
SELLER'S COSTS								**BUYER'S COSTS**	
				BUYER'S INSURABLE INTEREST*					

Cost, Insurance and Freight (...named port of destination)

In Cost, Insurance and Freight, the seller/exporter/manufacturer clears the goods for export and is responsible for delivering the goods past the ship's rail at the port of shipment (not destination).

The seller is responsible for paying for the costs associated with transport of the goods to the named port of destination. However, once the goods pass the ship's rail at the port of shipment, the buyer assumes responsibility for risk of loss or damage as well as any additional transport costs.

The seller is also responsible for procuring and paying for marine insurance in the buyer's name for the shipment.

The Cost and Freight term is used only for ocean or inland waterway transport.

The "named port of destination" in Cost and Freight and all "C" terms is do-

mestic to the buyer.

Normal payment terms for Cost and Freight transactions include cash in advance, open account, and letters of credit.

*Insurance Note

While the seller is responsible for procuring and paying for insurance cover during the voyage to the named port of destination, the buyer may exercise prudence and purchase additional insurance coverage.

Examples

CIF Cost Insurance and Freight Hong Kong

CIF Cost, Insurance and Freight Port of New York

CIF
Cost, Insurance and Freight (. . . named port of destination)

Incoterm Category

CIF is a "C" Incoterm where the seller is responsible for contracting and paying for carriage and insurance of the goods, but not responsible for additional costs or risk of loss or damage to the goods once they have been shipped. C terms evidence "shipment" (as opposed to "arrival") contracts.

Modes of Transport Covered

Used only for ocean or inland waterway transport.

Seller's Responsibilities (summary)

1. **Goods**—Provide the goods, commercial invoice or electronic message, and other documentation as required by the sales contract.
2. **Licenses and Customs Formalities**—Obtain at own risk and cost any export licenses and authorizations and carry out all export formalities and procedures.
3. **Carriage and Insurance**—Contract for and pay costs of carriage by sea or inland waterway and insurance for 110 percent of the value of the contract to the named port of destination. The insurance policy must allow the buyer to make claim directly from the insurer. Deliver the insurance document to the buyer.
4. **Delivery**—Deliver the goods on board the named vessel at the named port and at the date or within the time period stipulated in the sales contract.
5. **Risk Transfer**—Assume all risks of loss or damage to the goods until they have passed over the ship's rail at the port of shipment.
6. **Costs**—Pay all costs of carriage and insurance until the goods have been delivered to the named port of shipment and passed over the ship's rail, plus costs of loading, carriage to the port of destination and normal unloading. Also to pay all costs relating to export including duties, taxes and customs formalities.
7. **Notice to the Buyer**—Provide sufficient notice to the buyer that the goods have been delivered on board the named vessel.
8. **Proof of Delivery, Transport Documents**—Provide the buyer with a transport document that will allow the buyer to claim the goods at the destination and (unless otherwise agreed) allow the buyer to sell the goods while in transit through the transfer of the transport document or by notification to the sea carrier.
9. **Checking, Packing, Marking**—Pay all costs associated with checking the quality and quantity of the goods to be in conformity with the sales contract. Provide appropriate packing (unless the goods are traditionally delivered unpackaged) as required for the transport of the goods, to the extent that the buyer has made transport circumstances known to the seller prior to the execution of the sales contract. Provide marking appropriate to the packaging.
10. **Other**—Provide the buyer at the buyer's request, risk and cost any and all assistance in securing documentation originating in the country of export or of origin required for import and for transshipment.

Buyer's Responsibilities (summary)

1. **Payment**—Pay for the goods as provided in the sales contract.
2. **Licenses and Customs Formalities**—Obtain and pay costs of all import licenses and authorizations and carry out all import formalities.
3. **Carriage and Insurance**—No obligation to the seller to pay for carriage or insurance.
4. **Taking Delivery**—Take delivery of the goods at the port of destination as provided in the sales contract.
5. **Risk Transfer**—Assume all risk of loss or damage from the time the goods have passed over the ship's rail at the port of shipment.
6. **Costs**—Pay all supplemental costs for the goods once they have passed over the ship's rail at the port of shipment, including unloading, lighterage and wharfage at the port of destination. Pay all costs relating to import formalities including duties, taxes and other charges including transshipment.
7. **Notice to Seller**—If, according to the sales contract, the buyer is able to specify a time for shipping and/or specify a port of destination, to give the seller sufficient notice.
8. **Proof of Delivery, Transport Document**—Accept the seller's transport document so long as it is in conformity with the sales contract.
9. **Inspection(s)**—Pay for the costs of pre-shipment inspection except inspections required by the country of export.
10. **Other**—Pay costs of securing documentation from the country of origin or export as required for import. Reimburse seller such costs. Provide information necessary to obtain insurance.

INCOTERMS

INCOTERMS

CPT
Carriage Paid To (. . . named port of destination)

SELLER →   BUYER ⇢

Seller/ Exporter Premises	Export Documents Formalities	Delivered at named place of: Frontier/Terminal/Quay	Loading Port of Shipment	Onboard Ship's Rail	Onboard Ship's Rail	Discharging Port of Arrival	Delivery at named place of destination: Frontier/Terminal/Quay	Import Documents Formalities	Buyer/ Importer Premises
SELLER'S RISKS								BUYER'S RISKS	
SELLER'S COSTS								BUYER'S COSTS	

BUYER'S and SELLER'S INSURABLE INTEREST*

Carriage Paid To (...named port of destination)

In Carriage Paid To, the seller/exporter/manufacturer clears the goods for export, delivers them to the carrier, and is responsible for paying for carriage to the named port of destination. However, once the seller delivers the goods to the carrier, the buyer becomes responsible for all additional costs.

In Incoterms 2000 the seller is also responsible for the costs of unloading, customs clearance, duties, and other costs if such costs are included in the cost of carriage such as in small package courier delivery.

The seller is not responsible for procuring and paying for insurance cover.

The CPT term is valid for any form of transport including multimodal.

The "named port of destination" in CPT and all "C" terms is domestic to the buyer, but is not necessarily the final delivery point.

The Carriage Paid To term is often used in sales where the shipment is by air freight, containerized ocean freight, courier shipments of small parcels, and in "ro-ro" (roll-on, roll-off) shipments of motor vehicles.

A "carrier" can be a shipping line, airline, trucking firm, railway or also an individual or firm who undertakes to procure carriage by any of the above methods of transport including multimodal. Therefore, a person, such as a freight forwarder, can act as a "carrier" under this term.

If subsequent carriers are used for the carriage to the agreed destination, the risk passes when the goods have been delivered to the first carrier.

*Insurance Note

While neither the buyer nor seller have obligation for providing insurance during the main voyage, both may have "insurable interest" and prudence may dictate purchase of insurance coverage.

CPT
Carriage Paid To (. . . named port of destination)

Incoterm Category

CPT is a "C" Incoterm where the seller is responsible for contracting and paying for carriage of the goods, but not responsible for additional costs or risk of loss or damage to the goods once they have been shipped. C terms evidence "shipment" (as opposed to "arrival") contracts.

Modes of Transport Covered

All modes of transport including multimodal.

Seller's Responsibilities (summary)

1. **Goods**—Provide the goods, commercial invoice or electronic message, and other documentation as required by the sales contract.

2. **Licenses and Customs Formalities**—Obtain at own risk and cost any export licenses and authorizations and carry out all export formalities and procedures.

3. **Carriage and Insurance**—Contract for and pay all costs of carriage to the agreed point at the named place of destination. No obligation to provide insurance.

4. **Delivery**—Deliver the goods to the carrier (or first of multiple carriers) for carriage to the named port of destination within the time period stipulated in the sales contract.

5. **Risk Transfer**—Assume all risks of loss or damage to the goods until they have been delivered to the carrier or first of multiple carriers.

6. **Costs**—Pay all costs until the goods have been delivered to the carrier plus costs of loading, carriage to the port of destination and normal unloading. Also to pay all costs related to ex-

port including duties, taxes and customs formalities. Pay the costs of unloading, customs clearance, duties, and other costs if such costs are included in the cost of carriage.

7. **Notice to the Buyer**—Provide sufficient notice to the buyer that the goods have been delivered to the carrier.

8. **Proof of Delivery, Transport Documents**—Provide the buyer with a transport document.

9. **Checking, Packing, Marking**—Pay all costs associated with checking the quality and quantity of the goods to be in conformity with the sales contract. Provide appropriate packing (unless the goods are traditionally delivered unpackaged) as required for the transport of the goods, to the extent that the buyer has made transport circumstances known to the seller prior to the execution of the sales contract. Provide marking appropriate to the packaging.

10. **Other**—Provide the buyer at the buyer's request, risk and expense any and all assistance in securing documentation originating in the country of export or of origin required for import and for transshipment (as necessary). Provide the buyer at the buyer's request information necessary to obtain insurance.

Buyer's Responsibilities (summary)

1. **Payment**—Pay for the goods as provided in the sales contract.

2. **Licenses and Customs Formalities**—Obtain and pay costs of all import licenses and authorizations and carry out all import formalities.

3. **Carriage and Insurance**—No obligation to the seller for either carriage or insurance.

4. **Taking Delivery**—Take delivery of the goods from the carrier at the port of destination as provided in the sales contract.

5. **Risk Transfer**—Assume all risk of loss or damage from the time the goods have been delivered to the carrier by the seller.

6. **Costs**—Pay all additional costs (not covered in the seller's contract of carriage in Seller's #6) for the goods once they have been delivered to the carrier, including unloading, lighterage and wharfage at the port of destination. Pay all costs relating to import formalities including duties, taxes and other charges including transshipment.

7. **Notice to Seller**—If, according to the sales contract, the buyer is able to specify a time for shipping and/or specify a port of destination, to give the seller sufficient notice.

8. **Proof of Delivery, Transport Document**—Accept the seller's transport document so long as it is in conformity with the sales contract.

9. **Inspection(s)**—Pay for the costs of pre-shipment inspection(s) except inspections required by the country of export.

10. **Other**—Pay all costs associated with securing documentation from the country of origin or export as required for import. Reimburse seller for costs in providing such documentation or assistance.

INCOTERMS

INCOTERMS

CIP
Carriage and Insurance Paid To (. . . named port of destination)

SELLER →
BUYER ⇢

Seller/Exporter Premises	Export Documents Formalities	Delivered at named place of: Frontier/Terminal/Quay	Loading Port of Shipment	Onboard Ship's Rail	Onboard Ship's Rail	Discharging Port of Arrival	Delivery at named place of destination: Frontier/Terminal/Quay	Import Documents Formalities	Buyer/Importer Premises
SELLER'S RISKS								BUYER'S RISKS	
SELLER'S COSTS								BUYER'S COSTS	
					BUYER'S INSURABLE INTEREST*				

Carriage and Insurance Paid To (...named port of destination)

In Carriage and Insurance Paid To, the seller/exporter clears the goods for export, delivers them to the carrier, and is responsible for paying for carriage and insurance to the named port of destination. However, once the goods are delivered to the carrier, the buyer is responsible for all additional costs.

In Incoterms 2000 the seller is also responsible for the costs of unloading, customs clearance, duties, and other costs if such costs are included in the cost of carriage such as in small package courier delivery.

The seller is responsible for procuring and paying for insurance cover.

The CIP term is valid for any form of transport including multimodal

The "named port of destination" in CIP and all "C" terms is domestic to the buyer, but is not necessarily the final delivery point.

The Carriage and Insurance Paid To term is often used in sales where the shipment is by air freight, containerized ocean freight, courier shipments of small parcels, and in "ro-ro" (roll-on, roll-off) shipments of motor vehicles.

A "carrier" can be a shipping line, airline, trucking firm, railway or also an individual or firm who undertakes to procure carriage by any of the above methods of transport including multimodal. Therefore, a person, such as a freight forwarder, can act as a "carrier" under this term.

If subsequent carriers are used for the carriage to the agreed destination, the risk passes when the goods have been delivered to the first carrier.

*Insurance Note

While the seller is responsible for insurance coverage during the main voyage, the buyer may have additional "insurable interest" and prudence may dictate purchase of additional coverage.

CIP
Carriage and Insurance Paid To (. . . named port of destination)

Incoterm Category

CIP is a "C" Incoterm where the seller is responsible for contracting and paying for carriage and insurance of the goods, but not responsible for additional costs or risk of loss or damage to the goods once they have been shipped. C terms evidence "shipment" (as opposed to "arrival") contracts.

Modes of Transport Covered

All modes of transport including multimodal.

Seller's Responsibilities (summary)

1. **Goods**—Provide the goods, commercial invoice or electronic message, and other documentation as required by the sales contract.

2. **Licenses and Customs Formalities**—Obtain at own risk and cost any export licenses and authorizations and carry out all export formalities and procedures.

3. **Carriage and Insurance**—Contract for and pay all costs of carriage and insurance to the named port of destination. The insurance policy or document must allow the buyer to make a claim directly from the insurer. Deliver the insurance document to the buyer.

4. **Delivery**—Deliver the goods to the carrier (or first of multiple carriers) for carriage to the named port of destination within the time period stipulated in the sales contract.

5. **Risk Transfer**—Assume all risks of loss or damage to the goods until they have been delivered to the carrier or first of multiple carriers.

6. **Costs**—Pay all costs until the goods have been delivered to the carrier, plus costs of loading, carriage, insurance to the named port of destination plus normal unloading. Also to pay all costs relating to export including duties, taxes and customs formalities. Pay the costs of unloading, customs clearance, duties, and other costs if such costs are included in the cost of carriage.

7. **Notice to the Buyer**—Provide sufficient notice to the buyer that the goods have been delivered to the carrier.

8. **Proof of Delivery, Transport Documents**—Provide the buyer with a transport document.

9. **Checking, Packing, Marking**—Pay all costs associated with checking the quality and quantity of the goods to be in conformity with the sales contract. Provide appropriate packing (unless the goods are traditionally delivered unpackaged) as required for the transport of the goods, to the extent that the buyer has made transport circumstances known to the seller prior to the execution of the sales contract. Provide marking appropriate to the packaging.

10. **Other**—Provide the buyer at the buyer's request, risk and expense any and all assistance in securing documentation originating in the country of export or of origin required for import and for transshipment (as necessary). Provide the buyer with information necessary to procure additional insurance.

Buyer's Responsibilities (summary)

1. **Payment**—Pay for the goods as provided in the sales contract.

2. **Licenses and Customs Formalities**—Obtain and pay costs of all import licenses and authorizations and carry out all import formalities.

3. **Carriage and Insurance**—No obligation to the seller for either carriage or insurance.

4. **Taking Delivery**—Take delivery of the goods from the carrier at the port of destination as provided in the sales contract.

5. **Risk Transfer**—Assume all risk of loss or damage from the time the goods have been delivered to the carrier by the seller.

6. **Costs**—Pay all additional costs (not covered in the seller's contract of carriage in Seller's #6) for the goods once they have been delivered to the carrier, including unloading, lighterage and wharfage at the port of destination. Pay all costs relating to import formalities including duties, taxes and other charges including transshipment.

7. **Notice to Seller**—If, according to the sales contract, the buyer is able to specify a time for shipping and/or specify a port of destination, to give the seller sufficient notice.

8. **Proof of Delivery, Transport Document**—Accept the seller's transport document so long as it is in conformity with the sales contract.

9. **Inspection(s)**—Pay for the costs of pre-shipment inspection(s) except inspections required by the country of export.

10. **Other**—Pay all costs associated with securing documentation from the country of origin or export required for import. Reimburse seller for costs in providing such documentation or assistance.

INCOTERMS

INCOTERMS

DAF
Delivered At Frontier (. . . named place)

SELLER → BUYER →

Seller/Exporter Premises	Export Documents Formalities	Delivered at named place of: Frontier/Terminal/Quay	Loading Port of Shipment	Onboard Ship's Rail	Onboard Ship's Rail	Discharging Port of Arrival	Delivery at named place of destination: Frontier/Terminal/Quay	Import Documents Formalities	Buyer/Importer Premises
EXAMPLE 1 SELLER'S RISKS				NOT APPLICABLE					
EXAMPLE 1 SELLER'S COSTS				NOT APPLICABLE					
EXAMPLE 2 SELLER'S RISKS									
EXAMPLE 2 SELLER'S COSTS									
							EXAMPLE 1 BUYER'S RISKS		
							EXAMPLE 1 BUYER'S COSTS		
						EXAMPLE 2 BUYER'S RISKS			
						EXAMPLE 2 BUYER'S COSTS			

Delivered At Frontier (...named place)

In Delivered At Frontier, the seller/exporter/manufacturer clears the goods for export and is responsible for making them available to the buyer at the named point and place at the frontier, not unloaded, and not cleared for import.

In the DAF term, naming the precise point, place, and time of availability at the frontier is very important as the buyer must make arrangements to unload and secure the goods in a timely manner.

Frontier can mean any frontier including the frontier of export.

The DAF term is valid for any mode of shipment, so long as the final shipment to the named place at the frontier is by land.

The seller is not responsible for procuring and paying for insurance cover.

Example 1

DAF Laredo, Texas. Seller is in Dallas, Texas, buyer is in Mexico City, Mexico. The shipment travels by truck from Dallas to the frontier at Laredo, Texas USA where the buyer takes possession and trucks the goods to Mexico City.

Example 2

DAF Basel Switzerland. Seller is in Dallas, Texas, buyer is in Bern Switzerland. The shipment travels by truck from Dallas to Port Arthur, by ship to Le Havre, France and then by rail to the frontier in Basel where the buyer takes possession and transports the goods to the city of Bern.

DAF
Delivered at Frontier (. . . named place)

Incoterm Category

DAF is a "D" Incoterm where the seller is responsible for all costs associated with delivering the goods to the named point and place of destination. "D" terms evidence "arrival" (as opposed to "shipment") contracts.

Modes of Transport Covered

Used for all modes of transport so long as the final shipment to the named place at the frontier is by land.

Seller's Responsibilities (summary)

1. **Goods**—Provide the goods, commercial invoice or electronic message, and other documentation as required by the sales contract.
2. **Licenses and Customs Formalities**—a) Obtain at own risk and cost any export licenses and authorizations required to enable the buyer to deal with export formalities at the named frontier. And, if transshipped, b) Carry out all export formalities and procedures required to bring the goods to the named frontier.
3. **Carriage and Insurance**—Contract for and pay all costs of carriage and transshipment (if necessary) to the named place. No obligation to provide insurance.
4. **Delivery**—Make the goods available to the buyer unloaded at the frontier at the named point and place and on the date or period specified in the sales contract.
5. **Risk Transfer**—Assume all risks of loss or damage to the goods until they have been made available to the buyer at the named point place and time at the frontier.
6. **Costs**—Pay all costs until the goods have been delivered at the frontier, including carriage, and all prior to delivery export formalities.
7. **Notice to the Buyer**—Provide sufficient notice of dispatch and projected arrival that the buyer can take appropriate action to arrange pick-up of the goods.
8. **Proof of Delivery, Transport Documents**—Provide the buyer with documentary evidence of delivery at the frontier. At the buyer's request, risk and cost, provide a through document of transport to the named place of destination.
9. **Checking, Packing, Marking**—Pay all costs associated with checking the quality and quantity of the goods to be in conformity with the sales contract. Provide appropriate packing (unless the goods are traditionally delivered unpackaged) as required for the transport of the goods, to the extent that the buyer has made transport circumstances known to the seller prior to the execution of the sales contract. Provide appropriate marking to the packaging.
10. **Other**—Provide the buyer at the buyer's request, risk and expense any and all assistance in securing documentation originating in the country of export or of origin required for import. Provide the buyer with information necessary to obtain insurance.

and pay costs of all import licenses and authorizations and carry out all import formalities.
3. **Carriage and Insurance**—No obligation to the seller for either carriage or insurance.
4. **Taking Delivery**—Take delivery of the goods once they are made available at the frontier.
5. **Risk Transfer**—Assume all risk of loss or damage from the time the goods have been delivered at the named point, place and time at the frontier.
6. **Costs**—Pay all costs for the goods once they have been delivered to the frontier including unloading. Pay all costs relating to import formalities including duties, taxes and formalities. Pay for transport from the frontier to the final destination.
7. **Notice to Seller**—If, according to the sales contract, the buyer is able to specify a time for and/or a place of delivery, to give the seller sufficient notice.
8. **Proof of Delivery, Transport Document**—Accept the seller's transport document so long as it is in conformity with the sales contract.
9. **Inspection(s)**—Pay for the costs of pre-shipment inspection(s) except inspections required by the country of export.
10. **Other**—Pay all costs associated with securing documentation from the country of origin or export required for import. Reimburse seller for costs in providing such documentation or assistance. Provide the seller with any authorizations, permits, documents or other information required for obtaining a through transport document.

Buyer's Responsibilities (summary)

1. **Payment**—Pay for the goods as provided in the sales contract.
2. **Licenses and Customs Formalities**—Obtain

INCOTERMS

INCOTERMS

DES
Delivered Ex Ship (. . . named port of destination)

SELLER →

BUYER ⇢

Seller/ Exporter Premises	Export Documents Formalities	Delivered at named place of: Frontier/Terminal/Quay	Loading Port of Shipment	Onboard Ship's Rail		Discharging Port of Arrival	Delivery at named place of destination: Frontier/Terminal/Quay	Import Documents Formalities	Buyer/ Importer Premises
SELLER'S RISKS					Onboard Ship's Rail		BUYER'S RISKS		
SELLER'S COSTS							BUYER'S COSTS		

Delivered Ex Ship (...named port of destination)

In Delivered Ex Ship, the seller/exporter/manufacturer clears the goods for export and is responsible for making them available to the buyer on board the ship at the named port of destination, not cleared for import.

The seller is thus responsible for all costs of getting the goods to the named port of destination prior to unloading.

The DES term is used only for shipments of goods by ocean or inland waterway or by multimodal transport where the final delivery is made on a vessel at the named port of destination.

All forms of payment are used in DES transactions.

Examples

DES Delivered Ex Ship Port of Calcutta
DES Delivered Ex Ship Port of New York

DES
Delivered Ex Ship (. . . named port of destination)

Incoterm Category

DES is a "D" Incoterm where the seller is responsible for all costs associated with delivering the goods to the named port of destination. "D" terms evidence "arrival" (as opposed to "shipment") contracts.

Modes of Transport Covered

Used only for ocean or inland waterway transport.

Seller's Responsibilities (summary)

1. **Goods**—Provide the goods, commercial invoice or electronic message, and other documentation as required by the sales contract.

2. **Licenses and Customs Formalities**—Obtain at own risk and cost any export licenses and authorizations and carry out all export formalities and procedures, including those associated with transshipment to the named port of destination.

3. **Carriage and Insurance**—Contract for and pay all costs of carriage and transshipment (if necessary) to the named place and port of destination. No obligation to provide insurance.

4. **Delivery**—Make the goods available to the buyer uncleared for import on board the vessel at the named place and port on the date or within the time period specified in the sales contract.

5. **Risk Transfer**—Assume all risks of loss or damage to the goods until they have been made available to the buyer at the named place and port.

6. **Costs**—Pay all costs until the goods have been delivered, including all export formalities, carriage and transshipment (if necessary) to the named place and port.

7. **Notice to the Buyer**—Provide sufficient notice of dispatch and projected arrival that the buyer can take appropriate action to arrange pick-up of the goods.

8. **Proof of Delivery, Transport Documents**—Provide the buyer with the delivery order and/or a transport document enabling the buyer to take delivery of the goods at the port of destination.

9. **Checking, Packing, Marking**—Pay all costs associated with checking the quality and quantity of the goods to be in conformity with the sales contract. Provide appropriate packing (unless the goods are traditionally delivered unpackaged) as required for the transport of the goods, to the extent that the buyer has made transport circumstances known to the seller prior to the execution of the sales contract. Provide marking appropriate to the packaging.

10. **Other**—Provide the buyer at the buyer's request, risk and expense any and all assistance in securing documentation originating in the country of export or of origin required for import. Provide the buyer with information necessary to obtain insurance.

Buyer's Responsibilities (summary)

1. **Payment**—Pay for the goods as provided in the sales contract.

2. **Licenses and Customs Formalities**—Obtain and pay costs of all import licenses and authorizations and carry out all import formalities.

3. **Carriage and Insurance**—No obligation to the seller for either carriage or insurance.

4. **Taking Delivery**—Take delivery of the goods once they are made available at the port.

5. **Risk Transfer**—Assume all risk of loss or damage from the time the goods have been made available at the port.

6. **Costs**—Pay all costs for the goods once they have been made available at the port including unloading. Pay all costs relating to import formalities including duties, taxes and other charges.

7. **Notice to Seller**—If, according to the sales contract, the buyer is able to specify a time for and/or a place of delivery, to give the seller sufficient notice.

8. **Proof of Delivery, Transport Document**—Accept the seller's transport document so long as it is in conformity with the sales contract.

9. **Inspection(s)**—Pay for the costs of pre-shipment inspection(s) except inspections required by the country of export.

10. **Other**—Pay all costs associated with securing documentation from the country of origin or export required for import. Reimburse seller for costs in providing such documentation or assistance.

INCOTERMS

INCOTERMS

DEQ
Delivered Ex Quay (. . . named port of destination)

SELLER → BUYER

Seller/ Exporter Premises	Export Documents Formalities	Delivered at named place of: Frontier/Terminal/Quay	Loading Port of Shipment	Onboard Ship's Rail	Onboard Ship's Rail	Quay at named place	On-carriage to final destination	Import Documents Formalities	Buyer/ Importer Premises
SELLER'S RISKS						BUYER'S RISKS			
SELLER'S COSTS						BUYER'S COSTS			

Delivered Ex Quay (...named port of destination)

In Delivered Ex Quay, the seller/exporter/manufacturer clears the goods for export and is responsible for making them available to the buyer on the quay (warf) at the named port of destination, not cleared for import.

The buyer, therefore, assumes all responsibilities for import clearance, duties, and other costs upon import as well as transport to the final destination. This is new for Incoterms 2000.

The DES term is used only for shipments of goods arriving at the port of destination by ocean or by inland waterway.

All forms of payment are used in DEQ transactions.

Examples
DEQ Delivered Ex Quay Alexandria Egypt
DEQ Delivered Ex Quay Stockholm Sweden

DEQ
Delivered ___x Quay (. . . named port of destination)

Incoterm Category

DEQ is a "D" Incoterm where the seller is responsible for all costs associated with delivering the goods to the quay (wharf) at the named port of destination. "D" terms evidence "arrival" (as opposed to "shipment") contracts.

Modes of Transport Covered

Used only for ocean or inland waterway transport.

Seller's Responsibilities (summary)

1. **Goods**—Provide the goods, commercial invoice or electronic message, and other documentation as required by the sales contract.

2. **Licenses and Customs Formalities**—Obtain at own risk and cost any export licenses and authorizations and carry out all export formalities and procedures, including those associated with transshipment to the named port of destination.

3. **Carriage and Insurance**—Contract for and pay all costs of carriage and transshipment (if necessary) to the named place, port and quay (wharf) of destination. No obligation to provide insurance.

4. **Delivery**—Make the goods available to the buyer at the named port and quay on the date or within the period specified in the sales contract.

5. **Risk Transfer**—Assume all risks of loss or damage to the goods until they have been made available to the buyer at the named port and quay (wharf).

6. **Costs**—Pay all costs until the goods have been

delivered, including carriage, unloading, all export and import formalities, duties and taxes and transshipment (if necessary) to the named port and quay (wharf).

7. **Notice to the Buyer**—Provide sufficient notice of dispatch and projected arrival that the buyer can take appropriate action to arrange pick-up of the goods.

8. **Transport Documents**—Provide the buyer with the delivery order and/or a transport document enabling the buyer to take possession at the port of destination.

9. **Checking, Packing, Marking**—Pay all costs associated with checking the quality and quantity of the goods to be in conformity with the sales contract. Provide appropriate packing (unless the goods are traditionally delivered unpackaged) as required for the transport of the goods, to the extent that the buyer has made transport circumstances known to the seller prior to the execution of the sales contract. Provide marking appropriate to the packaging.

10. **Other**—Pay all costs associated with securing documentation originating in the country of importation required to for import clearance of the goods. Provide the buyer with information necessary to obtain insurance.

Buyer's Responsibilities (summary)

1. **Payment**—Pay for the goods as provided in the sales contract.

2. **Licenses and Customs Formalities**—Obtain and pay costs of all import licenses and autho-

rizations and carry out all import formalities.

3. **Carriage and Insurance**—No obligation to the seller for either carriage or insurance.

4. **Taking Delivery**—Take delivery of the goods once they are made available at the quay.

5. **Risk Transfer**—Assume all risk of loss or damage from the time the goods have been made available at the quay wharf).

6. **Costs**—Pay all costs for the goods once they have been made available at the quay (wharf).

7. **Notice to Seller**—If, according to the sales contract, the buyer is able to specify a time for and/or a place of delivery, to give the seller sufficient notice.

8. **Proof of Delivery, Transport Document**—Accept the seller's delivery order or transport document so long as it is in conformity with the sales contract.

9. **Inspection(s)**—Pay for the costs of pre-shipment inspection(s) except inspections required by the country of export.

10. **Other**—Pay all costs associated with securing documentation from the country of origin or export required for import. Reimburse seller for costs in providing such documentation or assistance.

INCOTERMS

DDU
Delivered Duty Unpaid (. . . named place of destination)

SELLER →   BUYER ⇢

Seller/ Exporter Premises	Export Documents Formalities	Delivered at named place of: Frontier/Terminal/Quay	Loading Port of Shipment	Onboard Ship's Rail	Onboard Ship's Rail	Discharging Port of Arrival	Delivery at named place of destination: Frontier/Terminal/Quay	Import Documents Formalities	Buyer/ Importer Premises
SELLER'S RISKS								BUYER'S RISKS	
SELLER'S COSTS								BUYER'S COSTS	

Delivered Duty Unpaid (...named place of destination)

In Delivered Duty Unpaid, the seller/exporter/manufacturer clears the goods for export and is responsible for making them available to the buyer at the named place of destination, not cleared for import.

The seller, therefore, assumes all responsibilities for delivering the goods to the named place of destination, but the buyer assumes all responsibility for import clearance, duties, administrative costs, and any other costs upon import as well as transport to the final destination.

The DDU term can be used for any mode of transport. However, if the seller and buyer desire that delivery should take place on board a sea vessel or on a quay (wharf), the DES or DEQ terms are recommended.

All forms of payment are used in DDU transactions.

The DDU term is used when the named place of destination (point of delivery) is other than the seaport or airport.

Examples

DDU Delivered Duty Unpaid New York New York USA
DDU Delivered Duty Unpaid Hamburg Germany

DDU
Delivered Duty Unpaid (. . . named place of destination)

Incoterm Category

DES is a "D" Incoterm where the seller is responsible for all costs associated with delivering the goods to the named point and place of destination. "D" terms evidence "arrival" (as opposed to "shipment") contracts.

Modes of Transport Covered

All modes of transport including multimodal.

Seller's Responsibilities (summary)

1. **Goods**—Provide the goods, commercial invoice or electronic message, and other documentation as required by the sales contract.

2. **Licenses and Customs Formalities**—Obtain at own risk and cost any export licenses and authorizations and carry out all export formalities and procedures, including those associated with transshipment to the named port of destination.

3. **Carriage and Insurance**—Contract for and pay all costs of carriage and transshipment (if necessary) to the named destination. No obligation to provide insurance.

4. **Delivery**—Make the goods available to the buyer at the named destination on the date or within the period specified in the sales contract.

5. **Risk Transfer**—Assume all risks of loss or damage to the goods until they have been made available to the buyer at the named destination.

6. **Costs**—Pay all costs until the goods have been delivered to the named destination, including

carriage, all export formalities, export duties and taxes, and transshipment (if necessary) to the named destination.

7. **Notice to the Buyer**—Provide sufficient notice of dispatch and projected arrival that the buyer can take appropriate action to arrange pick-up of the goods.

8. **Proof of Delivery, Transport Documents**—Provide the buyer with the delivery order and/or a transport document enabling the buyer to take delivery at the named place of destination.

9. **Checking, Packing, Marking**—Pay all costs associated with checking the quality and quantity of the goods to be in conformity with the sales contract. Provide appropriate packing (unless the goods are traditionally delivered unpackaged) as required for the transport of the goods, to the extent that the buyer has made transport circumstances known to the seller prior to the execution of the sales contract. Provide marking appropriate to the packaging.

10. **Other**—Provide the buyer at the buyer's request, risk and expense any and all assistance in securing documentation originating in the country of export or of origin required for import. Provide the buyer with information necessary to obtain insurance.

Buyer's Responsibilities (summary)

1. **Payment**—Pay for the goods as provided in the sales contract.

2. **Licenses and Customs Formalities**—Obtain and pay costs of all import licenses, documen-

tation and authorizations and carry out all import formalities.

3. **Carriage and Insurance**—No obligation to the seller for either carriage or insurance.

4. **Taking Delivery**—Take delivery of the goods once they are made available at the named destination.

5. **Risk Transfer**—Assume all risk of loss or damage from the time the goods have been made available at the named place of destination.

6. **Costs**—Pay all costs for the goods once they have been made available at the named place of destination. Pay all costs relating to import formalities including duties, taxes and other charges.

7. **Notice to Seller**—If, according to the sales contract, the buyer is able to specify a time for and/or a place of delivery, to give the seller sufficient notice.

8. **Proof of Delivery, Transport Document**—Accept the seller's transport document so long as it is in conformity with the sales contract.

9. **Inspection(s)**—Pay for the costs of pre-shipment inspection(s) except inspections required by the country of export.

10. **Other**—Pay all costs associated with securing documentation from the country of origin or export required for import. Reimburse seller for costs in providing such documentation or assistance.

INCOTERMS

INCOTERMS

DDP
Delivered Duty Paid (. . . named place of destination)

SELLER →   BUYER →

Seller/ Exporter Premises	Export Documents Formalities	Delivered at named place of: Frontier/Terminal/Quay	Loading Port of Shipment	Onboard Ship's Rail	Onboard Ship's Rail	Discharging Port of Arrival	Delivery at named place of destination: Frontier/Terminal/Quay	Import Documents Formalities	Buyer/ Importer Premises
SELLER'S RISKS									**BUYER'S RISKS**
SELLER'S COSTS									**BUYER'S COSTS**

Delivered Duty Paid (...named place of destination)

In Delivered Duty Paid, the seller/exporter/manufacturer clears the goods for export and is responsible for making them available to the buyer at the named place of destination, cleared for import, but not unloaded from the transport vehicle.

The seller, therefore, assumes all responsibilities for delivering the goods to the named place of destination, including all responsibility for import clearance, duties, and other costs payable upon import.

The DDP term can be used for any mode of transport.

All forms of payment are used in DDP transactions.

The DDP term is used when the named place of destination (point of delivery) is other than the seaport or airport.

Examples
DDP Delivered Duty Paid Chicago USA
DDP Delivered Duty Paid VAT Unpaid Paris France

DDP
Delivered Duty Paid (. . . named place of destination)

Incoterm Category

DDP is a "D" Incoterm where the seller is responsible for all costs associated with delivering the goods to the named point and place of destination. "D" terms evidence "arrival" (as opposed to "shipment") contracts.

Modes of Transport Covered

All modes of transport including multimodal.

Seller's Responsibilities (summary)

1. **Goods**—Provide the goods, commercial invoice or electronic message, and other documentation as required by the sales contract.

2. **Licenses and Customs Formalities**—Obtain at own risk and cost any export and import licenses and authorizations and carry out all export and import formalities and procedures, including those associated with transshipment to the named port of destination.

3. **Carriage and Insurance**—Contract for and pay all costs of carriage and transshipment (if necessary) to the named destination. No obligation to provide insurance.

4. **Delivery**—Make the goods available to the buyer not unloaded at the named destination on the date or within the period specified in the sales contract.

5. **Risk Transfer**—Assume all risks of loss or damage to the goods until they have been made available to the buyer at the named destination.

6. **Costs**—Pay all costs until the goods have been delivered to the named destination, including carriage, all export and import formalities and transshipment (if necessary) to the named destination.

7. **Notice to the Buyer**—Provide sufficient notice of dispatch and projected arrival that the buyer can take appropriate action to arrange unloading of the goods.

8. **Proof of Delivery, Transport Documents**—Provide the buyer with the delivery order and/or a transport document enabling the buyer to take delivery at the named place of destination.

9. **Checking, Packing, Marking**—Pay all costs associated with checking the quality and quantity of the goods to be in conformity with the sales contract. Provide appropriate packing (unless the goods are traditionally delivered unpackaged) as required for the transport of the goods, to the extent that the buyer has made transport circumstances known to the seller prior to the execution of the sales contract. Provide appropriate marking to the packaging.

10. **Other**—Pay all costs associated with securing documentation necessary for to make the goods available to the buyer at the named place of destination. Provide the buyer with information necessary to obtain insurance.

Buyer's Responsibilities (summary)

1. **Payment**—Pay for the goods as provided in the sales contract.

2. **Licenses and Customs Formalities**—Provide the seller at the seller's request, risk and cost any and all assistance in securing licenses, documentation and authorizations necessary to import the goods.

3. **Carriage and Insurance**—No obligation to the seller for either carriage or insurance.

4. **Taking Delivery**—Take delivery of the goods once they are made available at the named destination.

5. **Risk Transfer**—Assume all risk of loss or damage from the time the goods have been made available at the named place of destination.

6. **Costs**—Pay all costs for the goods once they have been made available at the named place of destination.

7. **Notice to Seller**—If, according to the sales contract, the buyer is able to specify a time for and/or a place of delivery, to give the seller sufficient notice.

8. **Proof of Delivery, Transport Document**—Accept the seller's transport document so long as it is in conformity with the sales contract.

9. **Inspection(s)**—Pay for the costs of pre-shipment inspection(s) except inspections required by the country of export.

10. **Other**—Provide the seller, at the seller's request, risk and cost any and all assistance in securing import and other documentation necessary for the seller to make the goods available to buyer at the named destination.

Letters of Credit[1]

Letters of Credit Defined

A documentary credit is the written promise of a bank, undertaken on behalf of a buyer, to pay a seller the amount specified in the credit provided the seller complies with the terms and conditions set forth in the credit. The terms and conditions of a documentary credit revolve around two issues: (1) the presentation of documents that evidence title to goods shipped by the seller, and (2) payment.

In simple terms, banks act as intermediaries to collect payment from the buyer in exchange for the transfer of documents that enable the holder to take possession of the goods.

Documentary credits provide a high level of protection and security to both buyers and sellers engaged in international trade. The seller is assured that payment will be made by a party independent of the buyer so long as the terms and conditions of the credit are met. The buyer is assured that payment will be released to the seller only after the bank has received the title documents called for in the credit.

Documentary credits are so named because of the importance of documents in the transaction. Letter of credit (L/C) is the historic and popular term used for a documentary credit because such credits were and are transmitted in the form of a letter from the buyer's bank. Both "documentary credit" and "letter of credit" will be used for our discussions.

Types of Credits

There are a number of different types of standard and special documentary credits. Each type contains a variety of features designed to meet the different needs of buyers, sellers, or the banks involved.

For example, standard documentary credits can be either revocable (may be cancelled by the buyer), or irrevocable (noncancellable by the buyer), or confirmed (a second bank, in addition to the buyer's bank, guarantees payment) or unconfirmed (payment guaranteed only by the issuing bank). The most popular variation for sellers is the irrevocable confirmed credit because it cannot be cancelled by the buyer, and a second bank (usually the seller's bank) adds its guarantee of payment to that of the buyer's bank. Standard credits are discussed later in this section.

Specialized credits include revolving credits, red clause credits, standby credits, transferable credits, and back-to-back credits. These are also discussed later this section.

This section is designed as an introduction to letters of credit. It is not comprehensive. To learn more about letters of credit and other types of international payments see *A Short Course in International Payments*, also available from World Trade Press.

Limitations of Letters of Credit

Although documentary credits provide good protection and are the preferred means of payment in many international transactions, they do have limitations. They do not, for example, ensure that the goods actually shipped are as ordered nor do they insulate buyers and sellers from other disagreements or complaints arising from their relationship. It is up to the parties to settle questions of this nature between themselves.

Advantages, disadvantages, and issues for both buyer and seller will be discussed later in this section. Please note that these issues can have a significant impact on a given transaction. An incomplete understanding of the subject can be more dangerous than no knowledge at all.

Role of Banks

It is important to note, and not for the last time, that a fundamental principle of documentary credits is that banks deal in documents and not goods. Banks are responsible for issues relating to documents and the specific wording of the documentary credit as opposed to issues relating to the goods themselves.

Therefore, banks are not concerned if a shipment is in conformity with the documents, only that the documents are in conformity to the wording of the credit.

L/C

---

1. This section has been excerpted from the book *A Short Course in International Payments*, ISBN 1-885073-50-X, also by Edward G. Hinkelman and available from World Trade Press.

The Uniform Customs and Practice

Although documentary credits, in one form or another, have been in use for a long time, questions arose about how to effect transactions in a practical, fair, and uniform manner.

The Uniform Customs and Practice for Documentary Credits (UCP) is the internationally recognized codification of rules unifying banking practice regarding documentary credits. The UCP was developed by a working committee attached to the International Chamber of Commerce (ICC) in Paris. It is revised and updated from time to time; the current valid version is ICC publication No. 500. See the Resources Appendix for contact information for the ICC.

Parties to the Transaction

There are four main parties to a basic documentary letter of credit transaction. Note that each party has multiple names. The name used for each party to the transaction depends upon who is speaking. Businesspeople like to use the names buyer, seller, buyer's bank and seller's bank. The banks prefer to use the names applicant, beneficiary, issuing bank, and advising bank. The four parties are:

The Buyer (Applicant/Importer)

The buyer initiates the documentary credit process by applying to his bank to open a documentary credit naming the seller as the beneficiary. The buyer, therefore, may be called the buyer in commercial terms, the importer in economic terms, and the applicant in banking terms. They are all one and the same.

The Issuing (Buyer's) Bank

Upon instructions from the buyer, the issuing bank (typically the buyer's regular business bank) issues a documentary credit naming the seller as the beneficiary and sends it to the advising bank (typically the seller's bank).

The Advising (Seller's) Bank

Upon instructions from the issuing bank and the buyer, the advising bank (typically the seller's bank) advises the seller of the credit. The advising bank is typically the seller's regular business bank and is in the seller's country.

The Seller (Beneficiary/Exporter)

The seller receives notification (advice) of the credit from the advising bank, complies with the terms and conditions of the credit, and gets paid. The seller is the beneficiary of the documentary credit. The seller, therefore, may be called the seller in commercial terms, the exporter in economic terms, and the beneficiary in banking terms. They are all one and the same.

Basic Documentary Credit Procedure

The documentary credit procedure involves the step-by-step exchange of documents giving title to the goods for either cash or a contracted promise to pay at a later time. There are four basic groupings of steps in the procedure.

Issuance

Issuance describes the process of the buyer's applying for and opening a documentary credit at the issuing bank and the issuing bank's formal notification of the seller through the advising bank.

Amendment

Amendment describes the process whereby the terms and conditions of a documentary credit may be modified after the credit has been issued.

Utilization

Utilization describes the procedure for the seller's shipping of the goods, the transfer of documents from the seller to the buyer through the banks, and the transfer of the payment from the buyer to the seller through the banks (settlement).

Settlement

Settlement (a subpart of utilization) describes the different ways in which payment may be effected to the seller from the buyer through the banks.

Note: Issues relating to applying for a documentary credit, confirmed vs. unconfirmed credits, special types of credits, settlement, correspondent and confirming banks will be discussed after the basic procedure is explained.

Issuance

Procedure

Refer to the diagram on the facing page for each numbered step.

 Buyer and Seller

1. The buyer and seller agree on the terms of sale: (a) specifying a documentary credit as the means of payment, (b) naming an advising bank (usually the seller's bank), and (c) listing required documents.

 Buyer (Applicant/Importer)

2. The buyer applies to his bank (issuing bank) and opens a documentary credit naming the seller as beneficiary based on specific terms and conditions that are listed in the credit.

 Issuing (Buyer's) Bank

3. The issuing bank sends the documentary credit to the advising bank named in the credit.

 Advising (Seller's) Bank

4. The advising bank informs (advises) the seller of the documentary credit.

ISSUANCE

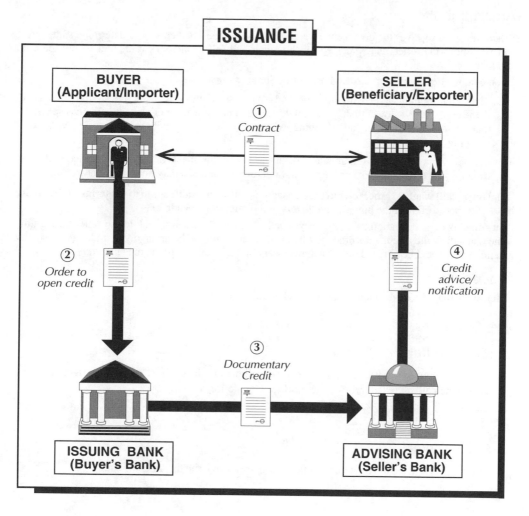

BUYER
(Applicant/Importer)

SELLER
(Beneficiary/Exporter)

① Contract

② Order to open credit

③ Documentary Credit

④ Credit advice/ notification

ISSUING BANK
(Buyer's Bank)

ADVISING BANK
(Seller's Bank)

Amendment

When the seller receives the documentary credit it must be examined closely to determine if the terms and conditions (1) reflect the agreement of the buyer and seller, and (2) can be met within the time stipulated.

Upon examination, the seller may find problems. Some examples:

1. The seller might disagree with the terms and conditions. For example, the transaction price listed in the credit may be lower than the originally agreed upon price, or perhaps the seller has specified that the total price is to include shipping, whereas the seller originally quoted a price without shipping.

2. The seller might find himself unable to meet specific requirements of the credit. For example, the time may be too short to effect shipment, or certain documents may not be available.

If the buyer still wants to proceed with the transaction, but with modification to the terms of the credit, he or she should contact the buyer immediately and request an amendment.

Amendments must be authorized by the buyer and issued by the issuing bank to the seller through the same channel as the original documentary letter of credit. This can be an involved undertaking so any amendments should be initiated only when necessary and as soon as a problem is identified.

Procedure

Refer to the diagram on the facing page for each numbered step.

Seller

1. The seller requests that the buyer make an amendment to the credit. This can be effected by a telephone call, a fax letter, or by face-to-face negotiation.

Buyer

2. If the buyer agrees, the buyer orders the issuing bank to issue the amendment.

Issuing Bank

3. The issuing bank amends the credit and notifies the advising bank of the amendment.

Advising Bank

4. The advising bank notifies seller of the amendment.

AMENDMENT

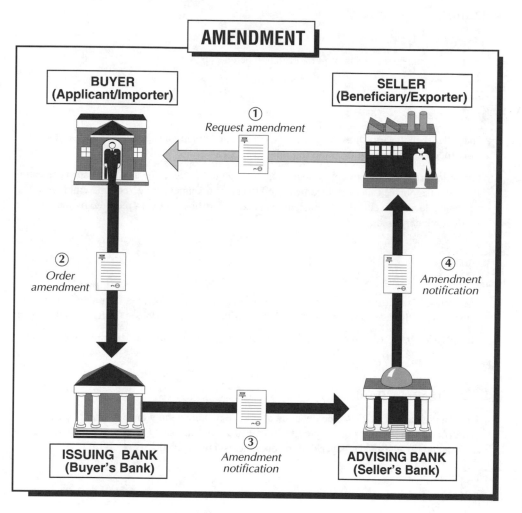

BUYER
(Applicant/Importer)

SELLER
(Beneficiary/Exporter)

① Request amendment

② Order amendment

④ Amendment notification

③ Amendment notification

ISSUING BANK
(Buyer's Bank)

ADVISING BANK
(Seller's Bank)

Utilization

Procedure

Refer to the diagram on the facing page for each numbered step.

 Seller

1. The seller (beneficiary) ships the goods to the buyer and obtains a negotiable transport document (negotiable bill of lading) from the shipping firm/agent.

2. The seller prepares and presents a document package to his bank (the advising bank) consisting of (a) the negotiable transport document, and (b) other documents (e.g., commercial invoice, insurance document, certificate of origin, inspection certificate, etc.) as required by the buyer in the documentary credit.

 Advising Bank

3. The advising bank (a) reviews the document package making certain the documents are in conformity with the terms of the credit and (b) pays the seller (based upon the terms of the credit).

4. The advising bank sends the documentation package by mail or by courier to the issuing bank.

 Issuing Bank

5. The issuing bank (a) reviews the document package making certain the documents are in conformity with the terms of the credit, (b) pays the advising bank (based upon the terms of the credit), and (c) advises the buyer that the documents have arrived.

 Buyer

6. The buyer (a) reviews the document package making certain the documents are in conformity with the terms of the credit, and (b) makes a cash payment (signs a sight draft) to the issuing bank, or if the collection order allows, signs an acceptance (promise to pay at a future date).

 Issuing Bank

7. The issuing bank sends the document package by mail or courier to the buyer who then takes possession of the shipment.

UTILIZATION

BUYER
(Applicant/Importer)

SELLER
(Beneficiary/Exporter)

① *Goods*

③ *Payment*

⑦ *Documents*

② *Documents*

⑥ *Payment*

④ *Documents*

⑤ *Payment*

ISSUING BANK
(Buyer's Bank)

ADVISING BANK
(Seller's Bank)

L/C

Settlement (Availability)

Settlement and availability refer to the availability of proceeds (funds) to the beneficiary (seller) after presentation of documents under the credit. Each of the following forms of payment availability must be specified in the original credit, and be accepted by the seller. For example, if the original agreement between the buyer and seller calls for a sight credit (immediate availability of funds to the seller) and a usance credit (funds available in 30, 60 or 90 days) is prescribed in the credit presented to the seller, the seller may reject the credit and the transaction.

The Sight Credit (Settlement by Payment)

In a sight credit (confirmed sight credit) the value of the credit is available to the beneficiary as soon as the terms and conditions of the credit have been met (as soon as the prescribed document package has been presented to and checked by the confirming bank). When foreign exchange is at issue, several days may pass between the time of beneficiary's presentation of documents and the actual transfer of funds to the beneficiary's account.

In a sight credit (unconfirmed), the value of the credit is made available to the beneficiary once the advising bank has received the funds from the issuing bank.

The Usance Credit (Settlement by Acceptance)

In a usance credit the beneficiary presents the required document package to the bank along with a time draft drawn on the issuing, advising, or a third bank for the value of the credit. Once the documents have made their way to the buyer and found to be in order, the draft is accepted by the bank upon which it is drawn (the draft is now called an acceptance) and it is returned to the seller who holds it until maturity.

The seller has the option of selling the acceptance by discounting its value. The discount charged will be in some proportion to the time to maturity of the draft and the perceived risk associated with its collection. The buyer pays the draft at maturity to its holder.

The Deferred Payment Credit (Settlement by Negotiation)

In a deferred payment credit the buyer accepts the documents and agrees to pay the bank after a set period of time. Essentially, this gives the buyer time (a grace period) between delivery of the goods and payment. The issuing bank makes the payment at the specified time, when the terms and conditions of the credit have been met.

Deferred payment credits are often used in transactions involving food or drugs that require inspection prior to import and approval by a government agency. In this case the bank will release the documents to the importer/buyer against a trust receipt. The bank holds the title documents to the goods and still owns the merchandise. Once the goods have been approved by the government agency, the bank transfers the titles documents to the buyer, charges the buyer's account, and pays the seller.

Opening a Documentary Credit

The Importance of Wording

The success or failure of a documentary credit transaction can turn upon the wording of the documentary credit itself. As such, the buyer (whose responsibility it is to open the credit) should adhere to the greatest extent possible to the terms and conditions of the original contractual agreement, keeping the specifications clear and concise and as simple as possible.

Refer to Documents

The buyer's instructions to the issuing bank should be given in clear, professional wording, and should pertain only to documentation, not to the goods themselves. It is very important to demand documents in the credit that clearly reflect the agreements reached.

Example 1: Require confirmation that goods are shipped by Conference vessel no more than twenty years old, rather than that the goods be shipped by Conference vessel no more than twenty years old.

Example 2: Require confirmation that the goods were packaged in double-strength, waterproof containers, rather than requiring that the goods be packaged in double-strength, waterproof containers.

Example 3: Require proof of notification to buyer (such as a copy of the cable or telex) that goods were shipped, rather than requiring that the buyer be notified that the goods were shipped.

Remember, the banks are concerned only with the documents presented, not with whether a party has complied with the contract clauses when they check compliance with the documentary credit terms.

Be Clear and Concise

The wording in a documentary credit should be simple but specific. The more detailed the documentary credit is, the more likely the seller will reject it as too difficult to fulfill. It is also more likely that the banks will find a discrepancy in the details, thus voiding the credit, even though simpler terms might have been found to be in compliance with the credit.

The buyer should, however, completely and precisely set forth the details of the agreement as it relates to credit terms and conditions and the presentation of documents.

Do Not Specify Impossible Documentation

The documentary credit should not require documents that the seller cannot obtain; nor should it call for details in a document that are beyond the knowledge of the issuer of the document. The documents specified should be limited to those required to smoothly and completely conclude an international sale of goods.

Documentary Credit Application

Procedure

Refer to the application form on the facing page for each numbered step.

 Buyer

1. **Beneficiary** Always write the seller's company name and address completely and correctly. A simple mistake here may result in the seller preparing inconsistent or improper documentation on the other end.

2. **Amount** State the actual amount of the credit. You may state a maximum amount in a situation where actual count or quantity is in question. You also may use the words APPROXIMATE, CIRCA, or ABOUT to indicate an acceptable 10 percent plus or minus amount from the stated amount. If you use such wording, you will need to be consistent and use it also in connection with the quantity as well.

3. **Validity Period** The validity and period for presentation of the documents following shipment of the goods should be sufficiently long to allow the exporter time to prepare the necessary documents and send them to the bank.

4. **Beneficiary's Bank** Either leave blank to indicate that the issuing bank may freely select the correspondent bank or name the seller's bank.

5. **Type of Payment Availability** Sight drafts, time drafts, or deferred payment may be used, as previously agreed to by the seller and buyer.

6. **Desired Documents** The buyer specifies which documents are needed. Buyer can list, for example, a bill of lading, a commercial invoice, a certificate of origin, certificates of analysis, and so on.

7. **Notify Address** An address is given for notification of the imminent arrival of goods at the port or airport of destination. This address can also be used for notification of damage to the shipment while en route. The buyer's business or shipping agent is most often used.

8. **Merchandise Description** A short, precise description of the goods is given, along with quantity. Note the comments in number two above concerning approximate amounts.

9. **Confirmation Order** If the foreign beneficiary (exporter) insists on having the credit confirmed by a bank in his or her country it will be so noted in this space.

Sender

Argentine Trading Company
Lavalle 1716, Piso 2
1048 Buenos Aires
Argentina

Our reference   AB/02

**Instructions
to open a Documentary Credit**

Buenos Aires, 30th September 19..
Place / Date

Please open the following

[X] irrevocable   [ ] revocable documentary credit

Argentine Bank Corporation
Documentary Credits
P.O. Box 1040

Buenos Aires, Argentina

Beneficiary

① American Import-Export Co., Inc.
123 Main Street
San Francisco, California
USA

Beneficiary's bank (if known)

④ US Domestic Bank
525 Main Street
San Francisco, CA   94105
USA

Amount
② US$1,250,000.--

Date and place of expiry
③ 25th November 19.. in San Francisco

Please advise this bank
[ ] by letter
[X] by letter, cabling main details in advance
[ ] by telex / telegram with full text of credit

Partial shipments
[X] allowed   [ ] not allowed

Transhipment
[ ] allowed   [X] not allowed

Terms of shipment (FOB, C & F, CIF)
CIF Buenos Aires

Despatch from / Taking in charge at
Oakland

For transportation to
Buenos Aires

Latest date of shipment
10th Nov. 19..

Documents must be presented not later than
③ 15 days after date of despatch

Beneficiary may dispose of the credit amount as follows ⑤

[X] at sight upon presentation of documents
[ ] after ....days, calculated from date of ....

[ ] by a draft due ....

drawn on   [ ] you   [ ] your correspondents

which you / your correspondents will please accept

against surrender of the following documents ⑥

[X] invoice   (....3......copies)

Shipping document
[X] sea: bill of lading, to order, endorsed in blank
[ ] rail: dublicate waybill
[ ] air: air consignment note
[ ]

[X] insurance policy, certificte covering the following risks: (................ copies)
   "all risks" including war up to
[ ] Additional documents final destination in
     Argentina
[X] Confirmation of the carrier that the ship is not more than 15 years old
[X] packing list (3 copies)

Notify address in bill of lading / goods addressed to ⑦

Argentine Trading Company
Lavalle 1716, Piso 2
1048 Buenos Aires   Argentina

Goods insured by   [ ] us   [X] seller

Goods ⑧

1,000 "Computers model 486 as per pro forma invoice
      no. 74/1853 dd 10th September 19.."

      at US$1,250.00 per unit

Your correspondents to advise beneficiary [ ] adding their confirmation [X] without adding their confirmation ⑨
Payments to be debited to our U.S. Dollars ....account no 10-32679150

NB. The applicable text is marked by [X]

Argentine Trading Company

Signature _____

For mailing please see overleaf

L/C

Details on Parties and Procedures

 ### The Buyer (Importer/Applicant)

Since a documentary credit is a pledge by the bank to make payment to the seller, the bank will want to evaluate the creditworthiness of the buyer. If the buyer's credit and relationship with the bank is excellent, the bank will issue a credit for the full value. If the buyer's relationship is good, but perhaps not excellent, the bank will require that the buyer pledge a percentage of the value of the documentary credit in cash funds. If the buyer's relationship with the bank is less established, the bank will require that they buyer pledge 100 percent of the value of the documentary credit in cash funds in advance.

It is essential that the application for the documentary credit be in conformity with the underlying sales contract between the buyer and the seller. The buyer's instructions to the issuing bank must be clear with respect to the type of credit, the amount, duration, required documents, shipping date, expiration date, and beneficiary.

 ### The Issuing (Buyer's) Bank

Upon receiving the buyer's application, the opening bank checks the credit of the applicant, determines whether cash security is necessary, and scrutinizes the contents of the application to see whether they generally are consistent with national and international banking and legal requirements. If the application is satisfactory to the bank, the buyer and the opening bank will sign an agreement to open a documentary credit. The credit must be written and signed by an authorized person of the issuing bank.

The issuing bank usually sends the original documentary credit to the seller (called the beneficiary) through an advising bank, which may be a branch or correspondent bank of the issuing (opening) bank. The seller may request that a particular bank be the advising bank, or the buyer's bank may select one of its correspondent banks in the seller's country.

L
/
C

The Advising (Seller's) Bank

Upon receipt of the credit from the issuing bank, the advising bank informs the seller that the credit has been issued.

The advising bank will examine the credit upon receipt. The advising bank, however, examines the terms of the credit itself; it does not determine whether the terms of the credit are consistent with those of the contract between the buyer and seller, or whether the description of goods is correctly stated in accordance with the contract. The advising bank then forwards the credit to the seller.

If the advising bank is simply "advising the credit," it is under no obligation or commitment to make payment, and it will so advise the seller. In some cases the advising bank confirms (adds its guarantee to pay) the seller. In this case it becomes the confirming bank.

If the advising bank confirms the credit it must pay without recourse to the seller when the documents are presented, provided they are in order and the credit requirements are met.

The Seller/Exporter/Beneficiary

In addition to assessing the reputation of the buyer prior to signing a sales contract, the seller should also assess the reputation of the buyer's (issuing) bank before agreeing to rely upon that bank for payment in a documentary credit. It is not unknown for sellers to receive fictitious documentary credits from non-existent banks and to realize their mistake after shipment.

The seller must carefully review all conditions the buyer has stipulated in the documentary credit. If the seller cannot comply with one or more of the provisions, or if the terms of the credit are not in accordance with those of the contract, the buyer should be notified immediately and asked to make an amendment to the credit.

The seller should also scrutinize the credit to make certain that it does not contain provisions that specify documents such as acceptance reports, progress reports, etc. that have to be signed or approved by the buyer. By refusing to sign such documents, the buyer can block payment.

After reaching agreement, the seller is well-advised to provide the buyer with a sample of the final product specified in the credit for confirmation of quality, suitability, etc.

Complying With the Documentary Credit

 Seller/Exporter/Beneficiary

Upon receipt of the documentary credit, the seller should immediately and carefully examine it to ensure it conforms with the original sales contract with the buyer and that all the conditions stated in the credit can be met. If any of its conditions have to be amended, which can be time-consuming, the seller should immediately contact the buyer.

Examining the Documentary Credit

The following is a checklist for the seller's examination of the credit:

1. The buyer's and seller's names and addresses are correct. ❏

2. The amount of the credit is in accordance with the contract, including unit prices, shipping charges, handling costs, and total invoice amounts. ❏

3. The merchandise description is consistent with the sales contract. ❏

4. The credit's payment availability agrees with the contract conditions. ❏

5. The shipping, expiration, and presentation dates allow sufficient time for processing the order, shipping the merchandise, and preparing the documents for presentation to the bank. ❏

6. Partial or transshipments are specified correctly. ❏

7. The point of dispatch, taking charge of the goods, loading on board, or of discharge at final destination are as agreed. ❏

8. Insurance coverage and party to pay charges are as agreed.

9. Instructions on whom the drafts are to be drawn, and in what tenor (maturity dates), are correct. ❏

10. The credit is confirmed or unconfirmed as agreed. ❏

11. There are no unacceptable conditions. ❏

12. The specified documents can be obtained in the form required. ❏

13. The issuing (or confirming) bank is known to the seller. ❏

Revocable vs. Irrevocable Documentary Credits

Documentary credits may be issued by the buyer and issuing bank as revocable or irrevocable. (The buyer must indicate either revocable or irrevocable on the application form to the issuing bank.) Each has a distinct advantage for buyers and sellers.

Revocable Credit

A revocable documentary credit gives the buyer and/or issuing bank the ability to amend or cancel the credit at any time right up to the moment of intended payment without approval by, or notice to, the seller. Revocable credits are, therefore, of great advantage to the buyer.

Revocable credits are, conversely, of great disadvantage to the seller as the credit may be canceled at any time, even while the goods are in transit, giving the seller no security whatsoever. Although revocable credits are sometimes used between affiliated firms, sellers are advised never to accept a revocable credit as a payment method.

Irrevocable Credit

An irrevocable documentary credit constitutes a firm contractual obligation on the part of the issuing bank to honor the terms of payment of the credit as issued. The buyer and issuing bank cannot amend or cancel the credit without the express approval of the seller.

Irrevocable credits are of advantage to the seller. As long as the seller complies with the terms of the credit, payment will be made by the issuing bank. Virtually all documentary credits issued today are irrevocable and so state on their face (on the face of the documentary credit itself). Sellers are advised to insist upon an irrevocable credit from the buyer.

Confirmed vs. Unconfirmed Documentary Credits

Payment under an irrevocable documentary credit is guaranteed by the issuing bank. However, from the seller's perspective, this guarantee may have limited value as the issuing bank may be (1) in a foreign country, (2) beholden to the buyer, (3) small and unknown to the seller, or (4) subject to unknown foreign exchange control restrictions. The seller, therefore, might wish that another, more local bank add its guarantee (confirmation) of payment to that of the issuing bank.

Within the category of irrevocable credits there are two further options for the buyer and seller. These are the irrevocable unconfirmed credit and the irrevocable confirmed credit. Once again, each has a distinct advantage for buyers and sellers.

Unconfirmed (or Advised) Documentary Credit

Under an unconfirmed documentary credit only the issuing bank assumes the undertaking to pay, thus payment is the sole responsibility of the issuing bank. An unconfirmed documentary credit will be communicated (advised) to the seller through a bank most likely located in the seller's country, and the related shipping and other documents will usually be presented to that bank for eventual payment. However, the final responsibility for payment rests with the issuing bank alone. The advising bank may or may not negotiate the seller's draft depending on the degree of political and financial risk anticipated in the issuing bank's country, as well as the credit standing of the issuing bank.

In dealing with a readily identifiable issuing bank in a developed country, an unconfirmed documentary credit is very probably an acceptable, safe instrument for most sellers. If you have any doubt about the issuing bank and its standing, you can check the name through a local bank with an international department.

L/C

Note: Some countries (most notably China) do not permit confirmation of letters of credit issued by their banks, deeming that the credit of their national financial institutions should not be questioned by others.

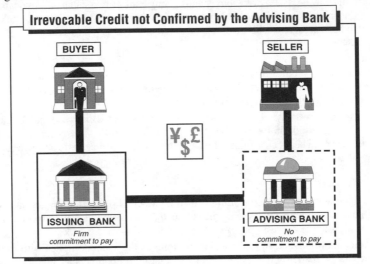

Confirmed Documentary Credit

Confirmed letters of credit carry the commitment to pay of both the issuing and the advising banks. The advising bank adds its undertaking to pay to that of the issuing bank, and its commitment is independent of that of the issuing bank. Therefore, when documents conforming to the requirements of the confirmed documentary credit are presented in a timely manner, the payment from the advising bank to the seller is final in all respects as far as the seller is concerned.

Confirmed, irrevocable letters of credit give the seller the greatest protection, since sellers can rely on the commitment of two banks to make payment. The confirming bank will pay even if the issuing bank cannot or will not honor the draft for any reason whatever. In accordance with the additional risk assumed by the banks, however, confirmed, irrevocable letters of credit are more expensive than unconfirmed letters of credit. Confirmed, irrevocable letters of credit are used most frequently in transactions involving buyers in developing countries.

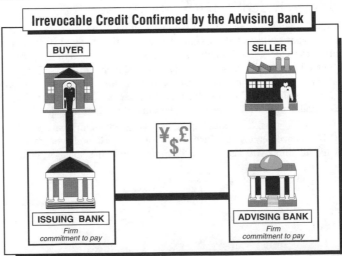

Special Letters of Credits

There are several special credits designed to meet the specific needs of buyers, suppliers, and intermediaries. Special credits involve increased participation by banks, so financing and service charges are higher. Each of the credits listed below is explained in greater detail in the pages that follow.

Standby Credit

Standby credits are often called nonperforming letters of credit because they are only used if the collection on a primary payment method is past due. Standby credits can be used to guarantee repayment of loans, fulfillment by subcontractors, and securing the payment for goods delivered by third parties.

Revolving Credit

This is a commitment on the part of the issuing bank to restore the credit to the original amount after it has been used or drawn down. This credit is used in cases where a buyer wishes to have certain quantities of the ordered goods delivered at specified intervals, such as in a multiple delivery contract.

Red Clause Credit

A red clause credit has a special clause (red clause) that authorizes the confirming bank to make advances to the beneficiary (seller) prior to the presentation of the shipping documents. In this credit the buyer, in essence, extends financing to the seller and incurs ultimate risk for all sums advanced under the credit.

Transferable Credit

A transferable credit is one where the original beneficiary transfers all or part of the proceeds of an existing credit to another party (typically the ultimate supplier of the goods). It is normally used by middlemen as a financing tool.

Back-to-BackCcredit

This is a new credit opened on the basis of an already existing, nontransferable credit. It is used by traders to make payment to the ultimate supplier. A trader receives a documentary credit from the buyer and then opens another documentary credit in favor of the ultimate supplier. The first documentary credit is used as collateral for the second credit. The second credit makes price adjustments from which comes the trader's profit.

L/C

Guide to Ocean Freight Containers

Introduction

The following Guide to Ocean Freight Container Specifications is provided courtesy of Hapag-Lloyd America Inc. The container specifications listed are virtually standardized world-wide. However, the possibility exists that individual container manufacturers and shipping lines will have container specifications which vary somewhat from those listed in this section. Be certain to inquire about precise specifications from your shipping line or forwarder when you arrange for a shipment.

Values / Details

All values listed in the tables are given in metric. Ft and lbs values are for easy reference only.

All details listed are nominal figures. Apart from the tolerances given on internal dimensions below the tare weight can vary +/- 2%.

General Information

External and Minimum Internal Dimensions

The following table gives the overall external dimensions as standardized in ISO 668 and the minimum internal dimensions and door openings for General Purpose Containers as standardized in ISO 1496-1.

	Length		Width		Height		
Dimensions	20' 6,058 mm	40' 12,192 mm	8' 2,438 mm	8'6" 2,438 mm	8'6" 2,438 mm	9'6" 2,896 mm
Minimum Internal Dimensions	5,867 mm 19'3"	11,998 mm 39' 4 3/8"	2,330 mm 7'7 3/4"	2,197 mm 7'2 1/2"	2,350 mm 7'8 1/2"	2,655 mm 8'8 1/2"
Minimun Door Opening Dimensions	-	-	2,286 mm 7'6"	2,134 mm 7'	2,261 mm 7'5"	2,566 mm 8'5"

Internal Dimensions

The internal dimensions and door openings of most containers exceed the above given dimensions. However, the dimensions mentioned on the following pages are nominal figures. Because of production tolerances a difference in measurements is possible:

Tolerances	Length	Width	Height
Maximum Difference	10 mm 3/8"	10 mm 3/8"	10 mm 3/8"

Maximum Gross Weights

20' containers:

24,000 kg (52,910 lbs) according to the latest issue of ISO 668;

30, 480 kg (67,200 lbs) valid for most Hapag-Lloyd 20' containers; exceeds ISO minimum standards.

40' containers:

30,480 kg (67,200 lbs).

Floor Loads

A container floor is capable of carrying a fork-lift truck with a maximum axle load of 5,460 kg (12,040 lbs), if the contact area per wheel is at least 142 cm2 (22 sq.in) (ISO 1496/I).

Concentrated Loads

When stowing heavy cargo in containers other than flats or platforms due care has to be taken that concentrated loads will not exceed the strength of the bottom construction of the container.

The maximum spreaded load should not exceed

—for 20' containers 4 ts per running meter in length (3' 3.5")

—for 40' containers 3 ts per running meter in length.

Gooseneck Tunnel on 40' Containers

All Hapag-Lloyd 40' containers are fitted with a Gooseneck tunnel to enable the transport on Gooseneck chassis.

Timber Treatment

Exposed timber is treated according to Australian requirements (exceptions: 40' flats and platforms).

General Purpose Container   20'

- Suitable for any general cargo.
- Containers may be equipped with liner bags suitable for bulk cargo, e.g. malt.
- Fork-lift pockets on a number of containers.
- Various lashing devices on the top and bottom longitudinal rails and the corner posts.
  Lashing devices have a permissible load of 1,000 kg (2,205 lbs) each.
- Note permissable weight limits for road and rail transport.

General Purpose Container   20'

Construction	Inside Dimensions			Door Opening		Weights			Capacity
	Length	Width	Height	Width	Height	Max. Gross	Tare	Max. Payload	
	mm ft	mm ft	mm ft	mm ft	mm ft	kg lbs	kg lbs	kg lbs	m³ cu.ft.
8'6" high									
Steel container with corrugated walls and wooden floor	5,895 19'4¹/₈"	2,350 7'8¹/₂"	2,392 7'10¹/₈"	2,340 7'8¹/₈"	2,292 7'6¹/₄"	30,480 67,200	2,250 4,960	28,230 62,240	33.2 1,172
	5,895 19'4"	2,350 7'8¹/₂"	2,385 7'9⁷/₈"	2,338 7'8"	2,292 7'6¹/₄"	24,000 52,910	2,250 4,960	21,750 47,950	33.2 1,172
	5,879 19'3³/₈"	2,330 7'7³/₄"	2,370 7'9¹/₄"	2,330 7'7³/₄"	2,290 7'6¹/₈"	24,000 52,910	2,250 4,960	21,750 47,950	33.0 1,165
	5,889 19'3⁷/₈"	2,346 7'8³/₈"	2,372 7'9³/₈"	2,330 7'7³/₄"	2,272 7'5¹/₂"	24,000 52,910	2,360 5,200	21,640 47,710	32.8 1,158
	5,885 19'4"	2,350 7'8¹/₂"	2,403 7'10⁵/₈"	2,338 7'8"	2,292 7'6¹/₄"	24,000 52,910	2,150 4,740	21,850 48,170	33.15 1,170
	5,884 19'3⁵/₈"	2,335 7'8"	2,390 7'10"	2,335 7'8"	2,292 7'6¹/₄"	24,000 52,910	2,200 4,850	21,800 48,060	33.1 1,169
	5,899 19'4¹/₄"	2,350 7'8¹/₂"	2,394 7'10¹/₄"	2,338 7'8"	2,280 7'5³/₄"	24,000 52,910	2,180 4,810	21,820 48,100	33.2 1,172
	5,891 19'3⁷/₈"	2,330 7'7³/₄"	2,376 7'9¹/₂"	2,330 7'7³/₄"	2,272 7'5¹/₂"	24,000 52,910	2,300 5,070	21,700 47,840	33.0 1,165
	5,880 19'3¹/₂"	2,330 7'7³/₄"	2,380 7'9⁵/₈"	2,330 7'7³/₄"	2,275 7'5¹/₂"	24,000 52,910	2,300 5,070	21,700 47,840	33.0 1,165

OCEAN

**O
C
E
A
N**

General Purpose Container   40'

- Suitable for any general cargo.
- Various lashing devices on the top and bottom longitudinal rails and the corner posts.
  Lashing devices have a permissible load of 1,000 kg (2,205 lbs) each.

- Note permissable weight limits for road and rail transport.

General Purpose Container   40'

Construction	Inside Dimensions			Door Opening		Weights			Capacity
	Length	Width	Height	Width	Height	Max. Gross	Tare	Max. Payload	
	mm ft	mm ft	mm ft	mm ft	mm ft	kg lbs	kg lbs	kg lbs	m³ cu.ft.
8'6" high									
Steel container with corrugated walls and wooden floor	12,029 39'5½"	2,350 7'8½"	2,392 7'10⅛"	2,340 7'8½"	2,292 7'6¼"	30,480 67,200	3,780 8,330	26,700 58,870	67.7 2,390
	12,024 39'5⅜"	2,350 7'8½"	2,387 7'10"	2,340 7'8⅛"	2,292 7'6¼"	30,480 67,200	3,810 8,400	26,670 58,800	67.7 2,390
	12,033 39'5¾"	2,350 7'8½"	2,394 7'10¼"	2,338 7'8"	2,280 7'5¾"	30,480 67,200	3,800 8,377	26,680 58,823	67.7 2,390

High Cube General Purpose Container   40'

9'6"
2.9m

- Especially for light, voluminous cargo and overheight cargo up to maximum 2.70 m (8'10¹/₄") (see table).

- Numerous lashing devices on the top and bottom longitudinal rails and the corner posts.

- Lashing devices have a permissible load of 1,000 kg (2,205 lbs) each.

- Consider overheight for inland transportation.

- Note permissable weight limits for road and rail transport.

High Cube General Purpose Container   40'

Construction	Inside Dimensions			Door Opening		Weights			Capacity
	Length	Width	Height	Width	Height	Max. Gross	Tare	Max. Payload	
	mm ft	mm ft	mm ft	mm ft	mm ft	kg lbs	kg lbs	kg lbs	m³ cu.ft.
9'6" high									
Steel container with corrugated walls and wooden floor	12,024 39'5³/₈"	2,350 7'8¹/₂"	2,697 8'10¹/₈"	2,340 7'8¹/₈"	2,597 8'6¹/₄"	30,480 67,200	4,020 8,860	26,460 58,340	76.3 2,694
	12,024 39'5³/₈"	2,350 7'8¹/₂"	2,697 8'10¹/₈"	2,338 7'8"	2,585 8'5³/₄"	30,480 67,200	4,020 8,860	26,460 58,340	76.3 2,694

Hardtop Container   20'

- This container type has been especially designed and developed for
  —heavy loads
  —high and excessively high loads
  —loading, e.g. by crane, through roof opening and door side.
- The steel roof of some series is lifted with fork-lift rings so that it can be removed by using a fork-lift. The weight of the steel roof is approx. 450 kg (990 lbs).
- With the roof removed and the door header swung out, it is much easier to load cargo using a crane via the door side.
- In case your cargo is overheight, the roof sections can be lashed to a sidewall inside the container using only some 13 cm (5 1/8") of space.
- If required, disposable tarpaulins can be provided for the transport which can be fastened to the walls on the outside using lashing devices.
- The capacity of the container floor exceeds the ISO 1496/1 standard by 33%, so that a fork-lift whose front axle weight does not exceed 7,280 kg (16,000 lbs) can be used inside.
- The hardtop container provides many lashing devices to fasten goods. The lashing devices on the corner posts and on the longitudinal rails of the roof and floor are capable of bearing loads of up to 2,000 kg (4,410 lbs) each, and those in the middle of the side walls up to 500 kg (1,100 lbs) each. Lashing to the side walls can only be done after the roof has been closed.
- This container type has been designed for heavy loads. While considering the technical data (including the permissible spreaded load limitations) please bear in mind the prevalent weight restrictions for land transport.
- Note permissable weight limits for road and rail transport.

Hardtop Container   20'

Construction	Inside Dimensions				Weights			Capacity
	Length	Width	Height		Max.	Tare	Max.	
			Middle	Side	Gross		Payload	
	mm ft	mm ft	mm ft	mm ft	kg lbs	kg lbs	kg lbs	m³ cu.ft.

8'6" high

Construction	Length	Width	Middle	Side	Gross	Tare	Payload	Capacity
Steel container with corrugated walls and wooden floor	5,886 19'3³/₄"	2,342 7'8¹/₈"	2,388 7'10"	2,313 7'7"	30,480 67,200	2,700 5,950	27,780 61,250	32.8 1,160
	5,886 19'3³/₄"	2,342 7'8¹/₈"	2,388 7'10"	2,313 7'7"	30,480 67,200	2,700 5,950	27,780 61,250	32.8 1,160
	5,886 19'3³/₄"	2,342 7'8¹/₈"	2,375 7'9¹/₂"	2,330 7'7³/₄"	30,480 67,200	2,590 5,710	27,890 61,490	32.8 1,160
	5,871 19'3¹/₈"	2,338 7'8"	2,390 7'10"	2,335 7'8"	24,000 52,910	2,580 5,690	21,420 47,220	32.8 1,158

Roof Opening

Door Opening

Hardtop Container Roof Openings   20'

Roof Openings		Door Openings					Roof Inside Container		
Length	Width	Width			Height		Reduced Width		
B Between Gusset Plates mm ft	C Max. Width mm ft	F Max. Width mm ft	G At Door Header mm ft	H Between Top Lon- gitudinal Rails mm ft	I Up to Door Header mm ft	K Up to Top Longitudi- nal Rail mm ft	Inside Width mm ft	Width of Roof Opening mm ft	Width of Door Opening mm ft
5,590 18'4"	2,208 7'2⁷/₈"	2,336 7'8"	1,896 6'2⁵/₈"	2,208 7'2⁷/₈"	2,276 7'5⁵/₈"	2,220 7'³/₈"	2,209 7'3"	2,142 7'¹/₄"	2,206 7'2⁷/₈"
5,590 18'4"	2,208 7'2⁷/₈"	2,336 7'8"	1,896 6'2⁵/₈"	2,208 7'2⁷/₈"	2,292 7'6¹/₄"	2,220 7'³/₈"	2,209 7'3"	2,142 7'¹/₄"	2,206 7'2⁷/₈"
5,590 18'4"	2,208 7'2⁷/₈"	2,336 7'8"	1,896 6'2⁵/₈"	2,208 7'2⁷/₈"	2,280 7'5³/₄"	2,231 7'3³/₄"	2,215 7'3¹/₈"	2,148 7'¹/₂"	2,212 7'3"
5,616 18'5¹/₈"	2,206 7'2⁷/₈"	2,335 7'8"	1,890 6'2³/₈"	2,206 7'2⁷/₈"	2,292 7'6¹/₄"	2,225 7'3¹/₂"	2,250 7'4¹/₂"	2,180 7'1³/₄"	2,250 7'4¹/₂"

OCEAN

Hardtop Container   40'

- The 40' hardtop container has particularly been constructed for:
  - —long loads which cannot be transport-ed in the 20' hardtop container
  - —heavy loads
  - —high and excessively high loads
  - —loading, e.g. by crane, through roof opening and door side.
- The roof can be removed by using a fork-lift. The weight of the steel roof is approx. 450 kg (990 lbs) each section.
- With the roof removed and the door-header swung out, it is much easier to load cargo using a crane via the door side.
- In case your cargo is overheight, the roof sections can be lashed to a sidewall inside the container using only some 13 cm (5 $1/_8$") of space.
- If required, disposable tarpaulins can be provided for the transport which can be fastened to the walls on the outside using lashing devices.
- The capacity of the container floor exceeds the ISO 1496/1 standard by 33%, so that a fork-lift whose front axle weight does not exceed 7,280 kg (16,000 lbs) can be used inside.

- The hardtop container provides many lashing devices to fasten goods. The lashing devices on the corner posts and on the longitudinal rails of the roof and floor are capable of bearing loads of up to 2,000 kg (4,410 lbs) each, and those in the middle of the side walls up to 500 kg (1,100 lbs) each. Lashing to the side walls can only be done after the roof has been closed.
- The roof can easily be raised by about 70 mm (2 $3/_4$"), using the roof locking devices so that the door-header can be swung out without removing the roof.
- This container type has been designed for heavy loads. While considering the technical data (including the permissible spreaded load limitations) please bear in mind the prevalent weight restrictions for land transport.
- Note permissable weight limits for road and rail transport.

OCEAN

Hardtop Container   40'

Construction	Inside Dimensions				Weights			Capacity
	Length	Width	Height		Max.	Tare	Max.	
			Middle	Side	Gross		Payload	
	mm ft	mm ft	mm ft	mm ft	kg lbs	kg lbs	kg lbs	m³ cu.ft.

8'6" high

Construction	Length mm/ft	Width mm/ft	Height Middle mm/ft	Height Side mm/ft	Gross kg/lbs	Tare kg/lbs	Payload kg/lbs	Capacity m³/cu.ft.
Steel container with corrugated walls and wooden floor	12,020 39'5¼"	2,342 7'8⅛"	2,388 7'10"	2,313 7'7"	30,480 67,200	4,700 10,360	25,780 56,840	67.2 2,374
	12,020 39'5¼"	2,342 7'8⅛"	2,388 7'10"	2,313 7'7"	30,480 67,200	4,700 10,360	25,780 56,840	67.2 2,374

Roof Opening

Door Opening

removable door header

Hardtop Container   40'

Roof Openings		Door Openings					Roof Inside Container		
Length	Width	Width			Height		Reduced Width		
B Between Gusset Plates mm ft	C Max. Width mm ft	F Max. Width mm ft	G At Door Header mm ft	H Between Top Lon- gitudinal Rails mm ft	I Up to Door Header mm ft	K Up to Top Longitudi- nal Rail mm ft	Inside Width mm ft	Width of Roof Opening mm ft	Width of Door Opening mm ft
11,724 38'5"	2,208 7'2⅞"	2,336 7'8"	1,896 6'2⅝"	2,208 7'2⅞"	2,292 7'6¼"	2,220 7'3⅜"	2,209 7'3"	2,142 7'⅜"	2,206 7'2⅞"
11,724 38'5"	2,208 7'2⅞"	2,336 7'8"	1,896 6'2⅝"	2,208 7'2⅞"	2,276 7'5⅝"	2,220 7'3⅜"	2,209 7'3"	2,142 7'⅜"	2,206 7'2⅞"

Open Top Container   20'

- Especially for:
  - overheight cargo
  - loading from top side, e.g. by crane
  - loading from door side, e.g. with cargo hanging from overhead tackle.
- Door header can be swung out on all open top containers.
- If required, disposable tarpaulins can be provided. For fastening tarpaulins, lashing bars are available on the outside of the walls. Using one way tarpaulins requires the corner castings to be accessible.
- Fork-lift pockets on a number of containers (please see footnote 1).
- The capacity of the floor for use of fort-lift trucks exceeds the ISO standards by 33% on all 20' open top containers.
- Numerous lashing devices are located on the top and bottom longitudinal rails and the corner posts. Lashing devices have a permissible load of 1,000 kg (2,205 lbs) each.
- Dimensions of roof and door openings are on the next page.
- Note permissable weight limits for road and rail transport.

Open Top Container Dimensions   20'

Construction	Inside Dimensions				Weights			Capacity
	Length	Width	Height		Max.	Tare	Max.	
			Middle	Side	Gross		Payload	
	mm ft	mm ft	mm ft	mm ft	kg lbs	kg lbs	kg lbs	m³ cu.ft.

8'6" high

Construction	Length	Width	Middle	Side	Gross	Tare	Payload	Capacity
Steel container with corrugated walls, removable tarpaulin and wooden floor	5,895 19'4"	2,350 7'8½"	2,394 7'10¼"	2,364 7'9"	24,000 52,910	2,100 4,630	21,900 48,280	32.45 1,146
	5,877 19'3³/₈"	2,335 7'8"	2,369 7'9¼"	2,309 7'6⁷/₈"	24,000 52,910	2,200 4,850	21,800 48,060	32.4 1,140
	5,895 19'4"	2,330 7'7³/₄"	2,329 7'7³/₄"	—	24,000 52,910	2,200 4,850	21,800 48,060	32.0 1,130
	5,888 19'3³/₄"	2,345 7'8¹/₈"	2,365 7'9"	2,315 7'7¹/₈"	30,480 67,200	2,250 4,960	28,230 62,240	32.0 1,130

Roll and Door Openings of Open Top Containers   20'

Types:

Door Openings:

Roof Openings:

Roof and Door Openings of Open Top Containers   20'

	Roof Openings					Door Openings				
	Length		Width			Width			Height	
Type	A Max. Length	B Between Gusset Plates	C Max. Width	D Front End between Gusset Plates	E Door End, between Gusset Plates	F Max. Width	G At Door Header	H Between Top Longitudinal Rails	I Up to Door Header	K Up to Top Longitudinal Rail
	mm ft	mm ft	mm ft	mm ft	mm ft	mm ft	mm ft	mm ft	mm ft	mm ft
Z	5,583 18'3³/₄"	5,488 18"	2,230 7'3³/₄"	1,928 6'3⁷/₈"	—	2,335 7'8"	1,928 6'3⁷/₈"	2,230 7'3³/₄"	2,291 7'6¹/₄"	2,194 7'2³/₈"
Z	5,660 18'6⁷/₈"	5,440 17'10¹/₈"	2,208 7'2⁷/₈"	1,860 6'1¹/₄"	—	2,335 7'8"	1,848 6³/₄"	2,208 7'2⁷/₈"	2,290 7'6¹/₈"	1,889 6'2³/₈"
Z	5,770 18'11¹/₈"	5,452 17'10⁵/₈"	2,232 7'3⁷/₈"	—	1,904 6'3"	2,305 7'6³/₄"	1,834 6¹/₈"	2,208 7'3⁷/₈"	2,218 7'3¹/₄"	2,033 6'8"
Z	5,415 17'9¹/₈"	5,360 17'7"	2,205 7'2³/₄"	—	1,880 6'2"	2,335 7'8"	1,880 6'2"	2,205 7'2³/₄"	2,280 7'5³/₄"	2,125 6'11⁵/₈"

O
C
E
A
N

Open Top Container   40'

- Especially for:
  - —overheight cargo
  - —loading from top side, e.g. by crane
  - —loading from door side, e.g. with cargo hanging from overhead tackle.
- Door header can be swung out on all open top containers.
- If required, disposable tarpaulins can be provided. For fastening tarpaulins, lashing bars are available on the outside of the walls. Using one way tarpaulins requires the corner castings to be accessible.

- The capacity of the floor for use of fort-lift trucks exceeds the ISO standards by 33% on all 40' open top containers.
- Numerous lashing devices are located on the top and bottom longitudinal rails and the corner posts.
  Lashing devices have a permissible load of 1,000 kg (2,205 lbs) each.
- Dimensions of roof and door openings follow in two pages.
- Note permissable weight limits for road and rail transport.

Open Top Container Dimensions   40'

Construction	Inside Dimensions				Weights			Capacity
	Length	Width	Height		Max.	Tare	Max.	
			Middle	Side	Gross		Payload	
	mm ft	mm ft	mm ft	mm ft	kg lbs	kg lbs	kg lbs	m³ cu.ft.

8'6" high

Construction	Length	Width	Middle	Side	Gross	Tare	Payload	Capacity
Steel container with corrugated walls, removable tarpaulin and wooden floor	12,023 39'5³/₈"	2,335 7'8"	2,378 7'9⁵/₈"	2,318 7'7¹/₄"	30,480 67,200	3,800 8,380	26,680 58,820	66.7 2,354
	12,038 39'5⁷/₈"	2,338 7'8"	2,363 7'9"	2,313 7'7¹/₈"	30,480 67,200	3,650 8,050	26,830 59,150	66.7 2,354
	12,025 39'5¹/₂"	2,330 7'7³/₄"	2,360 7'8⁷/₈"	2,325 7'7¹/₂"	30,480 67,200	3,890 8,580	26,590 58,620	66.0 2,330
	12,038 39'5⁷/₈"	2,336 7'8"	2,370 7'9¹/₄"	2,320 7'7¹/₄"	30,480 67,197	3,700 8,157	26,780 59,040	65.3 2,306
	12,029 39'5¹/₂"	2,342 7'8¹/₈"	2,376 7'9¹/₂"	2,326 7'7¹/₂"	30,480 67,200	3,810 8,400	26,670 58,800	65.5 2,310
	12,022 39'5¹/₄"	2,346 7'8³/₈"	2,365 7'9¹/₈"	2,315 7'7¹/₈"	30,480 67,200	3,740 8,250	26,740 58,950	65.3 2,306
	12,007 39'4³/₄"	2,315 7'7¹/₈"	2,362 7'9"	2,317 7'7¹/₄"	30,480 67,200	3,950 8,710	26,530 58,490	65.0 2,295
	12,005 39'4⁵/₈"	2,330 7'7³/₄"	2,380 7'9⁵/₈"	2,340 7'8¹/₈"	30,480 67,200	4,350 9,590	26,130 57,610	65.5 2,315

OCEAN

Roof and Door Openings of Open Top Containers   **40'**

Roof and Door Openings of Open Top Containers   40'

Type	Roof Openings					Door Openings				
	Length		Width			Width			Height	
	A Max. Length	B Between Gusset Plates	C Max. Width	D Front End between Gusset Plates	E Door End, between Gusset Plates	F Max. Width	G At Door Header	H Between Top Lon- gitudinal Rails	I Up to Door Header	K Up to Top Longitu- dinal Rail
	mm ft	mm ft	mm ft	mm ft	mm ft	mm ft	mm ft	mm ft	mm ft	mm ft
Z	11,800 38'8⅝"	11,317 37'1½"	2,205 7'2¾"	1,728 5'8"	—	2,335 7'8"	1,840 6'1½"	2,205 7'2¾"	2,287 7'6"	1,889 6'2⅜"
Z	11,787 38'8"	11,563 37'11¼"	2,208 7'2⅞"	1,850 6'⅞"	—	2,335 7'8"	1,844 6'⅝"	2,208 7'2⅞"	2,287 7'6"	1,896 6'2⅝"
X	11,917 39'1⅛"	10,837 35'6⅝"	2,128 6'11¾"	1,600 5'3"	1,816 5'11½"	2,330 7'7¾"	1,816 5'11½"	2,128 6'11⅞"	2,201 7'2⅝"	1,957 6'5"
Y	—	11,550 37'10⅝"	2,220 7'3⅜"	—	—	2,336 7'8"	1,845 6'⅝"	2,220 7'3⅜"	2,292 7'6¼"	2,125 6'11⅝"
Z	11,544 37'10½"	11,444 37'6½"	2,230 7'3¾"	—	1,885 6'2⅛"	2,336 7'8"	1,885 6'2⅛"	2,230 7'3¾"	2,280 7'5¾"	2,146 7'1½"
Z	11,550 37'10¾"	11,515 37'9⅜"	2,205 7'2¾"	—	1,880 6'2"	2,335 7'8"	1,880 6'2"	2,205 7'2¾"	2,280 7'5¾"	2,125 6'11⅝"
Y	—	11,379 37'4"	2,205 7'2¾"	—	—	2,315 7'7⅛"	1,855 6'1"	2,205 7'2¾"	2,266 7'5¼"	1,957 6'5"
X	11,825 38'9½"	11,496 37'8⅝"	2,100 6'10⅝"	1,774 5'9⅞"	1,774 5'9⅞"	2,335 7'8"	1,750 5'8⅞"	2,100 6'10⅝"	2,180 7'1¾"	2180 7'1¾"

Flat   40'

- Especially for heavy loads and overwidth cargo.
- Higher loadings possible.
- Strong bottom construction with fixed endwalls (which allow bracing and lashing of cargo as well as stacking).
- Gooseneck tunnel on both ends of 40' flats.
- Numerous very strong lashing devices on the corner posts, longitudinal rails and the floor. Lashing devices on the longitudinal rails and on the floor of 40' containers have a permissible load of 4,000 kg respectively (8,820 lbs) each.
- Maximum payload can only be used if distributed over the total floor area of the flat.
  If concentration of heavy load on a small part floor area is required please contact representative for stowage advice.
- Flats are delivered without stanchions. If stancions are required, please contact representative upon booking.
- Note permissable weight limits for road and rail transport.

OCEAN

Flat   40'

Construction	Inside Dimensions						Weights		
	Length of floor mm ft	Width between Corner Posts mm ft	Width of Floor mm ft	Width between Stanchions mm ft	Height mm ft	Height of Bottom mm ft	Max. Gross kg lbs	Tare kg lbs	Max. Payload kg lbs

8'6" high

Construction									
Steelframe with fixed endwalls and softwood floor	12,008 39'4³/₄"	11,712 38'5¹/₈"	2,318 7'7¹/₄"	2,232 7'3⁷/₈"	1,981 6'6"	610 2'	30,480 67,200	4,750 10,470	25,730 56,730
	11,990 39'4"	11,722 38'5¹/₂"	2,400 7'10¹/₂"	2,202 7'2³/₄"	1,981 6'6"	610 2'	30,480 67,200	5,100 11,240	25,380 55,960
	11,990 39'4"	11,758 38'6⁷/₈"	2,338 7'8"	2,228 7'3³/₄"	1,981 6'6"	610 2'	30,480 67,200	4,200 9,265	26,280 57,935
	12,010 39'4⁷/₈"	11,832 38'9⁷/₈"	2,228 7'3³/₄"	2,228 7'3³/₄"	1,981 6'6"	610 2'	30,480 67,200	4,200 9,265	26,280 57,935
	12,086 39'7⁷/₈"	11,826 38'9⁵/₈"	2,224 7'3¹/₂"	2,224 7'3¹/₂"	1,981 6'6"	610 2'	30,480 67,200	4,200 9,265	26,280 57,935
	12,010 39'4⁷/₈"	11,826 38'9⁵/₈"	2,244 7'4³/₈"	2,204 7'2³/₄"	1,981 6'6"	610 2'	30,480 67,200	4,200 9,265	26,280 57,935

9'6" high

Construction									
Steel container with collapsible endwalls and softwood floor	12,060 39'6³/₄"	11,660 38'3¹/₈"	2,365 7'9¹/₈"	2,200 7'2⁵/₈"	2,245 7'4³/₈"	648 2'1¹/₂"	45,000 99,210	5,700 12,570	39,300 86,640

Flat   20'

- Especially for heavy and overwidth cargo.
- Strong bottom construction with fixed endwalls (which allow bracing and lashing of cargo as well as stacking).
- Fork-lift pockets on a number of 20' flats
- Numerous very strong lashing devices on the corner posts, longitudinal rails and on the floor. Lashing devices on the longitudinal rails of 20' containers have a permissible load of 2,000 kg or 4,000 kg respectively (4,410 lbs or 8,820 lbs respectively) each.

- Maximum payload can only be used if distributed over the total floor area.
  If concentration of heavy load on a small part floor area is required please contact representative for stowage advice.
- Flats are delivered without stanchions. If stancions are required, please contact representative upon booking.
- Note permissable weight limits for road and rail transport.

Flat   20'

Construction	Inside Dimensions						Weights		
	Length of floor	Width between Corner Posts	Width of floor	Width between Stanchions	Height	Height of Bottom	Max. Gross	Tare	Max. Payload
	mm ft	mm ft	mm ft	mm ft	mm ft	mm ft	kg lbs	kg lbs	kg lbs
8' high									
Steelframe with fixed endwalls and softwood floor	5,918 19'5"	5,625 18'5³/₈"	2,398 7'10³/₈"	2,208 7'2⁷/₈"	2,172 7'1¹/₂"	265 10¹/₂"	24,000 52,910	2,800 6,170	21,200 46,740
8'6" high									
Steelframe with fixed endwalls and softwood floor	5,902 19'4³/₈"	5,700 18'8³/₈"	2,358 7'8⁷/₈"	2,235 7'4"	2,276 7'5⁵/₈"	315 1¹³/₈"	24,000 52,910	2,720 6,000	21,280 46,910
	5,980 19'7³/₈"	5,698 18'8³/₈"	2,230 7'3³/₈"	2,245 7'4³/₄"	2,255 7'4³/₄"	336 1¹¹/₄"	24,000 52,910	2,500 5,510	21,500 47,400
	5,962 19'6³/₄"	5,672 18'7¹/₄"	2,242 7'4¹/₄"	2,242 7'4¹/₄"	2,261 7'5"	330 1'1"	30,000 66,140	2,200 4,850	27,800 61,290
Steel container with collapsible endwalls and softwood floors.	5,956 19'6¹/₂"	5,658 18'6³/₄"	2,418 7'11¹/₈"	2,181 7'1⁷/₈"	2,320 7'7³/₈"	271 10⁵/₈"	33,050 72,860	3,045 6,710	30,005 66,150

Platform   20' / 40'

- Especially for heavy loads and oversized cargo.
- Strong bottom construction.
- Gooseneck tunnel on both ends of all 40' platforms.
- Numerous very strong lashing devices on the longitudinal rails. Lashing devices have a permissible load of 3,000 kg (6,615 lbs) each.
- Transport of heavy loads concentrated on a small load transfer area is possible. Contact your representative for details.

Platform Dimensions   20'

Construction	Dimensions			Weights		
	Length	Width	Height of bottom	Max. Gross	Tare	Max. Payload
	mm ft	mm ft	mm ft	kg lbs	kg lbs	kg lbs
1'1¼" high						
Steelframe with softwood floor	6,058 20'	2,438 8'	335 1'1¼"	24,000 52,910	2,100 4,630	21,900 48,280

Platform Dimensions   40'

Construction	Dimensions			Weights		
	Length	Width	Height of bottom	Max. Gross	Tare	Max. Payload
	mm ft	mm ft	mm ft	kg lbs	kg lbs	kg lbs
2' high						
Steelframe with softwood floor	12,192 40'	2,438 8'	610 2'	45,000 99,210"	4,200 9,260	40,800 89,950

OCEAN

O
C
E
A
N

Insulated Container　　　　20' / 40'

Porthole Type

- Especially for cargo which needs constant temperatures above or below freezing point.
- Walls in "sandwich-construction", with Polyurethane foam to provide maximum insulation.
- Temperature is controlled by ship's/terminal's cooling plant or "clip-on" unit.
- The air, delivered at the correct temperature, is circulated in the container through two aperatures in the front wall (supply air via the lower aperature, return air via the upper aperature).
- Possible temperatures inside the 20' containers, depending on specification of respective cooling device, from about +12°C to -25°C (+54°F to -14°F).
- Please note maximum stowage height in below table and as indicated by red line inside container in order to ensure proper ventilation.
- Possible temperatures inside the 40' containers, depending on specification of respective cooling device, from about +13°C to -22°C (+57°F to -8°F).
- Note permissable weight limits for road and rail transport.

Insulated Container   20'

Construction	Inside Dimensions			Door Opening		Weights			Capacity
	Length	Width	Max. Stowable Height	Width	Height	Max. Gross	Tare	Max. Payload	
	mm ft	mm ft	mm ft	mm ft	mm ft	kg lbs	kg lbs	kg lbs	m³ cu.ft.

8' high

Construction	Length	Width	Max. Stowable Height	Width	Height	Max. Gross	Tare	Max. Payload	Capacity
Steelframe. Walls: outside plywood, coated with GRP, inside GRP shell	5,652 18'6½"	2,235 7'4"	2,000 6'6¾"	2,235 7'4"	2,083 6'10"	20,320 44,800	2,500 5,510	17,820 39,290	26.35 930
	5,652 18'6½"	2,235 7'4"	2,000 6'6¾"	2,235 7'4"	2,083 6'10"	24,000 52,910	2,450 5,400	21,550 47,510	26.3 930
Steelframe. Walls outside and inside GRP.	5,652 18'6½"	2,235 7'8"	2,000 6'6¾"	2,218 7'3¼"	2,083 6'10"	20,320 44,800	2,633 5,800	17,687 39,000	26.3 930
Steelframe. Walls outside and inside stainless steel.	5,724 18'9⅜"	2,286 7'6"	2,014 6'7¼"	2,286 7'6"	2,067 6'9⅜"	24,000 52,910	2,550 5,620	21,450 47,290	26.4 933

Insulated Container   40'

Construction	Inside Dimensions			Door Opening		Weights			Capacity
	Length	Width	Max. Stowage Height	Width	Height	Max. Gross	Tare	Max. Payload	
	mm ft	mm ft	mm ft	mm ft	mm ft	kg lbs	kg lbs	kg lbs	m³ cu.ft.

8' high

Construction	Length	Width	Max. Stowage Height	Width	Height	Max. Gross	Tare	Max. Payload	Capacity
Steelframe. Walls: outside/inside: GRP coated plywood/stainless steel and aluminum/aluminum	11,750 38'6⅝"	2,250 7'4½"	2,080 6'9⅞"	2,250 7'4½"	2,180 7'1⅞"	30,480 67,200	4,650 10,250	25,830 56,950	58.4 2,060
	11,840 38'10⅛"	2,286 7'6"	2,120 6'11½"	2,286 7'6"	2,195 7'2⅜"	30,480 67,200	3,850 8,490	26,630 58,710	60.6 2,140

OCEAN

O C E A N

Ventilated Container   **20'**

- Especially for cargo that needs ventilation.
- Natural ventilation is provided by openings in top and bottom longitudinal rails. The labyrinth construction of these ventilation openings ensures weather-proofness.
- Numerous lashing devices on the top and bottom longitudinal rails and the corner

posts. Lashing devices have a permissible load of 1,000 kg (2,205 lbs) each.
- Note permissable weight limits for road and rail transport.

Ventilated Container   **20'**

Construction	Inside Dimensions			Door Opening		Weights			Capacity
	Length	Width	Height	Width	Height	Max. Gross	Tare	Max. Payload	
	mm ft	mm ft	mm ft	mm ft	mm ft	kg lbs	kg lbs	kg lbs	m³ cu.ft.
8'6" high									
Steelframe. Walls: plywood, coated with GRP, wooden floor.	5,930 19'5¹/₂"	2,358 7'8⁷/₈"	2,375 7'9¹/₂"	2,335 7'8"	2,292 7'6¹/₄"	24,000 52,910	2,400 5,290	21,600 47,620	33.7 1,190
Steel container with corrugated walls and wooden floor.	5,888 19'3³/₄"	2,346 7'8³/₈"	2,392 7'10¹/₈"	2,334 7'7⁷/₈"	2,290 7'6¹/₈"	30,480 67,200	2,400 5,290	28,080 61,910	33.0 1,167

Bulk Container   20'

OCEAN

- Especially for dry bulk cargos, e.g. malt.
- Three manholes for top loading of each container. Distance centerline to centerline manhole 1.83 m (6').
- One discharge opening in each door wing. On demand, short discharge tubes can be installed to move the cargo in desired directions.
- Fastening of linerbag possible.

- Fork-lift pockets on a number of the containers.
- Lashing devices on the top longitudinal rails.
- Roof openings 455 mm (18") discharge door openings 340 x 380 mm (13.5" x 15").
- Note permissable weight limits for road and rail transport.

Bulk Container   20'

Construction	Inside Dimensions			Door Opening		Weights			Capacity
	Length	Width	Height	Width	Height	Max. Gross	Tare	Max. Payload	
	mm ft	mm ft	mm ft	mm ft	mm ft	kg lbs	kg lbs	kg lbs	m³ cu.ft.
8'6" high									
Steelframe. Walls: plywood, coated with GRP.	5,934 19'5½"	2,358 7'8¾"	2,340 7'8⅛"	2,335 7'8"	2,292 7'6¼"	24,000 52,910	2,450 5,400	21,550 47,510	32.9 1,162
	5,931 19'5½"	2,358 7'8¾"	2,326 7'7⅝"	2,335 7'8"	2,292 7'6¼"	24,000 52,910	2,370 5,220	21,630 47,690	32.9 1,162

OCEAN

Refrigerated Container   20'

Temperature Controlled Container

- Especially for cargo that needs constant temperatures above or below freezing point.
- Controlled fresh-air supply is possible. Containers are ATO-approved (formerly SPRENGER).
- Walls in "sandwich-construction", with Polyurethane foam to provide maximum insulation.
- The reefer unit is a compact-design compressor unit with aircooled condenser. It switches automatically from cooling to heating operation (and vice versa), if a change of the outside temperatures makes it necessary.
- Please note maximum stowage height in below table and as indicated by red line inside container in order to ensure proper ventilation.
- Possible voltages:
  380V/50 Hz to 460 V/60Hz
  200 V/50 Hz to 220 V/60 Hz
- Refer to technical specifications and illustrations of electric plugs on refrigerated containers on page 355.
- Note permissable weight limits for road and rail transport.
- Permissable temperature setting:
  +25°C to -25°C (+77°F to -13°F).
- The set temperatures can be kept as long as the difference between outside and cargo temperatures does not exceed the following limits:
  for heating 42°C (76°F)
  for cooling 65°C (117°F).

Refrigerated Container   20'

Construction	Inside Dimensions				Door Opening		Weights			Capacity
	Length	Width	Height	Max. Stowable Height	Width	Height	Max. Gross	Tare	Max. Payload	
	mm ft	mm ft	mm ft	mm ft	mm ft	mm ft	kg lbs	kg lbs	kg lbs	m³ cu.ft.

8'6" high

Construction	Length	Width	Height	Max. Stow. Height	Width	Height	Max. Gross	Tare	Max. Payload	Capacity
Steelframe. Walls: outside plywood, coated with GRP, inside GRP, inside stainless steel	5,340 17'6¼"	2,200 7'2⅝"	2,254 7'4¾"	2,154 7'⅓⁄₄"	2,200 7'2⅝"	2,220 7'3⅜"	24,000 52,910	3,380 7,450	20,620 45,460	26.4 932
Steelframe. Walls outside and inside stainless steel	5,479 17'11⅝"	2,286 7'6"	2,257 7'4⅞"	2,157 7'⅞"	2,286 7'6"	2,220 7'3⅜"	30,480 67,200	3,160 6,970	27,320 60,230	28.3 1,000
	5,459 17'10⅞"	2,295 7'6⅛"	2,268 7'6"	2,168 7'1⅜"	2,291 7'6⅛"	2,259 7'4⅞"	30,480 67,200	3,050 6,720	27,430 60,480	28.4 1,003
	5,448 17'10½"	2,290 7'6⅛"	2,264 7'5⅛"	2,164 7'1⅛"	2,286 7'6"	2,260 7'5"	30,480 67,200	3,060 6,750	27,420 60,450	28.3 1,000

OCEAN

**O
C
E
A
N**

Refrigerated Container   40'

- Especially for cargo which needs constant temperatures above or below freezing point.
- Controlled fresh-air supply is possible. Containers are ATO-approved (formerly SPRENGER).
- Walls in "sandwich-construction", with Polyurethane foam to provide maximum insulation.
- The reefer unit is a compact-design compressor unit with aircooled condenser. It switches automatically from cooling to heating operation (and vice versa), if a change of the outside temperatures makes it necessary.
- Please note maximum stowage height in below table and as indicated by red line inside container in order to ensure proper ventilation.

- Possible voltages:
  380V/50 Hz to 460 V/60Hz
  200 V/50 Hz to 220 V/60 Hz
- Technical specifications and illustrations of electric plugs for refrigerated containers on page 355.
- Note permissable weight limits for road and rail transport.
- Possible temperature setting:
  +25°C to -25°C (+77°F to -13°F).
- Diesel generators are installed on some 40' containers to provide a power supply.
- The set temperatures can be kept as long as the difference between outside and cargo temperatures does not exceed the following limits:
  for heating 42°C (76°F)
  for cooling 60°C (108°F)

Refrigerated Container   40'

OCEAN

Construction	Inside Dimensions				Door Opening		Weights			Capacity
	Length	Width	Height	Max. Stowable Height	Width	Height	Max. Gross	Tare	Max. Payload	
	mm ft	mm ft	mm ft	mm ft	mm ft	mm ft	kg lbs	kg lbs	kg lbs	m³ cu.ft.

8' high

Construction	Length	Width	Height	Max. Stowable Height	Width	Height	Max. Gross	Tare	Max. Payload	Capacity
Steelframe. Walls: outside plywood, coated with GRP, inside GRP shell	11,141 36'4⁵/₈"	2,197 7'2¹/₂"	2,216 7'3¹/₄"	2,096 6'10¹/₂"	2,197 7'2¹/₂"	2,173 7'1¹/₂"	30,480 67,200	6,010 13,250	24,470 53,950	54.2 1,920
	11,141 36'4⁵/₈"	2,197 7'2¹/₂"	2,216 7'3¹/₄"	2,096 6'10¹/₂"	2,197 7'2¹/₂"	2,173 7'1¹/₂"	30,480 67,200	6,010 13,250	24,470 53,950	54.2 1,920
Steelframe. Walls: outside plywood coated with GRP, inside stainless steel	11,141 36'4⁵/₈"	2,197 7'2¹/₂"	2,216 7'3¹/₄"	2,096 6'10¹/₂"	2,197 7'2¹/₂"	2,173 7'1¹/₂"	30,480 67,200	6,010 13,250	24,470 53,950	54.2 1,920
	11,140 36'4⁵/₈"	2,226 7'3⁵/₈"	2,221 7'3³/₈"	2,101 6'10⁵/₈"	2,226 7'3⁵/₈"	2,173 7'1¹/₂"	30,480 67,200	6,010 13,250	24,470 53,950	55.0 1,945
Steelframe. Walls: outside aluminum, inside stainless steel	11,170 36'7³/₄"	2,286 7'6"	2,235 7'4"	2,115 6'11¹/₄"	2,286 7'6"	2,200 7'2⁵/₈"	30,480 67,200	5,200 11,460	25,280 55,740	57.3 2,023
	11,192 36'8⁵/₈"	2,286 7'6"	2,240 7'5¹/₄"	2,120 6'11¹/₂"	2,286 7'6"	2,195 7'2³/₈"	30,480 67,200	5,200 11,460	25,280 55,740	57.3 2,023
	11,572 37'11⁵/₈"	2,286 7'6"	2,254 7'4³/₄"	2,134 7'	2,286 7'6"	2,207 7'2⁷/₈"	30,480 67,200	4,400 9,700	26,080 57,500	59.64 2,106
Steelframe. Rails aluminum. Walls: outside aluminum, inside stainless steel	11,558 37'11"	2,286 7'6"	2,188 7'1⁷/₈"	2,068 6'9³/₈"	2,286 7'6"	2,161 7'1"	30,480 67,200	4,140 9,130	26,340 58,070	57.8 2,023

High Cube Refrigerated Container   40'

9'6"
2.9m

- Particularly suitable for voluminous light-weight cargoes (e.g., fruit, flowers, ferns).
- Especially for cargo that needs constant temperatures above or below freezing point.
- Controlled fresh-air supply is possible. Containers are ATO-approved (formerly SPRENGER).
- Walls in "sandwich-construction", with Polyurethane foam to provide maximum insulation.
- The reefer unit is a compact-design compressor unit with aircooled condenser. It switches automatically from cooling to heating operation (and vice versa), if a change of the outside temperatures makes it necessary.
- Possible voltages: 380V/50 Hz to 460 V/60Hz

- Technical specifications and illustrations of electric plugs for refrigerated containers on page 355.
- Note permissable weight limits for road and rail transport.
- Permissable temperature setting: +25°C to -25°C (+77°F to -13°F).
- The set temperatures can be kept as long as the difference between outside and cargo temperatures does not exceed the following limits:
for heating 42°C (76°F)
for cooling 60°C (108°F)

High Cube Refrigerated Container   40'

Construction	Inside Dimensions				Door Opening		Weights			Capacity
	Length	Width	Height	Max. Stowage Height	Width	Height	Max. Gross	Tare	Max. Payload	
	mm ft	mm ft	mm ft	mm ft	mm ft	mm ft	kg lbs	kg lbs	kg lbs	m³ cu.ft.

9'6" high — without Diesel Generator Set

Construction	Length	Width	Height	Max. Stowage Height	Width	Height	Max. Gross	Tare	Max. Payload	Capacity
Steelframes. Rails: Aluminum. Walls: outside aluminum, inside stainless steel.	11,634 38'2"	2,288 7'6¹/₈"	2,498 8'2³/₈"	2,378 7'9⁵/₈"	2,288 7'6¹/₈"	2,517 8'3¹/₈"	30,480 67,200	4,180 9,220	26,300 57,980	66.5 2348
	11,568 37'11³/₈"	2,290 7'6¹/₈"	2,509 8'2³/₄"	2,389 7'10"	2,290 7'6¹/₈"	2,473 8'1³/₈"	32,480 71,600	4,240 9,350	28,240 62,250	66.4 2,345
	11,580 37'11¹/₈"	2,288 7'6¹/₈"	2,498 8'2³/₈"	2,378 7'9⁵/₈"	2,288 7'6¹/₈"	2,517 8'3¹/₈"	30,480 67,200	4,180 9,220	26,300 57,980	66.2 2370
	11,580 37'11⁷/₈"	2,290 7'6¹/₈"	2,513 8'3"	2,393 7'10¹/₄"	2,290 7'6¹/₈"	2,522 8'3¹/₄"	30,480 67,200	4,180 9,220	26,300 57,980	67.0 2,370
	11,580 37'11⁷/₈"	2,286 7'6"	2,528 8'1¹/₂"	2,408 7'10³/₄"	2,286 7'6"	2,545 8'4¹/₈"	30,480 67,200	4,000 8,820	26,480 58,380	67.0 2,366
	11,580 37'11⁷/₈"	2,286 7'6"	2,515 8'3"	2,395 7'10¹/₄"	2,286 7'6"	2,535 8'3³/₄"	30,480 67,200	4,150 9,150	26,330 58,050	67.0 2,366
	11,580 37'11⁷/₈"	2,286 7'6"	2,515 8'3"	2,395 7'10¹/₄"	2,286 7'6"	2,535 8'3³/₄"	30,480 67,200	6,000 13,230	24,480 53,970	67.0 2,366
Steelframe. Walls outside and inside GRP.	11,575 37'11⁵/₈"	2,294 7'6¹/₄"	2,560 8'4³/₄"	2,440 8'	2,286 7'6"	2,570 8'5¹/₈"	32,500 71,650	4,300 9,480	28,200 62,170	68.0 2,400
	11,575 37'11⁵/₈"	2,294 7'6¹/₄"	2,560 8'4³/₄"	2,440 8'	2,286 7'6"	2,570 8'5¹/₈"	32,500 71,650	4,240 9,350	28,260 62,300	68.0 2,400
	11,578 37'11³/₄"	2,295 7'6³/₈"	2,550 8'4³/₈"	2,425 7'11¹/₂"	2,290 7'6¹/₈"	2,560 8'4³/₄"	30,480 67,200	4,640 10,230	25,840 56,970	67.8 2,394
	11,578 37'11³/₄"	2,295 7'6³/₈"	2,550 8'4³/₈"	2,425 7'11¹/₂"	2,290 7'6¹/₈"	2,560 8'4³/₄"	30,480 67,200	4,580 10,100	25,900 57,100	67.8 2,394

OCEAN

OCEAN

Tank Container   20'

- Separate tank fleets are available for:
  CHEMICAL PRODUCTS, e.g.:
  —Flammables
  —Oxidising agents
  —Toxic substances
  —Corrosives
     FOODSTUFFS, e.g.:
  —Alcohols
  —Fruit juices
  —Edible oils
  —Food additives
- Tanks must be filled to not less than 80% of their capacity to avoid dangerous surg/ swells during transport.
  Tanks must not be filled to 100% of their capacity. Sufficient ullage space shall be left—which must be determined depending on the thermal expansion of the product to be carried.
- Certain dangerous products must be carried in tanks having no openings below the surface level of the liquid. Such tanks must be discharged through a syphon pipe by either pressure or pumping.
- National road/rail weight limitations have to be maintained when arranging land transport.
- For the cleaning of tanks and disposal of residues tariff rules apply. Tanks moving in a dedicated service are exempted from such rules until the dedication is terminated.
- For more details contact your representative.

Electric Plugs

The following are electric plug configurations for refrigerated containers.

- Depending on power sources refrigerated containers are equipped with 1 or 2 plugs 380V/50Hz to 460V/60Hz (32 A), 200V/50Hz to 220V/60Hz (60A).
- There are fixed cables with a length of 15 m (49 ft).
- Couplings for adapters are available.
- Adapters are subject to corresponding safety regulations.

Earth Contact

all series

380/460 V plugs
- 4 poles according to CEE.
- According to ISO 1496-2 annex M.
- Earth contact in 3rd position according to socket.

Earth Contact

some series

200/220 V plugs
- 4 poles
- According to ISO 1496-2 annex O.
- Position of earth contact according to illustration.

OCEAN

Notes:

Guide to Air Freight Containers (ULDs)

Introduction
The following guide to air freight containers has been developed from materials supplied by the International Air Transport Association (IATA), air cargo carriers and container manufacturers. It should be noted that producing a truly comprehensive guide is a problematic task. While it would appear that there is a limited number of cargo aircraft operating the world, there are in fact, many aircraft types and many more aircraft cargo configurations. Each aircraft and configuration may require customized containers. The guide that follows contains illustrations and specifications of the most common containers in use today. Many of these containers can be used in multiple aircraft.

ULD (Unit Load Devices)
While in the ocean freight cargo business the word "container" is widely accepted, in the air freight cargo business the proper term is "unit load device", or more commonly ULD. However, both terms are used.

IATA
The International Air Transport Association (IATA) is the primary source of industry wide technical information for ULDs. Their "ULD Technical Manual" contains the specifications manufacturers usually follow in making containers for airlines. The book can be obtained from:
IATA
2000 Peel Street; Montreal, Quebec
Canada H3A 2R4
Tel: [1] (514) 985-6326; Fax: [1] (514) 844-7711
or
IATA
331 North Bridge Road; Suite 20-00;
Odeon Towers; Singapore 188720
Tel: [65] 331-0420; Fax: [65] 339-0855

Your Air Freight Forwarder
The practical source of information concerning ULDs for your shipment will most likely come from your air carrier or air freight forwarder. They will be best equipped to assist you in selecting the appropriate ULD for your needs.

Values / Details
All values listed in illustrations and tables are given in metric. Ft and lbs values are for easy reference only.

Openings / Doors
While airlines may be quite rigid about external dimensions and maximum gross weights, there are many styles of door openings that are permissible. ULD manufacturers produce products with hinged doors, folding aluminum panels as well as reinforced nylon curtains.

Pallets / Nettings
Pallets are in common use in most aircraft cargo configurations. All require the use of restraining devices. The most common type is a flexible netting of which there are numerous designs. Ask your air carrier or freight forwarder for details.

Maximum Gross Weights
Maximum gross weights vary from ULD type, ULD manufacturer, aircraft and air carrier. Be certain to confirm weight maximums.

ULD Markings
According to IATA all ULDs must carry the following marking information: 1) ULD Type Code, 2) Maximum Gross Weight (MGW) in kilograms and pounds and 3) The actual Tare Weight (TARE) in kilograms and pounds. Example:

UAK	1 2 3 4	XB
MGW	6,033 kg	13,300 lb
TARE	216 kg	476 lb

For marking non-structural aircraft containers MGW is optional. The actual TARE shall be the sum of the components aircraft pallet, net and container.

IATA ULD Identification Codes
Prior to October 1, 1993 the IATA Identification Code consisted of nine (9) alpha numeric elements in the following sequence:

Position	Character Type	Description
1	alphabetic	ULD Category
2	alphabetic	Base Dimensions
3	alphabetic	Contour or Compatibility
4,5,6,7	numeric	Serial Number
8,9	alpha-numeric	Owner/Registrant

Effective October 1, 1993 he IATA Identification Code consists of nine (9) or ten (10) alpha-numeric elements in the following sequence:

Position	Character Type	Description
1	alphabetic	ULD Category
2	alphabetic	Base Dimensions
3	alphabetic	Contour or Compatibility
4,5,6,7,8	(see Note below)	Serial Number
9, 10	alpha-numeric	Owner/Registrant

The serial number consists of four or five numerics.

A I R

ULD Type Code

IATA uses three letter codes (in upper case letters) to describe key characteristics of ULDs. Examples are AKE, DPN and RKE. Each of the three letter code positions describes particular characteristics of the ULD.

Position 1

The Position 1 letter describes the container as:

1. certified as to airworthiness or non-certified
2. structural unit or non-structural
3. fitted with equipment for refrigeration, insulation or thermal control (Thermal) or not fitted with refrigeration, insulation or thermal control
4. containers, pallets, nets, pallet/net/non-structural igloo assembly

The Code List for Position 1 is as follows:

A   Certified Aircraft Container
D   Non-Certified Aircraft Container
F   Non-Certified Aircraft Pallet
G   Non-Certified Aircraft Pallet Net
J   Thermal Non-Structural Igloo
H   Horse Stalls
K   Cattle Stalls
M   Thermal Non-Certified Aircraft Container
N   Certified Aircraft Pallet Net
P   Certified Aircraft Pallet
R   Thermal Certified Aircraft Container
U   Non-Structural Container
V   Automobile Transport Equipment

The following are obsolete codes that are still found on some older ULDs.

(B) Certified Main Deck Aircraft Container
(C) Non-Aircraft Container
(E) Non-Certified Main Deck Aircraft Container
(S) Structural Igloo— Solid Doors
(T) Structural Igloo—Other Closures
  (other than solid doors)

Position 2

The Position 2 letter describes the base dimensions of the container. For containers manufactured after October 1, 1990 the following code letters are used:

A   2,235 x 3,175 mm (88 x 125 in)
B   2,235 x 2,743 mm (88 x 108 in)
E   1,346 x 2,235 mm (53 x 88 in)
F   2,438 x 2,991 mm (96 x 117 ³/₄ in)
G   2,438 x 6,058 mm (96 x 238 ¹/₂ in)
H   2,438 x 9,125 mm (96 x 359 ¹/₄ in)
J   2,438 x 12,192 mm (96 x 480 in)
K   1,534 x 1,562 mm (60.4 x 61.5 in)
L   1,534 x 3,175 mm (60.4 x 125 in)
M   2,438 x 3,175 mm (96 x 125 in)
N   1,562 x 2,438 mm (61.5 x 96 in)
P   1,198 x 1,534 mm (47 x 60.4 in)
Q   1,534 x 2,438 mm (60.4 x 96 in)
R   2,438 x 4,938 mm (96 x 196 in)
X   Miscellaneous sizes largest dimension between 2,438 mm and 3,175 mm (between 96 in and 125 in)
Y   Miscellaneous sizes largest dimension 2,438 mm (96 in)
Z   Miscellaneous sizes largest dimension >3,175 (>125 in)

Position 3

The Position 3 letter describes the container's contour, fork lift capability, and in the case of pallets and nets, the restraint system into which the unit is classified. The Position 3 codes are extremely complex and are not within the scope of this publication. Refer to the IATA "ULD Technical Manual" for complete information.

Notes on ULD Guide

1. IATA (International Air Transport Association) and ATA (Air Transport Association of America) have different designations for air containers. For example: A US Type LD-3 is equivalent to the IATA Type 8 container. We list the IATA designation first and then the ATA designation second.
2. This guide lists and illustrates the primary air containers in use today. There are other types not listed that can be found in the IATA ULD Technical Manual.
3. Specifications listed in metric measures of kilos and millimeters (kg, mm) are official IATA specifications. Pounds and inches are listed only as a point of reference.
4. L x W x H = Length x Width x Height.
5. Specifications listed are taken from IATA's "ULD Technical Manual." In practice, these specifications (dimensions and weight) may vary according to special aircraft configurations and ULD manufacturers.
6. ULDs are generally classified as lower deck containers and upper deck containers. Lower deck containers generally have smaller base dimensions than upper deck containers as a result of the curvature of the airplane body.
7. Since a great deal of cargo is carried on commercial passenger flights, there are generally more lower deck than upper deck containers.

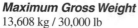

Main Deck Pallet with Net—IATA Type 1/1S—IATA Prefix: PG

2,438 mm
96 in

6,058 mm
238.5 in

2,438 mm
96 in

Maximum Gross Weight
13,608 kg / 30,000 lb

Volume
33.25 m³ / 1,174 ft³

Tare
400 kg / 882 lb

External Dimensions
(L x W x H)
6,058 mm x 2,438 mm x 2,438 mm
(238.5 in x 96 in x 96 in)

Aircraft Accepted For
DC10-30 Freighter, 747F

Main Deck Pallet with Net—IATA Type 2/2Q—IATA Prefix: PM

2,438 mm
96 in

3,175 mm
125 in

2,438 mm
96 in

Maximum Gross Weight
6,804 kg / 15,000 lb

Volume
17.16 m³ / 606 ft³

Tare
130 kg / 287 lb

External Dimensions
(L x W x H)
3,175 mm x 2,438 mm x 2,438 mm
(125 in x 96 in x 96 in)

Aircraft Accepted For
DC10-30 Freighter, 747F

A
I
R

Main Deck Pallet with Net—IATA Type 2H—IATA Prefix: PM

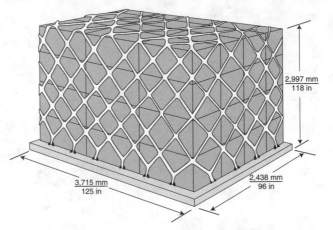

2,997 mm
118 in

3,715 mm
125 in

2,438 mm
96 in

Maximum Gross Weight
6,804 kg / 15,000 lb

Volume
21.16 m³ / 747 ft³

Tare
130 kg / 287 lb

External Dimensions
(L x W x H)
3,715 mm x 2,438 mm x 2,997 mm
(125 in x 96 in x 118in)

Aircraft Accepted For:
DC10-30 Freighter, 747F

Pallet with Net—IATA Type 2WA—IATA Prefix: PM

1,626 mm
64 in

3,175 mm
125 in

2,438 mm
96 in

Maximum Gross Weight
5,035 kg / 11,100 lb

Volume
15.8 m³ / 557 ft³

Tare
130 kg / 287 lb

External Dimensions
(L x W x H)
3,715 mm x 2,438 mm x 1,626 mm
(125 in x 96 in x 64 in)

Aircraft Accepted For:
DC10-30, Freighter, DC10-30, 747, 747F

Pallet with Net—IATA Type 5—IATA Prefix: PA

1,626 mm
64 in

3,175 mm
125 in

2,235 mm
88 in

Maximum Gross Weight
4,626 kg / 10,200 lb

Volume
9.91 m³ / 350 ft³

Tare
120 kg / 264 lb

External Dimensions
(L x W x H)
3,715 mm x 2,235 mm x 1,626 mm
(125 in x 88 in x 64 in)

Aircraft Accepted For:
DC10-30 Freighter, DC10-30
747, 747F, 777, 767-300

Lower Deck Pallet with Net—IATA Type 6—IATA Prefix: PL

1,626 mm
64 in

3,175 mm
125 in

1,534 mm
60.4 in

Maximum Gross Weight
3,175 kg / 7,000 lb

Volume
6.94 m³ / 245 ft³

Tare
90 kg / 198 lb

External Dimensions
(L x W x H)
3,175 mm x 1,534 mm x 1,626 mm
(125 in x 60.4 in x 64 in)

Aircraft Accepted For:
DC10, DC10-30 Freighter, 747, 777

AIR

Lower Deck Container—IATA Type 2BG—IATA Prefix: AMU

Maximum Gross Weight
6,033 kg / 13,300 lb

Volume
13.7 m³ / 480 ft³

Tare
200 kg / 440 lb

External Dimensions
(L x W x H)
3,175 mm x 2,438 mm x 1,626 mm
(125 in x 96 in x 64 in)

Aircraft Accepted For:
747, 747F

Main Deck Container—IATA Type 2/2Q—IATA Prefix: AMA

Maximum Gross Weight
6,804 kg / 15,000 lb

Volume
17.16 m³ / 606 ft³

Tare
260 kg / 572 lb

External Dimensions
(L x W x H)
3,175 mm x 2,438 mm x 2,438 mm
(125 in x 96 in x 96 in)

Aircraft Accepted For:
747F

Upper Deck Container—IATA Type 5—IATA Prefix AAK—ATA: LD-7

Maximum Gross Weight
6,033 kg / 13,300 lb

Volume
9.91 m³ / 350 ft³

Tare
200 kg / 440 lb

External Dimensions
(L x W x H)
3,175 mm x 2,235 mm x 1,626 mm
(125 in x 88 in x 64 in)

Aircraft Accepted For

Container—IATA Type 5—IATA Prefix AAP—ATA: LD-9

Maximum Gross Weight
6,033 kg / 13,300 lb

Volume
9.91 m³ / 350 ft³

Tare
200 kg / 440 lb

External Dimensions
(L x W x H)
3,175 mm x 2,235 mm x 1,626 mm
(125 in x 88 in x 64 in)

Aircraft Accepted For:
747, 747F, L1011

A
I
R

Lower Deck Container—IATA Type 6B—IATA Prefix: AQ—ATA: LD-8

Maximum Gross Weight
2,449 kg / 5,400 lb

Volume
6.94 m³ / 245 ft³

Tare
120 kg / 264 lb

External Dimensions
(L x W x H)
2,438 mm x 1,534 mm x 1,626 mm
(96 in x 60.4 in x 64 in)

Aircraft Accepted For:
777, 767

Lower Deck Container—IATA Type 6—IATA Prefix: ALF—ATA: LD-6

Maximum Gross Weight
3,175 kg / 7,000 lb

Volume
6.94 m³ / 245 ft³

Tare
180 kg / 397 lb

External Dimensions
(L x W x H)
3,175 mm x 1,534 mm x 1,626 mm
(125 in x 60.4 in x 64 in)

Aircraft Accepted For:
747, 747F, L1011

Lower Deck Container—IATA Type 8—IATA Prefix AK—ATA: LD-3

Maximum Gross Weight
1,588 kg / 3,500 lb

Volume
4.53 m³ / 160 ft³

Tare
70 kg / 154 lb

External Dimensions
(L x W x H)
1,562 mm x 1,534 mm x 1,626 mm
(61.5 in x 60.4 in x 64 in)

Aircraft Accepted For:
DC10-30 Freighter, DC10, 747, 777, 767

Lower Deck Container—IATA Type 8D—Prefix: APA—APA: LD-2

Maximum Gross Weight
1,225 kg / 2,700 lb

Volume
3.4 m³ / 120 ft³

Tare
60 kg / 132 lb

External Dimensions
(L x W x H)
1,194 mm x 1,534 mm x 1,626 mm
(47 in x 60.4 in x 64 in)

Aircraft Accepted For:
777, 767

Cargo Aircraft Specifications

DC 10-30 Freighter

Total Cargo Capacity	Total Cargo Volume
73,182 kg / 161,000 lb	452 m³ / 15,972 ft³

Main Deck Cargo Door (w x h)
350 cm x 255 cm / 140 in x 102 in
Lower Forward Cargo Door (w x h)
175 cm x 165 cm / 70 in x 66 in
Lower Rear Cargo Door (w x h)
175 cm x 165 cm / 70 in x 66 in
Types of Containers
Main Deck Pallet, LD-7, P9A, LD-11, LD-3

747 (400 Series)

Total Cargo Capacity	Total Cargo Volume
53,091 kg / 116,800 lb	159 m³ / 5,634 ft³

Bulk Cargo Door Dimensions (w x h)
111 cm x 119 cm / 44 in x 47in
Types of Containers
LD-7, P9A, LD-11, LD-3

747 (200 Series)

Total Cargo Capacity	Total Cargo Volume
48,091 kg / 105,800 lb	144 m³ / 5,123 ft³

Bulk Cargo Door Dimensions (w x h)
111 cm x 119 cm / 44 in x 47in
Types of Containers
LD-7, P9A, LD-11, LD-3

747 (100 Series)

Total Cargo Capacity	Total Cargo Volume
32,521 kg / 71,546 lb	115 m³ / 3,843 ft³

Bulk Cargo Door Dimensions (w x h)
111 cm x 119 cm / 44 in x 47in
Types of Containers
LD-7, P9A, LD-11, LD-3

767 (300 Series)

Total Cargo Capacity	Total Cargo Volume
33,062 kg / 72,736 lb	114 m³ / 4,030 ft³

Bulk Cargo Door Dimensions (w x h)
91 cm x 119 cm / 36 in x 47in
Types of Containers
LD-7, LD-8, LD-4, LD-3, LD-2

767 (200 Series)

Total Cargo Capacity	Total Cargo Volume
26,165 kg / 57,562 lb	92 m³ / 3,070 ft³

Bulk Cargo Door Dimensions (w x h)
91 cm x 119 cm / 36 in x 47in
Types of Containers
LD-8, LD-4, LD-3, LD-2

777

Total Cargo Capacity	Total Cargo Volume
54,685 kg / 120,306 lb	160 m³ / 5,720 ft³

Bulk Cargo Door Dimensions (w x h)
90 cm x 114 cm (left) x 122 cm (right)
35.7 in x 45.3 in (left) x 48.5 in (right)
Types of Containers
LD-7, LD-8, LD-4, LD-3, LD-2

757

Total Cargo Capacity	Total Cargo Volume
11,273 kg / 24,800lb	48 m³ / 1,698 ft³

Bulk Cargo Door Dimensions (w x h)
139 cm x 106 cm / 55 in x 42 in
Types of Containers

A 320

Total Cargo Capacity	Total Cargo Volume
9,125 kg / 20,074 lb	36 m³ / 1,270 ft³

Bulk Cargo Door Dimensions (w x h)
149 cm x 119 cm / 59 in x 47 in
Types of Containers

A 319

Total Cargo Capacity	Total Cargo Volume
6,800 kg / 14,960 lb	27 m³ / 975 ft³

Bulk Cargo Door Dimensions (w x h)
142 cm x 116 cm / 56 in x 46 in
Types of Containers

DC 10 (10 Series)

Total Cargo Capacity	Total Cargo Volume
43,636 kg / 96,000 lb	132 m³ / 4,678 ft³

Bulk Cargo Door Dimensions (w x h)
76 x 91 cm / 30 in x 36 in
Types of Containers
P9A, LD-11, LD-3

DC 10 (30 Series)

Total Cargo Capacity	Total Cargo Volume
27,727 kg / 61,000 lb	92 m³ / 3,280 ft³

Bulk Cargo Door Dimensions (w x h)
76 cm x 91 cm / 30 in x 36 in
Types of Containers
LD-7, P9A, LD-11, LD-3

727

Total Cargo Capacity	Total Cargo Volume
7,727 kg / 17,000 lb	40 m³ / 1,435 ft³

Bulk Cargo Door Dimensions (w x h)
139 cm x 106 cm / 55 in x 42 in

737 (300 Series)

Total Cargo Capacity	Total Cargo Volume
5,750 kg / 12,650 lb	30 m³ / 1,068 ft³

Bulk Cargo Door Dimensions (w x h)
114 cm x 86 cm / 45 in x 34 in

737 (200 Series)

Total Cargo Capacity	Total Cargo Volume
4,766 kg / 10,486 lb	24 m³ / 875 ft³

Bulk Cargo Door Dimensions (w x h)
114 cm x 86 cm / 45 in x 34 in

737 (500 Series)

Total Cargo Capacity	Total Cargo Volume
4,471 kg / 9,836 lb	23 m³ / 822 ft³

Bulk Cargo Door Dimensions (w x h)
114 cm x 86 cm / 45 in x 34 in

Resources for International Trade

BOOKS & DIRECTORIES

A Basic Guide to Exporting
Designed to help U.S. firms learn the costs and risks associated with exporting and to develop a strategy for exporting. Sources of assistance throughout the federal and state governments as well as the private sector. Available from: World Trade Press; 1450 Grant Ave., Ste. 204; Novato, CA 94945; USA; Tel: [1] (415) 898-1124 or [1] (800) 833-8586; Fax: [1] (415) 898-1080; http://www.worldtradepress.com.

Air Freight Directory
Directory of air freight motor carriers. Bimonthly. $60.00 per year. Available from: Air Cargo, Inc.; 1819 Bay Ridge Ave.; Annapolis, MD 21403; USA; Tel: [1] (410) 280-5578.

Black's Law Dictionary
Considered a standard in the field. Lists over 10,000 entries updated to reflect recent developments in the law. Includes pronunciation guides. By Henry Campbell Black. $25.95 Softcover. Abridged Sixth Edition. ISBN 0-314-88536-6. Available from: West Group; PO Box 64526; St. Paul, MN 55164-0526; USA; Tel: [1] (651) 687-7000; http://www.westgroup.com.

Breaking into the Trade Game: A Small Business Guide to Exporting
An information tool to assist America businesses develop international markets. Both a comprehensive how-to manual and reference book providing the reader with the contacts and resources to ease entry into markets around the world. Also highlights export success stories of small businesses. Available free from: Small Business Administration; 409 Third Street SW, Washington, DC 20416; USA; Tel: [1] (202) 205-7701. Also available from SBA regional offices in major U.S. cities.

19 Code of Federal Regulations (CFR)
Two volumes. Vol. 1 contains regulations of the U.S. Customs Services, Department of Treasury. Vol. 2 contains regulations of the International Trade Commission, International Trade Administration, Department of Commerce. Topics covered include packing and stamping, marking; customs financial and accounting procedure; customs bond; air commerce regulations; trademarks, trade names, and copyrights, etc. Available from: Superintendent of Documents; U.S. Government Printing Office; P.O.Box 371954; Pittsburgh, PA 15250-7954; USA; Tel: [1] (202) 512-1800.

Directory of United States Exporters
Directory of U.S. export firms, export executives, and products exported. Annual. $349.00. Available from: Journal of Commerce, 454 Marshall St.,Phillipsburg, NJ 08865; USA; Tel: [1] (212) 837-7000; http://www.joc.com.

Directory of United States Importers
Directory of U.S. import firms, import executives, and products imported. Annual. $349.00. Available from: Journal of Commerce; 454 Marshall St.,Phillipsburg, NJ 08865; USA; Tel: [1] (212) 837-7000; http://www.joc.com.

Directory of United States Importers and Exporters on diskette/tape
Directory of U.S. import and export firms, company executives, and products imported or exported on computer disk. Annual. $3,000.00 for both importers and exporters. Individual lists available for $1,695.00 each. Available from: Journal of Commerce; 454 Marshall St.,Phillipsburg, NJ 08865; USA; Tel: [1] (212) 837-7000; http://www.joc.com.

Documentary Credits, A Practical Guide
Assists the reader with document operations (letters of credit), particularly concerning the preparation and checking of documents. Provides examples of documents and checklist for submitting documents. Available from: Union Bank of Switzerland, UBS Tower; Aeschenvorstadt #1, CH-4402 Basel 4002, Switzerland; Tel: [41] (61) 288-2020. Union Bank of Switzerland; Swiss Bank Tower; 10 East 50th Street; New York, NY 10022; USA; Tel: [1] (212) 574-3000.

Europa World Year Book
Provides analytical, statistical, and directory information on each country's economic, social and political structure. Volume 1 covers international organizations and countries from A-J. Volume 2 covers countries from K-Z. Annual. Available from: Europa Publications Ltd., 18 Bedford Square, London WC1B 3JN; UK. Available in the U.S. from: Gale Research Inc.; 27500 Drake Rd.; Farmington Hills, MI 48331; USA; Tel: [1] (800) 877-GALE; Fax: [1] (800) 414-5043; http://www.galegroup.com.

Export Documentation
Describes the preparation of Export Documenta-

tion. Contains hundreds of samples of documents, By Donald Ewert and Richard Brown, Available from: International Trade Institute, Inc.; 5055 N. Main Street; Dayton, OH 45415; USA; Tel: [1] (937) 276-5995; Fax: [1] (937) 276-5920.

Export Sales and Marketing Manual

Step-by-step procedural manual for marketing U.S. products world-wide. The manual contains illustrations, flow charts, worksheets, and samples of export contracts, shipping documents, and effective international correspondence. By John Jague. Available from: Export Institute; 6901 West 84th St., Suite 157; P.O. Box 385883; Minneapolis; MN 55438; USA; Tel: [1] (612) 943-1505; Fax: [1] (612) 943-1535; http://www.exportinstitute.com; e-mail: jrj@exportinstitute.com. $315.00 Manual (bound or CD-ROM); no quarterly updates.

Exporters' Encyclopedia

A comprehensive reference manual detailing trade regulations, documentation requirements, transportation, key contacts, etc. for 180 world markets. Sections cover export order, markets and know-how, communication data, information sources and services, and transportation data. ISBN 1-56203-006-X. Annual. $525.00. Available from: Dun's Information Services; 3 Sylvan Way; Parsippany, NJ 07054; USA; Tel: [1] (800) 526-0651; http:www.dnb.com.

Export Shipping Manual

A reference manual used by exporters and freight forwarders as a source of country specific shipping document and import information. Updated weekly. Available from: Bureau of National Affairs (BNA); 1231 25th Street NW; Washington, DC 20037; USA; Tel [1] (202) 452-4200; http://www.bna.com.

Financing and Insuring Exports: Guide to Eximbank and FCIA Programs

A reference guide to Eximbank and FCIA programs for commercial bankers, other private lenders and exporters. Written for those who have some familiarity with Eximbank and FCIA programs and need to know how to apply for and administer the programs. Covers Eximbank's working capital guarantee, credit risk protection and lending programs. Also includes detailed case study. Available from: Office of Public Affairs; Export-Import Bank of the U.S.; 811 Vermont Ave. NW; Washington D.C. 20571; USA; Tel: [1] (202) 565-3946; Fax; [1] (202) 565-3380; http://www.exim.gov.

Foreign Exchange and Money Market Operations

Describes foreign exchange dealings and money market techniques. Covers currency and interest rate options as well as futures. Available from: Union Bank of Switzerland; UBS Tower; Aeschenvorstadt #1; CH-4002 Basel; Switzerland; Tel: [41] (61) 288-2020. In U.S., available from: Union Bank of Switzerland; Swiss Bank Tower; 10 East 50th Street, New York, NY 10022; USA; Tel: [1] (212) 574-3000.

Foreign Trade Zones Manual

A U.S. government reference manual for grantees, operators, and users of U.S. Foreign Trade Zones and customs brokers. Available from: Superintendent of Documents; U.S. Government Printing Office; P.O.Box 371954; Pittsburgh, PA 15250-7954; USA; Tel: [1] (202) 512-1800. When ordering, refer to GPO stock No. 048-002-00111-7 and Customs publication No. 559.

Gestures: The Do's and Taboo's of Body Language Around the World

A humorous and informative book on gestures and body language around the world. The first half of the book illustrates gestures and describes what each gestures means in different countries. The second half presents a country by country listing of gestures and body language. By Roger Axtell. ISBN 0-471-53672-5. Other books by Roger Axtell: *Do's and Taboos Around the World,* 2nd Edition; *Do's and Taboos of International Trade: A Small Business Primer; Do's and Taboos of Hosting International Visitors.* Available in many bookstores, also from the publisher: John Wiley and Sons, Inc.; Professional, Reference and Trade Group; 605 Third Avenue; New York, NY 10158; USA; Tel: [1] (212) 850-6000; http://www.wiley.com.

Global Road Warrior (book and CD-ROM)

Eighty-five country handbook for the international business traveler. Thousands of facts and tips for surviving and succeeding while "on the road internationally." Includes detailed "techno travel" information on Internet access, electrical requirements, and local support numbers for hardware and software vendors. Softcover, 665 pages, $29.95. Also available as a 100-country CD-ROM for both PC and Mac. Also $29.95. Available from: World Trade Press; 1450 Grant Ave., Ste. 204; Novato, CA 94945; USA; Tel: [1] (415) 898-1124 or (800) 833-8586; Fax: [1] (415) 898-1080; www.globalroadwarrior.com.

Global Trade-Directory of Major American Banks Doing Business Overseas

Lists about 100 American banks doing business overseas. Annual. Available from: North American Publishing Co.; 401 N. Broad Street; Philadelphia, PA 19108; USA; Tel: [1] (215) 238-5300; http://www.napco.com.

Global Trade-FMC-Licensed Foreign Freight Forwarders

Lists 200 independent ocean freight forwarders licensed by the Federal Maritime Commission. Annual. Available from: North American Publishing Co.; 401 N. Broad Street; Philadelphia, PA 19108; USA; Tel: [1] (215) 238-5300; http://www.napco.com.

Glossary of Finance and Debt: English-French-Spanish

A World Bank Glossary. 1991. Stock No. 11644. ISBN 0-8213-1644-3. $11.95. Books and electronic products by mail; PO Box 960; Herndon, VA 20172-0960; to order subscription items by mail: PO Box 7247-7956; Philadelphia, PA 19170; USA; Tel: [1] (703) 661-1580; Fax: [1] (703) 661-1501; http://www.worldbank.org; secure online ordering.

Harmonized Tariff Schedule of the United States (HTS or HTSUS)

(USA) An organized listing of goods and their duty rates which is used by U.S. Customs as the basis for classifying imported products and therefore establishing the duty to be charged and providing the U.S. Census with statistical information about imports and exports. The categorization of product listings in the HTSUS is based on the international Harmonized Commodity Description and Coding System developed under the auspices of the Customs Cooperation Council (Harmonized System, HS). Available from: Superintendent of Documents; U.S. Government Printing Office; P.O. Box 371954; Pittsburgh, PA 15250-7954; USA; Tel: [1] (202) 512-1800.

The Henry Holt International Desk Reference

A guide to information resources of the world's major trading nations. Organized by geographical region and country. Covers topics such as agriculture, banking, business development, imports and exports, laws, sales, and agents. By Gary McClain. ISBN 0-8050-1852-2. Available from: Henry Holt and Company, Inc.; 115 West 18th Street; New York, NY 10011; USA; Tel: [1] (212) 886-9200; http://www.henryholt.com.

Importer's Manual USA (3rd Edition)

A comprehensive reference for importing to the United States. Topics include U.S. Customs Entry and Clearance; International Banking, Letters of Credit; Foreign Exchange; International Law; Packing, Shipping and Insurance; and Commodity Index. Import how-to for 99 commodity groups. ISBN 1-885073-00-3. Hardbound, 860 pages, includes illustrations, photographs. $87.00. By Edward G. Hinkelman, Available from: World Trade Press; 1450 Grant Ave., Ste. 204; Novato, CA 94945; USA; Tel: [1] (415) 898-1124 or [1] (800) 833-8586; Fax: [1] (415) 898-1080; http://www.worldtrade-press.com.

Intercultural Interacting

Explains the elements of interacting with people from other cultures. Includes learning exercises. By V. Lynn Tyler. Available from: Culturegram; 1305 N Research Way; Orem, UT 84097; USA; Tel: [1] (801) 378-6528; toll free [1] (800) 528-6279; http://www.culturegram.com.

International Business Transactions

From the "In a Nutshell" series, a succinct exposition of the law for those who are not specialists in international trade. Traces legal aspects of an international business transaction from first idea to negotiated conclusion. By Ralph H. Folsom, Michael Wallace, John Spanogle, Jr. ISBN 0-314-06779-5. Available from: West Publishing Company; 50 W. Kellogg Blvd.; PO Box 64526; St. Paul, MN 55164; USA; Tel: [1] (651) 687-7000; http://www.westgroup.com.

Maritime Affairs: A World Handbook

Discussion of international maritime law, shipping, natural resources, etc. Includes a directory of international maritime organizations and publications. By Henry W. Dengenhardt. Published by Longman, 1986. Available from: Gale Research Inc.; 27500 Drake Rd.; Farmington Hills, MI 48331; USA; Tel: [1] (800) 877-GALE; Fax: [1] (800) 414-5043; http://www.galegroup.com.

Maritime Guide

Includes sections on dry and wet docks, a gazetteer, maps, postal and telecommunication addresses, call signs, and more, including shipbreakers listed by country. Annual. Available from: Lloyd's Register of Shipping; 71 Fenchurch Street; London EC3 M4BS; UK; Tel: [44] (0171) 709-9166.

Martindale-Hubbell Intl.Law Digest

Contains individual articles on the legal systems of countries around the world. Annual. Available from: Martindale-Hubbell; PO Box 1001; Summit, NJ 07902-1001; USA; Tel: [1] (908) 464-6800; [1] (800) 526-4902; http://www.martindale.com

National Trade Data Bank (NTDB)

(CD-ROM/WWW) Contains international economic and export promotion information supplied by 15 U.S. agencies. Data are updated monthly. The NTDB contains data from the Departments of Agriculture (Foreign Agricultural Service), Commerce (Bureau of the Census, Bureau of Economic Analysis, Office of Administration, and National Institute for Standards and Technology), Energy, Labor (Bureau of Labor Statistics), the Central Intelligence Agency, Eximbank, Federal Reserve System, U.S. International Trade Commission, Overseas Private Investment Corporation, Small Business Administration, the U.S. Trade Representative, and the University of Massachusetts. Source: U.S. Department of Commerce; Office of Business Analysis; HCHB Room 4883; Washington DC 20230; USA; Tel: [1] (202) 482-1986; http://www.stat-usa.gov.

Official Container Directory

Semiannual. $50.00. Available from: Advanstar Communications, Inc.; 7500 Old Oak Blvd.; Cleveland, OH 44130; USA; Tel: [1] (800) 225-4569 or [1] (216) 826-2839; Fax: (216) 891-2726; http://www.advanstar.com.

Official Export Guide

Gives comprehensive export information from source to market for shippers, freight forwarders, and transportation companies. Features marketing, shipping, and documentation information. Includes 197 country profiles with trade data to find new markets, surveys of major world ports, and Export Administration regulations. Available from: North American Publishing Co.; 401 N. Broad Street; Philadelphia, PA 19108; USA; Tel: [1] (215) 238-5300; http://www.napco.com.

Reference Book for World Traders

A looseleaf handbook covering information required for planning and executing exports and imports to and from all foreign countries; kept up to date by an amendment service. Includes sections covering exporting, free trade zones, and trade-related information on the countries of the world. Three volumes. $135.00 for master volume plus monthly supplements. Available from: Croner Publications, Inc.; 10951 Sorrento Valley Rd., Suite 1D; San Diego, CA 92121-1616; Tel: [1] (619) 546-1894; (800) 441-4033.; http://www.croner.com

Thompson Bank Directory, Intl. Edition

Lists banks located around the world with addresses of branches and other information. Biannual. $385.00. Available from: Thomson Financial Publishing; P.O. Box 668; Skokie, IL 60076-1253;

USA; Tel: [1] (800) 321-3373; http://www.tfp.com.

Trade Shows Worldwide

Details of conventions, conferences, trade shows and expositions. Five-year date and location information provided. U.S., Canada, and 60 other countries. Available from: Gale Research Inc.;27500 Drake Rd.; Farmington Hills, MI 48331; USA; Tel: [1] (800) 877-GALE; Fax: [1] (800) 414-5043; http://www.galegroup.com.

U.S. Customs House Guide

Comprehensive reference which provides information necessary to document, ship and distribute goods to market. Profiles of U.S. and Canadian ports. Updated harmonized tariff schedules, customs regulations and directories of services. Annual. Available from: North American Publishing Co.; 401 N. Broad Street; Philadelphia, PA 19108; USA; Tel: [1] (215) 238-5300; http://www.napco.com.

World Business Directory

Lists about 95,000 trade-oriented businesses in 150 countries. Names of executives are provided. By Meghan A. O'Meara and Kimberly A. Peterson, editors. Published jointly with the World Trade Centers Association. 1992. $395.00. Available from: Gale Research Inc.;27500 Drake Rd.; Farmington Hills, MI 48331; USA; Tel: [1] (800) 877-GALE; Fax:[1] (800) 414-5043; http://www.galegroup.com.

World Trade Resources Guide

A guide to resources on importing from and exporting to the major trading nations of the world. Kenneth Estell, Editor. Available from: Gale Research Inc.;27500 Drake Rd.; Farmington Hills, MI 48331; USA; Tel: [1] (800) 877-GALE; Fax: [1] (800) 414-5043; http://www.galegroup.com.

World Trade Almanac

Detailed economic, marketing, trade, cultural, legal & business travel surveys for the world's top 100 countries. Hardbound, 844 pages, includes 100 maps. Available from: World Trade Press; 1450 Grant Ave., Ste. 204; Novato, CA 94945; USA; Tel: [1] (415) 898-1124 or [1] (800) 833-8586; Fax: [1] (415) 898-1080; http://www.worldtrade-press.com.

Worldwide Corporate Tax Guide
Worldwide Personal Tax Guide

Summarizes the corporate tax systems in over 100 countries. Revised annually. Available from: Ernst and Young International; 787 Seventh Avenue; New York, NY 10019; USA; Tel: [1] (212) 773-3000; http://www.ey.com.

International Chamber of Commerce Publications

ICC Publishing; International Chamber of Commerce (ICC); 38 Cours Albert 1er; 75008 Paris, France; Tel: [33] (1) 49-53-28-28; Fax: [33] (1) 49-53-29-42; U.S. address: ICC Publishing, Inc.; 156 Fifth Avenue, Suite 417; New York, NY 10010; USA; Tel: [1] (212) 206-1150; Fax: [1] (212) 633-6025. Web: www.iccwbo.org / www.iccbooks.com.

Competition and Arbitration Law

Provides research on the powers and duties of arbitrators when they are confronted with the implementation of competition law. The study also covers national court decisions which have recognized the possibility for arbitrators to implement competition rules and which have established the conditions under which arbitrators can apply competition law. 250 pages. ICC Publication No. 480/3.

Documentary Credits: UP 500 and 400 Compared

This publication was developed as a vehicle from which to train managers, supervisors and practitioners of international trade in critical areas of the new UCP 500 Rules. It pays particular attention to those Articles that have been the source of litigation. 135 pages. Edited by Charles del Busto. ICC Publication No. 511.

Funds Transfer in International Banking

This publication describes the progress on EDI to date, analyzes the industrial community's financial EDI requirements and assesses the legal problems associated with EDI. It also discusses the impact of various EFT systems and regulations on capital adequacy and money laundering. Edited by Charles del Busto. 120 pages. ICC Publication No. 497.

Guide to Documentary Credit Operations

ICC's popular Guide to Documentary Credit Operations offers a total explanation of the documentary credit process. Each stage of the process is illstrated by colorful, easy-to-read diagrams and supported by concrete examples of how it applies in practice. ICC Publication No. 515a.

ICC Arbitration

A co-publication with Oceana. This revision of the original text details the history and workings of the world's foremost arbitration institutions, the ICC International Court of Arbitration. By Craig, Park, and Paulsson. 800 pages. ICC Publication No. 414/2.

ICC Model Commercial Agency Contract

New model form for negotiating agency agreements abroad which incorporates prevailing practice in international trade as well as principles generally recognized by domestic laws on agency agreements. 125 pages. ICC Publication No. 512.

Guide to the ICC Uniform Rules for Demand Guarantees

Intended to apply worldwide to the use of guarantees, bonds, and other payments arising on presentation of a written demand and other documents specified in the guarantee, and which are not conditional on proof of default by the principal in the underlying transaction. The Rules take into account the rights and obligations of all parties. 120 pages. ICC Publication No. 510.

Incoterms 2000

Defines the thirteen trading terms and specifies respective rights and obligations of buyer and seller in international transactions. 127 pages; ICC Publication No. 560a.

Key Words in International Trade

Contains more than 1,800 business words and expressions, translated into English, German, Spanish, French, and Italian. Separate alphabetical indexes are also included for all languages. 450 pages. ICC Publication No. 417/4.

Model Forms for Issuing Contact Guarantees

This publication provides a set of model forms for issuing contract guarantees, and offers practical help to facilitate procedures surrounding tender, performance and repayment guarantees issued in accordance with Uniform Rules for Contract Guarantees. 25 pages. ICC Publication No. 406.

Documentary Credit Operations

Uses a combination of graphs, charts and sample documents to illustrate the Documentary Credit process. An indispensable tool for import/export traders, bankers, training services, and anyone involved in a day-to-day operations. By Charles del Busto. ICC Publication No. 515.

Uniform Rules for Collections

This publication describes the conditions governing collections, including those for the presentation, payment and the acceptance terms. The Articles also specify the responsibility of the bank regarding protest, case of need and actions to protect the merchandise. An aid to everyday banking operations. (A revised, updated edition was published in 1995). ICC Publication No. 522.

RESOURCES

PERIODICALS & REPORTS

Background Notes

A series of publications by the U.S. State Department providing an overview of a country's history, people, political conditions, economy, and foreign relations. Also includes map of country and travel notes. Available from: Superintendent of Documents; U.S. Government Printing Office; P.O.Box 371954; Pittsburgh, PA 15250-7954; USA; Tel: [1] (202) 512-1800.

Business America

The official U.S. government trade magazine presents domestic and international business news. Each biweekly issue includes a "how to" article for new exporters, a discussion of U.S. trade policy, news of government actions that may affect trade, and a calendar of upcoming trade shows, exhibitions, fairs, and seminars. Published biweekly by the U.S Department of Commerce. $61.00/year. Order from the Government Printing Office; Superintendent of Documents; Mail Stop: SSOM; Washington, DC 20401; USA; Tel: [1] (202) 783-3288.

Commerce Business Daily (CBD)

A daily newspaper published by the U.S. Department of Commerce which lists government procurement invitations and contract awards, including foreign business opportunities and foreign government procurements. Available from: U.S. Department of Commerce; 14th St. and Constitution Ave.; Washington, DC 20230; USA; Tel: [1] (202) 482-0633; http://www.doc.gov.

Commercial News USA (CNUSA)

Provides exposure for U.S. products and services through an illustrated catalog and electronic bulletin boards. The catalog is distributed through U.S. embassies and consulates to business readers in 140 countries. Copies are provided to international visitors at trade events around the world. To be eligible, products must be at least 51 percent U.S. parts and 51 percent U.S. labor. The service helps U.S. firms identify potential export markets and make contacts leading to representation, distributorships, joint venture or licensing agreements, or direct sales. 10 times per year. Available from: Office of Administration; 725 17th Street NW; Washington, DC, 20503; USA; Tel: [1] (202) 395-7235; http://www.cnewsusa.com.

Economist

Current affairs and business magazine (they call it a newspaper). Includes reports, analysis, and comments on key events in business, finance, science and technology. Special editorial surveys focus on specific countries, industries or markets. Weekly. Available from: The Economist; 25 St. James; London SW1A 1HG; UK. In the U.S.: The Economist; 111 W. 57th Street, 9th Floor; New York, NY 10019; USA; [1] Tel: (800) 456-6086; http://www.economist.com.

Economist Intelligence Unit

A publishing company which sells research reports, country profiles, newsletters, and on-line information to help companies operate and expand abroad. Also sells individual country studies, quarterly country reports, and forecasts. Available from: Economist Intelligence Unit, Ltd.; 111 W. 57th Street, 9th Floor; New York, NY 10019; Tel: (212) 554-0600. U.K. address: 15 Regents St.; London SW1Y 4LR; UK; Tel: [44] (171) 830-1000.

The Exporter

Monthly reports on the business of exporting. Available from: Trade Data Reports; 90 John St., Ste. 505; New York, NY 10018; USA; Tel: [1] (212) 563-2772; Fax [1] (212) 587-1340; Fax: [1] (212) 587-1344; http://www.exporter.com.

Financial Times (of London)

Daily newspaper specifically for those in the economic and financial sector. Covers current news and information of financial and political issues. Also includes stock tables, graphs, and commentary. Available from: The Financial Times; Number One Southwark Bridge; London SE1 9HL; UK; Tel: [44] (0171) 873-3000.

Foreign Economic Trends (FET)

Reports prepared by U.S. embassies abroad to describe foreign country economic and commercial trends and trade and investment climates. Available from: Superintendent of Documents; U.S. Government Printing Office; P.O.Box 371954; Pittsburgh, PA 15250-7954; USA; Tel: [1] (202) 512-1800.

Foreign Labor Trends

A series of reports on specific countries of the world, providing an overview of the labor sector of a country's economy. Includes information on labor standards, conditions of employment, human resource development and labor relations. Available from: Superintendent of Documents; U.S. Government Printing Office; P.O.Box 371954; Pittsburgh, PA 15250-7954; USA; Tel: [1] (202) 512-1800.

Foreign Traders Index (FTI)

The U.S. and Foreign Commercial Service (US&FCS) headquarters compilation of overseas contact files, intended for use by domestic U.S. businesses. The FTI includes background information on foreign companies, address, contact person, sales figures, size of company, and products by SIC code. Available from: U.S. and Foreign Commercial Service; International Trade Administration; U.S. Department of Commerce; 14th St. and Constitution Ave.; Washington D.C. 20230; USA; Tel: [1] (202) 482-5777; Fax: [1] (202) 482-5013; http://www.doc.gov.

Global Business
The "how to" international business magazine for importers and exporters. Monthly. Available from: Trade Communications Inc.; 733 15th Street NW, Suite 1100; Washington, DC 20005; USA; Tel: [1] (202) 737-1060; Fax [1] (202) 783-5966; www.globalbusinessmag.com.

Global Trade
A trade publication for those involved in shipping. Gives information on ports, government regulations about transportation of certain materials, and other shipping topics. $45/year. Available from: North American Publishing Company; 401 N. Broad Street; Philadelphia, PA 19108; USA; Tel: [1] (215) 238-5300; http://www.napco.com.

International Journal of Purchasing and Materials Management
Articles on purchasing and materials management functions. Each issue includes some articles addressing international business or overseas business practices. Available from: National Association of Purchasing Management, Inc.; 2055 E. Centennial Circle; PO Box 22160; Tempe, AZ 85284-1898; USA; Tel: [1] (602) 752-6276; http://www.napm.org.

Journal of Commerce
Information on domestic and foreign economic developments plus export opportunities, shipyards, agricultural trade leads, and trade fair information. Feature articles on tariff and non-tariff barriers, licensing controls, joint ventures, and trade legislation in foreign countries. Daily. Available from: Journal of Commerce; 445 Marshall St.; Philliosburg, NJ 08865; USA; Tel: [1] (212) 837-7000: http://www.joc.com.

OAG Air Cargo Guide
A basic reference publication for shipping freight by air. It contains current domestic and international cargo flight schedules, including pure cargo, wide body, and combination passenger-cargo flights. Each monthly issue also contains information on air carriers' special services, labeling, airline and aircraft decodings, air carrier and freight forwarders directory, cargo charter information, Worldwide City Direc-

tory, small package services, interline air freight agreements, aircraft loading charts and more. Available from: Official Airline Guides, Inc.; Transportation Guides Division; 2000 Clearwater Drive; Oakbrook, IL 60523; USA; Tel: [1] (800) 323-3537; http://www.oag.com.

Overseas Business Reports (OBR)
Marketing studies of the U.S.'s major trading partners which provide export and economic outlooks, industrial trends, trade regulations, distribution and sales channels, transportation, and credit situation in individual countries. Superintendent of Documents; U.S. Government Printing Office; P.O.Box 371954; Pittsburgh, PA 15250-7954; USA; Tel: [1] (202) 512-1800.

Wall Street Journal
National and international finance and business. A more conservative tone. Also publishes a European and Asian edition as well as the Asian Wall Street Journal Weekly. $119/year, published weekdays. Available from: The Wall Street Journal; 200 Burnett Rd.; Chicopee, MA 01020; USA; Tel: [1] (800) JOURNAL; Fax: [1] (413) 592-4782; http://www.wsj.com.

World Trade Magazine
Provides information to help exporters increase global sales. $24.00/year (11 issues). Available from: from World Trade; 17702 Cowan, Suite 100; Irvine, CA 92714; USA; Tel: [1] (714) 798-3500; Fax: [1] (714) 798-3501; http://www.worldtrademag.com.

World Traders Data Reports (WTDR)
U.S. government fee-based service which provides a background report on a specific foreign firm, prepared by U.S. commercial officers overseas. WTDRs provide information about the type of organization, year established, relative size, number of employees, general reputation, language preferred, product lines handled, principal owners, financial references, and trade references. WTDRs include narrative information about the reliability of the foreign firm. Cost is $100 per report. Contact your nearest Department of Commerce District Office to order the report (or contact the U.S. Foreign and Commercial Service at [1] (202) 482-1171).

COUNTRY SERIES BOOKS

Business Profile Series

Booklets for 29 countries primarily in Asia and the Middle East. Provides overview of economy, facts and figures, business information, information for visitors and residents. Available free of charge from: Hong Kong and Shanghai Banking Corporation Limited; Group Public Affairs; Hongkong Bank; GPO Box 64, Hong Kong; Tel: [852] 2822-1111. United States address: Hongkong Bank Group; 140 Broadway; New York, NY 10005; USA; Tel: [1] (212) 658-2888.

Country Business Guides

Each book presents a comprehensive view of a country's business life, covering 25 topics important to the international business person. Included are chapters on the economy and natural resources, business formation, business entities, demographics, foreign investment, labor, business practices and etiquette, trade fairs, business law, industry reviews, business travel, personal and business taxation, opportunities, important addresses, maps and more. Available from: World Trade Press; 1450 Grant Ave., Ste. 204; Novato, CA 94945; USA; Tel: [1] (415) 898-1124 or [1] (800) 833-8586; Fax: [1] (415) 898-1080; http://www.worldtrade-press.com.

Culture Shock Series

A series of thirty country specific books devoted to helping the business person visiting or working in a particular country to wisely handle various cultural situations. Provides survival guide for expatriates and suggestions on dealing with culture shock. Available from: Graphic Arts Center Publishing Company; 3019 NW Yeon; Portland, OR 97210; USA; Tel: [1] (503) 226-2402; http://www.gacpc.com.

Doing Business in ...

Series includes countries from Antigua to Zimbabwe. Chapters cover investment climate, doing business, audit and accounting, taxation, and helpful appendix items. Available from any Price Waterhouse office in the United States free of charge. National Office: Price Waterhouse; 1251 Avenue of the Americas; New York, NY 10020; USA; Tel: [1] (212) 819-5000.

Doing Business In ...

Ernst and Young's International Business Series gives overview of the investment climate, taxation, forms of business organization, and business and accounting practices in specific countries. Available from: Ernst and Young International; 787 Seventh Avenue; New York, NY 10019; USA; Tel: [1] (212) 773-3000.

Country Profiles

Detailed and continually updated analysis of the financial, political, and economic climate in countries around the world. Available from: Economist Intelligence Unit, Ltd.; 111 W. 57th Street, 9th Floor; New York, NY 10019; USA; Tel: [1] (212) 554-0600. U.K. address: 15 Regents St.; London SW1Y 4LR; UK; Tel: [44] (171) 830-1000; http://www.ey.com.

Hints to Exporters Visiting ...

A series of concise and helpful booklets for those exporting to any almost any country around the world. Covers topics such as general country information, travel, economic factors, import and exchange control regulations. sources of market information and export services. £6.00/ each. Available from: DTI Export Publications; PO Box 55; Stratford-on-Avon; Warwickshire CV37 9GE; UK; Tel: [44] (1789) 296212.

Importing From ...

A buyer's manual for selecting suppliers, negotiating orders and arranging methods of payment for more profitable purchasing. Available from: Trade Media; Asian Sources Limited; GPO Box 12367; Hong Kong; Tel: [852] 2555-4777; Fax: [852] 873-0488. To order from the U.S. or Canada, call: [1] (847) 475-1900.

International Tax and Business Guides

Provide potential foreign investors with information about a country's environment including factors to consider when deciding to acquire an existing company or start a new one. Covers tax planning, employment and labor, financing, importing, exporting, and accounting. Deloitte Touche Tohmatsu; 555 12th Street, NW, Suite 500; Washington, DC 20004; Tel: [1] (202) 879-5381.

Passport to the World

Pocket-sized guides to the business, culture, etiquette and communication styles of a country. Designed to help businesspeople avoid cultural faux-pas, learn about a country's values and beliefs and develop an effective negotiating style. Twenty-four countries. Softcover, $6.95 each. Available from: World Trade Press; 1450 Grant Ave., Ste. 204; Novato, CA 94945; USA; Tel: [1] (415) 898-1124 or [1] (800) 833-8586; Fax: [1] (415) 898-1080; http:/www.worldtradepress.com.

TRADE ASSOCIATIONS

Air Transport Association of America (ATA)
The trade and service organization for the U.S. scheduled airlines. ATA acts on behalf of the airlines in activities ranging from improvement in air safety to planning for the airlines' role in national defense. ATA works with the airlines, the Government, and shippers in developing standards and techniques in all phases of air cargo. ATA is a source of information on cargo matters ranging from air freight packaging practices, automation, and freight lift capacity, data on air freight growth, and statistical data on air cargo services. Air Transport Association of America; 1301 Pennsylvania Ave. NW, Suite 1100; Washington, DC 20004-1707; USA; Tel: [1] (202) 626-4000; http://www.air-transport.org.

American Association of Exporters and Importers (AAEI)
A trade association which advises members of legislation regarding importing and exporting. Provides information to the international trade community and fights against protectionism. Hosts seminars and conferences for importers and exporters. Address: 11 W. 42nd St., 30th Floor; New York, NY 10036; USA; Tel: [1] (212) 944-2230; Fax: [1] (212) 382-2606; http://www.aaei.org.

Federation of International Trade Associations
Can assist you in locating an international trade association in your geographic area. Contact: Federation of International Trade Associations (FITA); 1851 Alexander Bell Drive; Reston, VA 22091; USA; Tel: [1] (703) 476-1352.

International Air Transport Association
The trade and service organization for airlines of more than 100 countries serving international routes. IATA activities on behalf of shippers in international air freight include development of containerization programs, freight handling techniques and, for some airlines, uniform rates and rules. For information: IATA; Route de l'Aeroport 33; PO Box 416; CH-1215 Geneva; 15 Airport; Switzerland; Tel: [41] (22) 799-2525; Fax: [41] (22) 798-3553.

International Civil Aviation Organization
The ICAO is an agency of the United Nations. It was organized to insure orderly worldwide technical development of civil aviation. For information: International Civil Aviation Organization; Document Sales Unit; 1000 Sherbrooke Street West, Suite 400; Montreal, PQ H3A 2R2; Canada; Tel: [1] (514) 285-8219

International Trade Association
A worldwide organization providing recognition and membership services to those who specialize in international trade. International Trade Association; 1224 North Nokomis, N.E.; Alexandria, MN 56308; USA Tel: [1] (320) 763-5101; Fax: [1] (320) 763-9290; www.iami.org.

International Trade Council
Conducts research and offers educational programs on topics such as market conditions abroad, transportation costs, and trade regulations. International Trade Council; 3114 Circle Hill Road, Alexandria, VA 22305; USA; Tel: [1] (703) 548-1234.

National Association of Export Companies
An information provider, support clearinghouse, forum, and advocate for those involved in exporting and servicing exporters. Provides networking opportunities, counseling, publications, seminars, etc. Address: PO Box 1330; Murray Hill Station; New York, NY 10156; USA; Tel: [1] (212) 725-3311; Fax: [1] (212) 725-3312.

National Association of Foreign Trade Zones
A U.S. based trade association of operators and users of U.S. Foreign Trade Zones. Address: National Association of Foreign Trade Zones; 1000 Connecticut Ave. NW, Suite 1001; Washington, DC 20036; USA; Tel: [1] (202) 331-1950; http://www.naftz.org.

National Customs Brokers and Freight Forwarders Association of America
A non-profit organization which serves as the trade organization of customs brokers and international freight forwarders in the U.S. Through ongoing communications with industry trade publications and the general media, the Association projects the industry's interests and objectives. Membership includes brokers and freight forwarders in 32 affiliated associations located at major ports throughout the U.S. Address: One World Trade Center, Suite 1153; New York, NY 10048; USA; Tel: [1] (212) 432-0050; Fax: [1] (212) 432-5709.

National Foreign Trade Council
Trade association that deals exclusively with U.S. public policy affecting international trade and investment. Membership consists of about 500 U.S. manufacturing corporations and service companies having international operations of interest. National Foreign Trade Council; 1625 K St. NW, Suite 1090; Washington, DC 20006; USA; Tel: [1] (202)

RESOURCES

887-0278; Fax: [1] (202) 452-8160; http://www.sbea.org

Small Business Exporters Association

A trade association representing small- and medium-size exporters. Small Business Exporters Association (SBEA); 1350 Beverly Rd.; McLean, VA; USA; Tel: [1] (703) 761-4140.

U.S. Chamber of Commerce, International Division

Represents American business. It lobbies the U.S. Government for specific trade policies and sponsors a number of conferences. Contact: U.S. Chamber of Commerce; International Division; 1615 H Street NW; Washington, DC 20062; Tel: [1] (202) 463-5460; Fax: [1] (202) 463-3114

U.S. Council for International Business

A membership organization which is the official U.S. affiliate of the International Chamber of Commerce. The council also oversees the Interstate Commerce Commission's Temporary Admission Carnet System. Provides a number of programs available for members: Court of Arbitration; Counterfeiting Intelligence Bureau; Institute of International Business and Law Practice; International Environmental Bureau. Address: United States Council for International Business; 1212 Avenue of the Americas, 21st Floor; New York, NY 10036; USA; Tel: [1] (212) 354-4480; Fax: [1] (212) 575-0327; http://www.uscib.org

World Trade Centers Association

Located around the world. World Trade Center members receive office support services, consultant services, conferences and reciprocal membership services at WTCs globally. Administers NETWORK, a trade lead data bank system. World Trade Centers Association (WCTA); One World Trade Center, Suite 7701; New York, NY 10048; USA; Tel: [1] (212) 432-2626; Fax: [1] (212) 488-0064; http://iserve.wtca.org.

OTHER INFORMATION SOURCES

Air Cargo, Inc. (ACI)

A ground service corporation established and jointly owned by the United States scheduled airlines. In addition to its airline owners, ACI also serves over 30 air freight forwarders and international air carriers. One of ACI's major functions is to facilitate the surface movement of air freight by negotiating and supervising the performance of a nationwide series of contracts under which trucking companies provide both local pickup and delivery service at airport cities and over-the-road truck service to move air freight to and from points not directly served by the airlines. ACI also makes available, in many cities, low cost, disposable containers for shippers' use. For further information: Air Cargo, Inc.; 1819 Bay Ridge Avenue; Annapolis, MD 21403; USA; Tel: [1] (410) 280-5578.

Export Hotline

The Export Hotline is a corporate and U.S. Department of Commerce sponsored nation-wide fax-retrieval system providing international trade information for U.S. business. Its purpose is to help find new markets for U.S. products and services. Contact at: [1] (800) USA-XPORT.

The Export Opportunity Hotline

Answers questions about getting started in exporting. Advice on product distribution; documentation; licensing and insurance; export financing; analyzing distribution options, export management firms; customs; currency exchange systems and travel requirements. Most services are free; some require a fee. Contact: The Small Business Foundation of America; 1155 15th Street NW; Washington, DC; USA; Tel: [1] (800) 243-7232.

World Trade Clubs

Local and regional based organizations around the world of importers, exporters, customs brokers, freight forwarders, attorneys, bankers, manufacturers and shippers. Each world trade club provides different services and activities, but many provide information services including data bases and libraries, educational services including seminars and regularly scheduled classes, meeting space, club atmosphere, dining, exhibit facilities, and trade missions. Most major cities in the world have World Trade Clubs. For a list of world trade clubs internationally contact: World Trade Center Association; One World Trade Center, Suite 7701; New York, NY 10048; USA; Tel: [1] (212) 432-2640; Fax: [1] (212) 488-0064;http://iserve.wtca.org.

World Trade Center Network

(Database) An electronic trading and communications services that connects user with over 160 World Trade Centers and more than 3,000 affiliates. Allows user to a advertise product around the world. Information available from: Network Headquarters; World Trade Centers Association; One World Trade Center, Suite 7701; New York, NY 10048; USA; Tel: [1] (212) 435-2552;http://iserve.wtca.org.

Web Resources

The following are internet websites that may be of interest to individuals and organizations involved in international trade. We offer this as a starting point for your research rather than as a comprehensive listing. As of February 15, 1999 these sites were accessible at no cost. Please note that the Internet is a very fluid medium and website addresses are subject to change.

General Travel Sites

Business Traveler Online   www.btonline.com
The online version of the monthly magazine for business travelers featuring country profiles, plus hotel, airline, and special perk information.

Center for Disease Control   www.cdc.gov
The U.S. Government's site for disease control and global immunization information.

Consular Information Sheets   http://travel.state.gov
U.S. Department of State country information sheets apprising travelers of current events and dangers affecting international travel safety. Also contact information for US consulates abroad.

Embassies and Consulates   http://travel.state.gov/links.html
Links to embassies and consulates worldwide.

Expedia Travel   www.expedia.com
Microsoft's online travel service featuring a fare finder, discounts, destination information, bulletin board, maps, global guidebook search, accommodations, transportation and travel merchandise.

Foreign Language for Travelers   www.travlang.com/languages
Foreign languages for travelers, dictionaries, worldwide hotels and currency exchange rates.

Global Road Warrior   www.globalroadwarrior.com
A 136-country travel and business information resource for the international business communicator and traveler. Contains pragmatic information on communications, mobile connectivity, business services, technical support, business culture, travel facts, color maps and city centers for each country.

iGo.com   www.igo.com
A major supplier of mobile connectivity products for business travelers. Print catalog also available.

Konexx   www.konexx.com
Comprehensive supplier of mobile connectivity products. Also has online tech support for products.

Magellan Geographix   www.maps.com
Specializing in maps, Magellan provides digital maps, travel guides and gear, an online map store, driving directions and an address locator.

Magellan's   www.magellans.com
A major mail order supplier of tech and non-tech travel products. Many mobile connectivity products. They also have an excellent print catalog you can order through their web site.

Lonely Planet Online   www.lonelyplanet.com
A travel guide to many destinations around the world, mostly aimed at the budget and adventure traveler, but with many helpful tips and insights useful to the businessperson.

Port Incorporated   www.port.com
Major supplier of mobile connectivity products.

Preview Travel   www.previewtravel.com
An online travel service with links to Fodor's destination guides, hotel and car reservations, farefinders, business travel information, a travel newswire and a travel store.

TeleAdapt   www.teleadapt.com
TeleAdapt is a major worldwide supplier of mobile connectivity products for the business traveler such as electrical and telephone plug adapters and much more.

WEBSITES

Travel Documents   **www.traveldocs.com**
A country-by-country listing of required travel documents and custom's information.

Travelocity   **www.travelocity.com**
Online travel service with air, hotel, and car reservations, maps, weather, currency converter, electronic ticketing, destination guide, consolidator fares, travel agency locator and travel headlines.

Walkabout Travel Gear   **www.walkabouttravelgear.com**
Supplier of mobile connectivity products. See photos of how the products work and order them online.

World Maps   **www.mapquest.com**
Create driving directions and maps, or purchase maps on this website.

World Time Information   **www.worldtime.com**
Features an interactive world atlas, information on local time worldwide and a public holiday database for countries around the world.

World Travel Guide   **www.wtgonline.com**
A extensive travel site with key information for most countries, including some business protocol and contact information.

International Trade Related Sites

A to Z Worldwide Gateway   **www.azairfreight.co.uk**
An air freight industry website containing listings of airlines, cargo handling agents, sales agents, airports, cargo agents, freight forwarders, couriers, services and supplies.

BizEurope   **www.bizeurope.com**
A business portal providing trade leads, company information and contacts, import and export information, individual country guides, a directory of World Trade Centers, and more.

Business Wire   **www.businesswire.com**
A newswire service listing the day's business headlines in industry-specific categories.

Cargo Ports of the World   **www.hal-pc.org/~nugent/port.html**
Provides links to ports and terminals around the world and contains information on vessel traffic and cargo types that individual ports allow.

Center for International Trade   **www.centretrade.com**
This helpful website for international trade includes rules, regulations, tariffs, trade opportunities, finance, management, transportation and resource information.

Dow Jones & Company   **www.dowjones.com**
Website includes indexes, business publications, financial information services, investor relations, Wall Street Journal services, press releases and a directory.

Export Today Online   **www.exporttoday.com**
The website of Export Today Magazine. Features interactive trade opportunities, editorial content from the magazine, news and trends in international trade, trade services and solutions, and a matchmaker service that helps link buyers with sellers and manufacturers with distributors.

Federation of Intl. Trade Associations   **www.fita.org**
An exhaustive website offering a massive database with over 1,000 links to websites related to international trade.

Global Index of Chambers of Commerce   **www.worldchambers.com**
A listing of chambers of commerce worldwide.

Global Information Network   **www.ginfo.net**
A search engine for industry news and resources.

International Business Resources   **http://ciber.bus.msu.edu/busres.htm**
Links to trade information. Includes regional and country information. Maintained by Michigan State University, USA, Center for International Business Education and Research.

International Chamber of Commerce (ICC) www.icc-ibcc.org/
The ICC represents businesses and chambers of commerce worldwide and facilitates contacts with intergovernmental organizations and other international bodies. The ICC also is the source of extremely important publications on international banking, letters of credit and mediation.

International Import Export Exchange   www.imex.com
Directory of trade associations, companies, products, import-export advice,and global markets.

International Monetary Fund (IMF)   www.imf.org
Official website of the IMF includes news releases, publications, fund rates, data standards and index.

Internet Service Providers   www.thelist.com
A listing of internet service providers (ISPs) and their service parameters within a specified country; listings include web links to the individual ISP sites.

The Journal of Commerce   www.joc.com
The daily Journal of Commerce online. Includes a plenitude of information about trade.

Nafta Home Page   www.nafta.net
An information site about the North American Free Trade Agreement provided by the U.S. Department of Commerce.

National Ass'n of Foreign Trade Zones   www.naftz.org
The official site of the National Association of FTZs, including descriptions of FTZs, how to establish one, case studies, event calendar, members and a listing of zones and subzones.

National Technical Information Service   www.ntis.com
The National Technical Information Service is the Federal Government's central source for the sale of scientific, technical, engineering, and related business information produced by or for the U.S. Government and complementary material from international sources.

Seaports of the World   www.seaportsinfo.com
A directory with links for seaports, port authorities and port industry info. for the Western Hemisphere.

Tradecompass   www.tradecompass.com
Large resource for electronic products and services that facilitate international commerce over the internet. Helps companies and individuals investigate trade, importing and exporting, sales, marketing, logistics, research and e-business.

Tradeport   www.tradeport.org
An international trade website funded by the California Export Assistance Center and the U.S. Department of Commerce provides information on trade leads, market and industry research, events and trade shows, trade tutorial and other information.

United Nations Online   www.un.org/
Official site of the United Nations.

World Trade Centers Association   http://iserve.wtca.org
A complete listing of world trade centers worldwide, their services and membership information.

World Trade Organization (WTO)   www.wto.org
Official website of the WTO contains trade topics, resources, and membership information.

World Trade Magazine   www.worldtrademag.com
Source of news and information for US companies doing business in the global marketplace. Core coverage areas include: banking, finance and insurance; cargo transportation and logistics; economic development; technology; international marketing and protocol; foreign exchange; tips on travel; cultural considerations; political risk analysis; and demographics.

World Trade Press   www.worldtradepress.com
Worldwide publisher of professional books, CD-ROMs and databases for international trade.

World Trade Zone   www.worldtradezone.com/
An international directory for products, sourcing, exporters, vendors, and international trade partners; contains over 200,000 companies. Register your company for a free directory listing.

WEBSITES

Country-Specific Sources

ARGENTINA

Fundacíon Invertir Argentina   www.invertir.com
The comprehensive web site covering topics related to doing business in Argentina.

Grippo Argentina Directory   www.grippo.com
A search engine for Argentina with links to other search engines. Links are usually in Spanish.

Trade Leads Online   www.tradeline.com.ar
A website for companies interested in exporting to or importing from Argentina and Mercosur countries.

AUSTRALIA

Austrade World Direct   www.austrade.gov.au
The Australian Trade Commission online; includes export and investment information, international business guide, general information, supplier database, Austrade offices, trade shows, importing from Australia and a link to the Australian stock exchange.

Australia Department of Foreign Affairs and Trade   www.dfat.gov.au
Searchable collection of detailed information on services, travel, trade policy, and foreign policy.

Web Wombat   www.webwombat.com.au/wombat
An Australian search engine, which includes a company search and trademark lookup.

AUSTRIA

Austrian Web-Index Search   http://infobase.netwing.at/webindex
An Austrian web index in German for 16 different categories including business.

Austrian Worldport   www.worldport.at/index.html
An index of company names and Austrian business information, including: marketing, legal, investment, business travel, addresses and on-line services.

BELGIUM

Belgian and Luxembourg Exports   www.belgiumexports.com
Overview of exporting and importing companies, links to importers and detailed company profiles.

EuroCommerce   www.eurocommerce.be
News, conferences, publications, and manifesto of the retail, wholesale and international trade representation to the European Union.

Scoot, the Belgium Business Directory   www.scoot.be
A quick find guide to companies, searchable by product, service, or company name, with identical local sites for the Netherlands and the United Kingdom.

Webwatch   www.webwatch.be
A Belgian search engine and directory.

BOLIVIA

Bolivian Law   natlaw.com/bolivia/links.htm
The National Law Center for Inter-American free trade provides links to Bolivia's Central Bank, Bolivian statistics, business information, general country information, industrial and commercial information and law.

Bolivia Web   **www.boliviaweb.com/**
This website for Bolivia includes business, communications, government, and travel links, as well as a chat room and classifieds.

BRAZIL

Brazil InfoNet   **www.brazilinfo.net/i**
A business directory with information and resources; includes economic statistics, government resources, trade shows, daily news, trade leads and trade zones.

BrazilBiz   **www.brazilbiz.com.br/english**
A Brazilian business to business directory for products and services; includes a business center for companies interested in buying, business opportunities as well as an international business directory.

Brazilian Web Resources   **www.brazilcham.com/brazweb.html**
A member directory searchable by name or product/service description; includes government sites, financial institutions and media.

Doing Business with Brazil   **www.brazil.org.uk/dbwb.html**
Information provided by the National Confederation of Brazilian Industry
including economic and trade policies, structure, and contacts.

Externa Brazil   **http://br.externa.com/**
A Mercosur business directory searchable by product or by company name; Externa supplies information for more than 45,000 Brazilian companies.

BULGARIA

Bulgaria.Com   **www.bulgaria.com/**
Business, services, travel, government, history, art, news, chat rooms and links are all included in this business and general information site.

Bulgarian Industrial Association   **www.bia-bg.com**
Directory for regional associations, branch chambers, economic focus, legal framework, investments, calendar, regulations, customs, tariffs and a Bulgarian company directory.

CANADA

Canada SME.COM   **http://canada.sme.com/**
Dedicated to small- and medium-size companies of Canada, presented with a collection of business related web site links.

Department of Foreign Affairs   **www.dfait-maeci.gc.ca/**
Official website of the Department of Foreign Affairs with links to trade, investment, market information, exporting programs and services, plus a directory.

Exporting Canada   **www.exportingcanadaonline.com/**
Sales resources and leads to help Canadian companies improve export business; lists export service firms, a trade database, government services, associations, publications and exporting tips.

Strategis   **http://strategis.ic.gc.ca/engdoc/main.html**
This website includes company directories; industry and professional associations; sector analysis and statistics; information on international trade, legislation, regulation, financial management, provinces and territories.

CHINA

Access China Business Online   **www.accesschina.com**
Website includes information about trade shows, tenders, trade leads for buying and selling, business reports and laws and regulations.

WEBSITES

BLI Internet Center for Chinese Products   www.buildlink.com
Build Link International provides listings of Chinese products, companies, investment opportunities, joint ventures, product bidding and general information.

China Company Database Register   www.wtdb.com/information/company.htm
Provides links to 4,000 import and export corporations and enterprises of ministries under state council; also lists the China offices of American companies.

China Today   www.chinatoday.com
Provides links to banking and finance, culture, diplomatic missions, government agencies and services, health, international trade, investment and business opportunities, products, legal services and law, mass media and publications, real estate and more.

COLOMBIA

Colombian Trade   www.coltrade.org
The Colombian Government Trade Bureau in Washington, DC USA supplies information on trade and economy, industrial sectors, commercial laws, trade agreements, trading with Colombia, news and events, trade shows. Also offers weblinks.

CUBA

LatinWorld - Cuba   www.latinworld.com/caribe/cuba
Links to Cuba including companies, exporters, organizations, products, services, economy, culture, government and politics, internet resources, news and travel.

CZECH REPUBLIC

Czech Information System   www.czis.cz/en
This site provides contacts to Czech companies, searchable by industry.

Economy.Cz   www.economy.cz
Business services and contacts online; includes information on economic and legal regulations, an economic overview and lists regional chambers of commerce.

DENMARK

Kraks Export Directory of Denmark   www.krak.dk/
An export directory and search engine; includes information about investing in Denmark, legal framework, organizations and media.

Invest in Denmark Agency   www.investindk.com
The Danish Agency for Trade and Industry provides news and information, facts and figures, Denmark investment information, company profiles and business networks and links.

ECUADOR

Ecuador   www.ecuador.org
A general educational site on Ecuador, with specific sections on economy and trade.

EGYPT

American Chamber of Commerce in Egypt   www.amcham.org.eg/BusinessMonthly/
Online business monthly publication; covers chamber's activities, committees, events, meetings, trade missions and more.

Egyptian Trading Directory   www.egtrade.comf
Egypt trade regulations including export controls and taxes, import controls and tariffs, licensing laws and price controls.

FINLAND

Contact Finland www.contactfinland.fi/
A guide to Finnish business services, organizations and authorities.

The Nordic Pages www.markovits.com/nordic/
The Nordic Pages provide resource links for Scandinavian countries, including Finland.

FRANCE

Business-in-Europe www.business-in-europe.com/
An extensive web directory of sites to assist in doing business in France. Includes: Ernst & Young report, website addresses, industry-by-industry guide, contacts in France as well as news.

France Companies www.france-companies.com/
Created in partnership with the French Ministry of Economy, Finance, and Industry, this website offers a directory of French companies, information on economic partners, business relations, international trade, job offers and searches and marketing in France.

FrancExport http://francexport.com/
This website lists a selection of links to small- and medium-sized companies chosen to help create contacts. The site is organized by industry and includes technology and business services.

GERMANY

Business Links to Germany www.integration.org/germany.htm
Economic news, databases, economic research, international economy, statistics, politics and public administration, economic organizations, trade fairs, basic facts, geography, travel information and dictionaries are all included on this extensive website.

DeTeMedien www.teleauskunft.de/
German Telekom posts a yellow-page directory comprising all of Germany.

Eule www.eule.de/
A German search engine in the German language.

German Business Center www.business-channel.de/
Business news, stock market, politics, economy, and private business news from Germany (in German).

Globis www.globis.de
A search engine that offers a supplier database searchable by company, brand name, or product; also contains a business center with economic and business information, and trade fairs taking place at the Hannover Convention Center.

BusinessLink www.businesslink.ch
A product and services search engine, convention guide and buyer contact list for Switzerland and Germany (in German).

GREECE

Hellenic Foreign Trade Board www.hepo.gr
Trade Board services, publications, economic and commercial offices, Greek investment information and Greek exports.

Go Greece www.gogreece.com
Internet directory of links to Greek travel, business, finance, education, news, government, and more.

GUATEMALA

Fundesa www.fundesa.guatemala.org
The Guatemalan Development Foundation is a non-profit, non-partisan organization of businesspersons from all sectors of Guatemala which promotes development of Guatemala. Provides information

WEBSITES

about its activities, investment and trade, tourism, resources and news.

Guatemala Online   **www.quetzalnet.com**
Website includes an exporter directory, newswatch, a phone-number converter, country profile, economic overview, Fundesa's business guidebook, traditional and non-traditional investment areas, business assistance and support institutions.

HONDURAS

Honduras Internet Directory   **www.hondirectorio.com**
Links to all manner of Honduras relatedinformation, including business, industry, and technology.

Hondu-Web   **www.marrder.com/hw**
Includes most of the contents from the book "Honduras Travel Guide." Also offers a link to import guidelines for Honduras, and a brief industrial overview.

In-Honduras   **www.in-honduras.com**
A search engine for Honduras.

HONG KONG

Hong Kong Trade Development Council   **www.tdc.org.hk**
The Hong Kong Trade Development Council (HKTDC) promotes Hong Kong's trade in goods and services. The website offers a products and services catalog, HKTDC business information, media information and more.

Hong Kong Search Engine   **www.chkg.com**
A search engine for Hong Kong sites.

Hong Kong's Stock Live   **http://www.int.quamnet.com**
This stock site includes daily quotes from the Hang Seng index with daily market reports.

HUNGARY

BusinessWeb Hungary   **www.businessweb.hu**
An online business guide to Hungary with access to an economic database with a free user name and password; the site supplies investors' information with country background information, and political and economic information.

Hungarian Yellowpages   **www.yellowpages.hu**
Hungarian yellow page search directory in Hungarian, English, and German.

INDIA

All India Site   **www.gadnet.com.imp_exp.htm**
An import/export index separated into categories: recreational/general and commercial/institutional.

India Business Directory   **http://indiaexpress.com/biz**
A business directory, investors' guide, classifieds, yellow pages and links to categories such as customs and tradition, faith and religion and technology.

IndiaMart   **www.indiamart.com**
A massive web directory with links to 60,000 Indian businesses (manufacture and exporters, importers and buyers and service providers), including foreign business, apparel and textiles, travel and tourism.

Commerce Net India   **www.commercenetindia.com**
A reference site on Indian trade and commerce, covering the Indian economy, taxation, legal system, stock market, and business news.

INDONESIA

Indonesia Yellow Pages www.yellowpages.co.id/
Yellow-page listings of Indonesian companies and businesses.

National Agency for Export Development www.nafed.go.id
The Ministry of Industry and Trade provides information on resources, trade fairs, offers, and links to other sources as well as maintaining a bulletin board dedicated to these topics.

IRAN

Business Resources www.neda.net/ibr
This website provides general information, business-related organizations, Iranian business index, fairs and exhibitions calendar and business publications.

Iranian Trade Association www.iraniantrade.org/about.htm
Daily updates, press releases, trade board publications, calendar, Iranian news, congressional directory, U.S. sanction watch, doing business with Iran, membership guest registry, advertising and other links provided by the U.S.-Iran Business Council.

IRELAND

Finfacts Irish Business and Finance www.finfacts.ie/
This website offers links to major Irish business sites including an Irish government site.

Irish Business Directory www.infosites.net/business/directory
A directory of Irish businesses by industry.

Industrial Development Agency www.idaireland.com
Information on investment in Ireland, with profiles on a range of service and manufacturing based industries, a directory of overseas companies currently doing business in Ireland, and statistics and demographics on the Irish labor force and local business environment.

Irish Finance Sector http://ireland.iol.ie/~rclapham/finance.html
An index for associations, banking, budgets and tax, government, investment, legal, life assurance, media and news, PLC's (corporations), securities, stock brokers, teletext and travel.

Swift Guide to Ireland http://swift.kerna.ie
A database of more than 3,000 sites sectioned by business category.

ISRAEL

AAI http://aai.business.israel.net
Channel for investment projects and business connections with companies, agencies and fine arts in Israel.

Globes Arena www.globes.co.il
Israel's Business in daily headlines, economic analysis and Tel Aviv stock exchange reports.

U.S.-Israel Business Networking www.std.com/neicc/contents.html
A resource guide to promote business between U.S. and Israel. Links to chambers of commerce, Israeli government, U.S. and local government programs, Israeli business and trade associations, economic development programs, finance and investments, academic institutions, research and reference materials and major trade fairs.

ITALY

ANIBO Italian Buyers http://anibo.com/members.html
The National Association of Italian Buying Offices provides a listing of member Italian purchasing agents with contact information, email links and some web links.

TRADE.IT www.trade.it
The home page of Italian manufacturing companies and their export partners, divided into ten sectors

WEBSITES

(English and Italian).

Trade World Italy Industry   www.italyindustry.com
An index of Italian companies searchable by product or industry, with product specific sub sites and free URL submission.

JAPAN

Global Window   www.anderson.ucla.edu/research/japan/mainfrm.htm
A guide to business success in Japan including information on business culture, consumers, economy, financial structure and institutions, legal and business travel tips.

Japan Export and Trade Consultants   www.jetc.com
Resources for developing your business in Japan; includes trade leads, directories of Japanese companies, business protocols, trade fairs, classifieds and business tips.

JETRO   www.jetro.go.jp
The Japan External Trade Organization is a non-profit, government-supported organization which promotes building trade and economic relationships; their website includes business information, useful links, JETRO forum.

KOREA

Business Korea Plaza   www.bizkorea.com
The Korean Exporters' Catalog; search for products offered by manufacturers and exporters from Korea.

Korea International Trade Association   www.kita.or.kr
KITA's website includes trade opportunities, a company directory, a digital catalog, trade information and Korean business information; offered in Korean and English.

KOTRA   www.kotra.or.kr
The Korea Trade and Investment Promotion Agency website; links to Korean products, export, trade fairs, investment guide and opportunities and a directory.

LEBANON

Business@Lebanon.com   www.lebanon.com/business
A website which includes links to Lebanon weekly business reports, the Beirut stock exchange, real estate, financial information, import-export, tour and hotel guide and a business directory.

Lebanon Index   www.lebindex.com
A search engine for Lebanon; categories include business and classifieds, embassies, holidays and tourism.

LIBYA

ArabNet   www.arab.net/libya
Overview, history, geography, business, culture, government and transport information about Libya.

MBendi   http://mbendi.co.za
A large electronic encyclopedia of business and communication information in Africa. Links to countries, companies, events, industries, organizations, personalities, stock exchanges, publications, projects, products and country-specific information.

MALAYSIA

Malaysia Online Business Yellow Pages   www.mol.com/companies
Links to Business Street (a new business site with searchable profiles), Malaysia Business Yellow Pages and other Malaysian websites.

WEBSITES

Malaysia Products www.malaysiaproducts.com
A site which includes a product index, company index, market place and more.

MEXICO

BANCOMEXT www.bancomext.com.mx
The Mexican Export Bank's website, includes a directory listing more than 8,000 Mexican companies.

Mexico Information Center www.mexico-trade.com
Export directory, business opportunities, export and investment offices in Mexico, trade leads, Mexican government agencies, resource centers, universities and research institutes, trade shows, news sources, NAFTA information regional and state information.

Mexico Online www.mexicool.com/business
Information on Mexican industry, trade leads, market size and other business information, including economic data, a business-to-business bulletin board with trade opportunities and a NAFTA center.

Mexico Connect www.mexconnect.com/mexbusboard/
Mexican Trade and Business Forum, listing Mexican products and services and providing a forum for business practices and problems of Mexican trade; refer to front page at www. mexconnect .com for general information on working and living in Mexico

MOROCCO

ArabNet www.arab.net/morocco
General country information, with culture, business and government links.

MBendi http://mbendi.co.za
A large electronic encyclopedia of business and communication information in Africa. Links to countries, companies, events, industries, organizations, personalities, stock exchanges, publications, projects, products and country-specific information.

Moroccan Resources on the Internet www.alakhawayn.ma/morocco
A collection of web links related to Morocco, collected by Al Akhawayn University, including links to business and industry.

Morocco - Casanet www.casanet.net.ma
Index of Moroccan websites, email addresses, classified ads, personal ads, events, business opportunities, Moroccan yellow pages and job offers (mostly in French).

NETHERLANDS

Holland Business www.hollandbusiness.nl
Business news, worldwide import and export contacts, company profiles, business contacts and information; the website publishes business requests, offers a subscription service and offers advertising opportunities.

Scoot, the Netherlands Business Directory www.scoot.nl
A quick find guide to companies, searchable by product, service, or company name, with identical local sites for Belgium and the United Kingdom.

The Dutch Export Site www.export.nl
A yellow-page directory of 4,000 plus Dutch exporting companies and their international business partners, including corporate identity, products, and services, searchable by country, business category or alphabetical name. Export information is also available.

NEW ZEALAND

National Business Review Online www.nbr.co.nz
A large business internet site. Includes instant news, share market, global update, politics and polls.

WEBSITES

New Zealand Business Directory   www.nzbd.co.nz
Directory of New Zealand businesses with a presence on the web.

Tradenz   www.tradenz.govt.nz
Information on trading, market information, export, services, markets, exporting, investing and importing.

NICARAGUA

Centramerica Nicaragua   www.directory.centramerica.com/
nicaragua_asp
Includes a business directory and links to economy, government, laws, demographics, news services, maps, related sites and events in Nicaragua.

NIGERIA

MBendi   http://mbendi.co.za
A large electronic encyclopedia of business and communication information in Africa, searchable by country; includes information on companies, events, industries, organizations, personalities, stock exchanges, publications, projects, products and country information.

Nigerian Business.Com   www.nigerianbusiness.com/index.html
Nigerian Business includes business news, a daily list of Nigerian equities and bonds, company profiles, stock exchange, a matching service and business sector information.

NORWAY

Norway Online Information Service   www.norway.org
Business information on this website includes links to the Norwegian Trade Council in North America, industry attaches, products made in Norway, oil production, the European Economic Area, the fishing industry, Norwegian shipping, the stock exchange, exchange rates, statistics and yellow pages.

ODIN   http://odin.dep.no/html/english
Official Documentation and Information from Norway is the central web server for the Norwegian government, the office of the Prime Minister and the ministries.

PAKISTAN

Pakistan Trade   http://alephx.org/paktrade/welcome.html
Trade information about the location of suppliers/buyers in Pakistan and the U.S. with a database of 50,000 Pakistani companies, listings of U.S. companies importing from Pakistan, investment opportunities and other business information.

Trade Index of Pakistan   www.PakistanBiz.com
Hosted by the Government of Pakistan, Trade Index offers buy and sell information, bulletin board services, a Pakistan web directory, domain name registration and the top ten clients.

PANAMA

Centramerica Panama   http://directory.centramerica.com
panama_asp
Includes a business directory and links to economy, government, laws, demographics, news services, maps, related sites and events in Panama.

PARAGUAY

Latinworld - Paraguay   www.latinworld.com/sur/paraguay
Latinworld provides links to business information in Paraguay, as well as North, Central and South American countries, the Caribbean, and Spain.

PERU

Peru Business and Economy Page   **www.latininvestor.com/country/peru.htm**
Links to Peruvian information sources: companies, economic and investment data, newspapers, government, financial, laws and regulations and Latin American news.

U.S. Embassy in Lima   **http://ekeko.rcp.net.pe/usa/wwwhmain.htm**
Links to USAID, agricultural service, consular section, commercial service and weekly topics.

PHILIPPINES

Filipino Directory Online   **www.filipino-directory.com**
A large website providing links for everything related to the Philippines including business and investment opportunities.

Philexport   **http://philexport.org**
An export oriented site for importers of products made in the Philippines. The database includes information for most products made in the Philippines.

Yehey Search Engine   **www.yehey.com.ph**
A Philippine search engine advertised as "Philippines at your Fingertips" includes business and technology as categories.

POLAND

Business Polska   **www.polska.net**
This site includes an investor's guide, business news on Poland, companies on the web, organizations, Warsaw Stock Exchange, market reports and a partner's forum.

Embassy of Poland Commercial Office   **http://pw1.netcom.com/~brhusa/index.html**
Provides information on laws and regulations, business and economy, news, customs tariff, directory of Polish companies, sector information, business opportunities and contact by email.

Poltrade   **www.poltrade.top.pl**
The Polish International Trade Forum supplies information on companies, services, trade board, search engines, Russia and CIS information, members' database, Polish products, chambers of commerce and contacts.

Polish Business   **business.poland.net/**
A directory of Polish businesses, organizations, institutions, and resources.

PORTUGAL

Business in Portugal   **www.portugaloffer.com**
Do business directly with Portuguese companies; contacts, products anservices offered by the nation's top 200 businesses so that you can find adsupplier, customer, agent, or partner in Portugal.

ROMANIA

Embassy of Romania   **www.roembus.org**
Information on consular services, embassy news, travel tips, trade and business, news and media, and links to other official Romanian sites.

Romanian American Chamber of Commerce **www.romamcc.org**
Romanian American Chamber of Commerce partnership and investment opportunities as well as business information sources.

RUSSIA

Russia at Your Fingertips   **www.publications-etc.com/russia**
News, services, business FAQs, conferences, exhibitions, associations, and companies of Russia; the on-line version of the monthly magazine: Russian Business and Trade Connections.

WEBSITES

Russia on the Net   **www.ru**

A Russian web directory and search engine for categories including business, companies, banks and finance, products and services, electronic commerce, news and references.

American Bank USA's Bookmarks   **www.aa.net/~russia/pbmarks.html**

An exhaustive listing of weblinks relating to Russia, broken into subject categories from A to Z.

Russia Today   **www.russiatoday.com**

Daily news and business updates concerning Russia and the CIS.

SAUDI ARABIA

ArabNet   **www.arab.net**

A large source of information for the Middle East, including Saudi Arabia.

U.S.-Saudi Arabian Business Council   **www.us-saudi-business.org**

Basic facts about Saudi Arabia, economy, doing business in Saudi Arabia, business regulations and procedures, joint venture opportunities, key contacts and certification procedures.

SINGAPORE

Singapore Connect   **http://sgconnect.com.sg**

Company database searchable by name, sector, or product; also features business leads and bulletin board, partner's program and "Business Times" online.

The Green Book   **www.thegreenbook.com**

The Singapore Industrial Directory directs users to chambers of commerce, news, the Singapore government, products and services, brand names, company information for 200,000 local companies and trade enquiries.

Singapore Trade Board Globalink   **www.tdb.gov.sg**

The government trade promotion site of Singapore featuring business matching, trade promotion, import and export information, foreign market information, information services, trade statistics, trade news and trade policy watch.

SLOVAKIA

Slovakia.net   **www.slovakia.net**

A Slovakian company directory, sorted by name.

Slovakia.Org   **www.slovakia.org**

An internet-based information site dedicated to presenting objective and non-partisan information about Slovak politics, society, history, culture, economy and links to government sites.

U.S. Embassy in Slovakia   **www.usis.sk**

The U.S. Embassy provides news, a daily Washington file, U.S. information service, commercial services, a contact list, USAID information, consular section and information about Slovakia.

SLOVENIA

Slovenia Yellow Pages   **http://yellow2.eunet.si/yellowpage/a/ index.html**

An internet directory of Slovenian businesses.

SOUTH AFRICA

ExiNet   **www.exinet.co.za/business.htm**

Links to trade, travel, web search, environment, events, professional services and yellow pages. Trade link includes manufacturers, exporters, importers and distributors, freight clearing and forwarding agents, investments and trade opportunities.

WEBSITES

South African Business Directory   http://iafrica.com/directories/business

A business directory searchable by sector or business name.

SPAIN

Camerdata Online   www.camerdata.es

Spanish chambers of commerce, Eurochambers, a Spanish company directory, a business information area, commercial offers and a business guide.

Spain Biz Point   www.spainbizpoint.com

An import and export directory for Spanish companies.

SPAINDUSTRY   www.spaindustry.com

A search engine for companies, trade leads, exporters and importers; search by economic activity, exported or imported products or by company name in five languages.

SWEDEN

SUNET Index of Swedish WWW Resources   www.sunet.se/sweden/main.html

A search engine of Swedish web pages searchable by category or by key words.

The Swedish Page - Svenska Sidor Online   www.svenska-sidor.com

A directory of Swedish sites including business, economy, government, politics, and education. Also, an address book.

Swedish Trade Council   www.swedishtrade.com/other

An informative website for the foreign company wishing to do business in Sweden; offers company search, an export directory, sector information, business news, investment advice, legal information, and a listing of relevant publications.

SWITZERLAND

SwissInfo   www.swissinfo.org

General Swiss information in eight languages, including an alphabetical listing of Swiss companies.

Swisstrade   www.swisstrade.com

Links to Swiss export services and companies, manufacturing pool and the Federal Office for Economic Development and Labor.

Swiss Search Engine   www.search.ch

A search engine offered in German, English, French and Italian languages; search all of Switzerland or by specific region.

TAIWAN

China Productivity Center (CPC)   www.cpc.org.tw

Homepage for the CPC, a statutory body in Taiwan. The CPC assists Taiwan enterprises to upgrade quality and productivity, gives Taiwan's enterprises competitiveness information and promotes economic growth. The CPC also publishes directories in English and guides to international trade in Chinese.

TAIMEX Directory   www.cens.com/cens/taimex.html

Taiwan's Leading Manufacturers' and Exporters' Directory includes links to more than 8,000 participants of the China External Trade Development Council's trade shows.

Taiwan Commerce   http://Taiwan-Commerce.com

The Taiwan Commerce search engine includes global trade, a trade bulletin board, business service, technology, world news, financial services and trade exhibition information.

TTnet   www.ttnet.net

An extensive databank of matching trade opportunities and trade information; enter keywords of products or companies.

WEBSITES

THAILAND

Department of Export Promotion   www.thaitrade.com
Information and links to business opportunities, trade fairs, pre-registration, trade associations, Thai exporters and special events.

Thai Trading   www.thaitrading.com
Trade news and a trade catalog with over 3,500 listings in 54 categories.

Thailand Board of Investment   www.boi.go.th
Offers information about investing in Thailand.

TURKEY

Business Turkey   www.businessturkey.com
An online bulletin board for business opportunities in Turkey, with listings for a long list of other countries as well.

TurkEx   www.turkex.com
The Turkish Foreign Trade Center provides a source of online information about Turkish importers and exporters, fairs and exhibitions and tourism.

UKRAINE

UkraineBiz   www.ukrainebiz.com
A free informational site describing services and products available for export to and from the Ukraine operated by the Center for Economic Initiative.

Welcome to Ukraine   www.ukraine.org
General Ukraine information with business contacts searchable by category.

UNITED ARAB EMIRATES (U.A.E.)

Go Dubai   www.godubai.com
A guide to Dubai and the United Arab Emirates, with information on travel facilities, a searchable database of companies, local business news, and more.

United Arab Emirates Internet Pages   www.uae-pages.com
Comprehensive collection of links to UAE based business, arts, education, government, science, and local newspapers

UNITED KINGDOM

British Export Directory   www.export.co.uk
A business directory of British companies with listings by company name or business classification; users must register company data in order to use the directory.

British Promotional Merchandise Association   www.martex.co.uk/bpma/prodfr.htm
A source directory of British promotional merchandise manufacturers and suppliers with listings by product category.

Scoot, the UK Business Directory   www.scoot.co.uk
A quick find guide to companies, searchable by product, service, or company name, with identical local sites for Belgium and Holland.

The Biz   www.thebiz.co.uk
Business information, products and services on the Internet as well as database listings for companies and organizations not yet on the internet.

UK Electronic Yellow Pages   www.eyp.co.uk
A yellow-page directory of businesses in the United Kingdom.

WEBSITES

UNITED STATES

American Export Register   **www.aernet.com**
A database of U.S. companies that export; listed by company or category.

Export Import Bank of the U.S.   **www.exim.gov**
Provides information regarding loans for U.S. exporters and purchasers of U.S. goods and services, and insurance against foreign buyer defaults.

Foreign Trade Statistics   **www.census.gov/foreign-trade/www**
The U.S. Census Bureau provides foreign trade statistics for the U.S.; includes country trade data, export classification assistance, profile of U.S. export companies, export seminars and more.

International Trade Administration   **www.ita.doc.gov**
A website by the U.S. Department of Commerce providing leads to exporters, trade development information, market access and compliance as well as import regulations.

Library of International Trade Resources   **www.litr.com**
U.S. trade statistics provided by the U.S. government.

Trade Information Center   **http://infoserv2.ita.doc.gov/tic.nsf**
Provides information about federal export assistance programs and country market information.

U.S. Council for Intl. Business   **www.uscib.org**
The U.S. division of the International Chamber of Commerce (ICC).

U.S. Customs Service   **www.customs.ustreas.gov**
Importing and exporting, traveler information, enforcement activities and news.

U.S. Department of Commerce   **www.doc.gov/bureaus**
The gateway for links to all the main bureaus within the Department of Commerce.

VENEZUELA

Trade Venezuela   **www.trade-venezuela.com**
An index of products and services for export; website includes a trade directory, business contacts, a Venezuelan diplomatic offices listing, Venezuelan links and international trade links.

Venezuelan Export Directory   **www.ddex.com**
A directory of exporters, products, services, engineering, tourism, business, chambers of commerce and embassies.

VIETNAM

Vietnam Access   **www.vietnamaccess.com**
Resources for business news, directories, law, trade fairs, exhibitions, investors, travel, importers and exporters seeking opportunities, contacts and trading and investment in Vietnam.

Vietpage   **www.vietpage.com**
Catalog and search engine for Vietnamese sites.

VVG Vietnam   **www.vvg-vietnam.com**
The Vietnam Venture Group provides web links in and about Vietnan.

WEBSITES

WEBSITES

Guide to Trade Documents[1]

Documents play a key role in international transactions. Both buyers and sellers need documents for bookkeeping, accounting, taxation, export and import formalities, as well as making payment using letters of credit and other documentary payment methods.

This section gives examples of the most common documents used in international trade. It is not an exhaustive listing. Specialized trades, special circumstances and different countries of origin and destination may require additional documentation. For more information contact your local logistics company representative or refer to *A Short Course in International Trade Documentation*, also by World Trade Press.

Following a general discussion of a) document categories, b) transport documents and c) documents and international payments; sample documents will be presented and defined, key elements listed, and cautions offered concerning important issues and common problems. Emphasis will be given to issues regarding letters of credit.

Document Categories

Documents for international trade fall into several overlapping categories:

Transaction Document(s)

The key transaction document is the invoice or commercial invoice. This document is used by all parties to the transaction for accounting and bookkeeping purposes. It is also required for export and import formalities as well as most banking and payment procedures.

Export Documents

These are documents required by the customs or national export authority of the country of export and vary greatly from country to country. Included are licenses, permits, export declarations, inspection certificates, commercial invoice and sometimes transport documents.

Transport Documents

These are documents issued by a shipping line, air cargo carrier, trucking company or freight forwarder that detail the terms of transport for cargo. The key transport document is the bill of lading.

Inspection Documents

These documents are generally issued by third party inspection firms at the request of the buyer to certify the quality and quantities of a shipment. Inspection documents are also issued to satisfy country export and import requirements.

Insurance Documents

These documents evidence insurance coverage of a shipment and can be in the form of a policy or a certificate.

Banking / Payment Documents

Banking and payment documents include letters of credit, amendments to letters of credit, various advices, plus virtually all the other documents used in trade (bills of lading, commercial invoice, insurance document, inspection certificates, etc.).

Import Documents

These are documents required by the customs authority of the country of import and vary greatly from country to country. The minimum documentation requirement is an entry form and a commercial invoice. However, many other forms may be required, especially if the imported merchandise is sensitive (e.g., animals, weapons, drugs, food), if the importer is requesting special tariff treatment under an import program (e.g., GSP, NAFTA) or if the import comes from certain countries.

Transport Documents

Bills of lading

A bill of lading is a document issued by a carrier to a shipper, signed by the captain, agent, or owner of a vessel, furnishing written evidence regarding receipt of the goods (cargo), the conditions on which transportation is made (contract of carriage), and the engagement to deliver goods at the prescribed port of destination to the lawful holder of the bill of lading.

A bill of lading is, therefore, both a receipt for merchandise and a contract to deliver it as freight. There are a number of different types of bills of

---

1. This section has been excerpted from the book Short Course in International Trade Documentation, ISBN 1-885073-59-3, also by Edward G. Hinkelman and available from World Trade Press.

lading and a number of issues that relate to them as a group of documents.

Straight bill of lading (non-negotiable)

A straight bill of lading indicates that the shipper will deliver the goods to the consignee. The document itself does not give title to the goods (making it "non-negotiable"). The consignee need only identify himself to claim the goods. A straight bill of lading is often used when payment for the goods has already been made in advance or in cases where the goods are shipped on open account. A straight bill of lading, therefore, cannot be transferred by endorsement.

Shipper's order bill of lading (negotiable)

A shipper's order bill of lading is a title document to the goods, issued "to the order of" a party, usually the shipper, whose endorsement is required to effect its negotiation. Because it is negotiable, it can be bought, sold, or traded while goods are in transit. These are highly favored for documentary credit transactions. The buyer usually needs the original or a copy as proof of ownership to take possession of the goods.

Blank endorsed negotiable bill of lading

A blank endorsed negotiable bill of lading is one that has been endorsed without naming an endorsee. In simple terms, the person in possession of the document may claim possession of the goods.

Air waybill

An air waybill is a form of bill of lading used for the air transport of goods and is not negotiable.

Clean bill of lading

A clean bill of lading is one where the carrier has noted that the merchandise has been received in apparent good condition (no apparent damage, loss, etc.) and that does not bear such notations as "Shipper's Load and Count," etc.

Most forms of documentary payment require a "clean" bill of lading in order for the seller to obtain payment. There are, however, some circumstances in some trades, in which transport documents with special clauses are acceptable.

Claused bill of lading

A claused bill of lading is one which contains notations that specify a shortfall in quantity or deficient condition of the goods and/or packaging. Opposite of clean bill of lading.

Originals

Some bills of lading are issued in "sets of originals." In documentary credit transactions the "full set" of original transport documents (one or more) must usually be presented for payment (especially if they are negotiable documents).

On board

An "on board" notation on a bill of lading means that the goods have in fact been loaded on board or shipped on a named vessel. This notation may be made by the carrier, his agent, the master of the ship, or his agent. Unless expressly authorized, the transport document issued by the carrier must reflect that it is "on board" in order for the seller to obtain payment under a documentary credit.

On deck

An "on deck" notation means that the goods have been secured on the deck of the vessel rather than in its hold, and therefore subject to wind and weather. Such a notation is generally not acceptable in documentary credit transactions unless specifically authorized. If the transport document shows that the goods are loaded on deck, any accompanying insurance document must show cover against "on deck" risks. Bear in mind, however, that certain dangerous cargo (including certain chemicals and live animals) are often carried on deck.

Documents and International Payments

Documents are an integral part of all international payment methods, including documentary letters of credit, documents against payment, and documents against acceptance.

The documents called for by a payment type will differ somewhat according to the nature of the goods and the countries of export and import. Some documents, however, such as the commercial invoice and a bill of lading, are specified in all transactions.

Consistency Among Documents

One of the major issues in the preparation, presentation, and verification of documentation by sellers, buyers, and banks in payment situations is consistency among the documents.

Example: In examining the documentation for a letter of credit transaction involving the sale of five pieces of machinery, the buyer noticed that the commercial invoice listed the net weight as 12,140 kilograms and the gross weight as 12,860 kilograms. The bill of lading, however, listed the gross weight as 9,612 kilograms. What happened to the other 3,248 kilograms? Did the seller make a mistake in preparing the commercial invoice? Did the shipping company make a mistake in preparing the bill of lading? Did the seller forget to ship one or more pieces of machinery? Did the shipping company misplace some machinery? Did someone steal the machinery?

In the above example, the seller should have noticed the inconsistency before forwarding the documents to the advising bank. The advising bank should have noticed the inconsistency before forwarding the documents to the issuing bank. The issuing bank should have noticed the inconsistency before forwarding the documents to the buyer. The buyer will most certainly reject this documentation.

Documentation Consistency Checklist

The following is a list of points of consistency buyers, sellers, and banks should all be aware of when preparing, presenting, and checking documents for documentary payment transactions:

1. Name and address of shipper
2. Name and address of buyer/consignee
3. Issuer name and address
4. Description of the goods, quantities, units
5. Country of origin of the goods
6. Country of destination of the goods
7. Invoice numbers, documentary credit numbers
8. Certifications
9. Legalizations
10. Shipping marks and numbers
11. Net weight, gross weight, volume
12. Number of crates, cartons, or containers

Ambiguity as to issuers of documents

If terms such as "first class," "well-known," "qualified," "independent," "official," "competent," or "local" are used in a documentary credit to refer to the issuer of a required document (e.g., inspection certificate or certificate of origin), banks are authorized to accept whatever documents are presented, provided that on their face they appear to be in compliance with the credit and were not issued and signed by the seller (beneficiary).

Originals

The originals of specified documents should be provided unless copies are called for or allowed. If more than one set of originals is required, the buyer should specify in the credit how many are necessary.

Unless otherwise noted in the documentary credit, banks are authorized to accept documents as originals, even if they were produced or appear to have been produced on a copy machine, by a computerized system, or are carbon copies, provided they have the notation "Original" and are, when necessary, signed.

Named carrier

A transport document must appear on its face to have been issued by a named carrier, or his agent. This does not mean that the applicant must name the carrier in the documentary credit application. It merely means that the transport document must indicate the name of the carrier.

Authentication

Unless otherwise noted in the documentary credit, banks are authorized to accept documents that are authenticated, validated, legalized, visaed, or certified so long as the document appears on its face to satisfy the requirement. This means that the banks are not responsible for the verification of the certification or authorized signature. Certificates must usually bear the signature of the issuer.

Signature

Banks are authorized to accept documents that have been signed by facsimile, perforated signature, stamp, symbol, or any other mechanical or electronic method.

Unspecified issuers or contents of documents

If the credit does not name a specific issuer or specific contents of a document (other than transport documents, insurance documents, and the commercial invoice), banks are authorized to accept documents as presented so long as the data contained in the documents are consistent with the credit and other stipulated documents.

Issuance date vs. documentary credit date

Unless otherwise noted in the documentary credit, banks are authorized to accept documents dated prior to the issuance date of the credit, so long as all other terms of the credit have been satisfied.

DOCUMENTS

Commercial Invoice

Definition

The commercial invoice is the key accounting document describing the commercial transaction between the buyer and the seller.

✔ Key Elements

The commercial invoice includes the following elements:

1. Name and address of seller
2. Name and address of buyer
3. Date of issuance
4. Invoice number
5. Order or contract number
6. Quantity and description of the goods
7. Unit price, total price, other agreed upon charges, and total invoice amount stated in the currency of the contract or letter of credit (e.g., US$, DM, ¥, etc.)
8. Shipping details including: weight of the goods, number of packages, and shipping marks and numbers
9. Terms of delivery and payment
10. Any other information as required in the sales contract or letter of credit (e.g., country of origin)

Cautions & Notes for Documentary Letters of Credit

In transactions involving a documentary letter of credit it is vitally important that the description of the goods in the commercial invoice correspond precisely to the description of goods in the credit.

The invoice amount should match exactly (or at least should not exceed) the amount specified in the credit. Banks have the right to refuse invoices issued for amounts in excess of the amount stated in the credit. For this, as well as other reasons, the invoice should be made out in the same currency as the credit.

The exception: when a documentary credit specifies "about" in relation to the currency amount and quantity of merchandise, in which case the invoice may specify an amount equal to plus or minus 10 percent of the stipulated amount of the credit.

Unless otherwise stipulated in the documentary credit, the commercial invoice must be made out in the name of the applicant (buyer). The exception: In a transferable documentary credit the invoice may be made out to a third party.

The buyer, seller, and bank(s) should all carefully check for discrepancies in the invoice. The details specified therein should not be inconsistent with those of any other documents, and should exactly conform to the specifications of the credit.

DOCUMENTS

Indonesia Coffee Export Co.
Jalan Sudirman
Jakarta 10420, Indonesia

INVOICE

June 27, 1998
Invoice No. 98-123456

American Caffeine Import Company
125 Main Street
Seattle, Washington

Description of goods:
15 metric tons of 60-kilo bags of New Crop D.P. Sumatra Mandheling Arabica
Grade 1 - Green Coffee - As per buyer's purchase order No. 1234

TOTAL CIF Seattle, Washington, USA US$65,000.00

Payment:	By irrevocable documentary letter of credit No. 1234567 dated May 27, 1998 of The American Import Bank, Seattle, Washington USA
Payment Terms:	At 120 days' sight, draft drawn on San Francisco International Bank, San Francisco, California, USA
Country of Origin:	Indonesia
Number of bags:	250 bags
Weights:	Gross 15,000 kilo, Net 15,000 kilo
Marks/No.:	USA Made in Indonesia No. 12345.67
Dispatch:	Through ABC Freight Services, by sea from Jakarta via Sea Maritime Steamship Line to Seattle

Indonesia Coffee Export Co.

Indonesia Coffee Export Company

DOCUMENTS

Marine/Ocean/Port-to-Port Bill of Lading

Definition

A marine bill of lading is a transport document covering port-to-port shipments of goods (for carriage of goods solely by sea).

✔ Key Elements

A completed marine bill of lading contains the following elements:

1. Name of carrier with a signature identified as that of carrier, or ship's master, or agent for or on behalf of either the carrier or ship's master
2. An indication or notation that the goods have been loaded "on board" or shipped on a named vessel. Also, the date of issuance or date of loading
3. An indication of the port of loading and the port of discharge
4. A sole original, or if issued in multiple originals, the full set of originals
5. The terms and conditions of carriage or a reference to the terms and conditions of carriage in another source or document
6. In a documentary letter of credit, no indication that the document is subject to a charter party and/ or an indication that the named vessel is propelled by sail only
7. Meets any other stipulations of the sales contract or documentary letter of credit

Cautions & Notes for Documentary Letters of Credits

If the document includes the notation "intended vessel" it must also contain an "on board" notation of a named vessel along with the date of loading, even if the named vessel is the same as the intended vessel.

If the document indicates a place where the goods were received by the carrier different from the port of loading, the document must also contain an "on-board" notation indicating the port of loading as named in the credit and the named vessel, along with the date.

If a documentary credit calls for a port-to-port shipment but does not call specifically for a marine bill of lading, the banks will accept a transport document, however named, that contains the above information. Banks will normally accept the following documents under this title: ocean bill of lading, combined transport bill of lading, short form bill of lading, or received for shipment bill of lading, provided it carries the notation "on board."

If the documents are drawn up "to the order of" the exporter or "to order" they must be endorsed.

If the documentary credit prohibits transshipment this document will be rejected if it specifically states that the goods will be transshipped.

Since this is a negotiable instrument, it may be endorsed and transferred to a third party while the goods are in transit.

DOCUMENTS

Bill of Lading

PAGE 2

Hapag-Lloyd

Carrier:
Hapag-Lloyd Container Linie GmbH, Hamburg

Multimodal Transport or Port to Port Shipment

Shipper:	Hapag-Lloyd Reference:	B/L-No.:
WATSON/SHAKLEY RICE INTERNATIONAL 8176 WILLOW STREET WINDSOR, CALIFORNIA CA 95492-9305	14013696	HLCUOAK980300049

Export References:

SHPR REF: JFC(UK) LTD
FWDR REF: SF01078226
C.H.B.NO: 5118

Consignee or Order:	Forwarding Agent: F.M.C.NO: 0087
TO THE ORDER BANK OF LLOYDS LONDON L/C# 3892XVGR012965	NALDUZAK ASSOCIATES, INC. 5088A DIAMOND HEIGHTS BLVD. SAN FRANCISCO, CA 94131-1605

Consignee's Reference:

Notify Address (Carrier not responsible for failure to notify, see clause 20 (1) hereof):	Place of Receipt:
CONNOLLY (UK) LIMITED #1 1000 NORTH CIRCLE ROAD EAST STAPLES CORNER LONDON NW2 7JP ENGLAND	

Pre-Carriage by:	Place of Receipt by Pre-Carrier:	Place of Delivery:

Ocean Vessel: 50E04	Port of Loading:
HEIDELBERG EXPRES	OAKLAND, CA

Port of Discharge:	Place of Delivery by On-Carrier:
THAMESPORT	

Container Nos., Seal Nos.; Marks and Nos.	Number and Kind of Packages; Description of Goods	Gross Weight (kg)	Measurement (cbm)
HLCU 2254295 SEAL: 136427	1 FCL/FCL 20' CONTAINER STC: 1420 PACKAGES MILLED RICE COMMODITY: 1006000000	43020# 19513K	

SHIPPED ON BOARD DATE: MAR/05/1998
PORT OF LOADING: OAKLAND, CA
VESSEL NAME: KOELN EXPRESS

SHIPMENT PURSUANT TO SC NO. 98-302
SHIPPER'S LOAD, STOWAGE AND COUNT
FREIGHT PREPAID - ORIGIN TERMINAL CHARGE PREPAID
NO S.E.D. REQUIRED, SECTION 30.39 FTSR, C.A.S. - JL.
THESE COMMODITIES, TECHNOLOGY OR SOFTWARE WERE EXPORTED FROM
THE UNITED STATES IN ACCORDANCE WITH THE EXPORT ADMINISTRATION
REGULATIONS. DIVERSION CONTRARY TO U.S. LAW PROHIBITED. NLR

Above Particulars as declared by Shipper. Without responsibility or warranty as to correctness by carrier (see clause 11(1) and 11(2))

ORIGINAL

Total No. of Containers/Packages received by the Carrier:	Shipper's declared value (see clause 7(1) and 7(2) hereof):	Received by the Carrier from the Shipper in apparent good order and condition (unless otherwise noted herein) the total number or quantity of Containers or other packages or units indicated in the box opposite entitled "Total No. of Containers/Packages received by the Carrier" for Carriage
1		

Movement	FCL/FCL		Currency		USD

subject to all the terms and conditions hereof **(including the Terms and Conditions on the Reverse hereof and the Terms and Conditions of the Carrier's Applicable Tariff)** from the Place of Receipt or the Port of Loading, whichever is applicable, to the Port of Discharge or the Place of Delivery, whichever is applicable. One original Bill of Lading, duly endorsed, must be surrendered by the Merchant to the Carrier in exchange for the Goods or a delivery order. In accepting this Bill of Lading the Merchant expressly accepts and agrees to all its terms and conditions whether printed, stamped or written, or otherwise incorporated, notwithstanding the non-signing of this Bill of Lading by the Merchant.

Charge	Rate	Basis	WT/MEA/VAL	Payment	Amount
THC	420.00	CTR	1	P	420.00
SEA	1530.00	CTR	1	P	1530.00
BAF	40.00	CTR	1	P	40.00
CAF	6.00	PCT	1530	P	91.80
THD	185.00	CTR	1	C	185.00

In Witness whereof the number of original Bills of Lading stated below all of this tenor and date has been signed, one of which being accomplished the others to stand void.

Place and Date of Issue:
CORTE MADERA, CA MAR/05/1998

Freight Payable at:	Number of original Bs/l:
CORTE MADERA, CA	3/3

For above named carrier
Hapag-Lloyd (America) Inc.
(as agent)

Allen Miller

Total Freight Prepaid	Total Freight Collect	Total Freight
2081.80	185.00	2266.80

DOCUMENTS

Non-Negotiable Sea Waybill

Definition

A non-negotiable sea waybill is a transport document covering port-to-port shipments. It is not a title document, is not negotiable and cannot be endorsed.

✔ Key Elements

A completed non-negotiable sea waybill contains the following elements:

1. Name of carrier with a signature identified as that of carrier, or ship's master, or agent for or on behalf of either the carrier or ship's master
2. An indication or notation that the goods have been loaded "on board" or shipped on a named vessel. Also, the date of issuance or date of loading
3. An indication of the port of loading and the port of discharge as specified in the original sales contract or documentary credit
4. A sole original, or if issued in multiple originals, the full set of originals
5. The terms and conditions of carriage or a reference to the terms and conditions of carriage in another source or document
6. In a documentary letter of credit, no indication that the document is subject to a charter party and/ or an indication that the named vessel is propelled by sail only
7. Meets any other stipulations of the sales contract or documentary credit

Cautions & Notes for Documentary Letters of Credit

If the document includes the notation "intended vessel" it must also contain an "on board" notation of a named vessel along with the date of loading, even if the named vessel is the same as the intended vessel.

If the document indicates a place where the goods were received by the carrier different from the port of loading, the document must also contain an "on-board" notation indicating the port of loading as named in the documentary letter of credit and the named vessel, along with the date.

If the documentary credit calls for a port-to-port shipment but does not call specifically for a marine bill of lading, the banks will accept a transport document, however named, that contains the above information. Banks will normally accept the following documents under this title: ocean bill of lading, combined transport bill of lading, short form bill of lading, or received for shipment bill of lading, provided it carries the notation "on board."

Because they are not title documents, sea waybills eliminate many of the inconveniences of a bill of lading and offer advantages in situations where the rigid security of a bill of lading is not required. Waybills reduce the opportunity for fraud—although they do by no means eliminate it—and they remove the problems of goods arriving ahead of documents (because they travel with the goods).

Sea waybills are appropriate for shipments between associated companies, for shipments to an agent for sale at destination on an open account basis, and for shipments between companies that have established mutual trust.

DOCUMENTS

Express Cargo Bill   PAGE 2   **Hapag-Lloyd**

Multimodal Transport or Port to Port Shipment

Carrier:
Hapag-Lloyd Container Linie GmbH, Hamburg

Shipper:

ABC WINE COMPANY
1234 SPAIN STREET
SONOMA, CA 96476

Hapag-Lloyd Reference: 10347784   **ECB-No.:** HLCU0AK980300071

Export References:

USS-NL-000-008

C.H.B.NO: 5118

Consignee:

DELAHAY WINE ENTERPRISES, LTD.
HAZELDONK 1408 - 1412
NL 4386 LH BREDA
THE NETHERLANDS

Forwarding Agent: F.M.C.NO: 0087

NALDUZAK ASSOCIATES, INC.
5088A DIAMOND HEIGHTS BLVD.
SAN FRANCISCO, CA 94131-1605

Consignee's Reference:

Notify Address (Carrier not responsible for failure to notify):

DELAHAY WINE ENTERPRISES, LTD.
HAZALDONK 1408 - 1412
NL 4386 LH BREDA
THE NETHERLANDS

Place of Receipt:

Pre-Carriage by:	Place of Receipt by Pre-Carrier:	Place of Delivery:
Ocean Vessel: 06E07 KOELN EXPRESS	**Port of Loading:** OAKLAND, CA	
Port of Discharge: ROTTERDAM	**Place of Delivery by On-Carrier:**	

Container Nos., Seal Nos., Marks and Nos.	Number and Kind of Packages Description of Goods	Gross Weight (kg)	Measurement (cbm)
HLCU 4073300 SEAL: 2902455 PO-DS: 3327-04G PO-C1: EL100093	1 X 40' CONTAINER SAID TO CONTAIN: 1246 CS CALIFORNIA WINES LESS THAN 14% ALCOHOL COMMODITY: 2204000000	19872 KGM	

SHIPPED ON BOARD DATE: MAR/06/1998
PORT OF LOADING: OAKLAND, CA
VESSEL NAME: KOELN EXPRESS

SHIPMENT PURSUANT TO SC NO. 98-500
SHIPPER'S LOAD, STOWAGE AND COUNT
FREIGHT COLLECT
PROTECT AGAINST EXTREME TEMPERATURES
THESE COMMODITIES LICENSED BY THE U.S. FOR ULTIMATE DESTINATION
THE NETHERLANDS. DIVERSION CONTRARY TO U.S. LAW PROHIBITED.

Above Particulars as declared by Shipper. Without responsibility or warranty as to correctness by carrier.   **RECEIPT**

Total No. of Containers/Packages received by the Carrier:	Shipper's declared value (see clause 7(1) and 7(2) hereof): 1

Movement	FCL/FCL		Currency	USD

Charge	Rate	Basis	WT/MEA/VAL	Payment	Amount
THC	500.00	CTR	1	C	500.00
SEA	1701.00	CTR	1	C	1701.00
BAF	80.00	CTR	1	C	80.00
CAF	21.00	PCT	1701	C	357.21
THC	343.00	CTR	1	C	167.33

RECEIVED by the Carrier from the Shipper in apparent good order and condition (unless otherwise noted herein) the total number or quantity of Containers or other packages or units indicated in the box opposite entitled "Total No. of Containers/Packages received by the Carrier" for Carriage subject to all the terms and conditions hereof (INCLUDING THE TERMS AND CONDITIONS ON THE REVERSE HEREOF AND THE TERMS AND CONDITIONS OF THE CARRIER'S APPLICABLE TARIFF) from the Place of Receipt or the Port of Loading, whichever is applicable, to the Port of Discharge or the Place of Delivery, whichever is applicable. In accepting this Express Cargo Bill the Merchant expressly accepts and agrees to all its terms and conditions whether printed, stamped or written, or otherwise incorporated, notwithstanding the non-signing of this Express Cargo Bill by the Merchant.

Place and Date of Issue:

CORTE MADERA, CA MAR/05/1998

Freight Payable at:

BARKING, U.K.

For above named carrier
Hapag-Lloyd (America) Inc.
(as agent)

Total Freight Prepaid	Total Freight Collect	Total Freight
	2805.54	2805.54

90116743

(left margin, vertical) Express Cargo Bill · Not Negotiable

(right margin, vertical) Express Cargo Bill · Not Negotiable

(far right margin, vertical) DOCUMENTS

Multimodal (Combined) Transport Document

Definition

A multimodal transport document is a bill of lading covering two or more modes of transport, such as shipping by rail and by sea.

✔ Key Elements

A completed multimodal transport document contains the following elements:

1. Name of carrier or multimodal transport operator with a signature identified as that of carrier, transport operator, or ship's master, or agent for or on behalf of either the carrier, transport operator, or ship's master

2. An indication that the shipment has been "dispatched," "taken in charge," or "loaded on board," along with a date

3. Indication of the place of receipt of the shipment that may be different from the place of actual loading "on board" and the place of delivery of the shipment, which may be different from the place of discharge

4. A sole original, or if issued in multiple originals, the full set of originals

5. The terms and conditions of carriage or a reference to the terms and conditions of carriage in another source or document other than the multimodal transport document

6. In a documentary letter of credit, no indication that the document is subject to a charter party and/ or an indication that the named vessel is propelled by sail only

7. Meets any other stipulations of the sales contract or documentary letter of credit

Cautions & Notes for Documentary Letters of Credit

In multimodal situations the contract of carriage and liability is for a combined transport from the place of shipment to the place of delivery. Thus, the document evidences receipt of goods and not shipment on board.

The date of issuance of the document is deemed to be the date of dispatch unless there is a specific date of dispatch, taking in charge, or loading on board, in which case the latter date is deemed to be the date of dispatch.

Even if a documentary letter of credit prohibits transshipment, banks will accept a multimodal transport document that indicates that transshipment will or may take place, provided that the entire carriage is covered by one transport document.

A combined transport document issued by a freight forwarder is acceptable unless the documentary letter of credit stipulates otherwise or unless the credit specifically calls for a "marine bill of lading." The issuing freight forwarder accepts carrier responsibility for performance of the entire contract of carriage and liability for loss or damage wherever and however it occurs.

As a rule, multimodal transport documents are not negotiable instruments.

Carrier:
Hapag-Lloyd Container Linie GmbH, Hamburg

Bill of Lading
Multimodal Transport or Port to Port Shipment

PAGE 2

Hapag-Lloyd

Shipper:	**Hapag-Lloyd Reference:**	**B/L-No.:**
WILSON COMMODITIES INTERNATIONAL 100 MEADOWCREEK DRIVE CORTE MADERA, CA 94125	10347484	HLCUOAK980204041

Export References:
REF#156008
REF#156008
C.H.B.NO: 12330

Consignee or Order:	**Forwarding Agent:** F.M.C.NO: 0953
ZAIDNERS INTERNATIONAL B.V. POSTBUS 27 4870 AA ETTEN-LEUR THE NETHERLANDS	NALDUZAK ASSOCIATES, INC. 5088A DIAMOND HEIGHTS BLVD. SAN FRANCISCO, CA 94131-1605 **Consignee's Reference:**

Notify Address (Carrier not responsible for failure to notify, see clause 20 (1) hereof)	**Place of Receipt:**
GARCIA ROTTERDAM B.V. POSTBUS 425 3200 AK SPIJKENISSE THE NTHERLANDS	FRESNO, CA

Pre-Carriage by:	**Place of Receipt by Pre-Carrier:** FRESNO, CA	**Place of Delivery:**
Ocean Vessel: 23E06 ROTTERDAM EXPRESS	**Port of Loading:** OAKLAND, CA	
Port of Discharge: ROTTERDAM	**Place of Delivery by On-Carrier:**	

Container Nos., Seal Nos., Marks and Nos.	Number and Kind of Packages; Description of Goods	Gross Weight (kg)	Measurement (cbm)
HLXU 4787302 SEAL: 3814	1 40' HC REEFER CONTAINER STC: 791 CARTONS OF RASPBERRIES SEEDLESS COMMODITY: 0811000003 MAINTAIN TEMPERATURE AT -18.0 CELSIUS OR LOWER	42857LBS	

SHIPPED ON BOARD DATE: FEB/17/1998
PORT OF LOADING: OAKLAND, CA
VESSEL NAME: CAPE HENRY

CARGO STOWED UNDER REFRIGERATION
SHIPPER'S LOAD, STOWAGE AND COUNT
FREIGHT COLLECT
THESE COMMODITIES, TECHNOLOGY OR SOFTWARE WERE EXPORTED FROM
THE UNITED STATES IN ACCORDANCE WITH THE EXPORT ADMINISTRATION
REGULATIONS.   DIVERSION CONTRARY TO U.S. LAW PROHIBITED. NLR

ORIGINAL

Above Particulars as declared by Shipper. Without responsibility or warranty as to correctness by carrier (see clause 11(1) and 11(2))

Total No. of Containers/Packages received by the Carrier:	Shipper's declared value (see clause 7(1) and 7(2) hereof):	
1		

Movement		FCL/FCL	Currency		USD
Charge	Rate	Basis	WT/MEA/VAL	Payment	Amount
OLF	490.00	CTR	1	C	490.00
THO	500.00	CTR	1	C	500.00
SEA	3805.00	CTR	1	C	3805.00
BAF	80.00	CTR	1	C	80.00
CAF	21.00	PCT	3805	C	799.05
THD	343.00	CTR	1	C	170.12

Place and Date of Issue	
CORTE MADERA, CA FEB/23/1998	
Freight Payable at: DESTINATION	**Number of original B/L:** 3/3

For above named carrier
Hapag-Lloyd (America) Inc.
(as agent)

Allen Miller

Total Freight Prepaid	Total Freight Collect	Total Freight
	5844.17	5844.17

90116721

Air Transport Document (Air Waybill)

Definition

An air waybill is a non-negotiable transport document covering transport of cargo from airport to airport.

✔ Key Elements

A completed air waybill contains the following elements:

1. Name of carrier with a signature identified as that of carrier or named agent for or on behalf of the carrier
2. An indication that the goods have been accepted for carriage. Also, the date of issuance or date of loading
3. In a documentary letter of credit, an indication of the actual date of dispatch if required by the documentary letter of credit, or, if the actual date of dispatch is not required by the credit, the issuance date of the document is deemed to be the date of shipment
4. An indication of the airport of departure and airport of destination
5. Appears on its face to be the original for consignor/shipper
6. The terms and conditions of carriage or a reference to the terms and conditions of carriage in another source or document
7. Meets any other stipulations of the sales contract or documentary letter of credit

Cautions & Notes for Documentary Letters of Credit

Information contained in the "for carrier use only" box concerning flight number and date are not considered to be the actual flight number and date.

Since air waybills are issued in three originals—one for the issuing carrier, one for the consignee (buyer), and one for the shipper (seller)—a documentary credit should not require presentation in more than one original. Nor should it call for a "full set of original air waybills."

The air waybill is not a negotiable document. It indicates only acceptance of goods for carriage.

The air waybill must name a consignee (who can be the buyer), and it should not be required to be issued "to order" and/or "to be endorsed." Since it is not negotiable, and it does not evidence title to the goods, in order to maintain some control of goods not paid for by cash in advance, sellers often consign air shipments to their sales agents, or freight forwarders' agents in the buyer's country.

The air waybill should not be required to indicate an "actual flight date" since IATA regulations specify that reservations requested by the shipper shall not be inserted under "Flight/Date."

Definitions

Master Air Waybill A shipper's contract of carriage with an airline.

House Air Waybill A shipper's contract of carriage with the logistics firm.

| 085 |BSL| 7260 2751 | | | | | | | | | | | 085-7260-2751 |

SWISS EXPORT LTD
AIRFREIGHT DIVISION
ZUERICH

NOT NEGOTIABLE
AIR WAYBILL
AIR CONSIGNMENT NOTE

swissair ✚

Issued by: Swiss Air Transport Co., Ltd., Zurich, Switzerland
Member of IATA (International Air Transport Association)

Copies 1, 2 and 3 of this Air Waybill are originals and have the same validity

Shipper's Name and Address / Shipper's account Number

Consignee's Name and Address / Consignee's account Number

IMPORT KONTOR
VIENNA

Phone: 633 7876

It is agreed that the goods described herein are accepted in apparent good order and condition (except as noted) for carriage SUBJECT O THE CONDITIONS OF CONTRACT ON THE REVERSE HEREOF. THE SHIPPER'S ATTENTION IS DRAWN TO THE NOTICE CONCERNING CARRIERS' LIMITATION OF LIABILITY. Shipper may increase such limitation of liability by declaring a higher value for carriage and paying a supplemental charge if required.

Issuing Carrier's Agent Name and City / Accounting information

FORWARDING LTD
BASLE

Agent's IATA Code / Account No.
81-4 0000

Airport of Departure (Addr. of the Carrier) and requested Routing
BSL-VIE

to	By first Carrier	Routing and Destination	to	by	to	by	Currency	CHGS Code	WT/VAL PPD COLL	Other PPD COLL	Declared Value for Carriage	Declared Value for Customs
VIE	SWISSAIR						SFR		CPP		NVD	

Airport of Destination	Flight/Date	For Carrier Use only Flight/Date	Amount of Insurance	INSURANCE - If carrier offers insurance and such insurance is requested in accordance with conditions on reverse hereof, indicate amount to be insured in figures in box marked amount of insurance.
VIENNA	SR436/8.7.			

Handling Information

No of Pieces RCP	Gross Weight	kg lb	Rate Class / Commodity Item No.	Chargeable Weight	Rate / Charge	Total	Nature and Quantity of Goods (incl. Dimensions or Volume)
8	200,6	K	C 6750	201	1.90	381.90	CHEMICALS NOT RESTRICTED CONTRACT No 100-15-2
8	200,6						

Prepaid	Weight Charge	Collect	Other Charges
		381.90	AWA 15.00

Valuation Charge

Tax

Total other Charges Due Agent
15.00

Shipper certifies that the particulars on the face hereof are correct and that insofar as any part of the consignment contains dangerous goods, such part is properly described by name and is in proper condition for carriage by air according to the applicable Dangerous Goods Regulations.

Total other Charges Due Carrier

SWISS EXPORT LTD / per Forwarding LTD

Signature of Shipper or his Agent

Total Prepaid	Total Collect
15.00	381.90

Currency Conversion Rates	cc charges in Dest. Currency	07.07.	BASLE	Forwarding LTD
		Executed on (Date)	at (Place)	Signature of Issuing Carrier or its Agent

For Carrier's Use only at Destination	Charges at Destination	Total collect Charges

085-7260 2751

No. 3 - ORIGINAL for SHIPPER

Form 30.301
Printed in the Fed. Rep. Germany - Bartsch Verlag, Munich-Ottobrunn 600j (III)

DOCUMENTS

Insurance Document (or Certificate)

Definition

A document indicating the type and amount of insurance coverage in force on a particular shipment. In documentary credit transactions the insurance document is used to assure the consignee that insurance is provided to cover loss of or damage to cargo while in transit.

✔ Key Elements

A completed insurance document includes the following elements:

1. The name of the insurance company
2. Policy number
3. Description of the merchandise insured
4. Points of origin and destination of the shipment. Coverage is indicated by the terms of sale. For example, for goods sold "FOB," coverage commences once the cargo, is on board the vessel and continues until the consignee takes possession at either the seaport or in-land port of destination.
5. Conditions of coverage, exclusions, and deductible, if applicable.
6. A signature by the insurance carrier, underwriter or agent for same
7. Indication that the cover is effective at the latest from the date of loading of the goods on board a transport vessel or the taking in charge of the goods by the carrier, as indicated by the transport document (bill of lading, etc.)
8. Statement of the sum insured
9. In a documentary letter of credit, specifies coverage for at least 110 percent of either: (a) the CIF or CIP value of the shipment, if such can be determined from the various documents on their face, otherwise, (b) the amount of the payment, acceptance or negotiation specified in the documentary credit, or (c) the gross amount of the commercial invoice
10. Is presented as the sole original, or if issued in more than one original, all the originals

Cautions & Notes

In documentary credit transactions the insurance currency should be consistent with the currency of the documentary credit.

Documentary credit transactions indicating CIF (Cost Insurance Freight) or CIP (Carriage and Insurance Paid) pricing should list an insurance document in their required documentation.

"Cover notes" issued by insurance brokers (as opposed to insurance companies, underwriters, or their agents) are not accepted in letter of credit transactions unless authorized specifically by the credit.

In Case of Loss or Shortfall

The consignee should always note on the delivery document any damage or shortfall prior to signing for receipt of the goods. The consignee has the responsibility to make reasonable efforts to minimize loss. This includes steps to prevent further damage to the shipment. Expenses incurred in such efforts are almost universally collectible under the insurance policy. Prompt notice of loss is essential.

The original copy of the insurance certificate is a negotiable document and is required in the filing of a claim.

Copies of documents necessary to support an insurance claim include the insurance policy or certificate, bill of lading, invoice, packing list, and a survey report (usually prepared by a claims agent).

$ _____
(sum insured)

CERTIFICATE OF MARINE INSURANCE
No. 473301

WASHINGTON INTERNATIONAL INSURANCE COMPANY
300 PARK BOULEVARD, SUITE 500, ITASCA, IL 60143-2625

This is to Certify, *That on the* _____ *day of* _____ 19 ___ , this Company

insured under Policy No. _____ *made for* _____

for the sum of _____ *Dollars,*

on _____

Valued at sum insured. Shipped on board the S/S or M/S _____ and/or following
steamer or steamers

at and from _____ , *via* _____
(Initial Point of Shipment)   (Port of Shipment)

to _____ *and it is understood and agreed, that in case of loss, the same*
(Port or Place of Destination)

is payable to the order of _____ *on surrender of this Certificate which conveys the right of collecting any such loss as fully as if the property were covered by a special policy direct to the holder hereof, and free from any liability for unpaid premiums. This certificate is subject to all the terms of the open policy, provided however, that the rights of a bona fide holder of this certificate for value shall not be prejudiced by any terms of the open policy which are in conflict with the terms of this certificate.*

SPECIAL CONDITIONS	MARKS & NUMBERS

NEW MERCHANDISE shipped subject to an UNDER DECK bill of lading insured–
  Against all risks of physical loss or damage from any external cause, irrespective of percentage, excepting those excluded by the F.C. & S., Nuclear Exclusion and S.R. & C.C. Warranties, arising during transportation between the points of shipment and of destination named herein.
  The above conditions apply only to New Approved Commodities, properly packed for export, as listed in the Master Policy to which this Certificate is made a part of. Commodities such as, but not limited to, Automobiles, Household Goods and Personal Effects, Wines, Liquors, Beer and Similar Spirits, are subject to further conditions and/or warranties of the policy.
  Non-approved commodities are subject to the F.P.A. conditions of the Master Policy unless broader conditions have been approved by these underwriters prior to attachment of risk and so endorsed hereon.

USED MERCHANDISE AND/OR ON DECK SHIPMENTS insured–
  Warranted free of particular average unless caused by the vessel being stranded, sunk, burnt, on fire or in collision, but including risk of jettison and/or washing overboard, irrespective of percentage.

DEDUCTIBLE	COUNTRY CODE

TERMS AND CONDITIONS–SEE ALSO BACK HEREOF

WAREHOUSE TO WAREHOUSE: This insurance attaches from the time the goods leave the Warehouse and/or Store at the place named in the Policy for the commencement of the transit and continues during the ordinary course of transit, including customary transhipment if any, until the goods are discharged overside from the overseas vessel at the final port. Thereafter the insurance continues whilst the goods are in transit and/or awaiting transit until delivered to final warehouse at the destination named in the Policy or until the expiry of 15 days (or 30 days if the destination to which the goods are insured is outside the limits of the port) whichever shall first occur. The time limits referred to above to be reckoned from midnight of the day on which the discharge overside of the goods hereby insured from the overseas vessel is completed. Held covered at a premium to be arranged in the event of transhipment, if any, other than as above and/or in the event of delay in excess of the above time limits arising from circumstances beyond the control of the Assured.
NOTE–IT IS NECESSARY FOR THE ASSURED TO GIVE PROMPT NOTICE TO THESE ASSURERS WHEN THEY BECOME AWARE OF AN EVENT FOR WHICH THEY ARE "HELD COVERED" UNDER THIS POLICY AND THE RIGHT TO SUCH COVER IS DEPENDENT ON COMPLIANCE WITH THIS OBLIGATION.
PERILS CLAUSE: Touching the adventures and perils which this Assurer is contented to bear and takes upon itself, they are of the seas, fires, assailing thieves, jettisons, barratry of the masters and mariners, and all other like perils, losses and misfortunes that have or shall come to the hurt, detriment or damage of the said goods and merchandise, or any part thereof, except as may be otherwise provided for herein or endorsed hereon.
SHORE CLAUSE: Where this insurance by its terms covers while on docks, wharves or elsewhere on shore, and/or during land transportation, it shall include the risks of collision, derailment, overturning or other accident to the conveyance, fire, lightning, sprinkler leakage, cyclones, hurricanes, earthquakes, floods (meaning the rising of navigable waters), and/or collapse or subsidence of docks or wharves, even though the insurance be otherwise F.P.A.
BOTH TO BLAME CLAUSE: Where goods are shipped under a Bill of Lading containing the so called "Both to Blame Collision" Clause, these Assurers agree as to all losses covered by this insurance, to indemnify the Assured for this Policy's proportion of any amount (not exceeding the amount insured) which the Assured may be legally bound to pay to the shipowners under such clause. In the event that such liability is asserted the Assured agrees to notify these Assurers who shall have the right at their own cost and expense to defend the Assured against such claim.
MACHINERY CLAUSE: When the property insured under this Policy includes a machine consisting when complete for sale or use of several parts, then in case of loss or damage covered by this insurance to any part of such machine, these Assurers shall be liable only for the proportion of the insured value of the part lost or damaged, or at the Assured's option, for the cost and expense, including labor and forwarding charges, of replacing or repairing the lost or damaged part, but in no event shall these Assurers be liable for more than the insured value of the complete machine.
LABELS CLAUSE: In case of damage affecting labels, capsules or wrappers, these Assurers, if liable therefor under the terms of this policy, shall not be liable for more than an amount sufficient to pay the cost of new labels, capsules or wrappers, and the cost of reconditioning the goods, but in no event shall these Assurers be liable for more than the insured value of the damaged merchandise.
DELAY CLAUSE: Warranted free of claim for loss of market or inherent vice or nature of the subject matter insured or for loss, damage or deterioration arising from delay, whether caused by a peril insured against or otherwise.
AMERICAN INSTITUTE CLAUSES: This insurance, in addition to the foregoing, is also subject to the following American Institute Cargo Clauses, current forms:

1. MARINE EXTENSION CLAUSES	4. CARRIER	7. INCHMAREE
2. DEVIATION	5. BILL OF LADING, ETC.	8. CONSTRUCTIVE TOTAL LOSS
3. CRAFT, ETC.	6. EXPLOSION	9. GENERAL AVERAGE

10. SOUTH AMERICA 60 DAY CLAUSE
11. S.R. & C.C. ENDORSEMENT
12. WAR RISK INSURANCE

PARAMOUNT WARRANTIES: THE FOLLOWING WARRANTIES SHALL BE PARAMOUNT AND SHALL NOT BE MODIFIED OR SUPERSEDED BY ANY OTHER PROVISION INCLUDED HEREIN OR STAMPED OR ENDORSED HEREON UNLESS SUCH OTHER PROVISION REFERS SPECIFICALLY TO THE RISKS EXCLUDED BY THESE WARRANTIES AND EXPRESSLY ASSUMES THE SAID RISKS:
F.C. & S.: Notwithstanding anything herein contained to the contrary, this insurance is warranted free from capture, seizure, arrest, restraint, detainment, confiscation, preemption, requisition or nationalization, and the consequences thereof or any attempt thereat, whether in time of peace or war and whether lawful or otherwise; also warranted free, whether in time of peace or war, from all loss, damage or expense caused by any weapon of war employing atomic or nuclear fission and/or fusion or other reaction or radioactive force or matter or by any mine or torpedo, also warranted free from all consequences of hostilities or warlike operations (whether there be a declaration of war or not), but this warranty shall not exclude collision or contact with aircraft, rockets or similar missiles or with any fixed or floating object (other than a mine or torpedo), stranding, heavy weather, fire or explosion unless caused directly (and independently of the nature of the voyage or service which the vessel concerned or, in the case of a collision, any other vessel involved therein, is performing) by a hostile act by or against a belligerent power; and for the purposes of this warranty 'power' includes any authority maintaining naval, military or air forces in association with a power.
Further warranted free from the consequences of civil war, revolution, rebellion, insurrection, or civil strife arising therefrom, or piracy.
NUCLEAR EXCLUSION: Notwithstanding anything to the contrary herein, it is hereby understood and agreed that this Policy shall not apply to any loss, damage or expense due to or arising out of, whether directly or indirectly, nuclear reaction, radiation, or radioactive contamination, regardless of how it was caused. However, subject to all provisions of this Policy, if this Policy insures against fire, then direct physical damage to the property insured located within the United States or Puerto Rico by fire directly caused by the above excluded perils, is insured, provided that the nuclear reaction, radiation, or radioactive contamination was not caused, whether directly or indirectly, by any of the perils excluded by the F.C. & S. Warranty of this Policy.
Nothing in this clause shall be construed to cover any loss, damage, liability or expense caused by nuclear reaction, radiation or radioactive contamination arising directly or indirectly from the fire mentioned above.
S.R. & C.C. Warranted free of loss or damage caused by or resulting from:
(a) strikes, lockouts, labor disturbances, riots, civil commotions, or the acts of any person or persons taking part in any such occurrences or disorders.
(b) vandalism, sabotage or malicious act, which shall be deemed also to encompass the act or acts of one or more persons, whether or not agents of a sovereign power, carried out for political, terroristic or ideological purposes and whether or not any loss, damage or expense resulting therefrom is accidental or intentional.
TIME FOR SUIT: No suit or action against this Assurer for the recovery of any claim by virtue of this insurance shall be sustained in any Court of Law or Equity unless commenced within one (1) year from the time loss occurred or, if such limitation is not valid by the law of the place where the policy is issued, within the shortest contractual period of limitation permitted by such law.

This Certificate is issued in Original and Duplicate, one of which being accomplished the other to stand null and void.

To support a claim local Revenue Laws may require this certificate to be stamped.

Not transferable unless countersigned

Countersigned _____

Paul D. Amstut
President

James P. Sheehy
Assistant Treasurer

ADDITIONAL CONDITIONS AND
INSTRUCTIONS TO CLAIMANTS ON REVERSE SIDE

ORIGINAL

W-13FF 6/97

DOCUMENTS

Certificate of Origin

Definition

A document issued by a certifying authority stating the country of origin of goods.

✔ Key Elements

A certificate of origin should include the following elements:

1. Key details (typically consignor, consignee, and description of goods) regarding the shipment. Also, such details to be in conformity with other documents (e.g., documentary credit, commercial invoice)
2. A statement of origin of the goods
3. The name, signature and/or stamp or seal of the certifying authority

A NAFTA Certificate of Origin includes the following elements:

1. Name and address of exporter
2. Blanket period of shipment (for multiple shipments of identical goods for a specified period of up to one year)
3. Name and address of importer
4. Name and address of producer
5. Description of goods
6. Harmonized System tariff classification number up to six digits
7. Preference criteria (one of six criteria of rules of origin of the goods)
8. Indication of whether the exporter is the producer of the goods
9. Regional Value Content indication
10. Country of origin of goods
11. Exporter company name, date and authorized signature

Cautions & Notes

If you are the buyer (importer) the import authority of your country may require a certificate of origin. If so, make certain that you require it of the seller in the form and content as specified by your country's customs authority.

A certificate of origin can be the key document required for obtaining special (reduced) tariff rates for imports from countries listed as beneficiaries to programs such as the GSP (Generalized Systems of Preferences) NAFTA (North American Free Trade Area).

In a documentary letter of credit buyers should avoid the use of such terms as "first class," "well-known," "qualified," "independent," "official," "competent," or "local" when referring to the certifying authority. It is preferable to name the required certifying authority. Use of vague terminology will result in the bank's acceptance of any relevant document that appears "on its face" to be in compliance with the documentary credit, so long as it was not issued and signed by the beneficiary (seller).

In certain countries the certificate of origin is prepared by the seller (beneficiary to the documentary credit) on a standard form and then certified (with a signature, stamp or seal) by the certifying authority.

Certifying authorities most often used are city and regional chambers of commerce and chambers of commerce and industry.

Exporteur
Exportateur
Esportatore
Exporter

MUELLER AG
Birsstrasse 26
4132 Muttenz / Switzerland

Empfänger
Destinataire
Destinatario
Consignee

ADILMA TRADING CORPORATION
27, Nihonbashi, Chiyoda-Ku

TOKYO 125 / Japan

Nr.
No.   201884

URSPRUNGSZEUGNIS
CERTIFICAT D'ORIGINE
CERTIFICATO D'ORIGINE
CERTIFICATE OF ORIGIN

SCHWEIZERISCHE EIDGENOSSENSCHAFT
CONFÉDÉRATION SUISSE
CONFEDERAZIONE SVIZZERA
SWISS CONFEDERATION

Ursprungsstaat
Pays d'origine
Paese d'origine   SWITZERLAND
Country of origin

Angaben über die Beförderung (Ausfüllung freigestellt)
Informations relatives au transport (mention facultative)
Informazioni riguardanti il trasporto (indicazione facoltativa)
Particulars of transport (optional declaration)

Bemerkungen
Observations
Osservazioni
Observations

LETTER OF CREDIT NR. 064204

Zeichen, Nummern, Anzahl und Art der Packstücke; Warenbezeichnung
Marques, numéros, nombre et nature des colis; désignation des marchandises
Marche, numeri, numero e natura dei colli; designazione delle merci
Marks, numbers, number and kind of packages; description of the goods

Nettogewicht
Poids net
Peso netto
Net weight
kg, l, m³
etc./ecc.

ADILMA TRADING   6 cases   CYLINDER-
VIA TOKYO   PRESS
NR. 1-6   COMPLETELY
ORDER 0-535/1   ASSEMBLED

12'140,0 kg

Bruttogewicht
Poids brut
Peso lordo
Gross weight

12'860,0 kg

Die unterzeichnete Handelskammer bescheinigt den Ursprung oben bezeichneter Ware
La Chambre de commerce soussignée certifie l'origine des marchandises désignées ci-dessus
La sottoscritta Camera di commercio certifica l'origine delle merci summenzionate
The undersigned Chamber of commerce certifies the origin of the above mentioned goods

Basel, 2 6. 04.

Basler Handelskammer
Chambre de Commerce de Bâle
Camera di Commercio di Basilea
Basle Chamber of Commerce

Inspection Certificate

Definition

A document issued by an authority indicating that goods have been inspected (typically according to a set of industry, customer, government, or carrier specifications) prior to shipment and the results of the inspection.

Inspection certificates are generally obtained from neutral testing organizations (e.g., a government entity or independent service company). In some cases the inspection certificate can come from the manufacturer or shipper, but not from the forwarder or logistics firm.

✔ Key Elements

An inspection certificate should include the following elements:

1. Key details (typically consignor, consignee, and description of goods) regarding the shipment. Also, such details to be in conformity with other documents (e.g., documentary credit, commercial invoice, etc.)
2. Date of the inspection
3. Statement of sampling methodology
4. Statement of the results of the inspection
5. The name, signature and/or stamp or seal of the inspecting entity

Cautions & Notes

In the case of certain countries and certain commodities the inspection certificate must be issued by an appropriate government entity.

In a documentary letter of credit buyers should avoid the use of such terms as "first class," "well-known," "qualified," "independent," "official," "competent," or "local" when referring to an acceptable inspection authority. It is preferable to agree beforehand as to a specific inspection organization or entity and for the buyer to name the required certifying organization or entity in the documentary credit.

Use of vague terminology (as above) will result in the bank's acceptance of any relevant document that appears "on its face" to be in compliance with the documentary credit, so long as it was not issued by the beneficiary (seller).

⊕SGS   SGS Supervise (Suisse) S.A.

May 10, 19..

Hardstrasse 1
Postfach 4149
CH-4002 Basel
Tel. (+41-61) 271 36 11
Fax (+41-61) 271 40 48
Telex : 962 457 SGS

Certificate No 1407/ 012488

BUYER	:	TA PING CO. LTD. YACHT BUILDING
		18-5, HARBOUR STREET, TAIPEI, TAIWAN
SELLER	:	SWISS EXPORT LTD. AIRFREIGHT DIVISION
		8008 ZUERICH, SWITZERLAND
LETTER OF CREDIT NBR.	:	FB-03-45786-9
GOODS	:	MACHINERY PARTS, as designated below
CONTRACT NBR.	:	FA12345WO79PE
IMPORT PERMIT NUMBER	:	TW-2395-497-0006, as declared
SERVICES REQUIRED	:	FINAL PRE-SHIPMENT INSPECTION

This is to certify that, at buyers' request and based on the specifications submitted to us, we have inspected the following goods:

1. MATERIAL DESIGNATION
   1 LOT ACCESSORIES AND SPARE PARTS FOR FOOD PROCESSING MACHINERY, as detailed in seller's commercial invoice and corresponding packing list both dated April 29. 19

2. INSPECTIONS PERFORMED AND FINDINGS
   - 2.1. Material identification for conformity with the specifications submitted to us.
   - 2.2. Visual inspection on workmanship, finish and condition.
   - 2.3. Quantitative and completeness checks.
   - 2.4. Dimensional checks at random, where applicable.
   - 2.5. Packing inspection: The packing, consisting of 5 plywood cases, is considered adequate to ship the goods by air to Taipei under normal conditions of transport and handling.
   - 2.6. Marking inspection: The shipping marks include: **SWISS EXPORT 0405/1-5**
   - 2.7. Loading details as per Air Waybill No. BSL 122077 issued by PANALPINA LTD BASLE-AIRPORT on 4 MAY ..

3. INSPECTION RESULTS AND CONCLUSION
   Based on the inspections performed, we certify the goods to be new, of good workmanship and finish, free from apparent damage or defect, and that the shipment is fully in compliance with the contract requirements in specification, quantity, quality, proper packing and marking.

5. DATE AND PLACE OF INSPECTION
   April 30, 19.. on seller's premises in Zurich, Switzerland with subsequent review of loading details.

This certificate is evidence of and reports on our findings at the time and place of inspection. It does not release buyers or sellers from their contractual obligations.

SGS SUPERVISE (SUISSE) SA
BASLE OFFICE, SWITZERLAND

As Member of SOCIETE GENERALE
DE SURVEILLANCE S.A. (SGS)
Geneva, Switzerland

DOCUMENTS

Shipper's Export Declaration (SED)

Definition

A document prepared by the shipper and presented to a government authority specifying goods exported along with their quantities, weight, value, and destination.

✔ Key Elements

Each country has its own export declaration form. Certain elements are likely to be required in the SED for all countries. The shipper's export declaration typically includes the following elements:

1. Name and address of seller
2. Name and address of buyer
3. Date of issuance
4. Export license number (if required, based upon country of export requirements and goods exported)
5. Country of origin of the goods shipped
6. Country of final destination of the goods
7. Quantity and description of the goods
8. Country of export statistical classification number (some countries do not require this information for shipments under a certain level)
9. Shipping details including: weight of the goods, number of packages, and shipping marks and numbers

Cautions & Notes

The shipper's export declaration is used by a nation's customs authority to control exports and compile trade statistics.

An SED is usually not required by the buyer in a documentary letter of credit transaction unless the buyer is responsible for export formalities.

Many nations impose strict controls on exports (e.g., high technology, armaments and drugs) and use the SED as a means of export control. Because many exports can be diverted to "unfriendly" nations and individuals, it is considered the responsibility of the exporter to know his cargo, destination, customer, end-use, and end-user.

Electronic Filing

Some nations (such as the United States) are in the process of instituting new procedures that will require exporters to submit their Shipper's Export Declarations electronically. This involves using a computer with a modem and specially designed forms software.

DOCUMENTS

FORM **7525-V** (1-1-88)   **SHIPPER'S EXPORT DECLARATION**   OMB No. 0607-0018

1a. EXPORTER'S *(Name and address including ZIP code)*

| ZIP CODE | 2. DATE OF EXPORTATION | 3. BILL OF LADING/AIR WAYBILL NO. |

b. EXPORTER'S EIN (IRS) NUMBER

c. PARTIES TO TRANSACTION
☐ Related   ☐ Non-related

4a. ULTIMATE CONSIGNEE

b. INTERMEDIATE CONSIGNEE

5. FORWARDING AGENT

6. POINT (STATE) OF ORIGIN OR FTZ NO.   7. COUNTRY OF ULTIMATE DESTINATION

8. LOADING PIER *(Vessel Only)*   9. MODE OF TRANSPORT *(Specify)*

10. EXPORTING CARRIER   11. PORT OF EXPORT

12. PORT OF UNLOADING *(VESSEL and AIR ONLY)*   13. CONTAINERIZED *(Vessel only)*
☐ Yes   ☐ No

14. SCHEDULE B DESCRIPTION OF COMMODITIES,
15. MARKS, NOS., AND KINDS OF PACKAGES   *(Use columns 17-19)*

D/F (16)	SCHEDULE B NUMBER (17)	CHECK DIGIT	QUANTITY – SCHEDULE B UNIT(S) (18)	SHIPPING WEIGHT *(Kilos)* (19)	VALUE (U.S. dollars, omit cents) *(Selling price or cost if not sold)* (20)

21. VALIDATED LICENSE NO./GENERAL LICENSE SYMBOL   22. ECCN *(When required)*

23. Duly authorized officer or employee   The exporter authorizes the forwarder named above to act as forwarding agent for export control and customs purposes.

24. I certify that all statements made and all information contained herein are true and correct and that I have read and understand the instructions for preparation of this document, set forth in the "Correct Way to Fill Out the Shipper's Export Declaration." I understand that civil and criminal penalties, including forfeiture and sale, may be imposed for making false or fraudulent statements herein, failing to provide the requested information or for violation of U.S. laws on exportation (13 U.S.C. Sec. 305; 22 U.S.C. Sec. 401; 18 U.S.C. Sec. 1001; 50 U.S.C. App. 2410).

Signature

Confidential - For use solely for official purposes authorized by the Secretary of Commerce (13 U.S.C. 301 (g).

Title

Export shipments are subject to inspection by U.S. Customs Service and/or Office of Export Enforcement

Date

25. AUTHENTICATION *(When required)*

The "Correct Way to Fill Out the Shipper's Export Declaration" is available from the Bureau of the Census, Washington, D.C. 20233.

DOCUMENTS

Packing List

Definition

A packing list is a document prepared by the shipper listing the kinds and quantities of merchandise in a particular shipment.

A copy of the packing list is often attached to the shipment itself and another copy sent directly to the consignee to assist in checking the shipment when received. Also called a bill of parcels.

✔ Key Elements

The packing list includes the following elements:

1. Name and address of seller
2. Name and address of buyer
3. Date of issuance
4. Invoice number
5. Order or contract number
6. Quantity and description of the goods
7. Shipping details including: weight of the goods, number of packages, and shipping marks and numbers
8. Quantity and description of contents of each package, carton, crate or container
9. Any other information as required in the sales contract or documentary credit (e.g., country of origin)

Cautions & Notes

The packing list is a more detailed version of the commercial invoice but without price information. The type of each container is identified, as well as its individual weight and measurements. The packing list is attached to the outside of its respective container in a waterproof envelope marked "Packing List" or "Packing List Enclosed," and is immediately available to authorities in both the countries of export and import.

Although not required in all transactions, it is required by some countries and some buyers.

DOCUMENTS